75

D0199802

Langenscheidt
Universal German Dictionary

German – English
English – German

completely revised edition

edited by the
Langenscheidt editorial staff

Langenscheidt

New York · Berlin · Munich · Vienna · Zurich

Project management:
Heike Pleisteiner

Lexicographical work:
Howard Atkinson, Martin Fellermayer, Stuart Fortey,
Heike Pleisteiner, Robin Sawers, Karin Weindl

This dictionary uses the standardised German spelling system
as of 2004.

This dictionary has been created with the help of dictionary
databases owned by HarperCollins Publishers Ltd.

Contents

How to use this dictionary

Where do I find what I am looking for?

The **Universal German Dictionary** contains over 36,000 references, which are listed **in alphabetical order**. The only exceptions to this strict rule are **phrasal verbs**, which are entered directly under the simple verb form. This means, to take an example, that **keep back**, **keep off**, **keep out**, **keep to** and **keep up** are all entered directly under **keep**. The entry for the word **keeper** follows the phrasal verbs, although strictly speaking it ought to come alphabetically between **keep back** and **keep off**.

The letters **ä**, **ö** and **ü** are treated on the same basis as **a**, **o** and **u**. Thus the entry for **träumen**, for example, comes between **Traum** and **traumhaft**.

For the **pronunciation** of German words, see the notes on pages 9–14.

How do I find what I am looking for?

The structure of the individual entries is the same for both sections of the dictionary.

Each entry is structured using Arabic numerals (1, 2, 3 etc.). These can differentiate between different **parts of speech** (noun, adjective, adverb, verb, etc.):

> **search 1.** *n* Suche *f* (*for* nach);
> *do a ~ for* IT suchen nach; *in*
> *~ of* auf der Suche nach **2.** *vi*
> suchen (*for* nach) **3.** *vt*
> durchsuchen

They can also differentiate between the different **meanings** of a word:

> **Druck 1.** *m* (-(e)s, Drücke)
> PHYS pressure; *fig* (*strain*)
> stress; *jdn unter ~ setzen*
> put sb under pressure **2.** *m*
> (-(e)s, -e) TYPO printing; (*product, typeface*) print

What can I find under each entry?

Look at the following entry:

> **cash 1.** *n* Bargeld *nt*; *in ~* bar; *~*
> *on delivery* per Nachnahme
> **2.** *vt* (*check*/*cheque*) einlösen

This example will serve to illustrate the main elements, which are itemised and explained below:

cash	the word itself in **bold print**
1.	Arabic numeral to differentiate between different parts of speech
n	part of speech (in this case, noun) in *italics*
Bargeld	German equivalent of the English word in standard script
nt	gender of the German equivalent (in this case, neuter) in *italics*
;	semi-colon used to separate the translation from the typical usages which follow
in ~	the expression *in cash* in **bold italics**
~	the swung dash as part of the expression stands for the main word **cash**
bar	German equivalent of the English expression in standard script
~ on delivery	the expression *cash on delivery* in **bold italics**
per Nachnahme	German equivalent of the English expression in standard script
2.	Arabic numeral to differentiate between different parts of speech
vt	part of speech (in this case, transitive verb) in *italics*

(check/ cheque)	typical object of the equivalent German expression (in this case, 'cash a *check/cheque*') placed within brackets and *italicised*
einlösen	German equivalent of the English word in standard script

Are all the entries structured in this way?

Every entry more or less follows the simple structure outlined above. The clear differentiation between various forms and meanings will lead you to the correct translation. In addition, the *italicised* information in brackets can denote a subject or object of the given word, or else it can indicate the general context in which the word is used:

> **break up 1.** *vi* aufbrechen; *(meeting, organisation)* sich auflösen; *(marriage)* in die Brüche gehen (...) **break down** *vi (car)* eine Panne haben; *(machine)* versagen; *(person)* zusammenbrechen

What is the purpose of the information in *italics*?

Information in *italics*, with or without brackets, often provides a more precise indication of the different meanings of a word. This information might refer to synonyms (words with a similar meaning), possible subjects and objects, etc. and is included in order to indicate which translation should be used in any given context.

Italics are also used to provide grammatical information, as well as to clarify the meaning and use of a word for which there is no direct translation:

> **Mehlspeise** *f sweet dish made from flour, eggs and milk*

> **Einwohnermeldeamt** *nt registration office for residents*

Translations of verbs are often followed by the prepositions which they take in *italics*. Equivalents are then given in standard script and the cases they take in *italics*.

> **inform** *vt* informieren (*of, about über + acc*); **keep sb ~ed** jdn auf dem Laufenden halten

For further information on the use of *italics*, you should refer to the **List of Abbreviations** on pages 15–16.

What is the purpose of cross-references?

Cross-references are always indicated by the → symbol. They usually refer you to another word of similar meaning or to an alternative spelling of the given word. When you look up the cross-referenced word, you will then find the translation(s) and other relevant information:

> **Januar** *m* (*-(s)*, *-e*) January; → **Juni**

> **Juni** *m* (*-(s)*, *-s*) June; **im ~** in June; **am 4. ~** on 4(th) June, on June 4(th) ; **Anfang/ Mitte/Ende ~** at the beginning/in the middle/at the end of June; **letzten/ nächsten ~** last/next June

> **homeopathic** *adj* (*US*) → **homoeopathic**

> **homoeopathic** *adj* homöopathisch

What is the purpose of the context indicators?

These help you to differentiate between the various meanings of a word and the contexts in which they are used:

> **dressing** *n* GAStR Dressing *nt*, Soße *f*; MED Verband *m*

The most common of these indicators are written in SMALL CAPITAL LETTERS and can be found in the **List of Abbreviations** on pages 15–16. Less common indicators are not abbreviated and are given in *italics*.

> **knight** *n* Ritter *m*; (*in chess*)
> Pferd *nt*, Springer *m*

How is the register of a word indicated?

This dictionary provides information on the following types of register: *fig* (figurative), *pej* (pejorative or derogatory), *fam* (familiar or informal) and *vulg* (vulgar). As far as possible, translations of words with such indicators have been chosen to reflect the same register. In other words, a vulgar German word or expression will be translated by a suitably vulgar English word or expression, and so on. These indicators can be found in the **List of Abbreviations** on pages 15–16.

What type of grammatical information can I find in this dictionary?

A list of the **Irregular German Verbs** contained in this dictionary can be found in the appendix on pages 596–599. Irregular verb forms are given in italics immediately after the verb and are also listed as separate entries:

> **schwimmen** (*schwamm, ge-schwommen*) *vi* swim
>
> **schwamm** *imperf of* **schwimmen**
>
> **geschwommen** *pp of* **schwimmen**

Irregular **plural forms**, as well as the **genitive forms**, are given after the relevant nouns:

> **Haus** *nt* (*-es, Häuser*) house;
> **nach** ~**e** home; **zu** ~**e** at
> home

The **List of Abbreviations** on pages 15–16 contains all the indicators for grammatical information used in this dictionary.

What can I find in the appendices?

In addition to the **Irregular German Verbs** mentioned above (pp. 596–599), the appendices also include chapters on **Numbers** (pp. 600–602), **European currency** (p. 603), the **States of Germany, Austria and Switzerland** (pp. 604–605), **Temperatures** (p. 606) and **Weights and measures** (pp. 607–608).

Notes on the pronunciation of German words

The rules governing the pronunciation of German words tend to be more straightforward than their English equivalents – and there are fewer exceptions. This means that you can apply these rules consistently without any great fear of being incorrect.

In order to help you understand the basic rules, we have divided our guidelines into the following sections: **consonants, vowels, stress.**

We have concentrated on those German sounds which follow different rules from their English equivalents and on those which do not exist in English at all.

Consonants

Silent consonants

The only silent consonant in German is **h**, which is silent or not depending on its position in a word. It is pronounced at the beginning of a word (as in **H**eld *hero*) but between two vowels (as in the name Jo**h**annes). It is silent when it comes between a vowel and a consonant (as in Fe**h**ler *mistake*) and when it comes at the end of a word (as in fro**h** *happy*).

When **h** is used in combination with other consonants (such as in **sch** and **ch**), different rules apply (see under **combinations of consonants**).

Single and double consonants

Most German single and double consonants are pronounced in the same way as their English equivalents.

The rules and examples below show **only** cases in which they are pronounced differently or (in the case of **ß**) do not exist in English at all.

conso-nant	rule	example
b	often pronounced **p** (as in the English **p**oet) at the end of a word, sometimes at the end of a syllable	hal<u>b</u> **Ab**stieg
c	pronounced **ts** (as in the English bi**ts**) pronounced **k** (as in the English **k**ite) in words of foreign derivation (most cases)	<u>C</u>D <u>C</u>annabis, <u>C</u>ola
d	often pronounced **t** (as in the English taxi) at the end of a word, sometimes at the end of a syllable	Lan<u>d</u> un<u>d</u> so weiter
g	often pronounced **k** (as in the English **k**ite) at the end of a word, sometimes at the end of a consonant; pronounced **ch** (as in the Scottish loch*) if the word ends in -ig	Zu<u>g</u> Flu<u>g</u>zeug lusti<u>g</u>
h	see **silent consonants** (above)	
j	usually pronounced **y** (as in the English **y**oung)	<u>J</u>oghurt
q	pronounced **kv** in combination with the vowel **u**	<u>Qu</u>iz
r	rolled at the back of the mouth (similarly to the Scottish **r** sound)	<u>r</u>und
s	pronounced **z** (as in the English **z**ebra) when it comes between two vowels	le<u>s</u>en

ß	pronounced **s** (as in the English six) never occurs at the beginning of a word	**Fu**ß**ball**
t	pronounced **ts** (as in the English bits) when followed by the letters -**ion**	**Intui**t**ion**
v	mostly pronounced **f** (as in the English fork) pronounced **v** (as in the English vote) in words of Greek or Latin derivation	**v**erstehen **V**eto
w	pronounced **v** (as in the English vote)	**w**o, **W**under
z	pronounced **ts** (as in the English bits)	**Z**unge

*   This sound does not commonly exist in English. It can best be described by comparing it to the sound made at the beginning of the word *human* in the phrase '**a h**uman being'.

Double consonants within one syllable always make the preceding vowel short (**Kra**bb**e, pa**dd**eln, ko**mm**en, gewi**nn**en, mu**ss, fe**tt)**

Combinations of consonants

In German, certain combinations of consonants (if they are pronounced as part of the same syllable) produce a sound which is not found in English. The most difficult for English native speakers is the following sound:

ch   This combination produces a guttural sound which can best be described by comparing it to the sound made at the beginning of the word *human* in the English phrase '**a h**uman being'. However, the sound can be pronounced in two slightly different basic ways, depending on the vowel sound which precedes it: in a word such as lachen (to laugh), it is produced at the back of the throat (as in Scottish loch*), whereas in ich (I) it is produced at the front of the mouth and sounds a little more like the English **sh** (as in fish).

The following consonant combinations also produce sounds different from their English equivalents:

chs	pronounced **ks** (as in the English kicks)	**Lachs, wachsen**
ng	always pronounced as in the English singer, never as in finger	**Hunger**
sch	always pronounced **sh** (as in the English shoe)	**Frosch, Schiff, verschwinden**
sp	at the beginning of a word or syllable, pronounced **shp** (as in the English phrase cash prize)	**Sport, verspätet**
st	at the beginning of a word or syllable, pronounced **sht** (as in the English phrase fish tank)	**Stein, verstehen**
th	always pronounced **t** (as in the English taxi)	**Thunfisch**
tsch	pronounced **ch** (as in the English chicken)	**Quatsch**
tz	pronounced **ts** (as in the English bits)	**Katze**

Vowels

Long and short vowel sounds

German vowel sounds can be long or short. Certain sounds (such as those produced by the letters **ä**, **ö** and **ü**) have no direct equivalent in English – in these cases we have given an approximation of the sound.

letter (-s)	vowel sound produced	example
a	short (close to the English fan)	**Hammer**
a, ah, aa	long (close to the English marmalade)	**Vater, Bahn, Aal**
ä	short (close to the English set)	**ändern**

ä, äh	long (close to the English bear)	**Käfig, ähnlich**
e	short (as in the English wet)	**endlich**
e, ee, eh	long (close to the English gay, but with no concluding y sound)	**edel, Fee, Fehler**
i	short (as in the English igloo)	**in, Kinn**
i, ie	long (as in the English feel)	**Kino, tief**
o	short (as in the English hop)	**kommen**
o, oo, oh	long (close to the English fold)	**los, Moos, Kohl**
oh	long (close to the English more)	**Ohr**
ö	short (close to the English flirt, but shorter)	**können**
ö	long (close to the English flirt)	**Löwe**
u	short (as in the English full)	**Mutter, unter**
u, uh	long (as in the English pool)	**tun, Kuh**
ü	short*	**dünn**
ü, üh	long (close to the English tune, but with a raised tongue)	**über, fühlen**

* There is really no English equivalent to this sound. The word **dünn**, for example can best be produced by pronouncing the English word **din** with pursed lips.

Diphthongs

A diphthong is in effect the combination of two vowel sounds. There are relatively few of these in German.

ei, ai	as in the English my	**fein, Haifisch**
au	as in the English now	**August**
eu, äu	as in the English toy	**neun, äußerst**

Stress

Most German words are stressed on the first syllable. The only major exception to this rule concerns words beginning with prefixes such as **be-**, **ent-** and **ver-**, which are usually stressed on the subsequent syllable (**be<u>ant</u>worten**, **Ent<u>täuschung</u>**, **ver<u>muten</u>**).

Additionally, some words of foreign (especially Latin) derivation are stressed on the final syllable (**Caf<u>é</u>**, **Elef<u>ant</u>**, **Sold<u>at</u>**, **Stat<u>ion</u>**).

Abbreviations

a.	also				(*Imperfekt*)
abbr	abbreviation		*impers*	impersonal
acc	accusative		*in cpds*	in compounds
acr	acronym		*indef*	indefinite
adj	adjective		*interj*	interjection
adv	adverb		*inv*	invariable
AGR	agriculture		*irr*	irregular
ANAT	anatomy		IT	IT, computing
art	article		*jdm*	jemandem
ART	fine arts		*jdn*	jemanden
ASTR	astronomy,		*jds*	jemandes
	astrology		*jmd*	jemand
AUTO	automobiles,		LAW	law
	traffic		LING	linguistics
AVIAT	aviation		*m*	masculine
BIO	biology		MATH	mathematics
BOT	botany		MED	medicine
Brit	British		METEO	meteorology
CHEM	chemistry		MIL	military
COMM	commerce		MUS	music
conj	conjunction		*n*	noun
contr	contraction		NAUT	nautical
dat	dative		*nom*	nominative
ELEC	electricity		*npl*	plural noun
esp	especially		*nsing*	singular noun
etw	etwas		*nt*	neuter
f	feminine		*num*	numeral
fam	familiar, informal		*or*	or
fig	figurative		*pej*	pejorative
FILM	film, cinema		PHOT	photography
FIN	finance		PHYS	physics
GASTR	gastronomy,		*pl*	plural
	cooking		POL	politics
gen	genitive		*pp*	past participle
hist	historically		*pref*	prefix
HIST	history		*prep*	preposition
imperf	past tense		*pron*	pronoun

pt	past tense	THEAT	theater/theatre
®	registered trade-mark	TV	television
		TYPO	typography, printing
RADIO	radio		
RAIL	railways	*US*	North American
REL	religion	*vaux*	auxiliary verb
sb	somebody	*vi*	intransitive verb
Scot	Scottish	*vr*	reflexive verb
sg	singular	*vt*	transitive verb
SPORT	sports	*vulg*	vulgar
sth	something	ZOOL	zoology
TECH	technology	~	swung dash
TEL	telecommunications	→	refer to

A

à *prep + acc* at ... each; **4 Tickets à 8 Euro** 4 tickets at 8 euros each

A *abbr* = Autobahn; ≈ M (Brit); ≈ I (US)

Aal *m* (-(e)s, -e) eel

ab 1. *prep + dat* from; **von jetzt ~** from now on; **Berlin ~ 16:30 Uhr** departs Berlin 16.30; **Seite 17** from page 17; **~ 18** from the age of 18 **2.** *adv* off; **links ~** to the left; **~ und zu** (or **an**) now and then (or again); **der Knopf ist ~** the button has come off

abbauen *vt* (tent) take down; (in number, degree) reduce

abbeißen *irr vt* bite off

abbestellen *vt* cancel

abbiegen *irr vi* turn off; (road) bend; **nach links/rechts ~** turn left/right; **Abbiegespur** *f* filter lane

Abbildung *f* illustration

abblasen *irr vt fig* call off

abblenden *vt, vi* AUTO (**die Scheinwerfer**) **~** dip (Brit) (or dim (US)) one's headlights; **Abblendlicht** *nt* dipped (Brit) (or dimmed (US)) headlights *pl*

abbrechen *irr vt* break off;

(building) pull down; (end) stop; (computer program) abort

abbremsen *vi* brake, slow down

abbringen *irr vt* **jdn von einer Idee ~** talk sb out of an idea; **jdn vom Thema ~** get sb away from the subject; **davon lasse ich mich nicht ~** nothing will make me change my mind about it

abbuchen *vt* to debit (von to)

abdanken *vi* resign

abdrehen 1. *vt* (gas, water) turn off; (light) switch off **2.** *vi* (ship, plane) change course

Abend *m* (-s, -e) evening; **am ~** in the evening; **zu ~ essen** have dinner; **heute/morgen/gestern ~** this/tomorrow/yesterday evening; **guten ~!** good evening; **Abendbrot** *nt* supper; **Abendessen** *nt* dinner; **Abendgarderobe** *f* evening dress (or gown); **Abendkasse** *f* box office; **Abendkleid** *nt* evening dress (or gown); **Abendkurs** *m* evening class; **Abendmahl** *nt* **das ~** (Holy) Communion; **abends** adv in the evening; **montags ~** on Monday evenings

Abenteuer nt (-s, -) adventure; **Abenteuerurlaub** m adventure holiday

aber conj but; (nevertheless) however; **oder ~** alternatively; **~ ja!** (but) of course; **das ist ~ nett von Ihnen** that's really nice of you

abergläubisch adj superstitious

abfahren irr vi leave (or depart) (nach for); (skier) ski down; **Abfahrt** f departure; (from motorway) exit; (in skiing) descent; (piste) run; **Abfahrtslauf** m (in skiing) downhill; **Abfahrtszeit** f departure time

Abfall m waste; (household) rubbish (Brit), garbage (US); **Abfalleimer** m rubbish bin (Brit), garbage can (US)

abfällig adj disparaging; **~ von jdm sprechen** make disparaging remarks about sb

abfärben vi (in the wash) run; fig rub off

abfertigen vt (parcel) prepare for dispatch; (at the border) clear; **Abfertigungsschalter** m (at airport) check-in desk

abfinden irr 1. vt pay off 2. vr **sich mit etw ~** come to terms with sth; **Abfindung** f (money) compensation; (for

employee) redundancy payment

abfliegen irr vi (plane) take off; (passenger also) fly off; **Abflug** m departure; (becoming airborne) takeoff; **Abflughalle** f departure lounge; **Abflugzeit** f departure time

Abfluss m drain; (of washbasin) plughole (Brit); **Abflussrohr** nt waste pipe; (outside) drainpipe

abfragen vt test; IT call up

abführen 1. vi MED have a laxative effect **2.** vt (tax, charges) pay; **jdn ~ lassen** take sb into custody; **Abführmittel** nt laxative

Abgabe f handing in; (of ball) pass; (charge) tax; (of statement) making; **abgabenfrei** adj tax-free; **abgabenpflichtig** adj liable to tax

Abgase pl AUTO exhaust fumes pl; **Abgas(sonder)untersuchung** f exhaust emission test

abgeben irr **1.** vt (luggage, key) leave (bei with); (homework etc) hand in; (heat) give off; (statement, judgment) make **2.** vr **sich mit jdm ~** associate with sb; **sich mit etw ~** bother with sth

abgebildet adj **wie oben ~** as shown above

abgehen irr vi (letters) go; (button etc) come off; (amount) be taken off;

(road) branch off; **von der Schule ~** leave school; **sie geht mir ab** I really miss her; **was geht denn hier ab?** fam what's going on here?

abgehetzt adj exhausted, shattered

abgelaufen adj (passport) expired; (time, period) up; **die Milch ist ~** the milk is past its sell-by date

abgelegen adj remote

abgemacht interj OK, it's a deal, that's settled, then

abgeneigt adj **einer Sache** dat **~ sein** be averse to sth; **ich wäre nicht ~, das zu tun** I wouldn't mind doing that

Abgeordnete(r) mf Member of Parliament

abgepackt adj prepacked

abgerissen adj **der Knopf ist ~** the button has come off

abgesehen adj **es auf jdn/ etw ~ haben** be after sb/sth; **~ von** apart from

abgespannt adj (person) exhausted, worn out

abgestanden adj stale; (beer) flat

abgestorben adj (plant) dead; (fingers) numb

abgestumpft adj (person) insensitive

abgetragen adj (clothes) worn

abgewöhnen vt **jdm etw ~** cure sb of sth; **sich etw ~**

give sth up

abhaken vt tick off; **das (Thema) ist schon abgehakt** that's been dealt with

abhalten irr vt (meeting) hold; **jdn von etw ~** keep sb away from sth; (prevent) keep sb from sth

abhanden adj **~ kommen** get lost

Abhang m slope

abhängen 1. vt (picture) take down; (trailer) uncouple; (pursuer) shake off **2.** irr vi **von jdm/etw ~** depend on sb/sth; **das hängt davon ab, ob ...** it depends (on) whether ...; **abhängig** adj dependent (von on)

abhauen irr **1.** vt (branch, arm etc) cut off **2.** vi fam clear off; **hau ab!** get lost!, beat it!

abheben irr **1.** vt (money) withdraw; (receiver, playing card) pick up **2.** vi (plane) take off; (rocket) lift off; (in card game) cut

abholen vt collect; (at station etc) meet; (with car) pick up; **Abholmarkt** m cash and carry

abhorchen vt MED listen to

abhören vt (vocabulary) test; (phone call) tap; (tape etc) listen to

Abitur nt (-s, -e) German school-leaving examination, ≈ A-levels (Brit), ≈ High School Diploma (US)

abkaufen vt **jdm etw ~** buy sth

from sb; **das kauf ich dir nicht ab!** *fam* I don't believe you

abklingen *irr vi* (*pain*) ease; (*effect*) wear off

abkommen *irr vi* get away; **von der Straße ~** leave the road; **von einem Plan ~** give up a plan; **vom Thema ~** stray from the point

Abkommen *nt* (-s, -) agreement

abkoppeln *vt* (*trailer*) unhitch

abkratzen 1. *vt* scrape off **2.** *vi fam* (*die*) kick the bucket, croak

abkühlen *vi, vr, vt* cool down

abkürzen *vt* (*word*) abbreviate; **den Weg ~** take a short cut; **Abkürzung** *f* (*of word*) abbreviation; (*path*) short cut

abladen *irr vt* unload

Ablage *f* (*for documents*) tray; (*for whole office*) filing system

Ablauf *m* drain; (*of events*) course; (*of deadline*) expiry; **ablaufen** *irr vi* (*liquid*) drain away; (*events*) happen; (*deadline, passport*) expire

ablegen 1. *vt* put down; (*clothes*) take off; (*habit*) get out of; (*exam*) take, sit; (*documents*) file away **2.** *vi* (*ship*) cast off

ablehnen 1. *vt* reject; (*invitation*) decline; (*be against*) disapprove of; (*applicant*) turn down **2.** *vi* decline

ablenken *vt* distract; **jdn von der Arbeit ~** distract sb from their work; **vom Thema ~** change the subject; **Ablenkung** *f* distraction

ablesen *vt* (*text, speech*) read; **das Gas/den Strom ~** read the gas/electricity meter

abliefern *vt* deliver

abmachen *vt* take off; (*date, price etc*) agree; **Abmachung** *f* agreement

abmelden 1. *vt* (*newspaper*) cancel; (*car*) take off the road **2.** *vr* give notice of one's departure; (*from hotel*) check out; (*member*) cancel one's membership

abmessen *irr vt* measure

abnehmen *irr vt* **1.** *vt* take off, remove; (*receiver*) pick up; (*driving licence*) take away; (*money*) get (*jdm etw* sb); (*purchase, fam:* believe) buy (*jdm from sb*) **2.** *vi* decrease; (*slim*) lose weight; TEL pick up the phone; **fünf Kilo ~** lose five kilos

Abneigung *f* dislike (*gegen* of); (*stronger*) aversion (*gegen* to)

abnutzen *vt, vr* wear out

Abonnement *nt* (-s, -s) subscription; **Abonnent(in)** *m(f)* subscriber; **abonnieren** *vt* subscribe to

abraten *irr vi* **jdm von etw ~** advise sb against sth

abräumen *vt* **den Tisch ~** clear the table; **das Ge-**

schirr ~ clear away the dishes; (*prize etc*) walk off with

Abrechnung *f* settlement; (*invoice*) calm

abregen *vr fam* calm (*or* cool) down; ***reg dich ab!*** take it easy

Abreise *f* departure; **abreisen** *vi* leave (*nach* for)

abreißen *irr* **1.** *vt* (*house*) pull down; (*sheet of paper*) tear off; ***den Kontakt nicht ~ lassen*** stay in touch **2.** *vi* (*button etc*) come off

abrunden *vt* **eine Zahl nach oben/unten ~** round a number up/down

abrupt *adj* abrupt

ABS *nt abbr* = **Antiblockiersystem**; AUTO ABS

Abs. *abbr* = **Absender**; from

absagen 1. *vt* cancel, call off; (*invitation*) turn down **2.** *vi* decline; **ich muss leider ~** I'm afraid I can't come

Absatz *m* COMM sales *pl*; (*in text*) paragraph; (*of shoe*) heel

abschaffen *vt* abolish, do away with

abschalten *vt, vi a. fig* switch off

abschätzen *vt* estimate; (*situation*) assess; **jdn ~** size sb up

abscheulich *adj* disgusting

abschicken *vt* send off

abschieben *irr vt* (*asylum seeker etc*) deport

Abschied *m* (*-(e)s, -e*) parting;

~ **nehmen** say good-bye (*von jdm* to sb); **Abschiedsfeier** *f* farewell party

Abschlagszahlung *f* interim payment

Abschleppdienst *m* AUTO breakdown service; **abschleppen** *vt* tow; **Abschleppseil** *nt* towrope; **Abschleppwagen** *m* breakdown truck (*Brit*), tow truck (*US*)

abschließen *irr vt* (*door*) lock; (*bring to an end*) conclude, finish; (*agreement, deal*) conclude; **Abschluss** *m* close, conclusion; (*of agreement, deal*) conclusion

abschmecken *vt* (*sample*) taste; (*with salt etc*) season

abschminken 1. *vr* take one's make-up off **2.** *vt fam sich dat etw* ~ get sth out of one's mind

abschnallen *vr* undo one's seatbelt

abschneiden *irr* **1.** *vt* cut off **2.** *vi* **gut/schlecht** ~ do well/badly

Abschnitt *m* (*of book, text*) section; (*of cheque, ticket*) stub

abschrauben *vt* unscrew

abschrecken *vt* deter, put off

abschreiben *irr vt* copy (*bei, von* from, off); (*give up on*) write off; COMM deduct

abschüssig *adj* steep

abschwächen *vt* lessen; (*statement, criticism*) tone

down

abschwellen *irr vi* (*inflammation*) go down; (*noise*) die down

absehbar *adj* foreseeable; **in ~er Zeit** in the foreseeable future; (*end, consequences*) foresee **2.** *vi* **von etw ~** refrain from sth

abseits 1. *adv* out of the way; SPORT offside **2.** *prep + gen* away from; **Abseits** *nt* SPORT offside; **Abseitsfalle** *f* SPORT offside trap

absenden *irr vt* send off; (*letter etc*) post; **Absender(in)** *m(f)* (*-s, -*) sender

absetzen *vt* (*glass, spectacles etc*) put down; (*passenger etc*) drop (off); COMM sell; FIN deduct; (*cancel*) drop **2.** *vr* (*leave*) clear off; (*mud etc*) be deposited

Absicht *f* intention; **mit ~** on purpose; **absichtlich** *adj* intentional, deliberate

absolut *adj* absolute

abspecken *vi fam* lose weight

abspeichern *vt* IT save

absperren *vt* block (*or close*) off; (*door*) lock; **Absperrung** *f* blocking (*or closing*) off; (*obstacle*) barricade

abspielen 1. *vt* (*CD etc*) play **2.** *vr* happen

abspringen *irr vi* jump down/off; (*participant*) drop out (*von of*)

abspülen *vt* rinse; (*dishes*)

wash (up)

Abstand *m* distance; (*time gap*) interval; **~ halten** keep one's distance

abstauben *vt, vi* dust; *fam* (*steal*) pinch

Abstecher *m* (*-s, -*) detour

absteigen *irr vi* (*from bicycle etc*) get off, dismount; (*at hotel*) stay in store

abstellen *vt* (*bag, tray etc*) put down; (*car*) park; (*light, machine etc*) turn (*or switch*) off; (*bad practice etc*) stop; **Abstellraum** *m* store room

Abstieg *m* (*-(e)s, -e*) (*from mountain*) descent; SPORT relegation

abstimmen 1. *vi* vote **2.** *vt* (*aims, dates*) fit in (*auf + acc* with); **Dinge aufeinander~** coordinate things **3.** *vr* come to an agreement (*or arrangement*)

abstoßend *adj* repulsive

abstrakt *adj* abstract

abstreiten *irr vt* deny

Abstrich *m* MED smear; **~e machen** cut back (*auf + dat* on); (*expect less*) lower one's sights

Absturz *m* fall; AVIAT, IT crash; **abstürzen** *vi* fall; AVIAT, IT crash

absurd *adj* absurd

Abszess *m* (*-es, -e*) abscess

abtauen *vt, vi* thaw; (*fridge*) defrost

Abtei *f* (*-, -en*) abbey

Abteil *nt* (*-(e)s, -e*) compartment

Abteilung f (in firm, department store) department; (in hospital) section

abtreiben irr **1.** vt (child) abort **2.** vi be driven off course; MED carry out an abortion; (pregnant woman) have an abortion; **Abtreibung** f abortion

abtrocknen vt dry

abwarten 1. vt wait for; **das bleibt abzuwarten** that remains to be seen **2.** vi wait

abwärts adv down

Abwasch m (-(e)s) washing-up; **abwaschen** irr vt (dirt) wash off; (dishes) wash (up)

Abwasser nt (-s, Abwässer) sewage

abwechseln vr alternate; **sich mit jdm ~** take turns with sb; **abwechselnd** adv alternately; **Abwechslung** f change; **zur ~** for a change

abweisen irr vt turn away; (application) turn down; **abweisend** adj unfriendly

abwesend adj absent; **Abwesenheit** f absence

abwiegen irr vt weigh (out)

abwischen vt (face, table etc) wipe; (dirt) wipe off

abzählen vt count; (money) count out

Abzeichen nt badge

abzeichnen 1. vt draw, copy; (document) initial **2.** vr stand out; fig (be imminent) loom

abziehen irr **1.** vt take off;

(bed) strip; (key) take out; (number, amount) take away, subtract **2.** vi go away

Abzug m (photo) print; (opening) vent; (of troops) withdrawal; (of amount) deduction; **nach ~ der Kosten** charges deducted; **abzüglich** prep + gen minus; **~ 20% Rabatt** less 20% discount

abzweigen 1. vi branch off **2.** vt set aside; **Abzweigung** f junction

Accessoires pl accessories pl

ach interj oh; **~ so!** oh, I see; **~ was!** (surprised) really?; (annoyed) don't talk nonsense

Achse f (-, -n) axis; AUTO axle

Achsel f (-, -n) shoulder; armpit

acht num eight; **heute in ~ Tagen** in a week('s time), a week from today

Acht f (-) **sich in ~ nehmen** be careful (vor + dat of), watch out (vor + dat for); **~ geben** take care (auf + acc of); **etw außer ~ lassen** disregard sth

achte(r, s) adj eighth; → **dritte**; **Achtel** nt (-s, -) (fraction) eighth; (liquid measure) eighth of a litre; (glass of wine) ≈ small glass

achten 1. vt respect **2.** vi pay attention (auf + acc to)

Achterbahn f big dipper, roller coaster

achthundert num eight hundred; **achtmal** adv eight

times

Achtung 1. f attention; (esteem) respect **2.** interj look out

achtzehn num eighteen; **achtzehnte(r, s)** adj eighteenth; → **dritte**; **achtzig** num eighty; **in den ~er Jahren** in the eighties; **achtzigste(r, s)** adj eightieth

Acker m (-s, Äcker) field

Action f (-, -s) fam action; **Actionfilm** m action film

Adapter m (-s, -) adapter

addieren vt add (up)

Adel m (-s) nobility; **adelig** adj noble

Ader f (-, -n) vein

Adjektiv nt (-s) adjective

Adler m (-s, -) eagle

adoptieren vt adopt; **Adoption** f (-, -en) adoption; **Adoptiveltern** pl adoptive parents pl; **Adoptivkind** nt adopted child

Adrenalin nt (-s) adrenalin

Adressbuch nt (-s) directory; (personal) address book; **Adresse** f (-, -n) address; **adressieren** vt address (an + acc to)

Advent m (-s, -) Advent; **Adventskranz** m Advent wreath

Adverb nt (-s) adverb

Aerobic nt (-s) aerobics sg

Affäre f (-, -n) affair

Affe m (-n, -n) monkey

Afghanistan nt (-s) Afghanistan

Afrika nt (-s) Africa; **Afrikaner(in)** m(f) (-s, -) African; **afrikanisch** adj African

After m (-s, -) anus

Aftershave nt (-(s), -s) aftershave

AG f (-, -s) abbr = **Aktiengesellschaft**; plc (Brit), corp. (US)

Agent(in) m(f) agent; **Agentur** f agency

aggressiv adj aggressive

Ägypten nt (-s) Egypt

ah interj ah, ooh

äh interj er, um; (disgusted) ugh

aha interj I see, aha

ähneln 1. vi + dat be like, resemble **2.** vr be alike (or similar)

ahnen vt suspect; **du ahnst es nicht!** would you believe it?

ähnlich adj similar (dat to); **jdm ~ sehen** be like sb; **Ähnlichkeit** f similarity

Ahnung f idea; (vague) suspicion; **keine ~!** no idea; **ahnungslos** adj unsuspecting

Ahorn m (-s, -e) maple

Aids nt (-) Aids; **aidskrank** adj suffering from Aids; **aidspositiv** adj tested positive for Aids; **Aidstest** m Aids test

Airbag m (-s, -s) AUTO airbag; **Airbus** m airbus

Akademie f (-, -n) academy; **Akademiker(in)** m(f) (-s, -) (university) graduate

akklimatisieren vr acclimatize oneself

Akkordeon nt (-s, -s) accordion

Akku m (-s, -s) (storage) battery

Akkusativ m accusative (case)

Akne f (-, -) acne

Akrobat(in) m(f) (-s, -en) acrobat

Akt m (-(e)s, -e) act; ART nude

Akte f (-, -n) file; **etw zu den ~n legen** a. fig file sth away; **Aktenkoffer** m briefcase

Aktie f (-, -n) share; **Aktiengesellschaft** f public limited company (Brit), corporation (US)

Aktion f campaign; (military, police) operation

Aktionär(in) m(f) (-s, -e) shareholder

aktiv adj active

aktualisieren vt update; **aktuell** adj (subject) topical; (modern) up-to-date; (problem) current; **nicht mehr ~** no longer relevant

Akupunktur f acupuncture

akustisch adj acoustic; **Akustik** f acoustics sg

akut adj acute

AKW nt (-s, -s) abbr = **Atomkraftwerk**, nuclear power station

Akzent m (-(e)s, -e) accent; (emphasis) stress; **mit starkem schottischen ~** with a strong Scottish accent

akzeptieren vt accept

Alarm m (-(e)s, -e) alarm; **Alarmanlage** f alarm system; **alarmieren** vt alarm; **die Polizei ~** call the police

Albanien nt (-s) Albania

Albatros m (-ses, -se) albatross

albern adj silly

Albtraum m nightmare

Album nt (-s, **Alben**) album

Algen pl algae pl, seaweed sg

Algerien nt (-s) Algeria

Alibi nt (-s, -s) alibi

Alimente pl maintenance sg

Alkohol m (-s, -e) alcohol; **alkoholfrei** adj non-alcoholic; **~es Getränk** soft drink; **Alkoholiker(in)** m(f) (-s, -) alcoholic; **alkoholisch** adj alcoholic

All nt (-s) universe

alle(r, s) **1.** pron all; **~ Passagiere** all passengers; **wir ~** all of us; **~ beide** both of us/you/them; **~ vier Jahre** every four years; **~ 100 Meter** every 100 metres; → **alles** **2.** adv fam finished

Allee f (-, -n) avenue

allein adj, adv alone; (unaided) on one's own, by oneself; **nicht ~** not only; **~ erziehende Mutter** single mother; **~ stehend** single, unmarried; **Alleinerziehende(r)** mf single mother/father/parent

allerbeste(r, s) adj very best

allerdings adv admittedly; (definitely) certainly, sure

(US)

allererste(r, s) *adj* very first; **zu allererst** first of all

Allergie *f* allergy; **Allergiker(in)** *m(f)* (*-s, -*) allergy sufferer; **allergisch** *adj* allergic (*gegen* to)

allerhand *adj inv fam* all sorts of; **das ist doch~!**(*reproaching*) that's the limit; **~!**(*praising*) that's pretty good

Allerheiligen *nt* (*-*) All Saints' Day

allerhöchste(r, s) *adj* very highest; **allerhöchstens** *adv* at the very most; **allerlei** *adj inv* all sorts of; **allerletzte(r, s)** *adj* very last; **allerwenigste(r, s)** *adj* very least

alles *pron* everything; **~ in allem** all in all; → **alle**

Alleskleber *m* (*-s, -*) all-purpose glue

allgemein *adj* general; **im Allgemeinen** in general

Alligator *m* (*-s, -en*) alligator

alljährlich *adj* annual

allmählich 1. *adj* gradual **2.** *adv* gradually

Allradantrieb *m* all-wheel drive

Alltag *m* everyday life; **alltäglich** *adj* everyday; (*average*) ordinary; (*life, walk etc*) daily

allzu *adv* all too

Allzweckreiniger *m* (*-s, -*) multi-purpose cleaner

Alpen *pl* **die ~** the Alps *pl*

Alphabet *nt* (*-(e)s, -e*) alphabet; **alphabetisch** *adj* alphabetical

Alptraum *m* → **Albtraum**

als *conj* (*comparison*) than; (*time*) when; **das Zimmer ist größer ~ das andere** this room is bigger than the other; **das Essen war billiger ~ ich erwartet hatte** the meal was cheaper than I expected (it to be); **~ Kind** as a child; **nichts ~ (Ärger)** nothing but (trouble); **anders ~** different from; **erst ~** only when; **~ ob** as if

also 1. *conj* so, therefore **2.** *adv, interj* so; **~ gut** (or **schön**)! okay then

alt *adj* old; **wie ~ sind Sie?** how old are you?; **28 Jahre ~** 28 years old; **vier Jahre älter** four years older

Altar *m* (*-(e)s, Altäre*) altar

Alter *nt* (*-s, -*) age; (*last period of life*) old age; **im ~ von** at the age of; **er ist in meinem ~** he's my age

alternativ *adj* alternative; (*concerned for the environment*) ecologically minded; (*farming*) organic; **Alternative** *f* alternative

Altersheim *nt* old people's home

Altglas *nt* used glass; **Altglascontainer** *m* bottle bank; **altmodisch** *adj* old-fashioned; **Altöl** *nt* used (or waste) oil; **Altpapier** *nt* waste paper; **Altstadt** *f* old town

Alt-Taste f Alt key

Alufolie f tin (or kitchen) foil

Aluminium nt (-s) aluminium (Brit), aluminum (US)

Alzheimerkrankheit f Alzheimer's (disease)

am contr of **an dem**; ~ **2. Januar** on January 2(nd); ~ **Morgen** in the morning; ~ **Strand** on the beach; ~ **Bahnhof** at the station; **was gefällt Ihnen ~ besten?** what do you like best?; ~ **besten bleiben wir hier** it would be best if we stayed here

Amateur(in) m(f) amateur

ambulant adj outpatient; **kann ich ~ behandelt werden?** can I have it done as an outpatient?; **Ambulanz** f (-, -en) ambulance; (in hospital) outpatients' department

Ameise f (-, -n) ant

amen interj amen

Amerika nt (-s) America; **Amerikaner(in)** m(f) (-s, -) American; **amerikanisch** adj American

Ampel f (-, -n) traffic lights pl

Amphitheater nt amphitheatre

Amsel f (-, -n) blackbird

Amt nt (-(e)s, Ämter) (governmental agency) office, department; (position) post; **amtlich** adj official; **Amtszeichen** nt TEL dialling tone (Brit), dial tone (US)

amüsant adj amusing; **amü-**

sieren 1. vt amuse **2.** vr enjoy oneself, have a good time

an 1. prep + dat ~ **der Wand** on the wall; ~ **der Themse** on the Thames; **alles ist ~ seinem Platz** everything is in its place; ~ **einem kalten Tag** on a cold day; ~ **Ostern** at Easter **2.** prep + acc ~ **die Tür klopfen** knock at the door; **ans Meer fahren** go to the seaside; ~ **die 40 Grad** nearly 40 degrees **3.** adv **von** ... ~ **from** ... on; **das Licht/Radio ist** ~ the light/radio is on

anal adj anal

analog adj analogous; IT analog

Analyse f (-, -n) analysis; **analysieren** vt analyse

Ananas f (-, - or -se) pineapple

anbaggern vt fam chat up (Brit), come on to (US)

Anbau m AGR cultivation; (building) extension; **anbauen** vt AGR cultivate; (garage etc) build on

anbehalten irr vt keep on

anbei adv enclosed; ~ **sende ich ...** please find enclosed ...

anbeten vt worship

anbieten irr **1.** vt offer **2.** vr volunteer

anbinden irr vt tie up

Anblick m sight

anbraten irr vt brown

anbrechen irr **1.** vt start; (reserves, savings) break into;

(bottle, packet) open **2.** vi start; *(day)* break; *(night)* fall

anbrennen irr vt, vi burn; **das Fleisch schmeckt angebrannt** the meat tastes burnt

anbringen irr vt *(along with one)* bring; *(fasten)* fix, attach

Andacht f (-, -en) devotion; *(church service)* prayers pl

andauern vi continue, go on; **andauernd** adj continual

Andenken nt (-s, -) memory; *(object)* souvenir

andere(r, s) adj other; *(not the same)* different; *(following)* next; **am ~n Tag** the next day; **von etw/jmd ~m sprechen** talk about sth/sb else; **unter ~m** among other things; **andererseits** adv on the other hand

ändern 1. vt alter, change **2.** vr change

andernfalls adv otherwise

anders adv differently *(als from)*; **jemand/irgendwo ~** someone/somewhere else; **sie ist ~ als ihre Schwester** she's not like her sister; **es geht nicht ~** there's no other way; **anders(he)rum** adv the other way round; **anderswo** adv somewhere else

anderthalb num one and a half

Änderung f change, alteration

andeuten vt indicate; *(indirectly)* hint at

Andorra nt (-s) Andorra

Andrang m **es herrschte großer Ber~** there was a huge crowd

androhen vt jdm etw ~ threaten sb with sth

aneinander adv at/on/to one another *(or* each other*)*; **~ denken** think of each other; **~ geraten** clash; **sich ~ gewöhnen** get used to each other; **~ legen** put together

Anemone f (-, -n) anemone

anerkennen irr vt *(country, certificate etc)* recognize; *(efforts etc)* appreciate; **Anerkennung** f recognition; *(of efforts etc)* appreciation

anfahren irr **1.** vt *(pedestrian)* run into; *(place, port)* stop *(or* call*)* at; *(goods)* deliver; **jdn ~** fig *(verbally)* jump on sb **2.** vi start; *(in car)* drive off

Anfall m MED attack; **anfällig** adj delicate; *(machine)* temperamental; **~ für** prone to

Anfang m (-(e)s, Anfänge) beginning, start; **zu/am ~** to start with; **~ Mai** at the beginning of May; **sie ist ~ 20** she's in her early twenties; **anfangen** irr vt, vi begin, start; **damit kann ich nichts ~** that's no use to me; **Anfänger(in)** m(f) (-s, -) beginner; **anfangs** adv at first; **Anfangsbuchstabe** m first *(or* initial*)* letter

anfassen 1. vt touch **2.** vi **kannst du mal mit ~?** can you give me a hand? **3.** vr **sich weich ~** feel soft

Anflug m AVIAT approach; (small amount) trace

anfordern vt demand; **Anforderung** f request (von for); (on sb or sth) demand

Anfrage f inquiry

anfreunden vr **sich mit jdm ~** make (or become) friends with sb

anfühlen vr feel; **es fühlt sich gut an** it feels good

Anführungszeichen pl quotation marks pl

Angabe f TECH specification; fam (swanking) showing off; (in tennis) serve; **~n** pl (information) particulars pl; **die ~n waren falsch** the information was wrong; angeben irr **1.** vt (name, reason) give; (temperature, time etc) indicate; (course, pace) set **2.** vi fam boast; SPORT serve; **Angeber(in)** m(f) ⟨-s, -⟩ fam show-off; **angeblich** adj alleged

angeboren adj inborn

Angebot nt offer; COMM supply (an + dat of); **~ und Nachfrage** supply and demand

angebracht adj appropriate

angebunden adj **kurz ~** curt

angeheitert adj tipsy

angehen irr **1.** vt concern; **das geht dich nichts an** that's none of your business; **ein Problem ~** tackle a problem;

was ihn angeht as far as he's concerned, as for him **2.** vi (fire) catch; fam (start) begin; **angehend** adj prospective

Angehörige(r) mf relative

Angeklagte(r) mf accused, defendant

Angel f ⟨-, -n⟩ fishing rod; (of door) hinge

Angelegenheit f affair, matter

Angelhaken m fish hook; **angeln 1.** vt catch **2.** vi fish; **Angeln** nt ⟨-s⟩ angling; fishing; **Angelrute** f ⟨-, -n⟩ fishing rod

angemessen adj appropriate, suitable

angenehm adj pleasant; **~!** pleased to meet you; **das ist mir gar nicht ~** I don't like the idea of that

angenommen 1. adj assumed **2.** conj **~, es regnet, was machen wir dann?** suppose it rains, what do we do then?

angesehen adj respected

angesichts prep + gen in view of, considering

Angestellte(r) mf employee

angetan adj **von jdm/etw ~ sein** be impressed by (or taken with) sb/sth

angewiesen adj **auf jdn/etw ~ sein** be dependent on sb/sth

angewöhnen vt **sich etw ~** get used to doing sth; **Angewohnheit** f habit

Angina f (-, Anginen) tonsillitis; **Angina Pectoris** f (-) angina

Angler(in) m(f) (-s, -) angler

Angora nt (-s) angora

angreifen irr vt attack; (with hand) touch; (harm) damage; **Angriff** m attack; **etw in ~ nehmen** get started on sth

Angst f (-, Ängste) fear; **~ haben** be afraid (or scared) (vor + dat of); **jdm ~ machen** scare sb; **ängstigen 1.** vt frighten **2.** vr worry (um, wegen + dat about); **ängstlich** adj nervous; (anxious) worried

anhaben irr vt (clothes) have on, wear; (light) have on

anhalten irr vi stop; (carry on) continue; **anhaltend** adj continuous; **Anhalter(in)** m(f) (-s, -) hitch-hiker; **per ~ fahren** hitch-hike

anhand prep + gen with; **~ von** by means of

anhängen vt hang up; RAIL (carriages) couple; (something extra) add (on); **jdm etw ~ fam** (blame) pin sth on sb; **Anhänger** m (-s, -) AUTO trailer; (on suitcase) tag; (jewellery) pendant; **Anhänger(in)** m(f) (-s, -) supporter; **Anhängerkupplung** f towbar; **anhänglich** adj affectionate; pej clinging

Anhieb m **auf ~** straight away; **das kann ich nicht auf ~ sa-**

gen I can't say offhand

anhimmeln vt worship, idolize

anhören 1. vt listen to **2.** vr sound; **das hört sich gut an** that sounds good

Animateur(in) m(f) host/hostess

Anis m (-es, -e) aniseed

Anker m (-s, -) anchor; **ankern** vt, vi anchor; **Ankerplatz** m anchorage

Ankleidekabine f changing cubicle

anklicken vt IT click on

anklopfen vi knock (an + acc on)

ankommen irr vi arrive; **bei jdm gut ~** go down well with sb; **es kommt darauf an** it depends (ob on whether); **darauf kommt es nicht an** that doesn't matter

ankotzen vt vulg **es kotzt mich an** it makes me sick

ankreuzen vt mark with a cross

ankündigen vt announce

Ankunft f (-, Ankünfte) arrival; **Ankunftszeit** f arrival time

Anlage f (tendency) disposition; (aptitude) talent; (park) gardens pl, grounds pl; (in letter etc) enclosure; (for CDs etc) stereo (system); TECH plant; FIN investment

Anlass m (-es, Anlässe) cause (zu for); (event) occasion; **aus diesem ~** for this reason; **anlassen** *irr vt (engine)* start; *(light, garment)* leave on; **Anlasser** *m (-s, -)* AUTO starter; **anlässlich** *prep + gen* on the occasion of

Anlauf *m* run-up; **anlaufen** *irr vi* begin; *(film)* open; *(window)* mist up; *(metal)* tarnish

anlegen 1. *vt* put *(an + acc against / on)*; *(jewellery)* put on; *(garden)* lay out; *(money)* invest; *(gun)* aim *(auf + acc* at); **es auf etw** *acc ~* be out for sth **2.** *vi (ship)* berth, dock **3.** *vr* **sich mit jdm ~** *fam* pick a quarrel with sb; **Anlegestelle** *f* moorings *pl*

anlehnen 1. *vt* lean *(an + acc* against); *(door)* leave ajar **2.** *vr* lean *(an + acc* against)

anleiern *vt* **etw ~** *fam* get sth going

Anleitung *f* instructions *pl*

Anliegen *nt (-s, -)* matter; *(question)* request

Anlieger(in) *m(f) (-s, -)* resident; **~ frei** residents only

anlügen *irr vt* lie to

anmachen *vt (fasten)* attach; *(light, TV etc)* switch on; *(salad)* dress; *fam (excite)* turn on; *fam (talk to)* chat up *(Brit)*, come on to *(US)*; *fam (attack verbally)* have a go at

Anmeldeformular *nt* application form; *(for registering with the authorities)* registration form; **anmelden 1.** *vt*

(visit etc) announce **2.** *vr (with doctor etc)* make an appointment; *(with the authorities, for course etc)* register; **Anmeldeschluss** *m* deadline for applications, registration deadline; **Anmeldung** *f* registration; *(request)* application

annähen *vt* **einen Knopf (an den Mantel) ~** sew a button on (one's coat)

annähernd *adv* roughly; **nicht ~** nowhere near

Annahme *f (-, -n)* acceptance; *(supposition)* assumption; **annehmbar** *adj* acceptable; **annehmen** *irr vt* accept; *(name)* take; *(child)* adopt; *(take as true)* suppose, assume

Annonce *f (-, -n)* advertisement

anöden *vt fam* bore stiff *(or* silly*)*

annullieren *vt* cancel

anonym *adj* anonymous

Anorak *m (-s, -s)* anorak

anpacken *vt (problem, task)* tackle; **mit ~** lend a hand

anpassen 1. *vt fig* adapt *(dat* to) **2.** *vr* adapt *(an + acc* to)

anpfeifen *irr vt* **das Spiel ~** start the game; **Anpfiff** *m* SPORT *(starting)* whistle; *(start)* kick-off; *fam (reprimand)* roasting

anprobieren *vt* try on

Anrede *f* form of address

anreden *vt* address

anregen vt stimulate; Anregung f stimulation; (idea) suggestion

Anreise f journey; **der Tag der ~** the day of arrival; anreisen vi arrive

Anreiz m incentive

anrichten vt (food) prepare; (damage) cause

Anruf m call; Anrufbeantworter m (-s, -) answering machine, answerphone; anrufen irr vt TEL call, phone, ring (Brit)

ans contr of **an das**

Ansage f announcement; (on answerphone) recorded message; ansagen 1. vt announce; **angesagt sein** be recommended; (fashionable) be the thing; **Spannung ist angesagt** we are in for some excitement 2. vr **er sagte sich an** he said he would come

anschaffen vt buy

anschauen vt look at

Anschein m appearance; **dem** (or **allem**) **~ nach** ... it looks as if ...; **den ~ erwecken, hart zu arbeiten** give the impression of working hard; anscheinend 1. adj apparent 2. adv apparently

anschieben irr vt **könnten Sie mir mal ~?** AUTO could you give me a push?

Anschlag m notice; (on sb or sth) attack; anschlagen irr 1. vt (poster) put up; (damage)

chip 2. vi (medicine etc) take effect; **mit etw an etw acc ~** bang sth against sth

anschließen irr 1. vt ELEC, TECH connect (an + acc to); (into socket) plug in 2. vi, vr (**sich**) **an etw acc ~** (building etc) adjoin sth; (happen after) follow sth 3. vr join (jdm/einer Gruppe sb/a group); anschließend 1. adj adjacent; (happening afterwards) subsequent 2. adv afterwards; **~ an** + acc following; Anschluss m ELEC, RAIL connection; (of water, gas etc) supply; **im ~ an** + acc following; **kein ~ unter dieser Nummer** TEL the number you have dialled has not been recognized; Anschlussflug m connecting flight

anschnallen 1. vt (skis) put on 2. vr fasten one's seat belt

Anschrift f address

anschwellen irr vi swell (up)

ansehen irr vt look at; (while sth happens) watch; **jdn/etw als etw ~** look on sb/sth as sth; **das sieht man ihm an** he looks it

an sein irr vi → **an**

ansetzen 1. vt (date) fix; (food) prepare 2. vi start, begin; **zu etw ~** prepare to do sth

Ansicht f view, opinion; (act of seeing) sight; **meiner ~ nach** in my opinion; **zur ~**

on approval; **Ansichtskarte** f postcard

ansonsten adv otherwise

Anspiel nt SPORT start of play; **anspielen** vi **auf etw acc ~** allude to sth; **Anspielung** f allusion (auf + acc to)

ansprechen irr **1.** vt speak to; (interest) appeal to **2.** vi **auf etw** acc ~ (patient) respond to sth; **ansprechend** adj attractive; **Ansprechpartner(in)** m(f) contact

anspringen irr vi AUTO start

Anspruch m claim; (entitlement) right (auf + acc to); **etw in ~ nehmen** take advantage of sth; **~ auf etw haben** be entitled to sth; **anspruchslos** adj undemanding; (life, accommodation etc) modest; **anspruchsvoll** adj demanding

Anstalt f (-, -en) institution

Anstand m decency; **anständig** adj decent; fig fam proper; (large) considerable

anstarren vt stare at

anstatt prep + gen instead of

anstecken 1. vt pin on; MED infect; **jdn mit einer Erkältung ~** pass one's cold on to sb **2.** vr **ich habe mich bei ihm angesteckt** I caught it from him **3.** vi fig be infectious; **ansteckend** adj infectious; **Ansteckungsgefahr** f danger of infection

anstehen irr vi queue (Brit), stand in line (US); (task

etc) be on the agenda

anstelle prep + gen instead of

anstellen 1. vt (radio, heating etc) turn on; (worker) employ; (undertake) do; **was hast du wieder angestellt?** what have you been up to now? **2.** vr queue (Brit), stand in line (US); fam **stell dich nicht so an!** stop making such a fuss

Anstoß m impetus; SPORT kick-off; **anstoßen** irr **1.** vt push; (with foot) kick **2.** vi knock, bump; (chink glasses) drink (a toast) (auf + acc to); **anstößig** adj offensive; (clothes etc) indecent

anstrengen 1. vt strain **2.** vr make an effort; **anstrengend** adj tiring

Antarktis f Antarctic

Anteil m share (an + dat in); **~ nehmen an** + dat sympathize with; take an interest in

Antenne f (-, -n) aerial

Antibabypille f **die ~** the pill; **Antibiotikum** nt (-s, Antibiotika) MED antibiotic

antik adj antique

Antilope f (-, -n) antelope

Antiquariat nt second-hand bookshop

Antiquitäten pl antiques pl; **Antiquitätenhändler(in)** m(f) antique dealer

antörnen vt fam turn on

Antrag m (-(e)s, Anträge) proposal; POL motion; (document) application form; **ei-**

nen ~ stellen auf + acc make
an application for
antreffen *irr vt* find
antreiben *irr vt* TECH drive;
(onto shore) wash up; *jdn
zur Arbeit ~* make sb work
antreten *irr vt eine Reise ~*
set off on a journey
Antrieb *m* TECH drive; *(motivation)* impetus
antun *irr vt jdm etwas ~* do
sth to sb; *sich dat etwas ~*
(commit suicide) kill oneself
Antwort *f* (-, -en) answer, reply; *um ~ wird gebeten*
RSVP *(répondez s'il vous
plaît)*; **antworten** *vi* answer,
reply; *jdm ~* answer sb; *auf
etw acc ~* answer sth
anvertrauen *vt jdm etw ~* entrust sb with sth
Anwalt *m* (-s, *Anwälte*), **Anwältin** *f* lawyer
anweisen *irr vt* instruct; *(flat,
job etc)* allocate *(jdm etw sth
to sb)*; **Anweisung** *f* instruction; *(for making payment)*
money order
anwenden *irr vt* use; *(law, rule)* apply; **Anwender(in)**
m(f) (-s, -) user; **Anwendung** *f* use; IT application
anwesend *adj* present; **Anwesenheit** *f* presence
anwidern *vt* disgust
Anwohner(in) *m(f)* (-s, -) resident
Anzahl *f* number *(an + dat* of); **anzahlen** *vt* pay a deposit
on; *100 Euro ~* pay 100 euros

as a deposit; **Anzahlung** *f*
deposit
Anzeichen *nt* sign; MED symptom
Anzeige *f* (-, -n) *(in newspaper)* advertisement; *(electronic)* display; *(made to the police)* report; **anzeigen** *vt*
(temperature, time) indicate,
show; *(electronically)* display; *(make known)* announce; *jdn/einen Autodiebstahl bei der Polizei ~*
report sb/a stolen car to
the police
anziehen *irr* **1.** *vt* attract;
(clothes) put on; *(screw, rope)* tighten **2.** *vr* get dressed;
anziehend *adj* attractive
Anzug *m* suit
anzüglich *adj* suggestive
anzünden *vt* light; *(house etc)*
set fire to
anzweifeln *vt* doubt
Aperitif *m* (-s, -s *(or* -e)*)* aperitif
Apfel *m* (-s, *Äpfel)* apple; **Apfelbaum** *m* apple tree; **Apfelkuchen** *m* apple cake; **Apfelmus** *nt* apple purée; **Apfelsaft** *m* apple juice; **Apfelsine** *f* orange; **Apfelwein** *m* cider
Apostroph *m* (-s, -e) apostrophe
Apotheke *f* (-, -n) chemist's
(shop) *(Brit)*, pharmacy
(US); **apothekenpflichtig**
adj only available at the
chemist's *(or* pharmacy)
Apotheker(in) *m(f)* (-s, -)

chemist (*Brit*), pharmacist (*US*)

Apparat *m* (-(*e*)*s*, -*e*) (piece of) apparatus; TEL telephone; RADIO, TV set; **am ~!** TEL speaking; **am ~ bleiben** TEL hold the line

Appartement *nt* (-*s*, -*s*) studio flat (*Brit*) (*or* apartment (*US*))

Appetit *m* (-(*e*)*s*, -*e*) appetite; **guten ~!** bon appétit

appetitlich *adj* appetizing

Applaus *m* (-*es*, -*e*) applause

Aprikose *f* (-, -*n*) apricot

April *m* (-(*s*), -*e*) April; → **Juni ~**, **~!** April fool!; **Aprilscherz** *m* (-*es*, -*e*) April fool's joke

apropos *adv* by the way; **~ Urlaub ...** while we're on the subject of holidays ...

Aquaplaning *nt* (-(*s*)) aquaplaning

Aquarell *nt* (-*s*, -*e*) watercolour

Aquarium *nt* aquarium

Äquator *m* equator

Araber(in) *m*(*f*) (-*s*, -) Arab; **arabisch** *adj* Arab; (*numeral*, *language*) Arabic; (*Sea*, *Desert*) Arabian

Arbeit *f* (-, -*en*) work; (*post*) job; (*product*) piece of work; **arbeiten** *vi* work; **Arbeiter(in)** *m*(*f*) (-*s*, -) worker; (*unskilled*) labourer; **Arbeitgeber(in)** *m*(*f*) (-*s*, -) employer; **Arbeitnehmer(in)** *m*(*f*) (-*s*, -) employee; **Arbeitsamt** *nt* job centre (*Brit*),

employment office (*US*); **Arbeitserlaubnis** *f* work permit; **arbeitslos** *adj* unemployed; **Arbeitslose(r)** *mf* unemployed person; **die ~n** *pl* the unemployed *pl*; **Arbeitslosengeld** *nt* (income--related) unemployment benefit, job-seeker's allowance (*Brit*); **Arbeitslosenhilfe** *f* (non-income related) unemployment benefit; **Arbeitslosigkeit** *f* unemployment; **Arbeitsplatz** *m* job; (*place*) workplace; **Arbeitsspeicher** *m* IT main memory; **Arbeitszeit** *f* working hours *pl*; **gleitende ~** flexible working hours *pl*, flexitime; **Arbeitszimmer** *nt* study

Archäologe *m* (-*n*, -*n*), **Archäologin** *f* archaeologist

Architekt(in) *m*(*f*) (-*en*, -*en*) architect; **Architektur** *f* architecture

Archiv *nt* (-*s*, -*e*) archives *pl*

arg **1.** *adj* bad; (*unpleasant*, *intense*) awful **2.** *adv* (*very*) terribly

Argentinien *nt* (-*s*) Argentina

Ärger *m* (-*s*) annoyance; (*stronger*) anger; (*difficulties*) trouble; **ärgerlich** *adj* angry; (*irritating*) annoying; **ärgern** **1.** *vt* annoy **2.** *vr* get annoyed

Argument *nt* (-*s*, -*e*) argument

Arktis *f* (-) Arctic

arm *adj* poor

Arm *m* (-(*e*)*s*, -*e*) arm; (*of ri-*

ver) branch

Armaturenbrett *nt* instrument panel; AUTO dashboard

Armband *nt* bracelet; **Armbanduhr** *f* (wrist)watch

Armee *f* (-, -n) army

Ärmel *m* (-s, -) sleeve; **Ärmelkanal** *m* (English) Channel

Armut *f* (-) poverty

Aroma *nt* (-s, *Aromen*) aroma; **Aromatherapie** *f* aromatherapy

arrogant *adj* arrogant

Arsch *m* (-es, *Ärsche*) *vulg* arse (*Brit*), ass (*US*); **Arschloch** *nt* *vulg* (*person*) arsehole (*Brit*), asshole (*US*)

Art *f* (-, -en) (*manner*) way; (*type*) kind, sort; (*of animal*) species; **nach ~ des Hauses** à la maison; **auf diese ~ (und Weise)** in this way; **das ist nicht seine ~** that's not like him

Arterie *f* (-, -n) artery

artig *adj* good, well-behaved

Artikel *m* (-s, -) (*product*) article, item; (*in newspaper*) article

Artischocke *f* (-, -n) artichoke

Artist(in) *m(f)* (-en, -en) (*circus*) performer

Arznei *f* medicine; **Arzt** *m* (-es, *Ärzte*) doctor; **Arzthelfer(in)** *m(f)* doctor's assistant; **Ärztin** *f* (female) doctor; **ärztlich** *adj* medical; **sich ~ behandeln lassen** undergo medical treatment

Asche *f* (-, -n) ashes *pl*; (*from cigarette*) ash; **Aschenbecher** *m* ashtray; **Aschermittwoch** *m* Ash Wednesday

Asiat(in) *m(f)* (-en, -en) Asian; **asiatisch** *adj* Asian; **Asien** *nt* (-s) Asia

Aspekt *m* (-(e)s, -e) aspect

Asphalt *m* (-(e)s, -e) asphalt

Aspirin® *nt* (-s, -) aspirin

aß *imperf of* **essen**

Ass *nt* (-es, -e) (*in card game, tennis*) ace

Assistent(in) *m(f)* assistant

Ast *m* (-(e)s, *Äste*) branch

Asthma *nt* (-s) asthma

Astrologie *f* astrology; **Astronaut(in)** *m(f)* (-en, -en) astronaut; **Astronomie** *f* astronomy

ASU *f* (-, -s) *abbr* = **Abgassonderuntersuchung**; exhaust emission test

Asyl *nt* (-s, -e) asylum; (*place*) home; (*for the homeless*) shelter; **Asylant(in)** *m(f)*, **Asylbewerber(in)** *m(f)* asylum seeker

Atelier *nt* (-s, -s) studio

Atem *m* (-s) breath; **atemberaubend** *adj* breathtaking; **Atembeschwerden** *pl* breathing difficulties *pl*; **atemlos** *adj* breathless; **Atempause** *f* breather

Athen *nt* Athens

Äthiopien *nt* (-s) Ethiopia

Athlet(in) *m(f)* (-en, -en) athlete

Atlantik *m* (-s) Atlantic

(Ocean)

Atlas m (- or Atlasses, Atlanten) atlas

atmen vt, vi breathe; **Atmung** f breathing

Atom nt (-s, -e) atom; **Atombombe** f atom bomb; **Atomkraftwerk** nt nuclear power station; **Atommüll** m nuclear waste; **Atomwaffen** pl nuclear weapons pl

Attentat nt (-(e)s, -e) assassination (auf + acc of); (unsuccessful) assassination attempt

Attest nt (-(e)s, -e) certificate

attraktiv adj attractive

Attrappe f (-, -n) dummy

ätzend adj fam revolting; (bad) lousy

au interj ouch!; **~ ja!** yeah

Aubergine f (-, -n) aubergine, eggplant (US)

auch conj also, too; even; (actually) really; **oder ~** or; **ich ~** so do I; **ich ~ nicht** me neither; **wer/was ~ immer** whoever/whatever; **ich gehe jetzt - ich ~** I'm going now - so am I; **das weiß ich ~ nicht** I don't know either

audiovisuell adj audiovisual

auf 1. prep + acc or dat on; **~ der Reise/dem Tisch** on the way/the table; **~ der Post*/ der Party** at the post office*/the party; **etw ~ den Tisch stellen** put sth on the table; **~ Deutsch** in German **2.** prep + acc (mountain, tree etc) up; (direction) to; (following) after; **~ eine Party gehen** go to a party; **bis ~ ihn** except for him; **~ einmal** suddenly; (simultaneously, in one go) at once **3.** adv open; **~ sein** fam be open; (person) be up; **~ und ab** up and down; **~!** come on!; **~ dass** so that

aufatmen vi breathe a sigh of relief

aufbauen vt (erect) put up; (develop) build up; (form) construct; (establish) found, base (auf + acc on); **sich eine Existenz ~** make a life for oneself

aufbewahren vt keep, store

aufbleiben irr vi (door, shop etc) stay open; (person) stay up

aufblenden vi, vt (die Scheinwerfer) **~** put one's headlights on full beam

aufbrechen irr **1.** vt break open **2.** vi burst open; (go) leave; (on journey) set off; **Aufbruch** m departure

aufdrängen 1. vt **jdm etw ~** force sth on sb **2.** vr intrude (jdm on sb); **aufdringlich** adj pushy

aufeinander adv on top of each other; **~ achten** look after each other; **~ schießen** shoot at each other; **~ vertrauen** trust each other; **~ folgen** follow one another;

~ prallen crash into one another

Aufenthalt m stay; (of train) stop; **Aufenthaltsgenehmigung** f residence permit; **Aufenthaltsraum** m lounge

aufessen irr vt eat up

auffahren irr vi (car) run (or crash) (auf + acc into); (get closer) drive up; **Auffahrt** f (of building) drive; (onto motorway) slip road (Brit), ramp (US); **Auffahrunfall** m rear-end collision; (several vehicles) pile-up

auffallen irr vi stand out; **jdm ~** strike sb; **das fällt gar nicht auf** nobody will notice; **auffallend** adj striking; **auffällig** adj conspicuous; (clothes, colour) striking

auffangen irr vt (ball) catch; (blow) cushion

auffassen irr vt understand; **Auffassung** f view; opinion; (interpretation) concept; (comprehension) grasp

auffordern vt (order) call upon; (request) ask

auffrischen vt (knowledge) brush up

aufführen 1. vt THEAT perform; (in table, index) list; (example) give 2. vr behave; **Aufführung** f THEAT performance

Aufgabe f job, task; (schoolwork) exercise; (giving up)

Aufgang m (steps) staircase

aufgeben irr 1. vt (job, smoking, plan etc) give up; (parcel) post; (luggage) check in; (order) place; (advertisement) insert; (puzzle, problem) set 2. vi give up

aufgehen irr vi (sun, dough) rise; (door, flower) open; (become clear) dawn (jdm on sb)

aufgelegt adj **gut / schlecht ~** in a good / bad mood

aufgeregt adj excited

aufgeschlossen adj open (-minded)

aufgeschmissen adj fam in a fix

aufgrund, auf Grund prep + gen on the basis of; (reason) because of

aufhaben irr **1.** vt (hat etc) have on; **viel ~** have a lot of homework to do **2.** vi (shop) be open

aufhalten irr **1.** vt (person) detain; (development) stop; (door, hand) hold open; (eyes) keep open **2.** vr (reside) live; (temporarily) stay

aufhängen irr vt hang up

aufheben irr vt (from ground etc) pick up; (not throw away) keep

aufholen 1. vt (time) make up **2.** vi catch up

aufhören vi stop; **~, etw zu tun** stop doing sth

aufklären vt (mystery etc) clear up; **jdn ~** enlighten sb; (about sex) tell sb the facts of life

Aufkleber m (-s, -) sticker

aufkommen irr vi (wind) come up; (doubt, feeling) arise; (fashion etc) appear on the scene; **für den Schaden ~** pay for the damage

aufladen irr vt load; (mobile phone etc) charge; **Ladegerät** nt charger

Auflage f edition; (of newspaper) circulation; (imposed on sb) condition

auflassen vt (hat, glasses) keep on; (door) leave open

Auflauf m crowd; (dish) bake

auflegen 1. vt (CD, make-up etc) put on; (receiver) put down **2.** vi TEL hang up

aufleuchten vi light up

auflösen 1. vt (in liquid) dissolve **2.** vr (in liquid) dissolve; **der Stau hat sich aufgelöst** traffic is back to normal; **Auflösung** f (of puzzle) solution; (of screen) resolution

aufmachen 1. vt open; (garment) undo **2.** vr set out (nach for)

aufmerksam adj attentive; **jdn auf etw akk ~ machen** draw sb's attention to sth; **Aufmerksamkeit** f attention; (concentration) attentiveness; (present) small token

aufmuntern vt encourage; (make happier) cheer up

Aufnahme f (-, -n) PHOT photo(graph); (in film) shot; (to

club, hospital etc) admission; (start) beginning; (on tape etc) recording; **Aufnahmeprüfung** f entrance exam; **aufnehmen** irr vt (to hospital, club etc) admit; (music) record; (begin) take up; (in list) include; (understand) take in; **mit jdm Kontakt ~** get in touch with sb

aufpassen vi pay attention; (be careful) take care; **auf jdn/etw ~** keep an eye on sb/sth

Aufprall m (-s, -e) impact; **aufprallen** vi **auf etw akk ~** hit sth, crash into sth

Aufpreis m extra charge

aufpumpen vt pump up

Aufputschmittel nt stimulant

aufräumen vt, vi clear away; (room) tidy up

aufrecht adj upright

aufregen 1. vt excite; (irritate) annoy **2.** vr get worked up; **aufregend** adj exciting; **Aufregung** f excitement

aufreißen vt (paper bag etc) tear open; (door) fling open; (person) fam pick up

Aufruf m AVIAT, IT call; (public request) appeal; **aufrufen** irr vt (request) call upon (zu for); (names) call out; AVIAT call; IT call up

aufrunden vt (amount) round up

aufs contr of **auf das**

Aufsatz m essay

aufschieben irr vt postpone;

(delay doing) put off; *(door)* slide open

Aufschlag *m (on price)* extra charge; *(in tennis)* service; **aufschlagen** *irr* **1.** *vt (book, eyes)* open; *(knee etc)* cut open; *(tent)* pitch, put up; *(camp)* set up **2.** *vi (in tennis)* serve; **auf etw ~** hit sth

aufschließen *irr* **1.** *vt* unlock, open up **2.** *vi (people in a row)* close up

aufschneiden *irr* **1.** *vt* cut open; *(bread, meat etc)* slice **2.** *vi* boast, show off

Aufschnitt *m (slices pl of)* cold meat; *(cheese)* (assorted) sliced cheeses *pl*

aufschreiben *irr vt* write down

Aufschrift *f* inscription; *(piece of paper)* label

Aufschub *m* delay; *(until a later date)* postponement

Aufsehen *nt (-s)* stir; **großes ~ erregen** cause a sensation; **Aufseher(in)** *m(f) (-s, -)* guard; *(in firm)* supervisor; *(in museum)* attendant; *(in park)* keeper

auf sein *irr → auf*

aufsetzen 1. *vt* put on; *(document)* draw up **2.** *vi (plane)* touch down

Aufsicht *f* supervision; *(in exam)* invigilation; **die ~ haben** be in charge

aufspannen *vt (umbrella)* put up

aufsperren *vt (mouth)* open

wide; *(door, flat)* unlock

aufspringen *irr vi* jump *(auf + acc* onto); *(stand up quickly)* jump up; *(door, suitcase)* spring open

aufstehen *vi* get up; *(door)* be open

aufstellen *vt* put up; *(in a row)* line up; *(candidate)* put up; *(list, schedule)* draw up; *(record)* set up

Aufstieg *m (-(e)s, -e) (up mountain)* ascent; *(progress)* rise; *(in career, sport)* promotion

Aufstrich *m* spread

auftanken *vt, vi (car)* tank up; *(plane)* refuel

auftauchen *vi* turn up; *(from water etc)* surface; *(question, problem)* come up

auftauen 1. *vt (food)* defrost **2.** *vi* thaw; *fig (person)* unbend

Auftrag *m (-(e)s, Aufträge)* COMM order; *(allocated work)* job; *(orders)* instructions *pl*; *(mission)* task; **im ~ von** on behalf of; **auftragen** *irr vt (ointment etc)* apply; *(meal)* serve

auftreten *irr vi* appear; *(problem)* come up; *(act)* behave; **Auftritt** *m (of actor)* entrance; *fig (argument)* scene

aufwachen *vi* wake up

aufwachsen *irr vi* grow up

Aufwand *m (-(e)s)* expenditure; *(costs also)* expense;

(exertion) effort; **aufwändig** *adj* costly; **das ist zu ~** that's too much trouble

aufwärmen *vt, vr* warm up

aufwärts *adv* upwards; **mit etw geht es ~** things are looking up for sth

aufwecken *vt* wake up

aufwendig *adj* → **aufwändig**

aufwischen *vt* wipe up; *(floor)* wipe

aufzählen *vt* list; **Aufzählungszeichen** *nt* bullet

aufzeichnen *vt* sketch; *(write)* jot down; *(on tape etc)* record; **Aufzeichnung** *f* *(written)* note; *(on tape etc)* recording; *(on film)* record

aufziehen *irr* **1.** *vt (drawer, curtains etc)* pull open; *(watch)* wind (up); *fam (make fun of)* tease; *(children)* bring up; *(animals)* rear **2.** *vi (storm)* come up

Aufzug *m* lift *(Brit)*, elevator *(US)*; *(clothes)* get-up; THEAT act

Auge *nt* (-s, -n) eye; **jdm etw aufs ~ drücken** *fam* force sth on sb; **ins ~ gehen** *fam* go wrong; **unter vier ~n** in private; **etw im ~ behalten** keep sth in mind; **Augenarzt** *m*, **Augenärztin** *f* eye specialist, eye doctor *(US)*; **Augenblick** *m* moment; **im ~** at the moment; **Augenbraue** *f* (-, -n) eyebrow; **Augenbrauenstift** *m* eyebrow pencil; **Augenfarbe** *f* eye colour;

seine ~ the colour of his eyes; **Augenlid** *nt* eyelid; **Augenoptiker(in)** *m(f)* (-s, -) optician; **Augentropfen** *pl* eyedrops *pl*; **Augenzeuge** *m*, **Augenzeugin** *f* eyewitness

August *m* (-(e)s *or* -, -e) August; → **Juni**

Auktion *f* auction

aus 1. *prep + dat (from inside)* out of; *(source)* from; *(material)* (made) of; **~ Berlin kommen** come from Berlin; **~ Versehen** by mistake; **~ Angst** out of fear **2.** *adv* out; *(ended)* finished, over; **ein/~** TECH on/off; **~ sein** *fam* SPORT be out; *(finished)* be over; **auf etw** *acc* **~ sein** be after sth; **von mir ~** as far as I'm concerned; **von mir ~!** I don't care; **zwischen uns ist es ~** we're finished; **Aus** *nt* (-) SPORT touch; *fig* end

ausatmen *vi* breathe out

ausbauen *vt (house, road)* extend; *(engine etc)* remove

ausbessern *vt* repair; *(clothes)* mend

ausbilden *vt* educate; *(apprentice etc)* train; *(skills)* develop; **Ausbildung** *f* education; *(of apprentice etc)* training; *(of skills)* development

Ausblick *m* view; *fig* outlook

ausbrechen *irr vi* break out; **in Tränen ~** burst into tears; **in Gelächter ~** burst out laughing

ausbreiten 1. vt spread (out); (arms) stretch out **2.** vr spread

Ausbruch m (of war, epidemic etc) outbreak; (of volcano) eruption; (of feelings) outburst; (from prison) escape

ausbuhen vt boo

Ausdauer f perseverance; SPORT stamina

ausdehnen vt stretch; fig (power) extend

ausdenken irr vt sich dat etw ~ come up with sth

Ausdruck 1. m (Ausdrücke pl) expression **2.** m (Ausdrucke pl) (from computer) print-out; **ausdrucken** vt IT print (out)

ausdrücken 1. vt (facts, feelings etc) express; (cigarette) put out; (lemon etc) squeeze **2.** vr express oneself; **ausdrücklich 1.** adj express **2.** adv expressly

auseinander adv apart; ~ **gehen** (people) separate; (opinions) differ; (object) fall apart; ~ **halten** tell apart; ~ **schreiben** write as separate words; ~ **setzen** explain; **sich** ~ **setzen** (with) take in at; (disagree) argue (mit with); **Auseinandersetzung** f (row) argument; (discussion) debate

Ausfahrt f (of train etc) departure; (from motorway, gara-

ge etc) exit

ausfallen irr vi (hair) fall out; (concert, class etc) be cancelled; (machine) break down; (electricity) be cut off; (well, badly etc) turn out; **groß/klein** ~ (clothes, shoes) be too big/too small

ausführen vt (order, task, plan) carry out; (person) take out; COMM export; (theory etc) explain

ausflippen vi fam freak out

Ausflug m excursion, outing; **Ausflugsziel** nt destination

Ausfluss m MED discharge

ausfragen vt question

Ausfuhr f (-, -en) export

ausführlich 1. adj detailed **2.** adv in detail

ausfüllen vt fill up; (questionnaire etc) fill in (or out)

Ausgabe f (money) expenditure; IT output; (of book) edition; (of magazine) issue

Ausgang m way out, exit; (at airport) gate; (conclusion) end; (outcome) result; „**kein** ~ " "no exit"

ausgeben irr **1.** vt (money) spend; (share out) distribute; **jdm etw** ~ (treat sb) buy sb sth **2.** vr **sich für etw/jdn** ~ pass oneself off as sth/sb

ausgebucht adj fully booked

ausgefallen adj unusual

ausgehen irr vi (in the evening etc) go out; (petrol, cof-

fee etc) run out; (*hair*) fall
out; (*fire, light etc*) go out;
(*well, badly etc*) turn out; **davon ~, dass** assume that;
ihm ging das Geld aus he
ran out of money

ausgelassen *adj* exuberant

ausgeleiert *adj* worn out

ausgenommen *conj, prep*
+ *gen or dat* except

ausgerechnet *adv* ~ **du** you
of all people; ~ **heute** today
of all days

ausgeschildert *adj* sign-
posted

ausgeschlafen *adj* **bist du
~?** have you had enough
sleep?

ausgeschlossen *adj* impossible, out of the question

ausgesprochen 1. *adj* out-
-and-out; (*strong*) marked **2.**
adv extremely; ~ **gut** really
good

ausgezeichnet *adj* excellent

ausgiebig *adj* (*use*) thorough;
(*meal*) substantial

ausgießen *irr vt* (*drink*) pour
out; (*jug, glass etc*) empty

ausgleichen *irr* **1.** *vt* even out
2. *vi* SPORT equalize

Ausguss *m* sink; (*waste pipe*)
outlet

aushalten *irr* **1.** *vt* bear, stand;
nicht auszuhalten sein be
unbearable **2.** *vi* hold out

aushändigen *vt* **jdm etw** ~
hand sth over to sb

Aushang *m* notice

Aushilfe *f* temporary help; (*in*
office) temp

auskennen *irr vr* know a lot
(*bei, mit* about); (*in a place*)
know one's way around

auskommen *irr vi* **gut/
schlecht mit jdm** ~ get on
well/badly with sb; **mit etw
~** get by with sth

Auskunft *f* (-, *Auskünfte*) information; (*particulars*) details *pl*; (*counter*) information desk; TEL (*directory*) enquiries *sg* (*Brit*), information
(*US*)

auslachen *vt* laugh at

ausladen *irr vt* (*luggage etc*)
unload; **jdn** ~ (*guest*) tell sb
not to come

Auslage *f* window display; **~n**
pl (*costs*) expenses

Ausland *nt* foreign countries
pl; im/ins ~ abroad; **Aus-
länder(in)** *m(f)* (-s, -) foreigner; **ausländerfeindlich**
adj hostile to foreigners, xen-
ophobic; **ausländisch** *adj*
foreign; **Auslandsgespräch**
nt international call; **Auslandskrankenschein** *m*
health insurance certificate
for foreign countries, ≈
E111 (*Brit*); **Auslands-
schutzbrief** *m* international
(*motor*) insurance cover
(*documents pl*)

auslassen *irr* **1.** *vt* leave out;
(*word etc also*) omit; (*do without*) skip; (*anger*) vent (*an
+ dat* on) **2.** *vr* **sich über
etw** *acc* ~ speak one's mind

about sth

auslaufen irr vi (liquid) run out; (tank etc) leak; (ship) leave port; (contract) expire

auslegen vt (goods) display; (money) lend; (text etc) interpret; (machine, building) design (für, auf + acc for)

ausleihen irr vt (to sb) lend; **sich** dat etw ~ borrow sth

ausloggen vi IT log out (or off)

auslösen vt (explosion, alarm) set off; (bring about) cause; **Auslöser** m (-s, -) PHOT shutter release

ausmachen vt (light, radio) turn off; (fire) put out; (date, price) fix; (arrange) agree; (proportion, amount etc) represent; (be significant) matter; **macht es ihnen etwas aus, wenn ...?** would you mind if ...?; **das macht mir nichts aus** I don't mind

Ausmaß nt extent

Ausnahme f (-, -n) exception; **ausnahmsweise** adv as an exception, just this once

ausnutzen vt (time, opportunity, influence) use; (person, sb's good nature) take advantage of

auspacken vt unpack

ausprobieren vt try (out)

Auspuff m (-(e)s, -e) TECH exhaust; **Auspuffrohr** nt exhaust (pipe); **Auspufftopf** m AUTO silencer (Brit), muffler (US)

ausrauben vt rob

ausräumen vt clear away; (cupboard, room) empty; (misgivings) put aside

ausrechnen vt calculate, work out

Ausrede f excuse

ausreden 1. vi finish speaking **2.** vt jdm etw ~ talk sb out of sth

ausreichend adj sufficient, satisfactory; (mark in school) ≈ D

Ausreise f departure; **bei der** ~ on leaving the country; **Ausreiseerlaubnis** f exit visa; **ausreisen** vi leave the country

ausreißen irr 1. vt tear out 2. vi come off; fam (abscond) run away

ausrenken vt sich dat den Arm ~ dislocate one's arm

ausrichten vt (message) deliver; (regards) pass on; **ich konnte bei ihr nichts** ~ I couldn't get anywhere with her; **jdm etw** ~ tell sb sth

ausrufen irr vt (over loudspeaker) announce; **jdn** ~ **lassen** page sb; **Ausrufezeichen** nt exclamation mark

ausruhen vi, vr rest

Ausrüstung f equipment

ausrutschen vi slip

ausschalten vt switch off; fig eliminate

Ausschau f ~ **halten** look out (nach for)

ausscheiden irr 1. vt MED

give off, secrete **2.** *vi* leave (*aus etw* sth); SPORT be eliminated

ausschlafen *irr* **1.** *vi*, *vr* have a lie-in **2.** *vt* sleep off

Ausschlag *m* MED rash; **den ~ geben** *fig* tip the balance; **ausschlagen** *irr* **1.** *vt* (*tooth*) knock out; (*invitation*) turn down **2.** *vi* (*horse*) kick out; **ausschlaggebend** *adj* decisive

ausschließen *irr* *vt* lock out; *fig* exclude; **ausschließlich 1.** *adv* exclusively **2.** *prep + gen* excluding

Ausschnitt *m* (*part*) section; (*of dress*) neckline; (*from newspaper*) cutting

Ausschreitungen *pl* riots *pl*

ausschütten *vt* (*liquid*) pour out; (*container*) empty

aussehen *irr* *vi* look; **krank ~** look ill; **gut ~** (*person*) be good-looking; (*thing*) be looking good; **es sieht nach Regen aus** it looks like rain; **es sieht schlecht aus** things look bad

aus sein *irr* *vi* → **aus**

außen *adv* outside; **nach ~** outwards; **von ~** from (the) outside; **Außenbordmotor** *m* outboard motor; **Außenminister(in)** *m(f)* foreign minister, Foreign Secretary (*Brit*); **Außenseite** *f* outside; **Außenseiter(in)** *m(f)* outsider; **Außenspiegel** *m* wing mirror (*Brit*), side mirror

(*US*)

außer 1. *prep + dat* except (for); **nichts ~** nothing but; **~ Betrieb** out of order; **sich sein** be beside oneself (*vor* with); **~ Atem** out of breath **2.** *conj* except; **~ wenn** unless; **~ dass** except; **außerdem** besides

äußere(r, s) *adj* outer, external

außergewöhnlich 1. *adj* unusual **2.** *adv* exceptionally; **~ kalt** exceptionally cold; **außerhalb** *prep + gen* outside

äußerlich *adj* external

äußern 1. *vt* express; (*display*) show **2.** *vr* give one's opinion; (*be visible*) show itself

außerordentlich *adj* extraordinary; **außerplanmäßig** *adj* unscheduled

äußerst *adv* extremely; **äußerste(r, s)** *adj* utmost; (*in distance*) farthest; (*date*) last possible

Äußerung *f* remark

aussetzen 1. *vt* (*child, animal*) abandon; (*reward*) offer; **ich habe nichts daran auszusetzen** I have no objection to it **2.** *vi* stop; (*take a break*) drop out; (*in game*) miss a turn

Aussicht *f* view; (*chance*) prospect; **aussichtslos** *adj* hopeless; **Aussichtsplattform** *f* observation platform; **Aussichtsturm** *m* observation tower

Aussiedler(in) *m(f)* (*-s, -*) émigré (*person of German descent from Eastern Europe*)

ausspannen 1. *vi* relax **2.** *vt* **er hat ihm die Freundin ausgespannt** *fam* he's nicked his girlfriend

aussperren 1. *vt* lock out **2.** *vr* lock oneself out

Aussprache *f* (*of words*) pronunciation; (*talk*) (frank) discussion; **aussprechen** *irr* **1.** *vt* pronounce; (*thoughts etc*) express **2.** *vr* talk (*über* + *acc* about) **3.** *vi* finish speaking

ausspülen *vt* rinse (out)

Ausstattung *f* (*in hospital, office etc*) equipment; (*in flat etc*) furnishings *pl*; (*in car*) fittings *pl*

ausstehen *irr* **1.** *vt* endure; **ich kann ihn nicht ~** I can't stand him **2.** *vi* (*debt etc*) be outstanding

aussteigen *irr vi* get out (*aus* of); **aus dem Bus/Zug ~** get off the bus/train; **Aussteiger(in)** *m(f)* dropout

ausstellen *vt* display; (*at trade fair, in museum etc*) exhibit; *fam* (*radio, heating etc*) switch off; (*cheque etc*) make out; (*passport etc*) issue; **Ausstellung** *f* exhibition

aussterben *irr vi* die out

ausstrahlen *vt* radiate; (*programme*) broadcast; **Ausstrahlung** *f* RADIO, TV broad-

cast; *fig* (*of person*) charisma

ausstrecken **1.** *vr* stretch out **2.** *vt* (*hand*) reach out (*nach* for)

aussuchen *vt* choose

Austausch *m* exchange; **austauschen** *vt* exchange (*gegen* for)

austeilen *vt* distribute; hand out

Auster *f* (*-, -n*) oyster; **Austernpilz** *m* oyster mushroom

austragen *irr vt* (*mail*) deliver; (*competition*) hold

Australien *nt* (*-s*) Australia; **Australier(in)** *m(f)* (*-s, -*) Australian; **australisch** *adj* Australian

austrinken *irr* **1.** *vt* (*glass*) drain; (*wine, coffee etc*) drink up **2.** *vi* finish one's drink

austrocknen *vi* dry out; (*river*) dry up

ausüben *vt* (*profession, sport*) practise; (*influence*) exert

Ausverkauf *m* sale; **ausverkauft** *adj* (*tickets, item*) sold out

Auswahl *f* selection, choice (*an + dat* of); **auswählen** *vt* select, choose

auswandern *vi* emigrate

auswärtig *adj* not local; (*relating to other countries*) foreign; **auswärts** *adv* out of town; SPORT **~ spielen** play away; **Auswärtsspiel** *nt* away match

auswechseln vt replace; SPORT substitute

Ausweg m way out

ausweichen irr vi get out of the way; **jdm/einer Sache ~** move aside for sb/sth; fig avoid sb/sth

Ausweis m (-es, -e) (for individual) identity card, ID; (for library etc) card; **ausweisen** irr 1. vt expel 2. vr prove one's identity; **Ausweiskontrolle** f ID check; **Ausweispapiere** pl identification documents pl

auswendig adv by heart

auswuchten vt AUTO (wheels) balance

auszahlen 1. vt (money) pay (out); (person) pay off 2. vr be worth it

auszeichnen 1. vt (special person) honour; COMM price 2. vr distinguish oneself

ausziehen irr 1. vt (clothes) take off 2. vr undress 3. vi (from flat) move out

Auszubildende(r) mf trainee

Auto nt (-s, -s) car; **~ fahren** drive; **Autoatlas** m road atlas; **Autobahn** f motorway (Brit), freeway (US); **Autobahnauffahrt** f motorway access road (Brit), on-ramp (US); **Autobahnausfahrt** f motorway exit (Brit), off-ramp (US); **Autobahngebühr** f toll; **Autobahnkreuz** nt motorway interchange; **Autobahnring** m motorway

ring (Brit), beltway (US); **Autobombe** f car bomb; **Autofähre** f car ferry; **Autofahrer(in)** m(f) driver, motorist; **Autofahrt** f drive

Autogramm nt (-s, -e) autograph

Automarke f make of car

Automat m (-en, -en) vending machine

Automatik f (-, -en) AUTO automatic transmission; **Automatikschaltung** f automatic gear change (Brit) (or shift (US)); **Automatikwagen** m automatic

automatisch 1. adj automatic 2. adv automatically

Automechaniker(in) m(f) car mechanic; **Autonummer** f registration (Brit) (or license (US)) number; **Autoradio** nt car radio; **Autoreifen** m car tyre (Brit), auto tire (US); **Autoreisezug** m Motorail train® (Brit), auto train (US); **Autorennen** nt motor racing; (single event) motor race; **Autoschlüssel** m car key; **Autotelefon** nt car phone; **Autounfall** m car accident; **Autoverleih** m, **Autovermietung** f car hire (Brit) (or rental (US)); (firm) car hire (Brit) (or rental (US)) company; **Autowaschanlage** f car wash; **Autowerkstatt** f car repair shop, garage; **Autozubehör** nt car accessories pl

Avocado f (-, -s) avocado

Axt f (-, Äxte) axe

Azubi m (-s, -s) f (-, -s) acr = **Auszubildende**; trainee

B

B abbr = **Bundesstraße**

Baby nt (-s, -s) baby; **Babybett** nt cot (Brit), crib (US); **Babyfläschchen** nt baby's bottle; **Babynahrung** f baby food; **Babysitter(in)** m(f) babysitter; **Babysitz** m child seat; **Babywickelraum** m baby-changing room

Bach m (-(e)s, Bäche) stream

Backblech nt baking tray (Brit), cookie sheet (US)

Backbord nt port (side)

Backe f (-, -n) cheek

backen (backte, gebacken) vt, vi bake

Backenzahn m molar

Bäcker(in) m(f) (-s, -) baker; **Bäckerei** f bakery; (selling bread) baker's (shop)

Backofen m oven; **Backpulver** nt baking powder

Backspace-Taste f IT backspace key

Backstein m brick

Backwaren pl bread, cakes and pastries pl

Bad nt (-(e)s, Bäder) bath; (in sea etc) swim; (resort) spa; **ein ~ nehmen** have (or take) a bath; **Badeanzug** m swimsuit, swimming costume (Brit); **Badehose** f swimming trunks pl; **Badekappe** f swimming cap; **Bademantel** m bathrobe; **Bademeister(in)** m(f) pool attendant; **Bademütze** f swimming cap

baden 1. vi have a bath; (in sea etc) swim, bathe (Brit) **2.** vt bath (Brit), bathe (US)

Baden-Württemberg nt (-s) Baden-Württemberg

Badeort m spa; **Badesachen** pl swimming things pl; **Badetuch** nt bath towel; **Badewanne** f bath (tub); **Badezimmer** nt bathroom

Badminton nt badminton

baff adj ~ **sein** fam be flabbergasted (or gobsmacked)

Bagger m (-s, -) excavator; **Baggersee** m artificial lake in quarry etc, used for bathing

Bahamas pl **die ~** the Bahamas pl

Bahn f (-, -en) railway (Brit), railroad (US); (racetrack) track; (for single runner) lane; ASTR orbit; **bahnbrechend** adj groundbreaking; **BahnCard®** f (-, -s) rail card (allowing 50% or 25% reduction on tickets); **Bahnfahrt** f railway (or railroad (US)) journey; **Bahn-**

hof *m* station; **am** (*or* **auf dem**) **~** at the station; **Bahnlinie** *f* railway (*Brit*) (*or* railroad (*US*)) line; **Bahnpolizei** *f* railway (*Brit*) (*or* railroad (*US*)) police; **Bahnsteig** *m* (*-s, -e*) platform; **Bahnstrecke** *f* railway (*Brit*) (*or* railroad (*US*)) line; **Bahnübergang** *m* level crossing (*Brit*), grade crossing (*US*)

Bakterien *pl* bacteria *pl*, germs *pl*

bald *adv* soon; almost; **bis ~!** see you soon (*or* later); **baldig** *adj* quick, speedy

Balkan *m* (*-s*) **der ~** the Balkans *pl*

Balken *m* (*-s, -*) beam

Balkon *m* (*-s, -s or -e*) balcony

Ball *m* (*-(e)s, Bälle*) ball; (*event*) dance, ball

Ballett *nt* (*-s*) ballet

Ballon *m* (*-s, -s*) balloon

Ballspiel *nt* ball game

Ballungsgebiet *nt* conurbation

Baltikum *nt* (*-s*) **das ~** the Baltic States *pl*

Bambus *m* (*-ses, -se*) bamboo; **Bambussprossen** *pl* bamboo shoots *pl*

banal *adj* banal; (*question, remark*) trite

Banane *f* (*-, -n*) banana

band *imperf of* **binden**

Band 1. *m* (*-(e)s, Bände*) (*book*) volume **2.** *nt* (*-(e)s, Bänder*) (*of fabric*) ribbon,

tape; (*in factory*) production line; (*for recording*) tape; ANAT ligament; **etw auf ~ aufnehmen** tape sth **3.** *f* (*-, -s*) (*musicians*) band

Bandage *f* (*-, -n*) bandage; **bandagieren** *vt* bandage

Bande *f* (*-, -n*) gang

Bänderriss *m* MED torn ligament

Bandscheibe *f* ANAT disc; **Bandwurm** *m* tapeworm

Bank 1. *f* (*-, Bänke*) bench **2.** *f* (*-, -en*) FIN bank

Bankautomat *m* cash dispenser; **Bankkarte** *f* bank card; **Bankkonto** *nt* bank account; **Bankleitzahl** *f* bank sort code; **Banknote** *f* banknote; **Bankverbindung** *f* banking (*or* account) details *pl*

bar *adj* **~es Geld** cash; **etw (in) ~ bezahlen** pay sth (in) cash

Bar *f* (*-, -s*) bar

Bär *m* (*-en, -en*) bear

barfuß *adj* barefoot

barg *imperf of* **bergen**

Bargeld *nt* cash; **bargeldlos** *adj* non-cash

Barkeeper *m* (*-s, -*), **Barmann** *m* barman, bartender (*US*)

barock *adj* baroque

Barometer *nt* (*-s, -*) barometer

barsch *adj* brusque

Barsch *m* (*-(e)s, -e*) perch

Barscheck *m* open (*or* uncrossed) cheque

Bart *m* (*-(e)s, Bärte*) beard

bärtig adj bearded

Barzahlung f cash payment

Basar m (-s, -e) bazaar

Baseballmütze f baseball cap

Basel nt (-s) Basle

Basilikum nt (-s) basil

Basis f (-, Basen) basis

Baskenland nt Basque region

Basketball m basketball

Bass m (-es, Bässe) bass

basta interj **und damit ~!** and that's that

basteln 1. vt make **2.** vi make things, do handicrafts

bat imperf of **bitten**

Batterie f battery; **batterie-betrieben** adj battery-powered

Bau 1. m (-(e)s) (constructing) building, construction; (organization) structure; (place) building site **2.** m (Baue pl) (of animal) burrow **3.** m (Bauten pl) (edifice) building; **Bauarbeiten** pl construction work sg; (on road) roadworks pl (Brit), roadwork (US); **Bauarbeiter(in)** m(f) construction worker

Bauch m (-(e)s, Bäuche) stomach; **Bauchnabel** m navel; **Bauchredner(in)** m(f) ventriloquist; **Bauchschmerzen** pl stomach-ache sg; **Bauchspeicheldrüse** f pancreas; **Bauchtanz** m belly dance; (activity) belly dancing; **Bauchweh** nt (-s) stomach-ache

Baudenkmal nt monument

bauen vt, vi build; TECH construct

Bauer m (-n or -s, -n) farmer; (in chess) pawn; **Bäuerin** f farmer; farmer's wife; **Bauernhof** m farm

baufällig adj dilapidated; **Baujahr** nt year of construction; **der Wagen ist ~ 2002** the car is a 2002 model, the car was made in 2002

Baum m (-(e)s, Bäume) tree

Baumarkt m DIY centre

Baumwolle f cotton

Bauplatz m building site; **Baustein** m (for building) stone; (toy) brick; fig element; **elektronischer ~** chip; **Baustelle** f building site; (on road) roadworks pl (Brit), roadwork (US); **Bauteil** nt prefabricated part; **Bauunternehmer(in)** m(f) building contractor; **Bauwerk** nt building

Bayern nt (-s) Bavaria

beabsichtigen vt intend

beachten vt pay attention to; (rule etc) observe; (ignore) ignore; **beachtlich** adj considerable

Beachvolleyball nt beach volleyball

Beamte(r) m (-n, -n), **Beamtin** f official; (employed by the state) civil servant

beanspruchen vt claim; (time, space) take up; **jdn ~** keep sb busy

beanstanden vt complain

about

beantragen vt apply for

beantworten vt answer

bearbeiten vt work; (material, data) process; CHEM treat; (case etc) deal with; (book etc) revise; fam (try to influence) work on; **Bearbeitungsgebühr** f handling (or service) charge

beatmen vt jdm ~ give sb artificial respiration

beaufsichtigen vt supervise; (in exam) invigilate

beauftragen vt instruct; jdn mit etw ~ give sb the job of doing sth

Becher m (-s, -) mug; (without handle) tumbler; (for yoghurt) pot; (made of cardboard) tub

Becken nt (-s, -) basin; (for washing) sink; (for swimming) pool; MUS cymbal; ANAT pelvis

bedanken vr say thank you; sich bei jdm für etw ~ thank sb for sth

Bedarf m (-(e)s) need (an + dat for); COMM demand (an + dat for); je nach ~ according to demand; bei ~ if necessary; **Bedarfshaltestelle** f request stop, flag stop (US)

bedauerlich adj regrettable; **bedauern** vt regret; (person) feel sorry for; **bedauernswert** adj regrettable; (person) unfortunate

bedeckt adj covered; (sky) overcast

bedenken irr vt consider; **Bedenken** nt (-s, -) (thought) consideration; (reservation) doubt; (moral doubt) scruples pl; **bedenklich** adj dubious; (condition, situation) serious

bedeuten vt mean; jdm nichts/viel ~ mean nothing/a lot to sb; **bedeutend** adj important; (large) considerable; **Bedeutung** f meaning; importance

bedienen 1. vt serve; (machine) operate **2.** vr (when eating) help oneself; **Bedienung** f service; (person) waiter/waitress; shop assistant; (supplement) service (charge); **Bedienungsanleitung** f operating instructions pl; **Bedienungshandbuch** nt instruction manual; **Bedingung** f condition; unter der ~, dass on condition that; unter diesen ~en under these circumstances

bedrohen vt threaten

Bedürfnis nt need

beeilen vr hurry

beeindrucken vt impress

beeinflussen vt influence

beeinträchtigen vt affect

beenden vt end; (complete) finish

beerdigen vt bury; **Beerdigung** f burial; (ceremony) funeral

Beere

Beere f (-, -n) berry; (for wine) grape

Beet nt (-(e)s, -e) bed

befahl imperf of **befehlen**

befahrbar adj passable; NAUT navigable; **befahren 1.** irr vt (road) use; (mountain pass) drive over; (river etc) navigate **2.** adj **stark/wenig ~** busy/quiet

Befehl m (-(e)s, -e) order; IT command; **befehlen** (befahl, befohlen) **1.** vt order; **jdm ~, etw zu tun** order sb to do sth **2.** vi give orders

befestigen vt fix; (with string, rope) attach; (with glue) stick

befeuchten vt moisten

befinden vr be

befohlen pp of **befehlen**

befolgen vt (advice etc) follow

befördern vt transport; (at work) promote; **Beförderung** f transport; (at work) promotion; **Beförderungsbedingungen** pl conditions pl of carriage

Befragung f questioning; (survey) opinion poll

befreundet adj friendly; **~ sein** be friends (mit jdm with sb)

befriedigen vt satisfy; **befriedigend** adj satisfactory; (mark for schoolwork) ≈ C; **Befriedigung** f satisfaction

befristet adj limited (auf + acc to)

befruchten vt fertilize; fig stimulate

Befund m (-(e)s, -e) findings pl; MED diagnosis

befürchten vt fear

befürworten vt support

begabt adj gifted, talented; **Begabung** f talent, gift

begann imperf of **beginnen**

begegnen vi meet (jdm sb), meet with (einer Sache dat sth)

begehen irr vt (offence) commit; (anniversary etc) celebrate

begehrt adj sought-after; (bachelor) eligible

begeistern 1. vt fill with enthusiasm; (stimulate) inspire **2.** vr **sich für etw ~** be/get enthusiastic about sth; **begeistert** adj enthusiastic

Beginn m (-(e)s) beginning; **zu ~** at the beginning; **beginnen** (begann, begonnen) vt, vi start, begin

beglaubigen vt certify; **Beglaubigung** f certification

begleiten vt accompany; **Begleiter(in)** m(f) companion; **Begleitung** f company; MUS accompaniment

beglückwünschen vt congratulate (zu on)

begonnen pp of **beginnen**

begraben irr vt bury; **Begräbnis** nt burial; (ceremony) funeral

begreifen irr vt understand

Begrenzung f boundary; fig restriction

Begriff m (-(e)s, -e) concept;

(*mental impression*) idea; **im ~ sein, etw zu tun** be on the point of doing sth; **schwer von ~ sein** be slow on the uptake

begründen vt justify; Begründung f explanation; (*vindication*) justification

begrüßen vt greet; (*guest*) welcome; Begrüßung f greeting; (*reception*) welcome

behaart adj hairy

behalten irr vt keep; (*keep in head*) remember; **etw für sich ~** keep sth to oneself

Behälter m (-s, -) container

behandeln vt treat; Behandlung f treatment

behaupten 1. vt claim, maintain **2.** vr assert oneself; Behauptung f claim

beheizen vt heat

behelfen irr vr **sich mit/ohne etw ~** make do with/without sth

beherbergen vt accommodate

beherrschen 1. vt (*situation, feelings*) control; (*instrument*) master **2.** vr control oneself; Beherrschung f control (*über + acc* of); **die ~ verlieren** lose one's self-control

behilflich adj helpful; **jdm ~ sein** help sb (*bei* with)

behindern vt hinder; (*traffic, view*) obstruct; Behinderte(r) mf disabled person; be-

hindertengerecht adj suitable for disabled people

Behörde f (-, -n) authority; **die ~n** pl the authorities pl

bei prep + dat (*place*) near, by; (*stay*) at; (*time*) at, on; (*in the course of*) during; (*circumstance*) in; **~m Friseur** at the hairdresser's; **~ uns zuhause** at our place; in our country; **~ Nacht** at night; **~ Tag** by day; **~ Nebel** in fog; **~ Regen findet die Veranstaltung im Saal statt** if it rains the event will take place in the hall; **etw ~ sich haben** have sth on one; **~m Fahren** while driving

beibehalten irr vt keep

Beiboot nt dinghy

beibringen irr vt **jdm etw ~** (*tell*) break sth to sb; (*instruct*) teach sb sth

beide(s) pron both; **meine ~n Brüder** my two brothers, both my brothers; **wir ~** both (or the two) of us; **keiner von ~n** neither of them; **alle ~** both (of them); **~s ist sehr schön** both are very nice; **30 ~** (*in tennis*) 30 all

beieinander adv together

Beifahrer(in) m(f) passenger; Beifahrerairbag m passenger airbag; Beifahrersitz m passenger seat

Beifall m (-(e)s) applause

beige adj inv beige

Beigeschmack m aftertaste

Beil nt (-(e)s, -e) axe

Beilage f GASTR side dish; vegetables pl; (of newspaper) supplement
beiläufig 1. adj casual 2. adv casually
Beileid nt condolences pl; (mein) herzliches ~ please accept my sincere condolences
beiliegend adj enclosed
beim contr of **bei dem**
Bein nt (-(e)s, -e) leg
beinah(e) adv almost, nearly
beinhalten vt contain
Beipackzettel m instruction leaflet
beisammen adv together; **Beisammensein** nt (-s) get-together
Beischlaf m sexual intercourse
beiseite adv aside; **etw ~ legen** (save) put sth by
Beispiel nt (-(e)s, -e) example; **sich** dat **an jdm/etw ein ~ nehmen** take sb/sth as an example; **zum ~** for example
beißen (biss, gebissen) 1. vt bite 2. vi bite; (smoke, acid) sting 3. vr (colours) clash
Beitrag m (-(e)s, Beiträge) contribution; (for membership) subscription; (for insurance) premium; **beitragen** irr vt, vi contribute (zu to)
bekannt adj well-known; (recognizable) familiar; **mit jdm ~ sein** know sb; ~ **geben** announce; **jdn mit jdm ma-**

chen introduce sb to sb; **Bekannte(r)** mf friend; (less close) acquaintance; **bekanntlich** adv as everyone knows; **Bekanntschaft** f acquaintance
bekiffen vr fam get stoned
beklagen vr complain
Bekleidung f clothing
bekommen irr 1. vt get; (letter, present etc) receive; (child) have; (train, cold) catch, get; **wie viel ~ Sie dafür?** how much is that? 2. vi **jdm ~** (food) agree with sb; **wir ~ schon** we're being served
beladen irr vt load
Belag m (-(e)s, Beläge) coating; (on teeth) plaque; (on tongue) fur
belasten vt load; (body) strain; (environment) pollute; fig (with worries etc) burden; COMM (account) debit; LAW incriminate
belästigen vt bother; (stronger) pester; (sexually) harass; **Belästigung** f annoyance; **sexuelle ~** sexual harassment
belebt adj (street etc) busy
Beleg m (-(e)s, -e) COMM receipt; (written evidence) proof; **belegen** vt (bread) spread; (seat) reserve; (course) register for; (claim, expenditure etc) prove
belegt adj TEL engaged (Brit), busy (US); (hotel) full;

bequem

(tongue) coated; **~es Brötchen** sandwich; **der Platz ist ~** this seat is taken; **Belegtzeichen** *nt* TEL engaged tone *(Brit)*, busy tone *(US)*

beleidigen *vt* insult; *(hurt feelings of)* offend; **Beleidigung** *f* insult; LAW slander; *(written)* libel

beleuchten *vt* light; *(light up)* illuminate; *fig* examine; **Beleuchtung** *f* lighting; *(lighting up)* illumination

Belgien *nt* (-s) Belgium; **Belgier(in)** *m(f)* (-s, -) Belgian; **belgisch** *adj* Belgian

belichten *vt* expose; **Belichtung** *f* exposure; **Belichtungsmesser** *m* (-s, -) light meter

Belieben *nt* **(ganz)** nach ~ (just) as you wish

beliebig 1. *adj* jedes ~e Muster any pattern; jeder ~e anyone **2.** *adv* ~ lange as long as you like; ~ viel as many *(or* much) as you like

beliebt *adj* popular

beliefern *vt* supply

bellen *vi* bark

Belohnung *f* reward

Belüftung *f* ventilation

belügen *irr vt* lie to

bemerkbar *adj* noticeable; **sich ~ machen** *(person)* attract attention; *(thing)* become noticeable; **bemerken** *vt* notice; *(say)* remark; **bemerkenswert** *adj* remarkable; **Bemerkung** *f* remark

bemitleiden *vt* pity

bemühen *vr* try (hard), make an effort; **Bemühung** *f* effort

bemuttern *vt* mother

benachbart *adj* neighbouring

benachrichtigen *vt* inform; **Benachrichtigung** *f* notification

benachteiligen *vt* (put at a) disadvantage; *(racially etc)* discriminate against

benehmen *irr vr* behave; **Benehmen** *nt* (-s) behaviour

beneiden *vt* envy; **jdn um etw ~** envy sb sth

Beneluxländer *pl* Benelux countries *pl*

benommen *adj* dazed

benötigen *vt* need

benutzen *vt* use; **Benutzer(in)** *m(f)* (-s, -) user; **benutzerfreundlich** *adj* user-friendly; **Benutzerhandbuch** *nt* user's guide; **Benutzerkennung** *f* user ID; **Benutzeroberfläche** *f* IT user / system interface

Benzin *nt* (-s, -e) AUTO petrol *(Brit)*, gas *(US)*; **Benzinkanister** *m* petrol *(Brit)* or gas *(US))* can; **Benzinpumpe** *f* petrol *(Brit)* (or gas *(US))* pump; **Benzintank** *m* petrol *(Brit)* (or gas *(US))* tank; **Benzinuhr** *f* fuel gauge

beobachten *vt* observe; **Beobachtung** *f* observation

bequem *adj* comfortable; *(excuse)* convenient; *(idle)* lazy;

machen Sie es sich ~ make yourself at home; Bequemlichkeit f comfort; laziness

beraten *irr* **1.** *vt* advise; (*plan etc*) discuss **2.** *vr* consult; (*at doctor's etc*) consultation

berauben *vt* rob

berechnen *vt* calculate; COMM charge; berechnend *adj* (*person*) calculating

berechtigen *vt* entitle (*zu* to); *fig* justify; berechtigt *adj* justified; *zu etw* ~ *sein* to be entitled to sth

bereden *vt* discuss

Bereich m (-(e)s, -e) area; (*sphere*) field

bereisen *vt* travel through

bereit *adj* ready; *zu etw* ~ *sein* be ready for sth; *sich* ~ *erklären, etw zu tun* agree to do sth

bereiten *vt* prepare; (*grief*) cause; (*pleasure*) give

bereitlegen *vt* lay out

bereitmachen *vr* get ready

bereits *adv* already

Bereitschaft f readiness; ~ *haben* (*doctor*) be on call

bereitstehen *vi* be ready

bereuen *vt* regret

Berg m (-(e)s, -e) mountain; (*smaller*) hill; *in die* ~*e fahren* go to the mountains; bergab *adv* downhill; bergauf *adv* uphill; Bergbahn f mountain railway (*Brit*) (or railroad (*US*))

bergen (*barg, geborgen*) *vt*

(*person*) rescue

Bergführer(in) m(f) mountain guide; Berghütte f mountain hut; bergig *adj* mountainous; Bergkette f mountain range; Bergschuh m climbing boot; Bergsteigen nt (-s) mountaineering; Bergsteiger(in) m(f) (-s, -) mountaineer; Bergtour f mountain hike

Bergung f rescue; (*of body, vehicle*) recovery

Bergwacht f (-, -en) mountain rescue service; Bergwerk nt mine

Bericht m (-(e)s, -e) report; berichten *vt*, *vi* report; berichtigen *vt* correct

Bermudadreieck nt Bermuda triangle; Bermudainseln pl Bermuda sg; Bermudashorts pl Bermuda shorts pl

Bernstein m amber

berüchtigt *adj* notorious, infamous

berücksichtigen *vt* take into account; (*application, applicant*) consider

Beruf m (-(e)s, -e) occupation; (*requiring academic training*) profession; (*skilled, self-employed*) trade; *was sind Sie von* ~? what do you do (for a living)?; beruflich *adj* professional

Berufsausbildung f vocational training; Berufsschule f vocational college; berufstätig *adj* employed; Be-

rufsverkehr *m* commuter traffic

beruhigen 1. *vt* calm **2.** *vr* (*person, situation*) calm down; **beruhigend** *adj* reassuring; **Beruhigungsmittel** *nt* sedative

berühmt *adj* famous

berühren 1. *vt* touch; (*emotionally*) move; (*be important for*) affect; (*subject*) mention, touch on **2.** *vr* touch

besaufen *irr vr fam* get plastered

beschädigen *vt* damage

beschäftigen 1. *vt* occupy; (*worker*) employ **2.** *vr sich mit etw* ~ occupy oneself with sth; (*problem etc*) deal with sth; **beschäftigt** *adj* busy, occupied; **Beschäftigung** *f* (*work*) employment; (*activity*) occupation; (*with problem etc*) preoccupation (*mit* with)

Bescheid *m* (-(e)s, -e) information; ~ **wissen** be informed (*or* know) (*über* + *acc* about); **ich weiß** ~ I know; **jdm** ~ **geben** (*or* **sagen**) let sb know

bescheiden *adj* modest

bescheinigen *vt* certify; (*confirm*) acknowledge; **Bescheinigung** *f* certificate; (*for money*) receipt

bescheißen *irr vt vulg* cheat (*um* out of)

beschimpfen *vt* swear at

Beschiss *m* (-es) **das ist** ~

vulg that's a rip-off; **beschissen** *adj vulg* shitty

beschlagnahmen *vt* confiscate

Beschleunigung *f* acceleration; **Beschleunigungsspur** *f* acceleration lane

beschließen *irr vt* decide on; (*conclude*) end; **Beschluss** *m* decision

beschränken 1. *vt* limit, restrict (*auf* + *acc* to) **2.** *vr* restrict oneself (*auf* + *acc* to); **Beschränkung** *f* limitation, restriction

beschreiben *irr vt* describe; (*paper*) write on; **Beschreibung** *f* description

beschuldigen *vt* accuse (*gen* of); **Beschuldigung** *f* accusation

beschummeln *vt, vi fam* cheat (*um* out of)

beschützen *vt* protect (*vor* + *dat* from)

Beschwerde *f* (-, -n) complaint; ~*n pl* (*illness*) trouble *sg*; **beschweren 1.** *vt* weight down; *fig* burden **2.** *vr* complain

beschwipst *adj* tipsy

beseitigen *vt* remove; (*problem*) get rid of; (*rubbish*) dispose of; **Beseitigung** *f* removal; (*of rubbish*) disposal

Besen *m* (-s, -) broom

besetzen *vt* (*house, country*) occupy; (*seat*) take; (*post*) fill; (*role*) cast; **besetzt** *adj* full; TEL engaged (*Brit*), busy

(US); *(seat)* taken; *(toilet)* engaged; **Besetztzeichen** *nt* engaged tone *(Brit)*, busy tone *(US)*

besichtigen *vt (museum)* visit; *(sights)* have a look at; *(town)* tour

besiegen *vt* defeat

Besitz *m (-es)* possession; *(objects)* property; **besitzen** *irr vt* own; *(quality)* have; **Besitzer(in)** *m(f) (-s, -)* owner

besoffen *adj fam* plastered

besondere(r, s) *adj* special; *(specific, more than usual)* particular; *(strange)* peculiar; **nichts ~s** nothing special; **Besonderheit** *f* special feature; *(unusual characteristic)* peculiarity; **besonders** *adv* especially, particularly; *(individually)* separately

besorgen *vt (obtain)* get *(jdm for sb)*; *(buy also)* purchase; *(task etc)* deal with

besprechen *irr vt* discuss; **Besprechung** *f* discussion; *(conference)* meeting

besser *adj* better; **es geht ihm ~** he feels better; **~ gesagt** or rather; **~ werden** improve; **bessern 1.** *vt* improve **2.** *vr* improve; *(person)* mend one's ways; **Besserung** *f* improvement; **gute ~!** get well soon

beständig *adj* constant; *(weather)* settled

Bestandteil *m* component

bestätigen *vt* confirm; *(receipt, letter)* acknowledge; **Bestätigung** *f* confirmation; *(of letter)* acknowledgement

beste(r, s) 1. *adj* best; **das ~ wäre, wir ...** it would be best if we ... **2.** *adv* **sie singt am ~n** she sings best; **so ist es am ~n** it's best that way; **am ~n gehst du gleich** you'd better go at once

bestechen *irr vt* bribe; **Bestechung** *f* bribery

Besteck *nt (-(e)s, -e)* cutlery

bestehen *irr* **1.** *vi* be, exist; *(continue)* last; **~ auf + dat** insist on; **~ aus** consist of **2.** *vt (test, exam)* pass; *(fight)* win

bestehlen *irr vt* rob

bestellen *vt* order; *(reserve)* book; *(regards, message)* pass on *(jdm to sb)*; *(person)* send for; **Bestellnummer** *f* order number; **Bestellung** *f* COMM order; *(action)* ordering

bestens *adv* very well

bestimmen *vt* determine; *(rules)* lay down; *(day, place)* fix; *(person to a post)* appoint; *(intend)* mean *(für for)*; **bestimmt 1.** *adj* definite; *(left unspecified)* certain; *(resolute)* firm **2.** *adv* definitely; *(know)* for sure; **Bestimmung** *f (rule)* regulation; *(intended use)* purpose

Best.-Nr. *abbr* = **Bestellnummer**; order number

bestrafen *vt* punish

bestrahlen vt illuminate; MED treat with radiotherapy

bestreiten irr vt (assertion etc) deny

Bestseller m (-s, -) bestseller

bestürzt adj dismayed

Besuch m (-(e)s, -e) visit; (person) visitor; ~ **haben** have visitors/a visitor; **besuchen** vt visit; (school, cinema etc) go to; **Besucher(in)** m(f) (-s, -) visitor; **Besuchszeit** f visiting hours pl

betäuben vt MED anaesthetize; **Betäubungsmittel** nt anaesthetic

Bete f (-, -n) **Rote** ~ beetroot

beteiligen 1. vr **sich an etw** dat ~ take part in sth, participate in sth **2.** vt **jdn an etw** dat ~ involve sb in sth; **Beteiligung** f participation; (portion) share; (number of people present) attendance

beten vi pray

Beton m (-s, -s) concrete

betonen vt stress; (give prominence to) emphasize; **Betonung** f stress; fig emphasis

Betr. abbr = **Betreff**; re

Betracht m in ~ **ziehen** take into consideration; **in** ~ **kommen** be a possibility; **nicht in** ~ **kommen** be out of the question; **betrachten** vt look at; ~ **als** regard as; **beträchtlich** adj considerable

Betrag m (-(e)s, Beträge) amount, sum; **betragen** irr **1.** vt amount (or come) to

2. vr behave

betreffen irr vt concern; (regulation etc) affect; **was mich betrifft** as for me; **betreffend** adj relevant, in question

betreten irr vt enter; (stage etc) step onto; „**Betreten verboten**" 'keep off/out'

betreuen vt look after; (party of tourists, department) be in charge of; **Betreuer(in)** m(f) (-s, -) (of invalid, old person) carer; (of child) child minder; (of party of tourists) groupleader

Betrieb m (-(e)s, -e) (company) firm; (buildings etc) plant; (of machine, factory) operation; (in shops etc) bustle; **außer** ~ **sein** be out of order; **in** ~ **sein** be in operation; **betriebsbereit** adj operational; **Betriebsrat** m works council; **Betriebssystem** nt IT operating system

betrinken irr vr get drunk

betroffen adj (upset) shaken; **von etw** ~ **werden/sein** be affected by sth

betrog imperf of **betrügen**; **betrogen** pp of **betrügen**

Betrug m (-(e)s) deception; LAW fraud; **betrügen** (betrog, betrogen) vt deceive; LAW defraud; (partner) cheat on; **Betrüger(in)** m(f) (-s, -) cheat

betrunken adj drunk

Bett nt (-(e)s, -en) bed; **ins** (or

zu) ~ **gehen** go to bed; **das** ~
machen make the bed; **Bett-**
bezug m duvet cover; **Bett-**
decke f blanket

betteln vi beg

Bettlaken nt sheet

Bettler(in) m(f) (-s, -) beggar

Bettsofa nt sofa bed; **Bett-**
tuch nt sheet; **Bettwäsche**
f bed linen; **Bettzeug** nt bedding

beugen 1. vt bend **2.** vr bend;
(yield) submit (dat to)

Beule f (-, -n) bump; (in car
etc) dent

beunruhigen vt, vr worry

beurteilen vt judge

Beute f (-) (of thief) booty,
loot; (of animal) prey

Beutel m (-s, -) bag

Bevölkerung f population

bevollmächtigt adj author-
ized (zu etw to do sth)

bevor conj before; **bevorste-**
hen irr vi (difficulties) lie
ahead; (danger) be immi-
nent; **jdm** ~ (surprise etc)
be in store for sb; **bevorste-**
hend adj forthcoming; **be-**
vorzugen vt prefer

bewachen vt guard; **bewacht**
adj **~er Parkplatz** supervised
car park (Brit), guarded
parking lot (US)

bewegen vt, vr move; **jdn da-**
zu ~, **etw zu tun** get sb to do
sth; **es bewegt sich etwas**
fig things are beginning to
happen; **Bewegung** f movement; PHYS motion; (inner)

emotion; (bodily) exercise;
Bewegungsmelder m (-s,
-) sensor (which reacts to
movement)

Beweis m (-es, -e) proof; (material, facts) evidence; **be-**
weisen irr vt prove; (demonstrate) show

bewerben irr vr apply (um
for); **Bewerbung** f application; **Bewerbungsunterla-**
gen pl application documents pl

bewilligen vt allow; (money)
grant

bewirken vt cause, bring
about

bewohnen vt live in; **Bewoh-**
ner(in) m(f) (-s, -) inhabitant; (of house) resident

bewölkt adj cloudy, overcast;
Bewölkung f clouds pl

bewundern vt admire; **be-**
wundernswert adj admirable

bewusst 1. adj conscious; (intentional) deliberate; **sich**
dat einer Sache gen ~ **sein**
be aware of sth **2.** adv con-
sciously; (intentionally) deliberately; **bewusstlos** adj
unconscious; **Bewusstlosig-**
keit f unconsciousness; **Be-**
wusstsein nt (-s) consciousness; **bei** ~ conscious

bezahlen vt pay; (goods, service) pay for; **sich bezahlt**
machen be worth it

Bezahlung f payment

bezeichnen vt (with sign etc)

mark; (give name to) call; (categorize) describe; **Bezeichnung** f name; (expression) term

beziehen irr **1.** vt (bed) change; (house, position) move into; (get) receive; (newspaper) take; **einen Standpunkt ~** fig take up a position **2.** vr refer (auf + acc to); **Beziehung** f (between two things) connection; (between lovers) relationship; (influential) **~en haben** have connections (or contacts); **in dieser ~** in this respect; **beziehungsweise** adv or; (more precisely) or rather

Bezirk m (-(e)s, -e) district

Bezug m (-(e)s, Bezüge) (for cushion etc) cover; (for pillow) pillowcase; **in ~ auf** + acc with regard to; **bezüglich** prep + gen concerning

bezweifeln vt doubt

BH m (-s, -s) bra

Bhf. abbr = **Bahnhof;** station

Biathlon m (-s, -s) biathlon

Bibel f (-, -n) Bible

Biber m (-s, -) beaver

Bibliothek f (-, -en) library

biegen (bog, gebogen) **1.** vt, vr bend **2.** vi turn (in + acc into); **Biegung** f bend

Biene f (-, -n) bee

Bier nt (-(e)s, -e) beer; **helles ~** ≈ lager (Brit), beer (US); **dunkles ~** ≈ brown ale (Brit), dark beer (US); **zwei**

~, bitte! two beers, please; **Biergarten** m beer garden; **Bierzelt** nt beer tent

bieten (bot, geboten) **1.** vt offer; (at auction) bid; **sich dat etw ~ lassen** put up with sth **2.** vr (opportunity) present itself (dat to)

Bikini m (-s, -s) bikini

Bild nt (-(e)s, -er) picture; (in one's mind) image; **PHOT** photo

bilden 1. vt form; (intellectually) educate; (rule, basis etc) constitute **2.** vr form; (learn) educate oneself

Bilderbuch nt picture book

Bildhauer(in) m(f) (-s, -) sculptor

Bildschirm m screen; **Bildschirmschoner** m (-s, -) screen saver; **Bildschirmtext** m viewdata, videotext

Bildung f formation; (knowledge, manners) education; **Bildungsurlaub** m educational holiday; (of employee) study leave

Billard nt billiards sg

billig adj cheap; (just) fair

Binde f (-, -n) bandage; (worn on arm) band; (for woman's period) sanitary towel (Brit), sanitary napkin (US)

Bindehautentzündung f conjunctivitis

binden (band, gebunden) vt tie; (book) bind; (sauce) thicken

Bindestrich m hyphen

Bindfaden m string

Bindung f bond, tie; (on ski) binding

Bio- in cpds bio-; **Biokost** f health food; **Biologie** f biology; **biologisch** adj biological; (cultivation) organic

Birke f (-, -n) birch

Birne f (-, -n) pear; ELEC (light) bulb

bis 1. prep + acc (space) to, as far as; (time) till, until; (at the latest) by; **Sie haben ~ Dienstag Zeit** you have until (or till) Tuesday; **~ Dienstag muss es fertig sein** it must be ready by Tuesday; **~ hierher** this far; **~ in die Nacht** into the night; **~ auf weiteres** until further notice; **~ bald/ gleich!** see you later/ soon; **~ auf etw** acc including sth; (excluding) except sth; **~ zu** up to; **von ... ~ ...** from ... to ... **2.** conj (numbers) to; (time) until, till

Bischof m (-s, Bischöfe) bishop

bisher adv up to now, so far

Biskuit nt (-(e)s, -s or -e) sponge

biss imperf of **beißen**

Biss m (-es, -e) bite

bisschen 1. adj ein **~** a bit of; **ein ~ Salz/Liebe** a bit of salt/love; **ich habe kein ~ Hunger** I'm not a bit hungry **2.** adv ein **~** a bit; **kein ~** not at all

bissig adj (dog) vicious; (re-

mark) cutting

Bit nt (-s, -s) IT bit

bitte interj please; (wie) **~?** (I beg your) pardon?; **~ (schön)!** (replying to thanks) you're welcome, that's alright; **hier, ~** here you are; **Bitte** f (-, -n) request; **(bat, gebeten)** vt, vi ask (um for)

bitter adj bitter

Blähungen pl MED wind sg

blamieren 1. vr make a fool of oneself **2.** vt jdn **~** make sb look a fool

Blankoscheck m blank cheque

Blase f (-, -n) bubble; MED blister; ANAT bladder

blasen (blies, geblasen) vi blow; **jdm einen ~** vulg give sb a blow job

Blasenentzündung f cystitis

blass adj pale

Blatt nt (-(e)s, Blätter) leaf; (of paper) sheet; **blättern** vi IT scroll; **in etw** dat **~** leaf through sth; **Blätterteig** m puff pastry; **Blattsalat** m green salad; **Blattspinat** m spinach

blau adj blue; fam (drunk) plastered; GASTR boiled; **~es** Auge black eye; **~er Fleck** bruise; **Blaubeere** f bilberry, blueberry; **Blaulicht** nt flashing blue light; **blaumachen** vi skip work; (pupil) skip school; **Blauschimmelkäse** m blue cheese

Blazer m (-s, -) blazer

Blech nt (-(e)s, -e) sheet metal; (for oven) baking tray (Brit), cookie sheet (US); **Blechschaden** m AUTO damage to the bodywork

Blei nt (-(e)s, -e) lead

bleiben (blieb, geblieben) vi stay; **lass das ~!** stop it; **das bleibt unter uns** that's (just) between ourselves; **mir bleibt keine andere Wahl** I have no other choice

bleich adj pale; **bleichen** vt bleach

bleifrei adj (petrol) unleaded; **bleihaltig** adj (petrol) leaded

Bleistift m pencil

Blende f (-, -n) PHOT aperture

Blick m (-(e)s, -e) look; (brief) glance; (from a place) view; **auf den ersten ~** at first sight; **einen ~ auf etw** acc **werfen** have a look at sth; **blicken** vi look; **sich ~ lassen** show up

blieb imperf of **bleiben**

blies imperf of **blasen**

blind adj blind; (glass etc) dull; **Blinddarm** m appendix; **Blinddarmentzündung** f appendicitis; **Blinde(r)** mf blind person / man / woman; **die ~n** pl the blind pl; **Blindenhund** m guide dog; **Blindenschrift** f braille

blinken vi (star, lights) twinkle; (brightly, briefly) flash;

AUTO indicate; **Blinker** m (-s, -) AUTO indicator (Brit), turn signal (US)

blinzeln vi blink

Blitz m (-es, -e) (flash of) lightning; PHOT flash; **blitzen** vi PHOT use a/the flash; **es blitzte und donnerte** there was thunder and lightning; **Blitzlicht** nt flash

Block m (-(e)s, Blöcke) block; (of paper) pad; **Blockflöte** f recorder; **Blockhaus** nt log cabin; **blockieren 1.** vt block **2.** vi jam; (wheels) lock; **Blockschrift** f block letters pl

blöd adj stupid; **blödeln** vi fam fool around

blond adj blond; (woman) blonde

bloß 1. adj (without covering) bare; (nothing more than) mere **2.** adv only; **geh mir ~ aus dem Weg** just get out of my way

blühen vi bloom; fig flourish

Blume f (-, -n) flower; (of wine) bouquet; **Blumenkohl** m cauliflower; **Blumenladen** m flower shop; **Blumenstrauß** m bunch of flowers; **Blumentopf** m flowerpot; **Blumenvase** f vase

Bluse f (-, -n) blouse

Blut nt (-(e)s) blood; **Blutbild** nt blood count; **Blutdruck** m blood pressure

Blüte f (-, -n) (part of plant) flower, bloom; (on tree) blos-

som; *fig* prime
bluten *vi* bleed
Blütenstaub *m* pollen
Bluter *m* (*-s, -*) MED haemophiliac; **Bluterguss** *m* haematoma; (*on skin*) bruise;
Blutgruppe *f* blood group;
blutig *adj* bloody; **Blutkonserve** *f* unit of stored blood;
Blutprobe *f* blood sample;
Blutspende *f* blood donation; **Bluttransfusion** *f*
blood transfusion; **Blutung**
f bleeding; **Blutvergiftung**
f blood poisoning; **Blutwurst** *f* black pudding (*Brit*),
blood sausage (*US*)
BLZ *abbr* = **Bankleitzahl**
Bob *m* (*-s, -s*) bob(sleigh)
Bock *m* (*-(e)s, Böcke*) (*deer*)
buck; (*sheep*) ram; (*stand*)
trestle; SPORT vaulting horse;
ich hab keinen ~ (drauf)
fam I don't feel like it
Boden *m* (*-s, Böden*) ground;
(*of room*) floor; (*of sea, barrel*) bottom; (*loft*) attic; **Bodennebel** *m* ground mist;
Bodenpersonal *nt* ground
staff; **Bodenschätze** *pl* mineral resources *pl*
Bodensee *m* **der** ~ Lake Constance
Body *m* (*-s, -s*) body; **Bodybuilding** *nt* (*-s*) bodybuilding
bog *imperf of* **biegen**
Bogen *m* (*-s, -*) curve; (*in architecture*) arch; (*weapon, for violin etc*) bow; (*of paper*)

sheet
Bohne *f* (*-, -n*) bean; **grüne ~n**
pl green (*or* French (*Brit*))
beans *pl*; **weiße ~n** *pl* haricot
beans (*US*); **Bohnenkaffee** *m*
real coffee; **Bohnensprosse**
f bean sprout
bohren *vt* drill; **Bohrer** *m* (*-s,
-*) drill
Boiler *m* (*-s, -*) water heater
Boje *f* (*-, -n*) buoy
Bolivien *nt* (*-s*) Bolivia
Bombe *f* (*-, -n*) bomb
Bon *m* (*-s, -s*) receipt; (*exchangeable for goods etc*)
voucher, coupon
Bonbon *nt* (*-s, -s*) sweet (*Brit*),
candy (*US*)
Bonus *m* (*- or -ses, -se or Boni*) bonus; (*in sport, school*)
bonus points *pl*; (*in insurance*) no-claims bonus
Boot *nt* (*-(e)s, -e*) boat; **Bootsverleih** *m* boat hire (*Brit*) (*or*
rental (*US*))
Bord *m* (*-(e)s, -e*) **an ~** (*eines
Schiffes*) on board (a ship);
an ~ gehen (*ship*) go on
board; (*plane*) board; **von
~ gehen** disembark; **Bordcomputer** *m* dashboard
computer
Bordell *nt* (*-s, -e*) brothel
Bordkarte *f* boarding card
Bordstein *m* kerb (*Brit*), curb
(*US*)
borgen *vt* borrow; **jdm etw ~**
lend sb sth; **sich** *dat* **etw ~**
borrow sth
Börse *f* (*-, -n*) stock exchange;

(*for coins*) purse

bös *adj* → **böse**; **bösartig** *adj* malicious; MED malignant

Böschung *f* slope; (*along river*) embankment

böse *adj* bad; (*stronger*) evil; (*wound*) angry; (*annoyed*) angry; **bist du mir ~?** are you angry with me?

boshaft *adj* malicious

Bosnien *nt* (-s) Bosnia; **Bosnien-Herzegowina** *nt* (-s) Bosnia-Herzegovina

böswillig *adj* malicious

bot *imperf of* **bieten**

botanisch *adj* **~er Garten** botanical gardens *pl*

Botschaft *f* message; POL embassy; **Botschafter(in)** *m(f)* ambassador

Botsuana *nt* (-s) Botswana

Bouillon *f* (-, -s) stock

Boutique *f* (-, -n) boutique

Bowle *f* (-, -n) punch

Box *f* (-, -en) (*container, for horse*) box; (*of stereo system*) speaker; (*in motor racing*) pit

boxen *vi* box; **Boxer** *m* (-s, -) (*dog, sportsman*) boxer; **Boxershorts** *pl* boxer shorts *pl*; **Boxkampf** *m* boxing match

Boykott *m* (-s, -e) boycott

brach *imperf of* **brechen**

brachte *imperf of* **bringen**

Brainstorming *nt* (-s) brainstorming

Branchenverzeichnis *nt* yellow pages® *pl*

Brand *m* (-(e)s, Brände) fire

Brandenburg *nt* (-s) Brandenburg

Brandsalbe *f* ointment for burns

Brandung *f* surf

Brandwunde *f* burn

brannte *imperf of* **brennen**

Brasilien *nt* (-s) Brazil

braten (*briet, gebraten*) *vt* roast; grill; fry; **Braten** *m* (-s, -) roast; (*uncooked*) joint; **Bratensoße** *f* gravy; **Brathähnchen** *nt* roast chicken; **Bratkartoffeln** *pl* fried potatoes *pl*; **Bratpfanne** *f* frying pan; **Bratspieß** *m* spit; **Bratwurst** *f* fried sausage; grilled sausage

Brauch *m* (-s, Bräuche) custom

brauchen *vt* need (*für, zu* for); (*patience, care etc*) require; (*time*) take; (*make use of*) use; **wie lange wird er ~?** how long will it take him?; **du brauchst es nur zu sagen** you only need to say; **das braucht (seine) Zeit** it takes time; **ihr braucht es nicht zu tun** you don't have (or need) to do it; **sie hätte nicht zu kommen ~** she needn't have come

brauen *vt* brew; **Brauerei** *f* brewery

braun *adj* brown; (*from sun*) tanned; **Bräune** *f* (-, -n) brownness; (*from sun*) tan; **Bräunungsstudio** *nt* tanning studio

Brause f (-, -n) (*apparatus*) shower; (*drink*) fizzy drink (*Brit*), soda (*US*)

Braut f (-, *Bräute*) bride; **Bräutigam** m (-*s*, -*e*) bridegroom

brav *adj* (*child*) good, well-behaved

bravo *interj* well done

brechen (*brach*, *gebrochen*) **1.** vt break; (*vomit*) bring up; **sich** *dat* **den Arm** ~ break one's arm **2.** vi break; (*when unwell*) vomit, be sick; **Brechreiz** m nausea

Brei m (-(*e*)s, -*e*) mush, pulp; (*oats*) porridge; (*for children*) pap

breit *adj* wide; (*shoulders*) broad; **zwei Meter** ~ two metres wide; **Breite** f (-, -*n*) breadth; (*in measurements*) width; GEO latitude; **der ~ nach** widthways; **Breitengrad** m (degree of) latitude

Bremen nt (-*s*) Bremen

Bremsbelag m brake lining; **Bremse** f (-, -*n*) brake; ZOOL horsefly; **bremsen 1.** vi brake **2.** vt (*car*) brake; *fig* slow down; **Bremsflüssigkeit** f brake fluid; **Bremslicht** nt brake light; **Bremspedal** nt brake pedal; **Bremsspur** f tyre marks pl; **Bremsweg** m braking distance

brennen (*brannte*, *gebrannt*) vi burn; (*house*, *forest*) be

on fire; **es brennt!** fire!; **mir ~ die Augen** my eyes are smarting; **das Licht ~ lassen** leave the light on; **Brennholz** nt firewood; **Brennnessel** f stinging nettle; **Brennspiritus** m methylated spirits pl; **Brennstab** m fuel rod; **Brennstoff** m fuel

Brett nt (-(*e*)s, -*er*) board; (*longer*) plank; (*for books etc*) shelf; (*for game*) board; **schwarzes** ~ notice board, bulletin board (*US*); **~er** pl skis pl; **Brettspiel** nt board game

Brezel f (-, -*n*) pretzel

Brief m (-(*e*)s, -*e*) letter; **Briefbombe** f letter bomb; **Brieffreund(in)** m(f) penfriend, pen pal; **Briefkasten** m letterbox (*Brit*), mailbox (*US*); **Briefmarke** f stamp; **Briefpapier** nt writing paper; **Brieftasche** f wallet; **Briefträger(in)** m(f) postman/-woman; **Briefumschlag** m envelope; **Briefwaage** f letter scales pl

briet *imperf of* **braten**

Brille f (-, -*n*) glasses pl; (*protective*) goggles pl; **Brilletui** nt glasses case

bringen (*brachte*, *gebracht*) vt bring; (*somewhere else*) take; (*go and come back with*) fetch; THEAT, FILM show; RADIO, TV broadcast; ~ **Sie mir bitte noch ein Bier** could you bring me another beer, please?; **jdn nach Hause ~** take sb home; **jdn dazu ~, etw zu tun** make sb do sth; **jdn auf eine Idee ~** give sb an idea

Brise f (-, -n) breeze
Brite m (-n, -n), **Britin** f British person, Briton; **er ist ~** he is British; **die ~n** the British; **britisch** adj British
Brocken m (-s, -) bit; (larger) lump, chunk
Brokkoli m broccoli
Brombeere f blackberry
Bronchitis f (-) bronchitis
Bronze f (-, -n) bronze
Brosche f (-, -n) brooch
Brot nt (-(e)s, -e) bread; loaf; **Brotaufstrich** m spread; **Brötchen** nt roll; **Brotzeit** f break; (food) snack; **~ machen** have a snack
Browser m (-s, -) IT browser
Bruch m (-(e)s, Brüche) (action) breaking; (crack etc; with hurry, tradition etc) break; MED rupture, hernia; (of bone) fracture; MATH fraction; **brüchig** adj brittle
Brücke f (-, -n) bridge
Bruder m (-s, Brüder) brother
Brühe f (-, -n) (clear) soup; (basis for soup) stock; pej (drink) muck; **Brühwürfel** m stock cube
brüllen vi roar; (bull) bellow; (in agony) scream (with pain)
brummen 1. vi (bear, person) growl; (mumble) mutter; (in-

sect) buzz; (engine, radio) drone **2.** vt growl
brünett adj brunette
Brunnen m (-s, -) fountain; (deep) well; (natural) spring
Brust f (-, Brüste) breast; (of man) chest; **Brustschwimmen** nt (-s) breaststroke; **Brustwarze** f nipple
brutal adj brutal
brutto adv gross
BSE nt (-) abbr = **bovine spongiforme Enzephalopathie**; BSE
Bube m (-n, -n) boy, lad; (playing card) jack
Buch nt (-(e)s, Bücher) book
Buche f (-, -n) beech (tree)
buchen vt book; (amount) enter
Bücherei f library
Buchfink m chaffinch
Buchhalter(in) m(f) accountant
Buchhandlung f bookshop
Büchse f (-, -n) tin (Brit), can; **Büchsenfleisch** nt tinned meat (Brit), canned meat; **Büchsenmilch** f tinned milk (Brit), canned milk; **Büchsenöffner** m tin opener (Brit), can opener
Buchstabe m (-ns, -n) letter; **buchstabieren** vt spell
Bucht f (-, -en) bay
Buchung f booking; COMM entry
Buckel m (-s, -) hump
bücken vr bend down
Buddhismus m (-) Bud-

dhism

Bude f (-, -en) (at market) stall; fam (flat) pad, place

Büfett nt (-s, -s) sideboard; **kaltes ~** cold buffet

Büffel m (-s, -) buffalo

Bügel m (-s, -) (for clothes) hanger; (on saddle) stirrup; (of glasses) sidepiece; (of ski-lift) T-bar; **Bügelbrett** nt ironing board; **Bügeleisen** nt iron; **Bügelfalte** f crease; **bügelfrei** adj non-iron; **bügeln** vt, vi iron

buh interj boo

Bühne f (-, -n) stage; **Bühnenbild** nt set

Bulgare m (-n, -n), **Bulgarin** f Bulgarian; **Bulgarien** nt (-s) Bulgaria; **bulgarisch** adj Bulgarian; **Bulgarisch** nt Bulgarian

Bulimie f (-) bulimia

Bulle m (-n, -n) bull; fam (policeman) cop

Bummel m (-s, -) stroll; **bummeln** vi stroll; (do things slowly) dawdle; (be idle) loaf around; **Bummelzug** m slow train

bums interj bang

bumsen vi vulg screw

Bund 1. m (-(e)s, Bünde) (of trousers, skirt) waistband; (between friends) bond; (organization) association; POL confederation; **der ~** fam (German military) the army **2.** nt (-(e)s, -e) bunch; (of straw etc) bundle

Bundes- in cpds Federal; (referring to Germany also) German; **Bundesbahn** f German railway company; **Bundeskanzler(in)** m(f) Chancellor; **Bundesland** nt state, Land; **Bundesliga** f **erste/ zweite ~** First / Second Division; **Bundespräsident(in)** m(f) President; **Bundesrat** m Upper House (of the German Parliament); (in Switzerland) Council of Ministers; **Bundesregierung** f Federal Government; **Bundesrepublik** f Federal Republic; **~ Deutschland** Federal Republic of Germany; **Bundesstraße** f ≈ A road (Brit), ≈ state highway (US); **Bundestag** m Lower House (of the German Parliament); **Bundeswehr** f (German) armed forces pl

Bündnis nt alliance

Bungalow m (-s, -s) bungalow

Bungeejumping nt (-s) bungee jumping

bunt 1. adj colourful; (programme etc) varied; **~e Farben** bright colours **2.** adv (paint) in bright colours; **Buntstift** m crayon, coloured pencil

Burg f (-, -en) castle

Bürger m(f) (-s, -) citizen; **bürgerlich** adj (rights, marriage etc) civil; (in social hierarchy) middle-class; pej bourgeois; **Bürgermeis-**

ter(in) *m(f)* mayor; **Bürger-
steig** *m (-(e)s, -e)* pavement
(*Brit*), sidewalk (*US*)
Büro *nt (-s, -s)* office; **Büro-
klammer** *f* paper clip
Bürokratie *f* bureaucracy
Bursche *m (-n, -n)* lad; (*man*)
guy
Bürste *f (-, -n)* brush; **bürsten**
vt brush
Bus *m (-ses, -se)* bus; (*long-
distance*) coach (*Brit*), bus;
Busbahnhof *m* bus station
Busch *m (-(e)s, Büsche)* bush;
shrub
Busen *m (-s, -)* breasts *pl*,
bosom
Busfahrer(in) *m(f)* bus driv-

er; **Bushaltestelle** *f* bus stop
Businessclass *f (-)* business
class
Busreise *f* coach tour (*Brit*),
bus tour
Bußgeld *nt* fine
Büstenhalter *m (-s, -)* bra
Busverbindung *f* bus con-
nection
Butter *f (-)* butter; **Butterbrot**
nt slice of bread and butter;
Buttermilch *f* buttermilk
Button *m (-s, -s)* badge (*Brit*),
button (*US*)
b. w. *abbr =* **bitte wenden**; pto
Byte *nt (-s, -s)* byte
bzw. *adv abbr =* **beziehungs-
weise**

C

ca. *adv abbr =* **circa**, approx
Cabrio *nt (-s, -s)* convertible
Café *nt (-s, -s)* café
Cafeteria *f (-, -s)* cafeteria
Call-Center *nt (-s, -s)* call centre
campen *vi* camp; **Camping** *nt
(-s)* camping; **Campingbus**
m (-ses, -se) camper; **Campingplatz** *m* campsite, camping
ground (*US*)
Cappuccino *m (-s, -)* cappuccino
Carving *nt (-s)* (*in skiing*)
carving; **Carvingski** *m* carving ski
CD *f (-, -s) abbr =* **Compact
Disc**; CD; **CD-Brenner** *m*

(-s, -) CD burner, CD writer;
CD-Player *m (-s, -)* CD play-
er; **CD-ROM** *f (-, -s) abbr =*
**Compact Disc Read Only
Memory**; CD-ROM; **CD-
-ROM-Laufwerk** *nt* CD-
-ROM drive, **CD-Spieler** *m*
CD player
Cello *nt (-s, -s or Celli)* cello
Celsius *nt* celsius; **20 Grad ~**
20 degrees Celsius, 68 de-
grees Fahrenheit
Cent *m (-, -s)* (*of dollar and
euro*) cent
Chamäleon *nt (-s, -s)* chame-
leon
Champagner *m (-s, -)* cham-
pagne

Champignon m (-s, -s) mushroom

Champions League f (-, -s) Champions League

Chance f (-, -n) chance; **die ~n stehen gut** the prospects are good

Chaos nt (-) chaos; **Chaot(in)** m(f) (-en, -en/-em/-en) disorganized person, scatterbrain; **chaotisch** adj chaotic

Charakter m (-s, -e) character; **charakteristisch** adj characteristic (für of)

Charisma nt (-s, Charismen or Charismata) charisma

charmant adj charming

Charterflug m charter flight; **chartern** vt charter

checken vt check; fam (understand) get

Check-in m (-s, -s) check-in; **Check-in-Schalter** m check-in desk

Chef(in) m(f) (-s, -s) boss; **Chefarzt** m, **Chefärztin** f senior consultant (Brit), medical director (US)

Chemie f (-) chemistry; **chemisch** adj chemical; **~e Reinigung** dry cleaning

Chemotherapie f chemotherapy

Chicorée m (-s) chicory

Chiffre f (-, -n) cipher; (in newspaper) box number

Chile nt (-s) Chile

Chili m (-s, -s) chilli

China nt (-s) China; **Chinakohl** m Chinese leaves pl (Brit), bok choy (US); **Chinarestaurant** nt Chinese restaurant; **Chinese** m (-n, -n) Chinese; **Chinesin** f (-, -nen) Chinese (woman); **sie ist ~** she's Chinese; **chinesisch** adj Chinese; **Chinesisch** nt Chinese

Chip m (-s, -s) IT chip; **Chipkarte** f smart card

Chips pl (snack) crisps pl (Brit), chips pl (US)

Chirurg(in) m(f) (-en, -en) surgeon

Chlor nt (-s) chlorine

Choke m (-s, -s) choke

Cholera f (-) cholera

Cholesterin nt (-s) cholesterol

Chor m (-(e), Chöre) choir; THEAT chorus

Choreografie f choreography

Christ(in) m(f) (-en, -en) Christian; **Christbaum** m Christmas tree; **Christi Himmelfahrt** f the Ascension (of Christ); **Christkind** nt baby Jesus; (bringing presents) ≈ Father Christmas, Santa Claus; **christlich** adj Christian

Chrom nt (-s) chrome; CHEM chromium

chronisch adj chronic

chronologisch 1. adj chronological **2.** adv in chronological order

Chrysantheme f (-, -n) chrysanthemum

circa adv about, approximate-

ly
City f (-) city centre, down-town (US)
Clementine f (-, -n) clementine
clever adj clever, smart
Clique f (-, -n) group; pej clique; *David und seine ~* David and his lot or crowd
Clown m (-s, -s) clown
Club m (-s, -s) club; **Cluburlaub** m club holiday (Brit), club vacation (US)
Cocktail m (-s, -s) cocktail; **Cocktailtomate** f cherry tomato
Cognac m (-s) cognac
Cola f (-, -s) Coke®, cola
Comic m (-s, -s) comic strip; (magazine) comic
Compact Disc f (-, -s) compact disc
Computer m (-s, -) computer; **Computerfreak** m computer nerd; **computergesteuert** adj computer-controlled; **Computergrafik** f computer graphics pl; **computerlesbar** adj machine-readable; **Computerspiel** nt computer game; **Computertomogra-**

fie f computer tomography, scan; **Computervirus** m computer virus
Container m (-s, -) (for transporting goods) container; (for refuse) skip
Control-Taste f control key
Cookie nt (-s, -s) IT cookie
cool adj fam cool
Cornflakes pl cornflakes pl
Couch f (-, -en) couch; **Couchtisch** m coffee table
Coupé nt (-s, -s) coupé
Coupon m (-s, -s) coupon
Cousin m (-s, -s) cousin; **Cousine** f cousin
Crack nt (-s) (drug) crack
Creme f (-, -s) cream; GASTR mousse
Creutzfeld-Jakob-Krankheit f Creutzfeld-Jakob disease, CJD
Croissant nt (-s, -s) croissant
Curry 1. m (-s) curry powder **2.** nt (-s) (dish) curry; **Currywurst** f fried sausage with ketchup and curry powder
Cursor m (-s, -) IT cursor
Cybercafé nt cybercafé; **Cyberspace** m (-) cyberspace

D

da 1. adv there; here; (time) then; *~ oben/drüben* up/ over there; *~, wo* where; *~ sein* be there; *ist jemand ~?* is there anybody there?;

ich bin gleich wieder ~ I'll be right back; *ist noch Brot ~?* is there any bread left?; *es ist keine Milch mehr ~* we've run out of milk; *~, bit-*

te! there you are; **~ kann man nichts machen** there's nothing you can do **2.** *conj* as
dabei *adv (position)* close to it; *(simultaneously)* at the same time; *(but)* though; ***sie hörte Radio und rauchte ~*** she was listening to the radio and smoking (at the same time); **~ fällt mir ein** ... that reminds me ...; **~ kam es zu einem Unfall** this led to an accident; **... und ~ hat er gar keine Ahnung** ... even though he has no idea; ***ich finde nichts ~*** I don't see anything wrong with it; ***es bleibt ~*** that's settled; **~ sein** be present; *(taking part)* be involved; ***ich bin ~!*** count me in; ***er war gerade ~ zu gehen*** he was just (*or* on the point of) leaving
dabeibleiben *irr vi* stick with it; ***ich bleibe dabei*** I'm not changing my mind
dabeihaben *irr vt* **er hat seine Schwester dabei** he's brought his sister; ***ich habe kein Geld dabei*** I haven't got any money on me
Dach *nt* (-(e)s, Dächer) roof; **Dachboden** *m* attic, loft; **Dachgepäckträger** *m* roofrack; **Dachrinne** *f* gutter
Dachs *m* (-es, -e) badger
dachte *imperf of* **denken**
Dackel *m* (-s, -) dachshund
dadurch 1. *adv (space)* through it; *(means)* in that

way; *(cause)* because of that, for that reason **2.** *conj* **~, dass** because; **~, dass er hart arbeitete** *(means)* by working hard
dafür *adv (in place of it)* instead; **~ habe ich 50 Euro bezahlt** I paid 50 euros for it; ***ich bin ~ zu bleiben*** I'm for (*or* in favour of) staying; **~ ist er ja da** that's what he's there for; **er kann nichts ~** he can't help it
dagegen *adv* against it; *(dissimilarity)* in comparison; *(exchange)* for it; ***ich habe nichts ~*** I don't mind
daheim *adv* at home
daher 1. *adv* from there; *(reason)* that's why **2.** *conj* that's why
dahin *adv* there; *(time)* then; *(past, used up)* gone; **bis ~** till then; *(place)* up to there; **bis ~ muss die Arbeit fertig sein** the work must be finished by then
dahinter *adv* behind it
dahinterkommen *vi* find out
Dahlie *f* dahlia
Dalmatiner *m* (-s, -) dalmatian
damals *adv* at that time, then
Dame *f* (-, -n) lady; *(card)* queen; *(game)* draughts *sg (Brit)*, checkers *sg (US)*; **Damenbinde** *f* sanitary towel *(Brit)*, sanitary napkin *(US)*; **Damenfriseur** *m* ladies' hairdresser; **Damen-**

kleidung *f* ladies' wear; **Damentoilette** *f* ladies' toilet (*or* restroom *US*)

damit 1. *adv* with it; (*as a result*) by that; **was meint er~?** what does he mean by that?; **genug ~!** that's enough **2.** *conj* so that

Damm *m* (*-(e)s, Dämme*) dyke; (*creating reservoir*) dam; (*in harbour*) mole; (*for railway, road*) embankment

Dämmerung *f* twilight; (*in morning*) dawn; (*in evening*) dusk

Dampf *m* (*-(e)s, Dämpfe*) steam; (*haze*) vapour; **Dampfbad** *nt* Turkish bath; **Dampfbügeleisen** *nt* steam iron; **dampfen** *vi* steam

dämpfen *vt* GASTR steam; (*sound*) deaden; (*enthusiasm*) dampen

Dampfer *m* (*-s, -*) steamer

Dampfkochtopf *m* pressure cooker

danach *adv* after that; (*time also*) afterwards; (*rules etc*) accordingly; **mir ist nicht ~** I don't feel like it; **~ sieht es aus** that's what it looks like

Däne *m* (*-n, -n*) Dane

daneben *adv* beside it; (*dissimilarity*) in comparison

Dänemark *nt* (*-s*) Denmark; **Dänin** *f* Dane, Danish woman/girl; **dänisch** *adj* Danish; **Dänisch** *nt* Danish

dank *prep + dat or gen* thanks to; **Dank** *m* (*-(e)s*) thanks *pl*; **vielen ~!** thank you very much; **jdm ~ sagen** thank sb; **dankbar** *adj* grateful; (*task*) rewarding; **danke** *interj* thank you, thanks; **nein~!** no, thank you; **~, gerne!** yes, please; **~, gleichfalls!** thanks, and the same to you; **danken** *vi* **jdm für etw ~** thank sb for sth; **nichts zu ~!** you're welcome

dann *adv* then; **bis ~!** see you (later); **~ eben nicht** okay, forget it, suit yourself

daran *adv* on it; (*fix*) to it; (*bang*) against it; **es liegt ~, dass ...** it's because ...

darauf *adv* on it; (*direction*) towards it; (*time*) afterwards; **es kommt ganz ~ an, ob ...** it all depends whether ...; **ich freue mich ~** I'm looking forward to it; **am Tag ~** the next day

darauffolgend *adj* (*day, year*) next, following

daraus *adv* from it; **was ist ~ geworden?** what became of it?

darin *adv* in it; **das Problem liegt ~, dass ...** the basic problem is that ...

Darlehen *nt* (*-s, -*) loan

Darm *m* (*-(e)s, Därme*) intestine; (*of sausage*) skin; **Darmgrippe** *f* gastroenteritis

darstellen *vt* represent; THEAT play; (*give account of*) de-

scribe; **Darsteller(in)** m(f)
actor/actress; **Darstellung**
f representation; (account)
description

darüber adv above it, over it;
(drive) over it; (amount)
more; (time) meanwhile;
(talk, argue, be pleased)
about it

darum adv (reason) that's
why; **es geht ~, dass ...**
the point (or thing) is that ...

darunter adv under it; over it;
(group) among them;
(amount) less; **was verstehen Sie ~?** what do you understand by that?

darunterfallen vi be included

das 1. art the; **er hat sich ~
Bein gebrochen** he's broken his leg; **vier Euro ~ Kilo**
four euros a kilo **2.** pron (that
(one), this (one)); **~ Auto da**
that car; **ich nehme ~ da**
I'll take that one; **~ heißt**
that is; **~ sind Amerikaner**
they're American **3.** pron
(thing) that, which; (person)
who, that; **~ Auto, ~ er kauf-
te** the car (that or which)
he bought; **~ Mädchen, ~
nebenan wohnt** the girl
who (or that) lives next door

da sein irr vi → **da**

dass conj that; **so ~** so that;
es sei denn, ~ unless; **ohne
~ er grüßte** without saying
hello

dasselbe pron the same

Datei f IT file; **Dateimanager**

m file manager

Daten pl data pl; **Datenbank** f
database; **Datenmiss-
brauch** m misuse of data;
Datenschutz m data protection; **Datenträger** m data
carrier; **Datenverarbeitung**
f data processing

datieren vt date

Dativ m dative (case)

Dattel f (-, -n) date

Datum nt (-s, Daten) date

Dauer f (-, -n) duration; (of
film, visit etc) length; **auf
die ~** in the long run; **für
die ~ von zwei Jahren** for
(a period of) two years; **Dauerauftrag** m FIN standing order; **dauerhaft** adj lasting;
(material) durable; **Dauerkarte** f season ticket; **dauern**
vi last; (require time) take;
**es hat sehr lange gedauert,
bis er ...** it took him a long
time to ...; **wie lange dauert
es denn noch?** how much
longer will it be?; **das dauert mir zu lange** I can't wait
that long; **dauernd 1.** adj
lasting; (continual) constant
2. adv always, constantly;
er lachte ~ he kept laughing;
unterbrich mich nicht ~
stop interrupting me; **Dauerwelle** f perm (Brit), permanent (US)

Daumen m (-s, -) thumb

Daunendecke f eiderdown

davon adv of it; (distance)
away; (separation) from it;

(reason) because of it; **ich hätte gerne ein Kilo ~** I'd like one kilo of that; **~ habe ich gehört** I've heard of it; (event) I've heard about it; **das kommt~, wenn ...** that's what happens when ...; **was habe ich ~?** what's the point?; **auf jeg ~** up and away; **davonlaufen** irr vi run away

davor adv in front of it; (time) before; **ich habe Angst ~** I'm afraid of it

dazu adv (in addition) on top of that, as well; (suitability) for it, for that purpose; **ich möchte Reis ~** I'd like rice with it; **und ~ noch** and in addition; **~ fähig sein, etw zu tun** be capable of doing sth; **wie kam es ~?** how did it happen?; **dazugehören** vi belong to it; **dazukommen** irr vi join sb; **kommt noch etwas dazu?** anything else?

dazwischen adv in between; (difference etc) between them; (in group) among them

dazwischenkommen irr vi **wenn nichts dazwischenkommt** if all goes well; **mir ist etwas dazwischengekommen** something has cropped up

dealen vi fam deal in drugs; **Dealer(in)** m(f) (-s, -) fam dealer, pusher

Deck nt (-(e)s, -s or -e) deck; **an ~** on deck

Decke f (-, -n) cover; (for bed) blanket; (for table) tablecloth; (of room) ceiling

Deckel m (-s, -) lid

decken 1. vt cover; (table) lay, set **2.** vr (interests) coincide; (statements) correspond **3.** vi lay (or set) the table

Decoder m (-s, -) decoder

defekt adj faulty; **Defekt** m (-(e)s, -e) fault, defect

definieren vt define; **Definition** f (-, -en) definition

deftig adj (prices) steep; **ein ~es Essen** a good solid meal

dehnbar adj flexible, elastic; **dehnen** vt, vr stretch

Deich m (-(e)s, -e) dyke

dein pron (as adj) your; **deine(r, s)** pron (as noun) yours, of you; **deinetwegen** adv because of you; (to please you) for your sake

deinstallieren vt (program) uninstall

Dekolleté nt (-s, -s) low neckline

Dekoration f decoration; (in shop) window dressing; **dekorativ** adj decorative; **dekorieren** vt decorate; (shop window) dress

Delfin m (-s, -e) dolphin

delikat adj (food) delicious; (problem) delicate

Delikatesse f (-, -n) delicacy

Delle f (-, -en) fam dent

Delphin m (-s, -e) dolphin

dem *dat sg of* **der/das**; **wie ~ auch sein mag** that is it may

demnächst *adv* shortly, soon

Demo *f* (-, -*s*) *fam* demo

Demokratie *f* (-, -*n*) democracy; **demokratisch** *adj* democratic

demolieren *vt* demolish

Demonstration *f* demonstration; **demonstrieren** *vt, vi* demonstrate

den 1. *art acc sg, dat pl of* **der**; **sie hat sich ~ Arm gebrochen** she's broken her arm **2.** *pron* him; (*thing*) that one; **~ hab ich schon ewig nicht mehr gesehen** I haven't seen him in ages **3.** *pron* (*person*) who, that, whom; (*thing*) which, that; **der Typ, auf ~ sie steht** the guy (who) she fancies; **der Berg, auf ~ wir geklettert sind** the mountain (that) we climbed

denkbar 1. *adj* **das ist ~** that's possible **2.** *adv* **~ einfach** extremely simple; **denken** (*dachte, gedacht*) **1.** *vt, vi* think (*über + acc* about); **an jdn/etw ~** think of sb/sth; (*recall, take into consideration*) remember sb/sth; **woran denkst Du?** what are you thinking about?; **denk an den Kaffee!** don't forget the coffee **2.** *vr* imagine; **das kann ich mir ~** I can (well) imagine

Denkmal *nt* (-*s*, *Denkmäler*) monument; **Denkmalschutz** *m* monument preservation; **unter ~ stehen** be listed

denn 1. *conj* for, because **2.** *adv* then; (*after comparative*) than; **was ist ~?** what's wrong?; **ist das ~ so schwierig?** is it really that difficult?

dennoch *conj* still, nevertheless

Deo *nt* (-*s*, -*s*), **Deodorant** *nt* (-*s*, -*s*) deodorant; **Deoroller** *m* roll-on deodorant; **Deospray** *m or nt* deodorant spray

Deponie *f* (-, -*n*) waste disposal site, tip

Depressionen *pl* an **~ leiden** suffer from depression *sg*; **deprimieren** *vt* depress

der 1. *art* the; (*dative*) to the; (*genitive*) of the; **~ arme Marc** poor Marc; **ich habe es ~ Kundin geschickt** I sent it to the client; **~ Vater ~ Besitzerin** the owner's father **2.** *pron* that (one), this (one); **~ mit ~ Brille** the one (*or* him) with the glasses; **~ schreibt nicht mehr** (*pen etc*) that one doesn't write any more **3.** *pron* (*person*) who, that; (*thing*) which, that; **jeder, ~ ...** anyone who ...; **er war ~ erste, ~ es erfuhr** he was the first

derart *adv* so; *(before adj)* such; **derartig** *adj* **ein ~er Fehler** such a mistake, a mistake like that

deren *gen of* **die 1.** *pron (person)* her; *(thing)* its; *(pl)* their **2.** *pron (person)* whose; *(thing)* of which

dergleichen *pron* **und ~ mehr** and the like, and so on; **nichts ~** no such thing

derjenige *pron* the one; **~, der** the one who *(or that)*

dermaßen *adv* so much; *(with adj)* so

derselbe *pron* the same (person/thing)

deshalb *adv* therefore; **~ frage ich ja** that's why I'm asking

Design *nt* (-s, -s) design; **Designer(in)** *m(f)* (-s, -) designer

Desinfektionsmittel *nt* disinfectant; **desinfizieren** *vt* disinfect

dessen *gen of* **der, das 1.** *pron (person)* his; *(thing)* its; **ich bin mir ~ bewusst** I'm aware of that **2.** *pron (person)* whose; *(thing)* of which

Dessert *nt* (-s, -s) dessert; **zum** *(or* **als)** **~** for dessert

destilliert *adj* distilled

desto *adv* **je eher, ~ besser** the sooner, the better

deswegen *conj* therefore

Detail *nt* (-s, -s) detail; **ins ~ gehen** go into detail

Detektiv(in) *m(f)* (-s, -e) detective

deutlich *adj* clear; *(difference)* distinct

deutsch *adj* German; **Deutsch** *nt* German; **auf ~** in German; **ins ~e übersetzen** translate into German; **Deutsche(r)** *mf* German; **Deutschland** *nt* Germany

Devise *f* (-, -n) motto; **~n** *pl* FIN foreign currency *sg*; **Devisenkurs** *m* exchange rate

Dezember *m* (-s) December; → **Juni**

dezent *adj* discreet

d.h. *abbr of* **das heißt**; i.e.

Dia *nt* (-s, -s) slide

Diabetes *m* (-, -) MED diabetes; **Diabetiker(in)** *m(f)* (-s, -) diabetic

Diagnose *f* (-, -n) diagnosis

diagonal *adj* diagonal

Dialekt *m* (-(e)s, -e) dialect

Dialog *m* (-(e)s, -e) dialogue; IT dialog

Dialyse *f* (-, -n) MED dialysis

Diamant *m* (-en, -en) diamond

Diaprojektor *m* slide projector

Diät *f* (-, -en) diet; **eine ~ machen** be on a diet; *(start)* go on a diet

dich *pron acc of* **du**; you; **~ (selbst)** yourself; **pass auf ~ auf** look after yourself; **reg ~ nicht auf** don't get upset

dicht 1. *adj* dense; *(fog)* thick;

(*weave*) close; (*shoes, boat etc*) watertight; (*traffic*) heavy **2.** *adv* ~ **an/bei** close to; ~ **bevölkert** densely populated

Dichter(in) *m(f)* (*-s, -*) poet; (*author*) writer

Dichtung *f* AUTO gasket; (*for tap etc*) washer; (*verse*) poetry

Dichtungsring *m* TECH washer

dick *adj* thick; (*person*) fat; **jdn** ~ **haben** be sick of sb; **Dickdarm** *m* colon; **Dickkopf** *m* stubborn (*or pigheaded*) person; **Dickmilch** *f* sour milk

die 1. *art* the; ~ **arme Sarah** poor Sarah **2.** *pron* (*sg*) that (one), this (one); (*pl*) these (ones); ~ **mit den langen Haaren** the one (*or* her) with the long hair; **ich nehme** ~ **da** I'll take that one/those **3.** *pron* (*person*) who, that; (*thing*) which, that; **sie war** ~ **erste,** ~ **es erfuhr** she was the first to know **4.** *pl* of **der, die, das**

Dieb(in) *m(f)* (*-(e)s, -e*) thief; **Diebstahl** *m* (*-(e)s, Diebstähle*) theft; **Diebstahlsicherung** *f* burglar alarm

diejenige *pron* the one; ~, **die** the one who (*or* that); ~**n** (*pl*) those *pl*, the ones

Diele *f* (*-, -n*) hall

Dienst *m* (*-(e)s, -e*) service; **außer** ~ retired; ~ **haben**

be on duty; **der** ~ **habende Arzt** the doctor on duty

Dienstag *m* Tuesday; → **Mittwoch**; **dienstags** *adv* on Tuesdays; → **mittwochs**

Dienstbereitschaft *f* ~ **haben** (*doctor*) be on call; **Dienstleistung** *f* service; **dienstlich** *adj* official; **er ist** ~ **unterwegs** he's away on business; **Dienstreise** *f* business trip; **Dienststelle** *f* department; **Dienstwagen** *m* company car; **Dienstzeit** *f* office hours *pl*; MIL period of service

diesbezüglich *adj* (*formal*) on this matter

diese(r, s) *pron* this (one); (*pl*) these; ~ **Frau** this woman; ~**r Mann** this man; ~**s Mädchen** this girl; ~ **Leute** these people; **ich nehme** ~/~**n**/~**s** I'll take this one; (*there*) I'll take that one; **ich nehme** ~ *pl* I'll take these (ones); (*there*) I'll take those (ones)

Diesel *m* (*-s, -*) AUTO diesel

dieselbe *pron* the same; **es sind immer** ~**n** it's always the same people

Dieselmotor *m* diesel engine; **Dieselöl** *nt* diesel (oil)

diesig *adj* hazy, misty

diesmal *adv* this time

Dietrich *m* (*-s, -e*) skeleton key

Differenz *f* (*-, -en*) difference

digital *adj* digital; **Digital-** in

cpds (camera, display etc)
digital

Diktat nt (-(e)s, -e) dictation

Diktatur f dictatorship

Dill m (-s) dill

DIN abbr = **Deutsche Indus-
trienorm**; DIN; ~ **A4** A4

Ding nt (-(e)s, -e) thing; **vor allen ~en** above all; **der Stand
der ~e** the state of affairs;
das ist nicht mein ~ fam
it's not my sort of thing (or
cup of tea); **Dingsbums** m
(-) fam thingy, thingummy-
bob

Dinosaurier m dinosaur

Diphtherie f diphtheria

Diplom nt (-(e)s, -e) diploma

Diplomat(in) m(f) (-en, -en)
diplomat

dir pron dat of **du**; (to) you;
hat er ~ geholfen? did he
help you?; **ich werde es ~ erklären** I'll explain it to you;
wasch ~ die Hände go and
wash your hands; **ein Freund
von ~** a friend of yours

direkt 1. adj direct; (question)
straight; **~e Verbindung**
through service **2.** adv directly; (straightaway) immediately; **~ am Bahnhof** right
next to the station; **Direktflug** m direct flight

Direktor(in) m(f) director;
(of school) headmaster/--
mistress (Brit), principal
(US)

Direktübertragung f live
broadcast

Dirigent(in) m(f) conductor;
dirigieren vt direct; MUS
conduct

Discman® m (-s, -s) Discman®

Diskette f disk, diskette; **Diskettenlaufwerk** nt disk drive

Diskjockey m (-s, -s) disc
jockey; **Disko** f (-, -s) fam
disco, club; **Diskothek** f (-,
-en) discotheque, club

diskret adj discreet

diskriminieren vt discriminate against

Diskussion f discussion; **diskutieren** vt, vi discuss

Display nt (-s, -s) display

disqualifizieren vt disqualify

Distanz f distance

Distel f (-, -n) thistle

Disziplin f (-, -en) discipline

dividieren vt divide (durch
by); **8 dividiert durch 2 ist
4** 8 divided by 2 is 4

DJ m (-s, -s) abbr = **Diskjockey**; DJ

doch 1. adv **das ist nicht
wahr! — ~!** that's not true
— yes it is; **nicht ~!** oh no;
er kommt ~ he will come,
won't he?; **er hat es ~ gemacht** he did it after all; **setzen Sie sich ~** do sit down,
please **2.** conj but

Doktor(in) m(f) doctor

Dokument nt document; **Dokumentarfilm** m documen-
tary (film); **dokumentieren**
vt document; **Dokument-
vorlage** f IT document tem-

plate

Dolch m (-(e)s, -e) dagger

Dollar m (-(s), -s) dollar

dolmetschen vt, vi interpret; **Dolmetscher(in)** m(f) (-s, -) interpreter

Dolomiten pl Dolomites pl

Dom m (-(e)s, -e) cathedral

Domäne f (-, -n) domain, province; IT detached

Dominikanische Republik f Dominican Republic

Domino nt (-s, -s) dominoes sg

Donau f (-) Danube

Döner m (-s, -), Döner Kebab m (-(s), -s) doner kebab

Donner m (-s, -) thunder; **donnern** vi **es donnert** it's thundering

Donnerstag m Thursday; → **Mittwoch**; **donnerstags** adv on Thursdays; → **mittwochs**

doof adj fam stupid

dopen vt dope; **Doping** nt (-s) doping; **Dopingkontrolle** f drugs test

Doppel nt (-s, -) duplicate; SPORT doubles sg; **Doppelbett** nt double bed; **Doppeldecker** m double-decker; **Doppelhaushälfte** f semi-detached house (Brit), duplex (US); **doppelklicken** vi double-click; **Doppelname** m double-barrelled name; **Doppelpunkt** m colon; **Doppelstecker** m two-way adaptor; **doppelt** adj

double; **in ˷er Ausführung** in duplicate; **Doppelzimmer** nt double room

Dorf nt (-(e)s, Dörfer) village

Dorn m (-(e)s, -en) BOT thorn

Dörrobst nt dried fruit

Dorsch m (-(e)s, -e) cod

dort adv there; **˷ drüben** over there; **dorther** adv from there

Dose f (-, -n) box; (for food) tin (Brit), can; (for beer) can

dösen vi doze

Dosenbier nt canned beer; **Dosenmilch** f canned milk, tinned milk (Brit); **Dosenöffner** m tin opener (Brit), can opener

Dotter m (-s, -), -(-s, -e) (egg) yolk

downloaden vt download

Downsyndrom nt (-(e)s, -e) MED Down's syndrome

Dozent(in) m(f) (-, -) lecturer

Dr. abbr = **Doktor**

Drache m (-n, -n) dragon; **Drachen** m (-s, -) (toy) kite; SPORT hang-glider; **Drachenfliegen** nt (-s) hang-gliding; **Drachenflieger(in)** m(f) (-s, -) hang-glider

Draht m (-(e)s, Drähte) wire; **Drahtseilbahn** f cable railway

Drama nt (-s, Dramen) drama; **dramatisch** adj dramatic

dran adv fam contr of **daran**; **gut ˷ sein** (rich) be well-off; (lucky) be fortunate; (healthy) be well; **schlecht ˷ sein** be in a bad way; **wer ist ˷?**

whose turn is it?; **ich bin ~** it's my turn; **bleib ~!** TEL hang on

drang *imperf of* **dringen**

Drang *m* (*-(e)s, Dränge*) urge (*nach* for); (*of circumstances etc*) pressure

drängeln *vt, vi* push

drängen 1. *vt* push; (*try to persuade*) urge **2.** *vi* be urgent; (*time*) press; **auf etw** *acc* **~** press for sth

drankommen *irr vi* **wer kommt dran?** who's turn is it?, who's next?

drauf *fam contr of* **darauf**; **gut/ schlecht ~ sein** be in a good/bad mood

Draufgänger(in) *m(f)* (*-s, -*) daredevil

draufkommen *irr vi* remember; **ich komme nicht drauf** I can't think of it

draufmachen *vi fam* **einen ~** go on a binge

draußen *adv* outside

Dreck *m* (*-(e)s*) dirt, filth; **dreckig** *adj* dirty, filthy

drehen 1. *vt, vi* turn; (*cigarette*) roll; (*film*) shoot **2.** *vr* turn; (*revolve*) rotate; **sich ~ um** (*concern*) be about

Drehstrom *m* three-phase current; **Drehtür** *f* revolving door; **Drehzahlmesser** *m* rev counter

drei *num* three; **~ viertel voll** three-quarters full; **es ist ~ viertel neun** it's a quarter to nine; **Drei** *f* (*-, -en*) three;

(*mark in school*) ≈ C; **Dreieck** *nt* triangle; **dreieckig** *adj* triangular; **dreifach 1.** *adj* triple **2.** *adv* three times; **dreihundert** *num* three hundred; **Dreikönigstag** *m* Epiphany; **dreimal** *adv* three times; **Dreirad** *nt* tricycle; **dreispurig** *adj* three-lane

dreißig *num* thirty; **dreißigste(r, s)** *adj* thirtieth; → **dritte**

Dreiviertelstunde *f* **eine ~** three quarters of an hour

dreizehn *num* thirteen; **dreizehnte(r, s)** *adj* thirteenth; → **dritte**

dressieren *vt* train

Dressing *nt* (*-s, -s*) (salad) dressing

Dressman *m* (*-s, Dressmen*) (male) model

Dressur *f* (*-, -en*) training

drin *fam contr of* **darin**; in it; **mehr war nicht ~** that was the best I could do

dringen (*drang, gedrungen*) *vi* (*water, light, cold*) penetrate (*durch* through, *in* + *acc* into); **auf etw** *acc* **~** insist on sth; **dringend, dringlich** *adj* urgent

drinnen *adv* inside

dritt *adv* **wir sind zu ~** there are three of us; **dritte(r, s)** *adj* third; **die Dritte Welt** the Third World; **3. September** 3(rd) September; **am 3. September** on 3(rd) Sep-

tember, on September 3(rd);
München, den 3. September Munich, September 3(rd); **Drittel** nt (-s, -) (*fraction*) third; **drittens** adv thirdly

Droge f (-, -n) drug; **drogenabhängig, drogensüchtig** adj addicted to drugs

Drogerie f chemist's (*Brit*), drugstore (*US*); **Drogeriemarkt** m discount chemist's (*Brit*) (or drugstore (*US*))

drohen vi threaten (*jdm* sb); **mit etw ~ setzen** threaten to do sth

dröhnen vi (*engine*) roar; (*voice, music*) boom; (*room*) resound

Drohung f threat

Drossel f (-, -n) thrush

drüben adv over there; on the other side

drüber fam contr of **darüber**

Druck 1. m (-(e)s, Drücke) PHYS pressure; fig (*strain*) stress; **jdn unter ~ setzen** put sb under pressure **2.** m (-(e)s, -e) TYPO printing; (*product, typeface*) print; **Druckbuchstabe** m block letter; **in ~n schreiben** print; **drucken** vt, vi print

drücken 1. vt, vi (*button, hand*) press; (*garment*) pinch; fig (*prices*) keep down; **jdm etw in die Hand ~** press sth into sb's hand **2.** vr **sich vor etw** dat **~** opt out of sth; **drückend** adj op-

pressive

Drucker m (-s, -) IT printer; **Druckertreiber** m printer driver

Druckknopf m press stud (*Brit*), snap fastener (*US*); **Drucksache** f printed matter; **Druckschrift** f block letters pl

drunten adv down there

drunter fam contr of **darunter**

Drüse f (-, -n) gland

Dschungel m (-s, -) jungle

du pron you; **bist ~ es?** is it you?; **wir sind per ~** we're on first-name terms

Dübel m (-s, -) Rawlplug®

ducken vt, vr duck

Dudelsack m bagpipes pl

Duett nt (-s, -e) duet

Duft m (-(e)s, Düfte) scent; **duften** vi smell nice; **es duftet nach ...** it smells of ...

dulden vt tolerate

dumm adj stupid; **Dummheit** f stupidity; (*act*) stupid thing; **Dummkopf** m idiot

dumpf adj (*sound*) muffled; (*memory*) vague; (*pain*) dull

Düne f (-, -n) dune

Dünger m (-s, -) fertilizer

dunkel adj dark; (*voice*) deep; (*suspicion*) vague; (*mysterious*) obscure; (*act*) dubious; **im Dunkeln tappen** fig be in the dark; **dunkelblau** adj dark blue; **dunkelblond** adj light brown;

dunkelhaarig *adj* dark-haired; **Dunkelheit** *f* darkness

dünn *adj* thin; (*coffee*) weak

Dunst *m* (*-es*, Dünste) haze; (*light fog*) mist; CHEM vapour

dünsten *vt* GASTR steam

Duo *nt* (*-s*, *-s*) duo

Dur *nt* (*-*) MUS major (key); **in G~** in G major

durch 1. *prep + acc* through; (*means*) by; (*time*) during; **~ Amerika reisen** travel across the USA; **er verdient seinen Lebensunterhalt ~ den Verkauf von Autos** he makes his living by selling cars **2.** *adv* (*meat*) cooked through, well done; **das ganze Jahr ~** all through the year, the whole year long; **darf ich bitte ~?** can I get through, please?

durchaus *adv* absolutely; **~ nicht** not at all

Durchblick *m* view; **den ~ haben** *fig* know what's going on; **durchblicken** *vi* look through; (*fam* understand (*bei etw*); **etw ~ lassen** *fig* hint at sth

Durchblutung *f* circulation

durchbrennen *irr vi* (*fuse*) blow; (*wire*) burn through; *fam* (*abscond*) run away

durchdacht *adj* **gut ~** well thought-out

durchdrehen 1. *vt* (*meat*) mince **2.** *vi* (*wheels*) spin; *fam* (*under stress*) crack up

durcheinander *adv* in a mess; *fam* (*person*) confused; **~ bringen** mess up; (*person*) confuse; **~ reden** talk all at the same time; **~ trinken** mix one's drinks; **Durcheinander** *nt* (*-s*) (*of people*) confusion; (*of things*) mess

Durchfahrt *f* way through; **„~ verboten!"** 'no thoroughfare'

Durchfall *m* MED diarrhoea

durchfallen *irr vi* fall through; (*in exam*) fail

durchfragen *vr* ask one's way

durchführen *vt* carry out

Durchgang *m* passage; SPORT round; (*in election*) ballot; **Durchgangsverkehr** *m* through traffic

durchgebraten *adj* well done

durchgefroren *adj* frozen to the bone

durchgehen *irr vi* go through (*durch etw* sth); (*horse*) break loose; (*make off*) run away; **durchgehend** *adj* (*train*) through; **~ geöffnet** open all day

durchhalten *irr* **1.** *vi* hold out **2.** *vt* (*pace*) keep up; **etw ~** (*not give up*) see sth through

durchkommen *irr vi* get through; (*patient*) pull through

durchlassen *irr vt* (*person*) let through; (*water*) let in

Durchlauf(wasser)erhitzer *m* (*-s*, *-*) instantaneous water heater

durchlesen *irr vt* read through

durchleuchten *vt* X-ray

durchmachen *vt* go through; (*development*) undergo; **die Nacht ~** make a night of it, have an all-nighter

Durchmesser *m* (*-s, -*) diameter

Durchreise *f* journey through; **auf der ~** passing through; (*goods*) in transit; **Durchreisevisum** *nt* transit visa

durchreißen *irr vt, vi* tear (in two)

durchs *contr of* **durch das**

Durchsage *f* (*-, -n*) announcement

durchschauen *vt* (*person, lie*) see through

durchschlagen *irr vr* struggle through

durchschneiden *irr vt* cut (in two)

Durchschnitt *m* average; **im ~** on average; **durchschnittlich 1.** *adj* average **2.** *adv* on average

durchsetzen 1. *vt* get through **2.** *vr* (*be successful*) succeed; (*assert oneself*) get one's way

durchsichtig *adj* transparent, see-through

durchstellen *vt* TEL put through

durchstreichen *irr vt* cross out

durchsuchen *vt* search (*nach* for); **Durchsuchung** *f* search

Durchwahl *f* direct dialling; (*number*) extension

durchziehen *irr vt* (*plan*) carry through

Durchzug *m* draught

dürfen (*durfte, gedurft*) *vi* **etw tun ~** (*permission*) be allowed to do sth; **darf ich?** may I?; **das darfst du nicht** (*tun*)! you mustn't do that; **was darf es sein?** what can I do for you?; **er dürfte schon dort sein** he should be there by now

dürr *adj* (*thin*) skinny

Durst *m* (*-(e)s*) thirst; **~ haben** be thirsty; **durstig** *adj* thirsty

Dusche *f* (*-, -n*) shower; **duschen** *vi, vr* have a shower; **Duschgel** *nt* shower gel

Düse *f* (*-, -n*) nozzle; TECH jet; **Düsenflugzeug** *nt* jet (aircraft)

düster *adj* dark; (*thoughts, future*) gloomy

Dutyfreeshop *m* (*-s, -s*) duty-free shop

duzen 1. *vt* address as 'du' **2.** *vr* **sich ~** (*mit jdm*) address each other as 'du', be on first-name terms

DVD *f* (*-, -s*) *abbr* = **Digital Versatile Disk**; DVD

dynamisch *adj* dynamic

Dynamo *m* (*-s, -s*) dynamo

E

Ebbe f (-, -n) low tide
eben 1. adj level; (even) smooth **2.** adv just; (confirming sth) exactly
ebenfalls adv also, as well; (reply) you too; **ebenso** adv just as; **~ gut** just as well; **~ viel** just as much
EC m (-, -s) abbr ≈ **Eurocityzug**
Echo nt (-s, -s) echo
echt adj (leather, gold) real, genuine; **ein ~er Verlust** a real loss
EC-Karte f ≈ debit card
Ecke f (-, -n) corner; MATH angle; **an der ~** at the corner; **gleich um die ~** just round the corner; **eckig** adj rectangular
Economyclass f (-) coach (class), economy class
Ecstasy f (-) (drug) ecstasy
Efeu m (-s) ivy
Effekt m (-(e)s, -e) effect
egal adj **das ist ~** it doesn't matter; **das ist mir ~** I don't care, it's all the same to me; **~ wie teuer** no matter how expensive
egoistisch adj selfish
ehe conj before
Ehe f (-, -n) marriage; **Ehefrau** f wife
ehemalig adj former; **ehemals** adv formerly

Ehemann m husband; **Ehepaar** nt married couple
eher adv (time) sooner; (preference) rather; (passing judgment) more; **je ~, desto besser** the sooner the better
Ehering m wedding ring
eheste(r, s) 1. adj (earliest) first **2.** adv **am ~n** (probably) most likely
Ehre f (-, -n) honour; **ehren** vt honour; **Ehrenwort** nt word of honour; **~!** I promise
ehrgeizig adj ambitious
ehrlich adj honest
Ei nt (-(e)s, -er) egg
Eiche f (-, -n) oak (tree); **Eichel** f (-, -n) acorn
Eichhörnchen nt squirrel
Eid m (-(e)s, -e) oath
Eidechse f (-, -n) lizard
Eierbecher m eggcup; **Eierstock** m ovary; **Eieruhr** f egg timer
Eifersucht f jealousy; **eifersüchtig** adj jealous (auf + acc of)
Eigelb nt (-(e)s, -) egg yolk
eigen adj own; (typical) characteristic (jdm of sb); (strange) peculiar; **eigenartig** adj peculiar; **Eigenschaft** f quality; CHEM, PHYS property
eigentlich 1. adj actual, real **2.** adv actually, really; **was denken Sie sich ~ dabei?**

what on earth do you think you're doing?

Eigentum *nt* property; **Eigentümer(in)** *m(f)* owner; **Eigentumswohnung** *f* owner-occupied flat (*Brit*), condominium (*US*)

eignen *vr* **sich ~ für** be suited for; **er würde sich als Lehrer ~** he'd make a good teacher

Eilbrief *m* express letter, special-delivery letter; **Eile** *f* (-) hurry; **eilen** *vi* (*letter, matter*) be urgent; **es eilt nicht** there's no hurry; **eilig** *adj* hurried; (*pressing*) urgent; **es ~ haben** be in a hurry

Eimer *m* (-s, -) bucket

ein *adv* **nicht ~ noch aus wissen** not know what to do; **~ - aus** (switch) on - off

ein(e) *art* a; an; **~ Mann** a man; **~ Apfel** an apple; **~e Stunde** an hour; **~ Haus** a house; **~ (gewisser) Herr Miller** a (certain) Mr Miller; **~es Tages** one day

einander *pron* one another, each other

einarbeiten 1. *vt* train **2.** *vr* get used to the work

einatmen *vt, vi* breathe in

Einbahnstraße *f* one-way street

einbauen *vt* build in; (*engine etc*) install, fit; **Einbauküche** *f* fitted kitchen

einbiegen *irr vi* turn (*in + acc* into)

einbilden *vt* **sich** *dat* **etw ~** imagine sth

einbrechen *irr vi* (*into house*) break in; (*roof etc*) fall in, collapse; **Einbrecher(in)** *m(f)* (-s, -) burglar

einbringen *irr* **1.** *vt* (*harvest*) bring in; (*profit*) yield; **jdm etw ~** bring (*or* earn) sb sth **2.** *vr* **sich in** *acc* **etw ~** make a contribution to sth

Einbruch *m* break-in, burglary; **bei ~ der Nacht** at nightfall

Einbürgerung *f* naturalization

einchecken *vt* check in

eincremen *vt, vr* put some cream on

eindeutig 1. *adj* clear, obvious **2.** *adv* clearly; **~ falsch** clearly wrong

eindringen *irr vi* force one's way in (*in + acc* -to); (*into house*) break in (*in + acc* -to); (*gas, water*) get in (*in + acc* -to)

Eindruck *m* impression; **großen ~ auf jdn machen** make a big impression on sb

eine(r, s) *pron* one; someone; **~r meiner Freunde** one of my friends; **~r nach dem andern** one after the other

eineiig *adj* (*twins*) identical

eineinhalb *num* one and a half

einerseits *adv* on the one hand

einfach 1. *adj* (*not complica-*

ted) simple; (person) ordinary; (food) plain; (not multiple) single; **~e Fahrkarte** single ticket (Brit), one-way ticket (US) **2.** adv simply; (single time) once

Einfahrt f (in car) driving in; (of train) arrival; (place) entrance

Einfall m idea; **einfallen** irr vi (light etc) fall in; (roof, house) collapse; **ihm fiel ein, dass ...** it occurred to him that ...; **ich werde mir etwas ~ lassen** I'll think of something; **was fällt Ihnen ein!** what do you think you're doing?

Einfamilienhaus nt detached house

einfarbig adj all one colour; (fabric etc) self-coloured

Einfluss m influence

einfrieren irr vi, vt freeze

einfügen vt fit in; add; IT insert; **Einfügetaste** f IT insert key

Einfuhr f (-, -en) import; **Einfuhrbestimmungen** pl import regulations pl

einführen vt introduce; (goods) import; **Einführung** f introduction

Eingabe f (of data) input; **Eingabetaste** f IT return (or enter) key

Eingang m entrance; **Eingangshalle** f entrance hall, lobby (US)

eingeben irr vt (data etc) enter, key in

eingebildet adj imaginary; (conceited) arrogant

Eingeborene(r) mf native

eingehen irr **1.** vi (letter, money) come in, arrive; (animal, plant) die; (fabric) shrink; **auf etw** acc **~** agree to sth; **auf jdn ~** respond to sb **2.** vt (contract) enter into; (bet) make; (risk) take

eingelegt adj (in vinegar) pickled

eingeschaltet adj (switched) on

eingeschlossen adj locked in; (in price) included

eingewöhnen vr settle in

eingießen irr vt pour

eingreifen irr vi intervene; **Eingriff** m intervention; (surgical) operation

einhalten irr vt (promise etc) keep

einhängen vt (**den Hörer**) **~** hang up

einheimisch adj (product, team) local; **Einheimische(r)** mf local

Einheit f unity; (measurement) unit; **einheitlich** adj uniform

einholen vt (car, person) catch up with; (lateness) make up for; (advice, permission) ask for

Einhorn nt unicorn

einhundert num one (or a) hundred

einig adj united; **sich** dat **~**

sein agree

einige 1. *pron pl* some; (*quite a few*) several **2.** *adj* some; **nach ~er Zeit** after some time; **~e hundert Euro** some hundred euros

einigen *vr* agree (*auf* + *acc* on)

einigermaßen *adv* fairly, quite; (*passably*) reasonably

einiges *pron* something; (*amount*) quite a bit; (*number*) a few things; **es gibt noch ~ zu tun** there's still a fair bit to do

Einkauf *m* purchase; **Einkäufe (machen)** (to do one's) shopping; **einkaufen 1.** *vt* buy **2.** *vi* go shopping; **Einkaufsbummel** *m* shopping trip; **Einkaufstasche** *f*, **Einkaufstüte** *f* shopping bag; **Einkaufswagen** *m* shopping trolley (*Brit*) (or cart (*US*)); **Einkaufszentrum** *nt* shopping centre (*Brit*) (or mall (*US*))

einklemmen *vt* jam; **er hat sich zu/at den Finger eingeklemmt** he got his finger caught

Einkommen *nt* (*-s, -*) income

einladen *irr vt* (*person*) invite; (*things*) load; **jdn zum Essen ~** take sb out for a meal; **ich lade dich ein** (*I'm paying*) it's my treat; **Einladung** *f* invitation

Einlass *m* (*-es, Einlässe*) admittance; **~ ab 18 Uhr** doors

open at 6 pm; **einlassen** *irr vr* **sich mit jdm/auf etw acc ~** get involved with sb/sth

einlenken *vr* settle down

einlegen *vt* (*film etc*) put in; (*food before cooking*) marinate; **eine Pause ~** take a break

einleiten *vt* start; (*measures*) introduce; (*birth*) induce; **Einleitung** *f* introduction; (*of birth*) induction

einleuchten *vi* **jdm ~** be (*or* become) clear to sb; **einleuchtend** *adj* clear

einloggen *vi* IT log on (*or* in)

einlösen *vt* (*cheque*) cash; (*voucher*) redeem; (*promise*) keep

einmal *adv* once; (*at earlier time*) before; (*in the future*) some day; (*to begin with*) first; **~ im Jahr** once a year; **noch ~** once more, again; **ich war schon ~ hier** I've been here before; **warst du schon ~ in London?** have you ever been to London?; **nicht ~** not even; **auf ~** suddenly; (*simultaneously, in one go*) at once; **einmalig** *adj* unique; (*occurring only once*) single; (*excellent*) fantastic

einmischen *vr* interfere (*in* + *acc* with)

Einnahme *f* (*-, -n*) (*money*) takings *pl*; (*of medicine*) taking; **einnehmen** *irr vt* (*medi-*

cine) take; (*money*) take in; (*attitude, space*) take up; **jdn für sich ~** win sb over

einordnen 1. *vt* put in order; (*categorize*) classify; (*documents*) file **2.** *vr* AUTO get in lane; **sich rechts/links ~** get into the right/left lane

einpacken *vt* pack (up)

einparken *vt, vi* park

einplanen *vt* allow for

einprägen *vt* **sich** *dat* **etw ~** remember (*or* memorize) sth

einräumen *vt* (*books, crockery*) put away; (*cupboard*) put things in

einreden *vt* **jdm/sich etw ~** talk sb/oneself into (believing) sth

einreiben *irr vt* **sich mit etw ~** rub sth into one's skin

einreichen *vt* hand in; (*application*) submit

Einreise *f* entry; **Einreisebestimmungen** *pl* entry regulations *pl*; **Einreiseerlaubnis** *f*, **Einreisegenehmigung** *f* entry permit; **einreisen** *vi* enter (*in ein Land* a country); **Einreisevisum** *nt* entry visa

einrenken *vt* (*arm, leg*) set

einrichten 1. *vt* (*house*) furnish; (*business etc*) establish, set up; (*fix*) arrange **2.** *vr* furnish one's home; (*get ready*) prepare oneself (*auf* + *acc* for); (*adjust*) adapt (*auf* + *acc* to); **Einrichtung** *f* (*in house*) furnishings *pl*; (*orga-*

nization) institution; (*swimming pool etc*) facility

eins *num* one; **Eins** *f* (-, -*en*) one; (*mark in school*) ≈ A

einsam *adj* lonely

einsammeln *vt* collect

Einsatz *m* (*component*) insert; (*of machine, troops etc*) use; (*in gambling*) stake; (*of one's life*) risk; MUS entry

einschalten *vt* ELEC switch on

einschätzen *vt* estimate, assess

einschenken *vt* pour

einschiffen *vr* embark (*nach* for)

einschlafen *irr vi* fall asleep, drop off; **mir ist der Arm eingeschlafen** my arm's gone to sleep

einschlagen *irr* **1.** *vt* (*window*) smash; (*teeth, skull*) smash in; (*path, direction*) take **2.** *vi* hit (*in etw acc* sth, *auf jdn* sb); (*lightning*) strike; (*film, song etc*) be a success

einschließen *irr vt* (*person*) lock in; (*object*) lock away; (*encircle*) surround; *fig* include; **einschließlich 1.** *adv* inclusive **2.** *prep* + *gen* including; **von Montag bis ~ Freitag** from Monday up to and including Friday, Monday through Friday (*US*)

einschränken 1. *vt* limit, restrict; (*reduce*) cut down **2.** *vr* cut down (on expenditure)

einschreiben *irr vr* register; (*for school*) enrol; **Einschreiben** *nt* (-s, -) registered letter; **etw per ~ schicken** send sth by special delivery

einschüchtern *vt* intimidate

einsehen *irr vt* (*understand*) see; (*error*) recognize; (*files*) have a look at

einseitig *adj* one-sided

einsenden *irr vt* send in

einsetzen **1.** *vt* put in; (*to a post*) appoint; (*money*) stake; (*machine, troops etc*) use **2.** *vi* (*rain etc*) set in; MUS enter, come in **3.** *vr* work hard; **sich für jdn/ etw ~** support sb/sth

Einsicht *f* insight; **zu der ~ kommen, dass ...** come to realize that ...

einsperren *vt* lock up

einspielen *vt* (*money*) bring in

einspringen *irr vi* (*help out*) step in (*für* for)

Einspruch *m* objection (*gegen* to)

einspurig *adj* single-lane

Einstand *m* (*in tennis*) deuce

einstecken *vt* pocket; ELEC plug in; (*letter*) post, mail (*US*); (*keys, passport etc*) take; (*accept*) swallow

einsteigen *irr vi* (*into car*) get in; (*onto bus, train, plane*) get on; (*in business, project etc*) get involved

einstellen **1.** *vt* (*end*) stop; (*de-* vice etc) adjust; (*camera*) focus; (*station, radio*) tune in; (*car, bicycle etc*) put; (*worker*) employ, take on **2.** *vr* **sich auf jdn/etw ~** adapt to sb/prepare oneself for sth; **Einstellung** *f* (*of device etc*) adjustment; (*of camera*) focusing; (*of worker*) taking on; (*opinion*) attitude

einstürzen *vi* collapse

eintägig *adj* one-day

eintauschen *vt* exchange (*gegen* for)

eintausend *num* one (*or* a) thousand

einteilen *vt* divide (up) (*in + acc* into); (*time*) organize

eintönig *adj* monotonous

Eintopf *m* stew

eintragen *irr* **1.** *vt* (*in list*) put down, enter **2.** *vr* put one's name down, register

eintreffen *irr vi* happen; (*person, train, letter etc*) arrive

eintreten *irr vi* enter (*in etw acc* sth); (*club, party*) join (*in etw acc* sth); (*event*) occur; **~ für** support; **Eintritt** *m* admission; **"~ frei"** 'admission free'; **Eintrittskarte** *f* (*entrance*) ticket; **Eintrittspreis** *m* admission charge

einverstanden **1.** *interj* okay, all right **2.** *adj* **mit etwas ~ sein** agree to sth, accept sth

Einwanderer *m*, **Einwanderin** *f* immigrant; **einwandern** *vi* immigrate

einwandfrei *adj* perfect,

flawless
Einwegflasche f non-returnable bottle; **Einwegwaschlappen** m disposable flannel (Brit) (or washcloth (US))
einweichen vt soak
einweihen vt (building) inaugurate, open; **jdn in etw** acc ~ let sb in on sth; **Einweihungsparty** f housewarming party
einwerfen irr vt (ball, remark etc) throw in; (letter) post, mail (US); (money) put in, insert; (window) smash
einwickeln vt wrap up; fig **jdn** ~ take sb in
Einwohner(in) m(f) (-s, -) inhabitant; **Einwohnermeldeamt** nt registration office for residents
Einwurf m (opening) slot; SPORT throw-in
Einzahl f singular
einzahlen vt pay in (auf ein Konto -to an account)
Einzel nt (-s, -) (in tennis) singles sg; **Einzelbett** nt single bed; **Einzelfahrschein** m single ticket (Brit), one-way ticket (US); **Einzelgänger(in)** m(f) loner; **Einzelhandel** m retail trade; **Einzelkind** nt only child
einzeln 1. adj individual; (not together) separate; (solitary) single; **~e ...** several ..., some ...; **der/die Einzelne** the individual; **im Einzelnen** in detail **2.** adv separately;

(pack, list) individually; ~ **angeben** specify; ~ **eintreten** enter one by one
Einzelzimmer nt single room; **Einzelzimmerzuschlag** m single-room supplement
einziehen irr **1.** vt **den Kopf** ~ duck **2.** vi (into house) move in
einzig 1. adj only; (solitary) single; (special) unique; **kein ~er Fehler** not a single mistake; **das Einzige** the only thing; **der/die Einzige** the only person **2.** adv only; **die ~ richtige Lösung** the only correct solution; **einzigartig** adj unique
Eis nt (-es, -) ice; (food) ice-cream; ~ **laufen** skate; **Eisbahn** f ice(-skating) rink; **Eisbär** m polar bear; **Eisbecher** m (ice-cream) sundae; **Eisberg** m iceberg; **Eiscafé** nt, **Eisdiele** f ice-cream parlour
Eisen nt (-s, -) iron; **Eisenbahn** f railway (Brit), railroad (US); **eisern** adj iron
eisgekühlt adj chilled; **Eishockey** nt ice hockey; **Eiskaffee** m iced coffee; **eiskalt** adj ice-cold; (temperature) freezing; **Eiskunstlauf** m figure skating; **Eissalat** m iceberg lettuce; **Eisschokolade** f iced chocolate; **Eisschrank** m fridge, ice-box (US); **Eistee** m iced tea; **Eiswürfel** m ice cube; **Eiszap-**

fen *m* icicle

eitel *adj* vain

Eiter *m* (-s) pus

Eiweiß *nt* (-es, -e) egg white; CHEM, BIO protein

ekelhaft, ek(e)lig *adj* disgusting, revolting; ekeln *vr* be disgusted (*vor + dat* at)

EKG *nt* (-s, -s) *abbr* = **Elektrokardiogramm**; ECG

Ekzem *nt* (-s, -e) MED eczema

Elastikbinde *f* elastic bandage; elastisch *adj* elastic

Elch *m* (-(e)s, -e) elk; (*North American*) moose

Elefant *m* elephant

elegant *adj* elegant

Elektriker(in) *m(f)* (-s, -) electrician; elektrisch *adj* electric; Elektrizität *f* electricity; Elektroauto *nt* electric car; Elektrogerät *nt* electrical appliance; Elektrogeschäft *nt* electrical shop; Elektroherd *m* electric cooker; Elektromotor *m* electric motor; Elektronik *f* electronics *sg*; elektronisch *adj* electronic; Elektrorasierer *m* (-s, -) electric razor

Element *nt* (-(e)s, -e) element

elend *adj* miserable; Elend *nt* (-(e)s) misery

elf *num* eleven; Elf *f* (-, -en) SPORT eleven

Elfenbein *nt* ivory

Elfmeter *m* SPORT penalty (kick)

elfte(r, s) *adj* eleventh; → **dritte**

Ell(en)bogen *m* elbow

Elster *f* (-, -n) magpie

Eltern *pl* parents *pl*

EM *f* *abbr* = **Europameisterschaft**; European Championship(s)

Email *nt* (-s, -s) enamel

E-Mail *f* (-, -s) IT e-mail; **jdm eine ~ schicken** e-mail sb, send sb an e-mail; **jdm etwas per ~ schicken** e-mail sth to sb; E-Mail-Adresse *f* e-mail address; e-mailen *vt* e-mail

Emoticon *nt* (-s, -s) emoticon

emotional *adj* emotional

empfahl *imperf of* **empfehlen**

empfand *imperf of* **empfinden**

Empfang *m* (-(e)s, Empfänge) (party; in hotel, office) reception; (of letter, goods) receipt; **in ~ nehmen** receive; empfangen (empfing, empfangen) *vt* receive; Empfänger(in) *m(f)* (-s, -) recipient; addressee 2. *m* TECH receiver; Empfängnisverhütung *f* contraception; Empfangshalle *f* reception area

empfehlen (empfahl, empfohlen) *vt* recommend; Empfehlung *f* recommendation

empfinden (empfand, empfunden) *vt* feel; empfindlich *adj* (person) sensitive; (spot) sore; (easily offended) touchy; (material) delicate

empfing *imperf of* **empfangen**

empfohlen *pp of* **empfehlen**
empfunden *pp of* **empfinden**
empört *adj* indignant (*über*
+ *acc* at)
Ende *nt* (-s, -n) end; (*of film,
novel*) ending; **am ~** at the
end; (*when all is said and done*) in the end; **~ Mai** at the
end of May; **~ der Achtzi-
gerjahre** in the late eighties;
sie ist ~ zwanzig she's in her
late twenties; **zu ~** over, finished; **enden** *vi* end; **der
Zug geht hier** this service (*or*
train) terminates here;
endgültig *adj* final; (*proof*)
conclusive
Endivie *f* endive
endlich *adj* at last, finally; (*in
the end*) eventually; **Endspiel** *nt* final; (*last round*) fi-
nals *pl*; **Endstation** *f* termi-
nus; **Endung** *f* ending
Energie *f* energy; **~ sparend**
energy-saving; **Energiebe-
darf** *m* energy requirement;
Energieverbrauch *m* energy
consumption
energisch *adj* (*firm*) forceful
eng **1.** *adj* narrow; (*clothes*)
tight; *fig* (*friendship, relationship*) close; **das wird ~**
fam (*deadline*) we're running
out of time, it's getting tight
2. *adv* **~ befreundet sein** be
close friends
engagieren **1.** *vt* engage **2.** *vr*
commit oneself, be commit-
ted (*für* to)
Engel *m* (-s, -) angel

England *nt* England; **Englän-
der(in)** *m(f)* (-s, -) English-
man/-woman; **die ~** *pl* the
English *pl*; **englisch** *adj*
English; GASTR rare; **Englisch** *nt* English; **ins ~e
übersetzen** translate into
English
Enkel *m* (-s, -) grandson; **Enkelin** *f* granddaughter
enorm *adj* enormous; *fig* tremendous
Entbindung *f* MED delivery
entdecken *vt* discover; **Entdeckung** *f* discovery
Ente *f* (-, -n) duck
entfernen **1.** *vt* remove; IT delete **2.** *vr* go away; **entfernt**
adj distant; **15 km von X ~**
15 km away from X; **20 km
voneinander ~** 20 km apart;
Entfernung *f* distance; **aus
der ~** from a distance
entführen *vt* kidnap; **Entfüh-
rer(in)** *m(f)* kidnapper; **Entführung** *f* kidnapping
entgegen **1.** *prep* + *dat* contrary to **2.** *adv* towards;
dem Wind ~ against the
wind; **entgegengesetzt** *adj*
(*direction*) opposite; (*view*)
opposing; **entgegenkom-
men** *irr vi* **jdm ~** come to
meet sb; *fig* accommodate
sb; **entgegenkommend** *adj*
(*traffic*) oncoming; *fig* oblig-
ing
entgegnen *vt* reply (*auf* + *acc*
to)
entgehen *irr vi* **jdm ~** escape

sb's notice; **sich** dat etw ~ **lassen** miss sth

entgleisen vi RAIL be derailed; fig (person) misbehave

Enthaarungscreme f hair remover

enthalten irr **1.** vt contain; (price) include **2.** vr abstain (gen from)

entkoffeiniert adj decaffeinated

entkommen irr vi escape

entkorken vt uncork

entlang prep + acc or dat ~ **dem Fluss, den Fluss** ~ along the river; **entlanggehen** irr vi walk along

entlassen irr vt (patient) discharge; (worker) dismiss

entlasten vt jdn~ relieve sb of some of his/her work

entmutigen vt discourage

entnehmen irr vt take (dat from)

entrahmt adj (milk) skimmed

entschädigen vt compensate; **Entschädigung** f compensation

entscheiden irr vt, vi, vr decide; **sich für/gegen etw** ~ decide on/against sth; **wir haben uns entschieden, nicht zu gehen** we decided not to go; **das entscheidet sich morgen** that'll be decided tomorrow; **entscheidend** adj decisive; (question, problem) crucial; **Entscheidung** f decision

entschließen irr vr decide

(zu, für on), make up one's mind; **Entschluss** m decision

entschuldigen 1. vt excuse **2.** vr apologize; **sich bei jdm für etw** ~ apologize to sb for sth **3.** vi **entschuldige!, ~ Sie!** (introducing question) excuse me; (apology) (I'm) sorry, excuse me (US); **Entschuldigung** f apology; (justification) excuse; **jdn um ~ bitten** apologize to sb; **~!** (colliding with sb) (I'm) sorry, excuse me (US); (introducing question) excuse me; (could you repeat that?) (I beg your) pardon?

entsetzlich adj dreadful, appalling

entsorgen vt dispose of

entspannen 1. vt (body) relax; POL (situation) ease **2.** vr relax; fam chill out; **Entspannung** f relaxation

entsprechen irr vi + dat correspond to; (requirements, wishes etc) comply with; **entsprechend 1.** adj appropriate **2.** adv accordingly **3.** prep + dat according to, in accordance with

entstehen vi (difficulties) arise; (town, building etc) be built; (work of art) be created

enttäuschen vt disappoint; **Enttäuschung** f disappointment

entweder conj ~ ... **oder** ... either ... or ...; ~ **oder!** take it or leave it

entwerfen irr vt (furniture, clothes) design; (plan, contract) draft

entwerten vt devalue; (ticket) cancel; **Entwerter** m (-s, -) ticket-cancelling machine

entwickeln vt, vr a. PHOT develop; (courage, energy) show, display; **Entwicklung** f development; PHOT developing; **Entwicklungshelfer(in)** m(f) (-s, -) development worker; **Entwicklungsland** nt developing country

Entwurf m outline; (of product) design; (of contract, novel etc) draft

entzückend adj delightful, charming

Entzug m withdrawal; (treatment) detox; **Entzugserscheinung** f withdrawal symptom

entzünden vr catch fire; MED become inflamed; **Entzündung** f MED inflammation

Epidemie f epidemic

Epilepsie f epilepsy

er pron he; (thing) it; **er ist** it's him; **wo ist mein Mantel? – ~ ist ...** where's my coat? – it's ...

Erbe 1. m (-n, -n) heir **2.** nt (-s) inheritance; fig heritage; **erben** vt inherit; **Erbin** f heiress; **erblich** adj hereditary

erbrechen irr vt, vr vomit; **Er-**

brechen nt vomiting

Erbschaft f inheritance

Erbse f (-, -n) pea

Erdapfel m potato; **Erdbeben** nt earthquake; **Erdbeere** f strawberry; **Erde** f (-, -) (planet) earth; (earth's surface) ground; **Erdgas** nt natural gas; **Erdgeschoss** nt ground floor (Brit), first floor (US); **Erdkunde** f geography; **Erdnuss** f peanut; **Erdöl** nt (mineral) oil; **Erdrutsch** m landslide; **Erdteil** m continent

ereignen vr happen, take place; **Ereignis** nt event

erfahren 1. irr vt learn, find out; (feeling) experience **2.** adj experienced; **Erfahrung** f experience

erfinden irr vt invent; **erfinderisch** adj inventive, creative; **Erfindung** f invention

Erfolg m (-(e)s, -e) success; (consequence) result; **~ versprechend** promising; **viel ~!** good luck; **erfolglos** adj unsuccessful; **erfolgreich** adj successful

erforderlich adj necessary

erforschen vt explore; (problem etc) investigate

erfreulich adj pleasing, pleasant; (news) good; **erfreulicherweise** adv fortunately

erfrieren irr vi freeze to death; (plants) be killed by frost

Erfrischung f refreshment

erfüllen 1. vt (room) fill; (request, wish etc) fulfil 2. vr come true

ergänzen 1. vt (remark) add; (collection etc) complete 2. vr complement one another; Ergänzung f completion; (thing added) supplement

ergeben 1. irr vt (amount) come to; (lead to) result in 2. irr vr surrender; (arise) result (aus from) 3. adj devoted; (unassuming) humble

Ergebnis nt result

ergreifen irr vt seize; (career) take up; (measure, opportunity) take; (fill with pity etc) move

erhalten irr vt receive; (building, custom etc) preserve; gut ~ sein be in good condition; erhältlich adj available

erheblich adj considerable

erhitzen vt heat (up)

erhöhen 1. vt raise; (in amount, degree) increase 2. vr increase

erholen vr recover; (relax) have a rest; erholsam adj restful; Erholung f recovery; (on holiday etc) relaxation, rest

erinnern 1. vt remind (an + acc of) 2. vr remember (an etw acc sth); Erinnerung f memory; (object) souvenir; (letter etc) reminder

erkälten vr catch a cold; erkältet adj (stark) ~ sein have a (bad) cold; Erkältung f cold

erkennen irr vt recognize; (discern, understand) see; ~, dass ... realize that ...; erkenntlich adj sich ~ zeigen show one's appreciation

Erker m (-s, -) bay

erklären vt explain; (announce) declare; Erklärung f explanation; (announcement) declaration

erkundigen vr enquire (nach about)

erlauben vt allow, permit; jdm ~, etw zu tun allow (or permit) sb to do sth; sich dat etw ~ permit oneself sth; ~ Sie(, dass ich rauche)? do you mind (if I smoke)?; was ~ Sie sich? what do you think you're doing?; Erlaubnis f permission

Erläuterung f explanation; (on text) comment

erleben vt experience; (pleasant time etc) have; (bad experience etc) go through; (scene etc) witness; (be still alive for) live to see; Erlebnis nt experience

erledigen vt (matter, task) deal with; fam (exhaust) wear out; fam (ruin) finish; erledigt adj finished; (sorted out) dealt with; fam (exhausted) whacked, knackered (Brit)

erleichtert adj relieved

Erlös m (-es, -e) proceeds pl

ermahnen vt (against sth)

warn

ermäßigt *adj* reduced; **Ermäßigung** *f* reduction

ermitteln 1. *vt* find out; (*culprit*) trace **2.** *vi* LAW investigate

ermöglichen *vt* make possible (*dat* for)

ermorden *vt* murder

ermüdend *adj* tiring

ermutigen *vt* encourage

ernähren 1. *vt* feed; (*family*) support **2.** *vr* support oneself; **sich ~ von** live on; **Ernährung** *f* food; **Ernährungsberater(in)** *m(f)* nutritional (*or* dietary) adviser

erneuern *vt* renew; (*to original condition*) restore; (*to good condition*) renovate; (*with new one*) replace

ernst 1. *adj* serious **2.** *adv* **jdn/etw ~ nehmen** take sb/sth seriously; **Ernst** *m* (*-es*) seriousness; **das ist mein ~** I'm quite serious; **im ~?** seriously?; **ernsthaft 1.** *adj* serious **2.** *adv* seriously

Ernte *f* (*-, -n*) harvest; **Erntedankfest** *nt* harvest festival (*Brit*), Thanksgiving (Day) (*US*); **ernten** *vt* harvest; (*praise etc*) earn

erobern *vt* conquer

eröffnen *vt* open; **Eröffnung** *f* opening

erogen *adj* erogenous

erotisch *adj* erotic

erpressen *vt* (*person*) blackmail; (*money etc*) extort; **Erpressung** *f* blackmail; (*of money*) extortion

erraten *irr vt* guess

erregen 1. *vt* excite; (*sexually*) arouse; (*make angry*) annoy; (*cause*) arouse **2.** *vr* get worked up by; **Erreger** *m* (*-s, -*) MED germ; virus

erreichbar ~ sein be within reach; (*person*) be available; **das Stadtzentrum ist zu Fuß / mit dem Wagen leicht ~** the city centre is within easy walking / driving distance; **erreichen** *vt* reach; (*train etc*) catch

Ersatz *m* (*-es*) replacement; (*temporary*) substitute; (*for loss etc*) compensation; **Ersatzreifen** *m* AUTO spare tyre; **Ersatzteil** *nt* spare (part)

erscheinen *irr vi* appear; (*give impression*) seem

erschöpft *adj* exhausted; **Erschöpfung** *f* exhaustion

erschrecken 1. *vt* frighten **2.** (*erschrak, erschrocken*) *vi* get a fright; **erschreckend** *adj* alarming; **erschrocken** *adj* frightened

erschwinglich *adj* affordable

ersetzen *vt* replace; (*expenses*) reimburse

erst *adv* first; (*initially*) at first; (*as recently as, merely*) only; (*no earlier than*) not until; **~ jetzt / gestern** only now / yesterday; **~ morgen**

not until tomorrow; **es ist ~ 10 Uhr** it's only ten o'clock; **~ recht** all the more; **~ recht nicht** even less

erstatten vt (costs) refund; **Bericht ~** report (**über** + acc on) **Anzeige gegen jdn ~** report sb to the police

erstaunlich adj astonishing; **erstaunt** adj surprised

erstbeste(r, s) adj **das ~ Hotel** any old hotel; **der Erstbeste** just anyone

erste(r, s) adj first; → **dritte** **zum ~n Mal** for the first time; **er wurde Erster** he came first; **auf den ~n Blick** at first sight

erstens adv first(ly), in the first place

ersticken vi (person) suffocate; **in Arbeit ~** be snowed under with work

erstklassig adj first-class

erstmals adv for the first time

erstrecken vr extend, stretch (**auf** + acc to; **über** + acc over)

ertappen vt catch

erteilen vt (advice, permission) give

Ertrag m (-(e)s, Erträge) yield; (profit) proceeds pl; **ertragen** irr vt (pain) bear, stand; (tolerate) put up with; **erträglich** adj bearable; (fairly good) tolerable

ertrinken irr vi drown

erwachsen adj grown-up; **~ werden** grow up; **Erwach-**

sene(r) mf adult, grown-up

erwähnen vt mention

erwarten vt expect; wait for; **ich kann den Sommer kaum ~** I can hardly wait for the summer

erwerbstätig adj employed

erwidern vt reply; (greeting, visit) return

erwischen vt fam catch (**bei etw** doing sth)

erwünscht adj desired; (person) welcome

Erz nt (-es, -e) ore

erzählen vt tell (**jdm etw** sb sth); **Erzählung** f story, tale

erzeugen vt produce; (electricity) generate; **Erzeugnis** nt product

erziehen irr vt bring up; (intellectually) educate; (animal) train; **Erzieher(in)** m(f) (-s, -) educator; (in kindergarten) (nursery school) teacher; **Erziehung** f upbringing; (intellectual) education

es pron it; (baby, animal) he/she; **ich bin ~** it's me; **~ ist kalt** it's cold; **~ gibt ...** there is ... / there are ...; **ich hoffe ~** I hope so; **ich kann ~** I can do it

Escape-Taste f IT escape key

Esel m (-s, -) donkey

Espresso m (-s, -) espresso

essbar adj edible; **essen** (aß, gegessen) vt eat; **zu Mittag/Abend ~** have lunch/dinner; **was gibt's zu ~?** what's for lunch/dinner?; **~**

gehen eat out; **Essen** nt (-s, -) meal; food

Essig m (-s, -e) vinegar; **Essiggurke** f gherkin

Esslöffel m dessert spoon; **Esszimmer** nt dining room

Estland nt Estonia

Etage f (-, -n) floor, storey; **in** (or **auf**) **der ersten ~** on the first (Brit) (or second (US)) floor; **Etagenbett** nt bunk bed

Etappe f (-, -n) stage

ethnisch adj ethnic

Etikett nt (-(e)s, -e) label

etliche pron pl several, quite a few; **etliches** pron quite a lot

etwa adv (approximation) about; (possibility) perhaps; (example) for instance

etwas 1. pron something; (with negative, question) anything; (small amount) a little; **~ Neues** something/anything new; **~ zu essen** something to eat; **~ Salz** some salt; **wenn ich noch ~ tun kann ...** if I can do anything else ... **2.** adv a bit, a little; **~ mehr** a little more

EU f (-) abbr = **Europäische Union;** EU

euch pron acc, dat of **ihr;** you, (to) you; **~ (selbst)** yourselves; **wo kann ich ~ treffen?** where can I meet you?; **sie schickt es ~** she'll send it to you; **ein Freund von ~** a friend of yours; **setzt ~ bitte** please sit down; **habt**

ihr ~ amüsiert? did you enjoy yourselves?

euer pron (as adj) your; **~ David** (at end of letter) Yours, David; **euere(r, s)** pron → **eure**

Eule f (-, -n) owl

eure(r, s) pron (as noun) yours; **das ist ~** that's yours; **euretwegen** adv because of you; (to please you) for your sake

Euro m (-, -) (currency) euro; **Eurocent** m eurocent; **Eurocity** m (-, -s), **Eurocityzug** m European Intercity train; **Europa** nt (-s) Europe; **Europäer(in)** m(f) (-s, -) European; **europäisch** adj European; **Europäische Union** European Union; **Europameister(in)** m(f) European champion; (team) European champions pl; **Europaparlament** nt European Parliament

Euter nt (-s, -) udder

evangelisch adj Protestant

eventuell 1. adj possible **2.** adv possibly, perhaps

ewig adj eternal; **er hat ~ gebraucht** it took him ages; **Ewigkeit** f eternity

Ex- in cpds ex-, former; **~frau** ex-wife; **~minister** former minister

exakt adj precise

Examen nt (-s, -) exam

Exemplar nt (-s, -e) specimen; (book) copy

Exil *nt* (-s, -e) exile
Existenz *f* existence; (*financial means*) livelihood, living; **existieren** *vi* exist
exklusiv *adj* exclusive; **exklusive** *adv, prep + gen* excluding
exotisch *adj* exotic
Experte *m* (-n, -n), **Expertin** *f* expert
explodieren *vi* explode; **Explosion** *f* explosion
Export *m* (-(e)s, -e) export; **exportieren** *vt* export

Express *m* (-es), **Expresszug** *m* express (train)
extra 1. *adj inv fam* separate; (*additional*) extra **2.** *adv* separately; (*for particular person or purpose*) specially; (*intentionally*) on purpose; **Extra** *nt* (-s, -s) extra
extrem 1. *adj* extreme **2.** *adv* extremely; **~ kalt** extremely cold
exzellent *adj* excellent
Eyeliner *m* (-s, -) eyeliner

F

fabelhaft *adj* fabulous, marvellous
Fabrik *f* factory
Fach *nt* (-(e)s, *Fächer*) compartment; (*area of knowledge*) subject; **Facharzt** *m*, **Fachärztin** *f* specialist; **Fachausdruck** *m* (-s, *Fachausdrücke*) technical term
Fächer *m* (-s, -) fan
Fachfrau *f* specialist, expert; **Fachmann** *m* (-leute pl) specialist, expert; **Fachwerkhaus** *nt* half-timbered house
Fackel *f* (-, -n) torch
fad(e) *adj* (*food*) bland; (*boring*) dull
Faden *m* (-s, *Fäden*) thread
fähig *adj* capable (*zu, gen of*); **Fähigkeit** *f* ability
Fahndung *f* search
Fahne *f* (-, -n) flag

Fahrausweis *m* ticket; **Fahrausweisautomat** *m* ticket machine; **Fahrausweiskontrolle** *f* ticket inspection
Fahrbahn *f* road; (*between lines*) lane
Fähre *f* (-, -n) ferry
fahren (*fuhr, gefahren*) **1.** *vt* drive; (*bicycle*) ride; (*convey*) drive, take; **50 km / h ~** drive at (*or do*) 50 kph **2.** *vi* go; (*in car*) drive; (*ship*) sail; (*depart*) leave; **mit dem Auto / Zug ~** go by car / train; **rechts ~!** keep to the right; **Fahrer(in)** *m(f)* (-s, -) driver; **Fahrerflucht** *f* **~ begehen** fail to stop after an accident; **Fahrersitz** *m* driver's seat
Fahrgast *m* passenger; **Fahrgeld** *nt* fare; **Fahrgemein-**

schaft f car pool; **Fahrkarte** f ticket

Fahrkartenautomat m ticket machine; **Fahrkartenschalter** m ticket office

fahrlässig adj negligent

Fahrlehrer(in) m(f) driving instructor; **Fahrplan** m timetable; **Fahrpreis** m fare; **Fahrpreisermäßigung** f fare reduction

Fahrrad nt bicycle; **Fahrradschloss** nt bicycle lock; **Fahrradverleih** m cycle hire (Brit) (or rental (US)); **Fahrradweg** m cycle path

Fahrschein m ticket; **Fahrscheinautomat** m ticket machine; **Fahrscheinentwerter** m ticket-cancelling machine

Fahrschule f driving school; **Fahrschüler(in)** m(f) learner (driver) (Brit), student driver (US)

Fahrstuhl m lift (Brit), elevator (US)

Fahrt f (-, -en) journey (short) trip; AUTO drive; **auf der ~ nach London** on the way to London; **nach drei Stunden** ~ after travelling for three hours; **gute ~!** I have a good trip; **Fahrtkosten** pl travelling expenses pl

fahrtüchtig f (person) fit to drive; (vehicle) roadworthy

Fahrtunterbrechung f break in the journey, stop

Fahrverbot nt ~ **erhalten/haben** be banned from driving;

Fahrzeug nt vehicle; **Fahrzeugbrief** m (vehicle) registration document; **Fahrzeughalter(in)** m(f) registered owner; **Fahrzeugpapiere** pl vehicle documents pl

fair adj fair

Fakultät f faculty

Falke m (-n, -n) falcon

Fall m (-(e)s, Fälle) (accident) fall; (instance, in law) case; **auf jeden ~, auf alle Fälle** in any case; (without fail) definitely; **auf keinen ~** on no account; **für den ~, dass ...** in case ...

Falle f (-, -n) trap

fallen (fiel, gefallen) vi fall; **etw ~ lassen** drop sth

fällig adj due

falls adv if; (allowing for eventuality) in case

Fallschirm m parachute; **Fallschirmspringen** nt parachuting, parachute jumping; **Fallschirmspringer(in)** m(f) parachutist

falsch adj wrong; (dishonest, not genuine) false; ~ **verbunden** sorry, wrong number; **fälschen** vt forge; **Falschgeld** nt counterfeit money; **Fälschung** f forgery, fake

Faltblatt nt leaflet

Falte f (-, -n) fold; (in skin) wrinkle; (in skirt) pleat; **falten** vt fold; **faltig** adj creased; (skin, face) wrinkled

Familie f family; **Familienangehörige(r)** mf family member; **Familienname** m surname; **Familienstand** m marital status

Fan m (-s, -s) fan

fand imperf of **finden**

fangen (fing, gefangen) **1.** vt catch **2.** vr (not fall) steady oneself; fig compose oneself

Fantasie f imagination

fantastisch adj fantastic

Farbbild nt colour photograph; **Farbe** f (-, -n) colour; (substance) paint; (for fabric) dye; **farbecht** adj colourfast; **färben** vt colour; (fabric, hair) dye; **Farbfilm** m colour film; **Farbfoto** nt colour photo; **farbig** adj coloured; **Farbkopierer** m colour copier; **Farbstoff** m dye; (for food) colouring

Farn m (-(e)s, -e) fern

Fasan m (-(e)s, -e(n)) pheasant

Fasching m (-s, -e) carnival, Mardi Gras (US); **Faschingsdienstag** m (-s, -e) Shrove Tuesday, Mardi Gras (US)

Faschismus m fascism

Faser f (-, -n) fibre

Fass nt (-es, Fässer) barrel; (for oil) drum

fassen **1.** vt (take hold of) grasp; (be able to contain) hold; (decision) take; (comprehend) understand; **nicht zu ~!** unbelievable **2.** vr com-

pose oneself; **Fassung** f (of jewel) mount; (of glasses) frame; (of lamp) socket; (of text) version; (self-control) composure; **jdn aus der ~ bringen** throw sb; **die ~ verlieren** lose one's cool

fast adv almost, nearly

fasten vi fast; **Fastenzeit** f **die ~** (Christian) Lent; (Muslim) Ramadan

Fast Food nt (-s) fast food

Fastnacht f carnival

faul adj (fruit, vegetables) rotten; (person) lazy; (excuse) lame; **faulen** vi rot

faulenzen vi do nothing, hang around; **Faulheit** f laziness

faulig adj rotten; (smell, taste) foul

Faust f (-, Fäuste) fist; **Fausthandschuh** m mitten

Fax nt (-, -(e)) fax; **faxen** vi, vt fax; **Faxgerät** nt fax machine; **Faxnummer** f fax number

FCKW nt (-, -s) abbr = **Fluorchlorkohlenwasserstoff**; CFC

Februar m (-(s), -e) February; → **Juni**

Fechten nt fencing

Feder f (-, -n) feather; (for writing) (pen-)nib; TECH spring; **Federball** m shuttlecock; (game) badminton; **Federung** f suspension

Fee f (-, -n) fairy

fegen vi, vt sweep

fehlen vi (from school etc) be

absent; **etw fehlt jdm** sb lacks sth; **was fehlt ihm?** what's wrong with him?; **du fehlst mir** I miss you; **es fehlt an ...** there's no...

Fehler m (-s, -) mistake, error; (defect, failing) fault; **Fehlermeldung** f IT error message

Fehlzündung f AUTO misfire

Feier f (-, -n) celebration; (get-together) party; **feierlich** adj solemn; **feiern** vt, vi celebrate, have a party; **Feiertag** m holiday; **gesetzlicher ~** public (or bank (Brit) or legal (US)) holiday

feig(e) adj cowardly

Feige f (-, -n) fig

Feigling m coward

Feile f (-, -n) file

fein adj fine; (gentleman, manners) refined

Feind(in) m(f) (-(e)s, -e) enemy; **feindlich** adj hostile

Feinkost f (-) delicacies pl; **Feinkostladen** m delicatessen

Feinwaschmittel nt washing powder for delicate fabrics

Feld nt (-(e)s, -er) field; (in chess) square; SPORT pitch; **Feldweg** m path across the fields

Felge f (-, -n) (wheel) rim

Fell nt (-(e)s, -e) fur; (of sheep) fleece

Fels m (-en, -en), **Felsen** m (-s, -) rock; (rock face) cliff; **felsig** adj rocky

feministisch adj feminist

Fenchel m (-s, -) fennel

Fenster nt (-s, -) window; **Fensterbrett** nt windowsill; **Fensterladen** m shutter; **Fensterplatz** m windowseat; **Fensterscheibe** f windowpane

Ferien pl holidays pl (Brit), vacation sg (US); **~ haben / machen** be / go on holiday (Brit) or vacation (US); **Ferienhaus** nt holiday (or vacation (US)) home; **Ferienkurs** m holiday (or vacation (US)) course; **Ferienlager** nt holiday camp (Brit), vacation camp (US); (for children in summer) summer camp; **Ferienort** m holiday (Brit) or vacation (US)) resort; **Ferienwohnung** f holiday flat (Brit), vacation apartment (US)

Ferkel nt (-s, -) piglet

fern adj distant, far-off; **von ~** from a distance; **Fernabfrage** f remote-control access; **Fernbedienung** f remote control; **Ferne** f distance; **aus der ~** from a distance

ferner adj, adv further; (in addition) besides

Fernflug m long-distance flight; **Ferngespräch** nt long-distance call; **ferngesteuert** adj remote-controlled; **Fernglas** nt binoculars pl; **Fernlicht** nt full beam (Brit), high beam (US)

fernsehen irr vi watch television; **Fernsehen** nt television; **im ~** on television; **Fernseher** m TV (set); **Fernsehkanal** m TV channel; **Fernsehprogramm** nt TV programme; (*magazine*) TV guide; **Fernsehserie** f TV series sg; **Fernsehturm** m TV tower

Fernstraße f major road; **Fernverkehr** m long-distance traffic

Ferse f (-, -n) heel

fertig adj ready; (*completed*) finished; (*task etc*) finish; **~ machen** (*task etc*) finish; **jdn ~ machen** (*criticize*) give sb hell; (*annoy*) drive sb mad; **sich ~ machen** get ready; **mit etw ~ werden** be able to cope with sth; **auf die Plätze, ~, los!** on your marks, get set, go!; **Fertiggericht** nt ready meal

fest adj firm; (*food*) solid; (*salary*) regular; (*shoes*) sturdy; (*sleep*) sound

Fest nt (-(e)s, -e) party; REL festival

Festbetrag m fixed amount

festbinden irr vt tie (an + dat to); **festhalten** irr **1.** vt hold onto **2.** vr hold on (an + dat to)

Festival nt (-s, -s) festival

festlegen 1. vt fix **2.** vr commit oneself

festlich adj festive

festmachen vt fasten; (*date*

etc) fix; **festnehmen** irr vt arrest

Festnetz nt TEL fixed-line network; **Festplatte** f IT hard disk

festsetzen vt fix

Festspiele pl festival sg

feststehen irr vi be fixed

feststellen vt establish; (*say*) remark

Festung f fortress

Festzelt nt marquee

Fete f (-, -n) party

fett adj (*person*) fat; (*food etc*) greasy; (*type*) bold; **Fett** nt (-(e)s, -e) fat; TECH grease; **fettarm** adj low-fat; **fettig** adj fatty; (*dirty*) greasy

fetzig adj fam (*music*) funky

feucht adj damp; (*air*) humid; **Feuchtigkeit** f dampness; (*of air*) humidity; **Feuchtigkeitscreme** f moisturizing cream

Feuer nt (-s, -) fire; **haben Sie ~?** have you got a light?; **Feueralarm** m fire alarm; **feuerfest** adj fireproof; **feuergefährlich** adj inflammable; **Feuerlöscher** m (-s, -) fire extinguisher; **Feuermelder** m (-s, -) fire alarm; **Feuertreppe** f fire escape; **Feuerwehr** f (-, -en) fire brigade; **Feuerwerk** nt fireworks pl; **Feuerzeug** nt (cigarette) lighter

Fichte f (-, -n) spruce

ficken vt, vi vulg fuck

Fieber nt (-s, -) temperature,

fever; **~ haben** have a high temperature; **Fieberthermometer** nt thermometer

fiel imperf of **fallen**

fies adj fam nasty

Figur f (-, -en) figure; (in chess) piece

Filet nt (-s, -s) fillet

Filiale f (-, -n) COMM branch

Film m (-(e)s, -e) film, movie; **filmen** vt, vi film

Filter m (-s, -) filter; **Filterkaffee** m filter coffee; **filtern** vt filter; **Filterpapier** nt filter paper

Filz m (-es, -e) felt; **Filzschreiber** m, **Filzstift** m felt(-tip) pen, felt-tip

Finale nt (-s, -) SPORT final

Finanzamt nt tax office; **finanziell** adj financial; **finanzieren** vt finance

finden (**fand, gefunden**) vt find; (have opinion) think; **ich finde nichts dabei, wenn ...** I don't see what's wrong if ...; **ich finde es gut/schlecht** I like/don't like it

fing imperf of **fangen**

Finger m (-s, -) finger; **Fingerabdruck** m fingerprint; **Fingernagel** m fingernail

Fink m (-en, -en) finch

Finne m (-n, -n), **Finnin** f Finn, Finnish man/woman; **finnisch** adj Finnish; **Finnisch** nt Finnish; **Finnland** nt Finland

finster adj dark; (suspicious)

dubious; (morose) grim; (thought) dark; **Finsternis** f darkness

Firewall f (-, -s) IT firewall

Firma f (-, **Firmen**) firm

Fisch m (-(e)s, -e) fish; **~e** pl ASTR Pisces sg; **fischen** vt, vi fish; **Fischer(in)** m(f) (-s, -) fisherman/-woman; **Fischerboot** nt fishing boat; **Fischgericht** nt fish dish; **Fischhändler(in)** m(f) fishmonger; **Fischstäbchen** nt fish finger (Brit) (or stick (US))

Fisole f (-, -n) French bean

fit adj fit; **Fitness** f (-) fitness; **Fitnesscenter** nt (-s, -) fitness centre

fix adj quick; **~ und fertig** exhausted

fixen vi fam shoot up; **Fixer(in)** m(f) (-s, -) fam junkie

FKK f abbr = **Freikörperkultur**; nudism; **FKK-Strand** m nudist beach

flach adj flat; (water, plate) shallow; **~er Absatz** low heel; **Flachbildschirm** m flat screen

Fläche f (-, -n) area; (of object) surface

Flagge f (-, -n) flag

flambiert adj flambé(ed)

Flamme f (-, -n) flame

Flasche f (-, -n) bottle; **eine ~ sein** fam be useless; **Flaschenöffner** m bottle opener; **Flaschenpfand** nt deposit

flatterhaft adj fickle; **flattern** vi flutter

flauschig adj fluffy

Flaute f (-, -n) calm; COMM recession

Flechte f (-, -n) plait; MED scab; BOT lichen; **flechten** (flocht, geflochten) vt plait; (wreath) bind

Fleck m (-(e)s, -e), **Flecken** m (-s, -) spot; (dirt) stain; **Fleckentferner** m (-s, -) stain remover; **fleckig** adj spotted; (with dirt) stained

Fledermaus f bat

Fleisch nt (-(e)s) flesh; (food) meat; **Fleischbrühe** f meat stock

Fleischer(in) m(f) (-s, -) butcher; **Fleischerei** f butcher's (shop)

fleißig adj diligent, hard-working

flexibel adj flexible

flicken vt mend; **Flickzeug** nt repair kit

Flieder m (-s, -) lilac

Fliege f (-, -n) fly; (clothing) bow tie

fliegen (flog, geflogen) vt, vi fly

Fliese f (-, -n) tile

Fließband nt conveyor belt; (system) production (or assembly) line; **fließen** (floss, geflossen) vi flow; **fließend** adj (speech, German) fluent; (transition) smooth; **~(es) Wasser** running water

flippig adj fam eccentric

flirten vi flirt

Flitterwochen pl honeymoon sg

flocht imperf of **flechten**

Flocke f (-, -n) flake

flog imperf of **fliegen**

Floh m (-(e)s, Flöhe) flea; **Flohmarkt** m flea market

Flop m (-s, -s) flop

Floskel f (-, -n) empty phrase

floss imperf of **fließen**

Floß nt (-es, Flöße) raft

Flosse f (-, -n) fin; (of swimmer) flipper

Flöte f (-, -n) flute; (held vertically) recorder

Fluch m (-(e)s, Flüche) curse; **fluchen** vi swear, curse

Flucht f (-, -en) flight; **flüchten** vi flee (vor + dat from); **flüchtig** adj **ich kenne ihn nur ~** I don't know him very well at all; **Flüchtling** m refugee

Flug m (-(e)s, Flüge) flight; **Flugbegleiter(in)** m(f) (-s, -) flight attendant; **Flugblatt** nt leaflet

Flügel m (-s, -) wing; MUS grand piano

Fluggast m passenger (on a plane); **Fluggesellschaft** f airline; **Flughafen** m airport; **Fluglotse** m air-traffic controller; **Flugnummer** f flight number; **Flugplan** m flight schedule; **Flugplatz** m airport; (small) airfield; **Flugschein** m plane ticket; **Flugschreiber** m flight recorder, black box; **Flugsteig** *m* (-s, -e) gate; **Flugticket** *nt* plane ticket; **Flugverbindung** *f* flight connection; **Flugverkehr** *m* air traffic; **Flugzeit** *f* flying time; **Flugzeug** *nt* plane; **Flugzeugentführung** *f* hijacking

Flunder *f* (-, -n) flounder

Fluor *nt* (-s) fluorine

Flur *m* (-(e)s, -e) hall

Fluss *m* (-es, Flüsse) river; (*movement*) flow

flüssig *adj* liquid; **Flüssigkeit** *f* liquid

flüstern *vt, vi* whisper

Flut *f* (-, -en) flood; (*in sea*) high tide; **Flutlicht** *nt* floodlight

Fohlen *nt* (-s, -) foal

Föhn *m* (-(e)s, -e) hairdryer; (*wind*) foehn; **föhnen** *vt* dry; (*at hairdresser's*) blow-dry

Folge *f* (-, -n) (*one after another*) series *sg*; (*belonging together*) sequence; (*of novel*) instalment; (*of TV series*) episode; (*consequence*) result; **~n haben** have consequences; **folgen** *vi* follow (*jdm* sb); (*do as told*) obey (*jdm* sb); **jdm ~ können** *fig* be able to follow sb; **folgend** *adj* following; **folgendermaßen** as follows; **folglich** *adv* consequently

Folie *f* foil; (*for projector*) transparency

Fön® *m* → **Föhn**

Fondue *nt* (-s, -s) fondue

fönen *vt* → **föhnen**

fordern *vt* demand

fördern *vt* promote; (*support*) help

Forderung *f* demand

Forelle *f* (-, -n) trout

Form *f* (-, -en) form; (*outer form*) shape; (*for casting*) mould; (*for baking*) baking tin (Brit) (or pan (US)); **in ~ sein** be in good form; **Formalität** *f* formality; **Format** *nt* format; **formatieren** *vt* (*disk*) format; (*text*) edit; **formen** *vt* form, shape; **förmlich** *adj* formal; (*proper*) real; **formlos** *adj* informal; **Formular** *nt* (-s, -e) form; **formulieren** *vt* formulate

forschen *vi* search (*nach* for); (*academic*) (do) research; **Forscher(in)** *m(f)* researcher; **Forschung** *f* research

Förster(in) *m(f)* (-s, -) forester; (*for animals*) gamekeeper

fort *adv* away; (*missing*) gone; **fortbewegen 1.** *vt* move away **2.** *vr* move; **Fortbildung** *f* further education; (*vocational*) further training; **fortfahren** *irr vi* go away; (*carry on*) continue; **fortgehen** *irr vi* go away; **fortgeschritten** *adj* advanced; **Fortpflanzung** *f* reproduction

Fortschritt *m* progress; **~e**

machen make progress; **fortschrittlich** *adj* progressive

fortsetzen *vt* continue; **Fortsetzung** *f* continuation; (*episode*) instalment; **~ folgt** to be continued

Foto 1. *nt* (*-s, -s*) photo **2.** *m* (*-s, -s*) camera; **Fotograf(in)** *m(f)* (*-en, -en*) photographer; **Fotografie** *f* photography; (*picture*) photograph; **fotografieren 1.** *vt* photograph **2.** *vi* take photographs; **Fotokopie** *f* photocopy; **fotokopieren** *vt* photocopy

Foul *nt* (*-s, -s*) foul

Foyer *nt* (*-s, -s*) foyer

Fr. *f abbr* = **Frau;** Mrs; (*unmarried, neutral*) Ms

Fracht *f* (*-, -en*) freight; NAUT cargo; **Frachter** *m* (*-s, -s*) freighter

Frack *m* (*-(e)s, Fräcke*) tails *pl*

Frage *f* (*-, -n*) question; **das ist eine ~ der Zeit** that's a matter (*or* question) of time; **das kommt nicht in ~** that's out of the question; **Fragebogen** *m* questionnaire; **fragen** *vt, vi* ask; **Fragezeichen** *nt* question mark; **fragwürdig** *adj* dubious

Franken 1. *m* (*-s, -s*) Swiss franc **2.** *nt* (*-s*) (*region*) Franconia

frankieren *vt* stamp; (*with machine*) frank

Frankreich *nt* (*-s*) France;

Franzose *m* (*-n, -n*), **Französin** *f* Frenchman / -woman; **die ~n** *pl* the French *pl*; **französisch** *adj* French; **Französisch** *nt* French

fraß *imperf of* **fressen**

Frau *f* (*-, -en*) woman; (*spouse*) wife; (*form of address*) Mrs; (*unmarried, neutral*) Ms; **Frauenarzt** *m*, **Frauenärztin** *f* gynaecologist

Fräulein *nt* young lady; (*old-fashioned form of address*) Miss

Freak *m* (*-s, -s*) *fam* freak

frech *adj* cheeky; **Frechheit** *f* cheek; **so eine ~!** what a cheek

Freeclimbing *nt* (*-s*) free climbing

frei *adj* free; (*road*) clear; (*worker*) freelance; (*on* ~**er Tag** a day off; **~e Arbeitsstelle** vacancy; **Zimmer ~** room(s) to let (*Brit*), room(s) for rent (*US*); **im Freien** in the open air

Freibad *nt* open-air (swimming) pool; **freiberuflich** *adj* freelance; **freig(i)ebig** *adj* generous; **Freiheit** *f* freedom; **Freikarte** *f* free ticket; **freilassen** *irr vt* (set) free

freilich *adv* of course

Freilichtbühne *f* open-air theatre; **freimachen** *vr* undress; **freinehmen** *irr vt* **sich** *dat* **einen Tag ~** take a day off; **Freisprechanlage** *f* hands-free phone; **Freistoß**

m free kick

Freitag *m* Friday; → **Mittwoch**; freitags *adv* on Fridays; → **mittwochs**

freiwillig *adj* voluntary

Freizeit *f* spare (or free) time; Freizeithemd *nt* sports shirt; Freizeitkleidung *f* leisure wear; Freizeitpark *m* leisure park

fremd *adj* (unfamiliar) strange; (of another country) foreign; (not one's own) someone else's; Fremde/n *mf* stranger; (from another country) foreigner; Fremdenführer(in) *m(f)* (tourist) guide; Fremdenverkehr *m* tourism; Fremdenverkehrsamt *nt* tourist information office; Fremdsprache *f* foreign language; Fremdsprachenkenntnisse *pl* knowledge *sg* of foreign languages; Fremdwort *nt* foreign word

Frequenz *f* RADIO frequency

fressen (fraß, gefressen) *vt, vi* (animal) eat; (person) guzzle

Freude *f* (-, -n) joy, delight; freuen 1. *vt* please; **es freut mich, dass ...** I'm pleased that ... 2. *vr* be pleased (**über** + *acc* about); **sich auf etw** *acc* ~ look forward to sth

Freund *m* (-(e)s, -e) friend; (in relationship) boyfriend; Freundin *f* friend; (in relationship) girlfriend; freundlich *adj* friendly; (helpful etc) kind; freundlicherweise *adv* kindly; Freundschaft *f* friendship

Frieden *m* (-s, -) peace; Friedhof *m* cemetery; friedlich *adj* peaceful

frieren (fror, gefroren) *vt, vi* freeze; **ich friere, es friert mich** I'm freezing

Frikadelle *f* rissole

Frisbeescheibe® *f* frisbee®

frisch *adj* fresh; (full of life) lively; **„~ gestrichen"** 'wet paint'; **sich ~ machen** freshen up; Frischhaltefolie *f* clingfilm® (Brit), plastic wrap (US); Frischkäse *m* cream cheese

Friseur *m*, Friseuse *f* hairdresser; frisieren 1. *vt* **jdn ~** do sb's hair 2. *vr* do one's hair; Frisör *m* (-s, -e), Frisöse *f* (-, -n) hairdresser

Frist *f* (-, -en) period; (last date) deadline; **innerhalb einer ~ von zehn Tagen** within a ten-day period; **eine ~ einhalten** meet a deadline; **die ~ ist abgelaufen** the deadline has expired; fristlos *adj* **~e Entlassung** dismissal without notice

Frisur *f* hairdo, hairstyle

frittieren *vt* deep-fry

Frl. *f abbr* = **Fräulein**; Miss

froh *adj* happy; **~e Weihnachten!** Merry Christmas

fröhlich *adj* happy, cheerful

Frontalzusammenstoß *m* head-on collision

fror *imperf of* **frieren**

Frosch m (-(e)s, Frösche) frog

Frost m (-(e)s, Fröste) frost; **bei ~** in frosty weather; **Frostschutzmittel** nt anti-freeze

Frottee nt terry(cloth); **frottieren** vr rub down; **Frottier(hand)tuch** nt towel

Frucht f (-, Früchte) fruit; (grain) corn; **Fruchteis** nt fruit-flavoured ice-cream; **fruchtig** adj fruity; **Fruchtsaft** m fruit juice; **Fruchtsalat** m fruit salad

früh adj, adv early; **heute ~** this morning; **um fünf Uhr ~** at five (o'clock) in the morning; **~ genug** soon enough; **früher 1.** adj earlier; (ex-) former **2.** adv formerly, in the past; **frühestens** adv at the earliest

Frühjahr nt, **Frühling** m spring; **Frühlingsrolle** f spring roll; **Frühlingszwiebel** f spring onion (Brit), scallion (US)

Frühschicht f **~ haben** be on the early shift

Frühstück nt breakfast; **frühstücken** vi have breakfast; **Frühstücksbüfett** nt breakfast buffet

frühzeitig adj early

Frust m (-s) fam frustration; **frustrieren** vt frustrate

Fuchs m (-es, Füchse) fox

fühlen vt, vi, vr feel

fuhr imperf of **fahren**

führen 1. vt lead; (business) run; (accounts) keep **2.** vi lead, be in the lead **3.** vr behave; **Führerschein** m driving licence (Brit), driver's license (US); **Führung** f leadership; (of company) management; MIL command; (in museum, town) guided tour; **in ~ liegen** be in the lead

füllen vt, vr fill; GASTR stuff

Füller m (-s, -), **Füllfederhalter** m (-s, -) fountain pen

Füllung f filling

Fund m (-(e)s, -e) find; **Fundbüro** nt lost property office (Brit), lost and found (US); **Fundsachen** pl lost property sg

fünf num five; **Fünf** f (-, -en) five; (mark in school) ≈ E; **fünfhundert** num five hundred; **fünfmal** adv five times; **fünfte(r, s)** adj fifth; → **dritte**; **Fünftel** nt (-s, -) fifth; **fünfzehn** num fifteen; **fünfzehnte(r, s)** adj fifteenth; → **dritte**; **fünfzig** num fifty; **fünfzigste(r, s)** adj fiftieth

Funk m (-s) radio; **über ~** by radio

Funke m (-ns, -n) spark; **funkeln** vi sparkle

Funkgerät nt radio set; **Funktaxi** nt radio taxi, radio cab

Funktion f function; **funktionieren** vi work, function

für prep + acc for; **was ~ (ein) ...?** what kind (or sort) of ...?; **Tag ~ Tag** day after day

Furcht f (-) fear; **furchtbar** adj terrible; **fürchten 1.** vt be afraid of, fear **2.** vr be afraid (*vor + dat* of); **fürchterlich** adj awful

füreinander adv for each other

fürs contr of **für das**

Fürst(in) m(f) (-en, -en) prince / princess; **Fürstentum** nt principality

Furunkel nt (-s, -) boil

Furz m (-es, -e) vulg fart; **furzen** vi vulg fart

Fuß m (-es, Füße) foot; (of glass, column etc) base; (of furniture) leg; **zu ~** on foot; **zu ~ gehen** walk; **Fußball** m football (Brit), soccer

Fußballmannschaft f football (Brit) (or soccer) team; **Fußballplatz** m football pitch (Brit), soccer field (US); **Fußballspiel** nt football (Brit) (or soccer) match; **Fußballspieler(in)** m(f) footballer (Brit), soccer player; **Fußboden** m floor; **Fußgänger(in)** m(f) (-s, -) pedestrian; **Fußgängerüberweg** m pedestrian crossing (Brit), crosswalk (US); **Fußgängerzone** f pedestrian precinct (Brit) (or zone (US)); **Fußgelenk** nt ankle; **Fußpilz** m athlete's foot; **Fußtritt** m kick; **jdm einen ~ geben** give sb a kick, kick sb; **Fußweg** m footpath

futsch adj fam broken; (in pieces) smashed; (lost, vanished) gone

Futter nt (-s, -) feed; (hay etc) fodder; (material) lining; **füttern** vt feed; (garment) line

Fuzzi m (-s, -s) fam guy

G

gab imperf of **geben**

Gabe f (-, -n) gift

Gabel f (-, -n) fork; **Gabelung** f fork

gaffen vi gape

Gage f (-, -n) fee

gähnen vi yawn

Galerie f gallery

Galle f (-, -n) gall; (organ) gall bladder; **Gallenstein** m gallstone

Galopp m (-s) gallop; **galoppieren** vi gallop

galt imperf of **gelten**

gammeln vi loaf (or hang) around

Gang m (-(e)s, Gänge) walk; (in plane) aisle; (of meal, events etc) course; (in building) corridor; (connecting way) passage; AUTO gear; **den zweiten ~ einlegen** change into second (gear); **etw in ~ bringen** get sth go-

ing; **Gangschaltung** f gears
pl; **Gangway** f (-, -s) AVIAT
steps pl; NAUT gangway
Gans f (-, *Gänse*) goose; **Gänseblümchen** nt daisy; **Gänsehaut** f goose pimples pl
(*Brit*), goose bumps pl (US)
ganz 1. adj whole; (*set etc*)
complete; ~ *Europa* all of
Europe; **sein ~es Geld** all
his money; **den ~en Tag** all
day; **die ~e Zeit** all the time
2. adv quite; (*totally*) completely; **es hat mir ~ gut gefallen** I quite liked it; ~
schön viel quite a lot; **ganz-
tägig** adj all-day; (*work, job*)
full-time
gar 1. adj done, cooked **2.** adv
at all; ~ **nicht/nichts/kei-
ner** not/nothing/nobody at
all; ~ **nicht schlecht** not
bad at all

Garage f (-, -n) garage
Garantie f guarantee; **garan-
tieren** vt guarantee
Garderobe f (-, -n) (*clothes*)
wardrobe; (*in theatre, muse-
um etc*) cloakroom
Gardine f curtain
Garn nt (-(e)s, -e) thread
Garnele f (-, -n) shrimp
garnieren vt decorate; (*food*)
garnish
Garten m (-s, *Gärten*) garden;
Gärtner(in) m(f) (-s, -) gar-
dener; **Gärtnerei** f market
garden (*Brit*), truck farm
(US)
Garzeit f cooking time

Gas nt (-es, -e) gas; ~ **geben**
AUTO accelerate; fig get a
move on; **Gasanzünder** m
gas lighter; **Gasheizung** f
gas heating; **Gasherd** m
gas stove, gas cooker (*Brit*);
Gaskocher m camping
stove; **Gaspedal** nt accelera-
tor, gas pedal (US)
Gasse f (-, -n) alley
Gast m (-es, *Gäste*) guest;
Gäste haben have guests;
Gästebett nt spare bed;
Gästebuch nt visitors' book;
Gästehaus nt guest house;
Gästezimmer nt guest room;
gastfreundlich adj hospitable; **Gastgeber(in)** m(f)
(-s, -) host/hostess; **Gasthaus** nt, **Gasthof** m inn;
Gastland nt host country
Gastritis f (-) gastritis
Gastronomie f catering trade
Gastspiel nt SPORT away
game; **Gaststätte** f restaurant; pub (*Brit*), bar; **Gast-
wirt(in)** m(f) landlord/-lady
Gaumen m (-s, -) palate
geb. 1. adj abbr = **geboren**; b.
2. adj abbr = **geborene**; née
→ **geboren**
Gebäck nt (-(e)s, -e) pastries
pl, biscuits pl (*Brit*), cookies
pl (US)
gebacken pp of **backen**
Gebärmutter f womb
Gebäude nt (-s, -) building
geben (**gab**, **gegeben**) **1.** vt, vi
give (*jdm etw* sb sth, sth to
sb); (*cards*) deal; **lass dir ei-**

ne Quittung ~ ask for a receipt **2.** *vt impers* **es gibt** there is / are; *(in the future)* there will be; **das gibt's nicht** I don't believe it **3.** *vr (person)* behave, act; **das gibt sich wieder** it'll sort itself out

Gebet *nt (-(e)s, -e)* prayer
gebeten *pp of* **bitten**
Gebiet *nt (-(e)s, -e)* area; *(British etc)* territory; *fig* field
gebildet *adj* educated; *(with book learning)* well-read
Gebirge *nt (-s, -)* mountains *pl*

Gebiss *nt (-es, -e)* teeth *pl*; *(false)* dentures *pl*; **gebissen** *pp of* **beißen**; **Gebissreiniger** *m* denture tablets *pl*
Gebläse *nt (-s, -)* fan, blower
geblasen *pp of* **blasen**
geblieben *pp of* **bleiben**
gebogen *pp of* **biegen**
geboren 1. *pp of* **gebären 2.** *adj* born; **Andrea Jordan, ~e Christian** Andrea Jordan, née Christian
geborgen 1. *pp of* **bergen 2.** *adj* secure, safe
geboten *pp of* **bieten**
gebracht *pp of* **bringen**
gebrannt *pp of* **brennen**
gebraten *pp of* **braten**
gebrauchen *vt* use; **Gebrauchsanweisung** *f* directions *pl* for use; **gebraucht** *adj* used; **etw ~ kaufen** buy sth secondhand; **Gebrauchtwagen** *m* secondhand (or

used) car
gebrochen *pp of* **brechen**
Gebühr *f (-, -en)* charge; *(for using road)* toll; *(for doctor, lawyer etc)* fee; **gebührenfrei** *adj* free of charge; *(number)* freefone® *(Brit)*, toll-free *(US)*; **gebührenpflichtig** *adj* subject to charges; **~e Straße** toll road
gebunden *pp of* **binden**
Geburt *f (-, -en)* birth; **gebürtig** *adj* **er ist ~er Schweizer** he is Swiss by birth; **Geburtsdatum** *nt* date of birth; **Geburtsjahr** *nt* year of birth; **Geburtsname** *m* birth name; *(of woman)* maiden name; **Geburtsort** *m* birthplace; **Geburtstag** *m* birthday; **herzlichen Glückwunsch zum ~!** Happy Birthday; **Geburtsurkunde** *f* birth certificate
Gebüsch *nt (-(e)s, -e)* bushes *pl*
gedacht *pp of* **denken**
Gedächtnis *nt* memory; **im ~ behalten** remember
Gedanke *m (-ns, -n)* thought; **sich dat über etw acc ~n machen** think about sth; *(anxiously)* be worried about sth; **Gedankenstrich** *m* dash
Gedeck *nt (-(e)s, -e)* place setting; *(on menu)* set meal
Gedenkstätte *f* memorial
Gedicht *nt (-(e)s, -e)* poem
Gedränge *nt (-s)* crush, crowd
gedrungen *pp of* **dringen**

Geduld f (-) patience; **geduldig** adj patient

gedurft pp of **dürfen**

geehrt adj **Sehr ~er Herr Young** Dear Mr Young

geeignet adj suitable

Gefahr f (-, -en) danger; **auf eigene ~** at one's own risk; **gefährden** vt endanger

gefahren pp of **fahren**

gefährlich adj dangerous

Gefälle nt (-s, -) gradient, slope

gefallen 1. pp of **fallen 2.** irr vi **jdm ~** please sb; **er/es gefällt mir** I like him/it; **sich** dat **etw ~ lassen** put up with sth

Gefallen m (-s, -) favour; **jdm einen ~ tun** do sb a favour

gefangen pp of **fangen**

Gefängnis nt prison

Gefäß nt (-es, -e) container, receptacle; ANAT, BOT vessel

gefasst adj composed, calm; **auf etw** acc **~ sein** be prepared (or ready) for sth

geflochten pp of **flechten**

geflogen pp of **fliegen**

geflossen pp of **fließen**

Geflügel nt (-s) poultry

gefragt adj in demand

gefressen pp of **fressen**

Gefrierbeutel m freezer bag; **Gefrierfach** nt freezer compartment; **Gefrierschrank** m (upright) freezer; **Gefriertruhe** f (chest) freezer

gefroren pp of **frieren**

Gefühl nt (-(e)s, -e) feeling

gefunden pp of **finden**

gegangen pp of **gehen**

gegeben pp of **geben**

gegebenenfalls adv if need be

gegen prep + acc against; (exchange) (in return) for; **~ 8 Uhr** about 8 o'clock; **Deutschland ~ England** Germany versus England; **etwas ~ Husten** something for coughs

Gegend f (-, -en) area; **hier in der ~** around here

gegeneinander adv against one another

Gegenfahrbahn f opposite lane; **Gegenmittel** nt remedy (**gegen** for); **Gegenrichtung** f opposite direction; **Gegensatz** m contrast; **im ~ zu** in contrast to; **gegensätzlich** adj conflicting; **gegenseitig** adj mutual; **sich ~ helfen** help each other

Gegenstand m object; (topic) subject

Gegenteil nt opposite; **im ~** on the contrary; **gegenteilig** adj opposite, contrary

gegenüber 1. prep + dat opposite; (with regard to person) to(wards) **2.** adv opposite; **gegenüberstehen** vt face; (problems) be faced with; **gegenüberstellen** vt confront (dat with); fig compare (dat with)

Gegenverkehr m oncoming traffic; **Gegenwart** f (-) present (tense)

gegessen *pp of* **essen**

geglichen *pp of* **gleichen**

geglitten *pp of* **gleiten**

Gegner(in) *m(f) (-s, -)* opponent

gegolten *pp of* **gelten**

gegossen *pp of* **gießen**

gegraben *pp of* **graben**

gegriffen *pp of* **greifen**

gehabt *pp of* **haben**

Gehalt 1. *m (-(e)s, -e)* content **2.** *nt (-(e)s, Gehälter)* salary

gehalten *pp of* **halten**

gehangen *pp of* **hängen**

gehässig *adj* spiteful, nasty

gehauen *pp of* **hauen**

gehbehindert *adj* **sie ist ~** she can't walk properly

geheim *adj* secret; **etw ~ halten** keep sth secret; **Geheimnis** *nt* secret; *(puzzling)* mystery; **geheimnisvoll** *adj* mysterious; **Geheimnummer** *f*, **Geheimzahl** *f (of credit card)* PIN number

geheißen *pp of* **heißen**

gehen *(ging, gegangen)* **1.** *vt, vi* go; *(on foot)* walk; *(function)* work; **über die Straße ~** cross the street **2.** *vi impers* **wie geht es (dir)?** how are you *(or* things)?; **mir/ ihm geht es gut** I'm/he's (doing) fine; **geht das?** is that possible?; **geht's noch?** can you still manage?; **es geht** not too bad, OK; **es geht um ...** it's about ...

Gehirn *nt (-(e)s, -e)* brain; Ge-

hirnerschütterung *f* concussion

gehoben *pp of* **heben**

geholfen *pp of* **helfen**

Gehör *nt (-(e)s)* hearing

gehorchen *vi* obey *(jdm* sb)

gehören 1. *vi* belong *(jdm* to sb); **wem gehört das Buch?** whose book is this?; **gehört es dir?** is it yours? **2.** *vr impers* **das gehört sich nicht** it's not done

Gehweg *m (-s, -e)* pavement *(Brit)*, sidewalk *(US)*

Geier *m (-s, -)* vulture

Geige *f (-, -n)* violin

geil *adj* randy *(Brit)*, horny *(US)*; *fam (wonderful)* fantastic

Geisel *f (-, -n)* hostage

Geist *m (-(e)s, -er)* spirit; *(phantom)* ghost; *(intellect)* mind; **Geisterbahn** *f* ghost train, tunnel of horror *(US)*; **Geisterfahrer(in)** *m(f)* person driving the wrong way on the motorway

geizig *adj* stingy

gekannt *pp of* **kennen**

geklungen *pp of* **klingen**

gekniffen *pp of* **kneifen**

gekommen *pp of* **kommen**

gekonnt 1. *pp of* **können 2.** *adj* skilful

gekrochen *pp of* **kriechen**

Gel *nt (-s, -s)* gel

Gelächter *nt (-s, -)* laughter

geladen 1. *pp of* **laden 2.** *adj* loaded; **ELEC** live; *fig* furious

gelähmt *adj* paralysed

Gelände nt (-s, -) land, terrain; (of factory, for sport) grounds pl; (being built on) site

Geländer nt (-s, -) railing; (on stairs) banister

Geländewagen m off-road vehicle

gelang imperf of **gelingen**

gelassen 1. pp of **lassen 2.** adj calm, composed

Gelatine f gelatine

gelaufen pp of **laufen**

gelaunt adj **gut/ schlecht ~** in a good/ bad mood

gelb adj yellow; (traffic light) amber, yellow (US); **gelblich** adj yellowish; **Gelbsucht** f jaundice

Geld nt (-(e)s, -er) money; **Geldautomat** m cash machine (or dispenser (Brit)), ATM (US); **Geldbeutel** m, **Geldbörse** f purse; **Geldschein** m (bank)note (Brit), bill (US); **Geldstrafe** f fine; **Geldstück** nt coin; **Geldwechsel** m exchange of money; **Geldwechselautomat** m, **Geldwechsler** m (-s, -) change machine

Gelee nt (-s, -s) jelly

gelegen pp of **liegen**

Gelegenheit f opportunity; (event) occasion

gelegentlich 1. adj occasional **2.** adv occasionally

Gelenk nt (-(e)s, -e) joint

gelernt adj skilled

gelesen pp of **lesen**

geliehen pp of **leihen**

gelingen (gelang, gelungen) vi succeed; **es ist mir gelungen, ihn zu erreichen** I managed to get hold of him

gelitten pp of **leiden**

gelogen pp of **lügen**

gelten (galt, gegolten) **1.** vt be worth; **jdm viel/ wenig ~** mean a lot/ not mean much to sb **2.** vi be valid; (in game etc) be allowed; **etw ~ lassen** accept sth

gelungen pp of **gelingen**

gemahlen pp of **mahlen**

Gemälde nt (-s, -) painting, picture

gemäß 1. prep + dat in accordance with **2.** adj appropriate (dat to)

gemein adj mean, nasty

Gemeinde f (-, -n) district, community; (church district) parish; (people in church) congregation

gemeinsam 1. adj joint, common **2.** adv together, jointly; **das Haus gehört uns beiden ~** the house belongs to both of us

Gemeinschaft f community

gemeint pp of **meinen**; **das war nicht so ~** I didn't mean it like that

gemessen pp of **messen**

gemieden pp of **meiden**

gemischt adj mixed

gemocht pp of **mögen**

Gemüse nt (-s, -) vegetables pl; **Gemüsehändler(in)**

m(f) greengrocer

gemusst *pp of* **müssen**

gemustert *adj* patterned

gemütlich *adj* comfortable, cosy; *(person)* good-natured, easy-going; **mach es dir ~** make yourself at home

genannt *pp of* **nennen**

genau 1. *adj* exact, precise **2.** *adv* exactly, precisely; **~ in der Mitte** right in the middle; **es mit etw ~ nehmen** be particular about sth; **~ genommen** strictly speaking; **ich weiß es ~** I know for certain (*or* for sure); **genauso** *adv* exactly the same (way); **~ gut/ viel/ viele Leute** just as well/ much/ many people (*wie* as)

genehmigen *vt* approve; **sich** *dat* **etw ~** indulge in sth; **Genehmigung** *f* approval

Generalkonsulat *nt* consulate general

Generation *f* generation

Genf *nt* (*-s*) Geneva; **~er See** Lake Geneva

genial *adj* brilliant

Genick *nt* (*-(e)s, -e*) (back of the) neck

Genie *nt* (*-s, -s*) genius

genieren *vr* feel awkward; **ich geniere mich vor ihm** he makes me feel embarrassed

genießen (*genoss, genossen*) *vt* enjoy

Genitiv *m* genitive (case)

genommen *pp of* **nehmen**

genoss *imperf of* **genießen**

genossen *pp of* **genießen**

genug *adv* enough

genügen *vi* be enough (*jdm* for sb); **danke, das genügt** thanks, that's enough (*or* that will do)

Genuss *m* (*-es, Genüsse*) pleasure; *(eating, drinking)* consumption

geöffnet *adj* (*shop etc*) open

Geografie *f* geography

Geologie *f* geology

Georgien *nt* (*-s*) Georgia

Gepäck *nt* (*-(e)s*) luggage (*Brit*), baggage; **Gepäckabfertigung** *f* luggage (*Brit*) (*or* baggage) check-in; **Gepäckannahme** *f* (*for forwarding*) luggage (*Brit*) (*or* baggage) office; (*for safekeeping*) left-luggage office (*Brit*), baggage checkroom (*US*); **Gepäckaufbewahrung** *f* left-luggage office (*Brit*), baggage checkroom (*US*); **Gepäckausgabe** *f* luggage (*Brit*) (*or* baggage) office; (*at airport*) baggage reclaim; **Gepäckband** *nt* luggage (*Brit*) (*or* baggage) conveyor; **Gepäckkontrolle** *f* luggage (*Brit*) (*or* baggage) check; **Gepäckstück** *nt* item of luggage (*Brit*) (*or* baggage); **Gepäckträger** *m* porter; (*fixed to bicycle*) carrier; **Gepäckwagen** *m* luggage van (*Brit*), baggage car (*US*)

gepfiffen pp of **pfeifen**

gepflegt adj well-groomed; (park) well looked after

gequollen pp of **quellen**

gerade 1. adj straight; (number) even **2.** adv exactly; (a short while ago) just; **warum ~ ich?** why me (of all people)?; **~ weil** precisely because; **~ noch** only just; **~ neben** right next to; **geradeaus** adv straight ahead

gerannt pp of **rennen**

Gerät nt (-(e)s, -e) device, gadget; (implement) tool; (radio, television) set; (gear) equipment

geraten 1. pp of **raten 2.** irr vi turn out; **gut/schlecht ~** turn out well/badly; **an jdn ~** come across sb; **in etw** acc **~** get into sth

geräuchert adj smoked

geräumig adj roomy

Geräusch nt (-(e)s, -e) sound; (unpleasant) noise

gerecht adj fair; (punishment, reward) just

gereizt adj irritable

Gericht nt (-(e)s, -e) LAW court; (food) dish

gerieben pp of **reiben**

gering adj small; (minor) slight; (temperature, price etc) low; (time) short; **geringfügig 1.** adj slight, minor **2.** adv slightly

gerissen pp of **reißen**

geritten pp of **reiten**

gern(e) adv willingly, gladly; **~**

haben, **~ mögen** like; **etw ~ tun** like doing sth; **~ geschehen** you're welcome

gerochen pp of **riechen**

Gerste f (-, -n) barley; **Gerstenkorn** nt (on eyelid) stye

Geruch m (-(e)s, Gerüche) smell

Gerücht nt (-(e)s, -e) rumour

gerufen pp of **rufen**

Gerümpel nt (-s) junk

gerungen pp of **ringen**

Gerüst nt (-(e)s, -e) (around building) scaffolding; fig framework (zu of)

gesalzen pp of **salzen**

gesamt adj whole, entire; (costs) total; (works) complete; **Gesamtschule** f ≈ comprehensive school

gesandt pp of **senden**

Gesäß nt (-es, -e) bottom

geschaffen pp of **schaffen**

Geschäft nt (-(e)s, -e) business; shop; (transaction) deal; **geschäftlich 1.** adj commercial **2.** adv on business; **Geschäftsführer(in)** m(f) managing director; (of shop) manager; **Geschäftsmann** m businessman; **Geschäftsreise** f business trip; **Geschäftszeiten** pl business (or opening) hours pl

geschehen (geschah, geschehen) vi happen

Geschenk nt (-(e)s, -e) present, gift; **Geschenkgutschein** m gift voucher; **Ge-**

schenkpapier *nt* giftwrap

Geschichte *f* (-, -n) story; (*matter*) affair; HIST history

geschickt *adj* skilful

geschieden **1.** *pp of* **scheiden 2.** *adj* divorced

geschienen *pp of* **scheinen**

Geschirr *nt* (-(e)s, -e) crockery; (*for cooking*) pots and pans *pl*; (*of horse*) harness; ~ **spülen** do (*or* wash) the dishes, do the washing-up (*Brit*); **Geschirrspülmaschine** *f* dishwasher; **Geschirrspülmittel** *nt* washing-up liquid (*Brit*), dishwashing liquid (*US*); **Geschirrtuch** *nt* tea towel (*Brit*), dish towel (*US*)

geschissen *pp of* **scheißen**

geschlafen *pp of* **schlafen**

geschlagen *pp of* **schlagen**

Geschlecht *nt* (-(e)s, -er) sex; LING gender; **Geschlechtskrankheit** *f* sexually transmitted disease, STD; **Geschlechtsverkehr** *m* sexual intercourse

geschlichen *pp of* **schleichen**

geschliffen *pp of* **schleifen**

geschlossen *adj* closed

Geschmack *m* (-(e)s, Geschmäcke) taste; **geschmacklos** *adj* tasteless; **Geschmack(s)sache** *f* **das ist** ~ that's a matter of taste; **geschmackvoll** *adj* tasteful

geschmissen *pp of* **schmeißen**

geschmolzen *pp of* **schmelzen**

geschnitten *pp of* **schneiden**

geschoben *pp of* **schieben**

Geschoss *nt* (-es, -e) (*storey*) floor

geschossen *pp of* **schießen**

Geschrei *nt* (-s) cries *pl*; *fig* fuss

geschrieben *pp of* **schreiben**

geschrie(e)n *pp of* **schreien**

geschützt *adj* protected

Geschwätz *nt* (-es) chatter; (*about other people*) gossip; **geschwätzig** *adj* talkative, gossipy

geschweige *adv* ~ (**denn**) let alone

geschwiegen *pp of* **schweigen**

Geschwindigkeit *f* speed; PHYS velocity; **Geschwindigkeitsbegrenzung** *f* speed limit

Geschwister *pl* brothers and sisters *pl*

geschwollen *adj* swollen; (*speech*) pompous

geschwommen *pp of* **schwimmen**

geschworen *pp of* **schwören**

Geschwulst *f* (-, Geschwülste) growth

Geschwür *nt* (-(e)s, -e) ulcer

gesehen *pp of* **sehen**

gesellig *adj* sociable; **Gesellschaft** *f* society; (*people with sb*) company

gesessen *pp of* **sitzen**

Gesetz nt (-es, -e) law; **gesetz-lich** adj legal; **gesetzwidrig** adj illegal

Gesicht nt (-(e)s, -er) face; (look) expression; **mach doch nicht so ein ~!** stop pulling such a face; **Ge-sichtscreme** f face cream; **Gesichtswasser** nt toner

gesoffen pp of **saufen**

gesogen pp of **saugen**

gespannt adj tense; (keen) eager; **ich bin ~, ob ...** I wonder if ...; **auf etw/jdn ~ sein** look forward to sth/to seeing sb

Gespenst nt (-(e)s, -er) ghost

gesperrt adj closed

gesponnen pp of **spinnen**

Gespräch nt (-(e)s, -e) talk, conversation; discussion; (by phone) call

gesprochen pp of **sprechen**

gesprungen pp of **springen**

Gestalt f (-, -en) form, shape; (person) figure

gestanden pp of **stehen**, **gestehen**

Gestank m (-(e)s) stench

gestatten vt permit, allow; **~ Sie?** may I?

Geste f (-, -n) gesture

gestehen irr vt confess

gestern adv yesterday; **~ Abend/Morgen** yesterday evening/morning

gestiegen pp of **steigen**

gestochen pp of **stechen**

gestohlen pp of **stehlen**

gestorben pp of **sterben**

gestört adj disturbed; (radio reception) poor

gestoßen pp of **stoßen**

gestreift adj striped

gestrichen pp of **streichen**

gestritten pp of **streiten**

gestunken pp of **stinken**

gesund adj healthy; **wieder ~ werden** get better; **Gesundheit** f health; **~!** bless you!

gesundheitsschädlich adj unhealthy

gesungen pp of **singen**

gesunken pp of **sinken**

getan pp of **tun**

getragen pp of **tragen**

Getränk nt (-(e)s, -e) drink; **Getränkeautomat** m drinks machine; **Getränkekarte** f list of drinks

Getreide nt (-s, -) cereals pl, grain

getrennt adj separate; **~ leben** live apart; **~ zahlen** pay separately

getreten pp of **treten**

Getriebe nt (-s, -) AUTO gearbox

getrieben pp of **treiben**

getroffen pp of **treffen**

getrunken pp of **trinken**

Getue nt fuss

geübt adj experienced

Gewähr f (-) guarantee

Gewalt f (-, -en) power; (influence) control; (brute strength) force; (brutality) violence; **mit aller ~** with all one's might; **gewaltig** adj tremendous; (mistake) huge

gewandt 1. pp of **wenden 2.** adj (physically) nimble; (talented) skilful; (practised) experienced

gewann imperf of **gewinnen**

gewaschen pp of **waschen**

Gewebe nt (-s, -) fabric; BIO tissue

Gewehr nt (-(e)s, -e) rifle, gun

Geweih nt (-(e)s, -e) antlers pl

gewellt adj (hair) wavy

gewendet pp of **wenden**

Gewerbe nt (-s, -) trade; **Gewerbegebiet** nt industrial estate (Brit) (or park (US)); **gewerblich** adj commercial

Gewerkschaft f trade union

gewesen pp of **sein**

Gewicht nt (-(e)s, -e) weight; fig importance

gewiesen pp of **weisen**

Gewinn m (-(e)s, -e) profit; (from gambling) winnings pl; **gewinnen** (gewann, gewonnen) **1.** vt win; (acquire) gain; (coal, oil) extract **2.** vi win; (profit) gain; **Gewinner(in** m)f (-s, -) winner

gewiss 1. adj certain **2.** adv certainly

Gewissen nt (-s, -) conscience; **ein gutes/schlechtes ~ haben** have a clear/bad conscience

Gewitter nt (-s, -) thunderstorm

gewogen pp of **wiegen**

gewöhnen 1. vt **jdn an etw** acc ~ accustom sb to sth **2.** vr **sich an jdn/etw ~** get

used (or accustomed) to sb/sth; **Gewohnheit** f habit; (tradition) custom; **gewöhnlich** adj usual; (average) ordinary; pej common; **wie ~** as usual; **gewohnt** adj usual; **etw ~ sein** be used to sth

Gewölbe nt (-s, -) vault

gewonnen pp of **gewinnen**

geworben pp of **werben**

geworden pp of **werden**

geworfen pp of **werfen**

Gewürz nt (-es, -e) spice; **Gewürznelke** f clove; **gewürzt** adj seasoned

gewusst pp of **wissen**

Gezeiten pl tides pl

gezogen pp of **ziehen**

gezwungen pp of **zwingen**

Gibraltar nt (-s) Gibraltar

Gicht f (-) gout

Giebel m (-s, -) gable

gierig adj greedy

gießen (goss, gegossen) vt pour; (flowers) water; (metal) cast; **Gießkanne** f watering can

Gift nt (-(e)s, -e) poison; **giftig** adj poisonous

Gigabyte nt gigabyte

Gin m (-s, -s) gin

ging imperf of **gehen**; **Gin Tonic** m (-(s), -s) gin and tonic

Gipfel m (-s, -) summit, peak; POL summit; fig (culmination) height

Gips m (-es, -e) a. MED plaster; **Gipsverband** m plaster cast

Giraffe f (-, -n) giraffe

Girokonto nt current account

(Brit), checking account (US)

Gitarre f (-, -n) guitar

Gitter nt (-s, -) bars pl

glänzen vi a. fig shine; **glänzend** adj shining; fig brilliant

Glas nt (-es, Gläser) glass; (for jam) jar; **Glascontainer** m bottle bank; **Glaser(in)** m(f) glazier; **Glasscheibe** f pane (of glass); **Glassplitter** m splinter of glass

Glasur f glaze; GASTR icing

glatt adj smooth; (floor, road etc) slippery; (lie) downright; **Glatteis** nt (black) ice

Glatze f (-, -n) bald head

glauben vt, vi believe (an + acc in); (have opinion) think; **jdm ~** believe sb

gleich 1. adj equal; (similar) same, identical; **es ist mir ~** it's all the same to me 2. adv equally; (immediately) straight away; (soon) in a minute; **~ groß/alt** the same size/age; **~ nach/an** right after/at; **Gleichberechtigung** f equal rights pl; **gleichen** (glich, geglichen) 1. vi **jdm/einer Sache ~** be like sb/sth 2. vr be alike; **gleichfalls** adv likewise; **danke ~!** thanks, and the same to you; **gleichgültig** adj indifferent; (immaterial) unimportant; **gleichmäßig** adj regular; (distribution) even, equal; **gleichzeitig** 1. adj simultaneous 2. adv at the same time

Gleis nt (-es, -e) track, rails pl; (area in station) platform

gleiten (glitt, geglitten) vi glide; (slip down) slide; **Gleitschirmfliegen** nt (-s) paragliding

Gletscher m (-s, -) glacier

glich imperf of **gleichen**

Glied nt (-(e)s, -er) (arm, leg) limb; (of chain) link; (male organ) penis; **Gliedmaßen** pl limbs pl

glitschig adj slippery

glitt imperf of **gleiten**

glitzern vi glitter; (stars) twinkle

Glocke f (-, -n) bell; **Glockenspiel** nt chimes pl

Glotze f (-, -n) fam (TV) box; **glotzen** vi fam stare

Glück nt (-(e)s) luck; (pleasure) happiness; **~ haben** be lucky; **viel ~!** good luck; **zum ~** fortunately; **glücklich** adj lucky; (pleased) happy; **glücklicherweise** adj fortunately; **Glückwunsch** m congratulations pl; **herzlichen ~ zur bestandenen Prüfung** congratulations on passing your exam; **herzlichen ~ zum Geburtstag!** Happy Birthday

Glühbirne f light bulb; **glühen** vi glow; **Glühwein** m mulled wine

GmbH f (-, -s) abbr = **Gesellschaft mit beschränkter Haftung**; ≈ Ltd (Brit), ≈

Inc (US)

Gokart m (-(s), -s) go-kart

Gold nt (-(e)s) gold; **golden** adj gold; fig golden; **Goldfisch** m goldfish; **Goldmedaille** f gold medal; **Goldschmied(in)** m(f) goldsmith

Golf 1. m (-(e)s, -e) gulf; **der ~ von Biskaya** the Bay of Biscay **2.** nt (-s) golf; **Golfplatz** m golf course; **Golfschläger** m golf club

Gondel f (-, -n) gondola; (of cable railway) cable-car

gönnen vt **ich gönne es ihm** I'm really pleased for him; **sich** dat **etw ~** allow oneself sth

goss imperf of **gießen**

gotisch adj Gothic

Gott m (-es, Götter) God; (deity) god; **Gottesdienst** m service; **Göttin** f goddess

Grab nt (-(e)s, Gräber) grave

graben (grub, gegraben) vt dig; **Graben** m (-s, Gräben) ditch

Grabstein m gravestone

Grad m (-(e)s, -e) degree; **wir haben 30 ~ Celsius** it's 30 degrees Celsius, it's 86 degrees Fahrenheit; **bis zu einem gewissen ~** up to a certain extent

Graf m (-en, -en) count; (in Britain) earl

Graffiti pl graffiti sg

Grafik f (-, -en) graph; (work of art) graphic; (illustration) diagram; **Grafikkarte** f IT

graphics card

Gräfin f (-, -nen) countess

Gramm nt (-s) gram(me)

Grammatik f grammar

Grapefruit f (-, -s) grapefruit

Graphik f → **Grafik**

Gras nt (-es, Gräser) grass

grässlich adj horrible

Gräte f (-, -n) (fish)bone

gratis adj, adv free (of charge)

gratulieren vi **jdm (zu etw) ~** congratulate sb (on sth); **(ich) gratuliere!** congratulations!

grau adj grey, gray (US); **grauhaarig** adj grey-haired

grausam adj cruel

gravierend adj (error) serious

greifen (griff, gegriffen) **1.** vt seize; **zu etw ~** fig resort to sth **2.** vi (rule etc) have an effect (bei on)

grell adj harsh

Grenze f (-, -n) boundary; (of country) border; (on sth) limit; **grenzen** vi border (an + acc on); **Grenzkontrolle** f border control

Grieche m (-n, -n) Greek; **Griechenland** nt Greece; **Griechin** f Greek; **griechisch** adj Greek; **Griechisch** nt Greek

Grieß m (-es, -e) GASTR semolina

griff imperf of **greifen**

Griff m (-(e)s, -e) grip; (of door etc) handle; **griffbereit** adj handy

Grill m (-s, -s) grill; (outdoors)

barbecue

Grille f (-, -n) cricket

grillen 1. vt grill **2.** vi have a barbecue; **Grillfest** nt, **Grillfete** f barbecue; **Grillkohle** f charcoal

grinsen vi grin; (mockingly) sneer

Grippe f (-, -n) flu; **Grippeschutzimpfung** f flu vaccination

grob adj coarse; (error, breach) gross; (estimate) rough

Grönland nt (-s) Greenland

groß 1. adj big, large; (person) tall; fig great; (letter) capital; (adult) grown-up; **im Großen und Ganzen** on the whole **2.** adv great; **großartig** adj wonderful

Großbritannien nt (-s) (Great) Britain

Großbuchstabe m capital letter

Größe f (-, -n) size; (of person) height; fig greatness; **welche ~ haben Sie?** what size do you take?

Großeltern pl grandparents pl; **Großhandel** m wholesale trade; **Großmarkt** m hypermarket; **Großmutter** f grandmother; **großschreiben** irr vt write with a capital letter; **Großstadt** f city; **Großvater** m grandfather; **großzügig** adj generous

Grotte f (-, -n) grotto

grub imperf of **graben**

Grübchen nt dimple

Grube f (-, -n) pit

grüezi interj (Swiss) hello

grün adj green; **~er Salat** lettuce; **~e Bohnen** French beans; **die Bananen sind noch zu ~** the bananas aren't ripe yet

Grund m (-(e)s, Gründe) reason; (earth's surface) ground; (of sea, container) bottom; (belonging to sb) land, property; **aus gesundheitlichen Gründen** for health reasons; **aus diesem ~** for this reason

gründen vt found; **Gründer(in)** m(f) founder

Grundgebühr f basic charge

gründlich adj thorough

grundsätzlich adj fundamental, basic; **sie kommt ~ zu spät** she's always late; **Grundschule** f primary school; **Grundstück** nt (land) estate; (for building on) site

Grüne(r) mf POL Green; **die ~n** the Green Party

Gruppe f (-, -n) group; **Gruppenermäßigung** f group discount; **Gruppenreise** f group tour

Gruß m (-es, Grüße) greeting; **viele Grüße** best wishes; **Grüße an** + acc regards to; **mit freundlichen Grüßen** Yours sincerely (Brit), Sincerely yours (US); **grüßen** vt greet; **grüß deine Mutter von mir** give your mother my regards; *Julia lässt (euch)* ~ Julia sends (you) her regards

gucken *vi* look

Gulasch *nt* (-(e)s, -e) goulash

gültig *adj* valid

Gummi *m or nt* (-(e)s, -s) rubber; **Gummistiefel** *m* wellington (boot) (*Brit*), rubber boot (*US*)

günstig *adj* favourable; (*price*) good

gurgeln *vi* gurgle; (*with mouthwash*) gargle

Gurke *f* (-, -n) cucumber; *saure* ~ gherkin

Gurt *m* (-(e)s, -e) belt

Gürtel *m* (-s, -) belt; GEO zone; **Gürtelrose** *f* shingles *sg*

gut 1. *adj* well; (*mark in school*) ≈ B; *sehr* ~ very good, excellent; (*mark in school*) ≈ A; *alles Gute!* all the best **2.** *adv* well; *~ gehen* (*business etc*) go well; *es geht ihm* ~ he's doing fine;

jdm ~ tun do sb good; *~ aussehend* good-looking; *~ gelaunt* in a good mood; *~ gemeint* well meant; *schon* ~! it's all right; *machs* ~! take care, bye

Gutachten *nt* (-s, -) report; **Gutachter(in)** *m(f)* (-s, -) expert

gutartig *adj* MED benign

Güter *pl* goods *pl*; **Güterzug** *m* goods train

gutgläubig *adj* trusting

Guthaben *nt* (-s) (credit) balance

gutmütig *adj* good-natured

Gutschein *m* voucher

Gutschrift *f* credit

Gymnasium *nt* ≈ grammar school (*Brit*), ≈ high school (*US*)

Gymnastik *f* exercises *pl*, keep-fit

Gynäkologe *m*, **Gynäkologin** *f* gynaecologist

Gyros *nt* (-, -) doner kebab

H

Haar *nt* (-(e)s, -e) hair; *um ein* ~ nearly; *sich dat die ~e schneiden lassen* have one's hair cut; **Haarbürste** *f* hairbrush; **Haarfestiger** *m* setting lotion; **Haargel** *nt* hair gel; **haarig** *adj* hairy; *fig* nasty; **Haarschnitt** *m* haircut; **Haarspange** *f* hair slide (*Brit*), barrette (*US*);

Haarspliss *m* split ends *pl*; **Haarspray** *nt* hair spray; **Haartrockner** *m* (-s, -) hairdryer; **Haarwaschmittel** *nt* shampoo

haben (*hatte, gehabt*) *vt*, *vaux* have; *Hunger/Angst* ~ be hungry/afraid; *Ferien* ~ be on holiday (*Brit*) (*or* vacation (*US*)); *welches Datum*

~ wir heute? what's the date today?; **ich hätte gerne ...** I'd like ...; **hätten Sie etwas dagegen, wenn ...?** would you mind if ...?; **was hast du denn?** what's the matter (with you)?

Haben nt COMM credit

Habicht m (-(e)s, -e) hawk

Hacke f (-, -n) hoe; (of foot, shoe) heel; **hacken** vt chop; (hole) hack; (soil) hoe; **Hacker(in)** m(f) (-s, -) IT hacker; **Hackfleisch** nt mince(d meat) (Brit), ground meat (US)

Hafen m (-s, Häfen) harbour; (larger) port; **Hafenstadt** f port

Hafer m (-s, -) oats pl; **Haferflocken** pl rolled oats pl

Haft f (-) custody; **haftbar** adj liable, responsible; **haften** vi stick; **~ für** be liable (or responsible) for; **Haftnotiz** f Post-it®; **Haftpflichtversicherung** f third party insurance; **Haftung** f liability

Hagebutte f (-, -n) rose hip

Hagel m (-s) hail; **hageln** vi impers hail

Hahn m (-(e)s, Hähne) cock; (for water) tap (Brit), faucet (US); **Hähnchen** nt cockerel; GASTR chicken

Hai(fisch) m (-(e)s, -e) shark

Haken m (-s, -) hook; (mark) tick

halb adj half; **~ eins** half past twelve; fam half twelve; **eine**

~e Stunde half an hour; **~ offen** half-open; **Halbfinale** nt semifinal; **halbieren** vt halve; **Halbinsel** f peninsula; **Halbjahr** nt half-year; **Halbmond** m ASTR half-moon; (symbol) crescent; **Halbpension** f half board; **halbtags** adv (work) part-time; **halbwegs** adv (fairly) reasonably; **Halbzeit** f half; (interval) half-time

half imperf of **helfen**; **Hälfte** f (-, -n) half

Halle f (-, -n) hall; **Hallenbad** nt indoor (swimming) pool

hallo interj hello, hi

Halogenlampe f halogen lamp

Hals m (-es, Hälse) neck; (inside) throat; **Halsband** nt (for animal) collar; **Halsentzündung** f sore throat; **Halskette** f necklace; **Hals-Nasen-Ohren-Arzt** m, **Hals-Nasen-Ohren-Ärztin** f ear, nose and throat specialist; **Halsschmerzen** pl sore throat sg; **Halstuch** nt scarf

halt 1. interj stop **2.** adv **das ist ~ so** that's just the way it is; **Halt** m (-(e)s, -e) stop; (grip) hold; (inner strength) stability

haltbar adj durable; (food) non-perishable; **Haltbarkeitsdatum** nt best-before date

halten (hielt, gehalten) **1.** vt keep; (grip) hold; **~ für** regard as; **~ von** think of; **den Elfmeter ~** save the penalty; **eine Rede ~** give (or make) a speech **2.** vi hold; (stay fresh) keep; (come to standstill) stop; **zu jdm ~** stand by sb **3.** vr (stay fresh) keep

Haltestelle f stop; **Halteverbot** nt **hier ist ~** you can't stop here

Haltung f (of body) posture; fig attitude; (self-control) composure

Hamburg nt (-s) Hamburg; **Hamburger** m (-s, -) GASTR hamburger

Hammelfleisch nt mutton

Hammer m (-s, **Hämmer**) hammer; fig fam (mistake) howler

Hämorr(ho)iden pl haemorrhoids pl, piles pl

Hamster m (-s, -) hamster

Hand f (-, **Hände**) hand; **jdm die ~ geben** shake hands with sb; **zu Händen von** attention; **Handarbeit** f (school subject) handicraft; **~ sein** be handmade; **Handball** m handball; **Handbremse** f handbrake; **Handbuch** nt handbook, manual; **Handcreme** f hand cream

Handel m (-s) trade; (deal) transaction; **handeln 1.** vi act; COMM trade; **~ von** be about **2.** vr impers **es handelt sich um ...** it's about ...

Handfeger m (-s, -) brush; **Handfläche** f palm; **Hand-**

gelenk nt wrist; **handgemacht** adj handmade; **Handgepäck** nt hand luggage (Brit) (or baggage)

Händler(in) m(f) (-s, -) dealer

handlich adj handy

Handlung f act, action; (of novel, film) plot

Handschellen pl handcuffs pl; **Handschrift** f handwriting; **Handschuh** m glove; **Handschuhfach** nt glove compartment; **Handtasche** f handbag, purse (US); **Handtuch** nt towel; **Handwerk** nt trade; **Handwerker** m (-s, -) workman

Handy nt (-s, -s) mobile (phone), cell phone (US)

Hang m (-(e)s, **Hänge**) slope; fig tendency

Hängematte f hammock

hängen 1. (hing, gehangen) vi hang; **an der Wand/ an der Decke ~** hang on the wall / from the ceiling; **an jdm ~** fig be attached to sb; **~ bleiben** get caught (an + dat on); fig get stuck (an + acc on) **2.** vt hang (an + acc on)

Hantel f (-, -n) dumbbell

Hardware f (-, -s) IT hardware

Harfe f (-, -n) harp

harmlos adj harmless

harmonisch adj harmonious

Harn m (-(e)s, -e) urine; **Harnblase** f bladder

hart adj hard; fig harsh; **~ gekocht** (egg) hard-boiled; **hartnäckig** adj stubborn

Haschisch nt (-) hashish

Hase m (-n, -n) hare

Haselnuss f hazelnut

Hass m (-es) hatred (auf + acc, gegen of), hate; **hassen** vt hate

hässlich adj ugly; (mean) nasty

Hast f (-) haste, hurry; **hastig** adj hasty

hatte imperf of **haben**

Haube f (-, -n) hood; (hat) cap; AUTO bonnet (Brit), hood (US)

hauchdünn adj (layer, slice) wafer-thin

hauen (haute, gehauen) vt hit

Haufen m (-s, -) pile; **ein ~ Geld** a lot of money

häufig 1. adj frequent **2.** adv frequently, often

Haupt- in cpds main; **Hauptbahnhof** m central (or main) station; **Haupteingang** m main entrance; **Hauptgericht** nt main course

Häuptling m chief

Hauptquartier nt headquarters pl; **Hauptrolle** f leading role; **Hauptsache** f main thing; **hauptsächlich** adv mainly, chiefly; **Hauptsaison** f high (or peak) season; **Hauptsatz** m main clause; **Hauptschule** f ≈ secondary school (Brit), ≈ junior high school (US); **Hauptstadt** f capital; **Hauptstraße** f main road; (in town centre) main street; **Hauptverkehrszeit** f rush hour

Haus nt (-es, Häuser) house; **nach ~e** home; **zu ~e** at home; **jdn nach ~e bringen** take sb home; **Hausarbeit** f housework; **Hausaufgabe** f homework; **~n** pl homework sg; **Hausbesitzer(in)** m(f) (-s, -) house owner; (renting out) landlord /-lady; **Hausbesuch** m home visit; **Hausflur** m hall; **Hausfrau** f housewife; **hausgemacht** adj homemade; **Haushalt** m household; POL budget

häuslich adj domestic

Hausmann m house-husband; **Hausmannskost** f good plain cooking; **Hausmeister(in)** m(f) caretaker (Brit), janitor (US); **Hausnummer** f house number; **Hausschlüssel** m front-door key; **Hausschuh** m slipper; **Haustier** nt pet; **Haustür** f front door

Haut f (-, Häute) skin; **Hautarzt** m, **Hautärztin** f dermatologist; **Hautausschlag** m skin rash; **Hautcreme** f skin cream; **Hautfarbe** f skin colour

Hawaii nt (-s) Hawaii

Hebamme f (-, -n) midwife

Hebel m (-s, -) lever

heben (hob, gehoben) vt raise, lift

Hebräisch nt (-) Hebrew

Hecht m (-(e)s, -e) pike

Heck nt (-(e)s, -e) (of boat)

stern; (of car) rear; **Heckan-
trieb** m rear-wheel drive

Hecke f (-, -n) hedge

Heckklappe f tailgate; **Heckscheibe** f rear window;
Heckscheibenheizung f
rear-window defroster

Hefe f (-, -n) yeast

Heft nt (-(e)s, -e) notebook, exercise book; (of magazine)
issue

heftig adj violent; (criticism,
argument) fierce

Heftklammer f paper clip;
Heftpflaster nt plaster
(Brit), Band-Aid® (US)

Heide f (-, -n) heath, moor;
Heidekraut nt heather

Heidelbeere f bilberry, blueberry

heidnisch adj (custom) pagan

heikel adj (matter) awkward;
(person) fussy

heil adj (thing) in one piece,
intact; **heilbar** adj curable

Heilbutt m (-(e)s, -e) halibut

heilen 1. vt cure **2.** vi heal

heilig adj holy; **Heiligabend**
m Christmas Eve; **Heilige(r)**
mf saint

Heilpraktiker(in) m(f) (-s, -)
non-medical practitioner

heim adv home; **Heim** nt (-(e),
-e) home

Heimat f (-, -en) home (town/
country)

heimfahren irr vi drive home;
Heimfahrt f journey home;
heimisch adj (population,
customs) local; (animal,

plant) native; **heimkommen**
irr vi come (or return) home

heimlich adj secret

Heimreise f journey home;
Heimspiel nt SPORT home
game; **Heimweg** m way
home; **Heimweh** nt (-s)
homesickness; ~ **haben** be
homesick

Heirat f (-, -en) marriage; **heiraten 1.** vi get married **2.** vt
marry; **Heiratsantrag** m
proposal; **er hat ihr einen ~
gemacht** he proposed to her

heiser adj hoarse

heiß adj hot; (discussion)
heated; **mir ist ~** I'm hot

heißen (hieß, geheißen) **1.** vi
be called; (have sense, consequence) mean; **ich heiße
Tom** my name is Tom; **wie
~ Sie?** what's your name?;
**wie heißt sie mit Nachna-
men?** what's her surname?;
wie heißt das auf Englisch?
what's that in English? **3.** vi
impers **es heißt** (people say)
it is said; **es heißt in dem
Brief ...** it says in the letter
...; **das heißt** that is

Heißluftherd m fan-assisted
oven

heiter adj cheerful; (weather)
bright

heizen vt heat; **Heizkissen** m
MED heated pad; **Heizkörper**
m radiator; **Heizöl** nt fuel oil;
Heizung f heating

Hektar nt (-s, -) hectare

Hektik f (-, -en) **nur keine ~!**

take it easy; **hektisch** *adj* hectic

Held *m* (-en, -en) hero; **Heldin** *f* heroine

helfen (*half, geholfen*) **1.** *vi* help (*jdm bei etw* sb with sth); (*thing*) be of use **2.** *vi impers* **es hilft nichts, du musst ...** it's no use, you have to ...; **Helfer(in)** *m(f)* helper; (*at work*) assistant

hell *adj* bright; (*colour*) light; (*complexion*) fair; **hellblau** *adj* light blue; **hellblond** *adj* ash-blond; **hellgelb** *adj* pale yellow; **hellgrün** *adj* light green; **Hellseher(in)** *m(f)* clairvoyant

Helm *m* (-(e)s, -e) helmet; **Helmpflicht** *f* compulsory wearing of helmets

Hemd *nt* (-(e)s, -en) shirt

hemmen *vt* check; (*hinder*) hamper; **gehemmt sein** *be inhibited*; **Hemmung** *f* inhibition; (*moral*) scruple

Henkel *m* (-s, -) handle

Henna *nt* (-s) henna

Henne *f* (-, -n) hen

Hepatitis *f* (-, *Hepatitiden*) hepatitis

her *adv* here; **wo ist sie ~?** where is she from?; **das ist zehn Jahre ~** that was ten years ago

herab *adv* down; **herablassend** *adj* (*remark*) condescending; **herabsehen** *irr vt* **auf jdn** look down on sb; **herabsetzen** *vt* reduce;

fig disparage

heran *adv* **näher~!** come closer; **herankommen** *irr vi* approach; **~ an** + *acc* be able to get at; *fig* be able to get hold of; **heranwachsen** *irr vi* grow up

herauf *adv* up; **heraufbeschwören** *irr vt* evoke; (*crisis, dispute etc*) cause; **heraufziehen** *irr* **1.** *vt* pull up **2.** *vi* approach; (*storm*) gather

heraus *adv* out; **herausbekommen** *irr vt* (*secret*) find out; (*puzzle*) solve; **herausbringen** *irr vt* bring out; **herausfinden** *irr vt* find out; **herausfordern** *vt* challenge; **Herausforderung** *f* challenge; **herausgeben** *irr vt* (*book*) edit; (*issue*) publish; **jdm zwei Euro ~** give sb two euros change; **herausholen** *vt* get out (*aus* of); **herauskommen** *irr vi* come out; **dabei kommt nichts heraus** nothing will come of it; **herausstellen** *vr* turn out (*als* to be); **herausziehen** *irr vt* pull out

Herbst *m* (-(e)s, -e) autumn, fall (*US*)

Herd *m* (-(e)s, -e) cooker, stove

Herde *f* (-, -n) herd; (*of sheep*) flock

herein *adv* in; **~!** come in; **hereinfallen** *irr vi* **wir sind auf einen Betrüger hereingefallen** we were taken in by a swindler; **hereinlegen** vt jdn ~ fig take sb for a ride

Herfahrt f journey here; **auf der ~** on the way here

Hergang m course (of events); **schildern Sie mir den ~** tell me what happened

Hering m (-s, -e) herring

herkommen irr vi come; **wo kommt sie her?** where does she come from?

Heroin nt (-s) heroin

Herpes m (-) MED herpes

Herr m (-(e)n, -en) (before name) Mr; (person) gentleman; (nobleman, God) Lord; **mein ~!** sir; **meine ~en!** gentlemen; **Sehr geehrte Damen und ~en** Dear Sir or Madam; **Herrentoilette** f men's toilet, gents

herrichten vt prepare

herrlich adj marvellous, splendid

Herrschaft f rule; power

herrschen vi rule; (exist) be

herstellen vt make; (industrially) manufacture; **Hersteller(in)** m(f) manufacturer; **Herstellung** f production

herüber adv over

herum adv around; (in a circle) round; **um etw ~** around sth; **du hast den Pulli falsch ~ an** you're wearing your sweater inside out; **anders ~** the other way round; **herumfahren** irr vi drive around; **herumkommen** irr vi **sie ist viel in der Welt he-** **rumgekommen** she's been around the world; **um etw ~** (avoid) get out of sth; **herumkriegen** vt talk round; **herumtreiben** irr vr hang around

herunter adv down; **heruntergekommen** adj (building, area) run-down; (person) down-at-heel; **herunterhandeln** vt get down; **herunterholen** vt bring down; **herunterkommen** irr vi come down; **herunterladen** irr vt IT download

hervor adv out; **hervorbringen** irr vt produce; (word) utter; **hervorheben** irr vt emphasize, stress; **hervorragend** adj excellent; **hervorrufen** irr vt cause, give rise to

Herz nt (-ens, -en) heart; (card suit) hearts pl; **von ganzem ~en** wholeheartedly; **sich dat etw zu ~en nehmen** take sth to heart; **Herzanfall** m heart attack; **Herzbeschwerden** pl heart trouble sg; **herzhaft** adj (meal) substantial; **~ lachen** have a good laugh; **Herzinfarkt** m heart attack; **Herzklopfen** nt (-s) MED palpitations pl; **ich hatte ~ (vor Aufregung)** my heart was pounding (with excitement); **herzkrank** adj **sie ist ~** she's got a heart condition; **herzlich** adj (reception, person) warm; **~en Glückwunsch**

congratulations

Herzog(in) m(f) (-s, Herzöge) duke / duchess

Herzschlag m heartbeat; (stopping) heart failure; **Herzschrittmacher** m pacemaker

Hessen nt (-s) Hessen

heterosexuell adj heterosexual

Hetze f (-, -n) rush; **hetzen** vt, vr rush

Heu nt (-(e)s) hay

heuer adv this year

heulen vi howl; (weep) cry

Heuschnupfen m hay fever

Heuschrecke f (-, -n) grasshopper; (larger) locust

heute adv today; **~ Abend/früh** this evening / morning; **~ Nacht** tonight; (just gone) last night; **~ in acht Tagen** a week (from) today; **sie hat bis ~ nicht bezahlt** she hasn't paid to this day; **heutig** adj **die ~e Zeitung/Generation** today's paper / generation; **heutzutage** adv nowadays

Hexe f (-, -n) witch; **Hexenschuss** m lumbago

hielt imperf of **halten**

hier adv here; **~ entlang** this way; **~ bleiben** stay here; **~ lassen** leave here; **ich bin auch nicht von ~** I'm a stranger here myself; **hierher** adv here; **das gehört nicht ~** that doesn't belong here; **hiermit** adv with this

hiesig adj local

hieß imperf of **heißen**

Hi-Fi-Anlage f hi-fi (system)

high adj fam high; **Highlife** nt (-s) high life; **~ machen** live it up; **Hightech** nt (-s) high tech

Hilfe f (-, -n) help; (financial, for those in need) aid; **~!** help!; **erste ~ leisten** give first aid; **um ~ bitten** ask for help; **hilflos** adj helpless; **hilfsbereit** adj helpful; **Hilfsmittel** nt aid

Himbeere f raspberry

Himmel m (-s, -) sky; REL heaven; **Himmelfahrt** f Ascension; **Himmelsrichtung** f direction; **himmlisch** adj heavenly

hin adv there; **~ und her** to and fro; **~ und zurück** there and back; **bis zur Mauer ~** up to the wall; **das ist noch lange ~** (in the future) that's a long way off

hinab adv down; **hinabgehen** irr vi go down

hinauf adv up; **hinaufgehen** irr vi, vt go up; **hinaufsteigen** irr vi climb (up)

hinaus adv out; **hinausgehen** irr vi go out; **~ über** + acc exceed; **hinauslaufen** irr vi run out; **~ auf** + acc come to, amount to; **hinausschieben** irr vi put off, postpone; **hinausschieben** irr vt throw out; (employee) fire, sack (Brit); **hinauszögern**

vr take longer than expected

hinbringen *vt* **ich bringe Sie hin** I'll take you there

hindern *vt* prevent; **jdn daran ~, etw zu tun** stop (or prevent) sb from doing sth; **Hindernis** *nt* obstacle

Hinduismus *m* Hinduism

hindurch *adv* through; **das ganze Jahr ~** throughout the year, all year round; **die ganze Nacht ~** all night (long)

hinein *adv* in; **hineingehen** *irr vi* go in; **~ in** + *acc* go into, enter; **hineinpassen** *vi* fit in; **~ in** + *acc* fit into

hinfahren *irr* **1.** *vi* go there **2.** *vt* take there; **Hinfahrt** *f* outward journey

hinfallen *irr vi* fall (down)

Hinflug *m* outward flight

hing *imperf of* **hängen**

hingehen *irr vi* go there; (*time*) pass; **hinhalten** *irr vt* hold out; (*keep waiting*) put off

hinken *vi* limp; **der Vergleich hinkt** the comparison doesn't work

hinlegen 1. *vt* put down **2.** *vr* lie down; **hinnehmen** *irr vt* fig put up with, take; **Hinreise** *f* outward journey; **hinsetzen** *vr* sit down; **hinsichtlich** *prep* + *gen* with regard to; **hinstellen 1.** *vt* put (down) **2.** *vr* stand

hinten *adv* at the back; (*in car*) in the back; (*sth / sb else*) behind

hinter *prep* + *dat or acc* behind; (*beyond, in order of importance*) after; **~ jdm her sein** be after sb; **etw ~ sich acc bringen** get sth over (and done) with; **Hinterachse** *f* rear axle; **Hinterbein** *nt* hind leg; **Hinterbliebene(r)** *mf* dependant; **hintere(r, s)** *adj* rear, back; **hintereinander** *adv* (*in a row*) one behind the other; (*in continuous sequence*) one after the other; **drei Tage ~** three days running (or in a row); **Hintergedanke** *m* ulterior motive; **hintergehen** *irr vt* deceive; **Hintergrund** *m* background; **hinterher** *adv* afterwards; **los, ~!** come on, after him / her / them; **Hinterkopf** *m* back of the head; **hinterlassen** *vt* leave; **jdm eine Nachricht ~** leave a message for sb; **hinterlegen** *vt* leave (*bei* with)

Hintern *m* (-, -) fam backside, bum

Hinterradantrieb *m* AUTO rear-wheel drive; **Hinterteil** *nt* back (part); (*of person*) behind; **Hintertür** *f* back door

hinüber *adv* over; **~ sein** fam (*broken*) be ruined; (*food*) have gone bad; **hinübergehen** *irr vi* go over

hinunter *adv* down; **hinuntergehen** *irr vi, vt* go down; hi-

nunterschlucken vt a. fig swallow

Hinweg m outward journey

hinwegsetzen vr **sich über etw** acc ~ ignore sth

Hinweis m (-es, -e) (suggestion) hint; (for user etc) instruction; **hinweisen** irr vi **jdn auf etw** acc ~ point sth out to sb

hinzu adv in addition; **hinzufügen** vt add

Hirn nt (-(e)s, -e) brain; (intellect) brains pl; **Hirnhautentzündung** f meningitis

Hirsch m (-(e)s, -e) deer; (meat) venison

Hirse f (-, -n) millet

Hirte m (-n, -n) shepherd

historisch adj historical

Hit m (-s, -s) MUS, IT hit; **Hitliste** f, **Hitparade** f charts pl

Hitze f (-) heat; **hitzebeständig** adj heat-resistant; **Hitzewelle** f heatwave; **hitzig** adj hot-tempered; (debate) heated; **Hitzschlag** m heatstroke

HIV nt (-(s), -(s)) abbr = **Human Immunodeficiency Virus**; HIV; **HIV-negativ** adj HIV-negative; **HIV-positiv** adj HIV-positive

H-Milch f long-life milk

hob imperf of **heben**

Hobby nt (-s, -s) hobby

Hobel m (-s, -) plane

hoch adj high; (tree, house) tall; (snow) deep; **der Zaun ist drei Meter** hoch the fence is three metres high; ~ **be-**

gabt extremely gifted; **das ist mir zu** ~ that's above my head; ~ **soll sie leben!, sie lebe** ~! three cheers for her; **4** ~ **2 ist 16** 4 squared is 16; **4** ~ **5** 4 to the power of 5

Hoch nt (-s, -s) METEO high; **hochachtungsvoll** adv Yours faithfully; **Hochbetrieb** m **es herrscht** ~ they/we are extremely busy; **Hochdeutsch** nt High German; **Hochgebirge** nt high mountains pl; **Hochhaus** nt high rise; **hochheben** irr vt lift (up); **Hochschule** f college; university; **Hochsommer** m midsummer; **Hochsprung** m high jump

höchst adv highly, extremely; **höchste(r, s)** adj highest; (very great) extreme; **höchstens** adv at the most; **Höchstgeschwindigkeit** f maximum speed

höchstwahrscheinlich adv very probably

Hochwasser nt high water; floods pl

Hochzeit f (-, -en) wedding; **Hochzeitsnacht** f wedding night; **Hochzeitsreise** f honeymoon; **Hochzeitstag** m wedding day; (yearly) wedding anniversary

hocken vi, vr squat, crouch

Hocker m (-s, -) stool

Hockey nt (-s) hockey

Hoden m (-s, -) testicle

Hof m (-(e)s, Höfe) yard; (surrounded by building) courtyard; (agricultural) farm; (royal) court

hoffen vi hope (auf + acc for); **ich hoffe es** I hope so; **hoffentlich** adv hopefully; **~ nicht** I hope not; **Hoffnung** f hope; **hoffnungslos** adj hopeless

höflich adj polite; **Höflichkeit** f politeness

hohe(r, s) adj → **hoch**

Höhe f (-, -n) height; (high land) hill; (of sum of money) amount; (flying height) altitude; **Höhenangst** f vertigo; **Höhensonne** f sun lamp

Höhepunkt m (of trip) high point; (of show etc) highlight; (sexual, of film) climax

höher adj, adv higher

hohl adj hollow

Höhle f (-, -n) cave

holen vt get, fetch; (collect) pick up; (breath) catch; **die Polizei ~** call the police; **jdn/etw ~ lassen** send for sb/sth

Holland nt Holland; **Holländer(in)** m(f) (-s, -) Dutchman/-woman; **holländisch** adj Dutch

Hölle f (-, -n) hell

Hologramm nt hologram

holperig adj bumpy

Holunder m (-s, -) elder

Holz nt (-es, Hölzer) wood; **Holzboden** m wooden floor; **hölzern** adj wooden; **holzig**

adj (stem) woody; **Holzkohle** f charcoal

Homebanking nt (-s) home banking, online banking; **Homepage** f (-, -s) home page; **Hometrainer** m exercise machine

homöopathisch adj homeopathic

homosexuell adj homosexual

Honig m (-s, -e) honey; **Honigmelone** f honeydew melon

Honorar nt (-s, -e) fee

Hopfen m (-s, -) hop; (in brewing) hops pl

hoppla interj whoops, oops

horchen vi listen (auf + acc to); (at door) eavesdrop

hören vt, vi hear; (by chance) overhear; (attentively: radio, music) listen to; **ich habe schon viel von Ihnen gehört** I've heard a lot about you; **Hörer** m TEL receiver; **Hörer(in)** m(f) listener; **Hörgerät** nt hearing aid

Horizont m (-(e)s, -e) horizon; **das geht über meinen ~** that's beyond me

Hormon nt (-s, -e) hormone

Hornhaut f hard skin; (of eye) cornea

Horoskop nt (-s, -e) horoscope

Hörsaal m lecture hall; **Hörsturz** m acute hearing loss

Hose f (-, -n) trousers pl (Brit), pants pl (US); (undergar-

ment) (under)pants *pl*; *eine ~* a pair of trousers/pants; *kurze ~* (pair of) shorts *pl*; **Hosenanzug** *m* trouser suit (*Brit*), pantsuit (*US*); **Hosenschlitz** *m* fly, flies (*Brit*); **Hosentasche** *f* trouser pocket (*Brit*), pant pocket (*US*); **Hosenträger** *m* braces *pl* (*Brit*), suspenders *pl* (*US*)

Hospital *nt* (*-s, Hospitäler*) hospital

Hotdog *nt or m* (*-s, -s*) hot dog

Hotel *nt* (*-s, -s*) hotel; *in welchem ~ seid ihr?* which hotel are you staying at?; **Hoteldirektor(in)** *m(f)* hotel manager; **Hotelkette** *f* hotel chain; **Hotelzimmer** *nt* hotel room

Hotline *f* (*-, -s*) hot line

Hubraum *m* cubic capacity

hübsch *adj* (*girl, child, dress*) pretty; (*man, woman*) good-looking, cute

Hubschrauber *m* (*-s, -*) helicopter

Huf *m* (*-(e)s, -e*) hoof; **Hufeisen** *nt* horseshoe

Hüfte *f* (*-, -n*) hip

Hügel *m* (*-s, -*) hill; **hügelig** *adj* hilly

Huhn *nt* (*-(e)s, Hühner*) hen; GASTR chicken; **Hühnchen** *nt* (*-s, -*) chicken; **Hühnerauge** *nt* corn; **Hühnerbrühe** *f* chicken broth

Hülle *f* (*-, -n*) cover; (*for ID*) case; (*cellophane*) wrapping

Hummel *f* (*-, -n*) bumblebee

Hummer *m* (*-s, -*) lobster; **Hummerkrabbe** *f* king prawn

Humor *m* (*-s*) humour; *~ haben* have a sense of humour; **humorvoll** *adj* humorous

humpeln *vi* hobble

Hund *m* (*-(e)s, -e*) dog; **Hundeleine** *f* dog lead (*Brit*), dog leash (*US*)

hundert *num* hundred; **hundertprozentig** *adj, adv* one hundred per cent; **hundertste(r, s)** *adj* hundredth

Hündin *f* bitch

Hunger *m* (*-s*) hunger; *~ haben/bekommen* be/get hungry; **hungern** *vi* go hungry; (*seriously, constantly*) starve

Hupe *f* (*-, -n*) horn; **hupen** *vi* sound one's horn

Hüpfburg *f* bouncy castle®; **hüpfen** *vi* hop; jump

Hürde *f* (*-, -n*) hurdle

Hure *f* (*-, -n*) whore

hurra *interj* hooray

husten *vi* cough; **Husten** *m* (*-s*) cough; **Hustenbonbon** *nt* cough sweet; **Hustensaft** *m* cough mixture

Hut *m* (*-(e)s, Hüte*) hat

hüten 1. *vt* look after 2. *vr* watch out; *sich ~, etw zu tun* take care not to do sth; *sich ~ vor* + *dat* beware of

Hütte *f* (*-, -n*) hut, cottage

Hyäne *f* (*-, -n*) hyena

Hydrant *m* hydrant

hygienisch *adj* hygienic

Hyperlink m (-s, -s) hyperlink
Hypnose f (-, -n) hypnosis;
Hypnotiseur(in) m(f) hypnotist; **hypnotisieren** vt
hypnotize

Hypothek f (-, -en) mortgage
hysterisch adj hysterical

I

IC m (-, -s) abbr = **Intercityzug**; Intercity (train)
ICE m (-, -s) abbr = **Intercityexpresszug**; German high-speed train
ich pron I; ~ **bin's** it's me; ~ **nicht** not me; **du und** ~ you and me; **hier bin** ~! here I am; ~ **Idiot!** stupid me
Icon nt (-s, -s) IT icon
ideal adj ideal; **Ideal** nt (-s, -e) ideal
Idee f (-, -n) idea
identifizieren vt, vr identify
identisch adj identical
Idiot(in) m(f) (-en, -en) idiot; **idiotisch** adj idiotic
Idol nt (-s, -e) idol
Idylle f (-, -n) idyll; **idyllisch** adj idyllic
Igel m (-s, -) hedgehog
ignorieren vt ignore
ihm pron dat sg of **er/es**; (to) him; (thing) (to) it; **wie geht es** ~? how is he?; **ein Freund von** ~ a friend of his
ihn pron acc sg of **er**; him; (thing) it
ihnen pron dat pl of **sie**; (to) them; **wie geht es** ~? how are they?; **ein Freund von** ~ a friend of theirs

Ihnen pron dat sg and pl of **Sie**; (to) you; **wie geht es** ~? how are you?; **ein Freund von** ~ a friend of yours
ihr 1. pron (2nd person pl) you; ~ **seid's** it's you **2.** pron (dat sg) of **sie**; (to) her; (thing) (to) it; **er schickte es** ~ he sent it to her; **er hat** ~ **die Haare geschnitten** he cut her hair; **wie geht es** ~? how is she?; **ein Freund von** ~ a friend of hers **3.** pron (as adj) her; (thing) its; (pl) their; ~ **Vater** her father; ~ **Auto** (several owners) their car
Ihr pron of **Sie**; (as adj) your; ~**(e) XY** (at end of letter) Yours, XY
ihre(r, s) pron (as noun, sg) hers; (pl) theirs; **das ist** ~/~**r/ihr(e)s** that's hers; (pl) that's theirs
Ihre(r, s) pron (as noun) yours; **das ist** ~/~**r/Ihr(e)s** that's yours
ihretwegen 1. adv (sg) because of her; (to please her) for her sake **2.** adv (pl) because of them; (to please them) for their sake;

Ihretwegen adv because of you; (to please you) for your sake

Ikone f (-, -n) icon

illegal adj illegal

Illusion f illusion; **sich** dat **~en machen** delude oneself; **illusorisch** adj illusory

Illustration f illustration

Illustrierte f (-n, -n) (glossy) magazine

im contr of **in dem**; **~ Bett** in bed; **~ Fernsehen** on TV; **~ Radio** on the radio; **~ Bus/Zug** on the bus/train; **~ Januar** in January; **~ Stehen** (while) standing up

Imbiss m (-es, -e) snack; **Imbissbude** f snack bar

Imbussschlüssel m hex key

immer adv always; **~ mehr** more and more; **~ wieder** again and again; **~ noch** still; **~ noch nicht** still not; **für ~** forever; **wenn ich ...** every time I ...; **~ schöner/trauriger** more and more beautiful/sadder and sadder; **was/wer/wo/wann (auch) ~** whatever/whoever/wherever/whenever; **immerhin** adv after all; **immerzu** adv all the time

Immigrant(in) m(f) immigrant

Immobilien pl property sg, real estate sg; **Immobilienmakler(in)** m(f) estate agent (Brit), realtor (US)

immun adj immune (gegen to); **Immunschwäche** f immunodeficiency; **Immunschwächekrankheit** f immune deficiency syndrome; **Immunsystem** nt immune system

impfen vt vaccinate; **Impfpass** m vaccination card; **Impfstoff** m vaccine; **Impfung** f vaccination

imponieren vi impress (jdm sb)

Import m (-(e)s, -e) import; **importieren** vt import

impotent adj impotent

imstande adj **~ sein** be in a position; (capable) be able

in 1. prep + acc in(to); to; **~ die Stadt** into town; **~ die Schule gehen** go to school **2.** prep + dat in; (with time) in; (in the course of) during; (before the end of) within; **~ der Stadt** in town; **~ der Schule** at school; **noch ~ dieser Woche** by the end of this week; **heute ~ acht Tagen** a week (from) today; **Dienstag ~ einer Woche** a week on Tuesday **3.** adv **~ sein** (fashionable) be in

inbegriffen adj included

indem conj **sie gewann, ~ sie mogelte** she won by cheating

Inder(in) m(f) (-s, -) Indian

Indianer(in) m(f) (-s, -) American Indian, Native American; **indianisch** adj American Indian, Native

American

Indien *nt* (-s) India

indirekt *adj* indirect

indisch *adj* Indian

individuell *adj* individual

Indonesien *nt* (-s) Indonesia

Industrie *f* industry; **Industrie-** *in cpds* industrial

ineinander *adv* in(to) one another (*or* each other)

Infarkt *m* (-(e)s, -e) heart attack

Infektion *f* infection; **Infektionskrankheit** *f* infectious disease; **infizieren 1.** *vt* infect **2.** *vr* be infected

Info *f* (-, -s) *fam* info

infolge *prep* + *gen* as a result of, owing to; **infolgedessen** *adv* consequently

Informatik *f* computer science; **Informatiker(in)** *m(f)* (-s, -) computer scientist

Information *f* information; **Informationsschalter** *m* information desk; **informieren 1.** *vt* inform; **falsch ~** misinform **2.** *vr* find out (*über* + *acc* about)

infrage *adv* **das kommt nicht ~** that's out of the question; **etw ~ stellen** question sth

Infrastruktur *f* infrastructure

Infusion *f* infusion

Ingenieur(in) *m(f)* engineer

Ingwer *m* (-s) ginger

Inhaber(in) *m(f)* (-s, -) owner; (*of licence*) holder

Inhalt *m* (-(e)s, -e) contents *pl*; (*of book etc*) content; MATH

volume; (*two-dimensional*) area; **Inhaltsangabe** *f* summary; **Inhaltsverzeichnis** *nt* table of contents

Initiative *f* initiative; **die ~ ergreifen** take the initiative

Injektion *f* injection

inklusive *adv, prep* inclusive (*gen* of)

inkonsequent *adj* inconsistent

Inland *nt* POL, COMM home; **im ~** at home; GEO inland; **Inlandsflug** *m* domestic flight; **Inlandsgespräch** *nt* national call

Inlineskates *pl* inline skates *pl*

innen *adv* inside; **Innenarchitekt(in)** *m(f)* interior designer; **Innenhof** *m* (inner) courtyard; **Innenminister(in)** *m(f)* minister of the interior, Home Secretary (*Brit*); **Innenseite** *f* inside; **Innenspiegel** *m* rearview mirror; **Innenstadt** *f* town centre; city centre

innere(r, s) *adj* inner; (*in body, own country*) internal; **Innere(s)** *nt* inside; (*middle*) centre; *fig* heart

innerhalb *adv, prep* + *gen* within; (*with space*) inside

innerlich *adj* internal; (*calm etc*) inner

innerste(r, s) *adj* innermost

Innovation *f* innovation

inoffiziell *adj* unofficial; (*party etc*) informal

ins contr of **in das**

Insasse m (-n, -n), **Insassin** f AUTO passenger; of (mental hospital, prison) inmate

insbesondere adv particularly, in particular

Inschrift f inscription

Insekt nt (-(e)s, -en) insect, bug (US); **Insektenschutzmittel** nt insect repellent; **Insektenstich** m insect bite

Insel f (-, -n) island

Inserat nt advertisement

insgesamt adv altogether, all in all

Insider(in) m(f) (-s, -) insider

insofern 1. adv in that respect; (therefore) (and) so **2.** conj if; ~ als in so far as

Installateur(in) m(f) plumber; electrician; **installieren** vt IT install

Instinkt m (-(e)s, -e) instinct

Institut nt (-(e)s, -e) institute

Institution f institution

Instrument nt instrument

Insulin nt (-s) insulin

Inszenierung f production

intakt adj intact

intellektuell adj intellectual

intelligent adj intelligent; **Intelligenz** f intelligence

intensiv adj intensive; (feeling, pain) intense; **Intensivkurs** m crash course; **Intensivstation** f intensive care unit

interaktiv adj interactive

interessant adj interesting; **Interesse** nt (-s, -n) interest;

~ **haben an** + dat be interested in; **interessieren 1.** vt interest **2.** vr be interested (für in)

Interface nt (-, -(-)) IT interface

Internat nt boarding school

international adj international

Internet nt (-s) Internet, Net; **im** ~ on the Internet; **im** ~ **surfen** surf the Net; **Internetcafé** nt Internetcafé, cybercafé; **Internetfirma** f dotcom company; **Internethandel** m e-commerce; **Internetseite** f web page

interpretieren vt interpret (als as)

Interpunktion f punctuation

Interregio m (-s, -s) regional train

Interview nt (-s, -s) interview; **interviewen** vt interview

intim adj intimate

intolerant adj intolerant

investieren vt invest

inwiefern adv in what way; (how far) to what extent; **inwieweit** adv to what extent

inzwischen adv meanwhile

Irak m (-(s)) **(der)** ~ Iraq

Iran m (-(s)) **(der)** ~ Iran

Ire m (-n, -n) Irishman

irgend adv ~ **so ein Idiot** some idiot; **wenn** ~ **möglich** if at all possible; **irgendein** pron, **irgendeine(r, s)** some; (with question, conditional clause; whichever) any; **irgendetwas** pron something; (with question, conditional clause) anything; **irgendjemand** pron somebody; (with question, conditional clause) anybody; **irgendwann** adv sometime; (whenever you like) any time; **irgendwie** adv somehow; **irgendwo** adv somewhere; (with question, conditional clause) anywhere

Irin f Irishwoman; **irisch** adj Irish; **Irland** nt Ireland

ironisch adj ironic

irre adj crazy, mad; (wonderful) terrific; **Irre(r)** mf lunatic; **irreführen** irr vt mislead; **irren** vi, vr be mistaken; **wenn ich mich nicht irre** if I'm not mistaken; **irrsinnig** adj mad, crazy; **Irrtum** m (-s, -tümer) mistake, error; **irrtümlich 1.** adj mistaken

2. adv by mistake

Ischias m (-) sciatica

Islam m (-s) Islam; **islamisch** adj Islamic

Island nt Iceland; **Isländer(in)** m(f) (-s, -) Icelander; **isländisch** adj Icelandic; **Isländisch** nt Icelandic

Isolierband nt insulating tape; **isolieren** vt isolate; ELEC insulate

Isomatte f thermomat, karrymat®

Israel nt (-s) Israel; **Israeli** m (-(s), -(s)) f (-, -(s)) Israeli; **israelisch** adj Israeli

IT f (-) abbr = **Informationstechnologie;** IT

Italien nt (-s) Italy; **Italiener(in)** m(f) (-s, -) Italian; **italienisch** adj Italian; **Italienisch** nt Italian

J

ja adv yes; **aber ~!** yes, of course; **~, wissen Sie ...** well, you know ...; **ich glaube ~** I think so; **~?** (on phone) hello?; **sag's ihr ~ nicht!** don't you dare tell her; **das sag ich ~** that's what I'm trying to say

Jacht f (-, -en) yacht; **Jachthafen** m marina

Jacke f (-, -n) jacket; (knitted) cardigan

Jackett nt (-s, -s or -e) jacket

Jagd f (-, -en) hunt; (activity) hunting; **jagen 1.** vi hunt **2.** vt (pursue) chase; **Jäger(in)** m(f) hunter

Jaguar m (-s, -e) jaguar

Jahr nt (-(e)s, -e) year; **ein halbes ~** six months pl; **Anfang der neunziger ~e** in the early nineties; **mit sechzehn ~en** at (the age of) sixteen; **Jahrestag** m anniversary; **Jahreszahl** f date, year; **Jahreszeit** f season; **Jahr-**

gang m (of wine) year, vintage; **der ~ 1989** (people) those born in 1989; **Jahrhundert** nt (-s, -e) century; **jährlich** adj yearly, annual; **Jahrmarkt** m fair; **Jahrtausend** nt millennium; **Jahrzehnt** nt decade

jähzornig adj hot-tempered

Jakobsmuschel f scallop

Jalousie f (venetian) blind

Jamaika nt Jamaica

jämmerlich adj pathetic

jammern vi moan

Januar m (-(s), -e) January; → **Juni**

Japan nt (-s) Japan; **Japaner(in)** m(f) (-s, -) Japanese; **japanisch** adj Japanese; **Japanisch** nt Japanese

jaulen vi howl

jawohl adv yes (of course)

Jazz m (-) jazz

je adv ever; (for every one) each; **~ nach** depending on; **~ nachdem** it depends; **~ schneller desto besser** the faster the better

Jeans f (-, -) jeans pl

jede(r, s) 1. indef num every; (considered singly) each; (whichever you like) any; **~s Mal** every time, each time; **~n zweiten Tag** every other day; **bei ~m Wetter** in any weather **2.** pron everybody; (every single one) each; **~r von euch/uns** each of you/us; **jedenfalls** adv in any case; **jederzeit** adv at

any time; **jedesmal** adv every time

jedoch adv however

jemals adv ever

jemand pron somebody; (with question or negative) anybody

Jemen m (-(s)) Yemen

jene(r, s) pron that (one), those pl

jenseits 1. adv on the other side **2.** prep + gen on the other side of; fig beyond

Jetlag m (-s) jet lag

jetzig adj present

jetzt adv now; **erst ~** only now; **~ gleich** right now; **bis ~** so far, up to now; **von ~ an** from now on

jeweils adv **~ zwei zusammen** two at a time; **zu ~ 5 Euro** at 5 euros each

Job m (-s, -s) job; **jobben** vi fam work, have a job

Jod nt (-(e)s) iodine

Joga nt (-s) yoga

joggen vi jog; **Jogging** nt (-s) jogging; **Jogginghose** f jogging pants pl

Jog(h)urt m or nt (-s, -s) yoghurt

Johannisbeere f **Schwarze ~** blackcurrant; **Rote ~** redcurrant

Joint m (-s, -s) fam joint

jonglieren vi juggle

Jordanien nt (-s) Jordan

Joule nt (-(s), -) joule

Journalist(in) m(f) journalist

Joystick m (-s, -s) IT joystick

jubeln *vi* cheer

Jubiläum *nt* (*-s, Jubiläen*) jubilee; (*date*) anniversary

jucken 1. *vi* itch 2. *vt* **es juckt mich am Arm** my arm is itching; **das juckt mich nicht** *fam* I couldn't care less; **Juckreiz** *m* itch

Jude *m* (*-n, -n*), **Jüdin** *f* Jew; **sie ist Jüdin** she's Jewish; **jüdisch** *adj* Jewish

Judo *nt* (*-(s)*) judo

Jugend *f* (*-*) youth; **Jugendherberge** *f* (*-, -n*) youth hostel; **jugendlich** *adj* youthful; **Jugendliche(r)** *mf* young person; **Jugendstil** *m* art nouveau; **Jugendzentrum** *nt* youth centre

Jugoslawien *nt* (*-s*) HIST Yugoslavia

Juli *m* (*-(s), -s*) July; → *Juni*

jung *adj* young

Junge *m* (*-n, -n*) boy

Junge(s) *nt* (*-n, -n*) young animal; **die ~n** *pl* the young

Jungfrau *f* virgin; ASTR Virgo

Junggeselle *m* (*-n, -n*) bachelor

Juni *m* (*-(s), -s*) June; **im ~ in** June; **am 4. ~** on 4(th) June, on June 4(th) ; **Anfang/ Mitte/ Ende ~** at the beginning/ in the middle/ at the end of June; **letzten/ nächsten ~** last/ next June

Jupiter *m* (*-s*) Jupiter

Jura *no article* (*subject*) law; **~ studieren** study law; **Jurist(in)** *m(f)* lawyer; **juristisch** *adj* legal

Justiz *f* (*-*) justice; **Justizminister(in)** *m(f)* minister of justice

Juwel *nt* (*-s, -en*) jewel; **Juwelier(in)** *m(f)* (*-s, -e*) jeweller

Jux *m* (*-es, -e*) joke, lark

K

Kabel *nt* (*-s, -*) ELEC wire; (*thick*) cable; **Kabelfernsehen** *nt* cable television

Kabeljau *m* (*-s, -e or -s*) cod

Kabine *f* cabin; (*at swimming pool*) cubicle

Kabrio *nt* (*-s, -s*) convertible

Kachel *f* (*-, -n*) tile; **Kachelofen** *m* tiled stove

Käfer *m* (*-s, -*) beetle, bug (*US*)

Kaff *nt* (*-s, -s*) dump, hole

Kaffee *m* (*-s, -s*) coffee; **~ kochen** make some coffee; **Kaffeekanne** *f* coffeepot; **Kaffeelöffel** *m* coffee spoon; **Kaffeemaschine** *f* coffee maker (*or machine*); **Kaffeetasse** *f* coffee cup

Käfig *m* (*-s, -e*) cage

kahl *adj* (*person, head*) bald; (*tree, wall*) bare

Kahn *m* (*-(e)s, Kähne*) boat; (*for goods*) barge

Kai m (-s, -e or -s) quay

Kaiser m (-s, -) emperor; **Kaiserin** f empress; **Kaiserschnitt** m MED caesarean (section)

Kajak nt (-s, -s) kayak

Kajüte f (-, -n) cabin

Kakao m (-s, -s) cocoa; (drink) (hot) chocolate

Kakerlake f (-, -n) cockroach

Kaki f (-, -s) kaki

Kaktee f (-, -n), **Kaktus** m (-, -se) cactus

Kalb nt (-(e)s, Kälber) calf; **Kalbfleisch** nt veal; **Kalbsbraten** m roast veal; **Kalbsschnitzel** nt veal cutlet; (in breadcrumbs) escalope of veal

Kalender m (-s, -) calendar; (book) diary

Kalk m (-(e)s, -e) lime; (in bones) calcium

Kalorie f calorie; **kalorienarm** adj low-calorie

kalt adj cold; **mir ist (es) ~** I'm cold; **kaltblütig** adj cold-blooded; **Kälte** f (-) cold; fig coldness

kam imperf of **kommen**

Kambodscha nt (-s) Cambodia

Kamel nt (-(e)s, -e) camel

Kamera f (-, -s) camera

Kamerad(in) m(f) (-en, -en) friend; (accompanying sb) companion

Kamerafrau f, **Kameramann** m camerawoman / -man

Kamille f (-, -n) camomile;

Kamillentee m camomile tea

Kamin m (-s, -e) (outside) chimney; (inside) fireplace

Kamm m (-(e)s, Kämme) comb; (of mountain) ridge; (of cock) crest; **kämmen** vr **sich ~, sich** dat **die Haare ~** comb one's hair

Kampf m (-(e)s, Kämpfe) fight; (in war) battle; (in sport etc) contest; fig struggle; **kämpfen** vi fight (für, um for); **Kampfsport** m martial art

Kanada nt (-s) Canada; **Kanadier(in)** m(f) (-s, -) Canadian; **kanadisch** adj Canadian

Kanal m (-s, Kanäle) canal; (ditch, on TV) channel; **der ~** the (English) Channel; **Kanalinseln** pl Channel Islands pl; **Kanaltunnel** m Channel Tunnel

Kanarienvogel m canary

Kandidat(in) m(f) (-en, -en) candidate

Kandis(zucker) m (-) rock candy

Känguru nt (-s, -s) kangaroo

Kaninchen nt rabbit

Kanister m (-s, -) can

Kännchen nt pot; **ein ~ Kaffee / Tee** a pot of coffee / tea; **Kanne** f (-, -n) jug; (for coffee) pot; (for milk) churn; (for watering plants) can

kannte imperf of **kennen**

Kante f (-, -n) edge

Kantine f canteen

Kanton m (-s, -e) canton

Kanu nt (-s, -s) canoe

Kanzler(in) m(f) (-s, -) chancellor

Kap nt (-s, -s) cape

Kapelle f chapel; MUS band

Kaper f (-, -n) caper

kapieren vt, vi fam understand; **kapiert?** got it?

Kapital nt (-s, -e or -ien) capital

Kapitän m (-s, -e) captain

Kapitel nt (-s, -) chapter

Kappe f (-, -n) cap

Kapsel f (-, -n) capsule

kaputt adj fam broken; (person) exhausted; **kaputtgehen** irr vi break; (shoes) fall apart; **kaputtmachen** vt break; (person) wear out

Kapuze f (-, -n) hood

Karaffe f (-, -n) carafe; (with stopper) decanter

Karambole f (-, -n) star fruit, carambola

Karamell m (-s) caramel, toffee

Karaoke nt (-(s)) karaoke

Karat nt (-s, -e) carat

Karate nt (-s) karate

Kardinal m (-s, Kardinäle) cardinal

Karfreitag m Good Friday

kariert adj checked; (paper) squared

Karies f (-) (tooth) decay

Karikatur f caricature

Karneval m (-s, -e or -s) carnival

Kärnten nt (-s) Carinthia

Karo nt (-s, -s) square; (card suit) diamonds pl

Karosserie f AUTO body (-work)

Karotte f (-, -n) carrot

Karpfen m (-s, -) carp

Karriere f (-, -n) career

Karte f (-, -n) (of country etc) map; (in restaurant) menu; (for theatre, train etc) ticket; **mit ~ bezahlen** pay by credit card; **~n spielen** play cards; **die ~n mischen/geben** shuffle/deal the cards

Kartei f card index; **Karteikarte** f index card

Kartenspiel nt card game; **Kartentelefon** nt cardphone; **Kartenvorverkauf** m advance booking

Kartoffel f (-, -n) potato; **Kartoffelbrei** m mashed potatoes pl; **Kartoffelchips** pl crisps pl (Brit), chips pl (US); **Kartoffelsalat** m potato salad

Karton m (-s, -s) cardboard; (container) (cardboard) box

Karussell nt (-s, -s) roundabout (Brit), merry-go-round

Kaschmir m (-s, e) cashmere

Käse m (-s, -) cheese; **Käsekuchen** m cheesecake; **Käseplatte** f cheeseboard

Kasino nt (-s, -s) casino

Kasper(l) m (-s, -) Punch; fig clown; **Kasperl(e)theater** nt Punch and Judy show

Kasse f (-, -n) (in shop) till, cash register; (in supermarket) checkout; (container) cashbox; (at theatre) box office; (at cinema) ticket office; (insurance scheme) health insurance; **Kassenbon** m (-s, -s), **Kassenzettel** m receipt

Kassette f (small) box; (tape) cassette; **Kassettenrekorder** m cassette recorder

kassieren 1. vt take **2.** vi **darf ich ~?** would you like to pay now?; **Kassierer(in)** m(f) cashier

Kastanie f chestnut

Kasten m (-s, **Kästen**) box; (for bodies) crate

Kat m abbr = **Katalysator**

Katalog m (-(e)s, -e) catalogue

Katalysator m AUTO catalytic converter

Katar nt (-s) Qatar

Katarr(h) m (-s, -e) catarrh

Katastrophe f (-, -n) catastrophe, disaster

Kategorie f (-, -n) category

Kater m (-s, -) tomcat; fam hangover

Kathedrale f (-, -n) cathedral

Katholik(in) m(f) Catholic; **katholisch** adj Catholic

Katze f (-, -n) cat

Kauderwelsch nt (-(s)) gibberish

kauen vt, vi chew

Kauf m (-(e)s, Käufe) purchase; (action) buying; **ein guter ~** a bargain; **etw in ~**

nehmen put up with sth; **kaufen** vt buy; **Käufer(in)** m(f) buyer; **Kauffrau** f businesswoman; **Kaufhaus** nt department store; **Kaufmann** m businessman; (retailer) shopkeeper (Brit), storekeeper (US)

Kaugummi m chewing gum

Kaulquappe f (-, -n) tadpole

kaum adv hardly, scarcely

Kaution f deposit; LAW bail

Kaviar m caviar

KB nt (-, -), **Kbyte** nt (-, -) abbr = **Kilobyte**; KB

Kebab m (-(s), -s) kebab

Kegel m (-s, -) skittle; (in tenpin bowling) pin; MATH cone; **Kegelbahn** f bowling alley; **kegeln** vi play skittles; (in tenpin bowling) bowl

Kehle f (-, -n) throat; **Kehlkopf** m larynx

kehren vt (with brush) sweep

Keilriemen m AUTO fan belt

kein pron no, not ... any; **ich habe ~ Geld** I have no money, I don't have money; **keine(r, s)** pron no one, nobody; (thing) not ... any, none; **~r von ihnen** none of them; (two people / things) neither of them; **ich will keins von beiden** I don't want either (of them); **keinesfalls** adv on no account, under no circumstances

Keks m (-es, -e) biscuit (Brit), cookie (US); **jdm auf den ~ gehen** fam get on sb's nerves

Keller m (-s, -) cellar; (storey) basement

Kellner m (-s, -) waiter; **Kellnerin** f waitress

Kenia nt (-s) Kenya

kennen (kannte, gekannt) vt know; **wir ~ uns seit 1990** we've known each other since 1990; ~ **lernen** get to know; **sich ~ lernen** get to know each other; (for the first time) meet

Kenntnis f knowledge; **seine ~se** his knowledge

Kennwort nt a. IT password; **Kennzeichen** nt mark, sign; AUTO number plate (Brit), license plate (US)

Kerl m (-s, -e) guy, bloke (Brit)

Kern m (-(e)s, -e) (of fruit) pip; (of peach, cherry etc) stone; (of nut) kernel; (of atom) nucleus; fig heart, core

Kernenergie f a. IT nuclear energy; **Kernkraft** f nuclear power; **Kernkraftwerk** nt nuclear power station

Kerze f (-, -n) candle; (in engine) plug

Ket(s)chup m or nt (-(s), -s) ketchup

Kette f (-, -n) chain; (jewellery) necklace

keuchen vi pant; **Keuchhusten** m whooping cough

Keule f (-, -n) club; GASTR leg; (of chicken also) drumstick

Keyboard nt (-s, -s) MUS keyboard

Kfz nt abbr = **Kraftfahrzeug**

Kfz-Brief nt ≈ logbook

Kfz-Steuer f ≈ road tax (Brit), vehicle tax (US)

Kichererbse f chick pea

kichern vi giggle

Kickboard® nt (-s, -s) micro scooter

Kicker m (-s, -) table football (Brit), foosball (US)

kidnappen vt kidnap

Kidney-Bohne f kidney bean

Kiefer 1. m (-s, -) jaw **2.** f (-, -n) pine

Kieme f (-, -n) gill

Kies m (-es, -e) gravel; **Kiesel** m (-s, -), **Kieselstein** m pebble

kiffen vi fam smoke pot

Kilo nt (-s, -(s)) kilo; **Kilobyte** nt kilobyte; **Kilogramm** nt kilogram; **Kilojoule** nt kilojoule; **Kilometer** m kilometre; **Kilometerstand** m ≈ mileage; **Kilowatt** nt kilowatt

Kind nt (-(e)s, -er) child; **sie bekommt ein ~** she's having a baby; **Kinderarzt** m, **Kinderärztin** f paediatrician; **Kinderbetreuung** f childcare; **Kinderbett** nt cot (Brit), crib (US); **Kinderfahrkarte** f child's ticket; **Kindergarten** m nursery school, kindergarten; **Kindergärtnerin** f nursery-school teacher; **Kindergeld** nt child benefit; **Kinderkrankheit** f children's illness;

Kinderkrippe f crèche (Brit); daycare center (US); **Kinderlähmung** f polio; **Kindermädchen** nt nanny (Brit), nurse/maid (US); **kindersicher** adj childproof; **Kindersicherung** f childproof safety catch; (on bottle) childproof cap; **Kindersitz** m child seat; **Kinderteller** m (in restaurant) children's portion; **Kinderwagen** m pram (Brit), baby carriage (US); **Kinderzimmer** nt children's (bed)room; **Kindheit** f childhood; **kindisch** adj childish; **kindlich** adj child-like

Kinn nt (-(e)s, -e) chin

Kino nt (-s, -s) cinema (Brit), movie theater (US); **ins ~ gehen** go to the cinema (Brit) (or to the movies (US))

Kiosk m (-(e)s, -e) kiosk

Kippe f fam cigarette end, fag end (Brit)

Kirche f (-, -n) church; **Kirchturm** m church tower; (pointed) steeple

Kirmes f (-, -sen) fair

Kirsche f (-, -n) cherry; **Kirschtomate** f cherry tomato

Kissen nt (-s, -) cushion; (on bed) pillow

Kiste f (-, -n) box; (trunk) chest

kitschig adj kitschy, cheesy

kitzelig adj a. fig ticklish; **kit-**zeln vt, vi tickle

Kiwi f (-, -s) kiwi (fruit)

Klage f (-, -n) complaint; LAW lawsuit; **klagen** vi complain (über + acc about, bei to); **kläglich** adj wretched

Klammer f (-, -n) (in text) bracket; (on documents) clip; (for washing) peg (Brit), clothespin (US); (on teeth) brace; **Klammeraffe** m fam at-sign, @; **klammern** vr cling (an + acc to)

klang imperf of **klingen**

Klang m (-(e)s, Klänge) sound

Klappbett nt folding bed

klappen vi impers (succeed) work; **es hat gut geklappt** it went well

klappern vi rattle; (pots and pans) clatter; **Klapperschlange** f rattlesnake

Klappstuhl m folding chair

klar adj clear; **sich dat im Klaren sein** be clear (über + acc about); **alles ~?** everything okay?

klären 1. vt (liquid) purify; (problem, issue) clarify **2.** vr clear itself up

Klarinette f (-, -n) clarinet

klarkommen irr vi **mit etw ~** cope with something; **kommst du klar?** are you managing all right?; **mit jdm ~** get along with sb; **klarmachen** vt **jdm etw ~** make sth clear to sb; **Klarsichtfolie** f clingfilm® (Brit), plastic wrap (US); **klarstellen** vt clarify

Klärung f (of problem, issue) clarification

klasse adj inv fam great, brilliant

Klasse f (-, -n) class; (year in school) form (Brit) or grade (US); **erster ~ reisen** travel first class; **in welche ~ gehst du?** which form (Brit) (or grade (US)) are you in?; **Klassenarbeit** f test; **Klassenlehrer(in)** m(f) class teacher; **Klassenzimmer** nt classroom

Klassik f classical period; classical music

Klatsch m (-(e)s, -e) (talk) gossip; **klatschen** vi (hit) smack; (after concert etc) applaud, clap; (talk) gossip; **klatschnass** adj soaking (wet)

Klaue f (-, -n) claw; fam (handwriting) scrawl

klauen vt fam pinch

Klavier nt (-s, -e) piano

Klebeband nt adhesive tape; **kleben 1.** vt stick (an + acc to) **2.** vi (unpleasantly) be sticky; **klebrig** adj sticky; **Klebstoff** m glue; **Klebstreifen** m adhesive tape

Klecks m (-es, -e) blob; (of ink) blot

Klee m (-s) clover

Kleid nt (-(e)s, -er) dress; **~er** pl clothes pl; **Kleiderbügel** m coat hanger; **Kleiderschrank** m wardrobe (Brit),

closet (US); **Kleidung** f clothing

klein adj small, little; (finger) little; **mein ~er Bruder** my little (or younger) brother; **als ich noch ~ war** when I was a little boy/ girl; **etw ~ schneiden** chop sth up; **Kleinanzeige** f classified ad; **Kleinbuchstabe** m small letter; **Kleinbus** m minibus; **Kleingeld** nt change; **Kleinigkeit** f trifle; (meal) snack; **Kleinkind** nt toddler; **kleinschreiben** vt write with a small letter; **Kleinstadt** f small town

Klempner(in) m(f) plumber

klettern vi climb

Klettverschluss m Velcro® fastening

klicken vi a. IT click

Klient(in) m(f) (-en, -en) client

Klima nt (-s, -s) climate; **Klimaanlage** f air conditioning; **klimatisiert** adj air-conditioned

Klinge f (-, -n) blade

Klingel f (-, -n) bell; **klingeln** vi ring

klingen (klang, geklungen) vi sound

Klinik f clinic; (non-specialist) hospital

Klinke f (-, -n) handle

Klippe f (-, -n) cliff; (in sea) reef; fig hurdle

Klischee nt (-s, -s) fig cliché

Klo nt (-s, -s) fam loo (Brit),

john (US); **Klobrille** f toilet seat; **Klopapier** nt toilet paper

klopfen vt, vi knock; (heart) thump

Kloß m (-es, Klöße) (in throat) lump; GASTR dumpling

Kloster nt (-s, Klöster) monastery; (for women) convent

Klub m (-s, -s) club

klug adj clever

knabbern vt, vi nibble

Knäckebrot nt crispbread

knacken vt, vi crack

Knall m (-(e)s, -e) bang; **Knallbonbon** nt cracker; **knallen** vi bang

knapp adj (in short supply) scarce; (victory) narrow; ~ **bei Kasse sein** be short of money; ~ **zwei Stunden** just under two hours

Knautschzone f AUTO crumple zone

kneifen (kniff, gekniffen) vt, vi pinch; (shirk) back out (vor + dat of)

Kneipe f (-, -n) fam pub (Brit), bar

Knete f (-) fam (money) dough; **kneten** vt knead; (shape) mould

knicken vt, vi break; (paper) fold

Knie nt (-s, -) knee; **in die ~ gehen** bend one's knees; **Kniebeuge** f knee bend; **Kniegelenk** nt knee joint; **Kniekehle** f back of the knee; **knien** vi kneel; **Knie**scheibe f kneecap; **Knieschoner** m (-s, -), **Knieschützer** m (-s, -) knee pad

kniff imperf of **kneifen**

knipsen 1. vt punch; PHOT snap **2.** vi PHOT take snaps

knirschen vi crunch; **mit den Zähnen ~** grind one's teeth

knitterfrei adj non-crease; **knittern** vi crease

Knoblauch m garlic; **Knoblauchbrot** nt garlic bread; **Knoblauchzehe** f clove of garlic

Knöchel m (-s, -) knuckle; (of foot) ankle

Knochen m (-s, -) bone; **Knochenbruch** m fracture; **Knochenmark** nt marrow

Knödel m (-s, -) dumpling

Knopf m (-(e)s, Knöpfe) button; **Knopfdruck** m **auf ~** at the touch of a bottom; **Knopfloch** nt buttonhole

Knospe f (-, -n) bud

knoten vt knot; **Knoten** m (-s, -) knot; MED lump

Know-how nt (-(s)) know-how, expertise

knurren vi (dog) growl; (stomach) rumble; (person) grumble

knusprig adj crisp; (biscuit) crunchy

knutschen vi fam smooch

k. o. adj inv SPORT knocked out; fig knackered

Koalition f coalition

Koch m (-(e)s, Köche) cook; **Kochbuch** nt cookery book, cookbook; **kochen** vt, vi cook; (water) boil; (coffee, tea) make; **Köchin** f cook; **Kochlöffel** m wooden spoon; **Kochnische** f kitchenette; **Kochplatte** f hotplate; **Kochrezept** nt recipe; **Kochtopf** m saucepan

Kode m (-s, -s) code

Köder m (-s, -) bait

Koffein nt (-s) caffeine; **koffeinfrei** adj decaffeinated

Koffer m (-s, -) (suit)case; **Kofferraum** m AUTO boot (Brit), trunk (US)

Kognak m (-s, -s) brandy

Kohl m (-(e)s, -e) cabbage

Kohle f (-, -n) coal; (made from wood) charcoal; fam (money) cash, dough; **Kohlehydrat** nt carbohydrate; **Kohlendioxid** nt carbon dioxide; **Kohlensäure** f (in drinks) fizz; **ohne ~** still, non-carbonated (US); **mit ~** sparkling, carbonated (US)

Kohlrabi m (-(s), -(s)) kohlrabi

Kohlrübe f swede (Brit), rutabaga (US)

Koje f (-, -n) cabin; (bed) bunk

Kokain nt (-s) cocaine

Kokosnuss f coconut

Kolben m (-s, -) TECH piston

Kolik f (-, -en) colic

Kollaps m (-es, -e) collapse

Kollege m (-n, -n), **Kollegin** f colleague

Köln nt (-s) Cologne

Kolonne f (-, -n) convoy

Kolumbien nt (-s) Columbia

Koma nt (-s, -s) coma

Kombi m (-s, -s) estate (car) (Brit), station wagon (US);
Kombination f combination; (reasoning) deduction; **kombinieren 1.** vt combine **2.** vi reason; (suspect) guess

Komfort m (-s) conveniences pl; (of guest, room etc) comfort

Komiker(in) m(f) comedian, comic; **komisch** adj funny

Komma nt (-s, -s) comma

kommen (kam, gekommen) vi come; (come closer) approach; (occur) happen; (reach, begin) get; (become visible) appear; (to school, prison etc) go; **zu sich ~** come round (or to); **zu etw ~** (get) acquire sth; (find time for) get round to sth; **wer kommt zuerst?** who's first?; **kommend** adj coming; **~e Woche** next week; **in den ~en Jahren** in the years to come

Kommentar m commentary; **kein ~** no comment

Kommilitone m (-n, -n), **Kommilitonin** f fellow student

Kommissar(in) m(f) inspector

Kommode f (-, -n) chest of drawers

Kommunikation f communication

Kommunion f REL communion

Kommunismus *m* communism

Komödie *f* comedy

kompakt *adj* compact

Kompass *m* (*-es*, *-e*) compass

kompatibel *adj* compatible

kompetent *adj* competent

komplett *adj* complete

Kompliment *nt* compliment; **jdm ein ~ machen** pay sb a compliment; **~!** congratulations

kompliziert *adj* complicated

Komponist(in) *m(f)* composer

Kompost *m* (*-(e)s*, *-e*) compost; **Komposthaufen** *m* compost heap

Kompott *nt* (*-(e)s*, *-e*) stewed fruit

Kompresse *f* (*-*, *-n*) compress

Kompromiss *m* (*-es*, *-e*) compromise

Kondition *f* condition; **sie hat eine gute ~** she's in good shape

Konditorei *f* cake shop; (*serving coffee etc*) café

Kondom *nt* (*-s*, *-e*) condom

Konfektionsgröße *f* size

Konferenz *f* conference

Konfession *f* religion; (*within Christianity*) denomination

Konfetti *nt* (*-(s)*) confetti

Konfirmation *f* REL confirmation

Konflikt *m* (*-(e)s*, *-e*) conflict

konfrontieren *vt* confront

Kongo *m* (*-s*) Congo

Kongress *m* (*-es*, *-e*) confer-

ence; **der ~** (*US parliament*) Congress

König *m* (*-(e)s*, *-e*) king; **Königin** *f* queen; **Königinpastete** *f* vol-au-vent; **königlich** *adj* royal; **Königreich** *nt* kingdom

Konkurrenz *f* competition

können (*konnte*, *gekonnt*) *vt, vi* be able to; (*poem, song*) know; **~ Sie Deutsch?** can (*or* do) you speak German?; **ich kann nicht kommen** I can't come; **das kann sein** that's possible; **ich kann nichts dafür** it's not my fault

konsequent *adj* consistent

konservativ *adj* conservative

Konserven *pl* tinned food *sg* (*Brit*), canned food *sg*; **Konservendose** *f* tin (*Brit*), can

konservieren *vt* preserve; **Konservierungsmittel** *nt* preservative

Konsonant *m* consonant

Konsul *m* (*-s*, *-n*) consul; **Konsulat** *nt* consulate

Kontakt *m* (*-(e)s*, *-e*) contact; **kontaktarm** *adj* **er ist ~** he lacks contact with other people; **kontaktfreudig** *adj* sociable; **Kontaktlinsen** *pl* contact lenses *pl*

Kontinent *m* continent

Konto *nt* (*-s*, *Konten*) account; **Kontoauszug** *m* (*bank*) statement; **Kontoinhaber(in)** *m(f)* account holder; **Kontonummer** *f* account number; **Kontostand** m balance

Kontrabass m double bass

Kontrast m (-(e)s, -e) contrast

Kontrolle f (-, -n) control; (checking) supervision; (at airport etc) passport control; **kontrollieren** vt control; (verify) check

Konzentration f concentration; **Konzentrationslager** nt HIST concentration camp; **konzentrieren** vt, vr concentrate

Konzept nt (-(e)s, -e) rough draft

Konzert nt (-(e)s, -e) concert; (piece of music) concerto; **Konzertsaal** m concert hall

koordinieren vt coordinate

Kopf m (-(e)s, Köpfe) head; **Kopfhörer** m headphones pl; **Kopfkissen** nt pillow; **Kopfsalat** m lettuce; **Kopfschmerzen** pl headache sg; **Kopfstütze** f headrest; **Kopftuch** nt headscarf

Kopie f copy; **kopieren** vt a. IT copy; **Kopierer** m (-s, -), **Kopiergerät** nt copier

Kopilot(in) m(f) co-pilot

Koralle f (-, -n) coral

Koran m (-s) REL Koran

Korb m (-(e)s, Körbe) basket; **jdm einen ~ geben** fig turn sb down

Kord m (-(e)s, -e) corduroy

Kordel f (-, -n) cord

Korinthe f (-e, -n) currant

Kork m (-(e)s, -e) cork; **Korken**

m (-s, -) cork; **Korkenzieher** m (-s, -) corkscrew

Korn nt (-(e)s, Körner) grain; **Kornblume** f cornflower

Körper m (-s, -) body; **Körperbau** m build; **körperbehindert** adj disabled; **Körpergeruch** m body odour; **körperlich** adj physical; **Körperverletzung** f physical injury

korrekt adj correct

Korrespondent(in) m(f) correspondent; **Korrespondenz** f correspondence

korrigieren vt correct

Kosmetik f cosmetics pl; **Kosmetikkoffer** m vanity case; **Kosmetiksalon** m beauty parlour

Kost f (-) food; (meals) board

kostbar adj precious; (dear) costly, expensive

kosten 1. vt cost **2.** vt, vi (sample) taste; **Kosten** pl costs pl, cost; (money spent) expenses pl; **auf ~ von** at the expense of; **kostenlos** adj free (of charge); **Kostenvoranschlag** m estimate

köstlich adj (food) delicious; **sich ~ amüsieren** have a marvellous time

Kostprobe f taster; fig sample; **kostspielig** adj expensive

Kostüm nt (-s, -e) costume; (jacket and skirt) suit

Kot m (-(e)s) excrement

Kotelett nt (-(e)s, -e or -s)

chop, cutlet

Koteletten pl sideboards pl (Brit), sideburns pl (US)

Kotflügel m AUTO wing

kotzen vi vulg puke, throw up

Krabbe f (-, -n) shrimp; (larger) prawn; (with pincers) crab

krabbeln vi crawl

Krach m (-(e)s, -s or -e) crash; (continuous) noise; fam (argument) row

Kraft f (-, Kräfte) strength; POL, PHYS force; (ability) power; **in ~ treten** come into effect; **Kraftausdruck** m swearword; **Kraftfahrzeug** nt motor vehicle; **Kraftfahrzeugbrief** m ≈ logbook; **Kraftfahrzeugschein** m vehicle registration document; **Kraftfahrzeugsteuer** f ≈ road tax (Brit), vehicle tax (US); **Kraftfahrzeugversicherung** f car insurance; **kräftig** adj strong; healthy; (colour) intense; strong; **Kraftstoff** m fuel; **Kraftwerk** nt power station

Kragen m (-s, -) collar

Krähe f (-, -n) crow

Kralle f (-, -n) claw; (on car) wheel clamp

Kram m (-(e)s) stuff

Krampf m (-(e)s, Krämpfe) cramp; (twitching) spasm; **Krampfader** f varicose vein

Kran m (-(e)s, Kräne) crane

Kranich m (-s, -e) ZOOL crane

krank adj ill, sick

kränken vt hurt

Krankengymnastik f physiotherapy; **Krankenhaus** nt hospital; **Krankenkasse** f health insurance; **Krankenpfleger** m (-s, -) (male) nurse; **Krankenschein** m health insurance certificate; **Krankenschwester** f nurse; **Krankenversicherung** f health insurance; **Krankenwagen** m ambulance; **Krankheit** f illness; (infectious) disease

Kränkung f insult

Kranz m (-es, Kränze) wreath

krass adj crass; fam (wonderful) wicked

kratzen vt, vi scratch; **Kratzer** m (-s, -) scratch

kraulen 1. vi (swim) do the crawl 2. vt (stroke) pet

Kraut nt (-(e)s, Kräuter) cabbage; **Kräuter** pl herbs pl; **Kräuterbutter** f herb butter; **Kräutertee** m herbal tea; **Krautsalat** m coleslaw

Krawatte f tie

kreativ adj creative

Krebs m (-es, -e) ZOOL crab; MED cancer; ASTR Cancer

Kredit m (-(e)s, -e) credit; **auf ~** on credit; **einen ~ aufnehmen** take out a loan; **Kreditkarte** f credit card

Kreide f (-, -n) chalk

Kreis m (-es, -e) circle; (administrative area) district

Kreisel m (-s, -) (toy) top; (on road) roundabout (Brit), traffic circle (US)

Kreislauf m MED circulation; fig (of nature etc) cycle; **Kreislaufstörungen** pl MED **ich habe ~** I've got problems with my circulation; **Kreisverkehr** m roundabout (Brit), traffic circle (US)

Kren m (-s) horseradish

Kresse f (-, -n) cress

Kreuz nt (-es, -e) cross; ANAT small of the back; (card suit) clubs pl; **mir tut das ~ weh** I've got backache; **Kreuzband** nt cruciate ligament; **Kreuzfahrt** f cruise; **Kreuzgang** m cloisters pl; **Kreuzotter** f (-, -n) adder; **Kreuzschlüssel** m AUTO wheel brace; **Kreuzschmerzen** pl backache sg; **Kreuzung** f crossroads sg; intersection; (animal, plant) cross; **Kreuzworträtsel** nt crossword (puzzle)

kriechen (kroch, gekrochen) vi crawl; (unobtrusively) creep; fig pej (vor jdm) ~ crawl (to sb)

Krieg m (-(e)s, -e) war

kriegen vt fam get; (rascal, bus etc) catch; **sie kriegt ein Kind** she's having a baby; **ich kriege noch Geld von dir** you still owe me some money

Krimi m (-s, -s) fam thriller; **Kriminalität** f criminality; **Kriminalpolizei** f detective force, ≈ CID (Brit), ≈ FBI

(US); **Kriminalroman** m detective novel; **kriminell** adj criminal

Krippe f (-, -n) manger; (Nativity scene) crib (Brit), crèche (US); (nursery) crèche (Brit), daycare center (US)

Krise f (-, -n) crisis

Kristall 1. m (-s, -e) crystal **2.** nt (-s) (glass) crystal

Kritik f criticism; (of film, book etc) review; **Kritiker(in)** m(f) critic; **kritisch** adj critical

kritzeln vt, vi scribble, scrawl

Kroate m (-n, -n) Croat; **Kroatien** nt (-s) Croatia; **Kroatin** f Croat; **kroatisch** adj Croatian; **Kroatisch** nt Croatian

kroch imperf of **kriechen**

Krokodil nt (-s, -e) crocodile

Krokus m (-, - or -se) crocus

Krone f (-, -n) crown

Kröte f (-, -n) toad

Krücke f (-, -n) crutch

Krug m (-(e)s, Krüge) jug; (for beer) mug

Krümel m (-s, -) crumb

krumm adj crooked

Kruste f (-, -n) crust

Kruzifix nt (-es, -e) crucifix

Kuba nt (-s) Cuba

Kübel m (-s, -) tub; (with handle) bucket

Kubikmeter m cubic metre

Küche f (-, -n) kitchen; (activity) cooking

Kuchen m (-s, -) cake; **Kuchengabel** f cake fork

Küchenmaschine f food processor; **Küchenpapier** nt kitchen roll; **Küchenschrank** m (kitchen) cupboard

Kuckuck m (-s, -e) cuckoo

Kugel f (-, -n) ball; MATH sphere; MIL bullet; (on Christmas tree) bauble; **Kugellager** nt ball bearing; **Kugelschreiber** m (ball-point) pen, biro® (Brit); **Kugelstoßen** nt (-s) shot put

Kuh f (-, Kühe) cow

kühl adj cool; **Kühlbox** f cool box; **kühlen** vt cool; **Kühler** m (-s, -) AUTO radiator; **Kühlerhaube** f AUTO bonnet (Brit), hood (US); **Kühlschrank** m fridge, refrigerator; **Kühltasche** f cool bag; **Kühltruhe** f freezer

Kuhstall m cowshed

Küken nt (-s, -) chick

Kuli m (-s, -s) fam pen, biro® (Brit)

Kulisse f (-, -n) scenery

Kult m (-(e)s, -e) cult; **Kultfigur** f cult figure

Kultur f culture; (way of life) civilization; **Kulturbeutel** m toilet bag (Brit), washbag; **kulturell** adj cultural

Kümmel m (-s, -) caraway seeds pl

Kummer m (-s) grief, sorrow

kümmern 1. vr sich um jdn ~ look after sb; sich um etw ~ see to sth 2. vt concern; das kümmert mich nicht that

doesn't worry me

Kumpel m (-s, -) fam mate, pal

Kunde m (-n, -n) customer; **Kundendienst** m after-sales (or customer) service; **Kunden(kredit)karte** f storecard, chargecard; **Kundennummer** f customer number

kündigen 1. vi hand in one's notice; (tenant) give notice that one is moving out; jdm ~ give sb his/her notice; (landlord) give sb notice to quit 2. vt (contract) terminate; jdm die Stellung ~ give sb his/her notice; **Kündigung** f (from job) dismissal; (of contract) termination; (of subscription) cancellation; (period of notification) notice

Kundin f customer; **Kundschaft** f customers pl

künftig adj future

Kunst f (-, Künste) art; (ability) skill; **Kunstausstellung** f art exhibition; **Kunstgewerbe** nt arts and crafts pl; **Künstler(in)** m(f) (-s, -) artist; **künstlerisch** adj artistic; **künstlich** adj artificial; **Kunststoff** m synthetic material; **Kunststück** nt trick; **Kunstwerk** nt work of art

Kupfer nt (-s, -) copper

Kuppel f (-, -n) dome

kuppeln vi AUTO operate the clutch; **Kupplung** f coupling; AUTO clutch

Kur f (-, -en) course of treatment; (at health resort) cure

Kür f (-, -en) SPORT free programme

Kurbel f (-, -n) winder

Kürbis m (-ses, -se) pumpkin

Kurierdienst m courier service

Kurort m health resort

Kurs m (-es, -e) course; FIN rate; (for foreign currency) exchange rate

kursiv 1. adj italic **2.** adv in italics

Kursleiter(in) m(f) course tutor; **Kursteilnehmer(in)** m(f) (course) participant

Kurve f (-, -n) curve; (in road) bend; **kurvenreich** adj (road) winding

kurz adj short; (with time also) brief; **~ vorher/darauf** shortly before/after; **kannst du ~ kommen?** could you come here for a minute?; **~ gesagt** in short; **kurzärmlig** adj short-sleeved; **kürzen** vt cut short; (in length) shorten; (salary) reduce; **kurzer-**

hand adv on the spot; **kurzfristig** adj short-term; **das Konzert wurde ~ abgesagt** the concert was called off at short notice; **Kurzgeschichte** f short story; **kürzlich** adv recently; **Kurznachrichten** pl news summary sg; **Kurzparkzone** f short-stay (Brit) (or short-term (US)) parking zone; **Kurzschluss** m ELEC short circuit; **kurzsichtig** adj short-sighted; **Kurzurlaub** m short holiday (Brit), short vacation (US)

Kusine f cousin

Kuss m (-es, Küsse) kiss; **küssen** vt, vr kiss

Küste f (-, -n) coast; (strip of land) shore; **Küstenwache** f coastguard

Kutsche f (-, -n) carriage; (enclosed) coach

Kuvert nt (-s, -s) envelope

Kuvertüre f (-, -n) coating

Kuwait nt (-s) Kuwait

KZ nt (-s, -s) abbr = **Konzentrationslager**; HIST concentration camp

L

Labor nt (-s, -e or -s) lab

Labyrinth nt (-s, -e) maze

lächeln vi smile; **Lächeln** nt (-s) smile; **lachen** vi laugh; **lächerlich** adj ridiculous

Lachs m (-es, -e) salmon

Lack m (-(e)s, -e) varnish; (co-

loured) lacquer; (for car) paint; **lackieren** vt varnish; (car) spray; **Lackschaden** m scratch (on the paintwork)

Ladegerät nt (battery) charger; **laden** (lud, geladen) vt a. IT load; (guest) invite; (mo-

bile phone etc) charge

Laden *m* (-s, Läden) shop; (*on window*) shutter; **Ladendieb(in)** *m(f)* shoplifter; **Ladendiebstahl** *m* shoplifting

Ladung *f* load; NAUT, AVIAT cargo

lag *imperf of* **liegen**

Lage *f* (-, -n) position, situation

Lager *nt* (-s, -) camp; COMM warehouse; TECH bearing; **Lagerfeuer** *nt* campfire; **lagern** *vt* store

Lagune *f* lagoon

lahm *adj* lame; (*dreary*) dull; **lähmen** *vt* paralyse; **Lähmung** *f* paralysis

Laib *m* (-s, -e) loaf

Laie *m* (-n, -n) layman

Laken *nt* (-s, -) sheet

Lakritze *f* (-, -n) liquorice

Lamm *nt* (-(e)s, Lämmer) (*also meat*) lamb

Lampe *f* (-, -n) lamp; (*in lamp*) bulb; **Lampenfieber** *nt* stage fright; **Lampenschirm** *m* lampshade

Lampion *m* (-s, -s) Chinese lantern

Land *nt* (-(e)s, Länder) land; (*nation*) country; (*German federal division*) state, Land; **auf dem ~e** in the country **Landebahn** *f* runway; **landen** *vt, vi* land

Länderspiel *nt* international (*match*)

Landesgrenze *f* national border, frontier; **Landeswäh**rung *f* national currency; **landesweit** *adj* nationwide

Landhaus *nt* country house; **Landkarte** *f* map; **Landkreis** *m* administrative region, ≈ district

ländlich *adj* rural

Landschaft *f* countryside; (*beautiful*) scenery; ART landscape; **Landstraße** *f* country road, B road (*Brit*)

Landung *f* landing; **Landungsbrücke** *f*, **Landungssteg** *m* gangway

Landwirt(in) *m(f)* farmer; **Landwirtschaft** *f* agriculture, farming; **landwirtschaftlich** *adj* agricultural

lang *adj* long; (*person*) tall; **ein zwei Meter ~er Tisch** a table two metres long; **den ganzen Tag ~** all day long; **langärmelig** *adj* long-sleeved; **lange** *adv* (for) a long time; **ich musste ~ warten** I had to wait (for) a long time; **ich bleibe nicht ~** I won't stay long; **es ist ~ her, dass wir uns gesehen haben** it's a long time since we saw each other; **Länge** *f* (-, -n) length; GEO longitude; **langen** *vi fam* be enough; *fam* (*with hand*) reach (*nach* for); **mir langt's** I've had enough

Langeweile *f* boredom

langfristig 1. *adj* long-term **2.** *adv* in the long term

Langlauf *m* cross-country skiing

langsam 1. *adj* slow **2.** *adv* slowly

Langschläfer(in) *m(f)* (-s, -) late riser

längst *adv* **das ist ~ fertig** that was finished a long time ago; **sie sollte ~ da sein** she should have been here long ago; **als sie kam, waren wir ~ weg** when she arrived we had long since left

Langstreckenflug *m* long-haul flight

Languste *f* (-, -n) crayfish, crawfish (US)

langweilen *vt* bore; **ich langweile mich** I'm bored; **langweilig** *adj* boring

Laos *nt* (-) Laos

Lappen *m* (-s, -) cloth, rag; (*for dusting*) duster

läppisch *adj* silly; (*amount of money*) ridiculous

Laptop *m* (-s, -s) laptop

Lärche *f* (-, -n) larch

Lärm *m* (-(e)s) noise

las *imperf of* **lesen**

Lasche *f* (-, -n) flap

Laser *m* (-s, -) laser; **Laserdrucker** *m* laser printer

lassen (ließ, gelassen) *vt* (*allow*) let; (*in a place, a condition*) leave; (*cease*) stop; **etw machen ~** have sth done; **sich** *dat* **die Haare schneiden ~** have one's hair cut; **jdn etw machen ~** make sb do sth; **lass das!** stop it!

lässig *adj* casual

Last *f* (-, -en) load; (*duty, obligation etc*) burden

Laster *nt* (-s, -) vice; *fam* truck, lorry (*Brit*)

lästern *vi* **über jdn/etw ~** make nasty remarks about sb/sth

lästig *adj* annoying; (*person*) tiresome

Last-Minute-Flug *m* last-minute flight; **Last-Minute-Ticket** *nt* last-minute ticket

Lastwagen *m* truck, lorry (*Brit*)

Latein *nt* (-s) Latin

Laterne *f* (-, -n) lantern; (*in street*) streetlight

Latte *f* (-, -n) slat; SPORT bar

Latz *m* (-es, Lätze) bib; **Lätzchen** *nt* bib; **Latzhose** *f* dungarees *pl*

lau *adj* (*wind, air*) mild

Laub *nt* (-(e)s) foliage; **Laubfrosch** *m* tree frog

Lauch *m* (-(e)s, -e) leeks *pl*; **eine Stange ~** a leek; **Lauchzwiebel** *f* spring onions *pl* (*Brit*), scallions *pl* (US)

Lauf *m* (-(e)s, **Läufe**) run; (*contest*) race; (*development*) course; **Laufbahn** *f* career; **laufen** (lief, gelaufen) *vi*, *vt* run; walk; (*function*) work; **mir läuft die Nase** my nose is running; **was läuft im Kino?** what's on at the cinema?; **wie läuft's so?** how are things?; **laufend** *adj* running; (*month, expenses*) current; **auf dem Laufenden sein/halten** be/keep up-to-date; **Läufer** m (-s, -) (carpet) rug; (in chess) bishop; **Läufer(in)** m(f) SPORT runner; **Laufmasche** f ladder (Brit), run (US); **Laufwerk** nt IT drive

Laune f (-, -n) mood; **gute/ schlechte ~ haben** be in a good/bad mood; **launisch** adj moody

Laus f (-, Läuse) louse

lauschen vi listen; (secretly) eavesdrop

laut 1. adj loud **2.** adv loudly; (read) aloud **3.** prep + gen or dat according to

läuten vt, vi ring

lauter adv fam nothing but

Lautsprecher m loudspeaker; **Lautstärke** f loudness; RADIO, TV volume

lauwarm adj lukewarm

Lava f (-, Laven) lava

Lavendel m (-s, -) lavender

Lawine f avalanche

leasen vt lease; **Leasing** nt (-s) leasing

leben vt, vi live; (not be dead) be alive; **wie lange ~ Sie schon hier?** how long have you been living here?; **von ... ~** (food etc) live on ...; (occupation, activity) make one's living from ...; **Leben** nt (-s, -) life; **lebend** adj living; **lebendig** adj alive; (full of live) lively; **lebensgefährlich** adj very dangerous; (injury) critical; **Lebensgefährte** m, **Lebensgefährtin** f

partner; **Lebenshaltungskosten** pl cost sg of living; **lebenslänglich** adj for life; **~ bekommen** get life; **Lebenslauf** m curriculum vitae (Brit), CV (Brit), resumé (US); **Lebensmittel** pl food sg; **Lebensmittelgeschäft** nt grocer's (shop); **Lebensmittelvergiftung** f food poisoning; **lebensnotwendig** adj vital; **Lebensretter(in)** m(f) rescuer; **Lebensstandard** m standard of living; **Lebenszeichen** nt sign of life

Leber f (-, -n) liver; **Leberfleck** m mole; **Leberpastete** f liver pâté

Lebewesen nt living being

lebhaft adj lively; (memory, impression) vivid

Lebkuchen m gingerbread

leblos adj lifeless

Leck nt leak

lecken 1. vi (container, ship) leak **2.** vt, vi lick

lecker adj delicious, tasty

Leder nt (-s, -) leather

ledig adj single

leer adj empty; (page) blank; (battery) dead; **leeren** vt, vr empty; **Leerlauf** m (gear) neutral; **Leerung** f emptying; (from postbox) collection

legal adj legal, lawful

legen 1. vt put, place; (eggs) lay **2.** vr lie down; (storm, excitement) die down; (pain, *feeling*) wear off

leger *adj* casual

Lehm *m* (-(e)s, -e) loam; (*for bricks etc*) clay

Lehne *f* (-, -n) arm(rest); back(rest); **lehnen** *vt*, *vr* lean

Lehrbuch *nt* textbook; **Lehre** *f* (-, -n) teaching; (*vocational*) apprenticeship; (*moral*) lesson; **lehren** *vt* teach; **Lehrer(in)** *m(f)* (-s, -) teacher; **Lehrgang** *m* course; **Lehrling** *m* apprentice; **lehrreich** *adj* instructive

Leibwächter(in) *m(f)* bodyguard

Leiche *f* (-, -n) corpse; **Leichenwagen** *m* hearse

leicht 1. *adj* light; (*task etc*) easy, simple; (*illness*) slight; **jdm ~ fallen** be easy for sb; **es ist sich dat ~ machen** take the easy way out **2.** *adv* easily; (*a bit*) slightly; **Leichtathletik** *f* athletics *sg*; **leichtsinnig** *adj* careless; (*stronger*) reckless

leid *adj* **jdn/etw ~ sein** be tired of sb/sth; **Leid** *nt* (-(e)s) grief, sorrow; **~ tun** → **leidtun**; **leiden** (*litt, gelitten*) *vi*, *vt* suffer (*an, unter* + *dat* from); **ich kann ihn/es nicht ~** I can't stand him/it; **Leiden** *nt* (-s, -) suffering; (*medical*) illness

Leidenschaft *f* passion; **leidenschaftlich** *adj* passionate

leider *adv* unfortunately; **wir**

müssen jetzt ~ gehen I'm afraid we have to go now; **~ ja/nein** I'm afraid so/not

leidtun *vi* **es tut mir/ihm ~** I'm/he's sorry; **er tut mir ~** I'm sorry for him

leihen (*lieh, geliehen*) *vt* **jdm etw ~** lend sb sth; **sich dat etw von jdm ~** borrow sth from sb; **Leihwagen** *m* hire car (*Brit*), rental car (*US*)

Leim *m* (-(e)s, -e) glue

Leine *f* (-, -n) cord; (*for washing*) line; (*for dog*) lead (*Brit*), leash (*US*)

Leinen *nt* (-s, -) linen; **Leinwand** *f* ART canvas; FILM screen

leise 1. *adj* quiet; (*music, steps etc*) soft **2.** *adv* quietly

Leiste *f* (-, -n) ledge; (*decorative*) strip; ANAT groin

leisten *vt* (*work*) do; (*accomplish*) achieve; **jdm Gesellschaft ~** keep sb company; **sich dat etw ~** (*as reward etc*) treat oneself to sth; **ich kann es mir nicht ~** I can't afford it

Leistenbruch *m* hernia

Leistung *f* performance; (*remarkable*) achievement

leiten *vt* lead; (*firm*) run; (*guide*) direct; ELEC conduct

Leiter *f* (-, -n) ladder

Leiter(in) *m(f)* (-s, -) (*of business*) manager

Leitplanke *f* (-, -n) crash barrier

Leitung *f* (*guidance*) direction; TEL line; (of firm) management; (for water) pipe; (for electricity) cable; **eine lange ~ haben** be slow on the uptake; **Leitungswasser** nt tap water

Lektion f lesson

Lektüre f (-, -n) reading; (books etc) reading matter

Lende f (-, -n) (meat) loin; (of beef) sirloin

lenken vt steer; (gaze) direct (auf + acc towards); **jds Aufmerksamkeit auf etw** acc ~ draw sb's attention to sth; **Lenker** m handlebars pl; **Lenkrad** nt steering wheel; **Lenkradschloss** nt steering lock; **Lenkstange** f handlebars pl

Leopard m (-en, -en) leopard

Lepra f (-) leprosy

Lerche f (-, -n) lark

lernen vt, vi learn; (for exam) study, revise

lesbisch adj lesbian

Lesebuch nt reader; **lesen** (las, gelesen) vi, vt read; (fruit) pick; **Leser(in)** m(f) reader; **leserlich** adj legible; **Lesezeichen** nt bookmark

Lettland nt Latvia

letzte(r, s) adj last; (definitive) final; (most recent) latest; **zum ~n Mal** for the last time; **am ~r Montag** last Monday; **in ~r Zeit** lately, recently; **letztens** adv recently

Leuchte f (-, -n) lamp, light; **leuchten** vi shine; (fire, dial)

glow; **Leuchter** m (-s, -) candlestick; **Leuchtreklame** f neon sign; **Leuchtstift** m highlighter; **Leuchtturm** m lighthouse

leugnen 1. vt deny **2.** vi deny everything

Leukämie f leukaemia (Brit), leukemia (US)

Leukoplast® nt (-(e)s, -e) Elastoplast® (Brit), Band-Aid® (US)

Leute pl people pl

Lexikon nt (-s, Lexika) encyclopaedia (Brit), encyclopedia (US)

Libanon m (-s) **der~** Lebanon

Libelle f dragonfly

liberal adj liberal

Libyen nt (-s) Libya

Licht nt (-(e)s, -er) light; **Lichtblick** m ray of hope; **lichtempfindlich** adj sensitive to light; **Lichtempfindlichkeit** f PHOT speed; **Lichthupe** f **die ~ betätigen** flash one's lights; **Lichtjahr** nt light year; **Lichtmaschine** f dynamo; **Lichtschalter** m light switch; **Lichtschranke** f light barrier; **Lichtschutzfaktor** m sun protection factor, SPF

Lichtung f clearing

Lid nt (-(e)s, -er) eyelid; **Lidschatten** m eyeshadow

lieb adj (kind) nice; (loved) dear; (lovely) sweet; **das ist ~ von dir** that's nice of you; **Lieber Herr X** Dear

Mr X; **Liebe** f (-, -n) love; **lieben** vt love; *(sexually)* make love to; **liebenswürdig** adj kind; **lieber** adv rather; *ich möchte ~ nicht* I'd rather not; *welches ist dir ~?* which one do you prefer?; → **gern**, **lieb**; **Liebesbrief** m love letter; **Liebeskummer** m ~ **haben** be lovesick; **Liebespaar** nt lovers pl; **liebevoll** adj loving; **Liebhaber(in)** m(f) (-s, -/-) lover; **lieblich** adj lovely; *(wine)* sweet; **Liebling** m darling; **Lieblings-** in cpds favourite; **liebste(r, s)** adj favourite; **liebsten** adv am ~ **esse ich** ... my favourite food is ...; *am ~ würde ich bleiben* I'd really like to stay

Liechtenstein nt (-s) Liechtenstein

Lied nt (-(e)s, -er) song; REL hymn

lief imperf of **laufen**

liefern vt deliver; *(provide)* supply; **Lieferung** f delivery

Liege f (-, -n) *(at doctor's)* couch; *(for overnight stay)* campbed; *(in garden)* lounger; **liegen** (lag, gelegen) vi lie; *(be situated)* be; *mir liegt nichts/ viel daran* it doesn't matter to me/ it matters a lot to me; *woran liegt es nur, dass ...?* why is it that ...?; *~ **bleiben*** *(person)* stay lying down; stay in bed; *(thing)* be left (behind); *~ **lassen*** *(for-*

get) leave behind; **Liegestuhl** m deck chair; **Liegestütz** m press-up *(Brit)*, push-up *(US)*; **Liegewagen** m RAIL couchette car

lieh imperf of **leihen**

ließ imperf of **lassen**

Lift m (-(e)s, -e or -s) lift, elevator *(US)*

Liga f (-, Ligen) league, division

light adj *(cola)* diet; *(food)* low-fat; low-calorie; *(cigarettes)* mild

Likör m (-s, -e) liqueur

lila adj inv purple

Lilie f lily

Limette f (-, -n) lime

Limo f (-, -s) fam fizzy drink *(Brit)*, soda *(US)*; **Limonade** f fizzy drink *(Brit)*, soda *(US)*; *(lemon-flavoured)* lemonade

Limone f (-, -n) lime

Limousine f (-, -n) saloon (car) *(Brit)*, sedan *(US)*; fam limo

Linde f (-, -n) lime tree

lindern vt relieve, soothe

Lineal nt (-s, -e) ruler

Linie f line; **Linienflug** m scheduled flight; **Linienrichter** m linesman; **liniert** adj ruled, lined

Linke f (-n, -n) left-hand side; *(hand)* left hand; POL left *(wing)*; **linke(r, s)** adj left; *auf der ~n Seite* on the left, on the left-hand side; **links** adv on the left; *~ **abbiegen***

turn left; **~ von** to the left of; **~ oben** at the top left; **Linksaußen** m left winger; **Linkshänder(in)** m(f) (-s, -) left-hander; **linksherum** adv to the left, anticlockwise; **Linksverkehr** m driving on the left

Linse f (-, -n) lentil; (*optical*) lens; **Linsensuppe** f lentil soup

Lippe f (-, -n) lip; **Lipgloss** nt lip gloss; **Lippenstift** m lipstick

lispeln vi lisp

List f (-, -en) cunning; (*ruse*) trick

Liste f (-, -n) list

Litauen nt (-s) Lithuania

Liter m or nt (-s, -) litre

literarisch adj literary; **Literatur** f literature

Litschi f (-, -s) lychee, litchi

litt imperf of **leiden**

live adv RADIO, TV live

Lizenz f licence

Lkw m (-(s), -(s)) abbr = **Lastkraftwagen**; truck, lorry (*Brit*)

Lob nt (-(e)s) praise; **loben** vt praise

Loch nt (-(e)s, Löcher) hole; **lochen** vt punch; **Locher** m (-s, -) (hole) punch

Locke f (-, -n) curl; **locken** vt lure; (*hair*) curl; **Lockenstab** m curling tongs pl (*Brit*), curling irons pl (*US*); **Lockenwickler** m (-s, -) curler

locker adj (*screw, tooth*) loose; (*posture*) relaxed; (*person*) easy-going; **lockern** vt, vr loosen

lockig adj curly

Löffel m (-s, -) spoon; **einen ~ Mehl zugeben** add a spoonful of flour

log imperf of **lügen**

Loge f (-, -n) THEAT box

logisch adj logical

Lohn m (-(e)s, Löhne) reward; (*for work*) pay, wages pl

lohnen vr be worth it; **es lohnt sich nicht zu warten** it's no use waiting

Lohnerhöhung f pay rise (*Brit*), pay raise (*US*); **Lohnsteuer** f income tax

Lokal nt (-(e)s, -e) restaurant; pub (*Brit*), bar

Lokomotive f locomotive

London nt (-s) London

Lorbeer m (-s, -en) laurel; **Lorbeerblatt** nt GASTR bay leaf

los adj loose; **~!** go on!; **jdn/ etw ~ sein** be rid of sb/sth; **was ist ~?** what's the matter?, what's up?; **dort ist nichts/ viel ~** there's nothing/a lot going on there

Los nt (-es, -e) lot, fate; (*in lottery etc*) ticket

löschen vt (*fire, light*) put out, extinguish; (*thirst*) quench; (*tape*) erase; (*data, line*) delete

lose adj loose

Lösegeld nt ransom

losen vi draw lots

lösen 1. vt (knot, screw etc) loosen; (puzzle) solve; CHEM dissolve; (ticket for train etc) buy **2.** vr (wallpaper, paint etc) come off; (sugar etc) dissolve; (problem, difficulty) (re)solve itself

losfahren irr vi leave; **losgehen** irr vi set out; (begin) start; **loslassen** irr vt let go

löslich adj soluble

Lösung f (liquid, of puzzle, problem) solution

loswerden irr vt get rid of

Lotterie f lottery; **Lotto** nt (-s) National Lottery; **~ spielen** play the lottery

Löwe m (-n, -n) ZOOL lion; ASTR Leo; **Löwenzahn** m dandelion

Luchs m (-es, -e) lynx

Lücke f (-, -n) gap

lud imperf of **laden**

Luft f (-, Lüfte) air; (of person) breath; (secret) reveal

lüften vt air; (secret) reveal

Luftfahrt f aviation; **Luftfeuchtigkeit** f humidity; **Luftfilter** m air filter; **Luftfracht** f air freight; **Luftmatratze** f airbed; **Luftpirat(in)** m(f) hijacker; **Luftpost** f air

mail; **Luftpumpe** f (bicycle) pump; **Luftröhre** f windpipe

Lüftung f ventilation

Luftverschmutzung f air pollution; **Luftwaffe** f air force; **Luftzug** m draught (Brit), draft (US)

Lüge f (-, -n) lie; **lügen** (log, gelogen) vi lie; **Lügner(in)** m(f) (-s, -) liar

Luke f (-, -n) hatch

Lumpen m (-s, -) rag

Lunchpaket nt packed lunch

Lunge f (-, -n) lungs pl; **Lungenentzündung** f pneumonia

Lupe f (-, -n) magnifying glass; **etw unter die ~ nehmen** fig have a close look at sth

Lust f (-, Lüste) joy, delight; (inclination) desire; **~ auf etw acc haben** feel like sth; **~ haben, etw zu tun** feel like doing sth

lustig adj amusing, funny; (jovial) cheerful

lutschen 1. vt suck **2.** vi **~ an** + dat suck; **Lutscher** m (-s, -) lollipop

Luxemburg nt (-s) Luxembourg

luxuriös adj luxurious

Luxus m (-) luxury

Lymphdrüse f lymph gland; **Lymphknoten** m lymph node

Lyrik f (-) poetry

M

machbar adj feasible

machen 1. vt (produce, cause) make; (carry out, accomplish) do; (cost) be; **das Essen/einen Fehler ~** make dinner/a mistake; **ein Foto ~** take a photo; **was machst du?** what are you doing?; (as job) what do you do (for a living)?; **das kann man doch nicht ~!** you can't do that; **das Bett ~** make the bed; **das Zimmer ~** (or tidy (up)) the room; **was macht das?** how much is that?; **das macht zwanzig Euro** that's twenty euros; **einen Spaziergang ~** go for a walk; **Urlaub ~** go on holiday; **eine Pause ~** take a break; **einen Kurs ~** take a course; **das macht nichts** it doesn't matter **2.** vr **sich an die Arbeit ~** get down to work

Macht f (-s, **Mächte**) power; **mächtig** adj powerful; fam enormous; **machtlos** adj powerless; **da ist man ~** there's nothing you can do (about it)

Mädchen nt girl; **Mädchenname** m maiden name

Made f (-, -n) maggot

Magazin nt (-s, -e) magazine

Magen m (-s, - or **Mägen**) stomach; **Magenbeschwerden** pl stomach trouble sg; **Magen-Darm-Infektion** f gastroenteritis; **Magengeschwür** nt stomach ulcer; **Magenschmerzen** pl stomachache sg

mager adj (meat) lean; (person) thin; (cheese, yoghurt) low-fat; **Magermilch** f skimmed milk; **Magersucht** f anorexia; **magersüchtig** adj anorexic

magisch adj magical

Magnet m (-s or -en, -en) magnet

mähen vt, vi mow

mahlen (mahlte, gemahlen) vt grind

Mahlzeit 1. f meal; (for baby) feed **2.** interj enjoy your meal

mahnen vt urge; **jdn schriftlich ~** send sb a reminder; **Mahngebühr** f fine; **Mahnung** f warning; (written) reminder

Mai m (-, -s) May; **~ Juni**; **Maifeiertag** m May Day; **Maiglöckchen** nt lily of the valley; **Maikäfer** m cockchafer

Mail f (-, -s) e-mail; **Mailbox** f IT mailbox; **mailen** vi, vt e-mail

Mais m (-es, -e) maize, corn (US); **Maiskolben** m corn

Mannschaft

cob; GASTR corn on the cob

Majestät f (-, -en) Majesty

Majonäse f (-, -n) mayonnaise

Majoran m (-s, -e) marjoram

Make-up nt (-s, -s) make-up

Makler(in) m(f) (-s, -) broker; (for houses etc) estate agent (Brit), realtor (US)

Makrele f (-, -n) mackerel

Makrone f (-, -n) macaroon

mal adv (in calculation) times, multiplied by; (in measurement) by; fam (in past) once; (in future) some day; **4 ~ 3 ist 12** 4 times 3 is (or equals) twelve; **da habe ich ~ gewohnt** I used to live there; **irgendwann ~ werde ich dort hinfahren** I'll go there one day

Mal nt (-(e)s, -e) time; (on skin) mark; **jedes ~** every time; **ein paar ~** a few times

Malaria f (-) malaria

Malaysia nt (-s) Malaysia

Malbuch nt colouring book

Malediven pl Maldives pl

malen vt, vi painting; **Maler(in)** m(f) (-s, -) painter; **Malerei** f painting; **malerisch** adj picturesque

Mallorca nt (-s) Majorca, Mallorca

malnehmen irr vt multiply (mit by)

Malta nt (-s) Malta

Malz nt (-es) malt; **Malzbier** nt malt beer

Mama f (-, -s) mum(my) (Brit), mom(my) (US)

man pron you; (formal) one; (unspecified person) someone, somebody; (unspecified persons) they, people pl; **wie schreibt ~ das?** how do you spell that?; **~ sagt, dass ...** they (or people) say that ...

managen vt fam manage; **Manager(in)** m(f) (-s, -) manager

manche(r, s) pron some; (large number) many; **~ Politiker** many politicians pl, many a politician; **manchmal** adv sometimes

Mandant(in) m(f) client

Mandarine f mandarin, tangerine

Mandel f (-, -n) almond; **~n** ANAT tonsils pl; **Mandelentzündung** f tonsillitis

Manege f (-, -n) ring

Mangel m (-s, Mängel) lack; (scarcity) shortage (an + dat of); (imperfection) defect, fault; **mangelhaft** adj (goods) faulty; (mark in school) ≈ E

Mango f (-, -s) mango

Manieren pl manners pl

Maniküre f (-, -n) manicure

manipulieren vt manipulate

Manko nt (-s, -s) deficiency

Mann m (-(e)s, Männer) man; (spouse) husband; **Männchen** nt **es ist ein ~** (animal) it's a he; **männlich** adj masculine; BIO male

Mannschaft f SPORT, fig team; NAUT, AVIAT crew

Mansarde f (-, -n) attic

Manschettenknopf m cuff-link

Mantel m (-s, *Mäntel*) coat

Mappe f (-, -n) briefcase; (*cardboard, plastic*) folder

Maracuja f (-, -s) passion fruit

Marathon m (-s, -s) marathon

Märchen nt (-s, -) fairy tale

Marder m (-s, -) marten

Margarine f margarine

Marienkäfer m ladybird (*Brit*), ladybug (*US*)

Marihuana nt (-s) marijuana

Marille f (-, -n) apricot

Marine f navy

marinieren vt marinate

Marionette f puppet

Mark nt (-(e)s) (*in bone*) marrow; (*from fruit*) pulp

Marke f (-, -n) (*of food, cigarettes etc*) brand; (*of car, cooker etc*) make; (*for letter*) stamp; (*for meal*) voucher, ticket; (*made of metal etc*) disc; (*of water level etc*) mark

markieren vt mark; **Markierung** f marking; (*sign*) mark

Markise f (-, -n) awning

Markt m (-(e)s, *Märkte*) market; **auf den ~ bringen** launch; **Markthalle** f covered market; **Marktlücke** f gap in the market; **Marktplatz** m market place; **Marktwirtschaft** f market economy

Marmelade f jam; (*orange*) marmalade

Marmor m (-s, -e) marble; **Marmorkuchen** m marble cake

Marokko nt (-s) Morocco

Marone f (-, -n) chestnut

Mars m (-) Mars

Marsch m (-(e)s, *Märsche*) march

Märtyrer(in) m(f) (-s, -) martyr

März m (-(es), -e) March; → **Juni**

Marzipan nt (-s, -e) marzipan

Maschine f machine; (*of car*) engine; **Maschinenbau** m mechanical engineering

Masern pl MED measles sg

Maske f (-, -n) mask; **Maskenball** m fancy-dress ball

Maskottchen nt mascot

maß imperf of **messen**

Maß nt (-es, -e) measure; (*restraint*) moderation; (*scale*) degree, extent; **~e** (*of person*) measurements; (*of room*) dimensions; **in gewissem / hohem ~e** to a certain / high degree

Mass f (-, -(en)) litre of beer

Massage f (-, -n) massage

Masse f (-, -n) mass; (*of people*) crowd; (*most*) majority; **massenhaft** adv masses (*or* loads) of; **Massenkarambolage** f pile-up; **Massenmedien** pl mass media pl

Masseur(in) m(f) masseur / masseuse

maßgeschneidert adj (*clothes*) made-to-measure

massieren vt massage

mäßig adj moderate

massiv *adj* solid; *fig* massive

maßlos *adj* extreme

Maßnahme *f* (-, -n) measure, step

Maßstab *m* rule, measure; *fig* standard; **im ~ von 1:5** on a scale of 1:5

Mast *m* (-(e)s, -e(n)) mast; ELEC pylon

Material *nt* (-s, -ien) material; (*for one's work*) materials *pl*; **materialistisch** *adj* materialistic

Materie *f* matter

Mathematik *f* mathematics *sg*; **Mathematiker(in)** *m(f)* mathematician

Matinee *f* (-, -n) ≈ matinee

Matratze *f* (-, -n) mattress

Matrose *m* (-n, -n) sailor

Matsch *m* (-(e)s) mud; (*snow*) slush; **matschig** *adj* (*ground*) muddy; (*snow*) slushy; (*fruit*) mushy

matt *adj* weak; (*not shiny*) dull; PHOT matt; (*in chess*) mate

Matte *f* (-, -n) mat

Matura *f* (-) Austrian school--leaving examination, ≈ A-levels (*Brit*), ≈ High School Diploma (*US*)

Mauer *f* (-, -n) wall

Maul *nt* (-(e)s, Mäuler) mouth; *fam* gob; **halt's ~!** shut your face (*or* gob); **Maulesel** *m* mule; **Maulkorb** *m* muzzle; **Maulwurf** *m* mole

Maurer(in) *m(f)* (-s, -) brick-layer

Mauritius *nt* (-) Mauritius

Maus *f* (-, Mäuse) mouse; **Mausefalle** *f* mousetrap; **Mausklick** *m* (-s, -s) mouse click; **Mauspad** *nt* (-s, -s) mouse mat (*or* pad); **Maustaste** *f* mouse key (*or* button)

Maut *f* (-, -en) toll; **Mautge-bühr** *f* toll; **mautpflichtig** *adj* **~e Straße** toll road, turn-pike (*US*); **Mautstelle** *f* toll-booth, tollgate; **Mautstraße** *f* toll road, turnpike (*US*)

maximal *adv* **ihr habt ~ zwei Stunden Zeit** you've got two hours at (the) most; **~ vier Leute** a maximum of four people

Mayonnaise *f* → **Majonäse**

Mazedonien *nt* (-s) Macedo-nia

MB *nt* (-, -), **Mbyte** *nt* (-, -) *abbr* = **Megabyte**; MB

Mechanik *f* mechanics *sg*; (*mechanism*) mechanics *pl*; **Mechaniker(in)** *m(f)* (-s, -) mechanic; **mechanisch** *adj* mechanical; **Mechanismus** *m* mechanism

meckern *vi* (*goat*) bleat; *fam* (*person*) moan

Mecklenburg-Vorpommern *nt* (-s) Mecklenburg-Western Pomerania

Medaille *f* (-, -n) medal

Medien *pl* media *pl*

Medikament *nt* medicine

Meditation *f* meditation; **me-ditieren** *vi* meditate

medium *adj* (*steak*) medium

Medizin f (-, -en) medicine (*gegen* for); **medizinisch** adj medical

Meer nt (-(e)s, -e) sea; **am ~** by the sea; **Meerenge** f straits pl; **Meeresfrüchte** pl seafood sg; **Meeresspiegel** m sea level; **Meerrettich** m horseradish; **Meerschweinchen** nt guinea pig

Megabyte nt megabyte

Mehl nt (-(e)s, -e) flour; **Mehlspeise** f sweet dish made from flour, eggs and milk

mehr 1. pron more; **~ will ich nicht ausgeben** I don't want to spend any more, that's as much as I want to spend; **was willst du ~?** what more do you want? 2. adv **immer ~ (Leute)** more and more (people); **~ als fünf Minuten** more than five minutes; **es ist kein Brot ~ da** there's no bread left; **nie ~** never again; **mehrdeutig** adj ambiguous; **mehrere** pron several; **mehreres** pron several things; **mehrfach** adj multiple; (*done again*) repeated; **Mehrfachstecker** m multiple plug; **Mehrheit** f majority; **mehrmals** adv repeatedly; **mehrsprachig** adj multilingual; **Mehrwertsteuer** f value added tax, VAT; **Mehrzahl** f majority; (*in grammar*) plural

meiden (*mied, gemieden*) vt avoid

Meile f (-, -n) mile

mein pron my; **meine(r, s)** pron mine

meinen vt, vi think; say; (*want to say, intend*) mean; **das war nicht so gemeint** I didn't mean it like that

meinetwegen adv because of me; (*to please me*) for my sake; (*for my part*) as far as I'm concerned

Meinung f opinion; **meiner ~ nach** in my opinion; **Meinungsumfrage** f opinion poll; **Meinungsverschiedenheit** f disagreement (*über + acc* about)

Meise f (-, -n) tit; **eine ~ haben** fam be crazy

Meißel m (-s, -) chisel

meist adv mostly; **meiste(r, s)** pron most; **die ~n (Leute)** most people; **die ~ Zeit** most of the time; **das ~ (davon)** most of it; **die ~n von ihnen** most of them; **meistens** adv mostly; (*largely*) for the most part

Meister(in) m(f) (-s, -) master; SPORT champion; **Meisterschaft** f championship; **Meisterwerk** nt masterpiece

melden 1. vt report 2. vr report; (*bei* to); (*in class*) put one's hand up; (*offer one's services*) volunteer; (*on phone, in response to advert etc*) answer; **Meldung** f announcement; (*account*) report; IT message

Melodie f tune, melody

Melone f (-, -n) melon

Memoiren pl memoirs pl

Menge f (-, -n) quantity; (of people) crowd; **eine ~** a lot (gen of)

Meniskus m (-, Menisken) meniscus

Mensa f (-, Mensen) canteen, cafeteria (US)

Mensch m (-en, -en) human being, man; (individual) person; **kein ~** nobody; **~!** wow!; (annoyed) bloody hell!; **Menschenmenge** f crowd; **Menschenrechte** pl human rights pl; **Menschenverstand** m **gesunder ~** common sense; **Menschheit** f humanity, mankind; **menschlich** adj human; (kind) humane

Menstruation f menstruation

Mentalität f mentality, mindset

Menthol nt (-s, -) menthol

Menü nt (-s, -s) set meal; IT menu; **Menüleiste** f IT menu bar

Merkblatt nt leaflet; **merken** vt notice; **sich dat etw ~** remember sth; **Merkmal** nt feature

Merkur m (-s) Mercury

merkwürdig adj odd

Messbecher m measuring jug

Messe f (-, -n) fair; REL mass

messen (maß, gemessen) **1.** vt measure; (temperature, pul-

se) take **2.** vr compete

Messer nt (-s, -) knife

Messing nt (-s) brass

Metall nt (-s, -e) metal

Meteorologe m, **Meteorologin** f meteorologist

Meter m or nt (-s, -) metre; **Metermaß** nt tape measure

Methode f (-, -n) method

Metzger(in) m(f) (-s, -) butcher; **Metzgerei** f butcher's (shop)

Mexiko nt (-s) Mexico

MEZ f abbr = **mitteleuropäische Zeit**; CET

miau interj miaow

mich pron acc of **ich**; me; **~ (selbst)** myself; **stell dich hinter ~** stand behind me; **ich fühle ~ wohl** I feel fine

mied imperf of **meiden**

Miene f (-, -n) look, expression

mies adj fam lousy

Miesmuschel f mussel

Mietauto nt → **Mietwagen**; **Miete** f (-, -n) rent; **mieten** vt rent; (car) hire (Brit), rent (US); **Mieter(in)** m(f) (-s, -) tenant; **Mietshaus** nt block of flats (Brit), apartment house (US); **Mietvertrag** m rental agreement; **Mietwagen** m hire car (Brit), rental car (US); **sich dat einen ~ nehmen** hire (Brit) (or rent (US)) a car

Migräne f (-, -n) migraine

Mikrofon nt (-s, -e) microphone

Mikrowelle f (-, -n), **Mikro-**

wellenherd m microwave (oven)

Milch f (-) milk; **Milcheis** nt ice-cream (made with milk); **Milchkaffee** m milky coffee; **Milchpulver** nt powdered milk; **Milchreis** m rice pudding; **Milchshake** m milk shake; **Milchstraße** f Milky Way

mild adj mild; (judge) lenient; (friendly) kind

Militär nt (-s) military, army

Milliarde f (-, -n) billion; **Milligramm** nt milligram; **Milliliter** m millilitre; **Millimeter** m millimetre; **Million** f million; **Millionär(in)** m(f) millionaire

Milz f (-, -en) spleen

Minderheit f minority

minderjährig adj underage

minderwertig adj inferior

Mindest- in cpds minimum; **mindeste(r, s)** adj least; **mindestens** adv at least

Mine f (-, -n) mine; (in pencil) lead; (in ballpoint pen) refill

Mineralwasser nt mineral water

Minibar f minibar; **Minigolf** nt miniature golf, crazy golf (Brit)

minimal adj minimal

Minimum nt (-s, Minima) minimum

Minirock m miniskirt

Minister(in) m(f) (-s, -) minister; **Ministerium** nt ministry; **Ministerpräsident(in)** m(f)

Minister President (Prime Minister of a Bundesland)

minus adv minus; **Minus** nt (-, -) deficit; **im ~ sein** be in the red; (account) be overdrawn

Minute f (-, -n) minute

Minze f (-, -n) mint

mir pron dat of **ich**; (to) me; **kannst du ~ helfen?** can you help me?; **kannst du es ~ erklären?** can you explain it to me?; **ich habe ~ einen neuen Rechner gekauft** I bought (myself) a new computer; **ein Freund von ~** a friend of mine

mischen vt mix; (cards) shuffle; **Mischung** f mixture (aus of)

missachten vt ignore; **Missbrauch** m abuse; (wrong use) misuse; **missbrauchen** vt misuse (zu for); (sexually) abuse; **Misserfolg** m failure; **Missgeschick** nt mishap; **misshandeln** vt ill-treat

Mission f mission

misslingen (misslang, misslungen) vi fail; **misstrauen** vt + dat distrust; **Misstrauen** nt (-s) mistrust, suspicion (gegenüber of); **misstrauisch** adj distrustful; (suspecting sth) suspicious; **Missverständnis** nt misunderstanding; **missverstehen** irr vt misunderstand

Mist m (-(e)s) fam rubbish; (from cows) dung; (as fertilizer) manure

Mistel f (-, -n) mistletoe

mit 1. prep + dat with; (by means of) by; **~ der Bahn** by train; **~ der Kreditkarte bezahlen** pay by credit card; **~ 10 Jahren** at the age of 10; **wie wärs ... ?** how about ...? **2.** adv along, too; **wollen Sie ~?** do you want to come along?

Mitarbeiter(in) m(f) employee

mitbekommen irr vt fam catch; (learn about) hear; (understand) get

mitbenutzen vt share

Mitbewohner(in) m(f) flatmate (Brit), roommate (US)

mitbringen irr vt bring along; **Mitbringsel** nt (-s, -) small present

miteinander adv with one another; (jointly) together

miterleben vt see (with one's own eyes)

Mitesser m (-s, -) blackhead

Mitfahrgelegenheit f ≈ lift, ride (US); **Mitfahrzentrale** f agency for arranging lifts

mitgeben irr vt jdm etw **~** give sb sth (to take along)

Mitgefühl nt sympathy

mitgehen irr vi go/come along

mitgenommen adj worn out, exhausted

Mitglied nt member

mithilfe prep + gen or **~ von** with the help of

mitkommen irr vi come along; (understand) follow

Mitleid nt pity; **~ haben mit** feel sorry for

mitmachen 1. vt take part in **2.** vi take part

mitnehmen irr vt take along; (tire) wear out, exhaust

mitschreiben irr **1.** vi take notes **2.** vt take notes

Mitschüler(in) m(f) schoolmate

mitspielen vi (in team) play; (in game) join in; **in einem Film/Stück ~** act in a film/play

Mittag m midday; **gestern ~** at midday yesterday, yesterday lunchtime; **zu ~ essen** have lunch; **Mittagessen** nt lunch; **mittags** adv at lunchtime, at midday; **Mittagspause** f lunch break

Mitte f (-, -n) middle; **~ Juni** in the middle of June; **sie ist ~ zwanzig** she's in her mid-twenties

mitteilen vt jdm etw **~** inform sb of sth; **Mitteilung** f notification

Mittel nt (-s -) means sg; (practical measure, way) method; MED remedy (gegen for)

Mittelalter nt Middle Ages pl; **mittelalterlich** adj medieval; **Mittelamerika** nt Central America; **Mitteleuropa** nt Central Europe; **Mittelfeld** nt midfield; **Mittelfinger** m middle finger; **mittelmäßig** adj mediocre; **Mittelmeer**

nt Mediterranean (Sea); **Mittelohrentzündung** *f* inflammation of the middle ear; **Mittelpunkt** *m* centre; *im ~ stehen* be the centre of attention

mittels *prep + gen* by means of

Mittelstürmer(in) *m(f)* striker, centre-forward

mitten *adv* in the middle; *~ auf der Straße / in der Nacht* in the middle of the street / night

Mitternacht *f* midnight

mittlere(r, s) *adj* middle; (*ordinary*) average

mittlerweile *adv* meanwhile

Mittwoch *m* (-s, -e) Wednesday; (*am*) ~ on Wednesday; (*am*) ~ **Morgen / Nachmittag / Abend** (on Wednesday morning / afternoon / evening; **diesen / letzten / nächsten** ~ this / last / next Wednesday; **jeden** ~ every Wednesday; *~ in einer Woche* a week on Wednesday, Wednesday week; **mittwochs** *adv* on Wednesdays; *~ abends* on Wednesday evenings

mixen *vt* mix; **Mixer** *m* (-s, -) (*kitchen appliance*) blender

mobben *vt* harass (*or* bully) (at work)

Möbel *nt* (-s, -) piece of furniture; *die ~ pl* the furniture *sg*; **Möbelpacker** *m* removal van

mobil *adj* mobile; **Mobiltelefon** *nt* mobile phone

möblieren *vt* furnish

mochte *imperf of* **mögen**

Mode *f* (-, -n) fashion

Model *nt* (-s, -s) model

Modell *nt* (-s, -e) model

Modem *nt* (-s, -s) IT modem

Mode(n)schau *f* fashion show

Moderator(in) *m(f)* presenter

modern *adj* modern; (*stylish*) fashionable; **modisch** *adj* fashionable

Modus *m* (-, *Modi*) IT mode; *fig* way

mögen (*mochte, gemocht*) *vt, vi* like; **ich möchte ...** I would like ...; **ich möchte lieber bleiben** I'd rather stay; **möchtest du lieber Tee oder Kaffee?** would you prefer tea or coffee?

möglich *adj* possible; *so bald wie* ~ as soon as possible; **möglicherweise** *adv* possibly; **Möglichkeit** *f* possibility; **möglichst** *adv* as ... as possible

Mohn *m* (-(e)s, -e) poppy; (*for cake etc*) poppy seed

Möhre *f* (-, -n), **Mohrrübe** *f* carrot

Mokka *m* (-s, -s) mocha

Moldawien *nt* (-s) Moldova

Molkerei *f* (-, -en) dairy

Moll *nt* (-) minor (key); *a~* A

minor

mollig adj cosy; (person) plump

Moment m (-(e)s, -e) moment; **im ~** at the moment; **einen ~ bitte!** just a minute; **momentan 1.** adj momentary **2.** adv at the moment

Monaco nt (-s) Monaco

Monarchie f monarchy

Monat m (-(e)s, -e) month; **sie ist im dritten ~** she's three months pregnant; **monatlich** adj, adv monthly; **~ 100 Euro zahlen** pay 100 euros a month (or every month); **Monatskarte** f monthly season ticket

Mönch m (-s, -e) monk

Mond m (-(e)s, -e) moon; **Mondfinsternis** f lunar eclipse

Mongolei f (-) **die ~** Mongolia

Monitor m IT monitor

monoton adj monotonous

Monsun m (-s, -e) monsoon

Montag m Monday; → **Mittwoch**; **montags** adv on Mondays; → **mittwochs**

Montenegro nt (-s) Montenegro

Monteur(in) m(f) (-s, -e) fitter; **montieren** vt assemble, set up

Monument nt (-(e)s, -e) monument

Moor nt (-(e)s, -e) moor

Moos nt (-es, -e) moss

Moped nt (-s, -s) moped

Moral f (-) morals pl; **moralisch** adj moral

Mord m (-(e)s, -e) murder; **Mörder(in)** m(f) (-s, -) murderer / murderess

morgen adv tomorrow; **~ früh** tomorrow morning

Morgen m (-s, -) morning; **am ~** in the morning; **Morgenmantel** m dressing gown; **Morgenmuffel** m **er ist ein ~** he's not a morning person; **morgens** adv in the morning; **um 3 Uhr ~** at 3 (o'clock) in the morning, at 3 am

Morphium nt (-s) morphine

morsch adj rotten

Mosaik nt (-s, -e(n)) mosaic

Mosambik nt (-s) Mozambique

Moschee f (-, -n) mosque

Moskau nt (-s) Moscow

Moskito m (-s, -s) mosquito; **Moskitonetz** nt mosquito net

Moslem m (-s, -s), **Moslime** f (-, -n) Muslim

Most m (-(e)s, -e) (unfermented) fruit juice; (fermented, from apples) cider

Motel nt (-s, -s) motel

motivieren vt motivate

Motor m engine; ELEC motor; **Motorboot** nt motorboat; **Motorenöl** nt engine oil; **Motorhaube** f bonnet (Brit), hood (US); **Motorrad** nt motorbike, motorcycle; **Motorradfahrer(in)** m(f) motorcyclist; **Motorroller** m (motor) scooter; **Motorschaden** m engine trouble

Motte f (-, -n) moth

Motto nt (-s, -s) motto

Mountainbike nt (-s, -s) mountain bike

Möwe f (-, -n) (sea)gull

Mücke f (-, -n) midge; (in the tropics) mosquito; **Mückenstich** m mosquito bite

müde adj tired

muffig adj (smell) musty; (face, person) grumpy

Mühe f (-, -n) trouble, pains pl; **sich** dat **große ~ geben** go to a lot of trouble

Mühle f (-, -n) mill; (for coffee) grinder

Mull m (-(e)s, -e) muslin; MED gauze

Müll m (-(e)s) rubbish (Brit), garbage (US); **Müllabfuhr** f rubbish (Brit) (or garbage (US)) disposal

Mullbinde f gauze bandage

Müllcontainer m waste container; **Mülleimer** m rubbish bin (Brit), garbage can (US); **Mülltonne** f dustbin (Brit), garbage can (US); **Müllwagen** m dustcart (Brit), garbage truck (US)

multikulturell adj multicultural

Multimedia- in cpds multimedia

Multiple-Choice-Verfahren nt multiple choice

multiple Sklerose f (-n, -n) multiple sclerosis

Multiplexkino nt multiplex (cinema)

multiplizieren vt multiply (mit by)

Mumie f mummy

Mumps m (-) mumps sg

München nt (-s) Munich

Mund m (-(e)s, Münder) mouth; **halt den ~!** shut up; **Mundart** f dialect; **Munddusche** f dental water jet

münden vi flow (in + acc into)

Mundgeruch m bad breath; **Mundharmonika** f (-, -s) mouth organ

mündlich adj oral

Mundschutz m mask; **Mundwasser** nt mouthwash

Munition f ammunition

munter adj lively

Münzautomat m vending machine; **Münze** f (-, -n) coin; **Münzeinwurf** m slot; **Münzrückgabe** f coin return; **Münztelefon** nt pay phone; **Münzwechsler** m change machine

murmeln vt, vi murmur, mutter

Murmeltier nt marmot

mürrisch adj sullen, grumpy

Muschel f (-, -n) mussel; (empty) shell

Museum nt (-s, Museen) museum

Musical nt (-s, -s) musical

Musik f music; **musikalisch** adj musical; **Musiker(in)** m(f) (-s, -) musician; **Musikinstrument** nt musical in-

strument; **musizieren** vi
play music
Muskat m (-(e)s) nutmeg
Muskel m (-s, -n) muscle;
Muskelkater m ~ **haben** be
stiff; **Muskelriss** m torn
muscle; **Muskelzerrung** f
pulled muscle; **muskulös**
adj muscular
Müsli nt (-s, -) muesli
Muslim(in) m(f) (-s, -s) Muslim
Muss nt (-) must
müssen (musste, gemusst) vi
must, have to; **er hat gehen
~** he (has) had to go; **sie
müsste schon längst hier
sein** she should have arrived
a long time ago; **du musst**

es nicht tun you don't have
to do it, you needn't do it;
ich muss mal I need to
got to the loo (Brit), I have
to go to the bathroom (US)
Muster nt (-s, -) pattern, design; (small quantity) sample
Mut m (-(e)s) courage; **jdm ~
machen** encourage sb; **mutig** adj brave, courageous
Mutter 1. f (-, Mütter) mother
2. f (-, -n) (for bolt) nut; **Muttersprache** f mother tongue;
Muttertag m Mother's Day;
Mutti f mum(my) (Brit),
mom(my) (US)
mutwillig adj deliberate
Mütze f (-, -n) cap
Myanmar nt (-s) Myanmar

N

na interj ~ **also!,** ~ **bitte!** see?,
what did I tell you?; ~ **ja** well;
~ **und?** so what?
Nabel m (-s, -) navel
nach prep + dat after; (direction) to; (consistent with) according to; ~ **zwei Stunden**
after two hours, two hours
later; **es ist fünf ~ sechs**
it's five past (Brit) (or after
(US)) six; **der Zug ~ London**
the train for (or to) London;
~ **rechts/links** to the right/
left; ~ **Hause** home; ~ **oben/
hinten/unten** up/back/
down; ~ **und ~** gradually
nachahmen vt imitate

Nachbar(in) m(f) (-n, -n)
neighbour; **Nachbarschaft**
f neighbourhood
nachdem conj after; (because) since; **je ~ (ob/wie)** depending on (whether/how)
nachdenken irr vi think
(über + acc about); **nachdenklich** adj thoughtful
nacheinander adv one after
another (or the other)
Nachfolger(in) m(f) (-s, -)
successor
nachforschen vt investigate
Nachfüllpack m refill pack
nachgeben irr vi give in (jdm
to sb)

nachgehen *irr vi* follow (*jdm sb*); (*investigate*) inquire (*einer Sache dat* into sth); **die Uhr geht (zehn Minuten) nach** this watch is (ten minutes) slow

nachher *adv* afterwards; **bis ~!** see you later

Nachhilfe *f* extra tuition

nachholen *vt* catch up with; (*what one has missed*) make up for

nachkommen *irr vi* follow; **einer Verpflichtung** *dat* ~ fulfil an obligation

nachlassen *irr* **1.** *vt* (*sum of money*) take off **2.** *vi* decrease, ease off; (*get worse*) deteriorate; **nachlässig** *adj* negligent, careless

nachlaufen *irr vi* run after, chase (*jdm sb*)

nachmachen *vt* imitate, copy (*jdm etw sth* from sb); (*fake*) counterfeit

Nachmittag *m* afternoon; **heute ~** this afternoon; **am ~** in the afternoon; **nachmittags** *adv* in the afternoon; **um 3 Uhr ~** at 3 (o'clock) in the afternoon, at 3 pm

Nachnahme *f* (-, -n) cash on delivery; **per ~** COD

Nachname *m* surname

Nachporto *nt* excess postage

nachprüfen *vt* check

nachrechnen *vt* check

Nachricht *f* (-, -en) (*piece of*) news *sg*; (*notification*) message; **Nachrichten** *pl* news *sg*

Nachsaison *f* off-season

nachschauen 1. *vi jdm* ~ gaze after sb **2.** *vt* check

nachschicken *vt* forward

nachschlagen *irr vt* look up

nachsehen *irr vt* check

nachsenden *irr vt* forward

Nachspeise *f* dessert

nächste(r, s) *adj* next; (*in space*) nearest

Nacht *f* (-, Nächte) night; **in der** ~ during the night; (*when dark*) at night; **Nachtclub** *m* nightclub; **Nachtdienst** *m* night duty; ~ **haben** (*chemist's*) be open all night

Nachteil *m* disadvantage

Nachtflug *m* night flight; **Nachthemd** *nt* nightdress; (*for men*) nightshirt

Nachtigall *f* (-, -en) nightingale

Nachtisch *m* dessert, sweet (*Brit*), pudding (*Brit*)

Nachtleben *nt* nightlife

nachträglich *adv* ~ **alles Gute zum Geburtstag!** Happy belated birthday

nachts *adv* at night; **um 11 Uhr** ~ at 11 (o'clock) at night, at 11 pm; **um 2 Uhr** ~ at 2 (o'clock) in the morning, at 2 am; **Nachtschicht** *f* night shift; **Nachttisch** *m* bedside table; **Nachtzug** *m* night train

Nachweis *m* (-es, -e) proof

Nachwirkung *f* after-effect

nachzahlen 1. *vi* pay extra **2.** *vt* **20 Euro ~** pay 20 euros extra

nachzählen *vt* check

Nacken *m* (-s, -) (nape of the) neck

nackt *adj* naked; (*facts*) plain, bare; **Nacktbadestrand** *m* nudist beach

Nadel *f* (-, -n) needle; (*with head*) pin

Nagel *m* (-s, *Nägel*) nail; **Nagelfeile** *f* nail-file; **Nagellack** *m* nail varnish (*or* polish); **Nagellackentferner** *m* (-s, -) nail-varnish (*or* nail-polish) remover; **Nagelschere** *f* nail scissors *pl*

nah(e) 1. *adj, adv* near(by); (*in time*) near; (*relative, friend*) close; **jdm ~e gehen** upset *sb*; **~e liegen** be obvious **2.** *prep + dat* near (to), close to; **Nähe** *f* (-) vicinity; **in der ~** nearby; **in der ~ von** near to

nähen *vt, vi* sew

nähere(r, s) *adj* (*explanation, investigation*) more detailed; **die ~ Umgebung** the immediate area; **Nähere(s)** *nt* details *pl*; **nähern** *vr* approach

nahezu *adv* virtually, almost

nahm *imperf of* **nehmen**

Nähmaschine *f* sewing machine; **Nähnadel** *f* (sewing) needle

nahrhaft *adj* nourishing, nutritious; **Nahrung** *f* food; **Nahrungsmittel** *nt* food

Naht *f* (-, *Nähte*) seam; MED stitches *pl*, suture; TECH join

Nahverkehr *m* local traffic

Nähzeug *nt* sewing kit

naiv *adj* naive

Name *m* (-ns, -n) name

nämlich *adv* that is to say, namely; (*because*) since

nannte *imperf of* **nennen**

Napf *m* (-(e)s, *Näpfe*) bowl, dish

Narbe *f* (-, -n) scar

Narkose *f* (-, -n) anaesthetic

Narzisse *f* (-, -n) narcissus

naschen *vt, vi* nibble

Nase *f* (-, -n) nose; **Nasenbluten** *nt* (-s) nosebleed; **~ haben** have a nosebleed; **Nasenloch** *nt* nostril; **Nasentropfen** *pl* nose drops *pl*

Nashorn *nt* rhinoceros

nass *adj* wet; **Nässe** *f* (-) wetness; **nässen** *vi* (*wound*) weep

Nation *f* (-, -en) nation; **national** *adj* national; **Nationalfeiertag** *m* national holiday; **Nationalhymne** *f* (-, -n) national anthem; **Nationalität** *f* nationality; **Nationalmannschaft** *f* national team; **Nationalspieler(in)** *m(f)* international (player)

NATO *f* (-) *abbr* = **North Atlantic Treaty Organization**; NATO, Nato

Natur *f* nature; **Naturkost** *f* health food; **natürlich 1.** *adj* natural **2.** *adv* naturally; (*certainly, obviously*) of course; **Naturpark** *m* nature reserve; **Naturschutz** *m* conservation; **Naturschutzgebiet** *nt* nature reserve; **Naturwissenschaft** *f* (natural) science; **Naturwissenschaftler(in)** *m(f)* scientist

Navigationssystem *nt* AUTO navigation system

n. Chr. *abbr* = *nach Christus*; AD

Nebel *m* (-s, -) fog, mist; **nebelig** *adj* foggy, misty; **Nebelscheinwerfer** *m* foglamp; **Nebelschlussleuchte** *f* AUTO rear foglight

neben *prep* + *acc or dat* next to; *(in addition to)* apart from, besides; **nebenan** *adv* next door; **nebenbei** *adv* at the same time; *(as an extra)* additionally; *(by the way)* incidentally; **nebeneinander** *adv* side by side; **Nebenfach** *nt* subsidiary subject

nebenher *adv* *(in addition)* besides; *(simultaneously)* at the same time; *(at the side)* alongside

Nebenkosten *pl* extra charges *pl*, extras *pl*; **nebensächlich** *adj* minor; **Nebensaison** *f* low season; **Nebenstelle** *f* *(of phone)* extension; **Nebenstraße** *f* side street; **Nebenwirkung** *f* side effect

neblig *adj* foggy, misty

necken *vt* tease

Neffe *m* (-n, -n) nephew

negativ *adj* negative; **Negativ**

nt PHOT negative

nehmen *(nahm, genommen)* *vt* take; **jdm etw ~** take sth (away) from sb; **den Bus/ Zug ~** take the bus/train; **jdn/etw ernst ~** take sb/sth seriously

neidisch *adj* envious

neigen *vi* **zu etw ~** tend towards sth; **Neigung** *f* slope; *(tendency)* inclination; *(interest)* liking

nein *adv* no

Nektarine *f* nectarine

Nelke *f* (-, -n) carnation; *(spice)* clove

nennen *(nannte, genannt)* *vt* name; *(by a name)* call

Neonlicht *nt* neon light; **Neonröhre** *f* neon tube

Nepal *nt* (-s) Nepal

Neptun *nt* (-s) Neptune

Nerv *m* (-s, -en) nerve; **jdm auf die ~en gehen** get on sb's nerves; **nerven** *vt* **jdn ~** *fam* get on sb's nerves; **Nervenzusammenbruch** *m* nervous breakdown; **nervös** *adj* nervous

Nest *nt* (-(e)s, -er) nest; *pej (place)* dump

nett *adj* nice; *(friendly)* kind; **sei so ~ und ...** do me a favour and ...

netto *adv* net

Netz *nt* (-es, -e) net; *(system)* network; *(electricity supply)* mains, power (US); **Netzanschluss** *m* mains connection; **Netzwerk** *nt* IT network

neu adj new; (languages, history) modern; **die ~esten Nachrichten** the latest news; **Neubau** m new building; **neuerdings** adv recently; **Neuerung** f innovation; (change) reform

Neugier f curiosity; **neugierig** adj curious (auf + acc about); **ich bin ~, ob ...** I wonder whether (or if) ...

Neuheit f novelty; **Neuigkeit** f news sg; **Neujahr** nt New Year; **prosit ~!** Happy New Year; **neulich** adv recently, the other day

neun num nine; **neunhundert** num nine hundred; **neunmal** adv nine times; **neunte(r, s)** adj ninth; → **dritte**; **Neuntel** nt (-s, -) (fraction) ninth; **neunzehn** num nineteen; **neunzehnte(r, s)** adj nineteenth; → **dritte**; **neunzig** num ninety; **in den ~er Jahren** in the nineties; **Neunzigerjahre** pl nineties pl; **neunzigste(r, s)** adj ninetieth

neureich adj nouveau riche

Neurologe m, **Neurologin** f neurologist; **Neurose** f (-, -n) neurosis; **neurotisch** adj neurotic

Neuseeland nt New Zealand

Neustart m IT restart, reboot

neutral adj neutral

neuwertig adj nearly new

Nicaragua nt (-s) Nicaragua

nicht 1. adv not; **er kommt ~** he doesn't come; (on this occasion) he isn't coming; **sie wohnt ~ mehr hier** she doesn't live here any more; **gar ~** not at all; **ich kenne ihn auch ~** I don't know him either; **noch ~** not yet; **~ berühren!** do not touch **2.** pref no-

Nichte f (-, -n) niece

Nichtraucher(in) m(f) non-smoker; **Nichtraucherzone** f non-smoking area

nichts pron nothing; **ich habe ~ gesagt** I didn't say anything; **~ sagend** meaningless; **macht ~** never mind

Nichtschwimmer(in) m(f) non-swimmer

nicken vi nod

Nickerchen nt nap

nie adv never; **~ wieder** (or **mehr**) never again; **fast ~** hardly ever

nieder 1. adj low; (in status) inferior **2.** adv down; **niedergeschlagen** adj depressed; **Niederlage** f defeat

Niederlande pl Netherlands pl; **Niederländer(in)** m(f) Dutchman/Dutchwoman; **niederländisch** adj Dutch; **Niederländisch** nt Dutch

Niederlassung f branch

Niederösterreich nt Lower Austria; **Niedersachsen** nt Lower Saxony

Niederschlag m METEO precipitation; rainfall

niedlich adj sweet, cute

niedrig adj low

niemals adv never

niemand pron nobody, no one; **ich habe ~en gesehen** I haven't seen anyone; **~ von ihnen** none of them

Niere f (-, -n) kidney; **Nierensteine** pl kidney stones pl

nieseln vi impers drizzle; **Nieselregen** m drizzle

niesen vi sneeze

Niete f (-, -n) (losing ticket) blank; pej (person) failure; TECH rivet

Nigeria nt (-s) Nigeria

Nikotin nt (-s) nicotine; **nikotinarm** adj low in nicotine

Nilpferd nt hippopotamus

nippen vi sip; **an etw** dat **~** sip sth

nirgends adv nowhere

Nische f (-, -n) niche

Nitrat nt nitrate

Niveau nt (-s, -s) level; **sie hat ~** she's got class

nobel adj generous; fam classy, posh

Nobelpreis m Nobel Prize

noch 1. adv still; (in addition) else; **wer kommt ~?** who else is coming?; **~ nie** never; **~ nicht** not yet; **immer ~** still; **~ einmal** (once) again; **am selben Tag** that (very) same day; **~ besser/mehr/ jetzt** even better/more/ now; **wie heißt sie ~?** what's her name again?; **~ ein Bier, bitte** another beer, please **2.** conj nor; **nochmal(s)** adv

again, once more

Nominativ m nominative (case)

Nonne f (-, -n) nun

Non-Stop-Flug m nonstop flight

Nord north; **Nordamerika** nt North America; **Norddeutschland** nt Northern Germany; **Norden** m (-s) north; **Nordeuropa** nt Northern Europe; **Nordirland** nt Northern Ireland; **nordisch** adj Nordic; **Nordkorea** nt (-s) North Korea; **nördlich** adj northern; (course, direction) northerly; **Nordost(en)** m northeast; **Nordpol** m North Pole; **Nordrhein-Westfalen** nt (-s) North Rhine-Westphalia; **Nordsee** f North Sea; **nordwärts** adv north, northwards; **Nordwest(en)** m northwest; **Nordwind** m north wind

nörgeln vi grumble

Norm f (-, -en) norm; (technical, industrial) standard

normal adj normal; **normalerweise** adv normally

Norwegen nt (-s) Norway; **Norweger(in)** m(f) Norwegian; **norwegisch** adj Norwegian; **Norwegisch** nt Norwegian

Not f (-, Nöte) need; poverty; (distress) hardship; (emergency situation) trouble; **zur ~** if necessary; (with little *to spare*) just about

Notar(in) *m(f)* public notary

Notarzt *m*, **Notärztin** *f* emergency doctor; **Notarztwagen** *m* emergency ambulance; **Notausgang** *m* emergency exit; **Notbremse** *f* emergency brake; **Notdienst** *m* emergency service, after-hours service; **notdürftig** *adj* scanty; (*rough and ready*) makeshift

Note *f* (-, -n) (*in school*) mark, grade (*US*); MUS note

Notebook *nt* (-(s), -s) IT notebook

Notfall *m* emergency; **notfalls** *adv* if necessary

notieren *vt* note down

nötig *adj* necessary; **etw ~ haben** need sth

Notiz *f* (-, -en) note; **Notizblock** *m* notepad; **Notizbuch** *nt* notebook

notlanden *vi* make a forced (*or* emergency) landing; **Notruf** *m* emergency call; **Notrufnummer** *f* emergency number; **Notrufsäule** *f* emergency telephone

notwendig *adj* necessary

Nougat *m or nt* (-s, -s) nougat

November *m* (-(s), -) November; → **Juni**

Nr. *abbr* = **Nummer**; No., no.

Nu *m* **im ~** in no time

nüchtern *adj* sober; (*sto-*

mach) empty

Nudel *f* (-, -n) noodle; **~n** *pl* (*Italian*) pasta *sg*; **Nudelsuppe** *f* noodle soup

null *num* zero; TEL O (*Brit*), zero (*US*); **~ Fehler** no mistakes; **~ Uhr** midnight; **Null** *f* (-, -en) nought; zero; *pej* (*person*) dead loss; **Nulltarif** *m* **zum ~** free of charge

Nummer *f* (-, -n) number; **nummerieren** *vt* number; **Nummernschild** *nt* AUTO number plate (*Brit*), license plate (*US*)

nun **1.** *adv* now; **von ~ an** from now on **2.** *interj* well; **~ gut!** all right, then; **es ist ~ mal so** that's the way it is

nur *adv* only; **nicht ~ ..., sondern auch ...** not only ..., but also ...

Nürnberg *nt* (-s) Nuremberg

Nuss *f* (-, *Nüsse*) nut; **Nussknacker** *m* (-s, -) nutcracker

Nutte *f* (-, -n) *fam* tart

nutz, nütze *adj* **zu nichts ~ sein** be useless; **nutzen, nützen 1.** *vi* (*zu etw* for sth); **was nützt es?** what use is it? **2.** *vt* be of use; **das nützt nicht viel** that doesn't help much; **Nutzen** *m* (-s, -) usefulness; (*financial*) profit; **nützlich** *adj* useful

Nylon *nt* (-s) nylon

O

o *interj* oh

Oase *f* (-, -n) oasis

ob *conj* if, whether; **so als ~** as if; **und ~!** you bet

obdachlos *adj* homeless

oben *adv* at the top; (*in pile, on cupboard etc*) on (the) top; (*in house*) upstairs; (*in text*) above; **da ~** up there; **von ~ bis unten** from top to bottom; **siehe ~** see above

Ober *m* (-s, -) waiter

obere(r, s) *adj* upper, top

Oberfläche *f* surface; **oberflächlich** *adj* superficial; **Obergeschoss** *nt* upper floor

oberhalb *adv, prep + gen* above

Oberkörper *m* upper body; **Oberlippe** *f* upper lip; **Oberösterreich** *nt* Upper Austria; **Oberschenkel** *m* thigh

oberste(r, s) *adj* very top, topmost

Oberteil *nt* top; **Oberweite** *f* bust/chest measurement

Objekt *nt* (-(e)s, -e) object

objektiv *adj* objective

Objektiv *nt* lens

obligatorisch *adj* compulsory, obligatory

Oboe *f* (-, -n) oboe

Observatorium *nt* observatory

Obst *nt* (-(e)s) fruit; **Obstku-**chen *m* fruit tart; **Obstsalat** *m* fruit salad

obwohl *conj* although

Ochse *m* (-n, -n) ox

ocker *adj* ochre

öd(e) *adj* waste; *fig* dull

oder *conj* or; **~ aber** or else; **er kommt doch, ~?** he's coming, isn't he?

Ofen *m* (-s, Öfen) oven; (*for heating*) heater; (*using coal etc*) stove; (*kitchen appliance*) cooker, stove; **Ofenkartoffel** *f* baked (*or* jacket) potato

offen 1. *adj* open; (*honest*) frank; (*job*) vacant **2.** *adv* frankly; **~ gesagt** to be honest

offenbar *adj* obvious; **offensichtlich** *adj* evident, obvious

öffentlich *adj* public; **Öffentlichkeit** *f* public

offiziell *adj* official

offline *adv* IT offline

öffnen *vt, vr* open; **Öffner** *m* (-s, -) opener; **Öffnung** *f* opening; **Öffnungszeiten** *pl* opening times *pl*

oft *adv* often; **schon ~** many times; **öfter** *adv* more often (*or* frequently); **öfters** *adv* often, frequently

ohne *conj, prep + acc* without; **~ weiteres** without a second thought; (without delay) immediately; **~ mich** count me out

Ohnmacht f (-machten pl) unconsciousness; **in ~ fallen** faint; **ohnmächtig** adj unconscious; **sie ist ~** she has fainted

Ohr nt (-(e)s, -en) ear; (faculty) hearing

Öhr nt (-(e)s, -e) eye

Ohrenarzt m, **Ohrenärztin** f ear specialist; **Ohrenschmerzen** pl earache; **Ohrentropfen** pl ear drops pl; **Ohrfeige** f slap (in the face); **Ohrläppchen** nt earlobe; **Ohrringe** pl earrings pl

oje interj oh dear

okay interj OK, okay

Ökoladen m health food store; **ökologisch** adj ecological; **~e Landwirtschaft** organic farming

ökonomisch adj economic; (money-saving) economical

Ökosystem nt ecosystem

Oktober m (-(s), -) October; → **Juni**

Öl nt (-(e)s, -e) oil; **Ölbaum** m olive tree; **ölen** vt oil; TECH lubricate; **Ölfarbe** f oil paint; **Ölfilter** m oil filter; **Ölgemälde** nt oil painting; **Ölheizung** f oil-fired central heating; **ölig** adj oily

oliv adj inv olive-green; **Olive** f (-, -n) olive; **Olivenöl** nt olive oil

Ölsardine f sardine in oil; **Öl-**

teppich m oil slick; **Ölwechsel** m oil change

Olympiade f Olympic Games pl; **olympisch** adj Olympic

Oma f, **Omi** f (-s, -s) grandma, gran(ny)

Omelett nt (-(e)s, -s), **Omelette** f omelette

Omnibus m bus

onanieren vi masturbate

Onkel m (-s, -) uncle

online adv IT online

OP m (-s, -s) abbr = **Operationssaal** m; operating theatre (Brit) (or room (US))

Opa m, **Opi** m (-s, -s) grandpa, grandad

Openairkonzert nt open-air concert

Oper f (-, -n) opera; (building) opera house

Operation f operation

Operette f operetta

operieren 1. vi operate **2.** vt operate on

Opernsänger(in) m(f) opera singer

Opfer nt (-s, -) sacrifice; (person) victim; **ein ~ bringen** make a sacrifice

Opium nt (-s) opium

Opposition f opposition

Optiker(in) m(f) (-s, -s) optician

optimal adj optimal, optimum

optimistisch adj optimistic

oral adj oral; **Oralverkehr** m oral sex

orange adj inv orange; **Orange** f (-, -n) orange; **Oran-**

genmarmelade f marmalade; **Orangensaft** m orange juice

Orchester nt (-s, -) orchestra

Orchidee f (-, -n) orchid

Orden m (-s, -) REL order; MIL decoration

ordentlich 1. adj respectable; (orderly) tidy, neat **2.** adv properly

ordinär adj common, vulgar; (joke) dirty

ordnen vt sort out; **Ordner** m (-s, -) (at events) steward; (for documents) file; **Ordnung** f order; (orderliness) tidiness; (**geht**) **in ~!** (that's) all right

Oregano m (-s) oregano

Organ nt (-s, -e) organ; voice

Organisation f organization; **organisieren 1.** vt organize; fam (obtain) get hold of **2.** vr organize

Organismus m organism

Orgasmus m orgasm

Orgel f (-, -n) organ

Orgie f orgy

orientalisch adj oriental

orientieren vr get one's bearings; **Orientierung** f orientation; **Orientierungssinn** m sense of direction

original adj original; (real) genuine; **Original** nt (-s, -e) original; **Originalfassung** f original version

originell adj original; (humorous) witty

Orkan m (-(e)s, -e) hurricane

Ort m (-(e)s, -e) place; (small town) village

Orthopäde m (-n, -n), **Orthopädin** f orthopaedist

örtlich adj local; **Ortschaft** f village, small town; **Ortsgespräch** nt local call; **Ortstarif** m local rate; **Ortszeit** f local time

Ost east; **Ostdeutschland** nt Eastern Germany; HIST East Germany; **Osten** m (-s) east

Osterei nt Easter egg; **Osterglocke** f daffodil; **Osterhase** m Easter bunny; **Ostermontag** m Easter Monday; **Ostern** nt (-, -) Easter; **an** (or **zu**) **~** at Easter; **frohe ~** Happy Easter

Österreich nt (-s) Austria; **Österreicher(in)** m(f) (-s, -) Austrian; **österreichisch** adj Austrian

Ostersonntag m Easter Sunday

Osteuropa nt Eastern Europe; **Ostküste** f east coast; **östlich** adj eastern; (course, direction) easterly; **Ostsee** f **die ~** the Baltic (Sea); **Ostwind** m east(erly) wind

Otter m (-s, -) otter

out adj fam out; **outen** vt out

oval adj oval

Overheadprojektor m overhead projector

Ozean m (-s, -e) ocean; **der Stille ~** the Pacific (Ocean)

Ozon nt (-s) ozone; **Ozonloch**

nt hole in the ozone layer;
Ozonschicht *f* ozone layer;

Ozonwerte *pl* ozone levels *pl*

P

paar *adj inv* **ein ~** a few; **ein ~ Mal** a few times; **ein ~ Äpfel** some apples
Paar *nt* (-(e)s, -e) pair; (*married*) couple
pachten *vt* lease
Päckchen *nt* package; (*of cigarettes*) packet; (*sent by post*) small parcel; **packen** *vt* pack; (*get hold of*) grasp, seize; *fam* (*succeed with*) manage; *fig* (*film, story etc*) grip; **Packpapier** *nt* brown paper; **Packung** *f* packet, pack (*US*); **Packungsbeilage** *f* package insert
Pädagoge *m* (-n, -n), **Pädagogin** *f* teacher; **pädagogisch** *adj* educational
Paddel *nt* (-s, -) paddle; **Paddelboot** *nt* canoe; **paddeln** *vi* paddle
Paket *nt* (-(e)s, -e) packet; (*sent by post*) parcel; **IT** package; **Paketbombe** *f* parcel bomb
Pakistan *nt* (-s) Pakistan
Palast *m* (-es, **Paläste**) palace
Palästina *nt* (-s) Palestine; **Palästinenser(in)** *m(f)* (-s, -) Palestinian
Palatschinken *pl* filled pancakes *pl*
Palette *f* (*of painter*) palette;

(*for moving goods*) pallet; (*variety*) range
Palme *f* (-, -n) palm (tree); **Palmsonntag** *m* Palm Sunday
Pampelmuse *f* (-, -n) grapefruit
pampig *adj fam* cheeky; (*food etc*) gooey
Panda(bär) *m* (-s, -s) panda
panieren *vt* GASTR coat with breadcrumbs; **paniert** *adj* breaded
Panik *f* panic
Panne *f* (-, -n) AUTO breakdown; (*mishap*) slip; **Pannendienst** *m*, **Pannenhilfe** *f* breakdown (*or* rescue) service
Pant(h)er *m* (-s, -) panther
Pantoffel *m* (-s, -n) slipper
Pantomime *f* (-, -n) mime
Panzer *m* (-s, -) MIL (*vehicle*) tank
Papa *m* (-s, -s) dad(dy), pa (*US*)
Papagei *m* (-s, -en) parrot
Papaya *f* (-, -s) papaya
Papier *nt* (-s, -e) paper; **~e** *pl* (*ID*) papers *pl*; (*official texts*) papers *pl*, documents *pl*; **Papierkorb** *m* wastepaper basket; **IT** recycle bin; **Papiertaschentuch** *nt* (pa-

per) tissue; **Papiertonne** f paper bank

Pappbecher m paper cup; **Pappe** f (-, -n) cardboard; **Pappkarton** m cardboard box; **Pappteller** m paper plate

Paprika m (-s, -s) (spice) paprika; (vegetable) pepper

Papst m (-(e)s, Päpste) pope

Paradeiser m (-s, -) tomato

Paradies nt (-es, -e) paradise

Paragliding nt (-s) paragliding

Paragraph m (-en, -en) paragraph; LAW section

parallel adj parallel

Paranuss f Brazil nut

Parasit m (-en, -en) parasite

parat adj ready; **etw ~ haben** have sth ready

Pärchen nt couple

Parfüm nt (-s, -s or -e) perfume

Park m (-s, -s or -e) park; **Parkanlage** f park; (around building) grounds pl; **Parkbank** f park bench

Parkdeck nt parking level; **parken** vt, vi park

Parkett nt (-s, -e) parquet flooring; THEAT stalls pl (Brit), parquet (US)

Parkhaus nt multi-storey car park (Brit), parking garage (US)

parkinsonsche Krankheit f Parkinson's disease

Parkkralle f AUTO wheel clamp; **Parklicht** nt parking

light; **Parklücke** f parking space; **Parkplatz** m parking space; (for many cars) car park (Brit), parking lot (US); **Parkscheibe** f parking disc; **Parkscheinautomat** m pay point; (issuing ticket) ticket machine; **Parkuhr** f parking meter; **Parkverbot** nt no-parking zone; **hier ist ~** you can't park here

Parlament nt parliament

Parmesan m (-s) Parmesan (cheese)

Partei f party

Parterre nt (-s, -s) ground floor (Brit), first floor (US)

Partitur f MUS score

Partizip nt (-s, -ien) participle

Partner(in) m(f) (-s, -) partner; **Partnerschaft** f partnership; **eingetragene ~** civil partnership; **Partnerstadt** f twin town

Party f (-, -s) party; **Partymuffel** m (-s, -) party pooper; **Partyservice** m catering service

Pass m (-es, Pässe) pass; (ID) passport

passabel adj reasonable

Passagier m (-s, -e) passenger

Passamt nt passport office; **Passbild** nt passport photo

passen vi (size) fit; (colour, style) go (zu with); (not answer) pass; **passt (es) dir morgen?** does tomorrow suit you?; **das passt mir gut** that suits me fine; pas-

send adj suitable; (in colour, style) matching; (appropriate) fitting; (time) convenient

passieren vi happen

passiv adj passive

Passkontrolle f passport control

Passwort nt password

Paste f (-, -n) paste

Pastete f (-, -n) pie; (small) vol-au-vent; (for spreading) pâté

Pastor, in m(f) (-s, -en) minister, vicar

Pate m (-n, -n) godfather; **Patenkind** nt godchild

Patient in m(f) patient

Patin f godmother

Patrone f (-, -n) cartridge

Patsche f (-, -n) (difficult situation) mess; **patschnass** adj soaking wet

pauschal adj (cost) inclusive; (judgment) sweeping; **Pauschale** f (-, -n), **Pauschalgebühr** f flat rate (charge); **Pauschalpreis** m flat rate; (for hotel, trip) all-inclusive price; **Pauschalreise** f package tour

Pause f (-, -n) break; THEAT interval; (in cinema) intermission; (when speaking) pause

Pavian m (-s, -e) baboon

Pavillon m (-s, -s) pavilion

Pay-TV nt (-s) pay-per-view television, pay TV

Pazifik m (-s) Pacific (Ocean)

PC m (-s, -s) abbr = **Personalcomputer**; PC

Pech nt (-s, -e) fig bad luck; ~ **haben** be unlucky; ~ **gehabt!** tough (luck)

Pedal nt (-s, -e) pedal

Pediküre f (-, -n) pedicure

Peeling nt (-s, -s) (facial/body) scrub

peinlich adj embarrassing, awkward; (conscientious) painstaking; **es war mir sehr ~** I was totally embarrassed

Peitsche f (-, -n) whip

Pelikan m (-s, -e) pelican

Pellkartoffeln pl potatoes pl boiled in their skins

Pelz m (-es, -e) fur; **pelzig** adj (tongue) furred

pendeln vi (train, bus) shuttle; (person) commute; **Pendelverkehr** m shuttle traffic; (for commuters) commuter traffic; **Pendler(in)** m(f) (-s, -) commuter

Penis m (-, -se) penis

Pension f (money) pension; (period) retirement; (building) guesthouse, B&B; **pensioniert** adj retired

Peperoni f (-, -) chilli

per prep + acc by, per; (each) per; (not later than) by

perfekt adj perfect

Periode f (-, -n) period

Perle f (-, -n) a. fig pearl

perplex adj dumbfounded

Person f (-, -en) person; **ein Tisch für drei ~en** a table for three; **Personal** nt (-s) staff, personnel; **Personalausweis** m identity card;

Personalien pl particulars pl; **Personenschaden** m injury to persons; **persönlich 1.** adj personal; (on letter) private **2.** adv personally; (oneself) in person; **Persönlichkeit** f personality

Peru nt (-s) Peru

Perücke f (-, -n) wig

pervers adj perverted

pessimistisch adj pessimistic

Pest f (-) plague

Petersilie f parsley

Petroleum nt (-s) paraffin (Brit), kerosene (US)

Pfad m (-(e)s, -e) path; **Pfadfinder** m (-s, -) boy scout; **Pfadfinderin** f girl guide

Pfahl m (-(e)s, Pfähle) post, stake

Pfand nt (-(e)s, Pfänder) security; (on bottle) deposit; (in game) forfeit; **Pfandflasche** f returnable bottle

Pfanne f (-, -n) (frying) pan; **Pfannkuchen** m pancake

Pfarrei f parish; **Pfarrer(in)** m(f) (-s, -) priest

Pfau m (-(e)s, -en) peacock

Pfeffer m (-s, -) pepper; **Pfefferkuchen** m gingerbread; **Pfefferminze** f (-e) peppermint; **Pfefferminztee** m peppermint tea; **Pfeffermühle** f pepper mill; **Pfefferstreuer** m (-s, -) pepper pot

Pfeife f (-, -n) whistle; (for tobacco, of organ) pipe; **pfeifen** (pfiff, gepfiffen) vt, vi whistle

Pfeil m (-(e)s, -e) arrow

Pferd nt (-(e)s, -e) horse; **Pferdeschwanz** m ponytail; **Pferdestall** m stable

pfiff imperf of **pfeifen**

Pfifferling m chanterelle

Pfingsten nt (-, -) Whitsun, Pentecost (US); **Pfingstmontag** m Whit Monday; **Pfingstsonntag** m Whit Sunday, Pentecost (US); **Pfingstrose** f peony

Pfirsich m (-s, -e) peach

Pflanze f (-, -n) plant; **pflanzen** vt plant; **Pflanzenfett** nt vegetable fat

Pflaster nt (-s, -) (for wound) plaster, Band Aid® (US); (on road) road surface, pavement (US)

Pflaume f (-, -n) plum

Pflege f (-, -n) care; (of patient) nursing; (of car, machine) maintenance; **pflegebedürftig** adj in need of care; **pflegeleicht** adj easy-care; fig easy to handle; **pflegen** vt look after; (patient) nurse; (relations) foster; (fingernails, face) take care of; (data) maintain; **Pflegepersonal** nt nursing staff; **Pflegeversicherung** f long-term care insurance

Pflicht f (-, -en) duty; SPORT compulsory section; **pflichtbewusst** adj conscientious; **Pflichtfach** nt compulsory subject

pflücken vt pick

Pforte f (-, -n) gate; **Pförtner(in)** m(f) (-s, -) porter

Pfosten m (-s, -) post

Pfote f (-, -n) paw

pfui interj ugh

Pfund nt (-(e)s, -e) pound

pfuschen vi fam be sloppy

Pfütze f (-, -n) puddle

Phantasie f → **Fantasie**; **phantastisch** adj → **fantastisch**

Phase f (-, -n) phase

Philippinen pl Philippines pl

Philosophie f philosophy

Photo nt → **Foto**

pH-neutral adj pH-balanced; **pH-Wert** m pH-value

Physalis f (-, Physalen) physalis

Physik f physics sg

physisch adj physical

Pianist(in) m(f) (-en, -en) pianist

Pickel m (-s, -) pimple; (tool) pickaxe

Picknick nt (-s, -e or -s) picnic; **ein ~ machen** have a picnic

piepsen vi chirp

piercen vt **sich die Nase ~ lassen** have one's nose pierced; **Piercing** nt (-s) (body) piercing

pieseln vi fam pee

Pik nt (-, -) (card suit) spades pl

pikant adj spicy

Pilger(in) m(f) pilgrim; **Pilgerfahrt** f pilgrimage

Pille f (-, -n) pill; **sie nimmt die ~** she's on the pill

Pilot(in) m(f) (-en, -en) pilot

Pilz m (-es, -e) mushroom; (poisonous) toadstool; MED fungus

PIN f (-, -s) PIN (number)

pingelig adj fam fussy

Pinguin m (-s, -e) penguin

Pinie f pine; **Pinienkern** m pine nut

pink adj shocking pink

pinkeln vi fam pee

Pinsel m (-s, -) (paint)brush

Pinzette f tweezers pl

Pistazie f pistachio

Piste f (-, -n) piste; AVIAT runway

Pistole f (-, -n) pistol

Pixel nt (-s) IT pixel

Pizza f (-, -s) pizza; **Pizzaservice** m pizza delivery service; **Pizzeria** f (-, Pizzerien) pizzeria

Pkw m (-(s), -(s)) abbr = **Personenkraftwagen**; car

Plakat nt poster

Plan m (-(e)s, Pläne) plan; (of town) map; **planen** vt plan

Planet m (-en, -en) planet; **Planetarium** nt planetarium

planmäßig adj scheduled

Plan(t)schbecken nt paddling pool; **plan(t)schen** vi splash around

Planung f planning

Plastik 1. f sculpture **2.** nt (-s) plastic; **Plastikfolie** f plastic film; **Plastiktüte** f plastic bag

Platin nt (-s) platinum

platsch interj splash

platt adj flat; fam (surprised)

flabbergasted; *fig (remarks etc)* flat, boring

Platte f (-, -n) PHOT, TECH, GASTR plate; *(stone slab)* flag; *(LP)* record; **Plattenspieler** m record player

Plattform f platform; **Plattfuß** m flat foot; *(on vehicle)* flat (tyre)

Platz m (-es, Plätze) place; *(in train, theatre etc)* seat; *(vacant area)* space, room; *(in town)* square; *(for sports)* playing field; **nehmen Sie ~** please sit down, take a seat; **ist dieser ~ frei?** is this seat taken?

Plätzchen nt spot; *(sweet food)* biscuit

platzen vi burst; *(bomb)* explode

Platzkarte f seat reservation; **Platzreservierung** f seat reservation; **Platzverweis** m **er erhielt einen ~** he was sent off; **Platzwunde** f laceration, cut

plaudern vi chat, talk

pleite adj *fam* broke; **Pleite** f (-, -n) bankruptcy; *fam (party, play etc)* flop

Plombe f (-, -n) lead seal; *(in tooth)* filling; **plombieren** vt *(tooth)* fill

plötzlich 1. adj sudden **2.** adv suddenly, all at once

plumps interj thud; *(in liquid)* plop

Plural m (-s, -e) plural

plus adv plus; **fünf ~ sieben**

ist zwölf five plus seven is *(or* are) twelve; **zehn Grad ~** ten degrees above zero; **Plus** nt (-, -) plus; FIN profit; *(benefit)* advantage

Plüsch m (-(e)s, -e) plush

Pluto m (-) Pluto

Po m (-s, -s) *fam* bottom, bum

Pocken pl smallpox sg

poetisch adj poetic

Pointe f (-, -n) punch line

Pokal m (-s, -e) goblet; SPORT cup

pökeln vt pickle

Pol m (-s, -e) pole

Pole m (-n, -n) Pole; **Polen** nt (-s) Poland

Police f (-, -n) *(insurance)* policy

polieren vt polish

Polin f Pole, Polish woman

Politik f politics sg; *(course of action)* policy; **Politiker(in)** m(f) politician; **politisch** adj political

Politur f polish

Polizei f police pl; **Polizeibeamte(r)** m, **Polizeibeamtin** f police officer; **Polizeirevier** nt, **Polizeiwache** f police station; **Polizist(in)** m(f) policeman / -woman

Pollen m (-s, -s) pollen; **Pollenflug** m (-s) pollen count

polnisch adj Polish; **Polnisch** nt Polish

Polo m (-s) polo; **Polohemd** nt polo shirt

Polterabend m party prior to a wedding, at which old

*crockery is smashed to bring
good luck*

Polyester m (-s, -) polyester

Polypen pl MED adenoids pl

Pommes frites pl chips pl
(*Brit*), French fries pl (*US*)

Pony 1. m (-s, -s) (*hairstyle*)
fringe (*Brit*), bangs pl (*US*)
2. nt (-s, -s) (*horse*) pony

Popcorn nt (-s) popcorn

Popmusik f pop (music)

populär adj popular

Pore f (-, -n) pore

Pornografie f pornography

Porree m (-s, -s) leeks pl; *eine
Stange ~* a leek

Portemonnaie, Portmonee
nt (-s, -s) purse

Portion f portion, helping

Porto nt (-s, -s) postage

Portrait, Porträt nt (-s, -s)
portrait

Portugal nt (-s) Portugal; **Portugiese** m (-n, -n) Portuguese; **Portugiesin** f (-,
-nen) Portuguese; **portugiesisch** adj Portuguese; **Portugiesisch** nt Portuguese

Portwein m (-(e)s, -e) port

Porzellan nt (-s, -e) china

Posaune f (-, -n) trombone

Position f position

positiv adj positive

Post® f (-, -en) post office; (*letters*) post (*Brit*), mail; **Post-
amt** nt post office; **Postan-
weisung** f postal order
(*Brit*), money order (*US*);
Postbank f German post office bank; **Postbote** m, **-bo-**

tin f postman / -woman

Posten m (-s, -) post, position

Poster nt (-s, -) poster

Postfach nt post-office box,
PO box; **Postkarte** f post-
card; **Postleitzahl** f postcode
(*Brit*), zip code (*US*)

Poststempel m postmark

Potenz f MATH power; (*of
man*) potency

PR f (-, -s) abbr = **Public Relations**; PR

prächtig adj splendid

prahlen vi boast, brag

Praktikant(in) m(f) trainee;
Praktikum nt (-s, Praktika)
practical training; **praktisch**
adj practical; **~er Arzt** general practitioner

Praline f chocolate

Prämie f (*for insurance*) premium; (*as recompense*) reward; (*from employer*) bonus

Präservativ nt condom

Präsident(in) m(f) president

Praxis f (-, Praxen) practice;
(*treatment room*) surgery;
(*of lawyer*) office

präzise adj precise, exact

predigen vt, vi preach; **Predigt** f (-, -en) sermon

Preis m (-es, -e) price; (*for
winner*) prize; **Preisaus-
schreiben** nt competition

Preiselbeere f cranberry

preisgünstig adj inexpensive; **Preisschild** nt price
tag; **Preisträger(in)** m(f)
prizewinner; **preiswert** adj

inexpensive

Prellung f bruise

Premiere f (-, -n) premiere, first night

Premierminister(in) m(f) prime minister, premier

Presse f (-, -n) press

pressen vt press

prickeln vi tingle

Priester(in) m(f) (-s, -) priest / (woman) priest

Primel f (-, -n) primrose

primitiv adj primitive

Prinz m (-en, -en) prince; **Prinzessin** f princess

Prinzip nt (-s, -ien) principle; **im~** basically; **aus~** on principle

privat adj private; **Privatfernsehen** nt commercial television; **Privatgrundstück** nt private property; **privatisieren** vt privatize; **Privatquartier** nt private accommodation

pro prep + acc per; **5 Euro Stück / Person** 5 euros each / per person; **Pro** nt (-s) pro

Probe f (-, -n) test; (small quantity) sample; THEAT rehearsal; **Probefahrt** f test drive; **eine ~ machen** go for a test drive; **Probezeit** f trial period; **probieren** vt, vi try; (wine, food) taste, sample

Problem nt (-s, -e) problem

Produkt nt (-(e)s, -e) product; **Produktion** f production;

(amount produced) output; **produzieren** vt produce

Professor(in) m(f) (-s, -en) professor

Profi m (-s, -s) pro

Profil nt (-s, -e) profile; (of tyre, sole of shoe) tread

Profit m (-(e)s, -e) profit; **profitieren** vi profit (von from)

Prognose f (-, -n) prediction; (of weather) forecast

Programm nt (-s, -e) programme; IT program; TV channel; **Programmheft** nt programme; **programmieren** vt program; **Programmierer(in)** m(f) (-s, -) programmer

Projekt nt (-(e)s, -e) project

Projektor m projector

Promenade f (-, -n) promenade

Promille nt (-(s), -) (blood) alcohol level; **0,8 ~** 0.08 per cent; **Promillegrenze** f legal alcohol limit

prominent adj prominent; **Prominenz** f VIPs pl, prominent figures pl; fam (celebrities) the glitterati pl

Propeller m (-s, -) propeller

prosit interj cheers

Prospekt m (-(e)s, -e) leaflet, brochure

prost interj cheers

Prostituierte(r) mf prostitute

Protest m (-(e)s, -e) protest

Protestant(in) m(f) Protestant; **protestantisch** adj Protestant

protestieren vi protest (*gegen* against)

Prothese f (-, -n) artificial arm / leg; (*false teeth*) dentures pl

Protokoll nt (-s, -e) (*of meeting*) minutes pl; IT protocol; (*given to police*) statement

protzen vi show off; **protzig** adj flashy

Proviant m (-s, -e) provisions pl

Provider m (-s, -) IT (service) provider

Provinz f (-, -en) province

Provision f COMM commission

provisorisch adj provisional

provozieren vt provoke

Prozent nt (-(e)s, -e) per cent

Prozess m (-(e)s, -e) process; LAW trial; (*lawsuit*) (court) case; **prozessieren** vi go to law (*mit* against)

Prozession f procession

Prozessor m (-s, -en) IT processor

prüde adj prudish

prüfen vt test; (*verify*) check; **Prüfung** f exam; (*verification*) check; *eine ~ machen* take an exam

Prügelei f fight; **prügeln 1.** vt beat **2.** vr fight

PS 1. abbr = **Pferdestärke**; hp **2.** abbr = **Postskript(um)**; PS

pseudo- pref pseudo; **Pseudonym** nt (-s, -e) pseudonym

pst interj ssh

Psychiater(in) m(f) (-s, -) psychiatrist; **psychisch** adj

psychological; (*illness*) mental; **Psychoanalyse** f psychoanalysis; **Psychologe** m (-n, -n), **Psychologin** f psychologist; **Psychologie** f psychology; **psychosomatisch** adj psychosomatic; **Psychoterror** m psychological intimidation; **Psychotherapie** f psychotherapy

Pubertät f puberty

Publikum nt (-s) audience; SPORT crowd

Pudding m (-s, -e or -s) blancmange

Pudel m (-s, -) poodle

Puder m (-s, -) powder; **Puderzucker** m icing sugar

Puerto Rico nt (-s) Puerto Rico

Pulli m (-s, -s), **Pullover** m (-s, -) sweater, pullover, jumper (*Brit*)

Puls m (-es, -e) pulse

Pulver nt (-s, -) powder; **Pulverkaffee** m instant coffee; **Pulverschnee** m powder snow

Pumpe f (-, -n) pump; **pumpen** vt pump; *fam* (*to sb*) lend; *fam* (*from sb*) borrow

Pumps pl court shoes pl (*Brit*), pumps pl (*US*)

Punk m (-s, -s) (*music, person*) punk

Punkt m (-(e)s, -e) point; (*in pattern*) dot; (*punctuation mark*) full stop (*Brit*), period (*US*); *~ zwei Uhr* at two o'clock sharp

pünktlich adj punctual, on time; **Pünktlichkeit** f punctuality

Punsch m (-(e)s, -e) punch

Pupille f (-, -n) pupil

Puppe f (-, -n) doll

pur adj pure; (absolute) sheer; (whisky) neat

Püree nt (-s, -s) puree; mashed potatoes pl

Puste f (-) fam puff; **außer ~ sein** be puffed; **pusten** vi blow; (pant) puff

Pute f (-, -n) turkey

Putz m (-es) (on wall) plaster

putzen vt clean; **sich dat die Nase ~** blow one's nose; **sich dat die Zähne ~** brush one's teeth; **Putzfrau** f cleaner; **Putzlappen** m cloth; **Putzmittel** nt cleaning agent, cleaner

Puzzle nt (-s, -s) jigsaw (puzzle)

Pyjama m (-s, -s) pyjamas pl

Pyramide f (-, -n) pyramid

Python m (-s, -s) python

Q

Quadrat nt square; **quadratisch** adj square; **Quadratmeter** m square metre

quaken vi (frog) croak; (duck) quack

Qual f (-, -en) pain, agony; (mental) anguish; **quälen 1.** vt torment **2.** vr struggle; (mentally) torment oneself; **Quälerei** f torture, torment

qualifizieren vt, vr qualify; (classify) label

Qualität f quality

Qualle f (-, -n) jellyfish

Qualm m (-(e)s) thick smoke; **qualmen** vt, vi smoke

Quantität f quantity

Quarantäne f (-, -n) quarantine

Quark m (-s) quark; fam (nonsense) rubbish

Quartett nt (-s, -e) quartet;

(card game) happy families sg

Quartier nt (-s, -e) accommodation

quasi adv more or less

Quatsch m (-es) fam rubbish; **quatschen** vi fam chat

Quecksilber nt mercury

Quelle f (-, -n) spring; (of river) source

quer adv crossways, diagonally; at right angles; **Querflöte** f flute; **Querschnitt** m cross section; **querschnittsgelähmt** adj paraplegic; **Querstraße** f side street

quetschen vt squash, crush; MED bruise; **Quetschung** f bruise

Queue m (-s, -s) (billiard) cue

quietschen vi squeal; (door, bed) squeak; (brakes)

screech
Quirl *m* (*-s*, *-e*) whisk
quitt *adj* quits, even
Quitte *f* (*-*, *-n*) quince

Quittung *f* receipt
Quiz *nt* (*-*, *-*) quiz
Quote *f* (*-*, *-n*) rate; COMM quota

R

Rabatt *m* (*-(e)s*, *-e*) discount
Rabbi *m* (*-(s)*, *-s*) rabbi; **Rabbiner** *m* (*-s*, *-*) rabbi
Rabe *m* (*-n*, *-n*) raven
Rache *f* (*-*) revenge, vengeance
Rachen *m* (*-s*, *-*) throat
rächen 1. *vt* avenge **2.** *vr* take (one's) revenge (*an + dat* on)
Rad *nt* (*-(e)s*, *Räder*) wheel; (*vehicle*) bike; **~ fahren** cycle; **mit dem ~ fahren** go by bike
Radar *m or nt* (*-s*) radar; **Radarfalle** *f* speed trap; **Radarkontrolle** *f* radar speed check
radeln *vi fam* cycle; **Radfahrer(in)** *m(f)* cyclist; **Radfahrweg** *m* cycle track (*or* path)
Radicchio *m* (*-s*) radicchio
radieren *vt* rub out, erase; **Radiergummi** *m* rubber (*Brit*), eraser; **Radierung** *f* ART etching
Radieschen *nt* radish
radikal *adj* radical
Radio *nt* (*-s*, *-s*) radio; **im ~ on** the radio
radioaktiv *adj* radioactive
Radiologe *m* (*-n*, *-n*) Radio-

login *f* radiologist
Radiowecker *m* radio alarm (clock)
Radkappe *f* AUTO hub cap
Radler(in) *m(f)* (*-s*, *-*) cyclist
Radler *m* (*-s*, *-*) ≈ shandy
Radlerhose *f* cycling shorts *pl*; **Radrennen** *nt* cycle racing; (*single event*) cycle race; **Radtour** *f* cycling tour; **Radweg** *m* cycle track (*or* path)
raffiniert *adj* crafty, cunning; (*sugar*) refined
Rafting *nt* (*-s*) white water rafting
Ragout *nt* (*-s*, *-s*) ragout
Rahm *m* (*-s*) cream
rahmen *vt* frame; **Rahmen** *m* (*-s*, *-*) frame
Rakete *f* (*-*, *-n*) rocket
rammen *vt* ram
Rampe *f* (*-*, *-n*) ramp
ramponieren *vt fam* damage, batter
Ramsch *m* (*-(e)s*, *-e*) junk
ran *fam contr of* **heran**
Rand *m* (*-(e)s*, *Ränder*) edge; (*of spectacles, cup etc*) rim; (*on paper*) margin; (*of dirt, under eyes*) ring; *fig* verge, brink
randalieren *vi* (go on the)

rampage

rang *imperf of* **ringen**

Rang *m* (-(e)s, Ränge) rank; (*in competition*) place; THEAT circle

rannte *imperf of* **rennen**

ranzig *adj* rancid

Rap *m* (-s, -s) MUS rap; **rappen** (*rl* MUS rap; **Rapper(in)** *m(f)* (-s, -) MUS rapper

rar *adj* rare, scarce

rasant *adj* quick, rapid

rasch *adj* quick

rascheln *vi* rustle

rasen *vi* (*rush*) race; (*behave wildly*) rave; **gegen einen Baum ~** crash into a tree

Rasen *m* (-s, -) lawn

rasend *adj* furious

Rasenmäher *m* (-s, -) lawn-mower

Rasierapparat *m* razor; (*electric*) shaver; **Rasiercreme** *f* shaving cream; **rasieren** *vt, vr* shave; **Rasierer** *m* shaver; **Rasiergel** *nt* shaving gel; **Rasierklinge** *f* razor blade; **Rasiermesser** *nt* (cutthroat) razor; **Rasierpinsel** *m* shaving brush; **Rasierschaum** *m* shaving foam

Rasse *f* (-, -n) race; (*animals*) breed

Rassismus *m* racism; **Rassist(in)** *m(f)* racist; **rassistisch** *adj* racist

Rast *f* (-, -en) rest, break; **~ machen** have a rest (*or* break); **Raststätte** *f* AUTO service area; (*café*) motor-

way (*Brit*) (*or* highway (*US*)) restaurant

Rasur *f* shave

Rat *m* (-(e)s, Ratschläge) (piece) of advice; **um ~ fragen** ask for advice

Rate *f* (-, -n) instalment; **etw auf ~n kaufen** buy sth in instalments (*Brit*), buy sth on the instalment plan (*US*)

raten (riet, geraten) *vt, vi* guess; (*recommend*) advise (*jdm* sb)

Rathaus *nt* town hall

Ration *f* ration

ratlos *adj* at a loss, helpless; **ratsam** *adj* advisable

Rätsel *nt* (-s, -) puzzle; (*word puzzle*) riddle; **das ist mir ein ~** it's a mystery to me; **rätselhaft** *adj* mysterious

Ratte *f* (-, -n) rat

rau *adj* rough, coarse; (*weather*) harsh

Raub *m* (-(e)s) robbery; (*stolen things*) loot, booty; **rauben** *vt* steal; **jdm etw ~** rob sb of sth; **Räuber(in)** *m(f)* (-s, -) robber; **Raubkopie** *f* pirate copy; **Raubmord** *m* robbery with murder; **Raubtier** *nt* predator; **Raubüberfall** *m* mugging; **Raubvogel** *m* bird of prey

Rauch *m* (-(e)s) smoke; (*from exhaust*) fumes *pl*; **rauchen** *vt, vi* smoke; **Raucher(in)** *m(f)* (-s, -) smoker

Räucherlachs *m* smoked salmon; **räuchern** *vt* smoke

rauchig *adj* smoky; **Rauch-melder** *m* smoke detector; **Rauchverbot** *nt* smoking ban; **hier ist ~** there's no smoking here

rauf *fam contr of* **herauf**

rauh *adj* → **rau**; **Rauhreif** *m* → **Raureif**

Raum *m* (-(e)s, **Räume**) space; (*part of building, space for a purpose*) room; (*district*) area

räumen *vt* clear; (*house, seat*) vacate; (*take away*) shift, move; (*into cupboard etc*) put away

Raumfähre *f* space shuttle; **Raumfahrt** *f* space travel; **Raumschiff** *nt* spacecraft, spaceship; **Raumsonde** *f* space probe; **Raumstation** *f* space station

Raupe *f* (-, -n) caterpillar

Raureif *m* hoarfrost

raus *fam contr of* **heraus, hinaus**; **~!** (get) out!

Rausch *m* (-(e)s, **Räusche**) intoxication; **einen ~ haben/kriegen** be/get drunk; **Rauschgift** *nt* drug; **Rauschgiftsüchtige(r)** *mf* drug addict

rausfliegen *irr vi fam* be kicked out

raushalten *irr vr fam* **halt du dich da raus!** you (just) keep out of it

räuspern *vr* clear one's throat

rausschmeißen *irr vt fam* throw out

Razzia *f* (-, **Razzien**) raid

reagieren *vi* react (**auf** + *acc* to); **Reaktion** *f* reaction

real *adj* real; **realisieren** *vt* (*danger, problem*) realize; (*plan, idea*) implement; **realistisch** *adj* realistic; **Realität** *f* (-, -en) reality; **Reality-TV** *nt* (-s) reality TV

Realschule *f* ≈ secondary school, junior high (school) (*US*)

rebellieren *vi* rebel

Rebhuhn *nt* partridge

rechnen 1. *vt, vi* calculate; **~ mit** expect; (*rely on*) count on **2.** *vr* pay off, turn out to be profitable; **Rechner** *m* (-s, -) calculator; (*larger*) computer; **Rechnung** *f* calculation(s); COMM bill (*Brit*), check (*US*); **die ~, bitte!** can I have the bill, please?; **das geht auf meine ~** this is on me

recht 1. *adj* right; **mir soll's ~ sein** it's alright by me; **mir ist es ~** I don't mind **2.** *adv* really, quite; (*correctly*) right(ly); **ich weiß nicht ~** I don't really know; **es geschieht ihm ~** it serves him right

Recht *nt* (-(e)s, -e) right; LAW law; **~ haben** be right; **jdm ~ geben** agree with sb

Rechte *f* (-n, -n) right-hand side; (*hand*) right hand; POL right (wing); **rechte(r, s)** *adj* right; **auf der ~n Seite**

on the right, on the right-hand side

Rechteck nt (-s, -e) rectangle; **rechteckig** adj rectangular

rechtfertigen 1. vt justify **2.** vr justify oneself

rechtlich adj legal; **rechtmäßig** adj legal, lawful

rechts adv on the right; **~ abbiegen** turn right; **~ von** to the right of; **~ oben** at the top right

Rechtsanwalt m, **-anwältin** f lawyer

Rechtschreibung f spelling

Rechtshänder(in) m(f) (-s, -) right-hander; **rechtsherum** adv to the right, clockwise; **rechtsradikal** adj POL extreme right-wing

Rechtsschutzversicherung f legal costs insurance

Rechtsverkehr m driving on the right

rechtswidrig adj illegal

rechtwinklig adj right-angled; **rechtzeitig 1.** adj timely **2.** adv in time

recyceln vt recycle; **Recycling** nt (-s) recycling

Redakteur(in) m(f) editor; **Redaktion** f editing; (people) editorial staff; (place) editorial office(s)

Rede f (-, -n) speech; (conversation) talk; **eine ~ halten** make a speech; **reden 1.** vi talk, speak **2.** vt say; (nonsense etc) talk; **Redewendung** f idiom; **Redner(in)**

m(f) speaker

reduzieren vt reduce

Referat nt (-s, -e) paper; **ein ~ halten** give a paper (über + acc on)

reflektieren vt reflect

Reform f (-, -en) reform; **Reformhaus** nt health food shop; **reformieren** vt reform

Regal nt (-s, -e) shelf; (piece of furniture) shelves pl

Regel f (-, -n) rule; MED period; **regelmäßig** adj regular; **regeln** vt regulate, control; (matter) settle; **Regelung** f regulation

Regen m (-s, -) rain; **Regenbogen** m rainbow; **Regenmantel** m raincoat; **Regenschauer** m shower; **Regenschirm** m umbrella; **Regenwald** m rainforest; **Regenwurm** m earthworm

Regie f direction

regieren vt, vi govern, rule; **Regierung** f government; (of monarch) reign

Region f region; **regional** adj regional

Regisseur(in) m(f) director

regnen vi impers rain; **regnerisch** adj rainy

regulär adj regular; **regulieren** vt regulate, adjust

Reh nt (-(e)s, -e) deer; (meat) venison

Reibe f (-, -n), **Reibeisen** nt grater; **reiben** (rieb, gerieben) vt rub; GASTR grate; **reibungslos** adj smooth

reich adj rich

Reich nt (-(e)s, -e) empire; (of king) kingdom

reichen 1. vi reach; (money, food etc) be enough, be sufficient (jdm for sb) **2.** vt hold out; (give) pass, hand; (serve) offer

reichhaltig adj ample, rich; **reichlich** adj (tip) generous; (meal) ample; **~ Zeit** plenty of time; **Reichtum** m (-s, -tümer) wealth

reif adj ripe; (person, judgment) mature

Reif 1. m (-(e)s) hoarfrost **2.** m (-(e)s, -e) ring, hoop

reifen vi mature; (fruit) ripen

Reifen m (-s, -) ring, hoop; (of car) tyre; **Reifendruck** m tyre pressure; **Reifenpanne** f puncture; **Reifenwechsel** m tyre change

Reihe f (-, -n) row; (of days etc) fam (number) series sg; **der ~ nach** one after the other; **er ist an der ~** it's his turn; **Reihenfolge** f order, sequence; **Reihenhaus** nt terraced house (Brit), row house (US)

Reiher m (-s, -) heron

rein 1. fam contr of **herein, hinein 2.** adj pure; (shirt, air) clean

Reinfall m fam letdown; **reinfallen** irr vi fam **auf etw** acc ~ fall for sth

reinigen vt clean; **Reinigung** f cleaning; (shop) (dry)

cleaner's; **Reinigungsmittel** nt cleaning agent, cleaner

reinlegen vt **jdn** ~ take sb for a ride

Reis m (-es, -e) rice

Reise f (-, -n) journey; (on ship) voyage; **Reiseapotheke** f first-aid kit; **Reisebüro** nt travel agent's; **Reisebus** m coach; **Reiseführer(in)** m(f) courier; (book) guide(book); **Reisegepäck** nt luggage (Brit), baggage; **Reisegesellschaft** f tour party; **Reiseleiter(in)** m(f) courier; **reisen** vi travel; **~ nach** go to; **Reisende(r)** mf traveller; **Reisepass** m passport; **Reisescheck** m traveller's cheque; **Reisetasche** f holdall (Brit), carryall (US); **Reiseveranstalter** m tour operator; **Reiseverkehr** m holiday traffic; **Reiseversicherung** f travel insurance; **Reiseziel** nt destination

reißen (riss, gerissen) vt, vi tear; (move) pull, drag

Reißnagel m drawing pin (Brit), thumbtack (US); **Reißverschluss** m zip (Brit), zipper (US); **Reißzwecke** f drawing pin (Brit), thumbtack (US)

reiten (ritt, geritten) vt, vi ride; **Reiter(in)** m(f) rider

Reiz m (-es, -e) stimulus; (delightfulness) charm; (appeal) attraction; **reizen** vt stimulate; (*make angry*) annoy; (*interest*) appeal to, attract; **reizend** *adj* charming; **Reizung** *f* irritation

Reklamation *f* complaint

Reklame *f* (-, -n) advertising; (*on TV*) commercial

reklamieren *vi* complain (*wegen* about)

Rekord *m* (-(e)s, -e) record

relativ 1. *adj* relative **2.** *adv* relatively

relaxen *vi* relax, chill out

Religion *f* religion; **religiös** *adj* religious

Remoulade *f* (-, -n) tartar sauce

Renaissance *f* renaissance, revival; HIST Renaissance

rennen (*rannte, gerannt*) *vt, vi* run; **Rennen** *nt* (-s, -) running; (*competition*) race; **Rennrad** *nt* racing bike

renommiert *adj* famous, noted (*wegen, für* for)

renovieren *vt* renovate; **Renovierung** *f* renovation

rentabel *adj* profitable

Rente *f* (-, -n) pension; **Rentenversicherung** *f* pension scheme

Rentier *nt* reindeer

rentieren *vr* pay, be profitable

Rentner(in) *m(f)* (-s, -) pensioner, senior citizen

Reparatur *f* repair; **Reparaturwerkstatt** *f* repair shop; AUTO garage; **reparieren** *vt* repair

Reportage *f* report; Repor-

ter(in) *m(f)* (-s, -) reporter

Republik *f* republic

Reservat *nt* (-(e)s, -e) nature reserve; **Reserve** *f* (-, -n) reserve; **Reservekanister** *m* spare can; **Reserverad** *nt* AUTO spare wheel; **Reservespieler(in)** *m(f)* reserve; **reservieren** *vt* reserve; **Reservierung** *f* reservation

resignieren *vi* give up; **resigniert** *adj* resigned

Respekt *m* (-(e)s) respect; **respektieren** *vt* respect

Rest *m* (-(e)s, -e) rest, remainder; (*left over*) remains *pl*

Restaurant *nt* (-s, -s) restaurant

restaurieren *vt* restore

restlich *adj* remaining

Resultat *nt* result

retten *vt* save, rescue

Rettich *m* (-s, -e) radish (*large white or red variety*)

Rettung *f* rescue; (*assistance*) help; (*medical team*) ambulance service; **Rettungsboot** *nt* lifeboat; **Rettungshubschrauber** *m* rescue helicopter; **Rettungsring** *m* lifebelt, life preserver (*US*); **Rettungswagen** *m* ambulance

Reue *f* (-) remorse; regret

revanchieren *vr* (*for help etc*) return the favour

Revolution *f* revolution

Rezept *nt* (-(e)s, -e) GASTR recipe; MED prescription; **rezeptfrei** *adj* over-the-counter, non-prescription

Rezeption f (at hotel) reception

rezeptpflichtig adj available only on prescription

Rhabarber m (-s) rhubarb

Rhein m (-s) Rhine; **Rheinland-Pfalz** nt (-) Rhineland-Palatinate

Rheuma nt (-s) rheumatism

Rhythmus m rhythm

richten 1. vt direct (auf + acc to); (weapon, camera) point (auf + acc at); (letter, inquiry) address (an + acc to) 2. vr **sich ~ nach** (rule etc) keep to; (fashion, example) follow; (vary according to) depend on

Richter(in) m(f) (-s, -) judge

Richtgeschwindigkeit f recommended speed

richtig 1. adj right, correct; (genuine) proper; **etw ~ stellen** correct sth 2. adv fam (very) really

Richtlinie f guideline

Richtung f direction; (trend) tendency

rieb imperf of **reiben**

riechen (roch, gerochen) vt, vi smell; **nach etw ~** smell of sth

rief imperf of **rufen**

Riegel m (-s, -) bolt; GASTR (of chocolate) bar

Riese m (-n, -n) giant; **Riesengarnele** f king prawn; **riesengroß** adj gigantic, huge; **Riesenrad** nt big

wheel; **riesig** adj enormous, huge

riet imperf of **raten ~**

Riff nt (-(e)s, -e) reef

Rind nt (-(e)s, -er) cow; (male) bull; GASTR beef; **~er** pl cattle pl

Rinde f (-, -n) (of tree) bark; (of cheese) rind; (of bread) crust

Rinderbraten m roast beef; **Rindfleisch** nt beef

Ring m (-(e)s, -e) ring; (round town) ring road; **Ringfinger** m ring finger; **ringsherum** adv round about

Rippe f (-, -n) rib

Risiko nt (-s, -s or Risiken) risk; **auf eigenes ~** at one's own risk; **riskant** adj risky; **riskieren** vt risk

riss imperf of **reißen**

Riss m (-es, -e) tear; (in wall, cup etc) crack; **rissig** adj cracked; (skin) chapped

ritt imperf of **reiten**

Ritter m (-s, -) knight

Rivale m (-n, -n), **Rivalin** f rival

Robbe f (-, -n) seal

Roboter m (-s, -) robot

robust adj robust

roch imperf of **riechen**

Rock m (-(e)s, Röcke) skirt

Rockmusik f rock (music)

Rodelbahn f toboggan run; **rodeln** vi toboggan

Roggen m (-s, -) rye; **Roggenbrot** nt rye bread

roh adj raw; (person) coarse,

crude; **Rohkost** f raw vegetables and fruit pl

Rohr nt (-(e)s, -e) pipe; **Röhre** f (-, -n) tube; (in cooker) oven; **Rohrzucker** m cane sugar

Rohstoff m raw material

Rokoko nt (-s) rococo

Rolle f (-, -n) roll; THEAT role

rollen vt, vi roll

Roller (-s, -) scooter

Rollerskates pl roller skates pl

Rollkragenpullover m polo-neck (Brit) (or turtleneck (US)) sweater; **Rollladen** m, **Rollo** m (-s, -s) (roller) shutters pl; **Rollschuh** m roller skate; **Rollstuhl** m wheelchair; **rollstuhlgerecht** adj suitable for wheelchairs; **Rolltreppe** f escalator

Roman m (-s, -e) novel

Romantik f romance; **romantisch** adj romantic

römisch-katholisch adj Roman Catholic

röntgen vt X-ray; **Röntgenaufnahme** f, **Röntgenbild** nt X-ray; **Röntgenstrahlen** pl X-rays pl

rosa adj inv pink

Rose f (-, -n) rose

Rosenkohl m (Brussels) sprouts pl

Rosé(wein) m rosé (wine)

rosig adj rosy

Rosine f raisin

Rosmarin m (-s) rosemary

Rost m (-(e)s, -e) rust; (for roasting) grill, gridiron; **Rostbratwurst** f grilled sausage; **rosten** vi rust; **rösten** vt roast, grill; (bread) toast; **rostfrei** adj rustproof; (steel) stainless; **rostig** adj rusty

rot adj red; **~ werden** blush; **~e Karte** red card; **~e Be(e)te** beetroot; **bei Rot über die Ampel fahren** jump the lights; **das Rote Kreuz** the Red Cross

Röteln pl German measles sg

rothaarig adj red-haired

rotieren vi rotate

Rotkehlchen nt robin; **Rotkohl** m, **Rotkraut** nt red cabbage; **Rotlichtviertel** nt red-light district; **Rotwein** m red wine

Rouge nt (-s, -s) rouge

Route f (-, -n) route

Routine f experience; (drudgery) routine

Rubbellos nt scratchcard; **rubbeln** vt rub

Rübe f (-, -n) turnip; **Gelbe ~** carrot; **Rote ~** beetroot

rüber fam contr of **herüber, hinüber**

Rubin m (-s, -e) ruby

rücken vt, vi move; **könntest du ein bisschen ~?** could you move over a bit?

Rücken m (-s, -) back; **Rückenlehne** f back(rest); **Rückenmark** nt spinal cord; **Rückenschmerzen** pl backache sg; **Rückenschwim-**

men *nt* (-s) backstroke; **Rück-
enwind** *m* tailwind

Rückerstattung *f* refund;
Rückfahrkarte *f* return tick-
et (*Brit*), round-trip ticket
(*US*); **Rückfahrt** *f* return
journey; **Rückfall** *m* relapse;
Rückflug *m* return flight;
Rückgabe *f* return; **rückgängig** machen **etw** ~ **machen**
cancel sth; **Rückgrat** *nt*
(-(e)s, -e) spine, backbone;
Rückkehr *f* (-, -en) return;
Rücklicht *nt* rear light;
Rückreise *f* return journey;
auf der ~ on the way back
Rucksack *m* rucksack, backpack; **Rucksacktourist(in)**
m(f) backpacker
Rückschritt *m* step back;
Rückseite *f* back; **siehe** ~
see overleaf
Rücksicht *f* consideration; ~
nehmen auf + *acc* show consideration for; **rücksichtslos** *adj* inconsiderate; (*driving*) reckless; **rücksichtsvoll** *adj* considerate
Rücksitz *m* back seat; **Rückspiegel** *m* AUTO rear-view
mirror; **Rückvergütung** *f* refund; **rückwärts** *adv* backwards, back; **Rückwärts-
gang** *m* AUTO reverse (gear);
Rückweg *m* return journey,
way back; **Rückzahlung** *f* re-
payment; **Rückzieher** *m* **einen** ~ **machen** back out
Ruder *nt* (-s, -) oar; (*at back of
boat*) rudder; **Ruderboot** *nt*

rowing boat (*Brit*), rowboat
(*US*); **rudern** *vt, vi* row
Ruf *m* (-(e)s, -e) call, cry; (*of
artist, company etc*) reputation; **rufen** (*rief, gerufen*)
vt, vi call; (*shout*) cry; **Ruf-
nummer** *f* telephone number
Ruhe *f* (-) rest; (*untroubled
state*) peace, quiet; (*stillness*)
calm; (*no talking*) silence;
lass mich in ~**!** leave me
alone; **ruhen** *vi* rest; **Ruhestand** *m* retirement; **im** ~
sein be retired; **Ruhetag** *m*
closing day; **montags** ~ **haben** be closed on Mondays
ruhig *adj* quiet; (*motionless*)
still; (*hand*) steady; (*composed, peaceful*) calm
Ruhm *m* (-(e)s) fame, glory
Rührei *nt* scrambled egg(s);
rühren **1.** *vt* move; (*with
spoon etc*) stir **2.** *vr* move;
(*speak*) say something; **rührend** *adj* touching, moving
Ruine *f* (-, -n) ruin; **ruinieren**
vt ruin
rülpsen *vi* burp, belch
rum *fam contr of* **herum**
Rum *m* (-s, -s) rum
Rumänien *nt* (-s) Romania
Rummel *m* (-s) hustle and
bustle; (*event*) fair; (*in the
media*) hype; **Rummelplatz**
m fairground
rumoren *vi* **es rumort in meinem Bauch / Kopf** my stomach is rumbling / my head is
spinning

Rumpf m (-(e)s, Rümpfe) ANAT trunk; AVIAT fuselage; NAUT hull

Rumpsteak nt rump steak

rund 1. adj round **2.** adv (approximately) around; **~ um etw** (a)round sth; **Runde** f (-, -n) round; (in race) lap; **Rundfahrt** f tour (durch of); **Rundfunk** m (organization) broadcasting service; **im ~** on the radio; **Rundgang** m tour (durch of); **Rundreise** f tour (durch of)

runter fam contr of **herunter, hinunter**; **runterscrollen** vt IT scroll down

runzeln vt **die Stirn ~** frown;

runzelig adj wrinkled

ruppig adj gruff

Ruß m (-es) soot

Russe m (-n, -n) Russian

Rüssel m (-s, -) (of elephant) trunk; (of pig) snout

Russin f Russian; **russisch** adj Russian; **Russisch** nt Russian; **Russland** nt Russia

Rüstung f (of knight) armour; (weapons etc) armaments pl

Rutsch m (-(e)s, -e) **guten ~ (ins neue Jahr)!** Happy New Year; **Rutschbahn** f, **Rutsche** f slide; **rutschen** vi slide; (accidentally) slip; **rutschig** adj slippery

rütteln vt, vi shake

S

s. abbr = **siehe**; see; **S.** abbr = **Seite**; p.

Saal m (-(e)s, Säle) hall; (for meetings) room

Saarland nt Saarland

sabotieren vt sabotage

Sache f (-, -n) thing; (situation, event) affair, business; (issue) matter; **bei der ~ bleiben** keep to the point; **sachkundig** adj competent; **Sachlage** f situation; **sachlich** adj (unemotional) matter-of-fact; (error, account) factual; **sächlich** adj LING neuter; **Sachschaden** m material damage

Sachsen nt (-s) Saxony; **Sachsen-Anhalt** nt (-s) Saxony-Anhalt

sacht(e) adv softly, gently

Sachverständige(r) mf expert

Sack m (-(e)s, Säcke) sack; pej bastard, bugger; **Sackgasse** f dead end, cul-de-sac

Safe m (-s, -s) safe

Safer Sex m safe sex

Safran m (-s, -e) saffron

Saft m (-(e)s, Säfte) juice; **saftig** adj juicy

Sage f (-, -n) legend

Säge f (-, -n) saw

sagen vt, vi say (jdm to sb),

tell (*jdm sb*); **wie sagt man ... auf Englisch?** what's ... in English?; **ich will dir mal was ~** let me tell you something

sägen vt, vi saw

sah imperf of **sehen**

Sahne f (-) cream; **Sahnetorte** f gateau

Saison f (-, -s) season; **außerhalb der ~** out of season

Saite f (-, -n) string

Sakko nt (-s, -s) jacket

Salami f (-, -s) salami

Salat m (-(e)s, -e) salad; (*vegetable*) lettuce; **Salatbar** f salad bar; **Salatschüssel** f salad bowl; **Salatsoße** f salad dressing

Salbe f (-, -n) ointment

Salbei m (-s) sage

Salmonellenvergiftung f salmonella (poisoning)

Salsamusik f salsa (music)

Salto m (-s, -s) somersault

Salz nt (-es, -e) salt; **salzarm** adj low-salt; **salzen** (*salzte, gesalzen*) vt salt; **salzig** adj salty; **Salzkartoffeln** pl boiled potatoes pl; **Salzstange** f pretzel stick; **Salzstreuer** m salt cellar (*Brit*) (or shaker (*US*)); **Salzwasser** nt salt water

Samba f (-, -s) samba

Samen m (-s, -) seed; (*of male*) sperm

sammeln vt collect; **Sammlung** f collection

Samstag m Saturday; → **Mitt-**

woch; **samstags** adv on Saturdays; → **mittwochs**

samt prep + dat (along) with, together with

Samt m (-(e)s, -e) velvet

sämtliche(r, s) adj all (the)

Sanatorium nt (-s, *Sanatorien*) sanatorium (*Brit*), sanitarium (*US*)

Sand m (-(e)s, -e) sand

Sandale f (-, -n) sandal

sandig adj sandy; **Sandkasten** m sandpit (*Brit*), sandbox (*US*); **Sandstrand** m sandy beach

sandte imperf of **senden**

sanft adj soft, gentle

sang imperf of **singen**

Sänger(in) m(f) (-s, -) singer

Sangria f (-, -s) sangria

sanieren vt redevelop; (*building*) renovate; (*business*) restore to profitability

sanitär adj sanitary; **~e Anlagen** pl sanitation

Sanitäter(in) m(f) (-s, -) ambulance man / woman, paramedic

sank imperf of **sinken**

Sardelle f anchovy

Sarg m (-(e)s, *Särge*) coffin

saß imperf of **sitzen**

Satellit m (-en, -en) satellite; **Satellitenfernsehen** nt satellite TV; **Satellitenschüssel** f fam satellite dish

satt adj full; (*colour*) rich, deep; **~ sein** (*after meal*) be full; **~ machen** be filling; **jdn/etw ~ sein** (or **haben**)

be fed up with sb/sth
Sattel m (-s, **Sättel**) saddle
Saturn m (-s) Saturn
Satz m (-es, **Sätze**) LING sentence; MUS movement; (in tennis) set; (of coffee) grounds pl; (leap) jump; COMM rate
Sau f (-, **Säue**) sow; pej dirty bugger
sauber adj clean; (ironic) fine; ~ **machen** clean; **Sauberkeit** f cleanness; (hygiene) cleanliness; **säubern** vt clean
saublöd adj fam really stupid, dumb
Sauce f (-, -n) sauce; (with meat) gravy
Saudi-Arabien nt (-s) Saudi Arabia
sauer adj sour; CHEM acid; fam (annoyed) cross; **saurer Regen** acid rain; **Sauerkirsche** f sour cherry; **Sauerkraut** nt sauerkraut; **säuerlich** adj slightly sour; **Sauerrahm** m sour cream; **Sauerstoff** m oxygen
saufen (soff, gesoffen) **1.** vt drink; fam (person) knock back **2.** vi drink; fam (person) booze
saugen (sog or saugte, gesogen or gesaugt) vt, vi suck; (with cleaner) vacuum, hoover (Brit); **Säugetier** nt mammal; **Säugling** m infant, baby
Säule f (-, -n) column, pillar
Saum m (-es, **Säume**) hem;

(join) seam
Sauna f (-, -s) sauna
Säure f (-, -n) acid
Saustall m pigsty; **Sauwetter** nt **was für ein ~** fam what lousy weather
Saxophon nt (-s, -e) saxophone
S-Bahn f suburban railway; **S-Bahn-Haltestelle** f, **S-Bahnhof** m suburban (train) station
scannen vt scan; **Scanner** m (-s, -) scanner
schäbig adj shabby
Schach nt (-s, -s) chess; (position) check; **Schachbrett** nt chessboard; **Schachfigur** f chess piece; **schachmatt** adj checkmate
Schacht m (-(e)s, **Schächte**) shaft
Schachtel f (-, -n) box
schade interj what a pity
Schädel m (-s, -) skull; **Schädelbruch** m fractured skull
schaden vt damage, harm (jdm sb); **das schadet nichts** it won't do any harm; **Schaden** m (-s, **Schäden**) damage; (to body) injury; (bad thing) disadvantage; **einen ~ verursachen** cause damage; **Schadenersatz** m compensation, damages pl; **schadhaft** adj faulty; damaged; **schädigen** vt damage; (person) do harm to, harm; **schädlich** adj harmful (für to); **Schadstoff** m harmful

substance; **schadstoffarm** *adj* low-emission

Schaf *nt* (-(e)s, -e) sheep; **Schäfer** *m* (-s, -) shepherd; **Schäferhund** *m* Alsatian (*Brit*), German shepherd; **Schäferin** *f* shepherdess

schaffen 1. *vt* (*schuf, geschaffen*) *vt* create; (*room*) make **2.** *vt* manage, do; (*complete*) finish; (*exam*) pass; **jdm zu ~ machen** give sb trouble

Schaffner(in) *m(f)* (-s, -) (*in bus*) conductor / conductress; **RAIL** guard

Schafskäse *m* sheep's (milk) cheese

schal *adj* (*drink*) flat

Schal *m* (-s, -e *or* -s) scarf

Schale *f* (-, -n) skin; (*removed*) peel; (*of nut, mussel, egg*) shell; (*container*) bowl, dish

schälen 1. *vt* peel; (*tomato, almonds*) skin; (*peas, eggs, nuts*) shell; (*grain*) husk **2.** *vr* peel

Schall *m* (-(e)s, -e) sound; **Schalldämpfer** *m* (-s, -) AUTO silencer (*Brit*), muffler (*US*); **Schallplatte** *f* record

Schalotte *f* (-, -n) shallot

schalten 1. *vt* switch **2.** *vi* AUTO change gear; **Schalter** *m* (-s, -) (*at post office, bank*) counter; (*electrical*) switch; **Schalterhalle** *f* main hall; **Schalthebel** *m* gear lever (*Brit*) (*or* shift (*US*)); **Schalt-jahr** *nt* leap year; **Schalt-**

Schutz substance

knüppel *m* gear lever (*Brit*) (or shift (*US*)); **Schaltung** *f* gear change (*Brit*), gearshift (*US*)

Scham *f* (-) shame; modesty; **schämen** *vr* be ashamed

Schande *f* (-) disgrace

Schanze *f* (-, -n) ski jump

Schar *f* (-, -en) (*of birds*) flock; (*of people*) crowd; **in ~en** in droves

scharf *adj* (*knife, criticism*) sharp; (*spicy*) hot; **auf etw acc ~ sein** *fam* be keen on sth

Schärfe *f* (-, -n) sharpness; (*severity*) rigour; PHOT focus

Scharlach *m* (-s) MED scarlet fever

Scharnier *nt* (-s, -e) hinge

Schaschlik *m or nt* (-s, -s) (shish) kebab

Schatten *m* (-s, -) shadow; **30 Grad im ~** 30 degrees in the shade; **schattig** *adj* shady

Schatz *m* (-es, *Schätze*) treasure; (*person*) love

schätzen *vt* estimate; (*object*) value; (*appreciate*) value, esteem; (*think*) reckon; **Schätzung** *f* estimate; (*action*) estimation; (*of object*) valuation; **schätzungsweise** *adv* roughly, approximately

schauen *vi* look; **ich schau mal, ob ...** I'll go and have a look whether ...; **schau, dass ...** see (to it) that ...

Schauer *m* (-s, -) (*rain*) shower; (*shiver*) shudder

Schaufel f (-, -n) shovel; ~ **und Besen** dustpan and brush; **schaufeln** vt shovel
Schaufenster nt shop window
Schaukel f (-, -n) swing; **schaukeln** vi rock; (on a swing) swing; **Schaukelstuhl** m rocking chair
Schaum m (-(e)s, Schäume) foam; (from soap) lather; (on beer) froth; **Schaumbad** nt bubble bath; **schäumen** vi foam; **Schaumfestiger** m (-s, -) styling mousse; **Schaumgummi** m foam (rubber); **Schaumwein** m sparkling wine
Schauplatz m scene
Schauspiel nt spectacle; THEAT play; **Schauspieler(in)** m(f) actor / actress
Scheck m (-s, -s) cheque; **Scheckheft** nt chequebook; **Scheckkarte** f cheque card
Scheibe f (-, -n) disc; (of bread, cheese etc) slice; (of glass) pane; **Scheibenwischer** m (-s, -) AUTO windscreen (Brit) (or windshield (US)) wiper
Scheich m (-s, -s) sheik(h)
Scheide f (-, -n) ANAT vagina
scheiden (schied, geschieden) vt separate; **sich ~ lassen** get a divorce; **sie hat sich von ihm ~ lassen** she divorced him; **Scheidung** f divorce
Schein m (-(e)s, -e) light; (ex-

ternal impression) appearance; (money) (bank)note; **scheinbar** adj apparent; **scheinen** (schien, geschienen) vi (sun) shine; (appear) seem; **Scheinwerfer** m (-s, -) floodlight; THEAT spotlight; AUTO headlight
Scheiß- in cpds vulg damned, bloody (Brit); **Scheiße** f (Brit) vulg shit, crap; **scheißegal** adj vulg **das ist mir ~** I don't give a damn (or toss); **scheißen** (schiss, geschissen) vi vulg shit
Scheitel m (-s, -) parting (Brit), part (US)
scheitern vi fail (an + dat because of)
Schellfisch m haddock
Schema nt (-s, -s or Schemata) scheme, plan; (drawing) diagram
Schenkel m (-s, -) thigh
schenken vt give; **er hat es mir geschenkt** he gave it to me (as a present); **sich** dat **etw ~** fam skip sth
Scherbe f (-, -n) broken piece, fragment
Schere f (-, -n) scissors pl; (large) shears pl; **eine ~** a pair of scissors / shears
Scherz m (-es, -e) joke
scheu adj shy
scheuen 1. vr **sich ~ vor** + dat be afraid of, shrink from **2.** vt shun **3.** vi (horse) shy
scheuern vt scrub; **jdm eine ~** fam slap sb in the face

Scheune f (-, -n) barn
scheußlich adj dreadful
Schi m (-s, -er) → **Ski**
Schicht f (-, -en) layer; (in society) class; (in factory etc) shift
schick adj stylish, chic
schicken 1. vt send **2.** vr hurry up
Schickimicki m (-(s), -s) fam trendy
Schicksal nt (-s, -e) fate
Schiebedach nt AUTO sunroof; **schieben** (schob, geschoben) vt, vi push; **die Schuld auf jdn ~** put the blame on sb; **Schiebetür** f sliding door
schied imperf of **scheiden**
Schiedsrichter(in) m(f) referee, umpire
schief 1. adj crooked **2.** adv crooked(ly); **~ gehen** fam go wrong
schielen vi squint
schien imperf of **scheinen**
Schienbein nt shin
Schiene f (-, -n) rail; MED splint
schießen (schoss, geschossen) **1.** vt shoot; (ball) kick; (goal) score; (photo) take **2.** vi shoot (auf + acc at)
Schiff nt (-(e)s, -e) ship; (in church) nave; **Schifffahrt** f shipping; **Schiffsreise** f voyage
schikanieren vt harass; (at school) bully
Schild 1. m (-(e)s, -e) (of war-

rior) shield **2.** nt (-(e)s, -er) sign; **was steht über dem ~?** what does the sign say?
Schilddrüse f thyroid gland
schildern vt describe
Schildkröte f tortoise; (living in water) turtle
Schimmel m (-s, -) mould; (animal) white horse; **schimmeln** vi go mouldy
schimpfen 1. vt tell off **2.** vi complain; **mit jdm ~** tell sb off; **Schimpfwort** nt swearword
Schinken m (-s, -) ham
Schirm m (-(e)s, -e) umbrella; (for sun) parasol, sunshade
schiss imperf of **scheißen**
Schlacht f (-, -en) battle; **schlachten** vt slaughter; **Schlachter(in)** m(f) (-s, -) butcher; **Schlachtfeld** nt battlefield
Schlaf m (-(e)s) sleep; **Schlafanzug** m pyjamas pl; **Schlafcouch** f bed settee
Schläfe f (-, -n) temple
schlafen (schlief, geschlafen) vi sleep; **schlaf gut!** sleep well! **hast du gut geschlafen?** did you sleep all right?; **er schläft noch** he's still asleep; **~ gehen** go to bed
schlaff adj slack; (weak) limp; (tired) exhausted
Schlafgelegenheit f place to sleep; **Schlaflosigkeit** f sleeplessness; **schläfrig** adj sleepy; **Schlafsack** m sleeping bag; **Schlaftablette** f

sleeping pill; **Schlafwagen**
m sleeping car, sleeper;
Schlafzimmer *nt* bedroom
Schlag *m* (-(e)s, **Schläge**)
blow; ELEC shock; **Schlagader** *f* artery; **Schlaganfall**
m MED stroke; **Schlagartig**
adj sudden; **Schlagbohrma-
schine** *f* hammer drill
schlagen (*schlug*, *geschlagen*)
1. *vt* hit; (*hit repeatedly, defeat*) beat; (*cream*) whip **2.**
vi (*heart*) beat; (*clock*)
strike; **mit dem Kopf gegen
etw ~** bang one's head
against sth **3.** *vr* fight
Schläger *m* (-s, -) SPORT bat;
racket; (*golf*) club; hockey
stick; (*person*) brawler;
Schlägerei *f* fight, brawl
schlagfertig *adj* quick-wit-
ted; **Schlagloch** *nt* pothole;
Schlagsahne *f* whipping
cream; (*beaten*) whipped
cream; **Schlagzeile** *f* headline; **Schlagzeug** *nt* drums
pl; (*in orchestra*) percussion
Schlamm *m* (-(e)s, -e) mud
schlampig *adj fam* sloppy
schlang *imperf of* **schlingen**
Schlange *f* (-, -n) snake; (*of
people*) queue (*Brit*), line
(*US*); **~ stehen** queue (*Brit*),
stand in line (*US*)
schlank *adj* slim
schlapp *adj* limp
Schlappe *f* (-, -n) *fam* setback
schlau *adj* clever, smart; (*wi-
ly*) crafty, cunning
Schlauch *m* (-(e)s, **Schläuche**)

hose; (*in tyre*) inner tube;
Schlauchboot *nt* rubber
dinghy
schlecht 1. *adj* bad; **mir ist ~** I
feel sick; **jdn ~ machen** run
sb down; **die Milch ist ~**
the milk has gone off **2.**
adv badly; **es geht ihm ~**
he's having a hard time;
(*health-wise*) he's not feeling
well; (*financially*) he's pretty
hard up
schleichen (*schlich, geschlichen*) *vi* creep
Schleier *m* (-s, -) veil
Schleife *f* (-, -n) IT, AVIAT, ELEC
loop; (*ribbon*) bow
Schleim *m* (-(e)s, -e) slime;
MED mucus; **Schleimer** *m*
(-s, -) *fam* creep; **Schleim-
haut** *f* mucous membrane
schlendern *vi* stroll
schleppen *vt* drag; (*car, ship*)
tow; (*carry*) lug; **Schlepplift**
m ski tow
Schleswig-Holstein *nt* (-s)
Schleswig-Holstein
Schleuder *f* (-, -n) catapult;
(*for washing*) spin-dryer;
schleudern 1. *vt* hurl; (*washing*) spin-dry **2.** *vi* AUTO
skid; **Schleudersitz** *m* ejec-
tor seat
schleunigst *adv* straight
away
schlich *imperf of* **schleichen**
schlicht *adj* simple, plain
schlichten *vt* (*dispute*) settle
schlief *imperf of* **schlafen**
schließen (*schloss, geschlos-*

sen) vt, vi, vr close, shut;
(*bring to an end*) close;
(*friendship, alliance, marriage*) enter into; (*deduce*) infer
(*aus from*); **Schließfach** nt
locker

schließlich adv finally;
(*when all is said and done*)
after all

schliff imperf of **schleifen**

schlimm adj bad; **schlimmer**
adj worse; **schlimmste(r, s)**
adj worst; **schlimmstenfalls**
adv at (the) worst

Schlips m (-es, -e) tie

Schlitten m (-s, -) sledge, toboggan; (*with horses*) sleigh;
Schlittenfahren nt (-s) tobogganing

Schlittschuh m ice skate; ~
laufen ice-skate

Schlitz m (-es, -e) slit; (*for
coin*) slot; (*on trousers*) flies
pl

schloss imperf of **schließen**

Schloss nt (-es, Schlösser)
lock; (*building*) castle

Schlosser(in) m(f) mechanic

Schlucht f (-, -en) gorge, ravine

schluchzen vi sob

Schluckauf m (-s) hiccups pl;
schlucken vt, vi swallow

schlug imperf of **schlagen**

schlüpfrig adj slippery; fig
risqué

schlürfen vt, vi slurp

Schluss m (-es, Schlüsse)
end; (*deduction*) conclusion;
am ~ at the end; **mit jdm** ~

machen finish (*or* split up)
with sb

Schlüssel m (-s, -) a. fig key;
Schlüsselbein nt collarbone; **Schlüsselblume** f
cowslip; **Schlüsselbund** m
bunch of keys; **Schlüsselloch** nt keyhole

Schlussfolgerung f conclusion; **Schlusslicht** nt tail-light; fig tail-ender;
Schlusspfiff m final whistle;
Schlussverkauf m clearance sale

schmal adj narrow; (*person,
book etc*) slim

Schmalz nt (-es, -e) dripping,
lard

schmatzen vi eat noisily

schmecken vt, vi taste (*nach*
of); **es schmeckt ihm** he
likes it; **lass es dir ~!** bon
appétit

Schmeichelei f flattery;
schmeichelhaft adj flattering; **schmeicheln** vi jdm ~
flatter sb

schmeißen (schmiss, geschmissen) vt fam chuck,
throw

schmelzen (schmolz, geschmolzen) vt, vi melt

Schmerz m (-es, -en)
(*sorrow*) grief; **~en haben**
be in pain; **~en im Rücken
haben** have a pain in one's
back; **schmerzen** vt, vi hurt;
Schmerzensgeld nt compensation; **schmerzhaft**,
schmerzlich adj painful;

Schmerzmittel *nt* painkiller; schmerzstillend *adj* painkilling; Schmerztablette *f* painkiller

Schmetterling *m* butterfly

schmieden *vt* forge; (*plans*) make

schmieren 1. *vt* smear; (*machine, bicycle etc*) lubricate, grease; (*person*) bribe 2. *vt*, *vi* (*write*) scrawl; Schmiergeld *nt* fam bribe; schmierig *adj* greasy; Schmiermittel *nt* lubricant; Schmierpapier *nt* scrap paper

Schminke *f* (-, -n) make-up; schminken *vr* put one's make-up on

schmiss *imperf of* schmeißen

schmollen *vi* sulk

schmolz *imperf of* schmelzen

Schmuck *m* (-(e)s, -e) jewellery (*Brit*), jewelry (*US*); (*ornament*) decoration; schmücken *vt* decorate

schmuggeln *vt*, *vi* smuggle

schmunzeln *vi* smile

schmusen *vi* (kiss and) cuddle

Schmutz *m* (-es) dirt, filth; schmutzig *adj* dirty

Schnabel *m* (-s, Schnäbel) beak, bill; (*for pouring*) spout

Schnake *f* (-, -n) mosquito

Schnäppchen *nt fam* bargain; schnappen 1. *vt* catch 2. *vi* nach Luft ~ gasp for

breath; Schnappschuss *m* PHOT snap(shot)

Schnaps *m* (-es, Schnäpse) schnapps

schnarchen *vi* snore

schnaufen *vi* puff, pant

Schnauzbart *m* moustache; Schnauze *f* (-, -n) snout, muzzle; (*for pouring*) spout; *fam* (mouth) trap; die ~ voll haben have had enough

schnäuzen *vr* blow one's nose

Schnecke *f* (-, -n) snail; Schneckenhaus *nt* snail's shell

Schnee *m* (-s) snow; Schneeball *m* snowball; Schneebrille *f* snow goggles *pl*; Schneeflocke *f* snowflake; Schneeglöckchen *nt* snowdrop; Schneegrenze *f* snowline; Schneekanone *f* snow thrower; Schneekette *f* AUTO snow chain; Schneemann *m* snowman; Schneematsch *m* slush; Schneepflug *m* snowplough; Schneeregen *m* sleet; Schneesturm *m* snowstorm, blizzard; Schneetreiben *nt* light blizzards *pl*; Schneewehe *f* snowdrift

Schneide *f* (-, -n) edge; (*part of knife*) blade; schneiden (*schnitt, geschnitten*) 1. *vt* cut; sich *dat* die Haare ~ lassen have one's hair cut 2. *vr* cut oneself; Schneider(in) *m(f)* (-s, -) tailor; dressmaker; **Schneidezahn** m incisor

schneien vi impers snow

schnell 1. adj quick, fast **2.** adv quickly, fast; **mach ~!** hurry up; **Schnelldienst** m express service; **Schnellhefter** m loose-leaf binder; **Schnellimbiss** m snack bar; **Schnellstraße** f expressway

schneuzen vr → **schnäuzen**

schnitt imperf of **schneiden**

Schnitt m (-(e)s, -e) cut; (where lines cross) intersection; (diagram) (cross) section; (of quantities) average; **Schnittblume** f cut flower; **Schnitte** f (-, -n) slice; (with filling) sandwich; **Schnittkäse** m cheese slices pl; **Schnittlauch** m chives pl; **Schnittstelle** f IT, fig interface; **Schnittwunde** f cut, gash

Schnitzel nt (-s, -) (of paper) scrap; GASTR escalope

schnitzen vt carve

Schnorchel m (-s, -) snorkel; **schnorcheln** vi go snorkelling, snorkel; **Schnorcheln** nt (-s) snorkelling

schnüffeln vi sniff

Schnuller m (-s, -) dummy (Brit), pacifier (US)

Schnulze f (-, -n) (film, novel) weepie

Schnupfen m (-s, -) cold

schnuppern vi sniff

Schnur f (-, Schnüre) string, cord; ELEC lead; **schnurlos**

adj cordless

Schnurrbart m moustache

schnurren vi purr

Schnürschuh m lace-up (shoe); **Schnürsenkel** m (-s, -) shoelace

schob imperf of **schieben**

Schock m (-(e)s, -e) shock; **unter ~ stehen** be in a state of shock; **schockieren** vt shock

Schokolade f chocolate; **Schokoriegel** m chocolate bar

Scholle f (-, -n) plaice; (on sea) ice floe

schon adv already; **ist er ~ da?** is he here yet?; **warst du ~ einmal da?** have you ever been there?; **ich war ~ einmal da** I've been there before; **~ damals** even then; **~ 1999** as early (or as long ago) as 1999

schön adj beautiful; (kind) nice; (woman) beautiful, pretty; (man) beautiful, handsome; (weather) fine; **~e Grüße** best wishes; **~es Wochenende** have a nice weekend

schonen 1. vt look after **2.** vr take it easy

Schönheit f beauty

Schonkost f light diet

Schöpfung f creation

Schoppen m (-s, -) glass (of wine)

Schorf m (-(e)s, -e) scab

Schorle f (-, -n) spritzer

Schornstein *m* chimney;
Schornsteinfeger(in) *m(f)*
(-s, -) chimney sweep

schoss *imperf of schießen*

Schoß *m* (-es, Schöße) lap

Schotte *m* (-n, -n) Scot, Scotsman; Schottin *f* Scot, Scotswoman; schottisch *adj*
Scottish, Scots; Schottland
nt Scotland

schräg *adj* slanting; *(roof)*
sloping; *(line)* diagonal;
fam (unconventional) wacky

Schrank *m* (-(e)s, Schränke)
cupboard; *(for clothes)*
wardrobe (Brit), closet (US)

Schranke *f* (-, -n) barrier

Schrankwand *f* wall unit

Schraube *f* (-, -n) screw;
schrauben *vt* screw;
Schraubenschlüssel *m*
spanner; Schraubenzieher
m (-s, -) screwdriver;
Schraubverschluss *m*
screw top, screw cap

Schreck *m* (-(e)s, -e), Schrecken *m* (-s, -) terror; *(momentary)* fright; *jdm einen
~ einjagen* give sb a fright;
schreckhaft *adj* jumpy;
schrecklich *adj* terrible,
dreadful

Schrei *m* (-(e)s, -e) scream;
(call) shout

Schreibblock *m* writing pad;
schreiben *(schrieb, geschrieben) vt, vi* write; spell;
wie schreibt man ...? how
do you spell ...?; Schreiben
nt (-s, -) writing; *(sent to*

sb) letter; Schreibfehler *m*
spelling mistake; schreibgeschützt *adj* write-protected; Schreibtisch *m*
desk; Schreibware *pl* stationery *sg*; Schreibwarenladen *m* stationer's

schreien *(schrie, geschrie(e)n)*
vt, vi scream; *(call)* shout

Schreiner(in) *m(f)* joiner;
Schreinerei *f* joiner's workshop

schrie *imperf of schreien*

schrieb *imperf of schreiben*

Schrift *f* (-, -en) *(by hand)*
handwriting; *(printing style)*
typeface; *(type)* font;
schriftlich **1.** *adj* written **2.**
adv in writing; *würden Sie
uns das bitte ~ geben?*
could we have that in writing, please?; Schriftsteller(in) *m(f)* (-s, -) writer

Schritt *m* (-(e)s, -e) step; *~ für
~* step by step; Schrittgeschwindigkeit *f* walking
speed; Schrittmacher *m*
MED pacemaker

Schrott *m* (-(e)s, -e) scrap
metal; *fig* rubbish

schrubben *vi, vt* scrub;
Schrubber *m* (-s, -) scrubbing brush

schrumpfen *vi* shrink

Schubkarren *m* (-s, -) wheelbarrow; Schublade *f* drawer

schuben *vt* shove, push

schüchtern *adj* shy

schuf *imperf of schaffen*

Schuh *m* (-(e)s, -e) shoe;

Schuhcreme f shoe polish;
Schuhgeschäft nt shoe
shop; Schuhgröße f shoe
size; Schuhlöffel m shoe-
horn; Schuhsohle f sole
Schulabschluss m school-
-leaving qualification
schuld adj wer ist ~ daran?
whose fault is it?; er ist ~
it's his fault, he's to blame;
Schuld f (-) guilt; (blame)
fault; ~ haben to be blame
(an + dat for); er hat ~ it's
his fault; schulden vt owe
(jdm etw sb sth); Schulden
pl debts pl; ~ haben be in
debt; ~ machen run up
debts; seine ~ bezahlen
pay off one's debts; schuldig
adj guilty (an + dat of); (proper) due; jdm etw ~ sein owe
sb sth
Schule f (-, -n) school; in der ~
at school; in die ~ gehen go
to school; Schüler(in) m(f)
(-s, -) pupil; (older) student;
Schüleraustausch m school
exchange; Schulfach nt subject; Schulferien pl school
holidays pl (Brit) (or vacation (US)); schulfrei adj
morgen ist ~ there's no
school tomorrow; Schul-
freund(in) m(f) schoolmate;
Schuljahr nt school year;
Schulkenntnisse pl ~ in
Französisch school(-level)
French; Schulklasse f class;
Schulleiter(in) m(f) headmaster / headmistress (Brit),

principal (US)
Schulter f (-, -n) shoulder
Schulung f (-) training; (event)
training course
Schund m (-(e)s) trash
Schuppe f (-, -n) (of fish)
scale; Schuppen pl dan-
druff sg
Schürfwunde f graze
Schürze f (-, -n) apron
Schuss m (-es, Schüsse) shot;
mit einem ~ Wodka with a
dash of vodka
Schüssel f (-, -n) bowl
Schuster(in) m(f) (-s, -)
shoemaker
Schutt m (-(e)s) rubble
Schüttelfrost m shivering fit;
schütteln vt, vr shake
schütten 1. vt pour; (sugar,
gravel etc) tip 2. vi impers
pour (down)
Schutz m (-es) protection (gegen, vor against, from); (place) shelter; jdn in ~ nehmen
stand up for sb; Schutzblech
nt mudguard
Schütze m (-n, -n) (in football) scorer; ASTR Sagittarius
schützen vt jdn gegen / vor
etw ~ protect sb against /
from sth; Schutzimpfung f
inoculation, vaccination
schwach adj weak; ~e Augen
poor eyesight sg; Schwäche
f (-, -n) weakness; Schwach-
stelle f weak point
Schwager m (-s, Schwäger)
brother-in-law; Schwägerin
f sister-in-law

Schwalbe f (-, -n) swallow; (in football) dive

schwamm imperf of **schwimmen**

Schwamm m (-(e)s, Schwämme) sponge

Schwan m (-(e)s, Schwäne) swan

schwanger adj pregnant; **im vierten Monat ~ sein** be four months pregnant; **Schwangerschaft** f pregnancy; **Schwangerschaftsabbruch** m abortion; **Schwangerschaftstest** m pregnancy test

schwanken vi sway; (prices, figures) fluctuate; (be uncertain) hesitate; (drunkard etc) stagger

Schwanz m (-es, Schwänze) tail; vulg (penis) cock

Schwarm m (-(e)s, Schwärme) swarm; fam (pop star etc) heartthrob; **schwärmen** vi swarm; **~ für** be mad about

schwarz adj black; **~ sehen** fam be pessimistic (für about); **mir wurde ~ vor Augen** everything went black; **Schwarzarbeit** f illicit work; **Schwarzbrot** nt black bread; **schwarzfahren** irr vi travel without a ticket; **Schwarzfahrer(in)** m(f) fare-dodger; **Schwarzmarkt** m black market; **Schwarzwald** m Black Forest; **schwarzweiß** adj black and white

schwatzen vi chatter; **Schwätzer(in)** m(f) (-s, -) chatterbox; (long-winded) gasbag; (about other people) gossip

schweben vi float; (upwards) soar

Schwede m (-n, -n) Swede; **Schweden** nt (-s) Sweden; **Schwedin** f Swede; **schwedisch** adj Swedish; **Schwedisch** nt Swedish

Schwefel m (-s) sulphur

schweigen (schwieg, geschwiegen) vi be silent; stop talking; **Schweigen** nt (-s) silence

Schwein nt (-(e)s, -e) pig; fam luck; fam (vile person) swine; **Schweinebraten** m roast pork; **Schweinefleisch** nt pork; **Schweinerei** f mess; (act) dirty trick

Schweiß m (-es) sweat

schweißen vt, vi weld

Schweißfüße pl sweaty feet pl

Schweiz f (-) **die ~** Switzerland; **Schweizer(in)** m(f) (-s, -) Swiss; **Schweizerdeutsch** nt Swiss German; **schweizerisch** adj Swiss

Schwelle f (-, -n) doorstep; a. fig threshold

schwellen vi swell (up); **Schwellung** f swelling

schwer 1. adj heavy; (task, life, question) difficult, hard; (illness, mistake) serious, bad **2.** adv (very) really; (injured *etc*) seriously, badly; **jdm ~ fallen** be difficult for sb; Schwerbehinderte(r) *mf* severely disabled person; **schwerhörig** *adj* hard of hearing

Schwert *nt* (-(e)s, -er) sword

Schwester *f* (-, -n) sister; MED nurse

schwieg *imperf of* **schweigen**

Schwiegereltern *pl* parents--in-law *pl*; Schwiegermutter *f* mother-in-law; Schwiegersohn *m* son-in-law; Schwiegertochter *f* daughter-in-law; Schwiegervater *m* father-in-law

schwierig *adj* difficult, hard; Schwierigkeit *f* difficulty; **in ~en kommen** get into trouble; **jdm ~en machen** make things difficult for sb

Schwimmbad *nt* swimming pool; Schwimmbecken *nt* swimming pool; schwimmen (*schwamm, geschwommen*) *vi* swim; (*drift, not sink*) float; *fig* be all at sea; Schwimmer(in) *m(f)* swimmer; Schwimmflosse *f* flipper; Schwimmflügel *m* water wing; Schwimmreifen *m* rubber ring; Schwimmweste *f* life jacket

Schwindel *m* (-s) dizziness; (*fit*) dizzy spell; (*deception*) swindle; schwindelfrei *adj* **nicht ~ sein** suffer from vertigo; **~ sein** have a head for heights; schwindlig *adj* dizzy; **mir ist ~** I feel dizzy

Schwips *m* **einen ~ haben** be tipsy

schwitzen *vi* sweat

schwoll *imperf of* **schwellen**

schwor *imperf of* **schwören**

schwören (*schwor, geschworen*) *vt, vi* swear; **einen Eid ~** take an oath

schwul *adj* gay

schwül *adj* close

Schwung *m* (-(e)s, *Schwünge*) swing; (*force when moving*) momentum; *fig* energy; *fam* (*quantity*) batch; **in ~ kommen** get going

Schwur *m* (-(e)s, *Schwüre*) oath

scrollen *vi* IT scroll

sechs *num* six; Sechs *f* (-, -en) six; (*mark in school*) ≈ F; sechshundert *num* six hundred; sechsmal *adv* six times; sechste(r, s) *adj* sixth; → **dritte**; Sechstel *nt* (-s, -) (*fraction*) sixth; sechzehn *num* sixteen; sechzehnte(r, s) *adj* sixteenth; → **dritte**; sechzig *num* sixty; **in den ~er Jahren** in the sixties; sechzigste(r, s) *adj* sixtieth

Secondhandladen *m* secondhand shop

See **1.** *f* (-, -n) sea; **an der ~** by the sea **2.** *m* (-s, -n) lake; **am ~** by the lake; Seehund *m* seal; Seeigel *m* sea urchin; seekrank *adj* seasick

Seele *f* (-, -n) soul

Seeleute pl seamen pl, sailors pl

seelisch adj mental, psychological

Seelöwe m sea lion; **Seemann** m sailor, seaman; **Seemeile** f nautical mile; **Seemöwe** f seagull; **Seepferdchen** nt sea horse; **Seerose** f water lily; **Seestern** m starfish; **Seezunge** f sole

Segel nt (-s, -) sail; **Segelboot** nt yacht; **Segelfliegen** nt (-s) gliding; **Segelflugzeug** nt glider; **segeln** vi, vi sail; **Segelschiff** nt sailing ship

sehbehindert adj partially sighted

sehen (sah, gesehen) vt, vi see; (in specific direction) look; **gut/ schlecht** ~ have good/bad eyesight; **kann ich das mal** ~? can I have a look at it?; **wir** ~ **uns morgen!** see you tomorrow; **Sehenswürdigkeiten** pl sights pl

Sehne f (-, -n) tendon; (on bow) string

sehnen vr long (nach for)

Sehnenzerrung f MED pulled tendon

Sehnsucht f longing; **sehnsüchtig** adj longing

sehr adv very; (with verbs) a lot, very much; **zu** ~ too much

seicht adj shallow

Seide f (-, -n) silk

Seife f (-, -n) soap; **Seifenoper** f soap (opera); **Seifenschale** f soap dish

Seil nt (-(e)s, -e) (metal) cable; **Seilbahn** f cable railway

sein (war, gewesen) vi, vaux be; **lass das** ~! leave that!; (sth annoying) stop that!; **das kann** ~ that's possible

sein pron his; her; its; **das ist** ~**e Tasche** that's his bag; **jeder hat** ~**e Sorgen** everyone has their problems; **seine(r, s)** pron his; hers; **das ist** ~**r/** ~**/** ~**s** that's his/hers/ its; **seinetwegen** adv because of him; (to please him) for his sake

seit conj since; (period) for; **er ist** ~ **Montag hier** he's been here since Monday; **er ist** ~ **einer Woche hier** he's been here for a week; ~ **langem** for a long time; **seitdem** adv, conj since

Seite f (-, -n) side; (in book) page; **zur** ~ **gehen** step aside; **Seitensprung** m affair; **Seitenstechen** nt (-s) ~ **haben/bekommen** have/ get a stitch; **Seitenstraße** f side street; **Seitenstreifen** m hard shoulder (Brit), shoulder (US); **seitenverkehrt** adj the wrong way round; **Seitenwind** m crosswind

seither adv since (then)

seitlich *adj* side

Sekretär(in) *m(f)* secretary

Sekt *m* (-(e)s, -e) sparkling wine

Sekte *f* (-, -n) sect

Sekunde *f* (-, -n) second; Sekundenkleber *m* (-s, -) superglue

selbst 1. *pron* **ich ~** I ... myself; **du/Sie ~** you ... yourself; **er ~** he ... himself; **sie ~** she ... herself; **they ...** themselves; **wir haben es ~ gemacht** we did it ourselves; **mach es ~** do it yourself; **von ~** by itself; **das versteht sich ja von ~** that goes without saying 2. *adv* even; **~ mir gefiel's** even I liked it

selbständig *adj* → **selbstständig**

Selbstauslöser *m* (-s, -) PHOT self-timer; Selbstbedienung *f* self-service; Selbstbefriedigung *f* masturbation; Selbstbeherrschung *f* self-control; Selbstbeteiligung *f* (*on insurance*) excess; selbstbewusst *adj* (self-)confident; selbstgemacht *adj* self-made; Selbstgespräch *nt* **~e führen** talk to oneself; selbstklebend *adj* self-adhesive; Selbstkostenpreis *m* cost price; Selbstlaut *m* vowel; Selbstmord *m* suicide; selbstsicher *adj* self-assured; selbstständig *adj* independent; (*working*) self-em-

ployed; selbstverständlich 1. *adj* obvious; **ich halte das für ~** I take that for granted 2. *adv* naturally; Selbstvertrauen *nt* self-confidence

Sellerie *m* (-s, -(s)) *f* (-, -n) celeriac; (*in sticks*) celery

selten 1. *adj* rare 2. *adv* seldom, rarely

seltsam *adj* strange; **~ schmecken/riechen** taste/smell strange

Semester *nt* (-s, -) semester; Semesterferien *pl* vacation sg

Seminar *nt* (-s, -e) seminar

Semmel *f* (-, -n) roll; Semmelbrösel *pl* breadcrumbs *pl*

Senat *m* (-(e)s, -e) senate

senden 1. (*sandte, gesandt*) *vt* send 2. *vt, vi* RADIO, TV broadcast; Sender *m* (-s, -) (*TV*) channel; (*radio*) station; (*apparatus*) transmitter; Sendung *f* RADIO, TV broadcast; (*single broadcast*) programme

Senf *m* (-(e)s, -e) mustard

Senior(in) *m(f)* senior citizen; Seniorenpass *m* senior citizen's travel pass

senken 1. *vt* lower 2. *vr* sink

senkrecht *adj* vertical

Sensation *f* (-, -en) sensation

sensibel *adj* sensitive

sentimental *adj* sentimental

separat *adj* separate

September *m* (-(s), -) September; → **Juni**

Serbien nt (-s) Serbia
Serie f series sg
seriös adj serious; (firm, people) respectable
Serpentine f hairpin (bend)
Serum nt (-s, Seren) serum
Server m (-s, -) IT server
servieren vt, vi serve
Serviette f napkin, serviette
Servolenkung f AUTO power steering
Sesam m (-s, -s) sesame seeds pl
Sessel m (-s, -) armchair; **Sessellift** m chairlift
Set m or nt (-s, -s) set; (under plate etc) tablemat
setzen 1. vt put; (sail) set **2.** vr settle; (person) sit down; ~ **Sie sich doch** please sit down
Seuche f (-, -n) epidemic
seufzen vi, vi sigh
Sex m (-es) sex; **sexistisch** adj sexist; **Sexualität** f sexuality; **sexuell** adj sexual
Seychellen pl Seychelles pl
sfr abbr = **Schweizer Franken**; Swiss franc(s)
Shampoo nt (-s, -s) shampoo
Shorts pl shorts pl
Shuttlebus m shuttle bus
sich pron himself; herself; itself; (plural) themselves; (after 'Sie') yourself; yourselves; (indefinite, after 'man') oneself; **er hat ~ ver-**

letzt he hurt himself; **sie kennen ~** they know each other; **sie hat ~ sehr gefreut** she was very pleased; **er hat ~ das Bein gebrochen** he's broken his leg
sicher adj safe (vor + dat from); (sure) certain (gen of); (method, source) reliable; (self-assured) confident; **aber ~!** of course, sure; **Sicherheit** f safety; (protective measures) FIN security; (sureness) certainty; (self-assurance) confidence; **mit ~** definitely; **Sicherheitsabstand** m safe distance; **Sicherheitsgurt** m seat belt; **sicherheitshalber** adv just to be on the safe side; **Sicherheitsnadel** f safety pin; **Sicherheitsvorkehrung** f safety precaution; **sicherlich** adv certainly; (in all likelihood) probably
sichern vt secure (gegen against); (guard) IT protect; (data) back up; **Sicherung** f securing; (on machine etc) safety device; (on gun) safety catch; ELEC fuse; IT back-up; **die ~ ist durchgebrannt** the fuse has blown
Sicht f (-) sight; (scene) view; **sichtbar** adj visible; **sichtlich** adj evident, obvious; **Sichtverhältnisse** pl visibility sg; **Sichtweite** f in/außer ~ within/out of sight
sie pron she; (plural) they;

(*accusative*) her; them; (*thing*) it; **da ist ~ ja** there she is; **da sind ~ ja** there they are; **ich kenne ~** I know her; I know them

Sie *pron* you

Sieb *nt* (-(*e*)*s*, -*e*) sieve; (*for tea*) strainer

sieben *num* seven; **siebenhundert** *num* seven hundred; **siebenmal** *adv* seven times; **siebte(r, s)** *adj* seventh; → **dritte**; **Siebtel** *nt* (-*s*, -) (*fraction*) seventh; **siebzehn** *num* seventeen; **siebzehnte(r, s)** *adj* seventeenth; → **dritte**; **siebzig** *num* seventy; **in den ~er Jahren** in the seventies; **siebzigste(r, s)** *adj* seventieth

Siedlung *f* (-, -*en*) housing estate (*Brit*) (or development (*US*))

Sieg *m* (-(*e*)*s*, -*e*) victory; **siegen** *vi* win; **Sieger(in)** *m(f)* (-*s*, -) winner; **Siegerehrung** *f* presentation ceremony

siezen *vt* address as 'Sie'

Signal *nt* (-*s*, -*e*) signal

Silbe *f* (-, -*n*) syllable

Silber *nt* (-*s*) silver; **Silberhochzeit** *f* silver wedding; **Silbermedaille** *f* silver medal

Silikon *nt* (-*s*, -*e*) silicone

Silvester *nt* (-*s*, -), **Silvesterabend** *m* New Year's Eve, Hogmanay (*Scot*)

Simbabwe *nt* (-*s*) Zimbabwe

simpel *adj* simple

simultan *adj* simultaneous

simsen *vt*, *vi fam* text

Sinfonie *f* (-, -*n*) symphony; **Sinfonieorchester** *nt* symphony orchestra

Singapur *nt* (-*s*) Singapore

singen (*sang, gesungen*) *vt*, *vi* sing; **richtig/falsch ~** sing in tune/out of tune

Single 1. *f* (-, -*s*) (*CD*) single **2.** *m* (-*s*, -*s*) (*person*) single

Singular *m* singular

sinken (*sank, gesunken*) *vi* sink; (*prices etc*) fall, go down

Sinn *m* (-(*e*)*s*, -*e*) (*of word, speech etc*) sense, meaning; **~ machen** make sense; **das hat keinen ~** it's no use; **sinnlich** *adj* sensuous; (*erotic*) sensual; (*perception*) sensory; **sinnlos** *adj* stupid; (*behaviour*) senseless; (*futile*) pointless; (*talk etc*) meaningless; **sinnvoll** *adj* meaningful; (*reasonable*) sensible

Sirup *m* (-*s*, -*e*) syrup

Sitte *f* (-, -*n*) custom

Situation *f* situation

Sitz *m* (-*es*, -*e*) seat; **sitzen** (*saß, gesessen*) *vi* sit; (*remark, blow*) strike home; (*what one has learnt*) have sunk in; **der Rock sitzt gut** the skirt is a good fit; **Sitzgelegenheit** *f* place to sit down; **Sitzplatz** *m* seat; **Sitzung** *f* meeting

Sizilien *nt* (-*s*) Sicily

Skandal m (-s, -e) scandal
Skandinavien nt (-s) Scandinavia
Skateboard nt (-s, -s) skateboard; **Skateboardfahrer(in)** m(f) skateboarder
Skelett nt (-s, -e) skeleton
skeptisch adj sceptical
Ski m (-s, -er) ski; ~ **laufen** (or **fahren**) ski; **Skianzug** m ski suit; **Skibrille** f ski goggles pl; **Skifahren** nt (-s) skiing; **Skigebiet** nt (-[e]s, -e) skiing area; **Skihose** f skiing trousers pl; **Skikurs** m skiing course; **Skiläufer(in)** m(f) skier; **Skilehrer(in)** m(f) ski instructor; **Skilift** m ski-lift
Skinhead m (-s, -s) skinhead
Skischuh m ski boot; **Skispringen** nt (-s, -n) ski jumping; **Skistiefel** m (-s, -) ski boot; **Skistock** m ski pole; **Skiurlaub** m skiing holiday (Brit) (or vacation (US))
Skizze f (-, -n) sketch
Skonto m or nt (-s, -s) discount
Skorpion m (-s, -e) ZOOL scorpion; ASTR Scorpio
Skulptur f (-, -en) sculpture
S-Kurve f double bend
Slalom m (-s, -s) slalom
Slip m (-s, -s) (pair of) briefs pl; **Slipeinlage** f panty liner
Slowakei f (-) Slovakia; **slowakisch** adj Slovakian; **Slowakisch** nt Slovakian
Slowenien nt (-s) Slovenia; **slowenisch** adj Slovenian;

Slowenisch nt Slovenian
Smiley m (-s, -s) smiley
Smog m (-s) smog; **Smogalarm** m smog alert
Smoking m (-s, -s) dinner jacket (Brit), tuxedo (US)
SMS 1. nt abbr = **Short Message Service 2.** f text message; **ich schicke dir eine** ~ I'll text you, I'll send you a text (message)
Snowboard nt (-s, -s) snowboard; **Snowboardfahren** nt (-s) snowboarding; **Snowboardfahrer(in)** m(f) snowboarder
so 1. adv so; (in this way) like this; (approximately) about; **fünf Euro oder** ~ five euros or so; ~ **ein** such a; ~ ... **wie** ... as ... as ...; **und** ~ **weiter** and so on; ~ **genannt** so-called; ~ **viel** as much (wie as); ~ **weit sein** be ready; ~ **weit wie** (or **als**) **möglich** as far as possible **2.** conj so; (before adjective) as
sobald conj as soon as
Socke f (-, -n) sock
Sodbrennen nt (-s) heartburn
Sofa nt (-s, -s) sofa
sofern conj if, provided (that)
soff imperf of **saufen**
sofort adv immediately, at once
Softeis nt soft ice-cream
Software f (-, -s) software
sog imperf of **saugen**
sogar adv even; **kalt,** ~ **sehr**

kalt cold, in fact very cold

Sohle f (-, -n) sole

Sohn m (-(e)s, Söhne) son

Soja f (-, Sojen) soya; **Sojasprossen** pl bean sprouts pl

solang(e) conj as long as

Solarium nt solarium

Solarzelle f solar cell

solche(r, s) pron such; **eine ~ Frau, solch eine Frau** such a woman, a woman like that; **~ Sachen** things like that, such things; **ich habe ~ Kopfschmerzen** I've got such a headache; **ich habe ~n Hunger** I'm so hungry

Soldat(in) m(f) (-en, -en) soldier

solidarisch adj showing solidarity

solid(e) adj solid; (life, person) respectable

Soll nt (-(s), -(s)) FIN debit; (amount of work) quota, target

sollen vi be supposed to; (obligation) shall, ought to; **soll ich?** shall I?; **du solltest besser nach Hause gehen** you'd better go home; **sie soll sehr reich sein** she's said to be very rich; **was soll das?** what's all that about?

Solo nt (-s, -) solo

Sommer m (-s, -) summer; **Sommerfahrplan** m summer timetable; **Sommerferien** pl summer holidays pl (Brit) (or vacation sg (US)); **sommerlich** adj summery; (clothes) summer; **Sommerreifen** m normal tyre; **Sommersprossen** pl freckles pl; **Sommerzeit** f summertime; (by the clock) daylight saving time

Sonderangebot nt special offer; **sonderbar** adj strange, odd; **Sondermüll** m hazardous waste

sondern conj but; **nicht nur ..., ~ auch** not only ..., but also

Sonderpreis m special price; **Sonderschule** f special school; **Sonderzeichen** nt IT special character

Song m (-s, -s) song

Sonnabend m Saturday; → **Mittwoch**; **sonnabends** adv on Saturdays; → **mittwochs**

Sonne f (-, -n) sun; **sonnen** vr sunbathe; **Sonnenaufgang** m sunrise; **Sonnenblume** f sunflower; **Sonnenbrand** m sunburn; **Sonnenbrille** f sunglasses pl, shades pl; **Sonnencreme** f sun cream; **Sonnendach** nt (of car) sunroof; **Sonnendeck** nt sun deck; **Sonnenmilch** f suntan lotion; **Sonnenöl** nt suntan oil; **Sonnenschein** m sunshine; **Sonnenschirm** m parasol, sunshade; **Sonnenstich** m sunstroke; **Sonnenstudio** nt solarium; **Sonnenuhr** f sundial; **Sonnenuntergang** m sunset; **sonnig** adj sunny

Sonntag m Sunday; → **Mittwoch**; **sonntags** adv on Sundays; → **mittwochs**

sonst adv also; (*if not*) otherwise, (or) else; (*at other times*) normally, usually; ~ **noch etwas?** anything else?; ~ **nichts** nothing else

sooft conj whenever

Sopran m (-s, -e) soprano

Sorge f (-, -n) worry; (*looking after*) care; **sich** dat **um jdn _n machen** be worried about sb; **sorgen 1.** vi **für jdn ~** look after sb; **für etw ~** take care of sth, see to sth **2.** vr worry (*um* about); **sorgfältig** adj careful

sortieren vt sort (out)

sosehr conj however much

Soße f (-, -n) sauce; (*with meat*) gravy

Soundkarte f IT sound card

Souvenir nt (-s, -s) souvenir

soviel conj as far as

soweit conj as far as

sowie conj as well as; (*with time*) as soon as

sowohl conj **~ ... als** (or **wie**) **auch** both ... and

sozial adj social; **Sozialhilfe** f income support (*Brit*), welfare aid (*US*); **Sozialismus** m socialism; **Sozialversicherung** f social security; **Sozialwohnung** f council flat (*Brit*), state-subsidized apartment (*US*)

Soziologie f sociology

sozusagen adv so to speak

Spachtel m (-s, -) spatula

Spag(h)etti pl spaghetti pl

Spalte f (-, -n) crack; (*in glacier*) crevasse; (*in text*) column

spalten vt, vr split

Spange f (-, -n) clasp; (*for hair*) hair slide (*Brit*), barrette (*US*)

Spanien nt (-s) Spain; **Spanier(in)** m(f) (-s, -) Spaniard; **spanisch** adj Spanish; **Spanisch** nt Spanish

spann imperf of **spinnen**

spannen 1. vt (*make taut*) tighten **2.** vi be tight

spannend adj exciting, gripping; **Spannung** f tension; ELEC voltage; fig suspense

Sparbuch nt savings book; (*account*) savings account; **sparen** vt, vi save

Spargel m (-s, -) asparagus; **Spargelsuppe** f asparagus soup

Sparkasse f savings bank; **Sparkonto** f savings account

spärlich adj meagre; (*clothing*) scanty

sparsam adj economical; **Sparschwein** nt piggy bank

Spaß m (-es, **Späße**) joke; (*pleasure*) fun; **es macht mir ~** I enjoy it, it's (great) fun; **viel ~!** have fun

spät adj, adv late; **zu ~ kommen** be late

Spaten m (-s, -) spade

später adj, adv later; **spätes-**

tens adv at the latest; **Spät-vorstellung** f late-night performance

Spatz m (-en, -en) sparrow

spazieren vi stroll, walk; ~ **gehen** go for a walk; **Spaziergang** m walk

Specht m (-(e)s, -e) woodpecker

Speck m (-(e)s, -e) bacon fat; ~ (streaky) bacon

Spedition f removal firm

Speiche f (-, -n) spoke

Speichel m (-s) saliva

Speicher m (-s, -) (in building) attic; IT memory; **speichern** vt (send to disk etc) save

Speise f (-, -n) food; (prepared) dish; **Speisekarte** f menu; **Speiseröhre** f gullet, oesophagus; **Speisesaal** m dining hall; **Speisewagen** m dining car

Spende f (-, -n) donation; **spenden** vt donate, give

spendieren vt jdm etw ~ treat sb to sth

Sperre f (-, -n) barrier; (on sb or sth) ban; **sperren** vt block; SPORT suspend; (exports etc) ban; **Sperrstunde** f closing time; **Sperrung** f closing

Spesen pl expenses pl

spezialisieren vr specialize (auf + acc on sth); **Spezialist(in)** m(f) specialist; **Spezialität** f speciality (Brit), specialty (US); **speziell 1.** adj special **2.** adv especially

Spiegel m (-s, -) mirror; **Spiegelei** nt fried egg (sunny-side up (US)); **spiegelglatt** adj very slippery; **Spiegelreflexkamera** f reflex camera

Spiel nt (-(e)s, -e) game; (activity) play(ing); (of playing cards) pack, deck; **Spielautomat** m gaming machine; (with cash payout) slot machine; **spielen** vt, vi play; (for money) gamble; THEAT perform, act; **Klavier** ~ play the piano; **spielend** adv easily; **Spieler(in)** m(f) (-s, -) player; (for money) gambler; **Spielfeld** nt (for football, hockey) field; (for basketball) court; **Spielfilm** m feature film; **Spielkasino** nt casino; **Spielplatz** m playground; **Spielraum** m room to manoeuvre; **Spielregel** f rule; *sich an die ~n halten* stick to the rules; **Spielsachen** pl toys pl; **Spielverderber(in)** m(f) (-s, -) spoilsport; **Spielzeug** nt toys pl; (single item) toy

Spieß m (-es, -e) spear; (for roasting) spit; **Spießer(in)** m(f) (-s, -) square, stuffy type; **spießig** adj square, uncool

Spikes pl SPORT spikes pl; AUTO studs pl

Spinat m (-(e)s, -e) spinach

Spinne f (-, -n) spider; **spinnen** (spann, gesponnen) vt, vi spin; fam talk rubbish;

be crazy; **du spinnst!** you must be mad; **Spinnwebe** f (-, -n) cobweb

Spion(in) m(f) (-s, -e) spy; **spionieren** vi spy; fig snoop around

Spirale f (-, -n) spiral; MED coil

Spirituosen pl spirits pl, liquor sg (US)

Spiritus m (-, -se) spirit

spitz adj (nose, chin) pointed; (pencil, knife) sharp; (angle) acute; **Spitze** f (-, -n) point; (of finger, nose) tip; (remark) taunt, dig; (in race etc) lead; (fabric) lace; **Spitzengeschwindigkeit** f top speed; **Spitzer** m (-s, -) pencil sharpener; **Spitzname** m nickname

Spliss m (-) split ends pl

sponsern vt sponsor; **Sponsor(in)** m(f) (-s, -en) sponsor

spontan adj spontaneous

Sport m (-(e)s, -e) sport; **~ treiben** do sport; **Sportanlage** f sports grounds pl; **Sportart** f sport; **Sportbekleidung** f sportswear; **Sportgeschäft** nt sports shop; **Sporthalle** f gymnasium, gym; **Sportlehrer(in)** m(f) (-s, -) sports instructor, PE teacher; **Sportler(in)** m(f) (-s, -) sportsman / -woman; **sportlich** adj sporting; (person) sporty; **Sportplatz** m playing field; **Sportverein** m sports club; **Sportwagen** m sports car

sprach imperf of **sprechen**

Sprache f (-, -n) language; (faculty) speech; **Sprachenschule** f language school; **Sprachkurs** m language course; **Sprachunterricht** m language teaching

sprang imperf of **springen**

Spray m or nt (-s, -s) spray

Sprechanlage f intercom; **sprechen** (sprach, gesprochen) vi, vt speak (jdn, mit jdm to sb); (converse) talk (mit to, über, von about); **~ Sie Deutsch?** do you speak German?; **kann ich bitte mit David ~?** (on phone) can I speak to David, please?; **Sprecher(in)** m(f) (-s, -) speaker; (on TV, radio) announcer; **Sprechstunde** f consultation; (of doctor) surgery hours pl; (of solicitor etc) office hours pl; **Sprechzimmer** nt consulting room

Sprichwort nt proverb

Springbrunnen m fountain

springen (sprang, gesprungen) vi jump; (glass) crack; (headfirst) dive

Sprit m (-(e)s, -e) fam petrol (Brit), gas (US)

Spritze f (-, -n) syringe; (jab) injection; (on hose) nozzle; **spritzen 1.** vt spray; MED inject **2.** vi splash; MED give injections

Spruch m (-(e)s, Sprüche) saying

Sprudel m (-s, -) sparkling

mineral water; (*sweet*) fizzy drink (*Brit*), soda (*US*); **sprudeln** vi bubble

Sprühdose f aerosol (can); **sprühen** vt, vi spray; *fig* sparkle; **Sprühregen** m drizzle

Sprung m (-(e)s, Sprünge) jump; (*Riss*) crack; **Sprungbrett** nt springboard; **Sprungschanze** f ski jump; **Sprungturm** m diving platforms pl

Spucke f (-) spit; **spucken** vt, vi spit

spuken vi (*ghost*) walk; *hier spukt es* this place is haunted

Spülbecken nt sink

Spule f (-, -n) spool; ELEC coil

Spüle f (-, -n) sink; **spülen** vt, vi rinse; (*after meal*) wash up; (*toilet*) flush; **Spülmaschine** f dishwasher; **Spülmittel** nt washing-up liquid (*Brit*), dishwashing liquid (*US*); **Spültuch** nt dishcloth; **Spülung** f (of toilet) flush

Spur f (-, -en) trace; (of feet, wheels) track; (followed by police etc) trail; (on road) lane; *die ~ wechseln* change lanes pl

spüren vt feel; (observe) notice; **Spürhund** m sniffer dog

Squash nt (-) squash; **Squashschläger** m squash racket

Sri Lanka nt (-s) Sri Lanka

Staat m (-(e)s, -en) state; **staatlich** adj state(-); (*Industry, museum etc*) state-run; **Staatsangehörigkeit** f nationality; **Staatsanwalt** m, **-anwältin** f prosecuting counsel (*Brit*), district attorney (*US*); **Staatsbürger(in)** m(f) citizen; **Staatsbürgerschaft** f nationality

Stab m (-(e)s, Stäbe) rod; (of cage, window) bar; **Stäbchen** nt chopstick; **Stabhochsprung** m pole vault

stabil adj stable; (furniture) sturdy

stach imperf of **stechen**

Stachel m (-s, -n) spike; (of animal) spine; (of insect) sting; **Stachelbeere** f gooseberry; **Stacheldraht** m barbed wire; **stachelig** adj prickly

Stadion nt (-s, Stadien) stadium

Stadt f (-, Städte) town; (large) city; *in der ~* in town; **Stadtautobahn** f urban motorway (*Brit*) (or expressway (*US*)); **Städtepartnerschaft** f twinning; **Stadtführer** m (booklet) city guide; **Stadtführung** f city sightseeing tour; **Stadthalle** f municipal hall; **städtisch** adj municipal; **Stadtmauer** f city wall(s); **Stadtmitte** f town / city centre, downtown (*US*); **Stadtplan** m (street) map; **Stadtrand** m outskirts pl; **Stadt-**

rundfahrt f city tour
stahl imperf of **stehlen**
Stahl m (-(e)s, Stähle) steel
Stall m (-(e)s, Ställe) stable; (for rabbit) hutch; (for pigs) pigsty; (for poultry) henhouse
Stamm m (-(e)s, Stämme) (of tree) trunk; (people) tribe; **stammen** vi **aus** come from; **Stammgast** m regular (guest); **Stammkunde** m, **Stammkundin** f regular (customer); **Stammtisch** m table reserved for regulars
stand imperf of **stehen**
Stand m (-(e)s, Stände) (of water, petrol) level; (posture) standing position; (situation) state; (in game) score; (at fair etc) stand
Standby-Betrieb m stand-by; **Standby-Ticket** nt stand-by ticket
Ständer m (-s, -) stand; fam (erection) hard-on
Standesamt nt registry office
ständig adj permanent; (uninterrupted) constant, continual
Standlicht nt sidelights pl (Brit), parking lights pl (US); **Standort** m position; **Standpunkt** m standpoint; **Standspur** f AUTO hard shoulder (Brit), shoulder (US)
Stange f (-, -n) stick; (long, round) pole; (metal) bar; (of cigarettes) carton

stank imperf of **stinken**
Stapel m (-s, -) pile
Star 1. m (-(e)s, -e) (bird) starling; MED cataract **2.** m (-s, -s) (in film etc) star
starb imperf of **sterben**
stark adj strong; (intense, big) heavy; (in measurements) thick; **Stärke** f (-, -n) strength; (dimension) thickness; (in washing, food) starch; **stärken** vt strengthen; (washing) starch; **Stärkung** f strengthening; (food) refreshment
starr adj stiff; (unyielding) rigid; (look) staring
starren vi stare
Start m (-(e)s, -e) start; AVIAT takeoff; **Startbahn** f runway; **starten** vt, vi start; AVIAT take off; **Startmenü** nt IT start menu
Station f stop; (on railway) station; (in hospital) ward; **stationär** adj stationary; **~e Behandlung** in-patient treatment; **jdn ~ behandeln** treat sb as an in-patient
Statistik f statistics pl
Stativ nt tripod
statt conj, prep + gen or dat instead of; **~ zu arbeiten** instead of working
stattfinden irr vi take place
Statue f (-, -n) statue
Statusleiste f, **Statuszeile** f IT status bar
Stau m (-(e)s, -e) (traffic) jam; **im ~ stehen** be stuck in a

traffic jam

Staub *m* (-(e)s) dust; ~ **wischen** dust; **staubig** *adj* dusty; **staubsaugen** *vt, vi* vacuum, hoover (*Brit*); **Staubsauger** *m* vacuum cleaner, hoover® (*Brit*); **Staubtuch** *nt* duster

Staudamm *m* dam

staunen *vi* be astonished (*über* + *acc* at)

Stausee *m* reservoir; **Stauung** *f* (*of water*) damming-up; (*of blood, traffic*) congestion

Stauwarnung *f* traffic report

Steak *nt* (-s, -s) steak

stechen (stach, gestochen) *vt, vi* (*with needle etc*) prick; (*with knife*) stab; (*with finger*) poke; (*bee*) sting; (*mosquito*) bite; (*sun*) burn; (*in card game*) trump; **Stechen** *nt* (-s, -) sharp pain, stabbing pain; **Stechmücke** *f* mosquito

Steckdose *f* socket; **stecken 1.** *vt* put; (*pin*) stick; (*in sewing*) pin **2.** *vi* (*not move*) be stuck; (*pin*) be (sticking); **der Schlüssel steckte** the key is in the door; **Stecker** *m* (-s, -) plug; **Stecknadel** *f* pin

Steg *m* (-s, -e) bridge

stehen (stand, gestanden) **1.** *vi* stand (*zu* by); (*with location, circumstance*) be; (*watch, machine, traffic*) have stopped; **was steht im** *Brief?* what does it say in the letter?; **jdm** (*gut*) ~ suit sb; ~ **bleiben** (*clock*) stop; ~ **lassen** leave **2.** *vi impers* **wie steht's?** SPORT what's the score?; **Stehlampe** *f* standard lamp (*Brit*), floor lamp (*US*)

stehlen (stahl, gestohlen) *vt* steal

Stehplatz *m* (*in concert etc*) standing ticket

Steiermark *f* (-) Styria

steif *adj* stiff

steigen (stieg, gestiegen) *vi* (*prices, temperature*) rise; (*person*) climb

steigern *vt, vr* increase

Steigung *f* incline, gradient

steil *adj* steep; **Steilhang** *m* steep slope; **Steilküste** *f* steep coast

Stein *m* (-(e)s, -e) stone; **Steinbock** *m* ZOOL ibex; ASTR Capricorn; **Steinbutt** *m* (-s, -e) turbot; **steinig** *adj* stony; **Steinschlag** *m* falling rocks *pl*

Stelle *f* (-, -n) place, spot; (*work*) post, job; (*department*) office; **ich an deiner** ~ if I were you; **stellen 1.** *vt* put; (*clock etc*) set (*auf* + *acc* to); (*make available*) provide **2.** *vr* (*to the police*) give oneself up; **sich schlafend** ~ pretend to be asleep; **Stellenangebot** *nt* job offer, vacancy; **stellenweise** *adv* in places; **Stellplatz** *m* parking space; **Stellung** f position; **zu etw ~ nehmen** comment on sth; **Stellvertreter(in)** m(f) representative; (as official post) deputy

Stempel m (-s, -) stamp; **stempeln** vt stamp; (postage stamp) cancel

sterben (starb, gestorben) vi die

Stereoanlage f stereo (system)

steril adj sterile; **sterilisieren** vt sterilize

Stern m (-(e)s, -e) star; **Sternbild** nt constellation; (in astrology) star sign, sign of the zodiac; **Sternfrucht** f star fruit; **Sternschnuppe** f (-, -n) shooting star; **Sternwarte** f (-e, -(e)n) observatory; **Sternzeichen** nt star sign, sign of the zodiac; **welches ~ bist du?** what's your star sign?

stets adv always

Steuer 1. nt (-s, -) AUTO steering wheel **2.** f (-, -n) tax; **Steuerberater(in)** m(f) tax adviser; **Steuerbord** nt starboard; **Steuererklärung** f tax declaration; **steuerfrei** adj tax-free; (goods) duty-free; **Steuerknüppel** m control column; AVIAT, IT joystick; **steuern** vt, vi steer; (plane) pilot; (development, volume) nt control; **steuerpflichtig** adj taxable; **Steuerung** f AUTO steering; (instru-

ments) controls pl; AVIAT piloting; fig control

Stich m (-(e)s, -e) (of insect) sting; (of mosquito) bite; (with knife) stab; (in sewing) stitch; (of colour) tinge; (in card game) trick; ART engraving; **Stichprobe** f spot check

sticken vt, vi embroider

Sticker m (-s, -) sticker

Stickerei f embroidery

stickig adj stuffy, close

Stiefbruder m stepbrother

Stiefel m (-s, -) boot

Stiefmutter f stepmother

Stiefmütterchen nt pansy

Stiefschwester f stepsister; **Stiefsohn** m stepson; **Stieftochter** f stepdaughter; **Stiefvater** m stepfather

stieg imperf of **steigen**

Stiege f (-, -n) steps pl

Stiel m (-(e)s, -e) handle; BOT stalk; **ein Eis am ~** an ice lolly (Brit), a Popsicle® (US)

Stier m (-(e)s, -e) ZOOL bull; ASTR Taurus; **Stierkampf** m bullfight; **Stierkämpfer(in)** m(f) bullfighter

stieß imperf of **stoßen**

Stift m (-(e)s, -e) (wooden) peg; (nail) tack; (for writing, drawing) pen; crayon; pencil

Stil m (-s, -e) style

still adj quiet; (motionless) still

stillen vt breast-feed

stillhalten irr vi keep still; **Stillleben** nt still life; **stillstehen** irr vi stand still

Stimme f (-, -n) voice; (in election) vote

stimmen vi be right; **stimmt!** that's right!; **hier stimmt was nicht** there's something wrong here; **stimmt so!** keep the change

Stimmung f mood; (in group etc) atmosphere

stinken (stank, gestunken) vi stink (nach of)

Stipendium nt scholarship; (as means of support) grant

Stirn f (-, -en) forehead; **Stirnhöhle** f sinus

Stock 1. m (-(e)s, Stöcke) stick; BOT stock **2.** m (Stockwerke pl) floor, storey; **Stockbett** nt bunk bed; **Stöckelschuhe** pl high-heels; **Stockwerk** nt floor; **im ersten ~** on the first floor (Brit), on the second floor (US)

Stoff m (-(e)s, -e) (fabric) material; (substance) matter; (of book etc) subject (matter); fam (drugs) stuff

stöhnen vi groan (vor with)

stolpern vi stumble, trip

stolz adj proud

stopp interj hold it!; (introducing new thought) hang on a minute!; **stoppen** vt, vi stop; (with watch) time; **Stoppschild** nt stop sign; **Stoppuhr** f stopwatch

Stöpsel m (-s, -) plug; (for bottle) cork

Storch m (-(e)s, Störche) stork

stören vt disturb; (hinder) interfere with; **darf ich dich kurz ~?** can I trouble you for a minute?; **stört es dich, wenn ...?** do you mind if ...?

stornieren vt cancel

Störung f disturbance; (on phone line) fault

Stoß m (-es, Stöße) push; (with fist, elbow) blow; (with foot) kick; (of books, washing) pile; **Stoßdämpfer** m (-s, -) shock absorber

stoßen (stieß, gestoßen) **1.** vt shove, push; (with a blow) knock; (with foot) kick; (head etc) bump **2.** vr bang oneself

Stoßstange f AUTO bumper

stottern vt, vi stutter

Strafe f (-, -n) punishment; SPORT penalty; (in prison) sentence; (money) fine; **strafen** vt punish; **Strafraum** m penalty area; **Strafstoß** m penalty kick; **Straftat** f (criminal) offence; **Strafzettel** m ticket

Strahl m (-s, -en) ray, beam; (of water) jet; **strahlen** vi radiate; fig beam

Strähne f (-, -n) strand; (white, coloured) streak

Strand m (-(e)s, Strände) beach; **am ~** on the beach; **Strandcafé** nt beach café

strapazieren vt be hard on; (person, nerves) be a strain on

Straße f (-, -n) road; (in town) street; **Straßenarbeiten** pl roadworks pl (Brit), road repairs pl (US); **Straßenbahn** f tram (Brit), streetcar (US); **Straßencafé** nt pavement café (Brit), sidewalk café (US); **Straßenfest** nt street party; **Straßenglätte** f slippery roads pl; **Straßenrand** m am ~ at the roadside; **Straßenschild** nt street sign; **Straßensperre** f roadblock; **Straßenverhältnisse** pl road conditions pl

Strategie f (-, -n) strategy
Strauch m (-(e)s, Sträucher) bush, shrub
Strauß 1. m (-es, Sträuße) bunch; (as gift) bouquet **2.** m (Sträuße pl) ostrich
Strecke f (-, -n) route; distance; RAIL line
strecken vt, vr stretch
streckenweise adv in parts; (occasionally) at times
Streich m (-(e)s, -e) trick, prank
streicheln vt stroke
streichen (strich, gestrichen) vt paint; (word etc) delete; (flight, race etc) cancel
Streichholz nt match; **Streichholzschachtel** f matchbox; **Streichkäse** m cheese spread
Streifen m (-s, -) stripe; (piece) strip; (movie) film
Streifenwagen m patrol car
Streik m (-(e)s, -s) strike; **streiken** vi be on strike
Streit m (-(e)s, -e) argument

(um, wegen about, over); **streiten** (stritt, gestritten) vi, vr argue (um, wegen about, over)
streng adj (look, appearance) severe; (teacher, measure) strict; (smell etc) sharp
Stress m (-es) stress; **stressen** vt stress (out); **stressig** adj fam stressful
Stretching nt (-s) SPORT stretching exercises pl
streuen vt scatter
strich imperf of **streichen**
Strich m (-(e)s, -e) line; **Stricher** m fam rent boy (Brit), boy prostitute; **Strichkode** m (-s, -s) bar code; **Stricherin** f fam hooker; **Strichpunkt** m semicolon
Strick m (-(e)s, -e) rope
stricken vt, vi knit; **Strickjacke** f cardigan; **Stricknadel** f knitting needle
Stripper(in) m(f) stripper; **Striptease** m (-) striptease
stritt imperf of **streiten**
Stroh nt (-(e)s) straw; **Strohdach** nt thatched roof; **Strohhalm** m (drinking) straw; **Strohhut** m straw hat
Strom m (-(e)s, Ströme) river; fig stream; ELEC current; **Stromanschluss** m connection; **Stromausfall** m power failure
strömen vi stream, pour; **Strömung** f current
Stromzähler m electricity meter

Strophe f (-, -n) verse

Strudel m (-s, -) (in river) whirlpool; (dessert) strudel

Struktur f structure; (of material) texture

Strumpf m (-(e)s, Strümpfe) stocking; sock; **Strumpfhose** f (pair of tights pl (Brit), pantyhose (US)

Stück nt (-(e)s, -e) piece; (some) bit; (of sugar) lump; THEAT play

Student(in) m(f) student; **Studentenausweis** m student card; **Studentenwohnheim** nt hall of residence (Brit), dormitory (US); **Studienabschluss** m qualification (at the end of a course of higher education); **Studienfahrt** f study trip; **Studienplatz** m university/college place; **studieren** vt, vi study; **Studium** nt studies pl; **während seines ~s** while he is/was studying

Stufe f (-, -n) step; (in development) stage

Stuhl m (-(e)s, Stühle) chair

stumm adj silent; MED dumb

stumpf adj blunt; (apathetic, not shiny) dull; **stumpfsinnig** adj dull

Stunde f (-, -n) hour; (in school etc) lesson; **eine halbe ~** half an hour; **Stundenkilometer** m **80 ~** 80 kilometres an hour; **stundenlang** adv for hours; **Stundenplan** m timetable;

stündlich adj hourly

Stuntman m (-s, Stuntmen) stuntman; **Stuntwoman** f (-, Stuntwomen) stuntwoman

stur adj stubborn; (stronger) pigheaded

Sturm m (-(e)s, Stürme) storm; **stürmen** vi (wind) blow hard; (rush) storm; **Stürmer(in)** m(f) striker, forward; **Sturmflut** f storm tide; **stürmisch** adj stormy; fig tempestuous; (time) turbulent; (lover) passionate; (applause, welcome) tumultuous; **Sturmwarnung** f gale warning

Sturz m (-es, Stürze) fall; POL overthrow; **stürzen 1.** vt hurl; POL overthrow; (container) overturn **2.** vi fall; (rush) dash; **Sturzhelm** m crash helmet

Stute f (-, -n) mare

Stütze f (-, -n) support; (person who helps) help; fam (for unemployed person) dole (Brit), welfare (US)

stutzig adj perplexed, puzzled; (distrustful) suspicious

Styropor® nt (-s) polystyrene (Brit), styrofoam (US)

subjektiv adj subjective

Substanz f (-, -en) substance

subtrahieren vt subtract

Subvention f subsidy; **subventionieren** vt subsidize

Suche f search (nach for); **auf**

der ~ nach etw sein be looking for sth; **suchen 1.** *vt* look for; IT search **2.** *vi* look, search (*nach* for); **Suchmaschine** *f* IT search engine

Sucht *f* (-, *Süchte*) mania; MED addiction; **süchtig** *adj* addicted; **Süchtige(r)** *mf* addict

Süd south; **Südafrika** *nt* South Africa; **Südamerika** *nt* South America; **Süddeutschland** *nt* Southern Germany; **Süden** *m* (-s) south; *im ~ Deutschlands* in the south of Germany; **Südeuropa** *nt* Southern Europe; **Südkorea** *nt* (-s) South Korea; **südlich** *adj* southern; (*course, direction*) southerly; **Südost(en)** *m* southeast; **Südpol** *m* South Pole; **Südstaaten** *pl* (*in USA*) the Southern States *pl*, the South *sg*; **südwärts** *adv* south, southwards; **Südwest(en)** *m* southwest; **Südwind** *m* south wind

Sultanine *f* sultana

Sülze *f* (-, -n) jellied meat

Summe *f* (-, -n) sum; (*altogether*) total

summen *vi*, *vt* hum; (*insect*) buzz

Sumpf *m* (-(e)s, *Sümpfe*) marsh; (*in the tropics*) swamp; **sumpfig** *adj* marshy

Sünde *f* (-, -n) sin

super *adj fam* super, great; **Super** *nt* (-s) four star (petrol) (*Brit*), premium (*US*); **Supermarkt** *m* supermarket

Suppe *f* (-, -n) soup; **Suppengrün** *nt* bunch of herbs and vegetables for flavouring soup; **Suppenwürfel** *m* stock cube

Surfbrett *nt* surfboard; **surfen** *vi* surf; *im Internet ~* surf the Internet; **Surfer(in)** *m(f)* (-s, -) surfer

Surrealismus *m* surrealism

süß *adj* sweet; **süßen** *vt* sweeten; **Süßigkeit** *f* sweet (*Brit*), candy (*US*); **süßsauer** *adj* sweet-and-sour; **Süßspeise** *f* dessert; **Süßstoff** *m* sweetener; **Süßwasser** *nt* fresh water

Sweatshirt *nt* (-s, -s) sweatshirt

Swimmingpool *m* (-s, -s) (swimming) pool

Sylvester *nt* → **Silvester**

Symbol *nt* (-s, -e) symbol; **Symbolleiste** *f* IT toolbar

Symmetrie *f* (-, -n) symmetry; **symmetrisch** *adj* symmetrical

sympathisch *adj* nice; *jdn ~ finden* like sb

Symphonie *f* (-, -n) symphony

Symptom *nt* (-s, -e) symptom (*für* of)

Synagoge *f* (-, -n) synagogue

synchronisiert *adj* (*film*) dubbed; **Synchronstimme** *f* dubbing voice

Synthesizer *m* (-s, -) MUS syn-

thesizer
Synthetik f (-, -en) synthetic (fibre); **synthetisch** adj synthetic

Syrien nt (-s) Syria

System nt (-s, -e) system; **systematisch** adj systematic; **Systemsteuerung** f IT control panel

Szene f (-, -n) scene

T

Tabak m (-s, -e) tobacco; **Tabakladen** m tobacconist's

Tabelle f table

Tablett nt (-s, -e) tray

Tablette f tablet, pill

Tabulator m tabulator, tab

Tacho(meter) m (-s, -) AUTO speedometer

Tafel f (-, -n) a. MATH table; (for notices) board; (in classroom) blackboard; (commemorative) plaque; **eine ~ Schokolade** a bar of chocolate

Tag m (-(e)s, -e) day; daylight; **guten ~!** good morning / afternoon; **am ~** during the day; **sie hat ihre ~e** she's got her period; **eines ~es** one day; **Tagebuch** nt diary; **tagelang** adj for days (on end); **Tagesanbruch** m daybreak; **Tagesausflug** m day trip; **Tagescreme** f day cream; **Tagesgericht** nt dish of the day; **Tageskarte** f day ticket; **die ~** (in restaurant) today's menu; **Tageslicht** nt daylight; **Tagesordnung** f agenda; **Tagestour** f day trip; **Tageszeitung** f daily newspaper; **täglich** adj, adv daily; **tags(über)** adv during the day; **Tagung** f conference

Tai Chi nt (-) tai chi

Taille f (-, -n) waist; **tailliert** adj fitted

Taiwan nt (-s) Taiwan

Takt m (-(e)s, -e) tact; MUS time

Taktik f (-, -en) tactics pl

Tal nt (-(e)s, Täler) valley

Talent nt (-(e)s, -e) talent; **talentiert** adj talented

Talkmaster(in) m(f) (-s, -) talk-show host; **Talkshow** f (-, -s) talkshow

Tampon m (-s, -s) tampon

Tandem nt (-s, -s) tandem

Tang m (-s, -e) seaweed

Tank m (-s, -s) tank; **Tankanzeige** f fuel gauge; **Tankdeckel** m fuel cap; **tanken** vi get some petrol (or gas (US)); AVIAT refuel; **Tanker** m (-s, -) (oil) tanker; **Tankstelle** f petrol station (Brit), gas station (US)

Tanne f (-, -n) fir; **Tannenzapfen** m fir cone

Tansania nt (-s) Tanzania

Tante f (-, -n) aunt; **Tante-Emma-Laden** m corner shop

(*Brit*), grocery store (*US*)

Tanz *m* (-es, *Tänze*) dance; **tanzen** *vt*, *vi* dance; **Tänzer(in)** *m(f)* dancer; **Tanzfläche** *f* dance floor; **Tanzkurs** *m* dancing course; **Tanzlehrer(in)** *m(f)* dancing instructor; **Tanzstunde** *f* dancing lesson

Tapete *f* (-, -n) wallpaper; **tapezieren** *vt*, *vi* wallpaper

Tarif *m* (-s, -e) tariff, (scale of) fares/charges *pl*

Tasche *f* (-, -n) bag; (*in trousers etc*) pocket; (*handbag*) bag (*Brit*), purse (*US*); **Taschen-** *in cpds* pocket; **Taschenbuch** *nt* paperback; **Taschendieb(in)** *m(f)* pickpocket; **Taschengeld** *nt* pocket money; **Taschenlampe** *f* torch (*Brit*), flashlight (*US*); **Taschenmesser** *nt* penknife; **Taschenrechner** *m* pocket calculator; **Taschentuch** *nt* handkerchief

Tasse *f* (-, -n) cup; *eine ~ Kaffee* a cup of coffee

Tastatur *f* keyboard; **Taste** *f* (-, -n) button; (*of piano, computer*) key; **Tastenkombination** *f* IT shortcut; **Tastentelefon** *nt* push-button telephone

tat *imperf of* **tun**

Tat *f* (-, -en) action

Tatar *nt* (-s, -s) raw minced beef

Täter(in) *m(f)* (-s, -) culprit

Tätigkeit *f* activity; (*job*) occupation

tätowieren *vt* tattoo; **Tätowierung** *f* tattoo (*an + dat* on)

Tatsache *f* fact; **tatsächlich 1.** *adj* actual **2.** *adv* really

Tau **1.** *nt* (-(e)s, -e) rope **2.** *m* (-(e)s) dew

taub *adj* deaf

Taube *f* (-, -n) pigeon, dove

taubstumm *adj* deaf-and-dumb; **Taubstumme(r)** *mf* deaf-mute

tauchen **1.** *vt* dip **2.** *vi* dive; NAUT submerge; **Tauchen** *nt* (-s) diving; **Taucher(in)** *m(f)* (-s, -) diver; **Taucheranzug** *m* diving (*or* wet) suit; **Taucherbrille** *f* diving goggles *pl*; **Tauchermaske** *f* diving mask; **Tauchkurs** *m* diving course

tauen *vi impers* thaw

Taufe *f* (-, -n) baptism; **taufen** *vt* baptize; (*name*) christen

taugen *vi* be suitable (*für* for); *nichts ~* be no good

Tausch *m* (-(e)s, -e) exchange; **tauschen** *vt* exchange, swap

täuschen **1.** *vt* deceive **2.** *vi* be deceptive **3.** *vr* be wrong; **täuschend** *adj* deceptive; **Täuschung** *f* deception; (*optical*) illusion

tausend *num* a thousand; *vier~* four thousand; *~ Dank!* thanks a lot; **tausendmal** *adv* a thousand times; **tausendste(r, s)** *adj* thousandth; **Tausendstel** *nt* (-s, -) thousandth

-) (*fraction*) thousandth
Tauwetter *nt* thaw
Taxi *nt* taxi; **Taxifahrer(in)** *m(f)* taxi driver; **Taxistand** *m* taxi rank (*Brit*), taxi stand (*US*)
Team *nt* (-s, -s) team; **Teamarbeit** *f* team work; **teamfähig** *adj* able to work in a team
Technik *f* technology; (*applied*) engineering; (*method, skill*) technique; **Techniker(in)** *m(f)* (-s, -) engineer; SPORT, MUS technician; **technisch** *adj* technical
Techno *m* (-s) MUS techno
Teddybär *m* teddy bear
Tee *m* (-s, -s) tea; **Teebeutel** *m* teabag; **Teekanne** *f* teapot; **Teelöffel** *m* teaspoon
Teer *m* (-(e)s, -e) tar
Teesieb *nt* tea strainer; **Teetasse** *f* teacup
Teich *m* (-(e)s, -e) pond
Teig *m* (-(e)s, -e) dough; **Teigwaren** *pl* pasta *sg*
Teil 1. *m* (-(e)s, -e) part; (*due to sb*) share; **zum ~** partly **2.** *nt* (-(e)s, -e) part; (*part of whole*) component; **teilen** *vt, vr* divide; (*with sb*) share (*mit* with); **20 durch 4 ~** divide 20 by 4
Teilnahme *f* (-, -n) participation (*an* + *dat* in); **teilnehmen** *irr vi* take part (*an* + *dat* in); **Teilnehmer(in)** *m(f)* (-s, -) participant
teils *adv* partly; **teilweise** *adv* partially, in part; **Teilzeit** *f* **~**

arbeiten work part-time
Teint *m* (-s, -s) complexion
Telefon *nt* (-s, -e) telephone; **Telefonanruf** *m*, **Telefonat** *nt* (tele)phone call; **Telefonanschluss** *m* telephone connection; **Telefonauskunft** *f* directory enquiries *pl* (*Brit*), directory assistance (*US*); **Telefonbuch** *nt* telephone directory; **Telefongebühren** *pl* telephone charges *pl*; **Telefongespräch** *nt* telephone conversation; **telefonieren** *vi* **ich telefoniere gerade (mit ...)** I'm on the phone (to ...); **telefonisch** *adj* telephone; (*notification*) by telephone; **Telefonkarte** *f* phonecard; **Telefonnummer** *f* (tele)phone number; **Telefonrechnung** *f* phone bill; **Telefonverbindung** *f* telephone connection; **Telefonzelle** *f* phone box (*Brit*), phone booth
Telegramm *nt* telegram; **Teleobjektiv** *nt* telephoto lens; **Teleshopping** *nt* (-s) teleshopping; **Teleskop** *nt* (-s, -e) telescope
Teller *m* (-s, -) plate
Tempel *m* (-s, -) temple
Temperament *nt* temperament; liveliness; **temperamentvoll** *adj* lively
Temperatur *f* temperature; **bei ~en von 30 Grad** at temperatures of 30 degrees
Tempo *nt* (-s, -s) speed; **Tem-**

polimit nt (-s, -s) speed limit

Tempotaschentuch® nt (paper) tissue, ≈ Kleenex®

Tendenz f tendency; intention

Tennis nt (-) tennis; Tennisball m tennis ball; Tennisplatz m tennis court; Tennisschläger m tennis racket; Tennisspieler(in) m(f) tennis player; Tennisturnier nt tennis tournament

Tenor m (-s, Tenöre) tenor

Teppich m (-s, -e) carpet; Teppichboden m (wall-to-wall) carpet

Termin m (-s, -e) date; (for finishing sth) deadline; (with doctor etc) appointment

Terminal nt (-s, -s) IT, AVIAT terminal

Terminkalender m diary; Terminplaner m appointment organizer, Filofax®; (pocket computer) personal digital assistant, PDA

Terrasse f (-, -n) terrace; (adjoining house) patio

Terror m (-s) terror; Terroranschlag m terrorist attack; terrorisieren vt terrorize; Terrorismus m terrorism; Terrorist(in) m(f) terrorist

Tesafilm® m ≈ sellotape® (Brit), ≈ Scotch tape® (US)

Test m (-s, -s) test

Testament nt will; das Alte/ Neue ~ the Old/New Testament

testen vt test; Testergebnis nt test results pl

Tetanus m (-) tetanus; Tetanusimpfung f (anti-)tetanus injection

teuer adj expensive, dear (Brit)

Teufel m (-s, -) devil; Teufelskreis m vicious circle

Text m (-(e)s, -e) text; (of song) words pl, lyrics pl; Textmarker m (-s, -) highlighter; Textverarbeitung f word processing

Thailand nt Thailand

Theater nt (-s, -) theatre; fam fuss; ins ~ gehen go to the theatre; Theaterkasse f box office; Theaterstück nt (stage) play

Theke f (-, -n) bar; (in shop) counter

Thema nt (-s, Themen) subject, topic; kein ~! no problem

Themse f (-) Thames

Theologie f theology

theoretisch adj theoretical; ~ stimmt das that's right in theory; Theorie f theory

Therapeut(in) m(f) therapist; Therapie f therapy; eine ~ machen undergo therapy

Thermalbad nt thermal bath; (resort) thermal spa; Thermometer nt (-s, -) thermometer; Thermoskanne f Thermos® (flask); Thermostat m (-(e)s, -e) thermostat

These f (-, -n) theory

Thron m (-(e)s, -e) throne

Thunfisch m tuna

Thüringen nt (-s) Thuringia

Thymian m (-s, -e) thyme

Tick m (-(e)s, -s) tic; (idiosyncrasy) quirk; (mania) craze; **ticken** vi tick; **er tickt nicht ganz richtig** he's off his rocker

Ticket nt (-s, -s) (plane) ticket

Tiebreak m (-s, -s) tie break(-er)

tief adj deep; (neckline, note, sun) low; **2 Meter ~** 2 metres deep; **Tief** nt (-s, -s) METEO low; (mood) depression; **Tiefdruck** m METEO low pressure; **Tiefe** f (-, -n) depth; **Tiefgarage** f underground car park (Brit) (or garage (US)); **tiefgekühlt** adj frozen; **Tiefkühlfach** nt freezer compartment; **Tiefkühlkost** f frozen food; **Tiefkühltruhe** f freezer; **Tiefpunkt** m low

Tier nt (-(e)s, -e) animal; **Tierarzt** m, **Tierärztin** f vet; **Tiergarten** m zoo; **Tierhandlung** f pet shop; **Tierheim** nt animal shelter; **tierisch** 1. adj animal 2. adv fam really; **~ ernst** deadly serious; **ich hatte ~ Angst** I was dead scared; **Tierkreiszeichen** nt sign of the zodiac; **Tierpark** m zoo; **Tierquälerei** f cruelty to animals; **Tierschützer(in)** m(f) (-s, -) animal rights campaigner; **Tierversuch** m animal experiment

Tiger m (-s, -) tiger

timen vt time; **Timing** nt (-s)

timing

Tinte f (-, -n) ink; **Tintenfisch** m cuttlefish; (small) squid; (with eight arms) octopus; **Tintenstrichringe** pl calamari pl

Tipp m (-s, -s) tip; **tippen** vt, vi tap; fam type; fam guess

Tirol nt (-s) Tyrol

Tisch m (-(e)s, -e) table; **Tischdecke** f tablecloth; **Tischtennis** nt table tennis; **Tischtennisschläger** m table-tennis bat

Titel m (-s, -) title; **Titelbild** nt cover picture; **Titelmusik** f theme music; **Titelverteidiger(in)** m(f) defending champion

Toast m (-(e)s, -s) toast; **toasten** vt toast; **Toaster** m (-s, -) toaster

Tochter f (-, Töchter) daughter

Tod m (-(e)s, -e) death; **Todesopfer** nt casualty; **Todesstrafe** f death penalty; **todkrank** adj terminally ill; (not life-threatening) seriously ill; **tödlich** adj deadly, fatal; **er ist ~ verunglückt** he was killed in an accident; **todmüde** adj fam dead tired; **todsicher** adj fam dead certain

Tofu m (-(s)) tofu, bean curd

Toilette f toilet, restroom (US); **Toilettenpapier** nt toilet paper

toi, toi, toi interj good luck

tolerant adj tolerant (gegen of)

toll adj mad; (activity) wild; fam (wonderful) great; **Tollwut** f rabies sg

Tomate f (-, -n) tomato; **Tomatenmark** nt tomato purée (Brit) (or paste (US)); **Tomatensaft** m tomato juice

Tombola f (-, -s) raffle, tombola (Brit)

Ton 1. m (-(e)s, -e) clay 2. m (Töne pl) sound; MUS note; (in voice) tone; (hue, nuance) shade

tönen 1. vi sound 2. vt shade; (hair) tint

Toner m (-s, -) toner; **Tonerkassette** f toner cartridge

Tonne f (-, -n) barrel; (weight) tonne, metric ton

Tontechniker(in) m(f) sound engineer

Tönung f hue; (for hair) rinse

Top nt (-s, -s) top

Topf m (-(e)s, Töpfe) pot

Töpfer(in) m(f) (-s, -) potter; **Töpferei** f pottery; (item) piece of pottery

Tor nt (-(e)s, -e) gate; SPORT goal; **ein ~ schießen** score a goal; **Torhüter(in)** m(f) goalkeeper

torkeln vi stagger

Torlinie f goal line

Tornado m (-s, -s) tornado

Torpfosten m goalpost; **Torschütze** m, **Torschützin** f (goal)scorer

Torte f (-, -n) cake; (fruit tart)

flan; (with layers of cream) gateau

Torwart(in) m(f) (-s, -e) goalkeeper

tot adj dead; **~er Winkel** blind spot

total adj total, complete; **Totalschaden** m complete write-off

Tote(r) mf dead man/woman; (body) corpse; **töten** vt, vi kill; **Totenkopf** m skull

totlachen vr kill oneself laughing

Toto m or nt (-s, -s) pools pl

totschlagen irr vt beat to death; **die Zeit ~** kill time

Touchscreen m (-s, -s) touch screen

Toupet nt (-s, -s) toupee

Tour f (-, -en) trip; (circular) tour

Tourismus m tourism; **Tourist(in)** m(f) tourist; **touristisch** adj tourist; pej touristy

traben vi trot

Tournee f (-, -n) tour

Tracht f (-, -en) traditional costume

Tradition f tradition; **traditionell** adj traditional

traf imperf of **treffen**

Trafik f (-, -en) tobacconist's

tragbar adj portable

träge adj sluggish, slow

tragen (trug, getragen) vt carry; (clothes, glasses, hair) wear; (name, fruit) bear; **Träger** m (-s, -) (on dress etc) strap; **Tragflügelboot**

nt hydrofoil

tragisch *adj* tragic; **Tragödie** *f* tragedy

Trainer(in) *m(f)* (-s, -) trainer, coach; **trainieren** *vt*, *vi* train; (*person also*) coach; (*exercise*) practise; **Training** *nt* (-s, -s) training; **Trainingsanzug** *m* tracksuit

Traktor *m* tractor

Trambahn *f* tram (Brit), streetcar (US)

trampen *vi* hitchhike; **Tramper(in)** *m(f)* hitchhiker

Träne *f* (-, -n) tear; **tränen** *vi* water; **Tränengas** *nt* teargas

trank *imperf of* **trinken**

Transfusion *f* transfusion

Transitverkehr *m* transit traffic; **Transitvisum** *nt* transit visa

Transplantation *f* transplant; (*of skin*) graft

Transport *m* (-(e)s, -e) transport; **transportieren** *vt* transport

Transvestit *m* (-en, -en) transvestite

trat *imperf of* **treten**

Traube *f* (-, -n) grape; bunch of grapes; **Traubensaft** *m* grape juice; **Traubenzucker** *m* glucose

trauen 1. *vi* jdm/*einer Sache* ~ trust sb/sth 2. *vr* dare 3. *vt* marry; *sich* ~ *lassen* get married

Trauer *f* (-) sorrow; (*for deceased person*) mourning

Traum *m* (-(e)s, *Träume*) dream; **träumen** *vt*, *vi* dream (*von* of, about); **traumhaft** *adj* dreamlike; *fig* wonderful

traurig *adj* sad (*über* + *acc* about)

Trauschein *m* marriage certificate; **Trauung** *f* wedding ceremony; **Trauzeuge** *m*, **Trauzeugin** *f* witness (*at wedding ceremony*), ≈ best man/maid of honour

Travellerscheck *m* traveller's cheque

treffen (*traf, getroffen*) 1. *vr* meet 2. *vt*, *vi* hit; (*remark*) hurt; (*friend etc*) meet; (*decision*) make; (*measures*) take; **Treffen** *nt* (-s, -) meeting; **Treffer** *m* (-s, -) goal; **Treffpunkt** *m* meeting place

treiben (*trieb, getrieben*) 1. *vt* drive; (*sport*) do 2. *vi* (*on water*) drift; (*plant*) sprout; (*tea, coffee*) be diuretic; **Treiber** *m* (-s, -) *IT* driver; **Treibhaus** *nt* greenhouse; **Treibstoff** *m* fuel

trennen 1. *vt* separate; (*split into parts*) divide 2. *vr* separate; *sich von jdm* ~ leave sb; *sich von etw* ~ part with sth; **Trennung** *f* separation

Treppe *f* (-, -n) stairs *pl*; (*outside*) steps *pl*

Tresen *m* (-s, -) bar; (*in shop*) counter

Tresor *m* (-s, -e) safe

Tretboot *nt* pedal boat; **treten** (*trat, getreten*) 1. *vi* step; ~ *nach* kick at 2. *vt* kick

treu adj (to partner) faithful; (customer, fan) loyal; **Treue** f (-) (in marriage) faithfulness; (of customer, fan) loyalty

Triathlon m (-s, -s) triathlon

Tribüne f (-, -n) stand; (for speaker) platform

Trick m (-s, -e or -s) trick; **Trickfilm** m cartoon

trieb imperf of **treiben**

Trieb m (-(e)s, -e) urge; (instinct) drive; (on tree etc) shoot; **Triebwerk** nt engine

Trikot nt (-s, -s) shirt, jersey

trinkbar adj drinkable; **trinken** (trank, getrunken) vt, vi drink; **einen ~ gehen** go out for a drink; **Trinkgeld** nt tip

Trinkhalm m (drinking) straw; **Trinkschokolade** f drinking chocolate; **Trinkwasser** nt drinking water

Trio nt (-s, -s) trio

Tritt m (-(e)s, -e) step; kick

Triumph m (-(e)s, -e) triumph; **triumphieren** vi triumph (über + acc over)

trivial adj trivial

trocken adj dry; **Trockenheit** f dryness; **trockenlegen** vt (baby) change; **trocknen** vt, vi dry; **Trockner** m (-s, -) dryer

Trödel m (-s) fam junk; **Trödelmarkt** m flea market

trödeln vi fam dawdle

Trommel f (-, -n) drum; **Trommelfell** nt eardrum; **trommeln** vt, vi drum

Trompete f (-, -n) trumpet

Tropen pl tropics pl

Tropf m (-(e)s, -e) MED drip; **am ~ hängen** be on a drip; **tröpfeln** vi drip; **es tröpfelt** it's drizzling; **tropfen** vt, vi drip; **Tropfen** m (-s, -) drop; **tropfenweise** adv drop by drop; **tropfnass** adj dripping wet; **Tropfsteinhöhle** f stalactite cave

tropisch adj tropical

Trost m (-es) consolation, comfort; **trösten** vt console, comfort; **trostlos** adj bleak; (conditions) wretched; **Trostpreis** m consolation prize

trotz prep + gen or dat in spite of; **Trotz** m (-es) defiance; **trotzdem 1.** adv nevertheless **2.** conj although; **trotzig** adj defiant

trüb adj dull; (liquid, glass) cloudy; fig gloomy

Trüffel f (-, -n) truffle

trug imperf of **tragen**

trügerisch adj deceptive

Truhe f (-, -n) chest

Trumpf m (-(e)s, Trümpfe) trump

Trunkenheit f intoxication; **~ am Steuer** drink driving (Brit), drunk driving (US)

Truthahn m turkey

Tschche m (-n, -n), **Tschechin** f Czech; **Tschechien** nt (-s) Czech Republic; **tschechisch** adj Czech;

Tschechisch nt Czech

Tschetschenien nt (-s) Chechnya

tschüs(s) interj bye

T-Shirt nt (-s, -s) T-shirt

Tube f (-, -n) tube

Tuberkulose f (-, -n) tuberculosis, TB

Tuch nt (-(e)s, Tücher) cloth; (for neck) scarf; (for head) headscarf

tüchtig adj competent; (hard-working) efficient

Tugend f (-, -en) virtue; **tugendhaft** adj virtuous

Tulpe f (-, -n) tulip

Tumor m (-s, -en) tumour

Tümpel m (-s, -) pond

tun (tat, getan) **1.** vt do; (sth somewhere) put; **was tust du da?** what are you doing?; **das tut man nicht** you shouldn't do that; **jdm etw ~** (harm) do sth to sb **2.** vi act; **so ~, als ob** act as if **3.** vr impers **es tut sich etwas/ viel** something/ a lot is happening

Tuner m (-s, -) tuner

Tunesien nt (-s) Tunisia

Tunfisch m tuna

Tunnel m (-s, -s or -) tunnel

Tunte f (-, -n) pej fam fairy

tupfen vt, vi dab; (with colour) dot; **Tupfen** m (-s, -) dot

Tür f (-, -en) door; **vor/ an der ~** at the door; **an die ~ gehen**

answer the door

Türke m (-n, -n) Turk; **Türkei** f (-) **die ~** Turkey; **Türkin** f Turk

Türkis m (-es, -e) turquoise

türkisch adj Turkish; **Türkisch** nt Turkish

Turm m (-(e)s, Türme) tower; (pointed church tower) steeple; (in chess) rook, castle

turnen vi do gymnastics; **Turnen** nt (-s) gymnastics sg, physical education, PE; **Turner(in)** m(f) gymnast; **Turnhalle** f gym(nasium); **Turnhose** f gym shorts pl

Turnier nt (-s, -e) tournament

Turnschuh m gym shoe, sneaker (US)

Türschild nt doorplate; **Türschloss** nt lock

tuscheln vt, vi whisper

Tussi f (-, -s) pej fam chick

Tüte f (-, -n) bag

TÜV m (-s, -s) acr = **Technischer Überwachungsverein**; ≈ MOT (Brit), vehicle inspection (US)

Tweed m (-s, -s) tweed

Typ m (-s, -en) type; (car) model; (man) guy, bloke

Typhus m (-) typhoid

typisch adj typical (für of); **ein ~er Fehler** a common mistake; **~ Marcus!** that's just like Marcus; **~ amerikanisch!** that's so American

U

u. a. *abbr* = **und andere(s)**; and others; = **unter anderem, unter anderen**; among other things

u. A. w. g. *abbr* = **um Antwort wird gebeten**; RSVP

U-Bahn *f* underground (*Brit*), subway (*US*)

übel *adj* bad; (*morally*) wicked; **mir ist~** I feel sick; **diese Bemerkung hat er mir ~ genommen** he took offence at my remark; **Übelkeit** *f* nausea

üben *vt, vi* practise

über *prep + dat or acc* (*throw, jump*) over; (*with position also*) above; (*from one side to the other*) across; (*farther up from*) above; (*route*) via; (*concerning*) about; (*quantity*) over, more than; **~ das Wochenende** over the weekend

überall *adv* everywhere

überbacken *adj* (**mit Käse**) ~ au gratin; **überbelichten** *vt* PHOT overexpose; **überbieten** *irr vt* outbid; (*be better than*) surpass; (*record*) break

Überbleibsel *nt* (-s, -) remnant

Überblick *m* overview; *fig* survey; (*understanding*) grasp (*über + acc* of)

überbuchen *vt* overbook;

Überbuchung *f* overbooking

übereinander *adv* on top of each other; (*talk etc*) about each other

übereinstimmen *vi* agree (*mit* with)

überfahren *irr vt* AUTO run over; **Überfahrt** *f* crossing

Überfall *m* robbery; MIL raid; (*on sb*) assault; **überfallen** *irr vt* attack; (*bank*) raid

überfällig *adj* overdue

überfliegen *irr vt* fly over; (*book*) skim through

überflüssig *adj* superfluous

überfordern *vt* demand too much of; (*strength etc*) overtax; **da bin ich überfordert** you've got me there

Überführung *f* flyover (*Brit*), overpass (*US*)

überfüllt *adj* overcrowded

Übergabe *f* handover

Übergang *m* crossing; (*change, passing*) transition; **Übergangslösung** *f* temporary solution, stopgap

übergeben *irr* 1. *vt* hand over 2. *vr* be sick, vomit

Übergepäck *nt* excess baggage

Übergewicht *nt* excess weight; (**10 Kilo**) ~ **haben** be (10 kilos) overweight

überglücklich *adj* overjoyed;

fam over the moon
überhaupt *adv* at all; in general

überheblich *adj* arrogant

überholen *vt* overtake; TECH overhaul; **Überholspur** *f* overtaking (Brit) (or passing (US)) lane; **überholt** *adj* outdated

überhören *vt* miss, not catch; (*deliberately*) ignore; **überladen 1.** *irr vt* overload **2.** *vt fig* cluttered; **überlassen** *irr vt* **jdm etw ~** leave sth to sb; **überlaufen** *irr vi* (*liquid*) overflow

überleben, *vi* survive; **Überlebende(r)** *mf* survivor

überlegen 1. *irr vt* **sich dat etw ~** think about sth; *er hat es sich dat anders überlegt* he's changed his mind **2.** *adj* superior (*dat* to); **Überlegung** *f* consideration

übermäßig *adj* excessive

übermorgen *adv* the day after tomorrow

übernächste(r, s) *adj* **~ Woche** the week after next

übernachten *vi* spend the night (*bei jdm* at sb's place); **Übernachtung** *f* overnight stay; **~ mit Frühstück** bed and breakfast

übernehmen *irr* **1.** *vt* take on; (*post, business*) take over **2.** *vr* take on too much

überprüfen *vt* check; **Überprüfung** *f* check; (*action*) checking

überqueren *vt* cross

überraschen *vt* surprise; **Überraschung** *f* surprise

überreden *vt* persuade; *er hat mich überredet* he talked me into it

überreichen *vt* hand over

überschätzen *vt* overestimate; **überschlagen** *irr* **1.** *vt* estimate **2.** *vr* somersault; (*car*) overturn; (*voice*) crack; **überschneiden** *irr vr* (*lines etc*) intersect; (*dates*) clash

Überschrift *f* heading

Überschwemmung *f* flood

übersehen *irr vt* look (out) over; (*ignore*) overlook

übersetzen *vt* translate (*aus* from, *in* + *acc* into); **Übersetzer(in)** *m(f)* (-s, -) translator; **Übersetzung** *f* translation

Übersicht *f* overall view; (*résumé*) survey; **übersichtlich** *adj* clear

überstehen *irr vt* get over

Überstunden *pl* overtime *sg*

überstürzt *adj* hasty

übertragbar *adj* transferable; MED infectious; **übertragen** *irr* **1.** *vt* transfer (*auf* + *acc* to); RADIO broadcast; (*disease*) transmit **2.** *vr* spread (*auf* + *acc* to) **3.** *adj* figurative; **Übertragung** *f* RADIO broadcast; (*of data*) transmission

übertreffen *irr vt* surpass

übertreiben *irr vt* exaggerate, overdo; **Übertreibung** *f* exaggeration; **übertrieben**

adj exaggerated, overdone

überwachen *vt* supervise; *(suspect)* keep under surveillance

überwand *imperf of* **überwinden**

überweisen *irr vt* transfer; *(patient)* refer *(an + acc* to); **Überweisung** *f* transfer; *(of patient)* referral

überwiegend *adv* mainly

überwinden *(überwand, überwunden)* **1.** *vt* overcome **2.** *vr* make an effort, force oneself; **überwunden** *pp of* **überwinden**

überzeugen *vt* convince; **Überzeugung** *f* conviction

überziehen *irr vt* cover; *(jacket etc)* put on; *(account)* overdraw; **die Betten frisch ~** change the sheets; **Überziehungskredit** *m* overdraft facility

üblich *adj* usual

übrig *adj* remaining; **ist noch Saft ~?** is there any juice left?; **für jdn etwas ~ haben** *fam* have a soft spot for sb; **die Übrigen** *pl* the rest *pl*; **im Übrigen** besides; **~ bleiben** be left (over); **übrigens** *adv* besides; *(incidentally)* by the way

Übung *f* practice; *(set of movements, task etc)* exercise

Ufer *nt* (-s, -) *(of river)* bank; *(of sea, lake)* shore; **am ~** on the bank/shore

Uhr *f* (-, *-en*) clock; watch; **wie**

viel ~ ist es? what time is it?; **1 ~** 1 o'clock; **20 ~** 8 o'clock, 8 pm; **Uhrzeit** *f* time (of day)

Ukraine *f* (-) **die ~** the Ukraine

UKW *abbr* = **Ultrakurzwelle**; VHF

Ulme *f* (-, *-n*) elm

Ultrakurzwelle *f* very high frequency; **Ultraschallaufnahme** *f* MED scan

um 1. *prep* + *acc (space)* (a)round; *(time)* at; **~ etw kämpfen** fight for sth **2.** *conj* (in order) to; **zu klug, ~ zu ...** too clever to ... **3.** *adv (approximately)* about; **die Ferien sind ~** the holidays are over; **die Zeit ist ~** time's up; → **umso**

umarmen *vt* embrace

Umbau *m* rebuilding; *(into sth)* conversion *(zu* into); **umbauen** *vt* rebuild; *(into sth)* convert *(zu* into)

umblättern *vt, vi* turn over

umbringen *irr vt* kill

umbuchen *vi* change one's reservation/flight

umdrehen *vt, vr* turn (round); *(retrace steps)* turn back; **Umdrehung** *f* turn; PHYS, AUTO revolution

umfahren *irr vt* knock down

umfallen *irr vi* fall over

Umfang *m* extent; *(of book)* size; *(of voice, instrument)* range; MATH circumference; **umfangreich** *adj* extensive

Umfrage *f* survey

Umgang m company; (with sb) dealings pl; **umgänglich** adj sociable; **Umgangssprache** f colloquial language, slang

Umgebung f surroundings pl; (social) environment; (friends, colleagues etc) people around one

umgehen 1. irr vi go round; ~ (**können**) mit (know how to) handle **2.** irr vt avoid; (problems) get round; **Umgehungsstraße** f bypass

umgekehrt 1. adj reverse; (contrary) opposite **2.** adv the other way round; **und** ~ and vice versa

umhören vr ask around; **umkehren 1.** vi turn back **2.** vt reverse; **umkippen 1.** vt tip over **2.** vi overturn; fig change one's mind; fam (faint) pass out

Umkleidekabine f changing cubicle (Brit), dressing room (US); **Umkleideraum** m changing room

umleiten vt divert; **Umleitung** f diversion

umrechnen vt convert (in + acc into); **Umrechnung** f conversion; **Umrechnungskurs** m rate of exchange

Umriss m outline

umrühren vi, vt stir

ums contr of **um das**

Umsatz m turnover

umschalten vi turn over

Umschlag m cover; (of book)

jacket; MED compress; (of letter) envelope

Umschulung f retraining

umsehen irr vr look around; (search) look out (nach for)

umso adv all the; ~ **mehr** all the more; ~ **besser** so much the better

umsonst adv in vain; (free) for nothing

Umstand m circumstance; **Umstände** pl fig fuss; **in anderen Umständen sein** be pregnant; **jdm Umstände machen** cause sb a lot of trouble; **unter diesen/keinen Umständen** under these/no circumstances; **unter Umständen** possibly; **umständlich** adj (method) complicated; (way of expressing oneself) long-winded; (person) ponderous

umsteigen irr vi change (trains/buses)

umstellen 1. vt (move) change round **2.** vr adapt (auf + acc to); **Umstellung** f change; (adapting) adjustment

Umtausch m exchange; **umtauschen** vt exchange; (currency) change

Umweg m detour

Umwelt f environment; **Umweltbelastung** f ecological damage; **Umweltschutz** m environmental protection; **Umweltschützer(in)** m(f) (-s, -) environmentalist; **Umweltverschmutzung** f pollution; **umweltverträglich** adj environment-friendly

umwerfen irr vt knock over; fig (change) upset; fig fam flabbergast

umziehen irr **1.** vt, vr change **2.** vi move (house); **Umzug** m procession; (to new house) move

unabhängig adj independent; **Unabhängigkeitstag** m Independence Day, Fourth of July (US)

unabsichtlich adv unintentionally

unangenehm adj unpleasant; **Unannehmlichkeit** f inconvenience; **~en** pl trouble sg

unanständig adj indecent; **unappetitlich** adj (food) unappetizing; (repulsive) off-putting; **unbeabsichtigt** adj unintentional; **unbedeutend** adj insignificant, unimportant; (error) slight

unbedingt 1. adj unconditional **2.** adv absolutely

unbefriedigend adj unsatisfactory; **unbegrenzt** adj unlimited; **unbekannt** adj unknown; **unbeliebt** adj unpopular; **unbemerkt** adj unnoticed; **unbequem** adj (chair, person) uncomfortable; **unbeständig** adj (weather) unsettled; (situation) unstable; (person) unreliable; **unbestimmt** adj indefinite; **unbewusst** adj uncon-

scious; **unbezahlt** adj unpaid; **unbrauchbar** adj useless

und conj and; **~ so weiter** and so on; **na ~?** so what?

undankbar adj (person) ungrateful; (task) thankless; **undenkbar** adj inconceivable; **undeutlich** adj indistinct; **undicht** adj leaky; **uneben** adj uneven; **unecht** adj (jewellery etc) fake; **unehelich** adj (child) illegitimate; **unendlich** adj endless; MATH infinite; **unentbehrlich** adj indispensable; **unentgeltlich** adj free (of charge)

unentschieden adj undecided; **~ enden** SPORT end in a draw

unerfreulich adj unpleasant; **unerlässlich** adj indispensable; **unerträglich** adj unbearable; **unerwartet** adj unexpected; **unfähig** adj incompetent; **~ sein, etw zu tun** be incapable of doing sth; **unfair** adj unfair

Unfall m accident; **Unfallstation** f casualty ward; **Unfallstelle** f scene of the accident; **Unfallversicherung** f accident insurance

unfreundlich adj unfriendly

Ungarn nt (-s) Hungary

Ungeduld f impatience; **ungeduldig** adj impatient

ungeeignet adj unsuitable

ungefähr 1. adj approximate **2.** adv approximately; **~ 10**

Kilometer about 10 kilometres; **wann ~?** about what time?; **wo ~?** whereabouts?

ungefährlich adj harmless; (involving no danger) safe

ungeheuer 1. adj huge **2.** adv fam enormously; **Ungeheuer** nt (-s, -) monster

ungehorsam adj disobedient (gegenüber to); **ungemütlich** adj unpleasant; (person) disagreeable; **ungenießbar** adj inedible; undrinkable; **ungenügend** adj unsatisfactory; (mark in school) ≈ F; **ungepflegt** adj (garden) untended; (appearance) unkempt; (hands) neglected; **ungerade** adj odd

ungerecht adj unjust; **ungerechtfertigt** adj unjustified; **Ungerechtigkeit** f injustice, unfairness

ungern adv reluctantly; **ungeschickt** adj clumsy; **ungeschminkt** adj without make-up; **ungesund** adj unhealthy; **ungewiss** adj uncertain; **ungewöhnlich** adj unusual

Ungeziefer nt (-s) vermin pl

ungezwungen adj relaxed

unglaublich adj incredible

Unglück nt (-(e)s, -e) misfortune; (in game, career etc) bad luck; (train or plane crash) disaster; **das bringt ~** that's unlucky; **~lich** adj unhappy; (unsuccessful) unlucky; (unfavou-

rable) unfortunate; **unglücklicherweise** adv unfortunately

ungültig adj invalid

ungünstig adj inconvenient

unheilbar adj incurable; **~ krank sein** be terminally ill

unheimlich 1. adj eerie **2.** adv fam incredibly

unhöflich adj impolite

uni adj plain

Uni f (-, -s) uni

Uniform f (-, -en) uniform

Universität f university

Unkenntnis f ignorance

unklar adj unclear

Unkosten pl expenses pl

Unkraut nt weeds pl

unlogisch adj illogical

unmissverständlich adj unambiguous

unmittelbar adj immediate; **~ darauf** immediately afterwards

unmöbliert adj unfurnished

unmöglich adj impossible

unnötig adj unnecessary

UNO f (-) acr = **United Nations Organization**; UN

unordentlich adj untidy; **Unordnung** f disorder

unpassend adj inappropriate; (time) inconvenient; **unpersönlich** adj impersonal; **unpraktisch** adj impractical

Unrecht nt wrong; **zu ~** wrongly; **~ haben, im ~ sein** be wrong

unregelmäßig adj irregular; **unreif** adj unripe; **unruhig**

adj restless; **~ schlafen** have a bad night

uns *pron* acc, dat of **wir**; us, (to) us; **~ (selbst)** (reflexive) ourselves; **sehen Sie ~?** can you see us?; **er schickte es ~** he sent it to us; **lasst~ in Ruhe** leave us alone; **ein Freund von ~** a friend of ours; **wir haben ~ hingesetzt** we sat down; **wir haben ~ amüsiert** we enjoyed ourselves; **wir mögen ~** we like each other

unscharf *adj* PHOT blurred, out of focus

unschlüssig *adj* undecided

unschuldig *adj* innocent

unser *pron* our; **unsere(r, s)** *pron* ours; **unseretwegen** *adv* because of us; (to please us) for our sake

unseriös *adj* dubious; **unsicher** *adj* uncertain; (lacking confidence) insecure

Unsinn *m* nonsense

unsterblich *adj* immortal; **~ verliebt** madly in love

unsympathisch *adj* unpleasant; **er ist mir ~** I don't like him

unten *adv* below; (in house) downstairs; (at lower end) at the bottom; **nach ~** down; **unter** *prep + acc or dat* under; below; (people) among; (time) during

Unterarm *m* forearm

Unterbewusstsein *nt* subconscious

unterbrechen *irr vt* interrupt; **Unterbrechung** *f* interruption; **ohne ~** nonstop

unterdrücken *vt* suppress; (people) oppress

untere(r, s) *adj* lower

untereinander *adv* (in space) one below the other; (reciprocally) each other; (person) themselves / yourselves / ourselves

Unterführung *f* underpass

untergehen *irr vi* go down; (sun also) set; (nation) perish; (world) come to an end; (by noise) be drowned out

Untergeschoss *nt* basement; **Untergewicht** *nt* (**10 Kilo**) **~ haben** be (10 kilos) underweight; **Untergrund** *m* foundation; POL underground; **Untergrundbahn** *f* underground (Brit), subway (US)

unterhalb *adv, prep + gen* below; **~ von** below

Unterhalt *m* maintenance; **unterhalten** *irr* **1.** *vt* maintain; (audience, guest) entertain **2.** *vr* talk; (have a good time) enjoy oneself; **Unterhaltung** *f* entertainment; talk, conversation

Unterhemd *nt* vest (Brit), undershirt (US); **Unterhose** *f* underpants *pl*; (for women) briefs *pl*

unterirdisch *adj* underground

Unterkiefer *m* lower jaw

Unterkunft f (-, -*künfte*) accommodation

Unterlage f document; (*for resting on when writing*) pad

unterlassen *irr vt* **es ~, etw zu tun** fail to do sth; (*hold back*) refrain from doing sth

unterlegen *adj* inferior (*dat* to); (*beaten*) defeated

Unterleib m abdomen

Unterlippe f lower lip

Untermiete f **zur ~ wohnen** be a subtenant; **Untermieter(in)** m(f) subtenant

unternehmen *irr vt* (*trip*) go on; (*attempt*) make; **etwas ~** do something (*gegen* about); **Unternehmen** nt (-s, -) undertaking; COMM company; **Unternehmensberater(in)** m(f) (-s, -) management consultant; **Unternehmer(in)** m(f) (-s, -) entrepreneur

Unterricht m (-(e)s, -e) lessons pl; **unterrichten** vt teach

unterschätzen vt underestimate

unterscheiden *irr* 1. vt distinguish (*von* from, *zwischen* + dat between) 2. vr differ (*von* from)

Unterschenkel m lower leg

Unterschied m (-(e)s, -e) difference; **im ~ zu dir** unlike you; **unterschiedlich** adj different

unterschreiben *irr vt* sign; **Unterschrift** f signature

Untersetzer m (-s, -) table-

mat; (*for glass*) coaster

unterste(r, s) adj lowest, bottom

unterstellen vr take shelter

unterstreichen *irr vt* a. fig underline

unterstützen vt support; **Unterstützung** f support

untersuchen vt MED examine; (*police*) investigate; **Untersuchung** f examination; (*by police*) investigation

Untertasse f saucer; **Unterteil** nt lower part, bottom; **Untertitel** m subtitle

untervermieten vt sublet

Unterwäsche f underwear

unterwegs adv on the way

unterzeichnen vt sign

untreu adj unfaithful; **unüberlegt 1.** adj ill-considered **2.** adv without thinking; **unüblich** adj unusual; **unverantwortlich** adj irresponsible

unverbindlich 1. adj not binding; (*reply*) noncommittal **2.** adv COMM without obligation

unverbleit adj unleaded; **unverheiratet** adj unmarried, single; **unvermeidlich** adj unavoidable; **unvernünftig** adj silly; **unverschämt** adj impudent; **unverständlich** adj incomprehensible; **unverträglich** adj (*food*) indigestible; **unverzüglich** adj immediate; **unvollständig** adj incomplete; **unvorsich-**

unwahrscheinlich 254

tig adj careless
unwahrscheinlich 1. adj improbable, unlikely **2.** adv fam incredibly
Unwetter nt thunderstorm
unwichtig adj unimportant
unwiderstehlich adj irresistible
unwillkürlich 1. adj involuntary **2.** adv instinctively
unwohl adj unwell, ill
unzählig adj innumerable, countless
unzerbrechlich adj unbreakable; **unzertrennlich** adj inseparable; **unzufrieden** adj dissatisfied; **unzugänglich** adj inaccessible; **unzumutbar** adj unacceptable; **unzutreffend** adj inapplicable; **unzuverlässig** adj unreliable
Update nt (-s, -s) IT update
üppig adj (meal) lavish; (vegetation) lush
uralt adj ancient, very old
Uran nt (-s) uranium
Uranus m (-) Uranus
Uraufführung f premiere
Urenkel m great-grandson; **Urenkelin** f great-granddaughter; **Urgroßeltern** pl great-grandparents pl; **Urgroßmutter** f great-grandmother; **Urgroßvater** m great-grandfather

Urheber(in) m(f) (-s, -) originator; (writer) author
Urin m (-s, -e) urine; **Urinprobe** f urine specimen
Urkunde f (-, -n) document
Urlaub m (-(e)s, -e) holiday (Brit), vacation (US); **im ~** on holiday (Brit), on vacation (US); **in ~ fahren** go on holiday (Brit) (or vacation (US)); **Urlauber(in)** m(f) (-s, -) holiday-maker (Brit), vacationer (US); **Urlaubsort** m holiday resort; **urlaubsreif** adj ready for a holiday (Brit) (or vacation (US)); **Urlaubszeit** f holiday season (Brit), vacation period (US)
Urologe m, **Urologin** f urologist
Ursache f cause (für of); **keine ~!** not at all; (in reply to apology) that's all right
Ursprung m origin; **ursprünglich 1.** adj original **2.** adv originally
Urteil nt (-s, -e) opinion; LAW verdict; (penalty) sentence; **urteilen** vi judge
Uruguay m (-s) Uruguay
Urwald m jungle
USA pl USA sg
User(in) m(f) (-s, -) IT user
usw. abbr = **und so weiter**; etc

V

vage *adj* vague

Vagina *f* (-, *Vaginen*) vagina

vakuumverpackt *adj* vacuum-packed

Valentinstag *m* St Valentine's Day

Vandalismus *m* vandalism

Vanille *f* (-) vanilla

variieren *vt, vi* vary

Vase *f* (-, -n) vase

Vater *m* (-s, *Väter*) father; **väterlich** *adj* paternal; **Vaterschaft** *f* fatherhood; LAW paternity; **Vatertag** *m* Father's Day; **Vaterunser** *nt das ~ (beten)* (to say) the Lord's Prayer

V-Ausschnitt *m* V-neck

v. Chr. *abbr* = **vor Christus**; BC

Veganer(in) *m(f)* (-s, -) vegan; **Vegetarier(in)** *m(f)* (-s, -) vegetarian; **vegetarisch** *adj* vegetarian

Veilchen *nt* violet

Velo *nt* (-s, -s) (*Swiss*) bicycle

Vene *f* (-, -n) vein

Venedig *nt* (-s) Venice

Venezuela *nt* (-s) Venezuela

Ventil *nt* (-s, -e) valve

Ventilator *m* ventilator

Venus *f* (-) Venus

Venusmuschel *f* clam

verabreden 1. *vt* arrange **2.** *vr* arrange to meet (*mit jdm* sb); **ich bin schon verabredet** I'm already meeting someone; **Verabredung** *f* arrangement; (*meeting*) appointment; (*with friend*) date

verabschieden 1. *vt* say goodbye to; (*law*) pass **2.** *vr* say goodbye

verachten *vt* despise; **verächtlich** *adj* contemptuous; (*deserving contempt*) contemptible; **Verachtung** *f* contempt

verallgemeinern *vt* generalize

Veranda *f* (-, *Veranden*) veranda, porch (*US*)

veränderlich *adj* changeable; **verändern** *vt, vr* change; **Veränderung** *f* change

veranlassen *vt* cause

veranstalten *vt* organize; **Veranstalter(in)** *m(f)* (-s, -) organizer; **Veranstaltung** *f* event; **Veranstaltungsort** *m* venue

verantworten 1. *vt* take responsibility for **2.** *vr sich für etw* ~ answer for sth; **verantwortlich** *adj* responsible (*für* for); **Verantwortung** *f* responsibility (*für* for)

verärgern *vt* annoy

verarschen *vt fam* take the piss out of (*Brit*), make a sucker out of (*US*)

Verb *nt* (-s, -en) verb

Verband m MED bandage; (*organization*) association; Verband(s)kasten m first-aid box; Verband(s)zeug nt dressing material

verbergen irr vt, vr hide (*vor* + *dat* from)

verbessern 1. vt improve; (*error, person speaking*) correct **2.** vr improve; (*when speaking*) correct oneself; Verbesserung f improvement; (*of error*) correction

verbiegen irr vt, vr bend

verbieten irr vt forbid; **jdm ~, etw zu tun** forbid sb to do sth

verbilligt adj reduced

verbinden irr **1.** vt connect; (*do or have at the same time*) combine; MED bandage; **können Sie mich mit ... ?** TEL can you put me through to ...?; **ich verbinde** TEL I'm putting you through; CHEM combine; Verbindung f connection

verbleit adj leaded

Verbot nt (-(e)s, -e) ban (*für, von* on); verboten adj forbidden; **es ist ~** it's not allowed; **es ist ~, hier zu parken** you're not allowed to park here; **Rauchen ~** no smoking

verbrannt adj burnt

Verbrauch m (-(e)s) consumption; verbrauchen vt use up; Verbraucher(in) m(f) (-s, -) consumer

Verbrechen nt (-s, -) crime;

Verbrecher(in) m(f) (-s, -) criminal

verbreiten vt, vr spread

verbrennen irr vt burn; Verbrennung f burning; (*in engine*) combustion

verbringen irr vt spend

verbunden adj **falsch ~** sorry, wrong number

Verdacht m (-(e)s) suspicion; verdächtig adj suspicious; verdächtigen vt suspect

verdammt interj fam damn

verdanken vt **jdm etw ~** owe sth to sb

verdarb imperf of **verderben**

verdauen vt a. fig digest; Verdauung f digestion

Verdeck nt (-(e)s, -e) top

verderben (verdarb, verdorben) **1.** vt spoil; (*morally*) ruin; (*morally*) corrupt; **ich habe mir den Magen verdorben** I've got an upset stomach **2.** vi (*food*) go off

verdienen vt earn; (*morally*) deserve; Verdienst **1.** m (-(e)s, -e) earnings pl **2.** nt (-(e)s, -e) merit; (*contribution*) service (*um* to)

verdoppeln vt double

verdorben 1. pp of **verderben 2.** adj spoilt; (*damaged*) ruined; (*morally*) corrupt

verdrehen vt twist; (*eyes*) roll; **jdm den Kopf ~** fig turn sb's head

verdünnen vt dilute

verdunsten vi evaporate

verdursten vi die of thirst

verehren vt admire; REL worship; **Verehrer(in)** m(f) (-s, -) admirer

Verein m (-(e)s, -e) association; (for sport, hobby) club

vereinbaren vt arrange; **Vereinbarung** f agreement, arrangement

vereinigen vt, vr unite; **Vereinigtes Königreich** nt United Kingdom; **Vereinigte Staaten (von Amerika)** pl United States sg (of America); **Vereinigung** f union; (organization) association; **Vereinte Nationen** pl United Nations pl

vereisen 1. vi (road) freeze over; (window) ice up 2. vt MED freeze

verfahren irr 1. vi proceed 2. vr get lost; **Verfahren** nt (-s, -) procedure; TECH method; LAW proceedings pl

verfallen irr vi decline; (ticket etc) expire; **~ in** + acc lapse into; **Verfallsdatum** nt expiry (Brit) (or expiration (US)) date; (of food) best-before date

verfärben vr change colour; (washing) discolour

Verfasser(in) m(f) (-s, -) author, writer; **Verfassung** f condition; POL constitution

verfaulen vi rot

verfehlen vt miss

Verfilmung f film (or screen) version

verfluchen vt curse

verfolgen vt pursue; POL persecute

verfügbar adj available; **verfügen** vi **über etw** acc **~** have sth at one's disposal; **Verfügung** f order; **jdm zur ~ stehen** be at sb's disposal

verführen vt tempt; (sexually) seduce; **verführerisch** adj seductive

vergangen adj past; **~e Woche** last week; **Vergangenheit** f past

Vergaser m (-s, -) AUTO carburettor

vergaß imperf of **vergessen**

vergeben irr vt forgive; (jdm etw sb for sth); **vergebens** adv in vain; **vergeblich** 1. adv in vain 2. adj vain, futile

vergehen irr 1. vi pass 2. vr **sich an jdm ~** indecently assault sb; **Vergehen** nt (-s, -) offence

vergessen (vergaß, vergessen) vt forget; **vergesslich** adj forgetful

vergeuden vt squander, waste

vergewaltigen vt rape; **Vergewaltigung** f rape

vergewissern vr make sure

vergiften vt poison; **Vergiftung** f poisoning

Vergissmeinnicht nt (-(e)s, -e) forget-me-not

Vergleich m (-(e)s, -e) comparison; LAW settlement; **im ~ zu** compared to (or with); **vergleichen** irr vt compare

(*mit* to, with)
Vergnügen *nt* (-s, -) pleasure; **viel ~!** enjoy yourself; **vergnügt** *adj* cheerful; **Vergnügungspark** *m* amusement park

vergriffen *adj* (*book*) out of print; (*product*) out of stock
vergrößern *vt* enlarge; (*in quantity*) increase; (*with lens*) magnify; **Vergrößerung** *f* enlargement; (*in quantity*) increase; (*with lens*) magnification; **Vergrößerungsglas** *nt* magnifying glass

verhaften *vt* arrest
verhalten *irr vr* behave; **Verhalten** *nt* (-s) behaviour
Verhältnis *nt* relationship (*zu* with); MATH ratio; **~se** *pl* circumstances *pl*, conditions *pl*; **im ~ von 1 zu 2** in a ratio of 1 to 2; **verhältnismäßig 1.** *adj* relative **2.** *adv* relatively
verhandeln *vi* negotiate (*über etw acc* sth); **Verhandlung** *f* negotiation
verheimlichen *vt* keep secret (*jdm* from sb)
verheiratet *adj* married
verhindern *vt* prevent; **sie ist verhindert** she can't make it
Verhör *nt* (-(e)s, -e) interrogation; (*in court*) examination
verhören 1. *vt* interrogate; (*in court*) examine **2.** *vr* mishear
verhungern *vi* starve to death
verhüten *vt* prevent; **Verhü-**

tung *f* prevention; (*with pill, condom etc*) contraception; **Verhütungsmittel** *nt* contraceptive

verirren *vr* get lost
Verkauf *m* sale; **verkaufen** *vt* sell; **zu ~** for sale; **Verkäufer(in)** *m(f)* seller; (*professional*) salesperson; (*in shop*) shop assistant (*Brit*), salesperson (*US*); **verkäuflich** *adj* for sale

Verkehr *m* (-s, -e) traffic; (*sexual*) intercourse; (*general use*) circulation; **verkehren** *vi* (*bus etc*) run; **~ mit** associate (*or* mix) with; **Verkehrsampel** *f* traffic lights *pl*; **Verkehrsamt** *nt* tourist information office; **Verkehrsfunk** *m* travel news *sg*; **Verkehrsinsel** *f* traffic island; **Verkehrsmeldung** *f* traffic report; **Verkehrsmittel** *nt* means *sg* of transport; **öffentliche ~** *pl* public transport *sg*; **Verkehrsschild** *nt* traffic sign; **Verkehrsunfall** *m* road accident; **Verkehrszeichen** *nt* traffic sign

verkehrt *adj* wrong; (*the wrong way round, inside out*); **du machst es ~** you're doing it wrong
verklagen *vt* take to court
verkleiden 1. *vt, vr* dress up (*als* as) **2.** *vr* dress up (*als* as); (*to avoid being recognized*) disguise oneself; **Verkleidung** *f* fancy dress

verkleinern vt reduce; (room, area etc) make smaller; **verkommen 1.** irr vi deteriorate; (person) go downhill **2.** adj (house etc) dilapidated; (morally) depraved; **verkraften** vt cope with

verkratzt adj scratched

verkühlen vr get a chill

verkürzen vt shorten

Verlag m (-(e)s, -e) publishing company

verlangen 1. vt demand; want; (price) ask; (expect) ask (von of); (person) ask for; (passport etc) ask to see; **~ Sie Herrn X** ask for Mr X **2.** vi **~ nach** ask for

verlängern vt extend; (passport, permit) renew; **Verlängerung** f extension; SPORT extra time; (of passport, permit) renewal; **Verlängerungsschnur** f extension cable; **Verlängerungswoche** f extra week

verlassen 1. irr vt leave **2.** irr vr rely (auf + acc on) **3.** adj desolate; (person) abandoned; **verlässlich** adj reliable

Verlauf m course; **verlaufen** irr **1.** vi (path, border) run (entlang along); (in time) pass; (colours) run **2.** vr get lost; (crowd) disperse

verlegen vt move; (lose) mislay; (book) publish **2.** adj embarrassed; **Verlegenheit** f embarrassment; (situation) difficulty

Verleih m (-(e)s, -e) hire company (Brit), rental company (US); **verleihen** irr vt lend; (commercially) hire (out) (Brit), rent (out) (US); (prize, medal) award

verleiten vt **jdn dazu ~, etw zu tun** induce sb to do sth

verlernen vt forget

verletzen vt injure; fig hurt; **Verletzte(r)** mf injured person; **Verletzung** f injury; (of law etc) violation

verlieben vr fall in love (in jdn with sb); **verliebt** adj in love

verlieren (verlor, verloren) vt, vi lose

verloben vr get engaged (mit to); **Verlobte(r)** mf fiancé / fiancée; **Verlobung** f engagement

verlor imperf of **verlieren**

verloren pp of **verlieren**

verlosen vt raffle; **Verlosung** f raffle

Verlust m (-(e)s, -e) loss

vermehren vt, vr multiply; (amount) increase

vermeiden irr vt avoid

vermeintlich adj supposed

vermieten vt rent (out), let (out) (Brit); (car) hire (out) (Brit), rent (out) (US); **Vermieter(in)** m(f) landlord / landlady

vermischen vt, vr mix

vermissen vt miss; **vermisst** adj missing; **jdn als ~ melden** report sb missing

Vermögen nt (-s, -) fortune

vermuten vt suppose; (sth bad) suspect; **vermutlich 1.** adj probable **2.** adv probably; **Vermutung** f supposition; (of sth bad) suspicion

vernachlässigen vt neglect

vernichten vt destroy; **vernichtend** adj fig crushing; (look) withering; (criticism) scathing

Vernunft f (-) reason; **vernünftig** adj sensible; (price) reasonable

veröffentlichen vt publish

verordnen vt MED prescribe; **Verordnung** f order; MED prescription

verpachten vt lease (out) (an + acc to)

verpacken vt pack; (in paper) wrap up

Verpackung f packaging

verpassen vt miss

verpflegen vt feed; **Verpflegung** f feeding; food; (in hotel) board

verpflichten 1. vt oblige; (employ) engage **2.** vr commit oneself (etw zu tun to doing sth)

verpfuschen vt fam make a mess of; vulg fuck up

verprügeln vt beat up

verraten irr **1.** vt betray; (secret) divulge; **aber nicht ~!** but don't tell anyone **2.** vr give oneself away

verrechnen 1. vt ~ **mit** set off against **2.** vr miscalculate;

Verrechnungsscheck m crossed cheque (Brit), check for deposit only (US)

verregnet adj rainy

verreisen vi go away (nach to); **sie ist (geschäftlich) verreist** she's away (on business); **verrenken** vt contort; MED dislocate; **sich** dat **den Knöchel ~** sprain (or twist) one's ankle; **verringern** vt reduce

verrostet adj rusty

verrückt adj mad, crazy; **es macht mich ~** it's driving me mad

versagen vi fail; **Versagen** nt (-s) failure; **Versager(in)** m(f) (-s, -) failure

versalzen irr vt put too much salt in / on

versammeln vt, vr assemble, gather; **Versammlung** f meeting

Versand m (-(e)s) dispatch; (in company) dispatch department; **Versandhaus** nt mail-order company

versäumen vt miss; (not do) neglect; **~, etw zu tun** fail to do sth

verschätzen vr miscalculate

verschenken vt give away; (chance) waste

verschicken vt send off

verschieben irr vt postpone, put off; (push) move

verschieden adj different; (several) various; **sie sind ~ groß** they are of different sizes; **Verschiedene** pl various people / things pl; **Verschiedenes** various things pl

verschimmelt adj mouldy

verschlafen irr **1.** vt sleep through; fig miss **2.** vi, vr oversleep

verschlechtern vr deteriorate, get worse; Verschlechterung f deterioration

verschließbar adj lockable; **verschließen** irr vt close; (with key) lock

verschlimmern 1. vt make worse **2.** vr get worse

verschlossen adj locked; fig reserved

verschlucken 1. vt swallow **2.** vr choke (an + dat on)

Verschluss m lock; (on dress) fastener; PHOT shutter; (bung) stopper

verschmutzen vt get dirty; (environment) pollute

verschnaufen vi **ich muss mal** ~ I need to get my breath back

verschneit adj snow-covered

verschnupft adj ~ **sein** have a cold; fam be peeved

verschonen vt spare (jdn mit etw sb sth)

verschreiben irr vt MED prescribe; **verschreibungspflichtig** adj available only on prescription

verschwand imperf of **verschwinden**

verschweigen irr vt keep secret; **jdm etw** ~ keep sth from sb

verschwenden vt waste; Verschwendung f waste

verschwiegen adj discreet; (place) secluded

verschwinden (verschwand, verschwunden) vi disappear, vanish; **verschwinde!** get lost!; verschwunden pp of **verschwinden**

Versehen nt (-s, -) **aus** ~ by mistake; versehentlich adv by mistake

versenden irr vt send off

versetzen 1. vt transfer; (jewellery etc) pawn; fam (on a date) stand up **2.** vr **sich in jdn** (or **jds Lage**) ~ put oneself in sb's place

verseuchen vt contaminate

versichern vt insure; (confirm) assure; **versichert sein** be insured; Versichertenkarte f health-insurance card; Versicherung f insurance; Versicherungskarte f **grüne** ~ green card (Brit), insurance document for driving abroad; Versicherungspolice f insurance policy

versilbert adj silver-plated

versinken irr vi sink

versöhnen 1. vt reconcile **2.** vr become reconciled

versorgen 1. vt provide, supply (mit with); (family) look after **2.** vr look after oneself; Versorgung f provision; (care) maintenance; (money) benefit

verspäten vr be late; **verspätet** adj late; **Verspätung** f delay; **(eine Stunde)** ~ **haben** be (an hour) late

versprechen irr **1.** vt promise **2.** vr **ich habe mich versprochen** I didn't mean to say that

Verstand m mind; (common) sense; **den ~ verlieren** lose one's mind; **verständigen 1.** vt inform **2.** vr communicate; (agree) come to an understanding; **Verständigung** f communication; **verständlich** adj understandable; **Verständnis** nt understanding (für of); (compassion) sympathy; **verständnisvoll** adj understanding

Verstärker m (-s, -) amplifier

verstauchen vt sprain

Versteck nt (-(e)s, -e) hiding place; ~ **spielen** play hide-and-seek; **verstecken** vt, vr hide (vor + dat from)

verstehen irr irr **1.** vt understand; **falsch** ~ misunderstand **2.** vr get on (mit with)

verstellbar adj adjustable; **verstellen 1.** vt move; (clock) adjust; (obstruct) block; (voice, handwriting) disguise **2.** vr pretend, put on an act

verstopfen vt block up; MED constipate; **Verstopfung** f obstruction; MED constipation

Verstoß m infringement, violation (gegen of)

Versuch m (-(e)s, -e) attempt; (scientific) experiment; **versuchen** vt try

vertauschen vt exchange; (by mistake) mix up

verteidigen vt defend

verteilen vt distribute

Vertrag m (-(e)s, Verträge) contract; POL treaty

vertragen irr **1.** vt stand, bear **2.** vr get along (with each other); (be reconciled) make it up

vertrauen vi jdm/einer Sache ~ trust sb/sth; **Vertrauen** nt (-s) trust (in + acc in, zu in); to sb) have no faith; **ich hab's ihm im ~ gesagt** I told him in confidence; **vertraulich** adj confidential; **vertraut** adj **sich mit etw ~ machen** familiarize oneself with sth

vertreten irr vt represent; (opinion) hold; **Vertreter(in)** m(f) (-s, -) representative

Vertrieb m (-(e)s, -e) sales department

verunglücken vi have an accident; **tödlich ~** be killed in an accident

verursachen vt cause

verurteilen vt condemn

verwackeln vt (photo) blur

verwählen vr dial the wrong number

verwalten vt manage; (offi-

cials) administer; **Verwalter(in)** *m(f)* (*-s, -*) manager; **Verwaltung** *f* management; (*by officials*) administration
verwandt *adj* related (*mit* to); **Verwandte(r)** *mf* relative, relation; **Verwandtschaft** *f* relationship; (*people*) relations *pl*
verwarnen *vt* warn; SPORT caution
verwechseln *vt* confuse (*mit* with); (*for sb or sth else*) mistake (*mit* for)
verweigern *vt* refuse
verwenden *vt* use; **Verwendung** *f* use
verwirklichen *vt* realize; **sich selbst ~** fulfil oneself
verwirren *vt* confuse; **Verwirrung** *f* confusion
verwöhnen *vt* spoil
verwunderlich *adj* surprising; **Verwunderung** *f* astonishment
verwüsten *vt* devastate
verzählen *vr* miscount
verzehren *vt* consume
Verzeichnis *nt* (*of books, products*) catalogue; (*in book*) index; *irr* Directory
verzeihen (*verzieh, verziehen*) *vt, vi* forgive (*jdm etw* sb for sth); **~ Sie bitte, ...** excuse me, ...; **~ Sie die Störung** sorry to disturb you; **Verzeihung** *f ~!* sorry; **~, ...** excuse me, ...; (*jdn*) **um ~ bitten** apologize (to sb)
verzichten *vi* **auf etw** *acc* **~** do

without sth; (*abandon*) give sth up
verzieh *imperf of* **verzeihen**
verziehen *pp of* **verzeihen**
verziehen *irr* **1.** *vt* (*child*) spoil; **das Gesicht ~** pull a face **2.** *vr* go out of shape; (*go away*) disappear
verzieren *vt* decorate
verzögern 1. *vt* delay **2.** *vr* be delayed; **Verzögerung** *f* delay
verzweifeln *vi* despair (*an* + *dat* of); **verzweifelt** *adj* desperate; **Verzweiflung** *f* despair
Vetter *m* (*-s, -n*) cousin
vgl. *abbr* = **vergleiche**; cf
Viagra® *nt* (*-s*) Viagra®
Vibrator *m* (*-s, -en*) vibrator; **vibrieren** *vi* vibrate
Video *nt* (*-s, -s*) video; **auf ~ aufnehmen** video; **Videoclip** *m* (*-s, -s*) video clip; **Videofilm** *m* video; **Videogerät** *nt* video (recorder); **Videokamera** *f* video camera; **Videokassette** *f* video (cassette); **Videorekorder** *m* video recorder; **Videospiel** *nt* video game; **Videothek** *f* (*-, -en*) video library
Vieh *nt* (*-(e)s*) cattle
viel 1. *pron* a lot (of), lots of; **~ Arbeit** a lot of work, lots of work; **~e Leute** a lot of people, lots of people, many people; **zu ~** too much; **zu ~e** too many; **sehr ~** a great deal of; **sehr ~e** a great

many; **ziemlich ~/~e** quite a lot of; **nicht ~** not much, not a lot of; **nicht ~e** not many, not a lot of; **sie sagt nicht ~** she doesn't say a lot; **gibt es ~?** is there much?, is there a lot?; **gibt es ~e?** are there many?, are there a lot? **2.** adv a lot; **er geht ~ ins Kino** he goes a lot to the cinema; **sehr ~** a great deal; **ziemlich ~** quite a lot; **~ besser** much better; **~ teurer** much more expensive; **~ zu ~** far too much

vielleicht adv perhaps; **~ ist sie krank** perhaps she's ill, she might be ill; **weißt du ~, wo er ist?** do you know where he is (by any chance)?

vielmals adv many times; **danke vielmals** many thanks; **vielmehr** adv rather; **vielseitig** adj very varied; (person, device) versatile

vier num four; **auf allen ~en** on all fours; **unter ~ Augen** in private, privately; **Vier** f (-, -en) four; (mark in school) ≈ D; **Vierbettzimmer** nt four-bed room; **Viereck** nt (-(e)s, -e) four-sided figure; square; **viereckig** adj four-sided; square; **vierfach** adj **die ~e Menge** four times the amount; **vierhundert** num four hundred; **viermal** adv four times; **vierspurig** adj four-lane

viert adv **wir sind zu ~** there

are four of us; **vierte(r, s)** adj fourth; → **dritte**

Viertel nt (-s, -) (of town) quarter, district; (fraction) quarter; (of wine etc) quarter-litre; **~ vor/nach drei** a quarter to/past three; **viertel drei** a quarter past two; **drei viertel drei** a quarter to three; **Viertelfinale** nt quarter-final; **vierteljährlich** adj quarterly; **Viertelstunde** f quarter of an hour

vierzehn num fourteen; **in ~ Tagen** in two weeks, in a fortnight (Brit); **vierzehntägig** adj two-week, fortnightly (Brit); **vierzehnte(r, s)** adj fourteenth; → **dritte**; **vierzig** num forty; **vierzigste(r, s)** adj fortieth

Vietnam nt (-s) Vietnam

Vignette f motorway (Brit) (or freeway (US)) permit

Villa f (-, Villen) villa

violett adj purple

Violine f violin

Virus m or nt (-, Viren) virus

Visitenkarte f card

Visum nt (-s, Visa or Visen) visa

Vitamin nt (-s, -e) vitamin

Vitrine f (-, -n) (glass) cabinet; (in museum etc) display case

Vogel m (-s, Vögel) bird; **vögeln** vi, vt vulg

Voicemail f (-, -s) voice mail

Vokal m (-s, -e) vowel

Volk nt (-(e)s, Völker) people pl; (community) nation;

Volksfest nt festival; (with rides etc) funfair; **Volkshochschule** f adult education centre; **Volkslied** nt folksong; **Volksmusik** f folk music; **volkstümlich** adj popular; (traditional; (art) folk

voll adj full (von of); ~ **machen** fill (up); ~ **tanken** fill up; **Vollbremsung** f eine ~ **machen** slam on the brakes; **vollends** adv completely

Vollgas nt **mit** ~ at full throttle; ~ **geben** step on it

völlig 1. adj complete **2.** adv completely

volljährig adj of age; **Vollkaskoversicherung** f fully comprehensive insurance; **vollklimatisiert** adj fully air-conditioned; **vollkommen 1.** adj perfect; **~er Unsinn** complete rubbish **2.** adv completely

Vollkornbrot nt wholemeal (Brit) (or whole wheat (US)) bread

Vollmacht f (-, -en) authority; (document) power of attorney

Vollmilch f full-fat milk (Brit), whole milk (US); **Vollmilchschokolade** f milk chocolate; **Vollmond** m full moon; **Vollnarkose** f general anaesthetic; **Vollpension** f full board

vollständig adj complete

Vollwaschmittel nt all-purpose washing powder; **Voll-**

wertkost f wholefood; **vollzählig** adj complete

Volt nt (-, -) volt

Volumen nt (-s, -) volume

vom contr of **von dem**; (with space, time, cause) from; **ich kenne sie nur ~ Sehen** I only know her by sight

von prep + dat (with space, time) from; (replacing genitive, consisting of) of; (passive) by; **ein Freund ~ mir** a friend of mine; **~ mir aus** fam if you like; **~ wegen!** no way; **voneinander** adv from each other

vor prep + dat or acc before; (in space) in front of; **fünf ~ drei** five to three; **~ 2 Tagen** 2 days ago; **~ Wut/Liebe** with rage/love; **~ allem** above all

vorangehen irr vi go ahead; **einer Sache** dat ~ precede sth; **vorankommen** irr vi make progress

voraus adv **jdm** ~ **sein** be ahead of sb; **im Voraus** in advance; **vorausfahren** irr vi drive on ahead; **vorausgesetzt** conj provided (that); **Voraussage** f prediction; (for weather) forecast; **voraussagen** vt predict; **voraussehen** irr vt foresee; **voraussetzen** vt assume; **Voraussetzung** f requirement, prerequisite; **voraussichtlich 1.** adj expected **2.** adv probably; **vorauszahlen** vt pay in advance

vorbei *adv* past, over, finished; **vorbeibringen** *irr vt* drop by (*or* in); **vorbeifahren** *irr vi* drive past; **vorbeigehen** *irr vi* pass by, go past; (*elapse, end*) pass; **vorbeikommen** *irr vi* drop by; **vorbeilassen** *irr vt* **kannst du die Leute ~?** would you let these people pass?; **lässt du mich bitte mal vorbei?** can I get past, please?

vorbereiten 1. *vt* prepare **2.** *vr* get ready (*auf + acc, für* for); **Vorbereitung** *f* preparation

vorbestellen *vt* book in advance; (*meal*) order in advance; **Vorbestellung** *f* booking, reservation

vorbeugen *vi* prevent (*dat* sth); **vorbeugend** *adj* preventive; **Vorbeugung** *f* prevention

Vorbild *nt* (role) model; **vorbildlich** *adj* model, ideal

Vorderachse *f* front axle; **vordere(r, s)** *adj* front; **Vordergrund** *m* foreground; **Vorderradantrieb** *m* AUTO front-wheel drive; **Vorderseite** *f* front; **Vordersitz** *m* front seat; **Vorderteil** *m or nt* front (part)

vordrängen *vr* push forward

voreilig *adj* hasty, rash; **~e Schlüsse ziehen** jump to conclusions; **voreingenommen** *adj* biased

vorenthalten *irr vt* **jdm etw ~**

withhold sth from sb

vorerst *adv* for the moment

vorfahren *irr vi* drive on ahead; **vor das Haus ~** drive up to the house; **fahren Sie bis zur Ampel vor** drive as far as the traffic lights

Vorfahrt *f* AUTO right of way; **~ achten** give way (*Brit*), yield (*US*); **Vorfahrtsschild** *nt* give way (*Brit*) (*or* yield (*US*)) sign; **Vorfahrtsstraße** *f* major road

Vorfall *m* incident

vorführen *irr vt* demonstrate; (*film*) show; THEAT perform

Vorgänger(in) *m(f)* predecessor

vorgehen *irr vi* go on ahead; (*to the front*) go forward; (*take action*) act, proceed; (*clock, watch*) be fast; (*be more important*) take precedence; (*happen*) go on; **Vorgehen** *nt* (-s) procedure

Vorgesetzte(r) *mf* superior

vorgestern *adv* the day before yesterday

vorhaben *irr vt* plan; **hast du schon was vor?** have you got anything on?; **ich habe vor, nach Rom zu fahren** I'm planning to go to Rome

vorhalten *irr vt* **jdm etw ~** accuse sb of sth

Vorhand *f* forehand

vorhanden *adj* existing; available

Vorhang *m* curtain

Vorhängeschloss *nt* padlock

Vorhaut f foreskin

vorher adv before; **zwei Tage ~** two days before; **~ essen wir** we'll eat first; **Vorhersage** f forecast; **vorhersehen** irr vt foresee

vorhin adv just now, a moment ago

vorig adj previous; (week etc) last

vorkommen irr vi come forward; (take place) happen; (appear) seem (to be); **sich** dat **dumm ~** feel stupid

Vorlage f model

vorlassen irr vt **jdn~** let sb go first

vorläufig adj temporary

vorlesen irr vt read out

vorletzte(r, s) adj last but one; **am ~n Samstag** (on) the Saturday before last

Vorliebe f preference

vormachen irr vt **kannst du es mir ~?** can you show me how to do it?; **jdm etwas~** fig fool sb

Vormittag m morning; **am~in** the morning; **heute~** this morning; **vormittags** adv in the morning; **um 9 Uhr~** at 9 (o'clock) in the morning, at 9 am

vorn(e) adv in front; **von~anfangen** start at the beginning; **nach~** to the front; **weiter~** further up; **von~bis hinten** from beginning to end

Vorname m first name; **wie**

heißt du mit ~ what's your first name?

vornehm adj distinguished; (behaviour) refined; (clothes, hotel etc) elegant

vornehmen irr vt **sich** dat **etw ~** start on sth; **sich** dat ~, **etw zu tun** decide to do sth

vornherein adv **von ~** from the start

Vorort m suburb

vorrangig adj priority

Vorrat m stock, supply; **vorrätig** adj in stock; **Vorratskammer** f pantry

Vorrecht nt privilege; **Vorruhestand** m early retirement; **Vorsaison** f early season

Vorsatz m intention; **vorsätzlich** adj intentional; LAW premeditated

Vorschau f preview; (for film) trailer

Vorschlag m suggestion, proposal; **vorschlagen** irr vt suggest, propose; **ich schlage vor, dass wir gehen** I suggest we go

vorschreiben irr vt stipulate; **jdm etw ~** dictate sth to sb

Vorschrift f regulation, rule; instruction; **vorschriftsmäßig** adj correct

Vorsicht f care; **~!** look out; (on sign) caution; **~ Stufe!** mind the step; **vorsichtig** adj careful; **vorsichtshalber** adv just in case

Vorsorge f precaution; (stopping) prevention; **Vorsorge-**

vorsorglich 268

untersuchung *f* checkup; vorsorglich *adv* as a precaution

Vorspeise *f* starter

vorstellen *vt* (*person*) introduce, put forward; (*in front of sth else*) put in front; **sich dat etw ~** imagine sth; Vorstellung *f* (*to sb*) introduction; THEAT performance; (*concept*) idea; Vorstellungsgespräch *nt* interview

vortäuschen *vt* feign

Vorteil *m* advantage (*gegenüber* over); **die Vor- und Nachteile** the pros and cons; vorteilhaft *adj* advantageous

Vortrag *m* (-(e)s, Vorträge) talk (*über* + *acc* on); (*academic*) lecture; **einen ~ halten** give a talk

vorüber *adv* over; vorübergehen *irr vi* pass; vorübergehend **1.** *adj* temporary **2.** *adv* temporarily, for the time being

Vorurteil *nt* prejudice

Vorverkauf *m* advance booking

vorverlegen *vt* bring forward

Vorwahl *f* TEL dialling code (*Brit*), area code (*US*)

Vorwand *m* (-(e)s, Vorwände) pretext, excuse; **unter dem ~, dass** with the excuse that

vorwärts *adv* forward; **~ gehen** *fig* progress; Vorwärtsgang *m* AUTO forward gear

vorweg *adv* in advance; vorwegnehmen *irr vt* anticipate

vorwerfen *irr vt* **jdm etw ~** accuse sb of sth

vorwiegend *adv* mainly

Vorwort *nt* preface

Vorwurf *m* reproach; **sich dat Vorwürfe machen** reproach oneself; **jdm Vorwürfe machen** accuse sb; vorwurfsvoll *adj* reproachful

vorzeigen *vt* show

vorzeitig *adj* premature, early

vorziehen *irr vt* prefer

vorzüglich *adj* excellent

vulgär *adj* vulgar

Vulkan *m* (-s, -e) volcano; Vulkanausbruch *m* volcanic eruption

W

Waage *f* (-, -n) scales *pl*; ASTR Libra; waagerecht *adj* horizontal

wach *adj* awake; **~ werden** wake up; Wache *f* (-, -n) guard

Wachs *nt* (-es, -e) wax

wachsen (wuchs, gewachsen) *vi* grow

wachsen *vt* (*skis*) wax

Wachstum *nt* growth

Wächter(in) *m(f)* (-s, -) guard; (*of car park*) attendant

wackelig *adj* wobbly; *fig* shaky; **Wackelkontakt** *m* loose connection; **wackeln** *vi* (*chair*) be wobbly; (*tooth, screw*) be loose; **mit dem Kopf ~** waggle one's head

Wade *f* (-, -*n*) ANAT calf

Waffe *f* (-, -*n*) weapon

Waffel *f* (-, -*n*) waffle; (*biscuit, for ice cream*) wafer

wagen *vt* risk; *es ~, etw zu tun* dare to do sth

Wagen *m* (-*s*, -) AUTO car; RAIL carriage; **Wagenheber** *m* (-*s*, -) jack; **Wagentyp** *m* model, make

Wahl *f* (-, -*en*) choice; POL election

wählen 1. *vt* choose; TEL dial; POL vote for; (*as president, to board etc*) elect 2. *vi* choose; TEL dial; POL vote; **Wähler(in)** *m(f)* (-*s*, -) voter; **wählerisch** *adj* choosy

Wahlkampf *m* election campaign; **wahllos** *adv* at random; **Wahlwiederholung** *f* redial

Wahnsinn *m* madness; **~!** amazing!; **wahnsinnig** 1. *adj* insane, mad 2. *adv fam* incredibly

wahr *adj* true; *das darf doch nicht ~ sein!* I don't believe it; *nicht ~?* that's right, isn't it?

während 1. *prep + gen* during 2. *conj* while; **währenddessen** *adv* meanwhile, in the meantime

Wahrheit *f* truth

wahrnehmbar *adj* noticeable, perceptible; **wahrnehmen** *irr vt* perceive

Wahrsager(in) *m(f)* (-*s*, -) fortune-teller

wahrscheinlich 1. *adj* probable, likely 2. *adv* probably; *ich komme ~ zu spät* I'll probably be late; **Wahrscheinlichkeit** *f* probability

Währung *f* currency

Wahrzeichen *nt* symbol

Wal *m* (-(*e*)*s*, -*e*) whale

Wald *m* (-(*e*)*s*, *Wälder*) wood; (*extensive*) forest; **Waldbrand** *m* forest fire; **Waldlauf** *m* cross-country run; **Waldsterben** *nt* (-*s*) forest dieback

Wales *nt* (-) Wales; **Waliser(in)** *m(f)* (-*s*, -) Welshman/ Welshwoman; **walisisch** *adj* Welsh; **Walisisch** *nt* Welsh

Walkman® *m* (-*s*, -*s*) walkman®, personal stereo

Wallfahrt *f* pilgrimage; **Wallfahrtsort** *m* place of pilgrimage

Walnuss *f* walnut

Walross *nt* (-*es*, -*e*) walrus

wälzen 1. *vt* roll; (*books*) pore over; (*problems*) deliberate on 2. *vr* wallow; (*in pain*) roll about; (*in bed*) toss and turn

Walzer *m* (-*s*, -) waltz

Wand *f* (-, *Wände*) wall

Wandel *m* (-*s*) change; **wandeln** *vt, vr* change

Wanderer m (-s, -), **Wanderin** f hiking; **Wanderkarte** f hiking map; **wandern** vi hike; (gaze) wander; (thoughts) stray; **Wanderschuh** m walking shoe; **Wanderstiefel** m hiking boot; **Wanderung** f hike; **eine ~ machen** go on a hike; **Wanderweg** m walking (or hiking) trail; **Wandschrank** m built-in cupboard (Brit), closet (US)

wandte imperf of **wenden**

Wange f (-, -n) cheek

wann adv when; **seit ~ ist sie da?** how long has she been here?; **bis ~ bleibt ihr?** how long are you staying?

Wanne f (-, -n) (bath) tub

Wappen nt (-s, -) coat of arms

war imperf of **sein**

warb imperf of **werben**

Ware f (-, -n) product; **~n** goods pl; **Warenhaus** nt department store; **Warenprobe** f sample; **Warensendung** f consignment; **Warenzeichen** nt trademark

warf imperf of **werfen**

warm adj warm; (meal) hot; **~ laufen** warm up; **mir ist es zu ~** I'm too warm; **Wärme** f (-, -n) warmth; **wärmen 1.** vt warm; (food) warm (or heat) up **2.** vi (clothes, sun) be warm **3.** vr warm up; (by holding each other) keep each other warm; **Wärmflasche** f hot-water bottle

Warnblinkanlage f AUTO

warning flasher; **Warndreieck** nt AUTO warning triangle; **warnen** vt warn (vor + dat about, of); **Warnung** f warning

Warteliste f waiting list; **warten 1.** vi wait (auf + acc for); **warte mal!** wait (or hang on) a minute **2.** vt TECH service

Wärter(in) m(f) attendant

Wartesaal m, **Wartezimmer** nt waiting room

Wartung f service; (action) servicing

warum adv why

Warze f (-, -n) wart

was 1. pron vt AUTO what; **~ kostet das?** what does it cost?, how much is it?; **~ für ein Auto ist das?** what kind of car is that?; **~ für eine Farbe/Größe?** what colour/size?; fam **~?**, what?; **~ ist/gibt's?** what is it?, what's up? **2.** pron **du weißt, ~ ich meine** you know what I mean; (auch) **immer** whatever **3.** fam something; **soll ich dir ~ mitbringen?** do you want me to bring you anything?

Waschanlage f AUTO car wash; **waschbar** adj washable; **Waschbecken** nt washbasin

Wäsche f (-, -n) washing; (dirty) laundry; **in der ~** in the wash; **Wäscheklammer** f clothes peg (Brit) (or pin (US)); **Wäscheleine** f clothesline

waschen (*wusch, gewaschen*)
1. *vt, vi* wash; **Waschen und
Legen** shampoo and set 2. *vr*
(have a) wash; **sich dat die
Haare ~** wash one's hair

Wäscherei *f* laundry; **Wäscheschleuder** *f* spin-drier;
Wäscheständer *m* clothes
horse; **Wäschetrockner** *m*
tumble-drier

Waschgelegenheit *f* washing
facilities *pl*; **Waschlappen** *m*
flannel (*Brit*), washcloth
(*US*); *fam* (person) wet blanket; **Waschmaschine** *f*
washing machine; **Wasch-
mittel** *nt*, **Waschpulver** *nt*
washing powder; **Wasch-
raum** *m* washroom; **Waschsalon** *m* (*-s, -s*) launderette
(*Brit*), laundromat (*US*);
Waschstraße *f* car wash

Wasser *nt* (*-s, -*) water; *flie-
Bendes ~* running water;
Wasserball *m* SPORT water
polo; **wasserdicht** *adj* watertight; (*fabric, watch*) waterproof; **Wasserfall** *m* wa-
terfall; **Wasserfarbe** *f* watercolour; **wasserfest** *adj* watertight, waterproof; **Wasserhahn** *m* tap (*Brit*), faucet
(*US*); **wässerig** *adj* watery;
Wasserkessel *m* kettle;
Wasserkocher *m* electric
kettle; **Wasserleitung** *f* water pipe; **wasserlöslich** *adj*
water-soluble; **Wassermann**
m ASTR Aquarius; **Wassermelone** *f* water melon; **Was-**

serrutschbahn *f* water
chute; **Wasserschaden** *m*
water damage; **wasser-
scheu** *adj* scared of water;
Wasserski *nt* water-skiing;
Wassersport *m* water sports
pl; **Wasserspülung** *f* flush;
wasserundurchlässig *adj*
watertight, waterproof;
Wasserverbrauch *m* water
consumption; **Wasserver-
sorgung** *f* water supply;
Wasserwerk *nt* waterworks
pl

waten *vi* wade

Watt 1. *nt* (*-(e)s, -en*) GEO mud
flats *pl* 2. *nt* (*-s, -*) ELEC watt

Watte *f* (*-, -n*) cotton wool;
Wattestäbchen *nt* cotton
bud, Q-tip® (*US*)

WC *nt* (*-s, -s*) toilet, restroom
(*US*); **WC-Reiniger** *m* toilet
cleaner

Web *nt* (*-s*) IT Web; **Webseite** *f*
IT web page

Wechsel *m* (*-s, -*) change;
SPORT substitution; **Wechselgeld** *nt* change; **wechselhaft** *adj* (*weather*) changeable; **Wechseljahre** *pl* menopause *sg*; **Wechselkurs** *m*
exchange rate; **wechseln** 1.
vt (*money*) change; (*looks*) exchange;
Geld ~ change some money;
(*into smaller coins or notes*)
get some change; **Euro in
Pfund ~** change euros into
pounds 2. *vi* change; **kannst
du ~?** can you change this?;
Wechselstrom *m* alternat-

ing current, AC; **Wechselstube** f bureau de change
Weckdienst m wake-up call
service; **wecken** vt wake
(up); **Wecker** m (-s, -) alarm
clock; **Weckruf** m wake-up
call

wedeln vi SKI wedel; **der
Hund wedelte mit dem
Schwanz** the dog wagged
its tail

weder conj **~ ... noch ...** neither ... nor ...

weg adv away; (leaving, removed) off; **er war schon ~**
he had already left (or gone);
Hände ~! hands off; **weit ~** a
long way away (or off)

Weg m (-(e)s, -e) way; (for
walking) path; (way travelled) route; **jdn nach dem ~
fragen** ask sb the way; **auf
dem ~ sein** be on the way

wegbleiben irr vi stay away;
wegbringen irr vt take away

wegen prep + gen or dat because of

wegfahren irr vi drive away;
(depart) leave; (on holiday)
go away; **Wegfahrsperre** f
AUTO (engine) immobilizer;
weggehen irr vi go away;
wegkommen irr vi get away;
fig **gut/schlecht ~** come off
well/badly; **weglassen** irr
vt leave out; **weglaufen** irr
vi run away; **weglegen** vt
put aside; **wegmüssen** irr
vi **ich muss weg** I've got
to go; **wegnehmen** irr vt

take away; **wegräumen** vt
clear away; **wegrennen** irr
vi run away; **wegschicken**
vt send away; **wegschmel-
ßen** irr vt throw away; **wegsehen** irr vi look away; **weg-
tun** irr vt put away

Wegweiser m (-s, -) signpost

wegwerfen irr vt throw away;
Wegwerfflasche f non-returnable bottle; **wegwi-
schen** vt wipe off; **wegziehen** irr vi move (away)

weh adj sore; **→ wehtun**

wehen vt, vi blow; (flag) flutter

Wehen pl labour pains pl

Wehrdienst m military service

wehren vr defend oneself

wehtun irr vi hurt; **jdm/sich
~** hurt sb/oneself

Weibchen nt **es ist ein ~** (animal) it's a she; **weiblich** adj
feminine; BIO female

weich adj soft; **~ gekocht**
(egg) soft-boiled

Weichspüler m (-s, -) (fabric)
softener

Weide f (-, -n) (tree) willow;
(field) meadow

weigern vr refuse; **Weigerung** f refusal

Weiher m (-s, -) pond

Weihnachten nt (-, -) Christmas; **Weihnachtsabend** m
Christmas Eve; **Weih-
nachtsbaum** m Christmas
tree; **Weihnachtsfeier** f
Christmas party; **Weih-**

nachtsferien pl Christmas holidays m (Brit), Christmas vacation sg (US); **Weihnachtsgeschenk** nt Christmas present; **Weihnachtslied** nt Christmas carol; **Weihnachtsmann** m Father Christmas, Santa (Claus); **Weihnachtstag** m **erster ~** Christmas Day; **zweiter ~** Boxing Day; **Weihnachtszeit** f Christmas season

weil conj because

Weile f (-) while, short time; **es kann noch eine ~ dauern** it could take some time

Wein m (-(e)s, -e) wine; (plant) vine; **Weinbrand** m brandy

weinen vt, vi cry

Weinglas nt wine glass; **Weinkarte** f wine list; **Weinkeller** m wine cellar; **Weinprobe** f wine tasting; **Weintraube** f grape

weise adj wise

Weise f (-, -n) manner, way; **auf diese (Art und) ~** this way

weisen (wies, gewiesen) vt show

Weisheit f wisdom; **Weisheitszahn** m wisdom tooth

weiß adj white; **Weißbier** nt ≈ wheat beer; **Weißbrot** nt white bread; **Weißkohl** m, **Weißkraut** nt (white) cabbage; **Weißwein** m white wine

weit 1. adj wide; (concept) broad; (journey, throw) long; (dress) loose; **wie ~ ist es ...?** how far is it ...?; **so ~ sein** be ready 2. adv far; **~ verbreitet** widespread; **~ gereist** widely travelled; **~ offen** wide open; **das geht zu ~** that's going too far, that's pushing it

weiter 1. adj (more distant) farther (away); (additional) further; **~e Informationen** further information sg 2. adv further; **~!** go on; (to people walking) move on; **~ nichts / niemand** nothing / nobody else; **und so ~** and so on; **Weiterbildung** f further training (or education); **weiterempfehlen** irr vt recommend; **weitererzählen** vt **nicht ~!** don't tell anyone; **weiterfahren** irr vi go on (nach to, bis as far as); **weitergeben** irr vt pass on; **weitergehen** irr vi go on; **weiterhelfen** irr vi **jdm ~** help sb

weiterhin adv **etw ~ tun** go on doing sth

weitermachen vt, vi continue; **weiterreisen** vi continue one's journey

weitgehend 1. adj considerable 2. adv largely; **weitsichtig** adj long-sighted; fig far-sighted; **Weitspringer(in)** m(f) long jumper; **Weitsprung** m long jump; **Weitwinkelobjektiv** nt PHOT wide-angle lens

Weizen *m (-s, -)* wheat; **Weizenbier** *nt ≈* wheat beer

welche(r, s) 1. *pron* what; (*when choosing*) which (one); ~ **Geschmacksrichtung willst du?** which flavour do you want?; ~**r ist es?** which (one) is it? **2.** *pron* (*relative; person*) who; (*relative; thing*) which, that; **zeig mir,** ~**r es war** show me which one of them it was **3.** *pron fam* some; **hast du Kleingeld? – ja, ich hab' ~s** have you got any change? – yes, I've got some

welk *adj* withered; **welken** *vi* wither

Welle *f (-, -n)* wave; **Wellengang** *m* waves *pl*; **starker ~** heavy seas *pl*; **Wellenlänge** *f* wavelength; **Wellenreiten** *nt* surfing; **Wellensittich** *m (-s, -e)* budgerigar, budgie

Welpe *m (-n, -n)* puppy

Welt *f (-, -en)* world; **auf der ~** in the world; **auf die ~ kommen** be born; **Weltall** *nt* universe; **weltbekannt** *adj*, **weltberühmt** *adj* world-famous; **Weltkrieg** *m* world war; **Weltmacht** *f* world power; **Weltmeister(in)** *m(f)* world champion; **Weltmeisterschaft** *f* world championship; (*in football*) World Cup; **Weltraum** *m* space; **Weltreise** *f* trip round the world; **Weltrekord** *m* world record; **Weltstadt** *f* metropolis; **weltweit** *adj* worldwide, global

wem *pron dat of* **wer**; who ... to, (to) whom; ~ **hast du's gegeben?** who gave it to?; ~ **gehört es?** who does it belong to?, whose is it?; ~ **auch immer es gehört** whoever it belongs to

wen *pron acc of* **wer**; who, whom; ~ **hast du besucht?** who did you visit?; ~ **möchten Sie sprechen?** who would you like to speak to?; ~ **auch immer du gesprochen hast** whoever you talked to

Wende *f (-, -n)* turning point; (*transformation*) change; **die ~** HIST the fall of the Berlin Wall; **Wendekreis** *m* AUTO turning circle

wenden (*wendete or wandte, gewendet or gewandt*) *vt, vi, vr* turn (round); (*by 180°*) make a U-turn; **sich an jdn ~** turn to sb; **bitte ~!** please turn over, PTO

wenig 1. *pron* little; ~**(e)** *pl* few; (*nur*) **ein (klein) ~** (just) a little (bit); **ein ~ Zucker** a little bit of sugar, a little sugar; **wir haben ~ Zeit** we haven't got much time; **zu ~** too little; *pl* too few; **nur ~ wissen** only a few know **2.** *adv* **er spricht ~** he doesn't talk much; ~ **bekannt** little known; **wenigstens** *adv* at least

wenn *conj* if; *(with time)* when; **wennschon** *adv* **na ~ so** what?

wer 1. *pron* who; **~ war das?** who was that?; **~ von euch?** which (one) of you? **2.** *pron* anybody who, anyone who; **~ das glaubt, ist dumm** anyone who believes that is stupid; **~ auch immer** whoever **3.** *pron* somebody, someone; anybody, anyone; **ist da ~?** is (there) anybody there?

Werbefernsehen *nt* TV commercials *pl*; **werben** *(warb, geworben)* **1.** *vt* win; **(member)** recruit **2.** *vi* advertise; **Werbespot** *m* **(-s, -s)** commercial; **Werbung** *f* advertising

werden *(wurde, geworden)* **1.** *vi* get, become; **alt / müde / reich ~** get old / tired / rich; **was willst du ~?** what do you want to be? **2.** *vaux (future)* will; *(definitely)* be going to; *(passive)* be; **er wird uns (schon) fahren** he'll drive us; **ich werde kommen** I'll come; **er wird uns abholen** he's going to pick us up; **wir ~ dafür bezahlt** we're paid for it; **er wird gerade diskutiert** he's being discussed

werfen *(warf, geworfen)* *vt* throw

Werft *f* **(-, -en)** shipyard, dockyard

Werk *nt* **(-(e)s, -e)** *(of art, lite-*rature etc) work; *(industrial)* *(mechanism)* works *pl*; **Werkstatt** *f* **(-, -stätten)** workshop; AUTO garage; **Werktag** *m* working day; **werktags** *adv* on weekdays, during the week; **Werkzeug** *nt* tool; **Werkzeugkasten** *m* toolbox

wert *adj* worth; **es ist etwa 50 Euro ~** it's worth about 50 euros; **das ist nichts ~** it's worthless; **Wert** *m* **(-(e)s, -e)** worth; FIN value; **~ legen auf** + *acc* attach importance to; **es hat doch keinen ~** *(sense)* it's pointless; **Wertangabe** *f* declaration of value; **Wertbrief** *m* insured letter; **Wertgegenstand** *m* valuable object; **wertlos** *adj* worthless; **Wertmarke** *f* token; **Wertpapiere** *pl* securities *pl*; **Wertsachen** *pl* valuables *pl*; **Wertstoff** *m* recyclable waste; **wertvoll** *adj* valuable

Wesen *nt* **(-s, -)** being; *(character)* nature

wesentlich 1. *adj* significant; *(substantial)* considerable **2.** *adv* considerably

weshalb *adv* why

Wespe *f* **(-, -n)** wasp

wessen *pron gen of* **wer**; whose

West west; **Westdeutschland** *nt* Western Germany; HIST West Germany

Weste *f* **(-, -n)** waistcoat *(Brit)*,

vest (US); (woollen) cardigan

Westen m (-s) west; **im ~ Englands** in the west of England; **Westeuropa** nt Western Europe; **Westküste** f west coast; **westlich** adj western; (course, direction) westerly; **Westwind** m west(erly) wind

weswegen adv why

Wettbewerb m competition; **Wettbüro** nt betting office; **Wette** f (-, -n) bet; **eine ~ abschließen** make a bet; **die ~ gilt!** you're on; **wetten** vt, vi bet (auf + acc on); **ich habe mit ihm gewettet, dass ...** I bet him that ...; **ich wette mit dir um 50 Euro** I'll bet you 50 euros; **~, dass?** wanna bet?

Wetter nt (-s, -) weather; **Wetterbericht** m, **Wettervorhersage** f weather forecast

Wettkampf m contest; **Wettlauf** m, **Wettrennen** nt race

WG f (-, -s) abbr = **Wohngemeinschaft**

Whirlpool® m (-s, -s) jacuzzi®

Whisky m (-s, -s) (Scottish) whisky; (Irish, American) whiskey

wichtig adj important

wickeln vt (string) wind (um round); (paper, scarf, blanket) wrap (um round); **ein Baby ~** change a baby's nappy (Brit) (or diaper US)

Wickelraum m baby-changing room; **Wickeltisch** m baby-changing table

Widder m (-s, -) ZOOL ram; ASTR Aries sg

wider prep + acc against

widerlich adj disgusting

widerrufen irr vt withdraw; (contract, order) cancel

widersprechen irr vi contradict (jdm sb); **Widerspruch** m contradiction

Widerstand m resistance; **widerstandsfähig** adj resistant (gegen to)

widerwärtig adj disgusting

widerwillig adj unwilling, reluctant

widmen 1. vt dedicate **2.** vr **sich jdm/etw ~** devote oneself to sb/sth; **Widmung** f dedication

wie 1. adv how; **~ viel** how much; **~ viele Menschen?** how many people?; **~ geht's?** how are you?; **~ das?** how come?; **~ bitte?** pardon?, sorry? (Brit) **2.** (so) **schön ~ ...** as beautiful as ...; **~ du weißt** as you know; **~ ich das hörte** when I heard that; **ich sah ~ er rauskam** I saw him coming out

wieder adv again; **~ ein(e) ...** another ...; **~ erkennen** recognize; **etw ~ gutmachen** make up for sth; **~ verwerten** recycle

wiederbekommen irr vt get back

wiederholen vt repeat; **Wie-**

derholung f repetition

Wiederhören nt TEL **auf ~** goodbye

wiederkommen irr vi come back

wiedersehen irr vt see again; (person) meet again; **Wiedersehen** nt (-s) reunion; **auf ~** goodbye

Wiedervereinigung f reunification

Wiege f (-, -n) cradle; **wiegen** (wog, gewogen) vt, vi weigh

Wien nt (-s) Vienna

wies imperf of **weisen**

Wiese f (-, -n) meadow

Wiesel nt (-s, -) weasel

wieso adv why

wievielmal adv how often; **wievielte(r, s)** adj **zum ~n Mal?** how many times?; **den Wievielten haben wir heute?** what's the date today?; **am Wievielten hast du Geburtstag?** which day is your birthday?

wieweit conj to what extent

wild adj wild

Wild nt (-(e)s) game

wildfremd adj fam **ein ~er Mensch** a complete (or total) stranger; **Wildleder** nt suede; **Wildpark** m game park; **Wildschwein** nt (wild) boar; **Wildwasserfahren** nt (-s) whitewater canoeing (or rafting)

Wille m (-ns, -n) will

willen prep + gen **um ... ~** for the sake of ...; **um Himmels**

~! for heaven's sake; (shocked) goodness me

willkommen adj welcome

Wimper f (-, -n) eyelash; **Wimperntusche** f mascara

Wind m (-(e)s, -e) wind

Windel f (-, -n) nappy (Brit), diaper (US)

windgeschützt adj sheltered from the wind; **windig** adj windy; fig dubious; **Windjacke** f windcheater; **Windmühle** f windmill; **Windpocken** pl chickenpox sg; **Windschutzscheibe** f AUTO windscreen (Brit), windshield (US); **Windstärke** f wind force; **Windsurfen** nt (-s) windsurfing; **Windsurfer(in)** m(f) windsurfer

Winkel m (-s, -) MATH angle; (in room) corner

winken vt, vi wave

Winter m (-s, -) winter; **Winterausrüstung** f AUTO winter equipment; **Winterfahrplan** m winter timetable; **winterlich** adj wintry; **Wintermantel** m winter coat; **Winterreifen** m winter tyre; **Winterschlussverkauf** m winter sales pl; **Wintersport** m winter sports pl

Winterzeit f (by the clock) winter time (Brit), standard time (US)

winzig adj tiny

wir pron we; **~ alle** all of us; **~ drei** the three of us; **~ sind's** it's us; **~ nicht** not us

Wirbel m (-s, -) whirl; (activity) hurly-burly; (about sb or sth) fuss; ANAT vertebra; **Wirbelsäule** f spine

wirken vi to be effective; (be successful) work; (appear to be) seem

wirklich adj real; **Wirklichkeit** f reality

wirksam adj effective; **Wirkung** f effect

wirr adj confused; **Wirrwarr** m (-s) confusion

Wirsing m (-s) savoy cabbage

Wirt m (-(e)s, -e) landlord; **Wirtin** f landlady

Wirtschaft f economy; (place) pub; **wirtschaftlich** adj economic; (not wasteful) economical

Wirtshaus nt pub

wischen vt, vi wipe; **Wischer** m (-s, -) wiper; **Wischlappen** m cloth

wissen (wusste, gewusst) vt know; **weißt du schon, ...?** did you know ...?; **woher weißt du das?** how do you know?; **das musst du selbst ~** that's up to you; **Wissen** nt (-s) knowledge

Wissenschaft f science; **Wissenschaftler(in)** m(f) (-s, -) scientist; (in the arts) academic; **wissenschaftlich** adj scientific; (in the arts) academic

Witwe f (-, -n) widow; **Witwer** m (-s, -) widower

Witz m (-(e)s, -e) joke; **mach keine ~e!** you're kidding!; **das soll wohl ein ~ sein** you've got to be joking; **witzig** adj funny

wo 1. adv where; **überall, ich hingehe** wherever I go **2.** conj **jetzt, ~ du da bist** now that you're here; **~ ich dich gerade spreche** while I'm talking to you; **woanders** adv somewhere else

wobei adv **~ mir einfällt ...** which reminds me ...

Woche f (-, -n) week; **während** (or **unter**) **der ~** during the week; **einmal die ~** once a week; **Wochenende** nt weekend; **am ~** at (Brit) (or on US) the weekend; **wir fahren übers ~ weg** we're going away for the weekend; **Wochenendhaus** nt weekend cottage; **Wochenkarte** f weekly (season) ticket; **wochenlang** adv for weeks (on end); **Wochenmarkt** m weekly market; **Wochentag** m weekday; **wöchentlich** adj, adv weekly

Wodka m (-s, -s) vodka

wodurch adv **~ unterscheiden sie sich?** what's the difference between them?; **~ hast du es gemerkt?** how did you notice?; **wofür** adv (relative) for which; (question) what ... for; **~ brauchst du das?** what do you need that for?

wog imperf of **wiegen**

woher *adv* where ... from; **wohin** *adv* where ... to

wohl *adv* well; at ease, comfortable; probably; certainly; **Wohl** *nt* (-(e)s) **zum ~!** cheers; **wohlbehalten** *adv* safe and sound; **wohlgemerkt** *adv* mind you; **Wohlstand** *m* prosperity, affluence

Wohnblock *m* block of flats (*Brit*), apartment house (*US*); **wohnen** *vi* live; **Wohngemeinschaft** *f* shared flat (*Brit*) (*or* apartment (*US*)); **ich wohne in einer ~** I share a flat (*or* apartment); **wohnhaft** *adj* resident; **Wohnküche** *f* kitchen-cum-living-room; **Wohnmobil** *nt* (-s, -e) camper, RV (*US*); **Wohnort** *m* place of residence; **Wohnsitz** *m* place of residence; **Wohnung** *f* flat (*Brit*), apartment (*US*); **Wohnungstür** *f* front door; **Wohnwagen** *m* caravan; **Wohnzimmer** *nt* living room

Wolf *m* (-(e)s, Wölfe) wolf

Wolke *f* (-, -n) cloud; **Wolkenkratzer** *m* skyscraper; **wolkenlos** *adj* cloudless; **wolkig** *adj* cloudy

Wolldecke *f* (woollen) blanket; **Wolle** *f* (-, -n) wool

wollen 1. *vaux* want; **sie wollte ihn nicht sehen** she didn't want to see him; **~ wir gehen?** shall we go?; **~ Sie bit-** te ... will (*or* would) you please ...; **2.** *vt* want; **ich lieber bleiben** I'd prefer to stay; **er will, dass ich aufhöre** he wants me to stop; **ich wollte, ich wäre/hätte ...** I wish I were/had ...; **3.** *vi* want to; **ich will nicht** I don't want to; **was du willst** whatever you like; **ich will nach Hause** I want to go home; **wo willst du hin?** where do you want to go?; (*to person heading somewhere*) where are you going?

Wolljacke *f* cardigan

womit *adv* what ... with; **~ habe ich das verdient?** what have I done to deserve that?

womöglich *adv* possibly

woran *adv* **~ denkst du?** what are you thinking of?; **~ ist er gestorben?** what did he die of?; **~ sieht man das?** how can you tell?

worauf *adv* **~ wartest du?** what are you waiting for?

woraus *adv* **~ ist das gemacht?** what is it made of?

Wort 1. *nt* (-(e)s, Wörter) word **2.** *nt* (-(e)s, -e) word; **mit anderen ~en** in other words; **jdn beim ~ nehmen** take sb at his/her word; **Wörterbuch** *nt* dictionary; **wörtlich** *adj* literal

worüber *adv* **~ redet sie?** what is she talking about?

worum *adv* **~ geht's?** what is it about?

worunter adv ~ **leidet er?** what is he suffering from?

wovon adv (relative) from which; ~ **redest du?** what are you talking about?; **wo-zu** adv (relative) to/for which; (question) what ... for/to; (for what reason) why; ~**?** what for?; ~ **brauchst du das?** what do you need it for?; ~ **soll das gut sein?** what's it for?; ~ **soll das** wünschenswert adj desirable

wurde imperf of **werden**

Wurf m (-s, Würfe) throw; ZOOL litter

Würfel m (-s, -) dice; MATH cube; **würfeln 1.** vi throw (the dice); (as game) play dice **2.** vt (number) throw; GASTR dice; **Würfelzucker** m lump sugar

Wrack nt (-(e)s, -s) wreck

wuchs imperf of **wachsen**

wühlen vi rummage; (animal) root; (mole) burrow

wund adj sore; **Wunde** f (-, -n) wound

Wunder nt (-s, -) miracle; **es ist kein ~** it's no wonder; **wunderbar** adj wonderful, marvellous; **Wunderkerze** f sparkler; **wundern 1.** vr be surprised (über + acc at) **2.** vt surprise; **wunderschön** adj beautiful; **wundervoll** adj wonderful

Wundsalbe f antiseptic ointment; **Wundstarrkrampf** m tetanus

Wunsch m (-(e)s, Wünsche) wish (nach for); **wünschen** vt wish; **jdm** dat **etw** ~ want sth; **ich wünsche dir alles Gute** I wish you all the best;

Wurm m (-(e)s, Würmer) worm

Wurst f (-, Würste) sausage; **das ist mir ~** fam I couldn't care less

Würstchen nt frankfurter

Würze f (-, -n) seasoning, spice

Wurzel f (-, -n) root

würzen vt season, spice; **würzig** adj spicy

wusch imperf of **waschen**

wusste imperf of **wissen**

wüst adj (untidy) chaotic; (party, life, person) wild; (place) desolate; fam (intense) terrible

Wüste f (-, -n) desert

Wut f (-) rage, fury; **ich habe eine ~ auf ihn** I'm really mad at him; **wütend** adj furious

WWW nt (-) abbr = **World Wide Web**; WWW

X, Y

X-Beine pl knock-knees pl;
x-beinig adj knock-kneed
x-beliebig adj ein ~es Buch
any book (you like)
x-mal adv umpteen times
Xylophon nt (-s, -e) xylophone

Yacht f (-, -en) yacht
Yoga m or nt (-(s)) yoga
Yuppie m (-s, -s) f (-, -s) yup-
pie

Z

Zacke f (-, -n) point; (of saw,
comb) tooth; (of fork) prong;
zackig adj (line etc) jagged;
fam (speed) brisk
zaghaft adj timid
zäh adj tough
Zahl f (-, -en) number; zahlbar
adj payable; zahlen vt, vi
pay; ~ bitte! could I have
the bill (Brit) (or check
(US)) please?; bar ~ pay
cash; zählen vt, vi count
(auf + acc on); ~ zu be one
of; Zahlenschloss nt com-
bination lock; Zähler m (-s,
-) counter; (for electricity,
water) meter; zahlreich adj
numerous; Zahlung f pay-
ment
zahm adj tame; zähmen vt
tame
Zahn m (-(e)s, Zähne) tooth;
Zahnarzt m, Zahnärztin f
dentist; Zahnbürste f toothbrush; Zahncreme f tooth-
paste; Zahnersatz m den-

tures pl; Zahnfleisch nt
gums pl; Zahnfleischbluten
nt bleeding gums pl; Zahn-
füllung f filling; Zahnklam-
mer f brace; Zahnpasta f,
Zahnpaste f toothpaste;
Zahnschmerzen pl tooth-
ache sg; Zahnseide f dental
floss; Zahnspange f brace;
Zahnstocher m (-s, -) toothpick
Zange f (-, -n) pliers pl; (for
sugar) tongs pl; ZOOL pincers
pl
zanken vi, vr quarrel
Zäpfchen nt ANAT uvula; MED
suppository
zapfen vt (beer) pull; Zapfsäule f petrol (Brit) (or gas
(US)) pump
zappeln vi wriggle; (be restless) fidget
zappen vi zap, channel-hop
zart adj soft; (meat etc) tender; (fine, weakly) delicate;
zartbitter adj (chocolate)

plain, dark

zärtlich adj tender, affectionate; **Zärtlichkeit** f tenderness; **~en** pl hugs and kisses pl

Zauber m (-s, -) magic; (magic power) spell; **Zauberei** f magic; **Zauberer** m (-s, -) magician; (entertainer) conjuror; **Zauberformel** f (magic) spell; **zauberhaft** adj enchanting; **Zauberin** f sorceress; **Zauberkünstler(in)** m(f) magician, conjuror; **Zaubermittel** nt magic cure; **zaubern** vi do magic; (entertainer) do conjuring tricks; **Zauberspruch** m (magic) spell

Zaun m (-(e)s, Zäune) fence

z. B. abbr = **zum Beispiel**; e.g., eg

Zebra nt (-s, -s) zebra; **Zebrastreifen** m zebra crossing (Brit), crosswalk (US)

Zechtour f pub crawl

Zecke f (-, -n) tick

Zehe f (-, -n) toe; (of garlic) clove; **Zehennagel** m toenail; **Zehenspitze** f tip of the toes

zehn num ten; **Zehnerkarte** f ticket valid for ten trips; **Zehnkampf** m decathlon; **Zehnkämpfer(in)** m(f) decathlete; **zehnmal** adv ten times; **zehntausend** num ten thousand; **zehnte(r, s)** adj tenth; → **dritte**; **Zehntel** nt (-s, -) tenth

Zeichen nt (-s, -) sign; (letter, numeral) character; **Zeichenblock** m sketch pad; **Zeichensetzung** f punctuation; **Zeichensprache** f sign language; **Zeichentrickfilm** m cartoon

zeichnen vt, vi draw; **Zeichnung** f drawing

Zeigefinger m index finger; **zeigen 1.** vt show; **sie zeigte uns die Stadt** she showed us around the town; **zeig mal!** let me see **2.** vi point (auf + acc to, at) **3.** vr show oneself; **es wird sich ~** time will tell; **Zeiger** m (-s, -) pointer; (of clock, watch) hand

Zeile f (-, -n) line

Zeit f (-, -en) time; **ich habe keine ~** I haven't got time; **lass dir ~** take your time; **von ~ zu ~** from time to time; **Zeitansage** f TEL speaking clock (Brit), correct time (US); **Zeitarbeit** f temporary work; **zeitgenössisch** adj contemporary, modern; **zeitgleich 1.** adj simultaneous **2.** adv at exactly the same time; **zeitig** adj early; **Zeitkarte** f season ticket; **zeitlich** adj (order) chronological; **es passt ~ nicht** it isn't a convenient time; **Zeitlupe** f slow motion; **Zeitplan** m schedule; **Zeitpunkt** m point in time; **Zeitraum** m period (of time)

Zeitschrift f magazine; (academic, scientific) periodical

Zeitung f newspaper; **es steht in der ~** it's in the paper(s); **Zeitungsartikel** m newspaper article; **Zeitungskiosk** m, **Zeitungsstand** m newsstand

Zeitunterschied m time difference; **Zeitverschiebung** f time lag; **Zeitvertreib** m (-(e)s, -e) **zum ~** to pass the time; **Zeitzone** f time zone

Zelle f (-, -n) cell

Zellophan® nt (-s) cellophane®

Zelt nt (-(e)s, -e) tent; **zelten** vi camp, go camping; **Zeltplatz** m campsite, camping site

Zement m (-(e)s, -e) cement

Zentimeter m or nt centimetre

Zentner m (-s, -) (metric) hundredweight; (in Germany) fifty kilos; (in Austria and Switzerland) one hundred kilos

zentral adj central; **Zentrale** f (-, -n) central office; TEL exchange; **Zentralheizung** f central heating; **Zentralverriegelung** f AUTO central locking; **Zentrum** m (-s, Zentren) centre

zerbrechen irr vt, vi break; **zerbrechlich** adj fragile

Zeremonie f (-, -n) ceremony

zerkleinern vt cut up; (roughly) chop up; **zerkratzen** vt scratch; **zerlegen** vt take to pieces; (meat) carve; (machi-

ne, engine) dismantle; **zerquetschen** vt squash; **zerreißen** irr 1. vt tear to pieces 2. vi tear

zerren 1. vt drag; **sich** dat **einen Muskel ~** pull a muscle 2. vi tug (an + dat at); **Zerrung** f MED pulled muscle

zerschlagen irr 1. vt smash 2. vr come to nothing

zerschneiden irr vt cut up

Zerstäuber m (-s, -) atomizer

zerstören vt destroy; **Zerstörung** f destruction

zerstreuen 1. vt scatter; (crowd) disperse; (doubts, fears) dispel 2. vr (crowd) disperse; **zerstreut** adj scattered; (person) absent-minded; (temporarily) distracted

zerteilen vt split up

Zertifikat nt (-(e)s, -e) certificate

Zettel m (-s, -) piece of paper; (message, reminder) note

Zeug nt (-(e)s, -e) fam stuff; (equipment) gear; **dummes ~** nonsense

Zeuge m (-n, -n), **Zeugin** f witness

Zeugnis nt certificate; (from school) report; (from former employer) reference

zickig adj fam touchy, bitchy

Zickzack m (-(e)s, -e) **im ~ fahren** zigzag (across the road)

Ziege f (-, -n) goat

Ziegel m (-s, -) brick; (on roof) tile

Ziegenkäse m goat's cheese

ziehen (*zog, gezogen*) **1.** *vt* draw; (*tug, drag*) pull; (*piece in game*) move; (*breed*) rear **2.** *vi* pull; (*go*) move; (*smoke, cloud etc*) drift; **den Tee ~ lassen** let the tea stand **3.** *vi impers* **es zieht** there's a draught **4.** *vr* (*meeting, speech*) drag on

Ziel *nt* (-(e)s, -e) (*of journey*) destination; SPORT finish; (*intention*) goal, aim; (*when taking aim*) aim (**auf** + *acc* at); **Zielgruppe** *f* target group; **ziellos** *adj* aimless; **Zielscheibe** *f* target

ziemlich 1. *adj* considerable; **ein ~es Durcheinander** quite a mess; **mit ~er Sicherheit** with some certainty **2.** *adv* rather, quite; **~ viel** quite a lot

zierlich *adj* dainty; (*woman*) petite

Ziffer *f* (-, -n) figure; **arabische/römische ~n** *pl* Arabic/Roman numerals *pl*; **Zifferblatt** *nt* dial, face

zig *adj fam* umpteen

Zigarette *f* cigarette; **Zigarettenautomat** *m* cigarette machine; **Zigarettenschachtel** *f* cigarette packet; **Zigarettenstummel** *m* cigarette end; **Zigarillo** *m* (-s, -s) cigarillo; **Zigarre** *f* (-, -n) cigar

Zimmer *nt* (-s, -) room; **haben Sie ein ~ für zwei Personen?** do you have a room for two?; **Zimmerlautstärke** *f* reasonable volume; **Zim-** mermädchen *nt* chambermaid; **Zimmermann** *m* carpenter; **Zimmerpflanze** *f* house plant; **Zimmerschlüssel** *m* room key; **Zimmerservice** *m* room service; **Zimmervermittlung** *f* accommodation agency

Zimt *m* (-(e)s, -e) cinnamon

Zink *nt* (-(e)s) zinc

Zinn *nt* (-(e)s) tin; (*alloy*) pewter

Zinsen *pl* interest *sg*

Zipfel *m* (-s, -) corner; (*pointed*) tip; (*of shirt*) tail; (*of sausage*) end; *fam* (*penis*) willy

zirka *adv* about, approximately

Zirkel *m* (-s, -) MATH (*pair of*) compasses *pl*

Zirkus *m* (-, -se) circus

zischen *vi* hiss

Zitat *nt* (-(e)s, -e) quotation (*aus* from); **zitieren** *vt* quote

Zitronat *nt* candied lemon peel; **Zitrone** *f* (-, -n) lemon; **Zitronenlimonade** *f* lemonade; **Zitronensaft** *m* lemon juice

zittern *vi* tremble (*vor* + *dat* with)

zivil *adj* civilian; (*price*) reasonable; **Zivil** *nt* (-s) plain clothes *pl*; MIL civilian clothes *pl*; **Zivildienst** *m* community service (*for conscientious objectors*)

zocken *vi fam* gamble

Zoff *m* (-s) *fam* trouble

zog *imperf of* **ziehen**

zögerlich *adj* hesitant; zögern *vi* hesitate

Zoll *m* (-(e)s, Zölle) customs *pl*; (*tax*) duty; Zollabfertigung *f* customs clearance; Zollamt *nt* customs office; Zollbeamte(r) *m*, Zollbeamtin *f* customs official; Zollerklärung *f* customs declaration; zollfrei *adj* duty-free; Zollgebühren *pl* customs duties *pl*; Zollkontrolle *f* customs check; Zöllner(in) *m(f)* customs officer; zollpflichtig *adj* liable to duty

Zone *f* (-, -n) zone

Zoo *m* (-s, -s) zoo

Zoom *nt* (-s, -s) zoom (shot); zoom (lens)

Zopf *m* (-(e)s, Zöpfe) plait (*Brit*), braid (*US*)

Zorn *m* (-(e)s) anger; zornig *adj* angry (*über etw acc* about sth, *auf jdn* with sb)

zu 1. *conj* (*with infinitive*) to 2. *prep + dat* (*direction, action*) to; (*place, time, price*) at; (*purpose*) for; **~r Post® gehen** go to the post office; **~ Hause** at home; **~ Weihnachten** at Christmas; **fünf Bücher ~ 20 Euro** five books at 20 euros each; **~m Fenster herein** through the window; **~ meiner Zeit** in my time 3. *adv* too; **~ viel** too much; **~ wenig** not enough 4. *adj fam* shut; **Tür ~!** shut the door!

zuallererst *adv* first of all; zu-

allerletzt *adv* last of all

Zubehör *nt* (-(e)s, -e) accessories *pl*

zubereiten *vt* prepare; Zubereitung *f* preparation

zubinden *irr vt* do (*or* tie) up

Zucchini *pl* courgettes *pl* (*Brit*), zucchini *pl* (*US*)

züchten *vt* (*animals*) breed; (*plants*) grow

zucken *vi* jerk; (*convulsively*) twitch; **mit den Schultern ~** shrug (one's shoulders)

Zucker *m* (-s, -) sugar; MED diabetes *sg*; Zuckerdose *f* sugar bowl; zuckerkrank *adj* diabetic; Zuckerrohr *nt* sugar cane; Zuckerwatte *f* candy-floss (*Brit*), cotton candy (*US*)

zudecken *vt* cover up

zudrehen *vt* turn off

zueinander *adv* to one other; (*as part of verb*) together; **~ halten** stick together

zuerst *adv* first; (*at the start*) at first; **~ einmal** first of all

Zufahrt *f* access; (*of house*) drive(way); Zufahrtsstraße *f* access road; (*onto motorway*) slip road (*Brit*), ramp (*US*)

Zufall *m* chance; (*event*) coincidence; **durch ~** by accident; **so ein ~!** what a coincidence; **zufällig** 1. *adj* chance 2. *adv* by chance; **weißt du ~, ob ...?** do you happen to know whether ...?

zufrieden *adj* content(ed);

(with sth) satisfied; **sich mit etw ~ geben** settle for sth; **lass sie** leave her alone (or in peace); **sie ist schwer ~ zu stellen** she is hard to please; **Zufriedenheit** f contentment; (with sth) satisfaction

zufügen vt add (dat to); **jdm Schaden/Schmerzen ~** cause sb harm/pain

Zug m (-(e)s, Züge) RAIL train; (air) draught; (tug) pull; (in chess) move; (of character) trait; (on cigarette) puff, drag; (swallow) gulp

Zugabe f extra; (at concert etc) encore

Zugabteil nt train compartment

Zugang m access; „**kein ~!**" 'no entry'

Zugauskunft f train information/desk; **Zugbegleiter(in)** m(f) guard (Brit), conductor (US)

zugeben irr vt admit; **zugegeben** adv admittedly

zugehen irr vi 1. vi (door, cupboard etc) shut; **auf jdn/ etw ~** walk towards sb/sth; **dem Ende ~** be coming to a close 2. vi impers happen; **es ging lustig zu** we/they had a lot of fun

Zügel m (-s, -) rein

Zugführer(in) m(f) guard (Brit), conductor (US)

zugig adj draughty

zügig adj speedy

Zugluft f draught

Zugpersonal nt train staff

zugreifen irr vi fig seize the opportunity; (when eating) help oneself; **~ auf + acc** IT access

Zugrestauraunt nt dining car, diner (US)

Zugriffsberechtigung f IT access right

zugrunde adv **~ gehen** perish; **~ gehen an + dat** die of; **Zugschaffner(in)** m(f) ticket inspector; **Zugunglück** nt train crash

zugunsten prep + gen or dat in favour of

Zugverbindung f train connection

zuhaben irr vi be closed

zuhalten irr vt **sich dat die Nase** ~ hold one's nose; **sich dat die Ohren** ~ hold one's hands over one's ears; **die Tür** ~ hold the door shut

Zuhause nt (-s) home

zuhören vi listen (dat to); **Zuhörer(in)** m(f) listener

zukleben vt seal

zukommen irr vi come up (auf + acc to); **jdm etw ~ lassen** give/send sb sth; **etw auf sich** acc **~ lassen** take sth as it comes

Zukunft f (-, Zukünfte) future; **zukünftig** 1. adj future 2. adv in future

zulassen irr vt (let in) admit; (allow) permit; (car) license; fam (not open) keep shut;

zulässig *adj* permissible, permitted

zuletzt *adv* finally, at last

zuliebe *adv* **jdm ~** for sb's sake

zum *contr of* **zu dem; ~ dritten Mal** for the third time; **~ Trinken** for drinking

zumachen 1. *vt* shut; *(clothes)* do up **2.** *vi* shut

zumindest *adv* at least

zumuten *vt* **jdm etw ~** expect sth of sb **2.** *vr* **sich** *dat* **zu viel ~** overdo things

zunächst *adv* first of all; **~ einmal** to start with

Zunahme *f* (-, -n) increase

Zuname *m* surname, last name

zünden *vt, vi* AUTO ignite; fire; **Zündholz** *nt* match; **Zündkabel** *f* AUTO ignition cable; **Zündkerze** *f* AUTO spark plug; **Zündschloss** *nt* ignition lock; **Zündschlüssel** *m* ignition key; **Zündung** *f* ignition

zunehmen *irr* **1.** *vi* increase; *(person)* put on weight **2.** *vt* **5 Kilo ~** put on 5 kilos

Zunge *f* (-, -n) tongue

Zungenkuss *m* French kiss

zunichte *adv* **~ machen** ruin

zunutze *adv* **sich** *dat* **etw ~ machen** make use of sth

zuparken *vt* block

zur *contr of* **zu der**

zurechtfinden *irr* *vr* find one's way around; **zurechtkommen** *irr* *vi* cope *(mit*

etw with sth); **zurechtmachen 1.** *vt* prepare **2.** *vr* get ready

Zürich *nt* (-s) Zurich

zurück *adv* back

zurückbekommen *irr* *vt* get back; **zurückblicken** *vi* look back *(auf + acc* at); **zurückbringen** *irr* *vt* bring back; *(somewhere else)* take back; **zurückerstatten** *vt* refund; **zurückfahren** *irr* *vi* go back; **zurückgeben** *irr* *vt* give back; **zurückgehen** *irr* *vi* go back; *(in time)* date back *(auf + acc* to)

zurückhalten *irr* **1.** *vt* hold back; *(hinder)* prevent **2.** *vr* hold back; **zurückhaltend** *adj* reserved

zurückholen *vt* fetch back; **zurückkommen** *irr* *vi* come back; **auf etw** *acc* **~** return (or get back) to sth; **zurücklassen** *irr* *vt* leave behind; **zurücklegen** *vt* put back; *(money)* put by; *(keep in reserve)* keep back; *(distance)* cover; **zurücknehmen** *irr* *vt* take back; **zurückrufen** *irr* *vt* call back; **zurückschicken** *vt* send back; **zurückstellen** *vt* put back; **zurücktreten** *irr* *vi* step back; *(from office)* retire; **zurückverlangen** *vt* **etw ~** ask for sth back; **zurückzahlen** *vt* pay back

zurzeit *adv* at present

Zusage *f* promise; *(of invitation)* acceptance; **zusagen**

1. *vt* promise **2.** *vi* accept; **jdm ~** (*please*) appeal to sb
zusammen *adv* together
Zusammenarbeit *f* collaboration; **zusammenarbeiten** *vi* work together
zusammenbrechen *irr vi* collapse; (*mentally*) break down; **Zusammenbruch** *m* collapse; (*mental*) breakdown
zusammenfassen *vt* summarize; (*bring together*) unite; **Zusammenfassung** *f* summary
zusammengehören *vi* belong together; **zusammenhalten** *irr vi* stick together
Zusammenhang *m* connection; **im/aus dem ~** in/out of context; **zusammenhängen** *irr vi* be connected; **zusammenhängend** *adj* coherent; **zusammenhang(s)-los** *adj* incoherent
zusammenklappen *vi, vt* fold up; **zusammenlegen 1.** *vt* fold up **2.** *vi* club together; **zusammennehmen** *irr* **1.** *vt* summon up; **alles zusammengenommen** all in all **2.** *vr* pull oneself together; *fam* get a grip, get one's act together; **zusammenpassen** *vi* go together; (*people*) be suited; **zusammenrechnen** *vt* add up
Zusammensein *nt* (*-s*) get-together
zusammensetzen 1. *vt* put

together **2.** *vr* **sich ~ aus** be composed of; **Zusammensetzung** *f* composition
Zusammenstoß *m* crash, collision; **zusammenstoßen** *irr vi* crash (*mit* into)
zusammenzählen *vt* add up
zusammenziehen *irr vi* (*into flat etc*) move in together
Zusatz *m* addition; **Zusatzgerät** *nt* attachment; **IT** add-on; **zusätzlich 1.** *adj* additional **2.** *adv* in addition
zuschauen *vi* watch; **Zuschauer(in)** *m(f)* (*-s, -*) spectator; **die ~** *pl* **THEAT** the audience *sg*; **Zuschauertribüne** *f* stand
zuschicken *vt* send
Zuschlag *m* extra charge; (*on ticket*) supplement
zuschlagpflichtig *adj* subject to an extra charge; **RAIL** subject to a supplement
zuschließen *irr vt* lock up
zusehen *irr vi* watch (*jdm* sb); **~, dass** make sure that
zusichern *vt* **jdm etw ~** assure sb of sth
Zustand *m* state, condition
zustande *adv* **~ bringen** bring about; **~ kommen** come about
zuständig *adj* (*authority*) relevant; **~ für** responsible for
Zustellung *f* delivery
zustimmen *vi* agree (*einer Sache dat* to sth, *jdm* with sb); **Zustimmung** *f* approval
zustoßen *irr vi* *fig* happen

(*jdm* to sb)

Zutaten *pl* ingredients *pl*

zutrauen *vt* **jdm etw** ~ think sb is capable of sth; *das hätte ich ihm nie zugetraut* I'd never have thought he was capable of it; *ich würde es ihr* ~ (*sth negative*) I wouldn't put it past her; **Zutrauen** *nt* (*-s*) confidence (*zu* in); **zutraulich** *adj* trusting; (*animal*) friendly

zutreffen *irr vi* be correct; ~ *auf* + *acc* apply to; *Zutreffendes bitte streichen* please delete as applicable

Zutritt *m* entry; (*permission to enter*) access; *"~ verboten!"* 'no entry'

zuverlässig *adj* reliable; **Zuverlässigkeit** *f* reliability

Zuversicht *f* confidence; **zuversichtlich** *adj* confident

zuvor *adv* before; (*before anything else*) first; **zuvorkommen** *irr vi* **jdm** ~ beat sb to it

Zuwachs *m* (*-es, Zuwächse*) increase, growth; *fam* (*baby*) addition to the family

zuwider *adv* **es ist mir** ~ I hate (*or* detest) it

zuzüglich *prep* + *gen* plus

zwang *imperf of* **zwingen**

Zwang *m* (*-(e)s, -̈e*) (*inner urge*) compulsion; (*against will*) force; **zwängen** *vt, vr* squeeze (*in* + *acc* into); **zwanglos** *adj* informal

zwanzig *num* twenty; **zwan-**

zigste(r, s) *adj* twentieth;
→ *dritte*

zwar *adv* **und** ~ ... ..., to be precise; *das ist ~ schön, aber ...* it is nice, but ...

Zweck *m* (*-(e)s, -e*) purpose; **zwecklos** *adj* pointless

zwei *num* two; **Zwei** *f* (*-, -en*) two; (*mark in school*) ≈ B; **Zweibettzimmer** *nt* twin room; **zweideutig** *adj* ambiguous; (*indecent*) suggestive; **zweifach** *adj, adv* double

Zweifel *m* (*-s, -*) doubt; **zweifellos** *adv* undoubtedly; **zweifeln** *vi* doubt (*an etw dat* sth); **Zweifelsfall** *m* **im** ~ in case of doubt

Zweig *m* (*-(e)s, -e*) branch; **Zweigstelle** *f* branch

zweihundert *num* two hundred; **zweimal** *adv* twice; **zweisprachig** *adj* bilingual; **zweispurig** *adj* AUTO two-lane; **zweit** *adv* **wir sind zu** ~ there are two of us; **zweite(r, s)** *adj* second; → *dritte*; **zweitens** *adv* secondly; (*when listing*) second; **zweitgrößte(r, s)** *adj* second largest; **Zweitschlüssel** *m* spare key

Zwerg(in) *m(f)* (*-(e)s, -e*) dwarf

Zwetschge *f* (*-, -n*) plum

zwicken *vt* pinch

Zwieback *m* (*-(e)s, -e*) rusk

Zwiebel *f* (*-, -n*) onion; (*of flower*) bulb; **Zwiebelsuppe**

f onion soup

Zwilling *m (-s, -e)* twin; **~e** *pl* ASTR Gemini *sg*

zwingen *(zwang, gezwungen) vt* force

zwinkern *vi* blink; *(deliberately)* wink

zwischen *prep + acc or dat* between; **Zwischenablage** *f* IT clipboard; **zwischendurch** *adv* in between; **Zwischenlandung** *f* stopover; **Zwischenraum** *m* space;

Zwischenstopp *m (-s, -s)* stopover; **Zwischenzeit** *f in der ~* in the meantime

zwitschern *vt, vi* twitter, chirp

zwölf *num* twelve; **zwölfte(r, s)** *adj* twelfth; → *dritte*

Zylinder *m (-s, -)* cylinder; top hat; **Zylinderkopfdichtung** *f* cylinder-head gasket

zynisch *adj* cynical

Zypern *nt (-s)* Cyprus

A

a, an *art* ein/eine/ein; **~ man** ein Mann; **~ woman** eine Frau; **~n apple** ein Apfel; **he's ~ student** er ist Student; **three times ~ week** dreimal pro Woche/in der Woche

AA *abbr* = **Automobile Association**; *britischer Automobilklub*; ≈ ADAC *m*

aback *adv* **taken ~** erstaunt

abandon *vt* (*desert*) verlassen; (*give up*) aufgeben

abbey *n* Abtei *f*

abbreviation *n* Abkürzung *f*

abdication *n* Abdankung *f*

abdomen *n* Unterleib *m*

ability *n* Fähigkeit *f*; **able** *adj* fähig; **be ~ to do sth** etw tun können

aboard *adv, prep* an Bord + *gen*

abolish *vt* abschaffen

aborigine *n* Ureinwohner(in) *m(f)* (Australiens)

abortion *n* Abtreibung *f*

about 1. *adv* (*around*) herum, umher; (*approximately*) ungefähr; (*with time*) gegen; **be ~ to** im Begriff sein zu; **there are a lot of people ~** es sind eine Menge Leute da **2.** *prep* (*concerning*) über + *acc*; **there is nothing you can do ~ it** da kann man nichts machen

above 1. *adv* oben; **children aged 8 and ~** Kinder ab 8 Jahren; **on the floor ~** ein Stockwerk höher **2.** *prep* über; **40 degrees ~** 40 Grad; **~ all** vor allem **3.** *adj* obig

abroad *adv* im Ausland; **go ~** ins Ausland gehen

absent *adj* abwesend; **be ~** fehlen; **absent-minded** *adj* zerstreut

absolute *adj* absolut; (*rubbish*) vollkommen, total; **absolutely** *adv* absolut; (*true, stupid*) vollkommen; **~!** genau!; **you're ~ right** du hast/Sie haben völlig Recht

absorb *vt* absorbieren; *fig* (*information*) in sich aufnehmen; **absorbed ~ in sth** in etw vertieft; **absorbent** *adj* absorbierend; **~ cotton** (*US*) Watte *f*; **absorbing** *adj* faszinierend, fesselnd

abstract *adj* abstrakt

abundance *n* Reichtum *m* (of an + *dat*)

abuse **1.** n (*rude language*) Beschimpfungen pl; (*mistreatment*) Missbrauch m **2.** vt (*misuse*) missbrauchen; **abusive** adj beleidigend

AC 1. abbr = **alternating current**; Wechselstrom m **2.** abbr = **air conditioning**; Klimaanlage f

a / c abbr = **account**; Kto.

academic 1. n Wissenschaftler(in) m(f) **2.** adj wissenschaftlich

accelerate vi (*car etc*) beschleunigen; (*driver*) Gas geben; **acceleration** n Beschleunigung f; **accelerator** n Gas(pedal) nt

accent n Akzent m

accept vt annehmen; (*agree to*) akzeptieren; (*responsibility*) übernehmen; **acceptable** adj annehmbar

access n Zugang m; IT Zugriff m; **accessible** adj (leicht) zugänglich / erreichbar; **accessory** n Zubehörteil nt; **access road** n Zufahrtsstraße f

accident n Unfall m; **by ~** zufällig; **accidental** adj unbeabsichtigt; (*meeting*) zufällig; (*death*) durch Unfall; **accident-prone** adj vom Pech verfolgt

acclimatize vt **~ oneself** sich gewöhnen (to an + acc)

accommodate vt unterbringen; **accommodation**, s n Unterkunft f

accompany vt begleiten

accomplish vt erreichen

accord n of one's own ~ freiwillig; **according to** prep nach, laut + dat

account n (in bank etc) Konto nt; (*narrative*) Bericht m; **on ~ of** wegen; **on no ~** auf keinen Fall; **take into ~** berücksichtigen, in Betracht ziehen; **accountant** n Buchhalter(in) m(f); **account for** vt (*explain*) erklären; (*expenditure*) Rechenschaft ablegen für; **account number** n Kontonummer f

accurate adj genau

accusation n Anklage f, Beschuldigung f; **accuse** vt beschuldigen; LAW anklagen (of wegen gen); **accused** n LAW Angeklagte(r) mf

accustom vt gewöhnen (to an + acc); **accustomed** adj gewohnt; **get ~ to sth** sich an etw acc gewöhnen

ace 1. n Ass nt **2.** adj Star-

ache 1. n Schmerz m **2.** vi wehtun

achieve vt erreichen; **achievement** n Leistung f

acid 1. n Säure f **2.** adj sauer

acknowledge vt (*recognize*) anerkennen; (*admit*) zugeben; (*receipt of letter etc*) bestätigen; **acknowledgement** n Anerkennung f; (*of letter*) Empfangsbestätigung f acne *n* Akne *f*

acorn *n* Eichel *f*

acoustic *adj* (*pain*) akustisch; acoustics *npl* Akustik *f*

acquaintance *n* (*person*) Bekannte(r) *mf*

acquire *vt* erwerben, sich aneignen; acquisition *n* (*of skills etc*) Erwerb *m*; (*object*) Anschaffung *f*

across 1. *prep* über + *acc*; he lives ~ the street er wohnt auf der anderen Seite der Straße 2. *adv* hinüber, herüber; **100m** = 100m breit

act 1. *n* (*deed*) Tat *f*; LAW Gesetz *nt*; THEAT Akt *m*; be in the ~ of doing sth gerade dabei sein, etw zu tun 2. *vi* (*take action*) handeln; (*behave*) sich verhalten; THEAT spielen; **as** (*character*) fungieren als; (*thing*) dienen als 3. *vt* (*a part*) spielen

action *n* (*of play, novel etc*) Handlung *f*; (*in film etc*) Action *f*; MIL Kampf *m*; **take** ~ etwas unternehmen; **put a plan into** ~ einen Plan in die Tat umsetzen; action replay *n* SPORT, TV Wiederholung *f*

active *adj* aktiv; (*child*) lebhaft; activity *n* Aktivität *f*; (*occupation*) Beschäftigung *f*; (*organized event*) Veranstaltung *f*

actor *n* Schauspieler(in) *m*(*f*); actress *n* Schauspielerin *f*

actual *adj* wirklich; actually

adv eigentlich; (*said in surprise*) tatsächlich

acupuncture *n* Akupunktur *f*

acute *adj* (*pain*) akut; MATH (*angle*) spitz

ad *abbr* = **advertisement**

AD *abbr* = **Anno Domini**; nach Christi, n. Chr.

adapt 1. *vi* sich anpassen (*to* + *dat*) 2. *vt* anpassen (*to* + *dat*); (*rewrite*) bearbeiten (*for* für); adaptation *n* (*of book etc*) Bearbeitung *f*; adapter *n* ELEC Zwischenstecker *m*, Adapter *m*

add *vt* (*ingredient*) hinzufügen; (*numbers*) addieren; add up 1. *vi* (*make sense*) stimmen 2. *vt* (*numbers*) addieren

addicted *adj* ~ to alcohol/ drugs alkohol-/drogensüchtig

addition *n* Zusatz *m*; (*to bill*) Aufschlag *m*; MATH Addition *f*; **in** ~ außerdem, zusätzlich (*to* zu); additional *adj* zusätzlich, weiter; additive *n* Zusatz *m*; add-on *n* Zusatzgerät *nt*

address 1. *n* Adresse *f* 2. *vt* (*letter*) adressieren; (*person*) anreden

adequate *adj* (*appropriate*) angemessen; (*sufficient*) ausreichend

adhesive *n* Klebstoff *m*; adhesive tape *n* Klebstreifen *m*

adjacent *adj* benachbart

adjoining *adj* benachbart, Neben-

adjust 1. *vt* einstellen; (*put right also*) richtig stellen; (*speed, flow*) regulieren; (*in position*) verstellen **2.** *vi* sich anpassen (*to* + *dat*); **adjustable** *adj* verstellbar

admin *n fam* Verwaltung *f*; **administration** *n* Verwaltung *f*; POL Regierung *f*

admirable *adj* bewundernswert; **admiration** *n* Bewunderung *f*; **admire** *vt* bewundern

admission *n* (*entrance*) Zutritt *m*; (*to university etc*) Zulassung *f*; (*fee*) Eintritt *m*; **admission charge, admission fee** *n* Eintrittspreis *m*; **admit** *vt* (*let in*) hereinlassen (*to* + *acc*); (*to university etc*) zulassen; (*confess*) zugeben, gestehen; **be ~ted to hospital** ins Krankenhaus eingeliefert werden

adolescent *n* Jugendliche(r) *mf*

adopt *vt* (*child*) adoptieren; (*idea*) übernehmen; **adoption** *n* (*of child*) Adoption *f*; (*of idea*) Übernahme *f*

adorable *adj* entzückend; **adore** *vt* anbeten; (*person*) über alles lieben, vergöttern

adult 1. *adj* (*person*) erwachsen; (*film etc*) für Erwachsene **2.** *n* Erwachsene(r) *mf*

adultery *n* Ehebruch *m*

advance 1. *n* (*money*) Vor-

schuss *m*; (*progress*) Fortschritt *m*; **in ~** im Voraus; **book in ~** vorbestellen **2.** *vi* (*move forward*) vorrücken **3.** *vt* (*money*) vorschießen; **advance booking** *n* Reservierung *f*; THEAT Vorverkauf *m*; **advanced** *adj* (*modern*) fortschrittlich; (*course, study*) für Fortgeschrittene; **advance payment** *n* Vorauszahlung *f*

advantage *n* Vorteil *m*; **take ~ of** (*exploit*) ausnutzen; (*profit from*) Nutzen ziehen aus; **it's to your ~** es ist in deinem / Ihrem Interesse

adventure *n* Abenteuer *nt*; **adventure holiday** *n* Abenteuerurlaub *m*; **adventure playground** *n* Abenteuerspielplatz *m*

adverse *adj* (*conditions etc*) ungünstig; (*effect, comment etc*) negativ

advert *n* Anzeige *f*; **advertise 1.** *vt* (*in newspaper*) inserieren; (*job*) ausschreiben **2.** *vi* Reklame machen; **advertisement** *n* Werbung *f*; (*announcement*) Anzeige *f*; **advertising** *n* Werbung *f*

advice *n* Rat(schlag) *m*; **take my ~** hör auf mich; **advisable** *adj* ratsam; **advise** *vt* raten (*sb* jdm); **~ sb to do sth / not to do sth** jdm zuraten / abraten, etw zu tun

aerial 1. *n* Antenne *f* **2.** *adj*

Luft-
aerobics *nsing* Aerobic *nt*
aeroplane *n* Flugzeug *nt*
afaik *abbr* = **as far as I know**;
(*SMS*) ≈ soweit ich weiß
affair *n* (*matter, business*) Sache *f*, Angelegenheit *f*;
(*scandal*) Affäre *f*; (*love affair*) Verhältnis *nt*
affect *vt* (*influence*) (ein)wir-
ken auf + *acc*; (*health, organ*)
angreifen; (*move deeply*) berühren; (*concern*) betreffen;
affection *n* Zuneigung *f*; **affectionate** *adj* liebevoll
affluent *adj* wohlhabend
afford *vt* sich leisten; **I can't ~
it** ich kann es mir nicht leisten; **affordable** *adj* erschwinglich
Afghanistan *n* Afghanistan
nt
aforementioned *adj* oben genannt
afraid *adj* **be ~** Angst haben
(*of* vor + *dat*); **be ~ that ...**
fürchten, dass ...; **I'm ~ I don't
know** das weiß ich leider
nicht
Africa *n* Afrika *nt*; **African 1.**
adj afrikanisch **2.** *n* Afrika-
ner(in) *m(f)*; **African American, Afro-American** *n* Afro-
amerikaner(in) *m(f)*
after 1. *prep* nach; **ten ~ five**
(*US*) zehn nach fünf; **be ~
sb/ sth** (*following, seeking*)
hinter jdm/ etw her sein; **~
all** schließlich **2.** *conj* nachdem **3.** *adv* **soon ~** bald da-

nach; **aftercare** *n* Nachbe-
handlung *f*
afternoon *n* Nachmittag *m*; **in
the ~** nachmittags
afters *npl* Nachtisch *m*; **after-
-sales service** *n* Kundendienst *m*; **after-shave** (*lotion*) *n* Rasierwasser *nt*; **af-
ter-sun lotion** *n* After-Sun-
-Lotion *f*; **afterwards** *adv*
nachher; (*after that*) danach
again *adv* wieder; (*one more
time*) noch einmal; **~ and ~**
immer wieder; **the same ~
please** das Gleiche noch
mal bitte
against *prep* gegen; **~ my will**
wider Willen; **~ the law** un-
rechtmäßig, illegal
age 1. *n* Alter *nt*; (*period of
history*) Zeitalter *nt*; **at the
~ of four** im Alter von vier
(Jahren); **what ~ is she?,
what is her ~?** wie alt ist
sie?; **under ~** minderjährig
2. *vi* altern, alt werden; **aged
1.** *adj* **~ thirty** dreißig Jahre
alt; **a son ~ twenty** ein zwan-
zigjähriger Sohn **2.** *n* (*elderly*) betagt; **age group** *n* Al-
tersgruppe *f*; **age limit** *n* Al-
tersgrenze *f*
agency *n* Agentur *f*
agenda *n* Tagesordnung *f*
agent *n* COMM Vertreter(in)
m(f); (*for writer, actor etc*)
Agent(in) *m(f)*
aggression *n* Aggression *f*;
aggressive *adj* aggressiv
AGM *abbr* = **Annual General**

Meeting; JHV f

ago *adv* **two days ~** heute vor zwei Tagen; **not long ~** (erst) vor kurzem

agonize *vi* sich den Kopf zerbrechen (*over* über + acc); **agonizing** *adj* qualvoll; **agony** *n* Qual f

agree 1. *vt* (*date, price etc*) vereinbaren; **~ to do sth** sich bereit erklären, etw zu tun; **~ that ...** sich *dat* einig sein, dass ...; (*decide*) beschließen, dass ...; (*admit*) zugeben, dass ... **2.** *vi* (*have same opinion, correspond*) übereinstimmen (*with* mit); (*consent*) zustimmen; (*come to an agreement*) sich einigen (*about, on* auf + acc); (*food*) bekommen; **~ not ~ with sb** jdm nicht bekommen; **agreement** *n* (*agreeing*) Übereinstimmung f; (*contract*) Abkommen nt, Vereinbarung f

agricultural *adj* landwirtschaftlich, Landwirtschafts-; **agriculture** *n* Landwirtschaft f

ahead *adv* **be ~** führen, vorne liegen; **~ of** vor + dat; **be 3 metres ~** 3 Meter Vorsprung haben

aid 1. *n* Hilfe f; **in ~ of** zugunsten + gen; **with the ~ of** mithilfe + gen **2.** *vt* helfen + dat; (*support*) unterstützen

Aids *n acr* = **acquired immune deficiency syndrome**; Aids nt

aim 1. *vt* (*gun, camera*) richten (*at* auf + acc) **2.** *vi* **~ at** (*with gun etc*) zielen auf + acc; *fig* abzielen auf + acc; **~ to do sth** beabsichtigen, etw zu tun **3.** *n* Ziel nt

air 1. *n* Luft f; **in the open ~** im Freien **2.** *vt* lüften; **air** *n* AUTO Airbag m; **air-conditioned** *adj* mit Klimaanlage; **air-conditioning** *n* Klimaanlage f; **aircraft** *n* Flugzeug nt; **airfield** *n* Flugplatz m; **air force** *n* Luftwaffe f; **airline** *n* Fluggesellschaft f; **airmail** *n* Luftpost f; **by ~** mit Luftpost; **airplane** *n* (*US*) Flugzeug nt; **air pollution** *n* Luftverschmutzung f; **airport** *n* Flughafen m; **airsick** *adj* luftkrank; **airtight** *adj* luftdicht; **air-traffic controller** *n* Fluglotse m, Fluglotsin f

aisle *n* Gang m; (*in church*) Seitenschiff nt; **~ seat** Sitz m am Gang

ajar *adj* (*door*) angelehnt

alarm 1. *n* (*warning*) Alarm m; (*bell etc*) Alarmanlage f **2.** *vt* beunruhigen; **alarm clock** *n* Wecker m; **alarmed** *adj* (*protected*) alarmgesichert; **alarming** *adj* beunruhigend

Albania *n* Albanien nt; **Albanian 1.** *adj* albanisch **2.** *n* (*person*) Albaner(in) m(f); (*language*) Albanisch nt

album *n* Album nt

alcohol *n* Alkohol m; **alco-**

hol-free *adj* alkoholfrei; **alcoholic 1.** *adj* (drink) alkoholisch **2.** *n* Alkoholiker(in) *m(f)*

ale *n* Ale *nt* (helles englisches Bier)

alert **1.** *adj* wachsam **2.** *n* Alarm *m* **3.** *vt* warnen (to vor + *dat*)

algebra *n* Algebra *f*

Algeria *n* Algerien *nt*

alibi *n* Alibi *nt*

alien *n* (foreigner) Ausländer(in) *m(f)*; (from space) Außerirdische(r) *mf*

alike *adj, adv* gleich; (similar) ähnlich

alive *adj* lebendig; **keep sth ~** etw am Leben erhalten; **he's still ~** er lebt noch

all **1.** *adj* (plural, every one of) alle; (singular, the whole of) ganz; **~ the children** alle Kinder; **~ the time** die ganze Zeit; **~ his life** sein ganzes Leben; **why me of ~ people?** warum ausgerechnet ich? **2.** *pron* (everything) alles; (everybody) alle; **~ of** ganz; **~ of them came** sie kamen alle **3.** *n* alles **4.** *adv* (completely) ganz; **it's ~ over** es ist ganz aus; **~ along** von Anfang an; **~ at once** auf einmal

allegation *n* Behauptung *f*; **alleged** *adj* angeblich

allergic *adj* allergisch (to gegen); **allergy** *n* Allergie *f*

alleviate *vt* (pain) lindern

alley *n* (enge) Gasse; (pas-

sage) Durchgang *m*; (bowling) Bahn *f*

alliance *n* Bündnis *nt*

alligator *n* Alligator *m*

all-night *adj* (café, cinema) die ganze Nacht geöffnet

allocate *vt* zuweisen, zuteilen (to *dat*)

allotment *n* (plot) Schrebergarten *m*

allow *vt* (permit) erlauben (sb jdm); (grant) bewilligen; (time) einplanen; **allow for** *vt* berücksichtigen; (cost etc) einkalkulieren; **allowance** *n* (from state) Beihilfe *f*; (from parent) Unterhaltsgeld *nt*

all right **1.** *adj* okay, in Ordnung; **I'm ~** mir geht's gut **2.** *adv* (satisfactorily) ganz gut **3.** *interj* okay

allusion *n* Anspielung *f* (to auf + *acc*)

all-wheel drive *n* AUTO Allradantrieb *m*

ally *n* Verbündete(r) *mf*; HIST Alliierte(r) *mf*

almond *n* Mandel *f*

almost *adv* fast

alone *adj, adv* allein

along **1.** *prep* entlang + *acc*; **~ the river** den Fluss entlang; (position) am Fluss entlang **2.** *adv* (onward) weiter; **~ with** zusammen mit; **all ~** die ganze Zeit; **alongside 1.** *prep* neben + *dat* **2.** *adv* (walk) nebenher

aloud *adv* laut

alphabet n Alphabet nt
Alps npl **the ~** die Alpen
already adv schon, bereits
Alsace n Elsass nt; **Alsatian 1.**
adj elsässisch **2.** n Elsäs-
ser(in) m(f); (Brit, dog)
Schäferhund m
also adv auch
altar n Altar m
alter vt ändern; **alteration** n
Änderung f; **~s** (to building)
Umbau m
alternate 1. adj abwechselnd
2. vi abwechseln (with mit);
alternating current n Wechselstrom m; **alternative 1.** adj
Alternativ- **2.** n Alternative f
although conj obwohl
altitude n Höhe f
altogether adv (in total) insgesamt; (entirely) ganz und
gar
aluminium, aluminum (US)
n Aluminium nt
always adv immer
am present of **be**; bin
am, a.m. abbr = **ante meridiem**; vormittags, morgens
amateur 1. n Amateur(in)
m(f) **2.** adj Amateur-; (theatre, choir) Laien-
amazed adj erstaunt (at über
+ acc); **amazing** adj erstaunlich
Amazon n **~** (**river**) Amazo-
nas m
ambassador n Botschafter m
ambiguity n Zweideutigkeit
f; **ambiguous** adj zweideutig

ambition n Ambition f; (ambitious nature) Ehrgeiz m;
ambitious adj ehrgeizig
ambulance n Krankenwagen
m
America n Amerika nt;
American 1. adj amerikanisch **2.** n Amerikaner(in)
m(f); **native ~** Indianer(in)
m(f)
amiable adj liebenswürdig
amicable adj freundlich; (relations) freundschaftlich
amnesia n Gedächtnisverlust
m
among(st) prep unter + acc
amount 1. n (quantity) Menge
f; (of money) Betrag m; **a
large/small ~ of ...** ziemlich
viel/wenig ... **2.** vi **~ to** (total)
sich belaufen auf + acc
amp, ampere n Ampere nt
amplifier n Verstärker m
Amtrak® n amerikanische Ei-
senbahngesellschaft
amuse vt amüsieren; (entertain) unterhalten; **amused**
adj **I'm not ~** das finde ich
gar nicht lustig; **amusement**
n (enjoyment) Vergnügen nt;
(recreation) Unterhaltung f;
amusement park n Vergnügungspark m; **amusing** adj
amüsant
an art ein(e)
anaemic adj blutarm
anaesthetic n Narkose f;
(substance) Narkosemittel
nt
analyse, analyze vt analysie-

ren; **analysis** n Analyse f

anatomy n Anatomie f; (structure) Körperbau m

ancestor n Vorfahr m

anchor 1. n Anker m **2.** vt verankern

anchovy n Sardelle f

ancient adj alt; fam (person, clothes etc) uralt

and conj und

Andorra n Andorra nt

anemic adj (US) → **anaemic**

anesthetic n (US) → **anaesthetic**

angel n Engel m

anger 1. n Zorn m **2.** vt ärgern

angina, angina pectoris n Angina Pectoris f

angle n Winkel m; fig Standpunkt m

angling n Angeln nt

angry adj verärgert; (stronger) zornig; **be ~ with sb** auf jdn böse sein

angular adj eckig; (face) kantig

animal n Tier nt; **animal rights** npl Tierrechte pl

animated adj lebhaft; **~ film** Zeichentrickfilm m

aniseed n Anis m

ankle n (Fuß)knöchel m

annex n Anbau m

anniversary n Jahrestag m

announce vt bekannt geben; RADIO, TV ansagen; **announcement** n Bekanntgabe f; (official) Bekanntmachung f; RADIO, TV Ansage f; **announcer** n RADIO, TV

annoy vt ärgern; **annoyance** n Ärger m; **annoyed** adj ärgerlich; **be ~ with sb (about sth)** sich über jdn (über etw) ärgern; **annoying** adj lästig, nervig

annual 1. adj jährlich **2.** n Jahrbuch nt

anonymous adj anonym

anorak n Anorak m; (Brit) fam pej Freak m

anorexia n Magersucht f; **anorexic** adj magersüchtig

another adj, pron (different) ein(e) andere(r, s); (additional) noch eine(r, s); **let me put it ~ way** lass es mich anders sagen

answer 1. n Antwort f (to auf + acc) **2.** vi antworten; (on phone) sich melden **3.** vt (person) antworten + dat; (letter, question) beantworten; (telephone) gehen an + acc, abnehmen; (door) öffnen; **answering machine, answerphone** n Anrufbeantworter m

ant n Ameise f

Antarctic n Antarktis f; **Antarctic Circle** n südlicher Polarkreis

antelope n Antilope f

antenna n ZOOL Fühler m; RADIO Antenne f

anti- pref Anti-, anti-; **antibiotic** n Antibiotikum nt

anticipate vt (expect: trouble, question) erwarten, rechnen mit; **anticipation** n Erwartung f

anticlimax n Enttäuschung f; **anticlockwise** adv entgegen dem Uhrzeigersinn; **antifreeze** n Frostschutzmittel nt

Antipodes npl Australien und Neuseeland

antiquarian adj ~ **bookshop** Antiquariat nt

antique 1. n Antiquität f **2.** adj antik; **antique shop** n Antiquitätengeschäft nt

antiseptic 1. n Antiseptikum nt **2.** adj antiseptisch

antlers npl Geweih nt

anxiety n Sorge f (about um); **anxious** adj besorgt (about um); (apprehensive) ängstlich

any 1. adj (in question: untranslated) **do you have ~ money?** hast du Geld?; (with negative) **I don't have ~ money** ich habe kein Geld; (whichever one likes) **take ~ card** nimm irgendeine Karte **2.** pron (in question) **do you want ~?** (singular) willst du etwas (davon)?; (plural) willst du welche?; (with negative) **I don't have ~** ich habe keine/keinen/keins; (whichever one likes) **you can take ~ of them** du kannst jede(n, s) beliebige(n) nehmen **3.** adv (in question) **are there ~ more strawberries?** gibt es noch Erdbeeren?; **can't you work**

~ faster? kannst du nicht schneller arbeiten?; (with negative) **not ~ longer** nicht mehr; **this isn't ~ better** das ist auch nicht besser; anybody pron (whoever one likes) irgendjemand; (everyone) jeder; (in question) jemand; **anyhow** adv **I don't want to talk about it, not now ~** ich möchte nicht darüber sprechen, jedenfalls nicht jetzt; **if I can help you ~** wenn ich Ihnen irgendwie helfen kann; **they asked me not to go, but I went ~** sie baten mich, nicht hinzugehen, aber ich bin trotzdem hingegangen; anyone pron (whoever one likes) irgendjemand; (everyone) jeder; (in question) jemand; **isn't there ~ you can ask?** gibt es denn niemanden, den du fragen kannst?; **anyplace** adv (US) (direction) irgendwohin; (everywhere) überall; **anything** pron (whatever one likes, in question) (irgend)etwas; (everything) alles; **~ else?** sonst noch etwas?; **~ but that** alles, nur das nicht; **she didn't tell me ~** sie hat mir nichts gesagt; **anytime** adv jederzeit; **anyway** adv **I didn't want to go there ~** ich wollte da sowieso nicht hingehen; **thanks ~** trotzdem danke; **~, as I was saying, ...** jedenfalls, wie ich schon sagte, ...; **anywhere** *adv* irgendwo; *(direction)* irgendwohin; *(everywhere)* überall

apart *adv* auseinander; **~ from** außer; **live ~** getrennt leben

apartment *n* Wohnung *f*; **apartment block** *n* Wohnblock *m*

ape *n* (Menschen)affe *m*

aperitif *n* Aperitif *m*

aperture *n* Öffnung *f*; PHOT Blende *f*

apologize *vi* sich entschuldigen; **apology** *n* Entschuldigung *f*

apostrophe *n* Apostroph *m*

appalled *adj* entsetzt (*at* über + *acc*);**appalling** *adj* entsetzlich

apparatus *n* Apparat *m*; *(piece of apparatus)* Gerät *nt*

apparent *adj (obvious)* offensichtlich (*to* für); *(seeming)* scheinbar; **apparently** *adv* anscheinend

appeal 1. *vi* (dringend) bitten (*for* um, *to* + *acc*); LAW Berufung einlegen; **~ to sb** *(be attractive)* jdm zusagen **2.** *n* Aufruf *m* (*for* an + *acc*); LAW Berufung *f*; *(attraction)* Reiz *m*; **appealing** *adj* ansprechend, attraktiv

appear *vi* erscheinen; THEAT auftreten; *(seem)* scheinen; **appearance** *n* Erscheinen *nt*; THEAT Auftritt *m*; *(look)* Aussehen *nt*

appendicitis *n* Blinddarm-

entzündung *f*; **appendix** *n* Blinddarm *m*; *(to book)* Anhang *m*

appetite *n* Appetit *m*; *fig (desire)* Verlangen *nt*; **appetizing** *adj* appetitlich

applause *n* Beifall *m*, Applaus *m*

apple *n* Apfel *m*; **apple juice** *n* Apfelsaft *m*; **apple pie** *n* gedeckter Apfelkuchen *m*; **apple puree**, **apple sauce** *n* Apfelmus *nt*; **apple tart** *n* Apfelkuchen *m*; **apple tree** *n* Apfelbaum *m*

appliance *n* Gerät *nt*; **applicable** *adj* anwendbar; *(on forms)* zutreffend; **applicant** *n* Bewerber(in) *m(f)*; **application** *n* *(request)* Antrag *m* (*for* auf + *acc*); *(for job)* Bewerbung *f* (*for* um);**application form** *n* Anmeldeformular *nt*; **apply 1.** *vi (be relevant)* zutreffen (*to* auf + *acc*); *(for job etc)* sich bewerben (*for* um) **2.** *vt (cream, paint etc)* auftragen; *(put into practice)* anwenden; *(brakes)* betätigen

appoint *vt (to post)* ernennen; **appointment** *n* Verabredung *f*; *(at doctor, hairdresser etc, in business)* Termin *m*; **by ~** nach Vereinbarung

appreciate 1. *vt (value)* zu schätzen wissen; *(understand)* einsehen **2.** *vi (increase in value)* im Wert steigen; **appreciation** *n* *(esteem)*

Anerkennung f, Würdigung f

apprehensive adj ängstlich

approach 1. vi sich nähern **2.** vt (place) sich nähern + dat; (person) herantreten an + acc

appropriate adj passend; (to occasion) angemessen; (remark) treffend; **appropriately** adv passend; (expressed) treffend

approval n (show of satisfaction) Anerkennung f; (permission) Zustimmung f (of zu); **approve 1.** vt billigen **2.** vi **~ of sth/sb** etw billigen/von jdm etwas halten; **I don't ~** ich missbillige das

approx = **approximately**; ca.; **approximate** adj ungefähr; **approximately** adv ungefähr, circa

apricot n Aprikose f

April n April m; → **September**

apron n Schürze f

aptitude n Begabung f

aquaplaning n AUTO Aquaplaning nt

aquarium n Aquarium nt

Aquarius n ASTR Wassermann m

Arab n Araber(in) m(f); **Arabian** adj arabisch; **Arabic 1.** n (language) Arabisch nt **2.** adj arabisch

arbitrary adj willkürlich

arcade n Arkade f; (shopping arcade) Einkaufspassage f

arch n Bogen m

archaeologist, archeologist (US) n Archäologe m, Archäologin f; **archaeology, archeology** (US) n Archäologie f

archaic adj veraltet

archbishop n Erzbischof m

architect n Architekt(in) m(f); **architecture** n Architektur f

archive(s) n(pl) Archiv nt

archway n Torbogen m

Arctic n Arktis f; **Arctic Circle** n nördlicher Polarkreis

are present of **be**

area n (region, district) Gebiet nt, Gegend f; (amount of space) Fläche f; (part of building etc) Bereich m, Zone f; fig (field) Bereich m; **the London ~** der Londoner Raum; **area code** n (US) Vorwahl f

aren't contr of **are not**

Argentina n Argentinien nt

argue vi streiten (about, over über + acc); **~ that...** behaupten, dass ...; **~ for/against ...** sprechen für/gegen ...; **argument** n (reasons) Argument nt; (quarrel) Streit m; **have an ~** sich streiten

Aries nsing ASTR Widder m

arise vi sich ergeben, entstehen; (problem, question, wind) aufkommen

aristocracy n (class) Adel m; **aristocrat** n Adlige(r) m(f); **aristocratic** adj aristokratisch, adlig

arm 1. *n* Arm *m*; *(sleeve)* Ärmel *m*; *(of armchair)* Armlehne *f* 2. *vt* bewaffnen; **armchair** *n* Lehnstuhl *m*
armed *adj* bewaffnet
armpit *n* Achselhöhle *f*
arms *npl* Waffen *pl*
army *n* Armee *f*
A road *n* *(Brit)* ≈ Bundesstraße *f*
aroma *n* Duft *m*, Aroma *nt*;
aromatherapy *n* Aromatherapie *f*
arose *pt of* **arise**
around 1. *adv* herum, umher; *(present)* hier (irgendwo); *(approximately)* ungefähr; *(with time)* gegen; **he's ~ somewhere** er ist hier irgendwo in der Nähe **2.** *prep* *(surrounding)* um ... (herum); *(about in)* in ... herum
arr. *abbr* = **arrival, arrives,** Ank.
arrange *vt* *(put in order)* (an-)ordnen; *(artistically)* arrangieren; *(agree to: meeting etc)* vereinbaren, festsetzen; *(organize)* planen; **~ that ...** es so einrichten, dass ...; **we ~d to meet at eight o'clock** wir haben uns für acht Uhr verabredet; **arrangement** *n* *(layout)* Anordnung *f*, *(agreement)* Vereinbarung *f*, Plan *m*; **make ~s** Vorbereitungen treffen
arrest 1. *vt* *(person)* verhaften **2.** *n* Verhaftung *f*

arrival *n* Ankunft *f*; **new ~** *(person)* Neuankömmling *m*; **arrivals** *n* *(airport)* Ankunftshalle *f*; **arrive** *vi* ankommen *(at* bei, in + *dat)*; **~ at a solution** eine Lösung finden
arrogant *adj* arrogant
arrow *n* Pfeil *m*
arse *n vulg* Arsch *m*
art *n* Kunst *f*; **~s** *pl* Geisteswissenschaften *pl*
artery *n* Schlagader *f*, Arterie *f*
art gallery *n* Kunstgalerie *f*, Kunstmuseum *nt*
arthritis *n* Arthritis *f*
artichoke *n* Artischocke *f*
article *n* Artikel *m*; *(object)* Gegenstand *m*
artificial *adj* künstlich, Kunst-
artist *n* Künstler(in) *m(f)*; **artistic** *adj* künstlerisch
as 1. *adv* *(like)* wie; *(in role of)* als; **such ~** *(for example)* wie etwa ...; **~ ... ~** so ... wie; **~ soon ~ he comes** sobald er kommt; **twice ~ much** zweimal so viel; **~ for ... was ...** betrifft; **~ of ...** *(time)* ab ... + *dat* **2.** *conj* *(since)* da, weil; *(while)* als, während; **~ if, ~ though** als ob; **leave it ~ it is** lass es wie (wie es ist); **~ it were** sozusagen
asap *acr* = **as soon as possible;** möglichst bald
ash *n* *(dust)* Asche *f*; *(tree)* Esche *f*

ashamed *adj* beschämt; **be ~ (of sb/sth)** sich (für jdn/etw) schämen

ashore *adv* an Land

ashtray *n* Aschenbecher *m*

Asia *n* Asien *nt*; **Asian 1.** *adj* asiatisch **2.** *n* Asiat(in) *m(f)*

aside *adv* beiseite, zur Seite; **~ from** (*esp, US*) außer

ask *vt, vi* fragen; (*question*) stellen; (*request*) bitten um; **~ sb the way** jdn nach dem Weg fragen; **~ sb to do sth** jdn darum bitten, etw zu tun; **ask for** *vt* bitten um

asleep *adj, adv* **be ~** schlafen; **fall ~** einschlafen

asparagus *n* Spargel *m*

aspirin *n* Aspirin® *nt*

ass *n a. fig* Esel *m*; (*US*) *vulg* Arsch *m*

assassinate *vt* ermorden; **assassination** *n* Ermordung *f*

assault 1. *n* Angriff *m*; LAW Körperverletzung *f* **2.** *vt* überfallen, herfallen über + *acc*

assemble 1. *vt* (*parts*) zusammensetzen **2.** *vi* sich versammeln; **assembly** *n* (*of people*) Versammlung *f*; **assembly hall** *n* Aula *f*; **assertion** *n* Behauptung *f*

assess *vt* einschätzen; **assessment** *n* Einschätzung *f*

asset *n* Vermögenswert *m*; *fig* Vorteil *m*; **~s** *pl* Vermögen *nt*

assign *vt* zuweisen; **assignment** *n* Aufgabe *f*; (*mission*) Auftrag *m*

assist *vt* helfen + *dat*; **assistance** *n* Hilfe *f*; **assistant** *n* Assistent(in) *m(f)*, Mitarbeiter(in) *m(f)*; (*in shop*) Verkäufer(in) *m(f)*

associate 1. *n* (*partner*) Partner(in) *m(f)*, Teilhaber(in) *m(f)* **2.** *vt* verbinden (*with* mit); **association** *n* (*organization*) Verband *m*, Vereinigung *f*; **in~ with...** in Zusammenarbeit mit ...

assorted *adj* gemischt; **assortment** *n* Auswahl *f* (*of* an + *dat*); (*of sweets*) Mischung *f*

assume *vt* annehmen (*that ... dass ...*); (*role, responsibility*) übernehmen; **assumption** *n* Annahme *f*

assurance *n* Versicherung *f*; (*confidence*) Zuversicht *f*; **assure** *vt* (*say confidently*) versichern + *dat*; **be ~d of sth** einer Sache sicher sein

asterisk *n* Sternchen *nt*

asthma *n* Asthma *nt*

astonished *adj* erstaunt (*at* über); **astonishing** *adj* erstaunlich; **astonishment** *n* Erstaunen *nt*

astound *vt* sehr erstaunen; **astounding** *adj* erstaunlich

astray *adv* **go ~** (*letter etc*) verloren gehen; (*person*) vom Weg abkommen

astrology *n* Astrologie *f*

astronaut *n* Astronaut(in) *m(f)*

astronomy *n* Astronomie *f*

asylum n (home) Anstalt f; (political asylum) Asyl nt; **asylum seeker** n Asylbewerber(in) m(f)

at prep (place) ~ **the door** an der Tür; ~ **home** zu Hause; ~ **John's** bei John; ~ **school** in der Schule; ~ **the theatre/ cinema** im Theater / Kino; ~ **lunch/work** beim Essen / bei der Arbeit; (direction) **point** ~ **sb** auf jdn zeigen; **he looked** ~ **me** er sah mich an; (time) ~ **2 o'clock** um 2 Uhr; ~ **Easter/Christmas** zu Ostern / Weihnachten; ~ **the moment** im Moment; ~ **(the age of) 16** im Alter von 16 Jahren, mit 16; (price) ~ **£5 each** zu je 5 Pfund; (speed) ~ **20 mph** mit 20 Meilen pro Stunde

ate pret of **eat**

athlete n Athlet(in) m(f); (track and field) Leichtathlet(in) m(f); **~'s foot** Fußpilz m; **athletic** adj sportlich; (build) athletisch; **athletics** npl Leichtathletik f

Atlantic n **the ~** (**Ocean**) der Atlantik

atlas n Atlas m

ATM abbr = **automated teller machine**; Geldautomat m

atmosphere n Atmosphäre f, Stimmung f

atom n Atom nt; **atom(ic) bomb** n Atombombe f; **atomic** adj Atom-; ~ **energy** Atomenergie f; ~ **power**

Atomkraft f

A to Z® n Stadtplan m (in Buchform)

atrocious adj grauenhaft; **atrocity** n Grausamkeit f; (deed) Gräueltat f

attach vt befestigen, anheften (to an + dat); **be ~ed to sb/ sth** an jdm / etw hängen; **attachment** n (affection) Zuneigung f; IT Attachment nt, Anhang m

attack 1. vt, vi angreifen **2.** n Angriff m + acc (on auf m); MED Anfall m

attempt 1. n Versuch m **2.** vt versuchen

attend vt (go to) teilnehmen an + dat; (lectures, school) besuchen **2.** vi (be present) anwesend sein; **attend to** vi sich kümmern um; (customer) bedienen; **attendance** n (presence) Anwesenheit f; **attendant** n (in car park etc) Wächter(in) m(f); (in museum) Aufseher(in) m(f)

attention n Aufmerksamkeit f; (your) ~ **please** Achtung!; **pay** ~ **to sth** etw beachten; **pay** ~ **to sb** jdm aufmerksam zuhören

attic n Dachboden m; (lived in) Mansarde f

attitude n (mental) Einstellung f (to, towards zu); (more general, physical) Haltung f

attorney n (US, lawyer) Rechtsanwalt m, Rechtsanwältin f

attract vt anziehen; (attention) erregen; **be ~ed to** or **by sb** sich zu jdm hingezogen fühlen; **attraction** n Anziehungskraft f; (thing) Attraktion f; **attractive** adj attraktiv; (thing, idea) reizvoll

aubergine n Aubergine f

auction 1. n Versteigerung f, Auktion f **2.** vt versteigern

audience n Publikum nt; RADIO Zuhörer pl; TV Zuschauer pl

audio adj Ton-

audition 1. n Probe f **2.** vi THEAT vorspielen, vorsingen

auditorium n Zuschauerraum m

August n August m; → **September**

aunt n Tante f

au pair n Aupairmädchen nt, Aupairjunge m

Australia n Australien nt; **Australian 1.** adj australisch **2.** n Australier(in) m(f)

Austria n Österreich nt; **Austrian 1.** adj österreichisch **2.** n Österreicher(in) m(f)

authentic adj echt; (signature) authentisch; **authenticity** n Echtheit f

author n Autor(in) m(f); (of report etc) Verfasser(in) m(f)

authority n (power, expert) Autorität f; **the authorities** pl die Behörden pl; **authorize** vt (permit) genehmigen

auto n (US) Auto nt

autograph n Autogramm nt

automatic 1. adj automatisch; **~ gear change** (Brit), **~ gear shift** (US) Automatikschaltung f **2.** n (car) Automatikwagen m

automobile n (US) Auto(mobil) nt; **autotrain** n (US) Autoreisezug m

autumn n (Brit) Herbst m

auxiliary 1. adj Hilfs- **2.** n Hilfskraft f

availability n (of product) Lieferbarkeit f; (of resources) Verfügbarkeit f; **available** adj erhältlich; (existing) vorhanden; (product) lieferbar; (person) erreichbar; **be/ make ~ to sb** jdm zur Verfügung stehen / stellen

avalanche n Lawine f

Ave abbr = **avenue**

avenue n Allee f

average 1. n Durchschnitt m; **on ~** im Durchschnitt **2.** adj durchschnittlich

aviation n Luftfahrt f

avocado n Avocado f

avoid vt vermeiden; (sb) jdm aus dem Weg gehen; **avoidable** adj vermeidbar

awake 1. vi aufwachen **2.** adj wach

award 1. n (prize) Preis m; (for bravery etc) Auszeichnung f **2.** vt zuerkennen (to sb jdm); (present) verleihen (to sb jdm)

aware adj bewusst; **be ~ of sth** sich dat einer Sache gen bewusst sein; **I was not ~ that ...**

es war mir nicht klar, dass ... **away** adv weg; **look** ~ wegsehen; **he's** ~ er ist nicht da; (on a trip) er ist verreist; (from school, work) er fehlt; SPORT **they are (playing)** ~ sie spielen auswärts; (with distance) **three miles** ~ drei Meilen (von hier) entfernt

awful adj schrecklich, furchtbar; **awfully** adv furchtbar

awkward adj (clumsy) ungeschickt; (embarrassing) peinlich; (difficult) schwierig

awning n Markise f

awoke pt of **awake**

awoken pp of **awake**

ax (US), **axe** n Axt f

axle n TECH Achse f

B

BA abbr = **Bachelor of Arts**
babe n fam Baby nt; (affectionate) Schatz m, Kleine(r) mf
baby n Baby nt; (of animal) Junge(s) nt; fam (affectionate) Schatz m, Kleine(r) mf; **have a** ~ ein Kind bekommen; **baby carriage** n (US) Kinderwagen m; **baby food** n Babynahrung f; **baby shower** n (US) Party für die werdende Mutter; **baby-sit** vi babysitten; **baby-sitter** n Babysitter(in) m(f)

bachelor n Junggeselle m; **Bachelor of Arts / Science** erster akademischer Grad, ≈ Magister / Diplom; **bachelorette** n Junggesellin f; **bachelorette party** n (US) Junggesellinnenabschied; **bachelor party** n (US) Junggesellenabschied

back 1. n (of person, animal)

Rücken m; (of house, coin etc) Rückseite f; (of chair) Rückenlehne f; (of car) Rücksitz m; (of train) Ende nt; SPORT (defender) Verteidiger(in) m(f); **at the** ~ **of** ..., **in** ~ **of** (inside) hinten in ...; (outside) hinter ...; **to front** verkehrt herum **2.** vt (support) unterstützen; (car) rückwärts fahren **3.** vi (go backwards) rückwärts gehen or fahren **4.** adj Hinter-; **~ wheel** Hinterrad nt **5.** adv zurück; **they're** ~ sie sind wieder da; **back down** vi nachgeben; **back up 1.** vi (car etc) zurücksetzen **2.** vt (support) unterstützen; IT sichern; (car) zurückfahren

backache n Rückenschmerzen pl; **backbone** n Rückgrat nt; **backdoor** n Hintertür f; **backfire** vi (plan) fehlschlagen; AUTO fehlzünden;

background n Hintergrund m; backhand n SPORT Rückhand f; backlog n (of work) Rückstand m; backpack n (US) Rucksack m; backpacker n Rucksacktourist(in) m(f); backpacking n Rucksacktourismus m; back seat n Rücksitz m; backside n fam Po m; back street n Seitenstraßchen nt; backstroke n Rückenschwimmen nt; back-up n (support) Unterstützung f; ~ (copy) IT Sicherungskopie f; backward adj (region) rückständig; ~ movement Rückwärtsbewegung f; backwards adv rückwärts; backyard n Hinterhof m

bacon n Frühstücksspeck m

bacteria npl Bakterien pl

bad adj schlecht, schlimm; (smell) übel; **I have a ~ back** mir tut der Rücken weh; **I'm ~ at maths/ sport** ich bin schlecht in Mathe/Sport; **go ~** schlecht werden, verderben

badge n Abzeichen nt

badger n Dachs m

badly adv schlecht; ~ wounded schwer verwundet; need sth ~ etw dringend brauchen; bad-tempered adj schlecht gelaunt

bag n (small) Tüte f; (larger) Beutel m; (handbag) Tasche f; **it's not my ~** fam das ist nicht mein Ding

baggage n Gepäck nt; baggage (re)claim n Gepäckrückgabe f

baggy adj (zu) weit; (trousers, suit) ausgebeult

bagpipes npl Dudelsack m

Bahamas npl the ~ die Bahamas pl

bail n (money) Kaution f

bait n Köder m

bake vt, vi backen; baked beans npl weiße Bohnen in Tomatensoße; baked potato n in der Schale gebackene Kartoffel, Ofenkartoffel f; baker n Bäcker(in) m(f); bakery n Bäckerei f; baking powder n Backpulver nt

balance n 1. ~ (equilibrium) Gleichgewicht nt 2. vt (make up for) ausgleichen; balance sheet n Bilanz f

balcony n Balkon m

bald adj kahl; **be ~** eine Glatze haben

Balkans npl the ~ der Balkan, die Balkanländer pl

ball n Ball m; **have a ~** fam sich prima amüsieren

ballet n Ballett nt; ballet dancer n Balletttänzer(in) m(f)

balloon n (Luft)ballon m

ballot n (geheime) Abstimmung

ballpoint (pen) n Kugelschreiber m

ballroom n Tanzsaal m

Baltic adj ~ Sea Ostsee f; the ~ States die baltischen Staaten pl

ten

bamboo n Bambus m; **bamboo shoots** npl Bambussprossen pl

ban 1. n Verbot nt **2.** vt verbieten

banana n Banane f; **he's ~s** er ist völlig durchgeknallt; **banana split** n Bananensplit nt

band n (group) Gruppe f; (of criminals) Bande f; (pop, rock etc) Band f; (strip) Band nt

bandage 1. n Verband m; (elastic) Bandage f **2.** vt verbinden

B & B abbr = **bed and breakfast**

bang 1. n (noise) Knall m; (blow) Schlag m **2.** vt, vi knallen; (door) zuschlagen, zuknallen; **banger** n (Brit) fam (firework) Knallkörper m; (sausage) Würstchen nt; (old car) Klapperkiste f

bangs npl (US, von Frisur) Pony m

banish vt verbannen

banister(s) n (Treppen)geländer nt

bank n FIN Bank f; (of river etc) Ufer nt; **bank account** n Bankkonto nt; **bank balance** n Kontostand m; **bank card** n Bankkarte f; **bank code** n Bankleitzahl f; **bank holiday** n gesetzlicher Feiertag

bankrupt vt ruinieren; **go ~** Pleite gehen

bank statement n Kontoauszug m

baptism n Taufe f; **baptize** vt taufen

bar 1. n (for drinks) Bar f; (less smart) Lokal nt; (rod) Stange f; (of chocolate etc) Riegel m, Tafel f; (of soap) Stück nt; (counter) Theke f **2.** prep außer; **~ none** ohne Ausnahme

barbecue n (device) Grill m; (party) Barbecue nt, Grillfete f; **have a ~** grillen

bar code n Strichkode m

bare adj nackt; **~ patch** kahle Stelle; **barefoot** adj, adv barfuß; **bareheaded** adj, adv ohne Kopfbedeckung; **barely** adv kaum; (with age) knapp

bargain 1. n (cheap offer) günstiges Angebot, Schnäppchen nt; (transaction) Geschäft nt; **what a ~** das ist aber günstig! **2.** vi (ver)handeln

barge n (for freight) Lastkahn m; (unpowered) Schleppkahn m

bark 1. n (of tree) Rinde f; (of dog) Bellen nt **2.** vi (dog) bellen

barley n Gerste f

barmaid n Bardame f; **barman** n Barkeeper m

barn n Scheune f

barometer n Barometer nt

baroque adj barock, Barock-

barracks npl Kaserne f

barrel n (of tree) Fass nt; **barrel organ**

n Drehorgel *f*

barrier *n* (*obstruction*) Absperrung *f*; (*across road etc*) Schranke *f*

bartender *n* (*US*) Barkeeper *m*

base 1. *n* Basis *f*; (*of lamp, pillar etc*) Fuß *m*; MIL Stützpunkt *m* **2.** *vt* gründen (*on* auf + *acc*); **be ~d on sth** auf etw *dat* basieren

baseball *n* Baseball *m*; **baseball cap** *n* Baseballmütze *f*

basement *n* Kellergeschoss *nt*

bash *fam* **1.** *n* Schlag *m*, Party *f* **2.** *vt* hauen

basic *adj* einfach; (*fundamental*) Grund-; (*importance, difference*) grundlegend; (*in principle*) grundsätzlich; **basically** *adv* im Grunde; **basics** *npl* the ~ das Wesentliche

basil *n* Basilikum *nt*

basin *n* (*for washing, valley*) (Wasch)becken *nt*

basis *n* Basis *f*; **on the ~ of** aufgrund + *gen*; **on a monthly ~** monatlich

basket *n* Korb *m*; **basketball** *n* Basketball *m*

Basque 1. *n* (*person*) Baske *m*, Baskin *f*; (*language*) Baskisch *nt* **2.** *adj* baskisch

bass 1. *n* MUS Bass *m*; ZOOL Barsch *m* **2.** *adj* MUS Bass-

bastard *n* *vulg* (*awful person*) Arschloch *nt*

bat *n* ZOOL Fledermaus *f*; SPORT (*cricket, baseball*)

Schlagholz *nt*; (*table tennis*) Schläger *m*

bath 1. *n* Bad *nt*; (*tub*) Badewanne *f*; **have a ~** baden **2.** *vt* (*child etc*) baden

bathe *vt, vi* (*wound etc*) baden; **bathing cap** *n* Badekappe *f*; **bathing costume**, **bathing suit** (*US*) *n* Badeanzug *m*

bathmat *n* Badevorleger *m*; **bathrobe** *n* Bademantel *m*; **bathroom** *n* Bad(ezimmer) *nt*; **bath towel** *n* Badetuch *nt*; **bathtub** *n* Badewanne *f*

baton *n* MUS Taktstock *m*; (*police*) Schlagstock *m*

batter 1. *n* Teig *m* **2.** *vt* heftig schlagen; **battered** *adj* übel zugerichtet; (*hat, car*) verbeult; (*wife, baby*) misshandelt

battery *n* ELEC Batterie *f*; **battery charger** *n* Ladegerät *nt*

battle *n* Schlacht *f*; *fig* Kampf *m* (*for* um); **battlefield** *n* Schlachtfeld *nt*

Bavaria *n* Bayern *nt*

bay *n* (*of sea*) Bucht *f*; (*on house*) Erker *m*; (*tree*) Lorbeerbaum *m*; **bay leaf** *n* Lorbeerblatt *nt*; **bay window** *n* Erkerfenster *nt*

BBC *abbr* = **British Broadcasting Corporation**; BBC *f*

BC *abbr* = **before Christ**; vor Christi Geburt, v. Chr.

be 1. *vi* (*become*) werden; (*be situated*) liegen, sein; **she's French** sie ist Französin; **he wants to ~ a doctor** er will Arzt werden; **I'm too hot** mir ist zu warm; **she's not well** (health) ihr geht's nicht gut; **the book is 5 dollars** (cost) das Buch kostet 5 Dollar; **how much is that altogether?** was macht das zusammen?; **how long have you been here?** wie lange sind Sie schon da?; **have you ever been to Rome?** warst du/ waren Sie schon einmal in Rom?; **there is/are** es gibt, es ist/sind; **there are two left** es sind noch zwei übrig **2.** *vaux* (passive) werden; **he was run over** er ist überfahren worden, er wurde überfahren; (continuous tenses) **I was walking on the beach** ich ging am Strand spazieren; **they're coming tomorrow** sie kommen morgen; (infinitive: intention, obligation) **the car is to ~ sold** das Auto soll verkauft werden; **you are not to mention it** du darfst es nicht erwähnen

beach *n* Strand *m*; **beachwear** *n* Strandkleidung *f*

bead *n* (of glass, wood etc) Perle *f*; (drop) Tropfen *m*

beak *n* Schnabel *m*

beam *n* (of wood etc) Balken *m*; (of light) Strahl *m* **2.** *vi* (smile etc) strahlen

bean *n* Bohne *f*; **bean curd** *n*

Tofu *m*

bear 1. *vt* (carry) tragen; (tolerate) ertragen **2.** *n* Bär *m*; **bearable** *adj* erträglich

beard *n* Bart *m*

beat 1. *vt* (subject; (as punishment) prügeln; **~ sb at tennis** jdn im Tennis schlagen **2.** *n* (of heart, drum etc) Schlag *m*; MUS Takt *m*; **beat up** *vt* zusammenschlagen; **beaten** *pp* of **beat**; **of the ~ track** abgelegen

beautiful *adj* schön; (splendid) herrlich; **beauty** *n* Schönheit *f*; **beauty spot** *n* (place) lohnendes Ausflugsziel

beaver *n* Biber *m*

became *pt* of **become**

because 1. *adv, conj* weil **2.** *prep* **~ of** wegen + *gen or dat*

become *vt* werden; **what's ~ of him?** was ist aus ihm geworden?

bed *n* Bett *nt*; (in garden) Beet *nt*; **bed and breakfast** *n* Übernachtung *f* mit Frühstück; **bedding** *n* Bettzeug *nt*; **bed linen** *n* Bettwäsche *f*; **bedroom** *n* Schlafzimmer *nt*; **bed-sit(ter)** *n* *fam* möblierte Einzimmerwohnung; **bedspread** *n* Tagesdecke *f*; **bedtime** *n* Schlafenszeit *f*

bee *n* Biene *f*

beech *n* Buche *f*

beef *n* Rindfleisch *nt*; **beefburger** *n* Hamburger *m*;

beef tomato n Fleischtomate f

beehive n Bienenstock m

been pp of **be**

beer n Bier nt

beetle n Käfer m

beetroot n Rote Bete

before 1. prep vor; *the year ~ last* vorletztes Jahr; *the day ~ yesterday* vorgestern **2.** conj bevor **3.** adv (of time) vorher; *have you been there ~?* waren Sie schon einmal dort?; beforehand adv vorher

beg 1. vt ~ **sb to do sth** jdn inständig bitten, etw zu tun **2.** vi (beggar) betteln (for um)

began pt of **begin**

beggar n Bettler(in) m(f)

begin vt, vi anfangen, beginnen; **beginner** n Anfänger(in) m(f); **beginning** n Anfang m; **begun** pp of **begin**

behalf n **on ~ of, in ~ of** (US) im Namen / Auftrag von; **on my ~** für mich

behave vi sich benehmen; **behavior** (US), **behaviour** n Benehmen nt

behind 1. prep hinter **2.** adv hinten; *be ~ with one's work* mit seiner Arbeit im Rückstand sein **3.** n fam Hinterteil nt

beige adj beige

being n (existence) Dasein nt; (person) Wesen nt

Belarus n Weißrussland nt

belch 1. n Rülpser m **2.** vi rülpsen

Belgian 1. adj belgisch **2.** n Belgier(in) m(f); **Belgium** n Belgien nt

belief n Glaube m (in an + acc); (conviction) Überzeugung f; *it's my ~ that ...* ich bin der Überzeugung, dass ...; **believe** vt glauben; **believe in** vi glauben an + acc

bell n (church) Glocke f; (bicycle, door) Klingel f; **bellboy** n (esp, US) Page m

bellows npl (for fire) Blasebalg m

belly n Bauch m; **bellyache 1.** n Bauchweh nt; **belly button** n fam Bauchnabel m; **bellyflop** n fam Bauchklatscher m

belong vi gehören (to sb jdm); (to club) angehören + dat; **belongings** npl Habe f

below 1. prep unter **2.** adv unten

belt 1. n (round waist) Gürtel m; (safety belt) Gurt m **2.** vi fam (go fast) rasen, düsen; **beltway** n (US) Umgehungsstraße f

bench n Bank f

bend 1. n Biegung f; (in road) Kurve f **2.** vt (curve) biegen; (head, arm) beugen **3.** vi sich biegen; (person) sich beugen; **bend down** vi sich bücken

beneath 1. prep unter **2.** adv darunter

beneficial adj gut, nützlich (to

für); **benefit 1.** *n (advantage)*
Vorteil *m*; *(profit)* Nutzen *m*;
for your/his ~ deinetwe-
gen/seinetwegen; **unem-**
ployment ~ Arbeitslosengeld *nt* **2.** *vt* gut tun + *dat*
3. *vi* Nutzen ziehen *(from*
aus)

Benelux *n* Beneluxländer *pl*

bent 1. *pt, pp of* **bend 2.** *adj*
krumm; *fam* korrupt

Bermuda 1. *n the ~s pl* die
Bermudas *pl* **2.** *adj ~* **shorts**
pl Bermudashorts *pl*

berry *n* Beere *f*

beside *prep* neben; **~ the**
sea/lake am Meer/See;
besides 1. *prep* außer **2.**
adv außerdem

best 1. *adj* beste(r, s); **my ~**
friend mein bester *or* engster
Freund; **the ~ thing (to do)**
would be to ... das Beste wäre zu ...; *(on food packaging)*
~ before ... mindestens haltbar bis ... **2.** *n* der/die/das
Beste; **all the ~** alles Gute;
make the ~ of it das Beste
daraus machen **3.** *adv* am
besten; **I like this ~** das
mag ich am liebsten; **~-**
before date *n* Mindesthalt-
barkeitsdatum *nt*; **best man**
n Trauzeuge *m*

bet 1. *vt, vi* wetten *(on* auf
+ *acc)*; **you ~** *fam* und ob!;
I ~ he'll be late er kommt
mit Sicherheit zu spät **2.** *n*
Wette *f*

betray *vt* verraten

better *adj, adv* besser; **get ~**
(healthwise) sich erholen,
wieder gesund werden; *(im-*
prove) sich verbessern; **I'm**
much ~ today es geht mir
heute viel besser; **you'd**
go du solltest lieber gehen;
a change for the ~ eine
Wendung zum Guten

between 1. *prep* zwischen;
(among) unter; **~ you and**
me, ... unter uns gesagt, ...
2. *adv (in)* dazwischen

beverage *n (formal)* Getränk
nt

beware *vt ~ of sth* sich vor etw
+ *dat* hüten; **'~ of the dog'**
„Vorsicht, bissiger Hund!"

beyond 1. *prep (place)* jenseits + *gen*; *(time)* über ... hinaus; *(out of reach)* außerhalb + *gen*; **it's ~ me** da habe
ich keine Ahnung, da bin ich
überfragt **2.** *adv* darüber hinaus

bias *n (prejudice)* Vorurteil *nt*,
Voreingenommenheit *f*; **bi-**
ased *adj* voreingenommen

bib *n* Latz *m*

Bible *n* Bibel *f*

bicycle *n* Fahrrad *nt*

bid 1. *vt (offer)* bieten **2.** *n (at-*
tempt) Versuch *m*; *(offer)*
Gebot *nt*

big *adj* groß; **it's no ~ deal**
fam es ist nichts Besonde-
res; **big dipper** *n (Brit)*
Achterbahn *f*; **bigheaded**
adj eingebildet

bike *n fam* Rad *nt*

bikini n Bikini m

bilberry n Heidelbeere f

bilingual adj zweisprachig

bill n (account) Rechnung f; (US, banknote) Banknote f; POL Gesetzentwurf m; ZOOL Schnabel m; **billfold** n (US) Brieftasche f

billiards nsing Billard nt

billion n Milliarde f

bin n Behälter m; (rubbish bin) Mülleimer m; (for paper) Papierkorb m

bind vt binden; (bind together) zusammenbinden; (wound) verbinden; **binding** n (ski) Bindung f; (book) Einband m

binge n fam (drinking) Sauferei f; **go on a ~** auf Sauftour gehen

bingo n Bingo nt

binoculars npl Fernglas nt

biological adj biologisch; **biology** n Biologie f

birch n Birke f

bird n Vogel m; (Brit fam (girl, girlfriend) Tussi f; **bird watcher** n Vogelbeobachter(in) m(f)

birth n Geburt f; **birth certificate** n Geburtsurkunde f; **birthday** n Geburtstag m; **happy ~** herzlichen Glückwunsch zum Geburtstag; **birthday card** n Geburtstagskarte f; **birthday party** n Geburtstagsfeier f; **birthplace** n Geburtsort m

biscuit n (Brit) Keks m

bisexual adj bisexuell

bishop n Bischof m; (in chess) Läufer m

bit 1. pt of **bite 2.** n (piece) Stück(chen) nt; IT Bit nt; (a ~ (of ...) (small amount) ein bisschen ...; **a ~ tired** etwas müde; **~ by ~** allmählich; (time) **for a ~** ein Weilchen; **quite a ~** (a lot) ganz schön viel

bitch n (dog) Hündin f; pej (woman) Miststück nt, Schlampe f; **son of a ~** (US) vulg Hurensohn m, Scheißkerl m; **bitchy** adj gemein, zickig

bite 1. vt, vi beißen **2.** n Biss m; (mouthful) Bissen m; (insect) Stich m; **have a ~** eine Kleinigkeit essen; **bitten** pp of **bite**

bitter 1. adj bitter; (memory etc) schmerzlich **2.** n (Brit, beer) halbdunkles Bier; **bitter lemon** n Bitter Lemon m

black adj schwarz; **blackberry** n Brombeere f; **blackbird** n Amsel f; **blackboard** n (Wand)tafel f; **black box** n AVIAT Flugschreiber m; **blackcurrant** n Schwarze Johannisbeere; **black eye** n blaues Auge; **Black Forest** n Schwarzwald m; **blackmail 1.** n Erpressung f **2.** vt erpressen; **black market** n Schwarzmarkt m; **blackout** n MED Ohnmacht f; **have a ~** ohnmächtig werden; **black**

bloodsports

pudding n ≈ Blutwurst f; **Black Sea** n **the** ~ das Schwarze Meer; **blacksmith** n Schmied(in) m(f); **black tie** n Abendanzug m, Smoking m; **is it a** ~? ist/besteht da Smokingzwang?

bladder n Blase f

blade n (of knife) Klinge f; (of propeller) Blatt nt; (of grass) Halm m

blame 1. n Schuld f **2.** vt ~ **sth on sb** jdm die Schuld an etw dat geben; **he is to** ~ er ist daran schuld

bland adj (taste) fade; (comment) nichts sagend

blank adj (page, space) leer, unbeschrieben; (look) ausdruckslos; ~ **cheque** Blankoscheck m

blanket n (Woll)decke f

blast 1. n (of wind) Windstoß m; (of explosion) Druckwelle f **2.** vt (blow up) sprengen

blatant adj (undisguised) offen; (obvious) offensichtlich

blaze 1. vi lodern; (sun) brennen **2.** n (building) Brand m; (other fire) Feuer nt

bleach 1. n Bleichmittel nt **2.** vt bleichen

bleary adj (eyes) trübe, verschlafen

bleed vi bluten

bleep 1. n Piepton m **2.** vi piepen; **bleeper** n fam Piepser m

blend 1. n Mischung f **2.** vt mischen **3.** vi sich mischen;

blender n Mixer m

bless vt segnen; ~ **you!** Gesundheit!; **blessing** n Segen m

blew pt of **blow**

blind 1. adj blind; (corner) unübersichtlich; **turn a** ~ **eye to sth** bei etw ein Auge zudrücken **2.** n (for window) Rollo nt **3.** vt blenden; **blind alley** n Sackgasse f; **blind spot** n AUTO toter Winkel; fig schwacher Punkt

blink vi blinzeln; (light) blinken

bliss n (Glück)seligkeit f

blister n Blase f

blizzard n Schneesturm m

block 1. n (of wood, stone, ice) Block m, Klotz m; (of buildings) Häuserblock m; ~ **of flats** (Brit) Wohnblock m **2.** vt (road etc) blockieren; (pipe, nose) verstopfen; **blockage** n Verstopfung f; **blockbuster** n Knüller m; **block letters** npl Blockschrift f

bloke n (Brit) fam Kerl m, Typ m

blonde 1. adj blond **2.** n (person) Blondine f, blonder Typ

blood n Blut nt; **blood count** n Blutbild nt; **blood donor** n Blutspender(in) m(f); **blood group** n Blutgruppe f; **blood poisoning** n Blutvergiftung f; **blood pressure** n Blutdruck m; **blood sample** n Blutprobe f; **bloodsports**

npl Sportarten, bei denen
Tiere getötet werden; **bloody**
adj (Brit) fam verdammt,
Scheiß-; (literal sense) blutig

bloom 1. n Blüte f **2.** vi blühen

blossom 1. n Blüte f **2.** vi blühen

blouse n Bluse f; **big girl's ~**
fam Schwächling m, femininer Typ

blow 1. n Schlag m **2.** vi, vt
(wind) wehen, blasen; (person: trumpet etc) blasen; ~
one's nose sich dat die Nase
putzen; **blow out** vt (candle
etc) ausblasen; **blow up 1.**
vi explodieren **2.** vt sprengen; (balloon, tyre) aufblasen; PHOT (enlarge) vergrößern; **blow-dry** vt föhnen;
blowjob n fam **give sb a ~**
jdm einen blasen; **blown**
pp of **blow**

BLT n abbr = **bacon, lettuce
and tomato sandwich**; mit
Frühstücksspeck, Kopfsalat
und Tomate belegtes Sandwich

blue adj blau; fam (unhappy)
trübsinnig, niedergeschlagen; (film) pornografisch;
(joke) anzüglich; (language)
derb; **bluebell** n Glockenblume f; **blueberry** n Blaubeere f; **blue cheese** n Blauschimmelkäse m; **blues** npl
the ~ MUS der Blues; **have
the ~** fam niedergeschlagen
sein

blunder n Schnitzer m

blunt adj (knife) stumpf; fig
unverblümt; **bluntly** adv geradeheraus

blurred adj verschwommen,
unklar

blush vi erröten

board 1. n (of wood) Brett nt;
(committee) Ausschuss m;
(of firm) Vorstand m; **~ and
lodging** Unterkunft und
Verpflegung; **on ~** an Bord
2. vt (train, bus) einsteigen
in + acc; (ship) an Bord
+ gen gehen; **boarder** n Pensionsgast m, Internatsschüler(in) m(f); **board game** n
Brettspiel nt; **boarding
card, boarding pass** n
Bordkarte f, Einsteigekarte
f; **boarding school** n Internat nt; **board meeting** n Vorstandssitzung f; **boardroom**
n Sitzungssaal m (des Vorstands)

boast 1. vi prahlen (about mit)
2. n Prahlerei f

boat n Boot nt; (ship) Schiff
nt; **boatman** n (hirer) Bootsverleiher m; **boat race** n Regatta f

bob(sleigh) n Bob m

bodily 1. adj körperlich **2.** adv
(forcibly) gewaltsam; **body** n
Körper m; (dead) Leiche f;
(of car) Karosserie f; **bodybuilding** n Bodybuilding
nt; **bodyguard** n Leibwächter m; (group) Leibwache
f; **body jewellery** n Intimschmuck m; **body odour** n

Körpergeruch *m*; **body piercing** *n* Piercing *nt*; **bodywork** *n* Karosserie *f*

boil 1. *vt, vi* kochen **2.** *n* MED Geschwür *nt*; **boiler** *n* Boiler *m*; **boiling** *adj* (*water etc*) kochend (heiß); *I was ~ (hot)* mir war fürchterlich heiß; (*with rage*) ich kochte vor Wut; **boiling point** *n* Siedepunkt *m*

bold *adj* kühn, mutig; (*colours*) kräftig; (*type*) fett

Bolivia *n* Bolivien *f*

bomb 1. *n* Bombe *f* **2.** *vt* bombardieren

bond *n* (*link*) Bindung *f*

bone *n* (*link*) Bindung *f*

bone *n* Knochen *m*; (*of fish*) Gräte *f*

boner *n* (*US*) *fam* Schnitzer *m*; (*erection*) Ständer *m*

bonfire *n* Feuer *nt* (im Freien)

bonnet *n* (*Brit*) AUTO Haube *f*; (*for baby*) Häubchen *nt*

bonny *adj* (*esp Scot*) hübsch

bonus *n* Bonus *m*, Prämie *f*

boo 1. *vt* auspfeifen **2.** *vi* buhen **3.** *n* Buhruf *m*

book 1. *n* Buch *nt*; (*of tickets, stamps*) Heft *nt* **2.** *vt* (*ticket etc*) bestellen; (*hotel, flight etc*) buchen; *fully ~ed (up)* ausgebucht; (*performance*) ausverkauft; **book in** *vt* eintragen; *be ~ed in at a hotel* ein Zimmer in einem Hotel bestellt haben; **bookable** *adj* im Vorverkauf erhältlich; **bookcase** *n* Bücherregal *nt*;

booking *n* Buchung *f*; **booking office** *n* RAIL Fahrkartenschalter *m*; THEAT Vorverkaufsstelle *f*; **booklet** *n* Broschüre *f*; **bookmark** *n* a. IT Lesezeichen *nt*; **bookshelf** *n* Bücherbord *nt*; **bookshelves** Bücherregal *nt*; **bookshop**, **bookstore** *n* (*esp US*) Buchhandlung *f*

boom 1. *n* (*of business*) Boom *m*; (*noise*) Dröhnen *nt* **2.** *vi* (*business*) boomen; *fam* florieren

boomerang *n* Bumerang *m*

boost 1. *n* Auftrieb *m* **2.** *vt* (*production, sales*) ankurbeln; (*power, profits etc*) steigern; **booster** (*injection*) *f* Wiederholungsimpfung *f*

boot 1. *n* Stiefel *m*; (*Brit*) AUTO Kofferraum *m* **2.** *vt* IT laden, booten

booth *n* (*at fair etc*) Bude *f*; (*at trade fair etc*) Stand *m*

booze 1. *n* *fam* Alkohol *m* **2.** *vi* *fam* saufen

border *n* Grenze *f*; (*edge*) Rand *m*; **north/south of the Border** (*Brit*) in Schottland / England; **borderline** *n* Grenze *f*

bore 1. *pt of* **bear 2.** *vt* (*hole etc*) bohren; (*person*) langweilen **3.** *n* (*person*) Langweiler(in) *m(f)*; (*thing*) langweilige Sache *f*; **bored** *adj* **be ~** sich langweilen; **boredom** *n* Langeweile *f*; **boring** *adj* langweilig

born adj he was ~ in London
er ist in London geboren

borne pp of **bear**

borough n Stadtbezirk m

borrow vt borgen

Bosnia-Herzegovina n Bosnien-Herzegowina nt; **Bos-
nian 1.** adj bosnisch **2.** n Bos-
nier(in) m(f)

boss n Chef(in) m(f), Boss m

botanical adj botanisch; ~
garden(s) botanischer Garten

both 1. adj beide; ~ **the books**
beide Bücher **2.** pron (people) beide; (things) beides;
~ (of) **the boys** beide Jungs;
I like ~ of them ich mag sie
(alle) beide **3.** adv ~ **X and
Y** sowohl X als auch Y

bother 1. vt ärgern, belästigen;
it doesn't ~ me das stört
mich nicht; **he can't be
~ed with details** mit Details
gibt er sich nicht ab; **I'm not
~ed** das ist mir egal **2.** vi sich
kümmern (about um); **don't
~** (das ist) nicht nötig, lass
es! **3.** n (trouble) Mühe f; (annoyance) Ärger m

bottle 1. n Flasche f **2.** vt (in
Flaschen) abfüllen; **bottle
bank** n Altglascontainer m;
bottled adj **~ beer** Flaschenbier nt; **bot-
tleneck** n fig Engpass m;
bottle opener n Flaschenöffner m

bottom 1. n (of container) Boden m; (underside) Untersei-

te f; fam (of person) Po m; **at
the ~ of the sea** / **table** /
page auf dem Meeres-
grund / am   Tabellenende /
unten auf der Seite **2.** adj un-
terste(r, s); **be ~ of the
class** / **league** Klassenletz-
te(r) / Tabellenletzte(r) sein;
~ **gear** AUTO erster Gang

bought pt, pp of **buy**

bounce vi (ball) springen,
aufprallen; ~ **up and down**
(person)   herumhüpfen;
bouncy adj (ball) gut sprin-
gend; (person) munter;
bouncy castle n Hüpfburg
f

bound 1. pt, pp of **bind 2.**
adj (tied up) gebunden; be
(obliged) verpflichtet; **be ~
to do sth** (sure to) etw bestimmt tun (werden); (have
to) etw tun müssen; **it's ~
to happen** es muss so kommen; **be ~ for ...** auf dem
Weg nach ... sein; **boundary**
n Grenze f

bouquet n (flowers) Strauß
m; (of wine) Blume f

bow n (ribbon) Schleife f;
(instrument, weapon) Bogen
m **2.** vi sich verbeugen (to
vor); (with head) Verbeugung f;
(of ship) Bug m

bowels npl Darm m

bowl 1. n (basin) Schüssel f;
(shallow) Schale f; (for animal) Napf m **2.** vt, vi (in
cricket) werfen

bowling n Kegeln nt; **bowling**

break

alley n Kegelbahn f; **bowling green** n Rasen m zum Bowling-Spiel; **bowls** nsing (game) Bowling-Spiel nt

bow tie n Fliege f

box n Schachtel f; (cardboard) Karton m; (bigger) Kasten m; (space on form) Kästchen nt; THEAT Loge f; **boxer** n Boxer(in) m(f); **boxers, boxer shorts** npl Boxershorts pl; **boxing** n SPORT Boxen nt; **Boxing Day** n zweiter Weihnachtsfeiertag; **boxing gloves** npl Boxhandschuhe pl; **box office** n Kasse f

boy n Junge m

boycott 1. n Boykott m 2. vt boykottieren

boyfriend n (fester) Freund m; **boy scout** n Pfadfinder m

bra n BH m

brace n Armband nt

bracelet n Armband nt

braces npl (Brit) Hosenträger pl

bracket 1. n (in text) Klammer f; TECH Träger m 2. vt einklammern

brag vi angeben

brain n ANAT Gehirn nt; (mind) Verstand m; **~s pl** (intelligence) Grips m; **brainy** adj schlau, clever

brake 1. n Bremse f 2. vi bremsen; **brake fluid** n Bremsflüssigkeit f; **brake light** n Bremslicht nt; **brake pedal** n Bremspedal nt

branch n (of tree) Ast m; (of family, subject) Zweig m; (of firm) Filiale f, Zweigstelle f; **branch off** vi (road) abzweigen

brand n COMM Marke f

brand-new adj (funkel)nagelneu

brandy n Weinbrand m

brass n Messing nt; (Brit fam (money) Knete f; **brass band** n Blaskapelle f

brave adj tapfer, mutig

brawn n (strength) Muskelkraft f; GASTR Sülze f; **brawny** adj muskulös

Brazil n Brasilien nt; **Brazilian** 1. adj brasilianisch 2. n Brasilianer(in) m(f); **brazil nut** n Paranuss f

bread n Brot nt; **breadbin** (Brit), **breadbox** (US) n Brotkasten m; **breadcrumbs** npl Brotkrumen pl; GASTR Paniermehl m; breaded paniert; **breadknife** n Brotmesser nt

breadth n Breite f

break 1. n (fracture) Bruch m; (rest) Pause f; (short holiday) Kurzurlaub m; **give me a ~** hör auf damit! 2. vt (fracture) brechen; (in pieces) zerbrechen; (toy, device) kaputtmachen; (promise) nicht halten; (silence) brechen; (law) verletzen; (news) mitteilen (to sb jdm); **I broke my leg** ich habe mir das Bein gebrochen; **he broke it to her**

gently er hat es ihr schonend beigebracht **3.** vi (*come apart*) (auseinander) brechen; (*in pieces*) zerbrechen; (*toy, device*) kaputtgehen; (*day, dawn*) anbrechen; (*news*) bekannt werden; **break down** vi (*car*) eine Panne haben; (*machine*) versagen; (*person*) zusammenbrechen; **break in** vi (*burglar*) einbrechen; **break into** vt einbrechen in + *acc*; **break off** vi, vt abbrechen; **break out** vi ausbrechen; ~ *in a rash* einen Ausschlag bekommen; **break up 1.** vi aufbrechen; (*meeting, organisation*) sich auflösen; (*marriage*) in die Brüche gehen; (*couple*) sich trennen; *school breaks up on Friday* am Freitag beginnen die Ferien **2.** vt zerstören; (*marriage*) zerrütten; (*meeting*) auflösen; **breakable** adj zerbrechlich; **breakdown** n (*of car*) Panne f; (*of machine*) Störung f; (*of person, relations, system*) Zusammenbruch m; **breakdown service** n Pannendienst m; **breakdown truck** n Abschleppwagen m

breakfast n Frühstück nt; **have** ~ frühstücken

break-in n Einbruch m; **breakup** n (*of meeting, organisation*) Auflösung f; (*of marriage*) Zerrüttung f

breast n Brust f; **breastfeed** vt stillen; **breaststroke** n Brustschwimmen nt

breath n Atem m; *out of* ~ außer Atem; **breathalyse,** **breathalyze** vt (ins Röhrchen) blasen lassen; **breath-alyser, breathalyzer** n Promillemesser m; **breathe** vt, vi atmen; **breathe in** vt, vi einatmen; **breathe out** vt, vi ausatmen; **breathless** adj atemlos; **breath-taking** adj atemberaubend

bred pt, pp of **breed**

breed 1. n (*race*) Rasse f **2.** vi sich vermehren **3.** vt züchten; **breeder** n Züchter(in) m(f); fam Hetero m; **breeding** n (*of animals*) Züchtung f

breeze n Brise f

brevity n Kürze f

brew 1. vt (*beer*) brauen; (*tea*) kochen; **brewery** n Brauerei f

bribe 1. n Bestechungsgeld nt **2.** vt bestechen; **bribery** n Bestechung f

brick n Backstein m; **bricklayer** n Maurer(in) m(f)

bride n Braut f; **bridegroom** n Bräutigam m; **bridesmaid** n Brautjungfer f

bridge n Brücke f, Bridge nt

brief 1. adj kurz **2.** vt instruieren (*o* über + *acc*)

briefcase n Aktentasche f

briefs npl Slip m

bright adj hell; (*colour*) leuchtend; (*cheerful*) heiter; (*intelligent*) intelligent; (*idea*) glänzend; **brighten up 1.** *vt* aufhellen; (*person*) aufheitern **2.** *vi* sich aufheitern; (*person*) fröhlicher werden

brilliant *adj* (*sunshine, colour*) strahlend; (*person*) brillant; (*idea*) glänzend; (*Brit*) *fam* **it was ~** es war fantastisch

brim *n* Rand *m*

bring *vt* bringen; (*with one*) mitbringen; **bring about** *vt* herbeiführen, bewirken; **bring back** *vt* zurückbringen; (*memories*) wecken; **bring down** *vt* (*reduce*) senken; (*government etc*) zu Fall bringen; **bring in** *vt* hereinbringen; (*introduce*) einführen; **bring out** *vt* herausbringen; **bring up** *vt* (*child*) aufziehen; (*question*) zur Sprache bringen

bristle *n* Borste *f*

Brit *n fam* Brite *m*, Britin *f*; **Britain** *n* Großbritannien *nt*; **British 1.** *adj* britisch; **the ~ Isles** *pl* die Britischen Inseln *pl* **2.** *n* **the ~** *pl* die Briten *pl*

brittle *adj* spröde

broad *adj* breit; (*accent*) stark; **in ~ daylight** am helllichten Tag

B road *n* (*Brit*) ≈ Landstraße *f*

broadcast 1. *n* Sendung *f* **2.** *irr vt, vi* senden; (*event*) übertragen

broaden *vt* ~ **the mind** den

Horizont erweitern; **broad-minded** *adj* tolerant

broccoli *n* Brokkoli *pl*

brochure *n* Prospekt *m*, Broschüre *f*

broke 1. *pt of* **break 2.** *adj* (*Brit*) *fam* pleite; **broken** *pp of* **break**; **broken-hearted** *adj* untröstlich

broker *n* Makler(in) *m(f)*

bronchitis *n* Bronchitis *f*

brooch *n* Brosche *f*

broom *n* Besen *m*

Bros *abbr* = **brothers**; Gebr.

broth *n* Fleischbrühe *f*

brothel *n* Bordell *nt*

brother *n* Bruder *m*; **~s** *pl* COMM Gebrüder *pl*; **brother-in-law** *n* Schwager *m*

brought *pt, pp of* **bring**

brow *n* (*eyebrow*) (Augen-)braue *f*; (*forehead*) Stirn *f*

brown *adj* braun; **brown bread** *n* Mischbrot *nt*; (*wholemeal*) Vollkornbrot *nt*; **brownie** *n* GASTR Brownie *m*; (*Brit*) junge Pfadfinderin; **brown paper** *n* Packpapier *nt*; **brown rice** *n* Naturreis *m*; **brown sugar** *n* brauner Zucker

browse *vi* (*in book*) blättern; (*in shop*) herumschauen; **browser** *n* IT Browser *m*

bruise 1. *n* blauer Fleck *m*; ~ **one's arm** sich *dat* einen blauen Fleck (am Arm) holen

brush 1. *n* Bürste *f*; (*for sweeping*) Handbesen *m*;

(for painting) Pinsel m **2.** vt bürsten; (sweep) fegen; ~ **one's teeth** sich dat die Zähne putzen; **brush up** (French etc) auffrischen

Brussels sprouts npl Rosenkohl m, Kohlsprossen m

brutality n Brutalität f

BSc abbr = **Bachelor of Science**

BSE abbr = **bovine spongiform encephalopathy**; BSE f

bubble n Blase f; **bubble bath** n Schaumbad nt; **bubbly 1.** adj sprudelnd; (person) temperamentvoll **2.** n fam Schampus m

buck n (animal) Bock m; (US) fam Dollar m

bucket n Eimer m

buckle 1. n Schnalle f **2.** vi TECH sich verbiegen **3.** vt zuschnallen

bud n Knospe f

Buddhism n Buddhismus m; **Buddhist 1.** adj buddhistisch **2.** n Buddhist(in) m(f)

buddy n fam Kumpel m

budgie n fam Wellensittich m

buffalo n Büffel m

buffet n (food) (kaltes) Büfett nt

bug 1. n IT Bug m, Programmfehler m; (listening device) Wanze f; (US, insect) Insekt nt; fam (illness) Infektion f **2.** vt abhören

bugger 1. n vulg Scheißkerl m **2.** interj vulg Scheiße f; **bug-**

ger off vi (Brit) vulg abhauen, Leine ziehen

buggy® n (for baby) Buggy® m; (US, pram) Kinderwagen m

build vt bauen; **build up** vt aufbauen; **building** n Gebäude nt; **building site** n Baustelle f

built pt, pp of **build**; **built-in** adj (cupboard) Einbau-, eingebaut

bulb n BOT (Blumen)zwiebel f; ELEC Glühbirne f

Bulgaria n Bulgarien nt; **Bulgarian 1.** adj bulgarisch **2.** n (person) Bulgare m, Bulgarin f; (language) Bulgarisch nt

bulimia n Bulimie f

bulk n (size) Größe f; (greater part) Großteil m (of + gen); **in ~** en gros; **bulky** adj (goods) sperrig; (person) stämmig

bull n Stier m; **bulldog** n Bulldogge f; **bulldoze** vt planieren; **bulldozer** n Planierraupe f

bullet n Kugel f

bulletin n Bulletin nt; (announcement) Bekanntmachung f; MED Krankenbericht m; **bulletin board** n (US) IT schwarzes Brett

bullshit n fam Scheiß m

bully n Tyrann m

bum n fam (Brit, backside) Po m; (US, vagrant) Penner m

bumblebee n Hummel f

bump 1. n fam (swelling) Beule f; (road) Unebenheit f;

bust

(blow) Stoß *m* **2.** *vt* stoßen; **~ one's head** sich *dat* den Kopf anschlagen *(on an + dat)*; **bump into** *vt* stoßen gegen; *fam (meet)* (zufällig) begegnen + *dat*; **bumper 1.** *n* AUTO Stoßstange *f* **2.** *adj (edition etc)* Riesen-; *(crop etc)* Rekord-; **bumpy** *adj* holp(e)rig

bun *n* süßes Brötchen

bunch *n (of flowers)* Strauß *m*; *fam (of people)* Haufen *m*; **~ of keys** Schlüsselbund *m*

bundle *n* Bündel *nt*

bungee jumping *n* Bungee-jumping *nt*

bunk *n* Koje *f*; **bunk bed(s)** *n(pl)* Etagenbett *nt*

bunker *n* Bunker *m*

bunny *n* Häschen *n*

buoy *n* Boje *f*; **buoyant** *adj (floating)* schwimmend

burden *n* Last *f*

bureau *n* Büro *nt*; *(government department)* Amt *nt*; **bureaucracy** *n* Bürokratie *f*; **bureau de change** *n* Wechselstube *f*

burger *n* Hamburger *m*

burglar *n* Einbrecher(in) *m(f)*; **burglar alarm** *n* Alarmanlage *f*; **burglarize** *vt (US)* einbrechen in *+ acc*; **burglary** *n* Einbruch *m*; **burgle** *vt* einbrechen in *+ acc*

burial *n* Beerdigung *f*

burn 1. *vt* verbrennen; *(food,*

slightly) anbrennen; **~ one's hand** sich *dat* die Hand verbrennen **2.** *vi* brennen **3.** *n (injury)* Brandwunde *f*; *(on material)* verbrannte Stelle

burp 1. *vi* rülpsen **2.** *vt (baby)* aufstoßen lassen

bursary *n* Stipendium *nt*

burst 1. *vt* platzen lassen **2.** *vi* platzen; **~ into tears** in Tränen ausbrechen

bury *vt* begraben; *(in grave)* beerdigen; *(hide)* vergraben

bus *n* Bus *m*; **bus driver** *n* Busfahrer(in) *m(f)*

bush *n* Busch *m*

business *n* Geschäft *nt*; *(enterprise)* Unternehmen *nt*; *(concern, affair)* Sache *f*; **I'm here on ~** ich bin geschäftlich hier; **it's none of your ~** das geht dich nichts an; **business card** *n* Visitenkarte *f*; **business class** *n* AVIAT Businessclass *f*; **business hours** *npl* Geschäftsstunden *pl*; **businessman** *n* Geschäftsmann *m*; **business studies** *npl* Betriebswirtschaftslehre *f*; **businesswoman** *n* Geschäftsfrau *f*

bus service *n* Busverbindung *f*; **bus shelter** *n* Wartehäuschen *nt*; **bus station** *n* Busbahnhof *m*; **bus stop** *n* Bushaltestelle *f*

bust 1. *n* Büste *f* **2.** *adj (broken)* kaputt; **go ~** Pleite gehen

busy *adj* beschäftigt; (*street, place*) belebt; (*esp US, telephone*) besetzt; **~ signal** (*US*) Besetztzeichen *nt*

but 1. *conj* aber; (*only*) nur; **not this ~ that** nicht dies, sondern das **2.** *prep* (*except*) außer; **any colour ~ blue** jede Farbe, nur nicht blau; **nothing ~ ...** nichts als ...; **the last/next house ~ one** das vorletzte/übernächste Haus

butcher *n* Metzger(in) *m(f)*

butter *n* Butter *f*; **buttercup** *n* Butterblume *f*; **butterfly** *n* Schmetterling *m*

buttocks *npl* Gesäß *nt*

button 1. *n* Knopf *m* **2.** *vt* zuknöpfen; **buttonhole** *n* Knopfloch *nt*

buy 1. *n* Kauf *m* **2.** *vt* kaufen (*from* von); **buyer** *n* Käufer(in) *m(f)*

buzz 1. *n* Summen *nt*; **give sb a ~** *fam* jdn anrufen **2.** *vi* summen; **buzzer** *n* Summer *m*

by 1. *prep* (*cause, author*) von; (*means*) mit; (*beside, near*) bei, an; (*via*) durch; (*before*)

bis; (*according to*) nach; **go ~ train/bus/car** mit dem Zug/Bus/Auto fahren; **send ~ post** mit der Post® schicken; **a house ~ the river** ein Haus *or* beim Fluss; **~ her side** neben ihr, an ihrer Seite; **leave ~ the back door** durch die Hintertür rausgehen; **~ day/night** tags/nachts; **they'll be here ~ five** bis fünf Uhr müssten sie hier sein; **judge ~ appearances** nach dem Äußeren urteilen; **rise ~ 10%** um 10% steigen; **it missed me ~ inches** es hat mich um Zentimeter verfehlt; **divided/multiplied ~ 7** dividiert durch/multipliziert mit 7; **~ oneself** allein **2.** *adv* (*past*) vorbei; **rush ~** vorbeirasen

bye-bye *interj fam* Wiedersehen, tschüss

by-election *n* Nachwahl *f*; **bypass** *n* Umgehungsstraße *f*; MED Bypass *m*; **byroad** *n* Nebenstraße *f*; **bystander** *n* Zuschauer(in) *m(f)*

byte *n* Byte *nt*

C

C *abbr* = **Celsius**; C

c *abbr* = **circa**; ca

cab *n* Taxi *nt*

cabbage *n* Kohl *m*

cabin *n* NAUT Kajüte *f*; AVIAT

Passagierraum *m*; (*wooden house*) Hütte *f*; **cabin crew** *n* Flugbegleitpersonal *nt*; **cabinet** *n* Schrank *m*; (*for display*) Vitrine *f*; POL Kabinett

campus

nt

cable *n* ELEC Kabel *nt*; **cable-car** *n* Seilbahn *f*; **cable television**, **cablevision** (*US*) *n* Kabelfernsehen *nt*

cactus *n* Kaktus *m*

CAD *abbr* = **computer-aided design**; CAD *nt*

Caesarean *adj* ~ (**section**) Kaiserschnitt *m*

café *n* Café *nt*; **cafeteria** *n* Cafeteria *f*; **cafetiere** *n* Kaffeebereiter *m*

caffein(e) *n* Koffein *nt*

cage *n* Käfig *m*

Cairo *n* Kairo *nt*

cake *n* Kuchen *m*; **cake shop** *n* Konditorei *f*

calculate *vt* berechnen; (*estimate*) kalkulieren; **calculating** *adj* berechnend; **calculation** *n* Berechnung *f*; (*estimate*) Kalkulation *f*; **calculator** *n* Taschenrechner *m*

calendar *n* Kalender *m*

calf *n* Kalb *nt*; ANAT Wade *f*

California *n* Kalifornien *nt*

call **1.** *vt* rufen; (*name, describe as*) nennen; TEL anrufen; IT, AVIAT aufrufen; **what's this ~ed?** wie heißt das? **2.** *vi* (*shout*) rufen (*for help* um Hilfe); (*visit*) vorbeikommen; **~ at the doctor's** beim Arzt vorbeigehen; (*of train*) **~ at ...** in ... halten **3.** *n* (*shout*) Ruf *m*; TEL Anruf *m*; IT, AVIAT Aufruf *m*; **make a ~** telefonieren; **give sb a ~** jdn anrufen; **be on ~** Bereit-

schaftsdienst haben; **call back** *vt, vi* zurückrufen; **call for** *vt* (*come to pick up*) abholen; (*demand, require*) verlangen; **call off** *vt* absagen

call centre *n* Callcenter *nt*; **caller** *n* Besucher(in) *m(f)*; TEL Anrufer(in) *m(f)*

calm 1. *n* Stille *f*; (*also of person*) Ruhe *f*; (*of sea*) Flaute *f* **2.** *vt* beruhigen **3.** *adj* ruhig; **calm down** *vi* sich beruhigen

calorie *n* Kalorie *f*

calves *pl of* **calf**

Cambodia *n* Kambodscha *nt*

camcorder *n* Camcorder *m*

came *pt of* **come**

camel *n* Kamel *nt*

camera *n* Fotoapparat *m*, Kamera *f*

camomile *n* Kamille *f*

camouflage *n* Tarnung *f*

camp 1. *n* Lager *nt*; (*camping place*) Zeltplatz *m* **2.** *vi* zelten, campen **3.** *adj fam* theatralisch, tuntig

campaign 1. *n* Kampagne *f*; POL Wahlkampf *m* **2.** *vi* sich einsetzen (*for* / *against* für / gegen)

campbed *n* Campingliege *f*; **camper** *n* (*person*) Camper(in) *m(f)*; (*van*) Wohnmobil *nt*; **camping** *n* Zelten *nt*, Camping *nt*; **campsite** *n* Zeltplatz *m*, Campingplatz *m*

campus *n* (*of university*) Universitätsgelände *nt*, Campus *m*

can 1. *vaux* (*be able*) können; (*permission*) dürfen; **I ~not** *or* **~'t see** ich kann nichts sehen; **~ I go now?** darf ich jetzt gehen? **2.** *n* (*for food, beer*) Dose *f*; (*for water, milk*) Kanne *f*

Canada *n* Kanada *nt*; **Canadian 1.** *adj* kanadisch **2.** *n* Kanadier(in) *m(f)*

canal *n* Kanal *m*

canary *n* Kanarienvogel *m*

cancel *vt* (*plans*) aufgeben; (*meeting, game*) absagen; COMM (*order etc*) stornieren; IT löschen; AVIAT streichen; **be ~led** (*event, train, bus*) ausfallen; **cancellation** *n* Absage *f*; COMM Stornierung *f*; AVIAT gestrichener Flug

cancer *n* MED Krebs *m*; **Cancer** *n* ASTR Krebs *m*

candid *adj* (*person, conversation*) offen

candidate *n* (*for post*) Bewerber(in) *m(f)*; POL Kandidat(in) *m(f)*

candle *n* Kerze *f*; **candlelight** *n* Kerzenlicht *nt*; **candlestick** *n* Kerzenhalter *m*

candy *n* (*US*) Bonbon *nt*; (*quantity*) Süßigkeiten *pl*; **candy-floss** *n* (*Brit*) Zuckerwatte *f*

canned *adj* Dosen-

cannot *contr of* **can not**

canoe *n* Kanu *nt*; **canoeing** *n* Kanufahren *nt*

can opener *n* Dosenöffner *m*

canopy *n* Baldachin *m*; (*aw-*

ing) Markise *f*; (*over entrance*) Vordach *nt*

can't *contr of* **can not**

canteen *n* (*in factory*) Kantine *f*; (*in university*) Mensa *f*

canvas *n* (*for sails, shoes*) Segeltuch *nt*; (*for tent*) Zeltstoff *m*; (*for painting*) Leinwand *f*

canvass *vi* um Stimmen werben (*for* für)

canyon *n* Felsenschlucht *f*; **canyoning** *n* Canyoning *nt*

cap *n* Mütze *f*; (*lid*) Verschluss *m*, Deckel *m*

capability *n* Fähigkeit *f*; **capable** *adj* fähig; **be ~ of sth** zu etw fähig (*or* imstande) sein

capacity *n* (*of building, container*) Fassungsvermögen *nt*; (*ability*) Fähigkeit *f*; (*function*) **in his ~ as ...** in seiner Eigenschaft als ...

cape *n* (*garment*) Cape *nt*, Umhang *m*; GEO Kap *nt*

caper *n* (*for cooking*) Kaper *f*

capital *n* FIN Kapital *nt*; (*letter*) Großbuchstabe *m*; **~** (*city*) Hauptstadt *f*; **capitalism** *n* Kapitalismus *m*; **capital punishment** *n* die Todesstrafe

Capricorn *n* ASTR Steinbock *m*

capsule *n* Kapsel *f*

captain *n* Kapitän *m*; (*army*) Hauptmann *m*

captive *n* Gefangene(r) *mf*; **capture 1.** *vt* (*person*) fassen, gefangen nehmen; (*town etc*) einnehmen; IT (data) erfassen **2.** n Gefangennahme f; IT Erfassung f

car n Auto nt; (US) RAIL Wagen m

carambola n Sternfrucht f

caravan n Wohnwagen m; **caravan site** n Campingplatz m für Wohnwagen

caraway (seed) n Kümmel m

carbohydrate n Kohle(n)hydrat nt

car bomb n Autobombe f

carbon n Kohlenstoff m

carburettor, carburetor (US) n Vergaser m

card n Karte f; (material) Pappe f; **cardboard** n Pappe f; ~ **(box)** Karton m; (smaller) Pappschachtel f; **card game** n Kartenspiel nt

cardiac adj Herz-

cardigan n Strickjacke f

cardphone n Kartentelefon nt

care 1. n (worry) Sorge f; (carefulness) Sorgfalt f; (looking after things, people) Pflege f; **with** ~ sorgfältig; (cautiously) vorsichtig; **take** ~ (watch out) vorsichtig sein; (in address) ~ **of** bei; **take.~ of** sorgen für, sich kümmern um **2.** vi **I don't** ~ es ist mir egal; ~ **about sth** Wert auf etw acc legen; **he ~s about her** sie liegt ihm am Herzen; **care for** vt (look after) sorgen für, sich kümmern um; (like) mögen

career n Karriere f, Laufbahn f; **careers advisor** n Berufsberater(in) m(f)

carefree adj sorgenfrei; **careful, carefully** adj, adv sorgfältig; (cautious, cautiously) vorsichtig; **careless, carelessly** adj, adv nachlässig; (driving etc) leichtsinnig; (remark) unvorsichtig; **carer** n Betreuer(in) m(f), Pfleger(in) m(f); **caretaker** n Hausmeister(in) m(f); **careworker** n Pfleger(in) m(f)

car-ferry n Autofähre f

cargo n Ladung f

car hire, car hire company n Autovermietung f

Caribbean 1. n Karibik f **2.** adj karibisch

caring adj mitfühlend; (parent, partner) liebevoll; (looking after sb) fürsorglich

car insurance n Kraftfahrzeugversicherung f

carnation n Nelke f

carnival n Volksfest nt; (before Lent) Karneval m

carol n Weihnachtslied nt

carp n (fish) Karpfen m

car park n (Brit) Parkplatz m; (multi-storey car park) Parkhaus nt

carpenter n Zimmermann m

carpet n Teppich m

car phone n Autotelefon nt; **carpool 1.** n Fahrgemeinschaft f; (vehicles) Fuhrpark m **2.** vi eine Fahrgemeinschaft bilden; **car rental**

Autovermietung f

carriage n (Brit) RAIL (coach) Wagen m; (compartment) Abteil nt; (horse-drawn) Kutsche f; (transport) Beförderung f; **carriageway** n (Brit, on road) Fahrbahn f

carrier n COMM Spediteur(in) m(f); **carrier bag** n Tragetasche f

carrot n Karotte f

carry vt tragen; (in vehicle) befördern; (have on one) bei sich haben; **carry on** 1. vi (continue) weitermachen 2. vt (continue) fortführen; ~ **on working** weiter arbeiten; **carry out** vt (orders, plan) ausführen, durchführen

carrycot n Babytragetasche f

carsick adj **he gets** ~ ihm wird beim Autofahren übel

cart n Wagen m, Karren m; (US, shopping trolley) Einkaufswagen m

carton n (Papp)karton m; (of cigarettes) Stange f

cartoon n Cartoon m or nt; (one drawing) Karikatur f; (film) (Zeichen)trickfilm m

cartridge n (film) Kassette f; (for gun, pen, printer) Patrone f; (for copier) Kartusche f

carve vt, vi (wood) schnitzen; (stone) meißeln; (meat) schneiden, tranchieren; **carving** n (in wood) Schnitzerei f, (in stone) Skulptur f, Carving nt

car wash n Autowaschanlage f

case n (crate) Kiste f; (box) Schachtel f; (for spectacles) Etui nt; (matter) LAW Fall m; **in** ~ falls; **in that** ~ in dem Fall; **in** ~ **of fire** im Brand; **it's a** ~ **of ...** es handelt sich hier um ...

cash 1. n Bargeld nt; **in** ~ bar; ~ **on delivery** per Nachnahme **2.** vt (check / cheque) einlösen; **cash desk** n Kasse f; **cash dispenser** n Geldautomat m; **cashier** n Kassierer(in) m(f); **cash machine** n (Brit) Geldautomat m

cashmere n Kaschmirwolle f

cash payment n Barzahlung f; **cashpoint** n (Brit) Geldautomat m

casing n Gehäuse nt

casino n Kasino nt

cask n Fass nt

casserole n Kasserole f; (food) Schmortopf m

cassette n Kassette f; **cassette recorder** n Kassettenrecorder m

cast 1. vt (throw) werfen; THEAT, FILM besetzen; (roles) verteilen **2.** n THEAT, FILM Besetzung f; MED Gipsverband m

caster n ~ **sugar** Streuzucker m

castle n Burg f

casual adj (arrangement, remark) beiläufig; (attitude, manner) (nach)lässig, zwanglos; (*dress*) leger; (*work, earnings*) Gelegenheits-; (*glance*) flüchtig; **~ wear** Freizeitkleidung *f*; **~ sex** Gelegenheitssex *m*; **casually** *adv* (*remark, say*) beiläufig; (*meet*) zwanglos; (*dressed*) leger

casualty *n* Verletzte(r) *mf*; (*dead*) Tote(r) *mf*; (*department in hospital*) Notaufnahme *f*

cat *n* Katze *f*; (*male*) Kater *m*

catalog (*US*), **catalogue** *n* Katalog *m*

cataract *n* Wasserfall *m*; MED grauer Star

catarrh *n* Katarr(h) *m*

catastrophe *n* Katastrophe *f*

catch 1. *n* (*fish etc*) Fang *m* **2.** *vt* fangen; (*thief*) fassen; (*train, bus etc*) nehmen; (*not miss*) erreichen; **~ a cold** sich erkälten; **~ fire** Feuer fangen; **I didn't ~ that** das habe ich nicht mitgekriegt; **catch up** *vt*, *vi* **~ with sb** jdn einholen; **~ on sth** etw nachholen; **catching** *adj* ansteckend

category *n* Kategorie *f*

cater *vi* die Speisen und Getränke liefern (*for* für); **cater for** *vt* (*customers*) eingestellt sein auf + *acc*; **catering** *n* Versorgung *f* mit Speisen und Getränken, Gastronomie *f*; **catering service** *n* Partyservice *m*

caterpillar *n* Raupe *f*

cathedral *n* Kathedrale *f*, Dom *m*

Catholic 1. *adj* katholisch **2.** *n* Katholik(in) *m(f)*

cat nap *n* (*Brit*) kurzer Schlaf; **cat's eyes** *npl* (*in road*) Katzenaugen *pl*, Reflektoren *pl*

catsup *n* (*US*) Ketschup *nt or m*

cattle *npl* Vieh *nt*

caught *pt*, *pp* of **catch**

cauliflower *n* Blumenkohl *m*; **cauliflower cheese** *n* Blumenkohl *m* in Käsesoße

cause 1. *n* (*origin*) Ursache *f* (*of* für); (*reason*) Grund *m* (*for* zu); (*purpose*) Sache *f*; **for a good ~** für wohltätige Zwecke; **no ~ for alarm/complaint** kein Grund zur Aufregung/Klage **2.** *vt* verursachen

causeway *n* Damm *m*

caution 1. *n* Vorsicht *f*; LAW, SPORT Verwarnung *f* **2.** *vt* (ver)warnen; **cautious** *adj* vorsichtig

cave *n* Höhle *f*

cavity *n* Hohlraum *m*; (*in tooth*) Loch *nt*

cayenne (pepper) *n* Cayennepfeffer *m*

CCTV *abbr* = **closed circuit television**; Videoüberwachungsanlage *f*

CD *abbr* = **Compact Disc**; CD *f*; **CD player** *n* CD-Spieler *m*; **CD-ROM** *abbr* = **Compact Disc Read Only Memory**; CD-ROM *f*

cease 1. vi aufhören **2.** vt beenden; **~ doing sth** aufhören, etw zu tun; **cease fire** n Waffenstillstand m

ceiling n Decke f

celebrate vt, vi feiern; **celebrated** adj gefeiert; **celebration** n Feier f; **celebrity** n Berühmtheit f, Star m

celeriac n (Knollen)sellerie f or f; **celery** n (Stangen)sellerie m or f

cell n Zelle f; (US) → **cellphone**

cellar n Keller m

cello n Cello nt

cellphone, cellular phone n Mobiltelefon nt, Handy nt

Celt n Kelte m, Keltin f; **Celtic 1.** adj keltisch **2.** n (language) Keltisch nt

cement n Zement m

cemetery n Friedhof m

cent n (of dollar, euro etc) Cent m

center n (US) → **centre**

centiliter (US), **centilitre** n Zentiliter m; **centimeter** (US), **centimetre** n Zentimeter m

central adj zentral; **Central America** n Mittelamerika nt; **Central Europe** n Mitteleuropa nt; **central heating** n Zentralheizung f; **centralize** vt zentralisieren; **central locking** n AUTO Zentralverriegelung f; **central reservation** n (Brit) Mittelstreifen m; **central station** n Haupt-

bahnhof m

centre 1. n Mitte f; (building, of city) Zentrum nt **2.** vt zentrieren; **centre forward** n SPORT Mittelstürmer m

century n Jahrhundert nt

ceramic adj keramisch

cereal n (any grain) Getreide nt; (breakfast cereal) Frühstücksflocken pl

ceremony n Feier f, Zeremonie f

certain adj sicher (of + gen); (particular) bestimmt; **for ~** mit Sicherheit; **certainly** adv sicher; (without doubt) bestimmt; **~!** aber sicher!; **~ not** ganz bestimmt nicht!

certificate n Bescheinigung f; (in school, of qualification) Zeugnis nt; **certify** vt, vi bescheinigen

cervical smear n Abstrich m

CFC abbr = **chlorofluorocarbon**; FCKW nt

chain 1. n Kette f **2.** vt ~ (up) anketten

chair n Stuhl m; (university) Lehrstuhl m; (armchair) Sessel m; (chairperson) Vorsitzende(r) mf; **chairlift** n Sessellift m; **chairman** n Vorsitzende(r) m; (of firm) Präsident m; **chairperson** n Vorsitzende(r) m; (of firm) Präsident(in) mf(f); **chairwoman** n Vorsitzende f; (of firm) Präsidentin f

chalet n (in mountains) Berghütte f; (holiday dwelling)

Ferienhäuschen nt

chalk n Kreide f

challenge 1. n Herausforderung f **2.** vt (person) herausfordern; (statement) bestreiten

chambermaid n Zimmermädchen nt

champagne n Champagner m

champion n SPORT Meister(in) m(f); **championship** n Meisterschaft f; **Champions League** n Champions League f

chance n (fate) Zufall m; (possibility) Möglichkeit f; (opportunity) Gelegenheit f; (risk) Risiko nt; **by** ~ zufällig; **he doesn't stand a** ~ **(of winning)** er hat keinerlei Chance(, zu gewinnen)

chancellor n Kanzler(in) m(f)

chandelier n Kronleuchter m

change 1. vt verändern; (alter) ändern; (money, wheel, nappy) wechseln; (exchange) (um)tauschen; ~ **one's clothes** sich umziehen; ~ **trains** umsteigen; ~ **gear** AUTO schalten **2.** vi sich ändern; (esp outwardly) sich verändern; (get changed) sich umziehen **3.** n Veränderung f; (alteration) Änderung f; (money) Wechselgeld nt; (coins) Kleingeld nt; **by** ~ zur Abwechslung; **can you give me** ~ **for £10?** können

Sie mir auf 10 Pfund herausgeben?; **change down** vi (Brit) AUTO herunterschalten; **change over** vi sich umstellen (to auf + acc); **change up** vi (Brit) AUTO hochschalten

changeable adj (weather) veränderlich, wechselhaft; **change machine** n Geldwechsler m; **changing room** n Umkleideraum m

channel n Kanal m; RADIO, TV Kanal m, Sender m; **the (English) Channel** der Ärmelkanal; **the Channel Islands** die Kanalinseln; **channel-hopping** n Zappen nt

chaos n Chaos nt; **chaotic** adj chaotisch

chap n (Brit) fam Bursche m, Kerl m

chapel n Kapelle f

chapped adj (lips) aufgesprungen

chapter n Kapitel nt

character n Charakter m, Wesen nt; (in a play, novel etc) Figur f; TYPO Zeichen nt; **he's a real** ~ er ist ein echtes Original; **characteristic** n typisches Merkmal

charcoal n Holzkohle f

charge 1. n (cost) Gebühr f; LAW Anklage f; **free of** ~ gratis, kostenlos; **be in** ~ **of** verantwortlich sein für **2.** vt (money) verlangen; LAW anklagen; (battery) laden

charity n (*institution*) wohltätige Organisation f; *a collection for* ~ eine Sammlung für wohltätige Zwecke; **charity shop** n *Geschäft einer 'charity', in dem freiwillige Helfer gebrauchte Kleidung, Bücher etc verkaufen*

charm 1. n Charme m **2.** vt bezaubern; **charming** adj reizend, charmant

chart n Diagramm nt; (*map*) Karte f; **the ~s** pl die Charts, die Hitliste

charter 1. n Urkunde f **2.** vt NAUT, AVIAT chartern; **charter flight** n Charterflug m

chase 1. vt jagen, verfolgen **2.** n Verfolgungsjagd f; (*hunt*) Jagd f

chassis n AUTO Fahrgestell nt

chat 1. vi plaudern; TEL chatten **2.** n Plauderei f; **chat up** vt anmachen, anbaggern; **chat room** n IT Chatroom m; **chat show** n Talkshow f

chauffeur n Chauffeur(in) m(f), Fahrer(in) m(f)

cheap adj billig; (*of poor quality*) minderwertig

cheat vt, vi betrügen; (*in school, game*) mogeln

Chechnya n Tschetschenien nt

check 1. vt (*examine*) überprüfen (*for* auf + acc); TECH (*adjustment etc*) kontrollieren; (*US, tick*) abhaken; AVIAT (*luggage*) einchecken; (*US, coat*) abgeben **2.** n (*examina-*

tion, restraint) Kontrolle f; (*US, restaurant bill*) Rechnung f; (*pattern*) Karo(muster) nt; (*US*) → **cheque**; **check in** vt, vi AVIAT einchecken; (*into hotel*) sich anmelden; **check out** vi sich abmelden, auschecken; **check up** vi nachprüfen; **~ on sb** Nachforschungen über jdn anstellen

checkers nsing (*US*) Damespiel nt

check-in n (*airport*) Check-in m; (*hotel*) Anmeldung f; **check-in desk** n Abfertigungsschalter m; **checking account** n (*US*) Scheckkonto nt; **check list** n Kontrollliste f; **checkout** n (*supermarket*) Kasse f; **checkout time** n (*hotel*) Abreise(zeit) f; **checkpoint** n Kontrollpunkt m; **checkroom** n (*US*) Gepäckaufbewahrung f; **checkup** n MED (ärztliche) Untersuchung

cheddar n Cheddarkäse m

cheek n Backe f, Wange f; (*insolence*) Frechheit f; **what a** ~ so eine Frechheit!; **cheekbone** n Backenknochen m; **cheeky** adj frech

cheer 1. n Beifallsruf m; **~s** (*when drinking*) prost!; (*Brit*) fam (*thanks*) danke!; (*Brit, goodbye*) tschüs **2.** vt zujubeln + dat **3.** vi jubeln; **cheer up 1.** vt aufmuntern **2.** vi fröhlicher werden;

cheerful *adj* fröhlich

cheese *n* Käse *m;* cheeseboard *n* Käsebrett *nt; (as course)* (gemischte) Käseplatte; cheesecake *n* Käsekuchen *m*

chef *n* Koch *m; (in charge of kitchen)* Küchenchef(in) *m(f)*

chemical 1. *adj* chemisch 2. *n* Chemikalie *f;* chemist *n (pharmacist)* Apotheker(in) *m(f); (industrial chemist)* Chemiker(in) *m(f);* ~'s *(shop)* Apotheke *f;* chemistry *n* Chemie *f*

cheque *n (Brit)* Scheck *m;* cheque account *n (Brit)* Girokonto *nt;* cheque book *n (Brit)* Scheckheft *nt;* cheque card *n (Brit)* Scheckkarte *f*

chequered *adj* kariert

cherish *vt (look after)* liebevoll sorgen für; *(hope)* hegen; *(memory)* bewahren

cherry *n* Kirsche *f;* cherry tomato *n* Kirschtomate *f*

chess *n* Schach *nt;* chessboard *n* Schachbrett *nt*

chest *n* Brust *f; (box)* Kiste *f;* ~ of drawers *n* Kommode *f*

chestnut *n* Kastanie *f*

chew *vt, vi* kauen; chewing gum *n* Kaugummi *m*

chick *n* Küken *nt;* chicken *n* Huhn *nt; (food: roast)* Hähnchen *nt; (coward)* Feigling *m;* chicken breast *n* Hühnerbrust *f;* chicken Kiev *n* paniertes Hähnchen, mit

Knoblauchbutter gefüllt; chickenpox *n* Windpocken *pl;* chickpea *n* Kichererbse *f*

chicory *n* Chicorée *f*

chief 1. *n (of department etc)* Leiter(in) *m(f); (boss)* Chef(in) *m(f); (of tribe)* Häuptling *m* 2. *adj* Haupt-; chiefly *adv* hauptsächlich

child *n* Kind *nt;* child allowance, child benefit *(Brit) n* Kindergeld *nt;* childhood *n* Kindheit *f;* childish *adj* kindisch; child lock *n* Kindersicherung *f;* childproof *adj* kindersicher; children *pl of* child; child seat *n* Kindersitz *m*

Chile *n* Chile *nt*

chill 1. *n* Kühle *f;* MED Erkältung *f* 2. *vt (wine)* kühlen; chill out *vi fam* relaxen; chilled *adj* gekühlt

chilli *n* Pepperoni *f; (spice)* Chili *m;* chilli con carne *n* Chili con carne *nt*

chilly *adj* kühl, frostig

chimney *n* Schornstein *m;* chimneysweep *n* Schornsteinfeger(in) *m(f)*

chimpanzee *n* Schimpanse *m*

chin *n* Kinn *nt*

china *n* Porzellan *nt*

China *n* China *nt;* Chinese 1. *adj* chinesisch 2. *n (person)* Chinese *m,* Chinesin *f; (language)* Chinesisch *nt;* Chinese leaves *npl* Chinakohl *m*

chip 1. *n (of wood etc)* Splitter

m; (damage) angeschlagene Stelle; IT Chip *m;* ~**s** *(Brit, potatoes)* Pommes frites *pl; (US, crisps)* Kartoffelchips *pl* **2.** *vt* anschlagen, beschädigen; **chippie** *fam,* **chip shop** *n* Frittenbude *f*

chiropodist *n* Fußpfleger(in) *m(f)*

chirp *vi* zwitschern

chisel *n* Meißel *m*

chives *npl* Schnittlauch *m*

chlorine *n* Chlor *m*

chocaholic, chocoholic *n* Schokoladenfreak *m;* **choc-ice** *n* Eis *nt* mit Schokoladenüberzug; **chocolate** *n* Schokolade *f; (chocolate-coated sweet)* Praline *f; a bar of* ~ eine Tafel Schokolade; *a box of* ~*s* eine Schachtel Pralinen; **chocolate cake** *n* Schokoladenkuchen *m*

choice 1. *n* Wahl *f; (selection)* Auswahl *f* **2.** *adj* auserlesen; *(product)* Qualitäts-

choir *n* Chor *m*

choke 1. *vi* sich verschlucken; SPORT die Nerven verlieren *f* **2.** *vt* erdrosseln **3.** *n* AUTO Choke *m*

cholera *n* Cholera *f*

cholesterol *n* Cholesterin *m*

choose *vt* wählen; *(pick out)* sich aussuchen; *there are* **three to** ~ *from* es stehen drei zur Auswahl

chop 1. *vt (zer)*hacken; *(meat etc)* klein schneiden **2.** *n (meat)* Kotelett *nt; get the*

~ gefeuert werden; **chopsticks** *npl* Essstäbchen *pl*

chorus *n* Chor *m; (in song)* Refrain *m*

chose, chosen *pt, pp* of **choose**

chowder *n (US)* dicke Suppe mit Meeresfrüchten

christen *vt* taufen; **christening** *n* Taufe *f;* **Christian 1.** *adj* christlich **2.** *n* Christ(in) *m(f);* **Christian name** *n (Brit)* Vorname *m*

Christmas *n* Weihnachten *pl;* **Christmas card** *n* Weihnachtskarte *f;* **Christmas carol** *n* Weihnachtslied *nt;* **Christmas Day** *n* der erste Weihnachtstag; **Christmas Eve** *n* Heiligabend *m;* **Christmas pudding** *n* Plumpudding *m;* **Christmas tree** *n* Weihnachtsbaum *m*

chronic *adj* MED chronisch

chubby *adj (child)* pummelig; *(adult)* rundlich

chuck *vt fam* schmeißen; **chuck in** *vt fam (job)* hinschmeißen; **chuck out** *vt fam* rausschmeißen; **chuck up** *vi fam* kotzen

chunk *n* Klumpen *m; (of bread)* Brocken *m; (of meat)* Batzen *m;* **chunky** *adj (person)* stämmig

Chunnel *n fam* Kanaltunnel *m*

church *n* Kirche *f;* **churchyard** *n* Kirchhof *m*

chute *n* Rutsche *f*

clam chowder

chutney n Chutney m
CIA abbr = **Central Intelligence Agency**; (US) CIA f
CID abbr = **Criminal Investigation Department**; (Brit) ≈ Kripo f
cider n ≈ Apfelmost m
cigar n Zigarre f; **cigarette** n Zigarette f
cinema n Kino nt
cinnamon n Zimt m
circa prep zirka
circle 1. n Kreis m **2.** vi kreisen; **circuit** n Rundfahrt f; (on foot) Rundgang m; (for racing) Rennstrecke f; ELEC Stromkreis m; **circular 1.** adj (kreis)rund, kreisförmig **2.** n Rundschreiben nt; **circulation** n (of blood) Kreislauf m; (of newspaper) Auflage f
circumstances npl (facts) Umstände pl; (financial condition) Verhältnisse pl; **in/ under the ~** unter den Umständen; **under no ~** auf keinen Fall
circus n Zirkus m
cissy n fam Weichling m
cistern n Zisterne f; (of WC) Spülkasten m
cite vt zitieren
citizen n Bürger(in) m(f); (of nation) Staatsangehörige(r) m(f); **citizenship** n Staatsangehörigkeit f
city n Stadt f; (large) Großstadt f; **the ~** (London's financial centre) die (Londo-

ner) City; **city centre** n Innenstadt f, Zentrum nt
civil adj (of town) Bürger-; (of state) staatsbürgerlich; (not military) zivil; **civil ceremony** n standesamtliche Hochzeit; **civil engineering** n Hoch- und Tiefbau m, Bauingenieurwesen nt; **civilian** n Zivilist(in) m(f); **civilization** n Zivilisation f, Kultur f; **civilized** adj zivilisiert, kultiviert; **civil partnership** n eingetragene Partnerschaft f; **civil rights** npl Bürgerrechte pl; **civil servant** n (Staats)beamte(r) m, (Staats)beamtin f; **civil service** n Staatsdienst m; **civil war** n Bürgerkrieg m
CJD abbr = **Creutzfeld-Jakob disease**; Creutzfeld-Jakob-Krankheit f
cl abbr = **centilitre(s)**; cl
claim 1. vt beanspruchen; (apply for) beantragen; (demand) fordern; (assert) behaupten (that dass) **2.** n (demand) Forderung f (for für); (right) Anspruch m (to auf + acc); **~ for damages** Schadenersatzforderung f; **make or put in a ~** (insurance) Ansprüche geltend machen; **claimant** n Antragsteller(in) m(f)
clam n Venusmuschel f; **clam chowder** n (US) dicke Muschelsuppe (mit Sellerie, Zwiebeln etc)

clap *vi* (Beifall) klatschen

claret *n* roter Bordeaux(wein)

clarify *vt* klären

clash 1. *vi* (physically) zusammenstoßen (with mit); (argue) sich auseinandersetzen (with mit); (fig (colours) sich beißen **2.** *n* Zusammenstoß *m*; (argument) Auseinandersetzung *f*

class 1. *n* Klasse *f* **2.** *vt* einordnen, einstufen

classic 1. *adj* (mistake, example etc) klassisch **2.** *n* Klassiker *m*; **classical** *adj* (music, ballet etc) klassisch

classification *n* Klassifizierung *f*; **classify** *vt* klassifizieren; **classified advertisement** Kleinanzeige *f*

classroom *n* Klassenzimmer *nt*

classy *adj fam* nobel, exklusiv

clause *n* LING Satz *m*; LAW Klausel *f*

claw *n* Kralle *f*

clay *n* Lehm *m*; (for pottery) Ton *m*

clean 1. *adj* sauber; ~ **driving licence** Führerschein ohne Strafpunkte **2.** *adv* (completely) glatt **3.** *vt* sauber machen; (carpet etc) reinigen; (window, shoes, vegetables) putzen; (wound) säubern; **clean up 1.** *vt* sauber machen **2.** *vi* aufräumen; **cleaner** *n* (person) Putzmann *m*, Putzfrau *f*; (substance) Putzmittel *nt*; **~'s** (firm) Reinigung *f*

cleanse *vt* reinigen; (wound) säubern; **cleanser** *n* Reinigungsmittel *nt*

clear 1. *adj* klar; (distinct) deutlich; (conscience) rein; (free, road etc) frei; **be ~ about sth** sich über etw im Klaren sein **2.** *adv* **stand ~** zurücktreten **3.** *vt* (road, room etc) räumen; (table) abräumen; LAW (find innocent) freisprechen (of von); **~** (fog, mist) sich verziehen; (weather) aufklaren; **clear away** *vt* wegräumen; (dishes) abräumen; **clear off** *vi fam* abhauen; **clear up 1.** *vi* (tidy up) aufräumen; (weather) sich aufklären **2.** *vt* (room) aufräumen; (litter) wegräumen; (matter) klären

clearance sale *n* Räumungsverkauf *m*; **clearing** *n* Lichtung *f*; **clearly** *adv* klar; (speak, remember) deutlich; (obviously) eindeutig; **clearway** *n* (Brit) Straße *f* mit Halteverbot

clench *vt* (fist) ballen; (teeth) zusammenbeißen

clergyman *n* Geistliche(r) *m*

clerk *n* (US) *n* (in office) Büroangestellte(r) *mf*; (US, salesperson) Verkäufer(in) *m(f)*

clever *adj* schlau, klug

cliché *n* Klischee *nt*

click 1. *vi* Klicken *nt*; IT Mausklick *m* **2.** *vi* klicken; **~ on sth** IT etw anklicken; **it ~ed** *fam* ich hab's/er hat's etc geschnallt; **they ~ed** sie haben sich gleich verstanden; **click on** vt IT anklicken

client n Kunde m, Kundin f; LAW Mandant(in) m(f)

cliff n Klippe f

climate n Klima m

climax n Höhepunkt m

climb 1. vi (person) klettern; (aircraft, sun) steigen; (road) ansteigen **2.** vt (mountain) besteigen; (tree etc) klettern auf + acc **3.** n Aufstieg m; **climbing** n Klettern nt, Bergsteigen nt; **climbing frame** n Klettergerüst nt

cling vi sich klammern (to an + acc); **cling film** n Frischhaltefolie f

clinic n Klinik f

clip 1. n Klammer f **2.** vt (fix) anklemmen (to an + acc); (fingernails) schneiden; **clippers** npl Schere f; (for nails) Zwicker m

cloak n Umhang m; **cloakroom** n (for coats) Garderobe f

clock n Uhr f; AUTO fam Tacho m; **round the ~** rund um die Uhr; **clockwise** adv im Uhrzeigersinn; **clockwork** n Uhrwerk nt

cloister n Kreuzgang m

clone 1. n Klon m **2.** vt klonen

close 1. adj nahe (to + dat); (friend, contact) eng; (resemblance) groß; **~ to the beach** in der Nähe des Strandes; **~ win** knapper Sieg; **on ~r ex-**

amination bei näherer or genauerer Untersuchung **2.** adv dicht; **he lives ~ by** er wohnt ganz in der Nähe **3.** vt schließen; (road) sperren; (discussion, matter) abschließen **4.** vi schließen **5.** n Ende nt; **close down 1.** vi schließen; (factory) stillgelegt werden **2.** vt (shop) schließen; (factory) stilllegen; **closed** adj (road) gesperrt; (shop etc) geschlossen; **closed circuit television** n Videoüberwachungsanlage f; **closely** adv (related) eng, nah; (packed, follow) dicht; (attentively) genau

closet n (esp US) Schrank m

close-up n Nahaufnahme f

closing adj **~ date** letzter Termin; (for competition) Einsendeschluss m; **~ time** (of shop) Ladenschluss m; (Brit, of pub) Polizeistunde f

clot 1. (blood) **~** Blutgerinnsel nt; fam (idiot) Trottel m **2.** vi (blood) gerinnen

cloth n (material) Tuch nt; (for cleaning) Lappen m

clothe vt ankleiden; **clothes** npl Kleider pl, Kleidung f; **clothes peg**, **clothespin** (US) n Wäscheklammer f; **clothing** n Kleidung f

clotted adj **~ cream** dicke Sahne (aus erhitzter Milch)

cloud n Wolke f; **cloudy** adj (sky) bewölkt; (liquid) trüb

clove n Gewürznelke f; **~ of**

garlic Knoblauchzehe f

clover n Klee m; **cloverleaf** n Kleeblatt nt

clown n Clown m

club n (weapon) Knüppel m; (society) Klub m, Verein m; (nightclub) Disko f; (golf club) Golfschläger m, Kreuz nt; **clubbing** n **go ~** in die Disko gehen; **club class** n AVIAT Businessclass f

clue n Anhaltspunkt m, Hinweis m; **he hasn't a ~** er hat keine Ahnung

clumsy adj unbeholfen, ungeschickt

clung pt, pp of **cling**

clutch n AUTO Kupplung f

cm abbr = **centimetre(s)**; cm

c/o abbr = **care of**; bei

Co abbr = **company**

coach 1. n (Brit, bus) Reisebus m; RAIL (Personen)wagen m; SPORT (trainer) Trainer(in) m(f) 2. vt Nachhilfeunterricht geben + dat; SPORT trainieren; **coach (class)** n AVIAT Economyclass f; **coach driver** n Busfahrer(in) m(f); **coach station** n Busbahnhof m; **coach trip** n Busfahrt f; (tour) Busreise f

coal n Kohle f

coalition n POL Koalition f

coast n Küste f; **coastguard** n Küstenwache f; **coastline** n Küste f

coat n Mantel m; (jacket) Jacke f; (on animals) Fell nt,

Pelz m; (of paint) Schicht f; **~ of arms** Wappen nt; **coathanger** n Kleiderbügel m; **coating** n Überzug m; (layer) Schicht f

cobble(stone)s npl Kopfsteine pl; (surface) Kopfsteinpflaster nt

cobweb n Spinnennetz nt

cocaine n Kokain nt

cock n Hahn m; vulg (penis) Schwanz m

cockle n Herzmuschel f

cockpit n (in plane, racing car) Cockpit nt; **cockroach** n Kakerlake f; **cocksure** adj todsicher; **cocktail** n Cocktail m; **cock-up** n (Brit) fam **make a ~ of sth** hier etw Mist bauen; **cocky** adj großspurig, von sich selbst überzeugt

cocoa n Kakao m

coconut n Kokosnuss f

cod n Kabeljau m

COD abbr = **cash on delivery**; per Nachnahme

code n Kode m

coffee n Kaffee m; **coffee bar** n Café nt; **coffee break** n Kaffeepause f; **coffee maker** n Kaffeemaschine f; **coffee pot** n Kaffeekanne f; **coffee shop** n Café nt; **coffee table** n Couchtisch m

coffin n Sarg m

coil n Rolle f; ELEC Spule f; MED Spirale f

coin n Münze f

coincide vi (happen together)

zusammenfallen (with mit);
coincidence n Zufall m
coke n Koks m; Coke® Cola f
cola n Cola f
cold 1. adj kalt; I'm ~ mir ist
kalt, ich friere 2. n Kälte f;
(illness) Erkältung f, Schnupfen m; catch a ~ sich erkälten; cold box n Kühlbox f;
coldness n Kälte f; cold
sore n Herpes m
coleslaw n Krautsalat m
collaborate vi zusammenarbeiten (with mit); collaboration n Zusammenarbeit f;
(of one party) Mitarbeit f
collapse 1. vi zusammenbrechen; (building etc) einstürzen 2. n Zusammenbruch
m; (of building) Einsturz m
collar n Kragen m; (for dog,
cat) Halsband nt; collarbone
n Schlüsselbein nt
colleague n Kollege m, Kollegin f
collect 1. vt sammeln; (fetch)
abholen 2. vi sich sammeln;
collect call n (US) R-Ge-
spräch nt; collected adj
(works) gesammelt; (person)
gefasst; collector n Samm-
ler(in) m(f); collection n
Sammlung f; REL Kollekte
f; (from postbox) Leerung f
college n (residential) College
nt; (specialist) Fachhoch-
schule f; (vocational) Berufsschule f; (US, university)
Universität f; go to ~ (US)
studieren

collide vi zusammenstoßen;
collision n Zusammenstoß
m
colloquial adj umgangs-
sprachlich
Cologne n Köln nt
colon n (punctuation mark)
Doppelpunkt m
colonial adj Kolonial-; colony n Kolonie f
color n (US), colour 1. n Farbe f; (of skin) Hautfarbe f 2.
vt anmalen; (bias) färben;
colour-blind adj farben-
blind; coloured adj farbig;
(biased) gefärbt; colour film
n Farbfilm m; colourful adj
lit, fig bunt; (life, past) bewegt; colouring n (in food
etc) Farbstoff m; (complexion) Gesichtsfarbe f; colour-
less adj farblos; colour pho-
to(graph) n Farbfoto nt; colour television n Farbfernse-
hen nt
column n Säule f; (of print)
Spalte f
comb 1. n Kamm m 2. vt kämmen; ~ one's hair sich kämmen
combination n Kombination
f; (mixture) Mischung f (of
aus); combine vt verbinden
(with mit); (two things) kombinieren
come vi kommen; (arrive) ankommen; (on list, in order)
stehen; (with adjective: become) werden; ~ and see
us besuchen Sie uns mal;

coming ich komm ja schon!; **~ first / second** erster / zweiter werden; **~ true** wahr werden; **~ loose** sich lockern; **the years to ~** die kommenden Jahre; **there's one more to ~** es kommt noch eins / noch einer; **how ...~?** *fam* wie kommt es, dass ...?; **~ to think of it** *fam* wo es mir gerade einfällt; **come across** *vi* (*find*) stoßen auf + *acc*; **come back** *vi* zurückkommen; **I'll ~ to that** ich komme darauf zurück; **come down** *vi* herunterkommen; (*rain, snow, price*) fallen; **come from** *vt* (*result*) kommen von; **where do you ~?** wo kommen Sie her?; **I ~ London** ich komme aus London; **come in** *vi* hereinkommen; (*arrive*) ankommen; **come off** *vi* (*button, handle etc*) abgehen; (*succeed*) gelingen; **~ well / badly** gut / schlecht wegkommen; **come on** *vi* (*progress*) vorankommen; **~!** komm!; (*hurry*) beeil dich!; (*encouraging*) los!; **come out** *vi* herauskommen; (*photo*) was werden; (*homosexual*) sich outen; **come round** *vi* (*visit*) vorbeikommen; (*regain consciousness*) wieder zu sich kommen; **come to** 1. *vi* (*regain consciousness*) wieder zu sich kommen 2. (*sum*) sich belaufen auf + *acc*;

when it comes to ... wenn es um ... geht; **come up** *vi* hochkommen; (*sun, moon*) aufgehen; **~ (for discussion)** zur Sprache kommen; **come up to** *vt* (*approach*) zukommen auf + *acc*; (*water*) reichen bis zu; (*expectations*) entsprechen + *dat*; **come up with** *vt* (*idea*) haben; (*solution, answer*) kommen auf + *acc*; **~ a suggestion** einen Vorschlag machen

comedian *n* Komiker(in) *m(f)*; **comedy** *n* Komödie *f*

come-on *n* **give sb the ~** *fam* jdn anmachen

comfort 1. *n* Komfort *m*; (*consolation*) Trost *m* 2. *vt* trösten; **comfortable** *adj* bequem; (*income*) ausreichend; (*temperature, life*) angenehm; **comfort station** *n* (*US*) Toilette *f*; **comforting** *adj* tröstlich

comic 1. *n* (*magazine*) Comic(heft) *nt*; (*comedian*) Komiker(in) *m(f)* 2. *adj* komisch

coming *adj* kommend; (*event*) bevorstehend

comma *n* Komma *nt*

command 1. *n* Befehl *m*; (*control*) Führung *f*; MIL Kommando *nt* 2. *vt* befehlen + *dat*

commemorate *vt* gedenken + *gen*; **commemoration** *n* **in ~ of** in Gedenken an + *acc*

comment **1.** n (remark) Bemerkung f; (note) Anmerkung f; (official) Kommentar m (on zu); **no ~** kein Kommentar **2.** vi sich äußern (on zu); **commentary** n Kommentar m (on zu); TV, SPORT Livereportage f; **commentator** n Kommentator(in) m(f); TV, SPORT Reporter(in) m(f)

commerce n Handel m; **commercial 1.** adj kommerziell; (training) kaufmännisch; (TV) TV **break** Werbepause f **2.** n TV Werbespot m

commission **1.** n Auftrag m; (fee) Provision f; (reporting body) Kommission f **2.** vt beauftragen

commit **1.** vt (crime) begehen **2.** vr ~ **oneself** (undertake) sich verpflichten (to zu); **commitment** n Verpflichtung f; POL Engagement nt

committee n Ausschuss m, Komitee nt

common **1.** adj (experience) allgemein, alltäglich; (shared) gemeinsam; (widespread, frequent) häufig; pej gewöhnlich, ordinär; **have sth in ~** etw gemein haben **2.** n (Brit, land) Gemeindewiese f; **commonly** adv häufig, allgemein; **commonplace** adj alltäglich; pej banal; **commonroom** n Gemeinschaftsraum m; **Commons** n (Brit) POL **the**

(**House of**) **~** das Unterhaus; **common sense** n gesunder Menschenverstand

communal adj gemeinsam; (of a community) Gemeinschafts-, Gemeinde-

communicate vi kommunizieren (with mit); **communication** n Kommunikation f, Verständigung f; **communicative** adj gesprächig

communion n (Holy) **Communion** Heiliges Abendmahl; (Catholic) Kommunion f

communism n Kommunismus m; **communist 1.** adj kommunistisch **2.** n Kommunist(in) m(f)

community n Gemeinschaft f; **community centre** n Gemeindezentrum nt; **community service** n LAW Sozialdienst m

commutation ticket n (US) Zeitkarte f; **commute** vi pendeln; **commuter** n Pendler(in) m(f)

compact **1.** adj kompakt **2.** n (for make-up) Puderdose f; (US, car) ≈ Mittelklassewagen m; **compact camera** n Kompaktkamera f; **compact disc** n Compact Disc f, CD f

companion n Begleiter(in) m(f)

company n Gesellschaft f; COMM Firma f; **keep sb ~** jdm Gesellschaft leisten;

company car n Firmenauto nt

comparable adj vergleichbar (*with, to* mit); **comparatively** adv verhältnismäßig; **compare** vt vergleichen (*with, to* mit); **~d with** or **to** im Vergleich zu; **beyond ~** unvergleichlich; **comparison** n Vergleich m; **in ~ with** im Vergleich mit (or zu)

compartment n RAIL Abteil nt; (*in desk etc*) Fach nt

compass n Kompass m; **~es** pl Zirkel m

compassion n Mitgefühl nt

compatible adj vereinbar (*with* mit); IT kompatibel; **we're not ~** wir passen nicht zueinander

compensate 1. vt (*person*) entschädigen (*for* für) 2. vi **~ for sth** Ersatz für etw leisten; (*make up for*) etw ausgleichen; **compensation** n Entschädigung f; (*money*) Schadenersatz m; LAW Abfindung f

compete vi konkurrieren (*for* um); SPORT kämpfen (*for* um); (*take part*) teilnehmen (*in* an + dat)

competence n Fähigkeit f; LAW Zuständigkeit f; **competent** adj fähig; LAW zuständig

competition n (*contest*) Wettbewerb m; COMM Konkurrenz f (*for* um); **competitive** adj (*firm, price, product*) konkurrenzfähig; **competitor** n COMM Konkurrent(in) m(f); SPORT Teilnehmer(in) m(f)

complain vi klagen; (*formally*) sich beschweren (*about* über + acc); **complaint** n Klage f; (*formal*) Beschwerde f; MED Leiden nt

complement vt ergänzen

complete 1. adj vollständig; (*finished*) fertig; (*failure, disaster*) total; (*happiness*) vollkommen; **are we ~?** sind wir vollzählig? 2. vt vervollständigen; (*form*) ausfüllen; **completely** adv völlig; **not ~ ...** nicht ganz ...

complex 1. adj (*task, theory etc*) kompliziert 2. n Komplex m

complexion n Gesichtsfarbe f, Teint m

complicated adj kompliziert; **complication** n Komplikation f

compliment n Kompliment nt; **complimentary** adj lobend; (*free of charge*) Gratis-; **~ ticket** Freikarte f

component n Bestandteil m

compose vt (*music*) komponieren; **~ oneself** sich zusammennehmen; **composed** adj gefasst; **be ~ of** bestehen aus; **composition** n (*of a group*) Zusammensetzung f; MUS Komposition f

comprehend vt verstehen; **comprehension** n Verständnis *nt*

comprehensive *adj* umfassend; **~ school** Gesamtschule *f*

comprise *vt* umfassen, bestehen aus

compromise 1. *n* Kompromiss *m* **2.** *vi* einen Kompromiss schließen

compulsory *adj* obligatorisch

computer *n* Computer *m*; **computer aided** *adj* computergestützt; **computer-controlled** *adj* rechnergesteuert; **computer game** *n* Computerspiel *nt*; **computer-literate** *adj* **be ~** mit dem Computer umgehen können; **computer scientist** *n* Informatiker(in) *m(f)*; **computing** *n* (*subject*) Informatik *f*

con *fam* **1.** *n* Schwindel *m* **2.** *vt* betrügen (*out of* um)

conceal *vt* verbergen (*from* vor + *dat*)

conceive *vt* (*imagine*) sich vorstellen; (*child*) empfangen

concentrate *vi* sich konzentrieren (*on* auf + *acc*); **concentration** *n* Konzentration *f*

concept *n* Begriff *m*

concern 1. *n* (*affair*) Angelegenheit *f*; (*worry*) Sorge *f*; **it's not my ~** das geht mich nichts an; **there's no cause for ~** kein Grund zur Beunruhigung **2.** *vt* (*affect*) angehen; (*have connection with*)

betreffen; (*be about*) handeln von; **those ~ed** die Betroffenen; **as far as I'm ~ed** was mich betrifft; **concerned** *adj* (*anxious*) besorgt; **concerning** *prep* bezüglich, hinsichtlich + *gen*

concert *n* Konzert *nt*; **~ hall** Konzertsaal *m*

concession *n* Zugeständnis *nt*; (*reduction*) Ermäßigung *f*

conclude *vt* (*end*) beenden, (ab)schließen; (*infer*) folgern (*from* aus); **~ that ...** zu dem Schluss kommen, dass ...; **conclusion** *n* Schluss *m*, Schlussfolgerung *f*

concrete 1. *n* Beton *m* **2.** *adj* konkret

concussion *n* Gehirnerschütterung *f*

condition *n* (*state*) Zustand *m*; (*requirement*) Bedingung *f*; **on ~ that ...** unter der Bedingung, dass ...; **~s** *pl* (*circumstances, weather*) Verhältnisse *pl*

conditioner *n* Weichspüler *m*; (*for hair*) Pflegespülung *f*

condo *n* → **condominium**

condolences *npl* Beileid *nt*

condom *n* Kondom *nt*

condominium *n* (*US, apartment*) Eigentumswohnung *f*

conduct 1. *n* (*behaviour*) Verhalten *nt* **2.** *vt* führen, leiten; (*orchestra*) dirigieren

cone *n* Kegel *m*; (*for ice cream*) Waffeltüte *f*; (*fir cone*) (Tannen)zapfen *m*

conference n Konferenz f

confess vt, vi **~ that ...** gestehen, dass ...; **confession** n Geständnis nt; REL Beichte f

confidence n Vertrauen nt (in zu); (assurance) Selbstvertrauen nt; **confident** adj (sure) zuversichtlich (that ... dass ...), überzeugt (of von); (self-assured) selbstsicher; **confidential** adj vertraulich

confine vt beschränken (to auf + acc)

confirm vt bestätigen; **confirmation** n Bestätigung f; REL Konfirmation f; **confirmed** adj (bachelor) eingefleischt

confuse vt verwirren; (sth with sth) verwechseln (with mit); (several things) durcheinanderbringen; **confused** adj (person) konfus, verwirrt; (account) verworren; **confusing** adj verwirrend; **confusion** n Verwirrung f; (of two things) Verwechslung f; (muddle) Chaos nt

congestion n Stau m

congratulate vt gratulieren (on zu); **congratulations** npl Glückwünsche pl; **~!** gratuliere!, herzlichen Glückwunsch!

congregation n REL Gemeinde f

congress n Kongress m; (US) **Congress** der Kongress; **congressman**, **congresswoman** n (US) Mitglied nt des Repräsentantenhauses

conjunction n LING Konjunktion f; **in ~ with** in Verbindung mit

connect 1. vt verbinden (with, to mit); ELEC, TECH (appliance etc) anschließen (to an + acc) **2.** vi (train, plane) Anschluss haben (with an + acc); **~ing flight** Anschlussflug m; **~ing train** Anschlusszug m; (link) Zusammenhang m; (for train, plane, electrical appliance) Anschluss m (with, to an + acc); (business etc) Beziehung f; **in ~ with** in Zusammenhang mit; **bad ~** TEL schlechte Verbindung; ELEC Wackelkontakt m; **connector** n IT (computer) Stecker m

conscience n Gewissen nt; **conscientious** adj gewissenhaft

conscious adj (act) bewusst; MED bei Bewusstsein

consecutive adj aufeinander folgend

consent 1. n Zustimmung f **2.** vi zustimmen (to dat)

consequence n Folge f, Konsequenz f; **consequently** adv folglich

conservation n Erhaltung f; (of buildings) Denkmalschutz m; (nature conservation) Naturschutz m; **conservation area** n Naturschutzgebiet nt; (in town) unter Denkmalschutz stehendes Gebiet

Conservative adj POL konservativ

conservatory n (greenhouse) Gewächshaus nt; (room) Wintergarten m

consider vt (reflect on) nachdenken über, sich überlegen; (take into account) in Betracht ziehen; (regard) halten für; **he is ~ed (to be)** ... er gilt als ...; **considerable** adj beträchtlich; **considerate** adj aufmerksam, rücksichtsvoll; **consideration** n (thoughtfulness) Rücksicht f; (thought) Überlegung f; **take sth into ~** etw in Betracht ziehen; **considering 1.** prep in Anbetracht + gen **2.** conj da

consist vi **~ of ...** bestehen aus

consistent adj (behaviour, process etc) konsequent; (statements) übereinstimmend; (argument) folgerichtig; (performance, results) beständig

consolation n Trost m; **console** vt trösten

consonant n Konsonant m

conspicuous adj auffällig, auffallend

conspiracy n Komplott nt

constable n (Brit) Polizist(in) m(f)

Constance n Konstanz nt; **Lake ~** der Bodensee

constant adj (continual) ständig, dauernd; (unchanging: temperature etc) gleich bleibend; **constantly** adv dauernd

consternation n (dismay) Bestürzung f

constituency n Wahlkreis m

constitution n Verfassung f; (of person) Konstitution f

construct vt bauen; **construction** n (process, result) Bau m; (method) Bauweise f; **under ~** im Bau befindlich; **construction site** n Baustelle f

consulate n Konsulat m

consult vt um Rat fragen; (doctor) konsultieren; (book) nachschlagen in + dat; **consultant** n MED Facharzt m, Fachärztin f; **consultation** n Beratung f; MED Konsultation f

consume vt verbrauchen; (food) konsumieren; **consumer** n Verbraucher(in) m(f)

contact 1. n (touch) Berührung f; (communication) Kontakt m; (person) Kontaktperson f; **be/keep in ~ (with sb)** (mit jdm) in Kontakt sein/bleiben **2.** vt sich in Verbindung setzen mit; **contact lenses** npl Kontaktlinsen pl

contagious adj ansteckend

contain vt enthalten; **container** n Behälter m; (for transport) Container m

contaminate vt verunreinigen; (chemically) verseuchen; **~d by radiation** strahlenverseucht, verstrahlt; **contamination** n Verunreinigung f; (by radiation) Verseuchung f

contemporary adj zeitgenössisch

contempt n Verachtung f; **contemptuous** adj verächtlich

content adj zufrieden

content(s) n pl Inhalt m

contest 1. n (Wett)kampf m (for um), (competition) Wettbewerb m 2. vt kämpfen um + acc; (dispute) bestreiten; **contestant** n Teilnehmer(in) m(f)

context n Zusammenhang m; **out of ~** aus dem Zusammenhang gerissen

continent n Kontinent m, Festland nt; **the Continent** (Brit) das europäische Festland, der Kontinent; **continental** adj kontinental; **~ breakfast** kleines Frühstück mit Brötchen und Marmelade, Kaffee oder Tee

continual adj (endless) ununterbrochen; (constant) dauernd, ständig; **continually** adv dauernd; (again and again) immer wieder; **continuation** n Fortsetzung f; **continue** 1. vi weitermachen (with mit); (esp talking) fortfahren (with mit); (travelling) weiterfahren; (state, conditions) fortdauern, anhalten 2. vt fortsetzen; **to be ~d** Fortsetzung folgt; **continuous** adj (endless) ununterbrochen; (constant) ständig

contraceptive n Verhütungsmittel nt

contract n Vertrag m

contradict vt widersprechen + dat; **contradiction** n Widerspruch m

contrary 1. adj Gegenteil nt; **on the ~** im Gegenteil 2. adj **~ to** entgegen + dat

contrast 1. n Kontrast m, Gegensatz m; **in ~ to** im Gegensatz zu 2. vt entgegensetzen

contribute vt, vi beitragen (to zu); (money) spenden (to für); **contribution** n Beitrag m

control 1. vt (master) beherrschen; (temper etc) im Griff haben; (esp) TECH steuern; **~ oneself** sich beherrschen 2. n Kontrolle f; (mastery) Beherrschung f; (of business) Leitung f; (esp) TECH Steuerung f; **~s** pl (knobs, switches etc) Bedienungselemente pl; (of machine) Steuerung f; **be out of ~** außer Kontrolle sein; **control knob** n Bedienungsknopf m; **control panel** n Schalttafel f

controversial adj umstritten

convalesce vi gesund werden; **convalescence** n Genesung f

convenience n (quality, thing) Annehmlichkeit f; **at your ~** wann es Ihnen passt; **with all modern ~s** mit allem Komfort; **convenience food** n Fertiggericht nt; **convenient** adj günstig, passend

convent n Kloster nt

convention n (custom) Konvention f; (meeting) Konferenz f; **conventional** adj herkömmlich, konventionell

conversation n Gespräch nt, Unterhaltung f

conversion n Umwandlung f (into in + acc); (of building) Umbau m (into zu); (calculation) Umrechnung f; **conversion table** n Umrechnungstabelle f; **convert** vt umwandeln; (person) bekehren; IT konvertieren; **~ into Euros** in Euro umrechnen; **convertible** n AUTO Kabrio nt

convey vt (carry) befördern; (feelings) vermitteln; **conveyor belt** n Förderband nt, Fließband nt

convict 1. vt verurteilen (of wegen) **2.** n Strafgefangene(r) mf; **conviction** n LAW Verurteilung f; (strong belief) Überzeugung f

convince vt überzeugen (of von); **convincing** adj überzeugend

cook 1. vt, vi kochen **2.** n Koch m, Köchin f; **cookbook** n Kochbuch nt; **cooker** n Herd

m; **cookie** n (US) Keks m; **cooking** n Kochen nt; (style of cooking) Küche f

cool 1. adj kühl, gelassen; fam (brilliant) cool, stark **2.** vt, vi (ab)kühlen; **~ it** reg dich ab **3.** n keep/lose one's **~** fam ruhig bleiben/durchdrehen; **cool down** vi abkühlen; (calm down) sich beruhigen

cooperate vi zusammenarbeiten, kooperieren; **cooperation** n Zusammenarbeit f, Kooperation f; **cooperative 1.** adj hilfsbereit **2.** n Genossenschaft f

cop n fam (policeman) Bulle m

cope vi zurechtkommen, fertig werden (with mit)

Copenhagen n Kopenhagen nt

copier n Kopierer m

copper n Kupfer nt; (Brit) fam (policeman) Bulle m; fam (coin) Kupfermünze f; **~s** Kleingeld nt

copy 1. n Kopie f; (of book) Exemplar nt **2.** vt kopieren; (imitate) nachahmen; **copyright** n Urheberrecht nt

coral n Koralle f

cord n Schnur f; (material) Kordsamt m

cordial adj freundlich

cordless adj (phone) schnurlos

core n Kern m; (of apple, pear) Kerngehäuse nt; **core**

business n Kerngeschäft nt

cork n (material) Kork m; (stopper) Korken m; corkscrew n Korkenzieher m

corn n Getreide nt, Korn nt; (US, maize) Mais m; (on foot) Hühnerauge nt; ~ on the cob (gekochter) Maiskolben; corned beef n Cornedbeef nt

corner 1. n Ecke f; (on road) Kurve f; sport Eckstoß m 2. vt in die Enge treiben; corner shop n Laden m an der Ecke

cornflakes npl Cornflakes pl; cornflour (Brit), cornstarch (US) n Maismehl nt

Cornish adj kornisch; ~ pasty mit Fleisch und Kartoffeln gefüllte Pastete; Cornwall n Cornwall nt

coronary n MED Herzinfarkt m

corporation n (US) COMM Aktiengesellschaft f

corpse n Leiche f

correct 1. adj (accurate) richtig; (proper) korrekt 2. vt korrigieren, verbessern; correction n (esp written) Korrektur f

correspond vi entsprechen (to dat); (two things) übereinstimmen; corresponding adj entsprechend

corridor n (in building) Flur m; (in train) Gang m

corrupt adj korrupt

cosmetic adj kosmetisch;

cosmetics npl Kosmetika pl; cosmetic surgery n Schönheitschirurgie f

cosmopolitan adj international; (attitude) weltoffen

cost 1. vt kosten 2. n Kosten pl; at all ~s, at any ~ um jeden Preis; ~ of living Lebenshaltungskosten pl; costly adj kostspielig

costume n THEAT Kostüm nt

cosy adj gemütlich

cot n (Brit) Kinderbett nt; (US) Campingliege f

cottage n kleines Haus; (country cottage) Landhäuschen nt; cottage cheese n Hüttenkäse m; cottage pie n Hackfleisch mit Kartoffelbrei überbacken

cotton n Baumwolle f; cotton candy n (US) Zuckerwatte f; cotton wool n (Brit) Watte f

couch n Couch f; (sofa) Sofa nt; (couchette) Liegewagen(platz) m

cough 1. vi husten 2. n Husten m; cough mixture n Hustensaft m; cough sweet n Hustenbonbon nt

could pt of can; könnte conditional könnte; ~ you come earlier? könntest du früher kommen?; couldn't contr of could not

council n POL Rat m; (local ~) Gemeinderat m; (town ~) Stadtrat m; council estate n Siedlung f des sozialen

Wohnungsbaus; **council house** *n* Sozialwohnung *f*; **council tax** *n* Gemeindesteuer *f*

count 1. *vt, vi* zählen; *(include)* mitrechnen **2.** *n* Zählung *f*; *(noble)* Graf *m*; **count on** *vt (rely on)* sich verlassen auf + *acc*; *(expect)* rechnen mit

counter *n (in shop)* Ladentisch *m*; *(in café)* Theke *f*; *(in bank, post office)* Schalter *m*; **counter attack 1.** *n* Gegenangriff *m* **2.** *vi* zurückschlagen; **counter-clockwise** *adv (US)* entgegen dem Uhrzeigersinn

counterfoil *n* (Kontroll)abschnitt *m*

counterpart *n* Gegenstück *nt (of* zu)

countess *n* Gräfin *f*

countless *adj* zahllos, unzählig

country *n* Land *nt*; **in the ~** auf dem Land(e); **in this ~** hierzulande; **country cousin** *n fam* Landei *nt*; **country dancing** *n* Volkstanz *m*; **countryman** *n (compatriot)* Landsmann *m*; **country music** *n* Countrymusic *f*; **country road** *n* Landstraße *f*; **countryside** *n* Landschaft *f*; *(rural area)* Land *nt*

county *n (Brit)* Grafschaft *f*; *(US)* Verwaltungsbezirk *m*; **county town** *n (Brit)* ≈ Kreisstadt *f*

couple *n* Paar *nt*; **a ~ of** ein paar

coupon *n (voucher)* Gutschein *m*

courage *n* Mut *m*

courgette *n (Brit)* Zucchini *f*

courier *n (for tourists)* Reiseleiter(in) *m(f)*; *(messenger)* Kurier *m*

course *n (of study)* Kurs *m*; *(for race)* Strecke *f*; NAUT, AVIAT Kurs *m*; *(at university)* Studiengang *m*; *(in meal)* Gang *m*; **of ~** natürlich; **in the ~ of** während

court *n* SPORT Platz *m*; LAW Gericht *m*

courtesy *n* Höflichkeit *f*; **~ bus/coach** (gebührenfreier) Zubringerbus

courthouse *n (US)* Gerichtsgebäude *nt*; **court order** *n* Gerichtsbeschluss *m*; **courtroom** *n* Gerichtssaal *m*

courtyard *n* Hof *m*

cousin *n (male)* Cousin *m*; *(female)* Cousine *f*

cover 1. *vt* bedecken *(in, with* mit); *(distance)* zurücklegen; *(loan, costs)* decken **2.** *n (for bed etc)* Decke *f*; *(of cushion)* Bezug *m*; *(lid)* Deckel *m*; *(of book)* Umschlag *m*; *(insurance)* ~ Versicherungsschutz *m*; **cover up** *vt* zudecken; *(error etc)* vertuschen; **coverage** *n* Berichterstattung *f* *(of* über + *acc*); **cover charge** *n* Kosten *pl* für ein Gedeck; **covering letter** *n*

Begleitbrief m; **cover story** n (newspaper) Titelgeschichte f

cow n Kuh f

coward n Feigling m; **cowardly** adj feig(e)

cowboy n Cowboy m

cozy adj (US) gemütlich

CPU n abbr = **central processing unit**; Zentraleinheit f

crab n Krabbe f

crabby adj mürrisch, reizbar

crack 1. n Riss m; (in pottery, glass) Sprung m; (drug) Crack nt; **have a ~ at sth** etw ausprobieren **2.** vi (pottery, glass) einen Sprung bekommen; (wood, ice etc) einen Riss bekommen; **get ~ing** fam loslegen **3.** vt (bone) anbrechen; (nut, code) knacken

cracker n (biscuit) Kräcker m; (Christmas cracker) Knallbonbon nt; **crackers** adj fam verrückt, bekloppt

crackle vi knistern; (telephone, radio) knacken; **crackling** n GASTR Kruste f (des Schweinebratens)

cradle n Wiege f

craft n Handwerk nt; (art) Kunsthandwerk nt; **craftsman** n Handwerker m

cram 1. vt stopfen (into in + acc); **be ~med with ...** mit ... voll gestopft sein **2.** vi (revise for exam) pauken (for für)

cramp n Krampf m

cranberry n Preiselbeere f

crane n (machine) Kran m; (bird) Kranich m

crap 1. n vulg Scheiße f; (rubbish) Mist m **2.** adj beschissen, Scheiß-

crash 1. vi einen Unfall haben; (two vehicles) zusammenstoßen; (plane, computer) abstürzen; (economy) zusammenbrechen; **~ into sth** gegen etw knallen **2.** vt einen Unfall haben mit **3.** n (car) Unfall m; (train) Unglück nt; (collision) Zusammenstoß m; AVIAT, IT Absturz m; (noise) Krachen nt; **crash barrier** n Leitplanke f; **crash course** n Intensivkurs m; **crash helmet** n Sturzhelm m

crate n Kiste f; (of beer) Kasten m

crater n Krater m

craving n starkes Verlangen, Bedürfnis nt

crawl 1. vi kriechen; (baby) krabbeln **2.** n (swimming) Kraul nt; **crawler lane** n Kriechspur f

crayfish n Languste f

crayon n Buntstift m

crazy adj verrückt (about nach)

cream 1. n (from milk) Sahne f, Rahm m; (polish, cosmetic) Creme f **2.** adj cremefarben; **cream cake** n (small) Sahnetörtchen nt; (big) Sahnetorte f; **cream cheese** n Frischkäse m; **creamer** n

Kaffeeweißer m; creamy adj sahnig

crease 1. n Falte f 2. vt falten; (untidy) zerknittern

create vt schaffen; (cause) verursachen; creative adj (person) kreativ; creature n Geschöpf nt

crèche n Kinderkrippe f

credible adj (person) glaubwürdig; credibility n Glaubwürdigkeit f

credit n FIN (amount allowed) Kredit m; (amount possessed) Guthaben nt; (recognition) Anerkennung f; ~s (of film) Abspann m; credit card n Kreditkarte f

creep vi kriechen; creeps n he gives me the ~ er ist mir nicht ganz geheuer; creepy adj (frightening) gruselig, unheimlich

crept pt, pp of creep

cress n Kresse f

crest n Kamm m; (coat of arms) Wappen nt

crew n Besatzung f, Mannschaft f

crib n (US) Kinderbett nt

cricket n (insect) Grille f; (game) Kricket nt

crime n Verbrechen nt; criminal 1. n Verbrecher(in) m(f) 2. adj kriminell, strafbar

crisis n Krise f

crisp adj knusprig; crisps npl (Brit) Chips pl; crispbread n Knäckebrot nt

criterion n Kriterium nt; crit-

ic n Kritiker(in) m(f); critical adj kritisch; critically adv kritisch; ~ ill/injured schwer krank / verletzt; criticism n Kritik f; criticize vt kritisieren

Croat n Kroate m, Kroatin f; Croatia n Kroatien nt; Croatian adj kroatisch

crockery n Geschirr nt

crocodile n Krokodil nt

crocus n Krokus m

crop n (harvest) Ernte f; crops npl Getreide nt

croquette n Krokette f

cross 1. n Kreuz nt; mark sth with a ~ etw ankreuzen 2. vt (road, river etc) überqueren; (legs) übereinander schlagen; it ~ed my mind es fiel mir ein; ~ one's fingers die Daumen drücken 3. adj ärgerlich, böse; cross out vt durchstreichen

crossbar n (of bicycle) Stange f; SPORT Querlatte f; cross-country adj ~ running Geländelauf m; ~ skiing Langlauf m; cross-eyed adj to be ~ schielen; crossing n (crossroads) (Straßen)kreuzung f; (for pedestrians) Fußgängerüberweg m; (on ship) Überfahrt f; crossroads nsing or pl Straßenkreuzung f; cross section n Querschnitt m; crosswalk n (US) Fußgängerüberweg m; crossword (puzzle) n Kreuzworträtsel nt

crouch vi hocken

crouton n Croûton m

crow n Krähe f

crowd 1. n Menge f 2. vi sich drängen (into in + acc; round um); **crowded** adj überfüllt

crown 1. n Krone f 2. vt krönen; **crown jewels** npl Kronjuwelen pl

crucial adj entscheidend

crude 1. adj primitiv; (humour, behaviour) derb, ordinär 2. n ~ (oil) Rohöl nt

cruel adj grausam (to zu, gegen); (unfeeling) gefühllos; **cruelty** n Grausamkeit f; ~ **to animals** Tierquälerei f

cruise 1. n Kreuzfahrt f 2. vi (ship) kreuzen; (car) mit Reisegeschwindigkeit fahren; **cruise liner** n Kreuzfahrtschiff nt; **cruise missile** n Marschflugkörper m

crumb n Krume f

crumble 1. vt, vi zerbröckeln 2. n mit Streuseln überbackenes Kompott

crumpet n weiches Hefegebäck zum Toasten (attractive woman) fam Schnecke f

crumple vt zerknittern; **crumple zone** n AUTO Knautschzone f

crunchy adj (Brit) knusprig

crusade n Kreuzzug m

crush 1. vt zerdrücken; (finger etc) quetschen; (spices, stone) zerstoßen 2. n **have a ~ on sb** in jdn verknallt sein; **crushing** adj (defeat, remark) vernichtend

crust n Kruste f; **crusty** adj knusprig

crutch n Krücke f

cry 1. vi (call) rufen; (scream) schreien; (weep) weinen 2. n (call) Ruf m; (louder) Schrei m

crypt n Krypta f

cu abbr = **see you**; (SMS, E-Mail) ≈ bis bald

cub n (animal) Junge(s) nt

Cuba n Kuba nt

cube n Würfel m

cubic adj Kubik-

cubicle n Kabine f

cuckoo n Kuckuck m

cucumber n Salatgurke f

cuddle 1. vt in den Arm nehmen; (amorously) schmusen mit 2. n Liebkosung f, Umarmung f; **have a ~** schmusen; **cuddly** adj verschmust; **cuddly toy** n Plüschtier nt

cuff n Manschette f; (US, trouser cuff) Aufschlag m; **cufflink** n Manschettenknopf m

cuisine n Kochkunst f, Küche f

cul-de-sac n (Brit) Sackgasse f

culprit n Schuldige(r) mf, Übeltäter(in) m(f)

cult n Kult m

cultivate vt AGR (land) bebauen; (crop) anbauen; **cultivated** adj (person) kultiviert, gebildet

cultural adj kulturell, Kultur-; **culture** n Kultur f; **cultured**

adj gebildet, kultiviert; **culture vulture** *fam* (*Brit*) *n* Kulturfanatiker(in) *m(f)*

cumbersome *adj* (*object*) unhandlich

cumin *n* Kreuzkümmel *m*

cunning 1. *adj* schlau; (*person a.*) gerissen

cup 1. Tasse *f*; (*prize*) Pokal *m*; *it's not his ~ of tea* das ist nicht sein Fall; **cupboard** *n* Schrank *m*; **cup final** *n* Pokalendspiel *nt*

curable *adj* heilbar

curb *n* (*US*) → **kerb**

curd *n* ~ **cheese, ~s** ≈ Quark *m*

cure 1. *n* Heilmittel *nt* (*for* gegen); (*process*) Heilung *f* **2.** *vt* heilen; GASTR (*salt*) pökeln; (*smoke*) räuchern

curious 1. *adj* neugierig; (*strange*) seltsam

curl 1. *n* Locke *f* **2.** *vi* sich kräuseln; **curly** *adj* lockig

currant *n* (*dried*) Korinthe *f*; (*red, black*) Johannisbeere *f*

currency *n* Währung *f*; **foreign ~** Devisen *pl*

current 1. *n* (*in water*) Strömung *f*; (*electric*) Strom *m* **2.** *adj* (*issue, affairs*) aktuell, gegenwärtig; (*expression*) gängig; **current account** *n* Girokonto *nt*; **currently** *adv* zur Zeit

curriculum *n* Lehrplan *m*; **curriculum vitae** *n* (*Brit*) Lebenslauf *m*

curry *n* Currygericht *nt*; **curry**

powder *n* Curry(pulver) *nt*

curse 1. *vi* (*swear*) fluchen (*at* auf + *acc*) **2.** *n* Fluch *m*

cursor *n* IT Cursor *m*

curtain *n* Vorhang *m*; *it was ~s for Benny* für Benny war alles vorbei

curve *n* Kurve *f*; **curved** *adj* gebogen

cushion *n* Kissen *nt*

custard *n* dicke Vanillesoße, die warm oder kalt zu vielen englischen Nachspeisen gegessen wird

custom 1. *n* Brauch *m*; (*habit*) Gewohnheit *f*; **customary** *adj* üblich; **custom-built** *adj* nach Kundenangaben gefertigt; **customer** *n* Kunde *m*, Kundin *f*; **customer loyalty card** *n* Kundenkarte *f*; **customer service** *n* Kundendienst *m*

customs *npl* (*organization, location*) Zoll *m*; *pass through ~* durch den Zoll gehen; **customs officer** *n* Zollbeamte(r) *m*, Zollbeamtin *f*

cut 1. *vt* schneiden; (*cake*) anschneiden; (*wages, benefits*) kürzen; (*prices*) heruntersetzen; *I ~ my finger* ich habe mir in den Finger geschnitten **2.** *n* Schnitt *m*; (*wound*) Schnittwunde *f*; (*reduction*) Kürzung *f* (*in gen*); *price/ tax ~* Preissenkung / Steuersenkung *f*; **cut back** *vt* (*workforce etc*) reduzieren;

cut down vt (*tree*) fällen; **~ on sth** etwas einschränken; **cut in** vi AUTO scharf einscheren; **cut off** vt abschneiden; (*gas, electricity*) abstellen; TEL **I was ~** ich wurde unterbrochen

cute adj putzig, niedlich; (*US, shrewd*) clever

cutlery n Besteck nt

cutlet n (*pork*) Kotelett n; (*veal*) Schnitzel nt

cut-price adj verbilligt

cutting 1. n (*from paper*) Ausschnitt m; (*of plant*) Ableger m 2. adj (*comment*) verletzend

CV abbr = **curriculum vitae**

cwt abbr = **hundredweight**; ≈ Zentner, Ztr.

cybercafé n Internetcafé nt;

cyberspace n Cyberspace m

cyclamen n Alpenveilchen nt

cycle 1. n Fahrrad nt 2. vi Rad fahren; **cycle lane, cycle path** n Radweg m; **cycling** n Radfahren nt; **cyclist** n Radfahrer(in) m(f)

cylinder n Zylinder m

cynical adj zynisch

cypress n Zypresse f

Cypriot 1. adj zypriotisch 2. n Zypriote m, Zypriotin f; **Cyprus** n Zypern nt

czar n Zar m; **czarina** n Zarin f

Czech 1. adj tschechisch 2. n (*person*) Tscheche m, Tschechin f; (*language*) Tschechisch nt; **Czech Republic** n Tschechische Republik, Tschechien nt

D

dab vt (*wound, nose etc*) betupfen (*with* mit)

dad(dy) n Papa m, Vati m; **daddy-longlegs** nsing (*Brit*) Schnake f; (*US*) Weberknecht m

daffodil n Osterglocke f

daft adj fam blöd, doof

daily 1. adj, adv täglich 2. n (*paper*) Tageszeitung f

dairy n (*on farm*) Molkerei f; **dairy products** npl Milchprodukte pl

daisy n Gänseblümchen nt

dam 1. n Staudamm m 2. vt

stauen

damage 1. n Schaden m; **~s** pl LAW Schadenersatz m 2. vt beschädigen; (*reputation, health*) schädigen, schaden + dat

damn 1. adj fam verdammt 2. vt (*condemn*) verurteilen; **~ (it)!** verflucht! 3. n **he doesn't give a ~** es ist ihm völlig egal

damp 1. adj feucht 2. n Feuchtigkeit f; **dampen** vt befeuchten

dance 1. n Tanz m; (*event*)

Tanzveranstaltung f **2.** vi tanzen; **dance floor** n Tanzfläche f; **dancer** n Tänzer(in) m(f); **dancing** n Tanzen nt

dandelion n Löwenzahn m

dandruff n Schuppen pl

Dane n Däne m, Dänin f

danger n Gefahr f; **be in ~** in Gefahr sein; **dangerous** adj gefährlich

Danish 1. adj dänisch **2.** n (language) Dänisch nt; **the ~ pl** die Dänen; **Danish pastry** n Plundergebäck nt

Danube n Donau f

dare vi **~ (to) do sth** es wagen, etw zu tun; **I didn't ~ ask** ich traute mich nicht, zu fragen; **how ~ you** was fällt dir ein!; **daring** adj (person) mutig; (film, clothes etc) gewagt

dark 1. adj dunkel; (gloomy) düster, trübe; (sinister) finster; **~ chocolate** Bitterschokolade f; **~ green/ blue** dunkelgrün/ dunkelblau **2.** n Dunkelheit f; **dark glasses** npl Sonnenbrille f; **darkness** n Dunkelheit nt

darling n Schatz m; (also favourite) Liebling m

dart n Wurfpfeil m; **darts** nsing (game) Darts nt

dash 1. vi stürzen, rennen **2.** vt **~ hopes** Hoffnungen zerstören **3.** n (in text) Gedankenstrich m; (of liquid) Schuss m; **dashboard** n Armaturenbrett nt

data npl Daten pl; **data bank,**

data base n Datenbank f; **data capture** n Datenerfassung f; **data processing** n Datenverarbeitung f; **data protection** n Datenschutz m

date 1. n Datum nt; (for meeting, delivery etc) Termin m; (with person) Verabredung f; (with girlfriend etc) Date nt; (fruit) Dattel f; **what's the ~ (today)?** der Wievielte ist heute?; **out of ~** adj veraltet; **up to ~** adj (news) aktuell; (fashion) zeitgemäß **2.** vt (letter etc) datieren; (person) gehen mit; **dated** adj altmodisch; **date of birth** n Geburtsdatum nt; **dating agency** n Partnervermittlung f

daughter n Tochter f; **daughter-in-law** n Schwiegertochter f

dawn 1. n Morgendämmerung f **2.** vi dämmern; **it ~ed on me** mir ging ein Licht auf

day n Tag m; **one ~** eines Tages; **by ~** bei Tage; **~ after ~, ~ by ~** Tag für Tag; **the ~ after/ before** am Tag danach/ zuvor; **the ~ before yesterday** vorgestern; **the ~ after tomorrow** übermorgen; **these ~s** heutzutage; **in those ~s** damals; **let's call it a ~** Schluss für heute!; **daydream 1.** n Tagtraum m **2.** vi (mit offenen Augen) träumen; **daylight** n Tageslicht nt; **daylight saving time**

Sommerzeit f; **day nursery** n Kindertagesstätte f; **day return** n (Brit) RAIL Tagesrückfahrkarte f; **daytrip** n Tagesausflug m

dazzle vt blenden

dead 1. adj ist; (limb) gestorben **2.** adv genau; fam total, völlig; ~ **tired** adj todmüde; ~ **slow** (sign) Schritt fahren; **dead end** n Sackgasse f; **deadline** n Termin m; (period) Frist f; ~ **for applications** Anmeldeschluss m; **deadly 1.** adj tödlich **2.** adv ~ **dull** todlangweilig

deaf adj taub; **deafen** vt taub machen; **deafening** adj ohrenbetäubend

deal 1. vt, vi (cards) geben, austeilen **2.** n (business ~) Geschäft nt; (agreement) Abmachung f; **it's a** ~ abgemacht!; **a good/great** ~ **of** ziemlich/sehr viel; **deal in** vt handeln mit; **deal with** vt (matter) sich beschäftigen mit; (book, film) behandeln; (successfully: person, problem) fertig werden mit; (matter) erledigen; **dealer** n COMM Händler(in) m(f); (drugs) Dealer(in) m(f)

dealt pt, pp of **deal**

dear 1. adj lieb, teuer; **Dear Sir or Madam** Sehr geehrte Damen und Herren; **Dear David** Lieber David **2.** n Schatz m; (as address) mein Schatz, Liebling; **dearly**

adv (love) (heiß und) innig; (pay) teuer

death n Tod m; (of project, hopes) Ende nt; ~**s** pl Todesfälle; (in accident) Todesopfer; **death certificate** n Totenschein m; **death penalty** n Todesstrafe f; **death toll** n Zahl f der Todesopfer

debatable adj fraglich; (question) strittig; **debate 1.** n Debatte f **2.** vt debattieren

debit 1. n Soll nt **2.** vt (account) belasten; **debit card** n Geldkarte f

debris n Trümmer pl

debt n Schuld f; **be in** ~ verschuldet sein

decade n Jahrzehnt nt

decaff n fam koffeinfreier Kaffee; **decaffeinated** adj koffeinfrei

decanter n Dekanter m, Karaffe f

decay 1. n Verfall m; (rotting) Verwesung f; (of tooth) Fäule f **2.** vi verfallen; (rot) verwesen; (wood) vermodern; (teeth) faulen; (leaves) verrotten

deceased n **the** ~ der/die Verstorbene

deceive vt täuschen

December n Dezember m; → **September**

decent adj anständig

decide 1. vt (question) entscheiden; (body of people) beschließen; **I can't** ~ **what to do** ich kann mich nicht entscheiden, was ich tun soll **2.** *vi* sich entscheiden; **~ on sth** (*in favour of sth*) sich für etw entscheiden; sich zu etw entschließen; **decided** *adj* entschieden; (*clear*) deutlich; **decidedly** *adv* entschieden

decimal *adj* Dezimal-; **decimal system** *n* Dezimalsystem *nt*

decipher *vt* entziffern

decision *n* Entscheidung *f* (*on über + acc*); (*of committee, jury etc*) Beschluss *m*; **make a ~** eine Entscheidung treffen; **decisive** *adj* entscheidend; (*person*) entscheidungsfreudig

deck *n* NAUT Deck *nt*; (*of cards*) Blatt *nt*; **deckchair** *n* Liegestuhl *m*

declaration *n* Erklärung *f*; **declare** *vt* erklären; (*state*) behaupten (*that* dass); (*at customs*) **have you anything to ~?** haben Sie etwas zu verzollen?

decline 1. *n* Rückgang *m* **2.** *vt* (*invitation, offer*) ablehnen **3.** *vi* (*become less*) sinken, abnehmen; (*health*) sich verschlechtern

decode *vt* entschlüsseln

decorate *vt* (aus)schmücken; (*wallpaper*) tapezieren; (*paint*) anstreichen; **decoration** *n* (*process*) Schmücken *nt*; (*wallpapering*) Tapezieren *nt*; (*paint-ing*) Anstreichen *nt*; **Christmas ~s** Weihnachtsschmuck *m*; **decorator** *n* Maler(in) *m(f)*

decrease 1. *n* Abnahme *f* **2.** *vi* abnehmen

dedicate *vt* widmen (*to sb* jdm); **dedicated** *adj* (*person*) engagiert; **dedication** *n* Widmung *f*; (*commitment*) Hingabe *f*, Engagement *nt*

deduce *vt* folgern, schließen (*from* aus, *that* dass)

deduct *vt* abziehen (*from* von); **deduction** *n* (*of money*) Abzug *m*; (*conclusion*) (Schluss)folgerung *f*

deed *n* Tat *f*

deep *adj* tief; **deepen** *vt* vertiefen; **deep-freeze** *n* Tiefkühltruhe *f*; (*upright*) Gefrierschrank *m*; **deep-fry** *vt* frittieren

deer *n* Reh *nt*; (*with stag*) Hirsch *m*

defeat 1. *n* Niederlage *f*; **admit ~** sich geschlagen geben **2.** *vt* besiegen

defect *n* Defekt *m*, Fehler *m*; **defective** *adj* fehlerhaft

defence *n* Verteidigung *f*; **defend** *vt* verteidigen; **defendant** *n* LAW Angeklagte(r) *mf*; **defender** *n* SPORT Verteidiger(in) *m(f)*; **defensive** *adj* defensiv

deficiency *n* Mangel *m*; **deficit** *n* Defizit *nt*

define *vt* (*word*) definieren; (*duties, powers*) bestimmen

definite adj (clear) klar, eindeutig; (certain) sicher; **it's** ~ es steht fest; **definitely** adv bestimmt; (in Definition) Definition f; PHOT Schärfe f

deflate vt die Luft ablassen aus

defrost vt (fridge) abtauen; (food) auftauen

degree n Grad m; (at university) akademischer Grad; **to a certain** ~ einigermaßen; **I have a** ~ **in chemistry** ≈ ich habe Chemie studiert

dehydrated adj (food) getrocknet, Trocken-; (person) ausgetrocknet

de-ice vt enteisen

delay 1. vt (postpone) verschieben, aufschieben; **be** ~**ed** (event) sich verzögern; **the train/flight was** ~**ed** der Zug/die Maschine hatte Verspätung **2.** vi warten; (hesitate) zögern **3.** n Verzögerung f; (of train etc) Verspätung f; **without** ~ unverzüglich; **delayed** adj (train etc) verspätet

delegation n Abordnung f; (foreign) Delegation f

delete vt (aus)streichen; IT löschen; **deletion** n Streichung f; IT Löschung f

deli n fam Feinkostgeschäft nt

deliberate adj (intentional) absichtlich; **deliberately** adv mit Absicht, extra

delicate adj (fine) fein; (fragile) zart; a. MED empfindlich;

(situation) heikel

delicatessen nsing Feinkostgeschäft nt

delicious adj köstlich, lecker

delight n Freude f; **delighted** adj sehr erfreut (with über + acc); **delightful** adj entzückend; (weather, meal etc) herrlich

deliver vt (goods) liefern (to sb jdm); (letter, parcel) zustellen; (speech) halten; (baby) entbinden; **delivery** n Lieferung f; (of letter, parcel) Zustellung f; (of baby) Entbindung f; **delivery van** n Lieferwagen m

delude vt täuschen; **don't** ~ **yourself** mach dir nichts vor; **delusion** n Irrglaube m

de luxe adj Luxus-

demand 1. vt verlangen (from von); (time, patience etc) erfordern **2.** n (request) Forderung f, Verlangen nt (for nach); COMM (for goods) Nachfrage f; **on** ~ auf Wunsch; **very much in** ~ sehr gefragt; **demanding** adj anspruchsvoll

demerara n ~ (sugar) brauner Zucker

demister n Defroster m

demo n fam Demo f

democracy n Demokratie f; **democrat** n Demokrat, Democrat (US) POL Demokrat(in) m(f); **democratic** adj demokratisch; **the Democratic Party** (US) POL die Demokratische

Partei

demolish vt abreißen; fig zerstören

demonstrate vt, vi demonstrieren, beweisen; **demonstration** n Demonstration f

denationalization n Privatisierung f

denial n Leugnung f; (official ~) Dementi nt

denim n Jeansstoff m; **denim jacket** n Jeansjacke f; **denims** npl Bluejeans pl

Denmark n Dänemark nt

denomination n REL Konfession f; COMM Nennwert m

dense adj dicht; fam (stupid) schwer von Begriff; **density** n Dichte f

dent 1. n Beule f, Delle f **2.** vt einbeulen

dental adj Zahn-; ~ **care** Zahnpflege f; ~ **floss** Zahnseide f; **dentist** n Zahnarzt m, Zahnärztin f; **dentures** npl Zahnprothese f; (full) Gebiss nt

deny vt leugnen, bestreiten; (refuse) ablehnen

deodorant n Deo(dorant) nt; ~ **spray** Deospray nt or m

depart vi abreisen; (bus, train) abfahren (for nach, from von); (plane) abfliegen (for nach, from von)

department n Abteilung f; (at university) Institut nt; POL (ministry) Ministerium nt; **department store** n Kaufhaus nt

departure n (of person) Weggang m; (on journey) Abreise f (for nach); (of train etc) Abfahrt f (for nach); (of plane) Abflug m (for nach); **departure lounge** n AVIAT Abflughalle f; **departure time** n AVIAT Abflugzeit f

depend vi it ~s es kommt darauf an (whether, ob); **depend on** vt (thing) abhängen von; (person: rely on) sich verlassen auf + acc; (person, area etc) angewiesen sein auf + acc; it ~s on the weather es kommt auf das Wetter an; **dependable** adj zuverlässig; **dependent** adj abhängig (on von)

deplorable adj bedauerlich

deport vt ausweisen, abschieben; **deportation** n Abschiebung f

deposit 1. n (down payment) Anzahlung f; (security) Kaution f; (for bottle) Pfand nt; (to bank account) Einzahlung f; (in river etc) Ablagerung f **2.** vt (put down) abstellen, absetzen; (to bank account) einzahlen; (sth valuable) deponieren; **deposit account** n Sparkonto nt

depot n Depot nt

depress vt (in mood) deprimieren; **depressed** adj (person) niedergeschlagen, deprimiert; ~ **area** Notstandsgebiet nt; **depressing** adj deprimierend; **depression** n (mood) Depression f; METEO Tief nt

deprive vt ~ **sb of sth** jdn einer Sache berauben; **deprived** adj (child) (sozial) benachteiligt

dept abbr = **department**; Abt.

depth n Tiefe f

deputy 1. adj stellvertretend, Vize-; ~ **Stellvertreter(in)** m(f); (US) POL Abgeordnete(r) mf

derail vt entgleisen lassen; **be ~ed** entgleisen

dermatitis n Hautentzündung f

derogatory adj abfällig

descend vt, vi hinabsteigen, hinuntergehen; (person) ~ or **be ~ed from** abstammen von; **descendant** n Nachkomme m; **descent** n (coming down) Abstieg m; (origin) Abstammung f

describe vt beschreiben; **description** n Beschreibung f

desert 1. n Wüste f **2.** vt verlassen; (abandon) im Stich lassen; **deserted** adj verlassen; (empty) menschenleer

deserve vt verdienen

design 1. n (plan) Entwurf m; (of vehicle, machine) Konstruktion f; (of object) Design nt; (planning) Gestaltung f **2.** vt entwerfen; (machine etc) konstruieren; **~ed for sb/sth** (intended) für jdn/ etw konzipiert; **designer** n

Designer(in) m(f); TECH Konstrukteur(in) m(f); **designer drug** n Designerdroge f

desirable n wünschenswert; (person) begehrenswert; **desire 1.** n Wunsch m (for nach); (esp sexual) Begierde f (for nach) **2.** vt wünschen; (ask for) verlangen; **if ~d** auf Wunsch

desk n Schreibtisch m; (reception ~) Empfang m; (at airport etc) Schalter m; **desktop publishing** n Desktoppublishing nt

despair 1. n Verzweiflung f (at über + acc) **2.** vi verzweifeln (of an + dat)

despatch → dispatch

desperate adj verzweifelt; (situation) hoffnungslos; **be ~ for sth** etw dringend brauchen, unbedingt wollen; **desperation** n Verzweiflung f

despicable adj verachtenswert; **despise** vt verachten

despite prep trotz + gen

dessert n Nachtisch m; **dessertspoon** n Dessertlöffel m

destination n (of person) (Reise)ziel nt; (of goods) Bestimmungsort m; **destine** vt **we're ~d for Hull** wir sind auf dem Weg nach Hull; **destiny** n Schicksal nt

destroy vt zerstören; (completely) vernichten; **destruction** n Zerstörung f; (complete) Vernichtung f; **de-structive** adj zerstörerisch, destruktiv

detach vt abnehmen; (from form etc) abtrennen; (free) lösen (from von); **detachable** adj abnehmbar; (from form etc) abtrennbar; **detached** adj (attitude) distanziert, objektiv; **~ house** Einzelhaus nt

detail (US) n Einzelheit f, Detail nt; **(further) ~s from ...** Näheres erfahren Sie bei ...; **go into ~** ins Detail gehen; **in ~** ausführlich; **detailed** adj detailliert, ausführlich

detain vt aufhalten; (police) in Haft nehmen

detect vt entdecken; (notice) wahrnehmen; **detective** n Detektiv(in) m(f); **detective story** n Detektivroman m, Krimi m

detergent n Reinigungsmittel nt; (soap powder) Waschmittel nt

deteriorate vi sich verschlechtern

determination n Entschlossenheit f; **determine** vt bestimmen; **determined** adj (fest) entschlossen

detest vt verabscheuen; **detestable** adj abscheulich

detour n Umweg m; (of traffic) Umleitung f

deuce n TENNIS Einstand m

devastate vt verwüsten; **devastating** adj verheerend

develop 1. vt entwickeln; (illness) bekommen **2.** vi sich entwickeln; **developing country** n Entwicklungsland nt; **development** n Entwicklung f; (of land) Erschließung f

device n Vorrichtung f, Gerät nt

devil n Teufel m

devoted adj liebend; (servant etc) treu ergeben; **devotion** n Hingabe f

devour vt verschlingen

dew n Tau m

diabetes n Diabetes m, Zuckerkrankheit f; **diabetic 1.** adj zuckerkrank, für Diabetiker **2.** n Diabetiker(in) m(f)

diagnosis n Diagnose f

diagonal adj diagonal

diagram n Diagramm nt

dial 1. n Skala f; (of clock) Zifferblatt nt **2.** vt TEL wählen; **dial code** n (US) Vorwahl f

dialect n Dialekt m

dialling code n (Brit) Vorwahl f; **dialling tone** n (Brit) Amtszeichen nt

dialogue, dialog (US) n Dialog m

dial tone n (US) Amtszeichen nt

dialysis n MED Dialyse f

diameter n Durchmesser m

diamond n Diamant m, Karo nt

diaper n (US) Windel f

diarrhoea n Durchfall m

diary n (Taschen)kalender m; (account) Tagebuch nt

dice npl Würfel pl

dictation n Diktat nt

dictator n Diktator(in) m(f);
dictatorship n Diktatur f

dictionary n Wörterbuch nt

did pt of **do**

didn't contr of **did not**

die vi sterben (of an + dat); (plant, animal) eingehen; (engine) absterben; **be dying to do sth** darauf brennen, etw zu tun; **I'm dying for a drink** ich brauche unbedingt was zu trinken; **die away** vi schwächer werden; (wind) sich legen; **die down** vi nachlassen; **die out** vi aussterben

diesel n (fuel, car) Diesel m

diet n. 1 Kost f; (special food) Diät f 2. vi eine Diät machen

differ vi (be different) sich unterscheiden; (disagree) anderer Meinung sein; **difference** n Unterschied m; **it makes no ~ (to me)** es ist (mir) egal; **it makes a big ~** es macht viel aus; **different** adj andere(r, s); (with pl) verschieden; **be quite ~** ganz anders sein (from als); (two people, things) völlig verschieden sein; **differentiate** vt, vi unterscheiden; **differently** adv anders (from als); (from one another) unterschiedlich

difficult adj schwierig; **I find it ~** es fällt mir schwer; **difficulty** n Schwierigkeit f

dig vt, vi (hole) graben; **dig in** vi fam (to food) reinhauen; **~!** greif(t) zu!; **dig up** vt ausgraben

digest vt verdauen; **digestion** n Verdauung f; **digestive** adj **~ biscuit** (Brit) Vollkornkeks m

digit n Ziffer f; **digital** adj digital; **digital camera** n Digitalkamera f

dignified adj würdevoll; **dignity** n Würde f

dilapidated adj baufällig

dill n Dill m

dilute vt verdünnen

dim 1. adj (light) schwach; (outline) undeutlich; (stupid) schwer von Begriff **2.** vt verdunkeln; (US) AUTO abblenden; **~med headlights** (US) Abblendlicht nt

dimen (US) Zehncentstück nt

dimension n Dimension f; **~s** pl Maße pl

diminish 1. vt verringern **2.** vi sich verringern

dimple n Grübchen nt

dine vi speisen; **dine out** vi außer Haus essen; **diner** n Gast m; RAIL Speisewagen m; (US) Speiselokal nt

dinghy n Ding(h)i nt; (inflatable) Schlauchboot nt

dining car n Speisewagen m; **dining room** n Esszimmer nt; (in hotel) Speiseraum m

dinner n Abendessen nt; (lunch) Mittagessen nt;

(*public*) Diner *nt*; **be at ~** beim Essen sein; **have ~** zu Abend/Mittag essen; **dinner jacket** *n* Smoking *m*; **dinnertime** *n* Essenszeit *f*

dinosaur *n* Dinosaurier *m*

dip 1. *vt* tauchen (*in* in + *acc*); ~ **(one's headlights)** (*Brit*) AUTO abblenden; ~**ped headlights** Abblendlicht *nt* **2.** *n* (*in ground*) Bodensenke *f*; (*sauce*) Dip *m*

diploma *n* Diplom *nt*

diplomatic *adj* diplomatisch

dipstick *n* Ölmessstab *m*

direct 1. *adj* direkt; (*cause, consequence*) unmittelbar; ~ **debit** (*mandate*) Einzugsermächtigung *f*; ~ **train** durchgehender Zug **2.** *vt* (*aim, send*) richten (*at, to* an + *acc*); (*film*) die Regie führen bei; (*traffic*) regeln; **direct current** *n* ELEC Gleichstrom *m*

direction *n* (*course*) Richtung *f*; FILM Regie *f*; **in the ~ of ...** in Richtung ...; ~**s** *pl* **for use** Gebrauchsanweisung *f*; ~**s** *pl* (*to a place*) Wegbeschreibung *f*

directly *adv* direkt; (*at once*) sofort

director *n* Direktor(in) *m(f)*, Leiter(in) *m(f)*; (*of film*) Regisseur(in) *m(f)*

directory *n* Adressbuch *nt*, Telefonbuch *nt*; ~ **enquiries** or (*US*) **assistance** TEL Auskunft *f*

dirt *n* Schmutz *m*, Dreck *m*; **dirt cheap** *adj* spottbillig; **dirty** *adj* schmutzig

disability *n* Behinderung *f*; **disabled 1.** *adj* behindert, Behinderten- **2.** *npl* **the ~** die Behinderten

disadvantage *n* Nachteil *m*; **at a ~** benachteiligt; **disadvantageous** *adj* nachteilig, ungünstig

disagree *vi* anderer Meinung sein; (*two people*) sich nicht einig sein; (*two reports*) nicht übereinstimmen; **disagreeable** *adj* unangenehm; (*person*) unsympathisch; **disagreement** *n* Meinungsverschiedenheit *f*

disappear *vi* verschwinden

disappoint *vt* enttäuschen; **disappointing** *adj* enttäuschend; **disappointment** *n* Enttäuschung *f*

disapprove *vi* missbilligen (*of* acc)

disarm 1. *vt* entwaffnen **2.** *vi* POL abrüsten; **disarmament** *n* Abrüstung *f*; **disarming** *adj* (*smile, look*) gewinnend

disaster *n* Katastrophe *f*; **disastrous** *adj* katastrophal

disbelief *n* Ungläubigkeit *f*

disc *n* Scheibe *f*, CD *f*; → **disk** ANAT Bandscheibe *f*

discharge 1. *n* MED Ausfluss *m* **2.** *vt* (*person*) entlassen; (*emit*) ausstoßen; MED ausscheiden

discipline *n* Disziplin *f*

disc jockey n Diskjockey m

disclose vt bekannt geben; (secret) enthüllen

disco n Disko f, Diskomusik f

discomfort n (slight pain) leichte Schmerzen pl; (unease) Unbehagen nt

disconnect vt (electricity, gas, phone) abstellen; (unplug) ~ the TV (from the mains) den Stecker des Fernsehers herausziehen; TEL **I've been ~ed** das Gespräch ist unterbrochen worden

discontinue vt einstellen; (product) auslaufen lassen

discotheque n Diskothek f

discount n Rabatt m

discover vt entdecken; discovery n Entdeckung f

discredit 1. vt in Verruf bringen 2. n Misskredit m

discreet adj diskret

discrepancy n Unstimmigkeit f, Diskrepanz f

discriminate v unterscheiden; ~ against sb jdn diskriminieren; discrimination n (different treatment) Diskriminierung f

discus n Diskus m

discuss vt diskutieren, besprechen; discussion n Diskussion f

disease n Krankheit f

disembark vi von Bord gehen

disgrace 1. n Schande f 2. vt Schande machen + dat; (family etc) Schande bringen über + acc; (less strong) bla-

mieren; disgraceful adj skandalös; **it's ~** es ist eine Schande

disguise 1. vt verkleiden; (voice) verstellen 2. n Verkleidung f

disgust 1. n Abscheu m; (physical) Ekel m 2. vt anekeln, anwidern; disgusting adj widerlich; (physically) ekelhaft

dish n Schüssel f; (food) Gericht nt; (crockery) Geschirr nt; **~es** pl do/wash the **~es** abwaschen; dishcloth n (for washing) Spültuch nt; (for drying) Geschirrtuch nt

dishearten vt entmutigen; **don't be ~ed** lass den Kopf nicht hängen!

dishonest adj unehrlich

dish towel n (US) Geschirrtuch nt; dish washer n Geschirrspülmaschine f

dishy adj (Brit) fam klasse, attraktiv

disillusioned adj desillusioniert

disinfect vt desinfizieren; disinfectant n Desinfektionsmittel nt

disk n IT (floppy) Diskette f; disk drive n Diskettenlaufwerk nt; diskette n Diskette f

dislike 1. n Abneigung f 2. vt nicht mögen; ~ doing sth etw ungern tun

dislocate vt MED verrenken, f

distinguish

ausrenken
dismal *adj* trostlos
dismantle *vt* auseinander
nehmen; *(machine)* demon-
tieren
dismay *n* Bestürzung *f*; **dismayed** *adj* bestürzt
dismiss *vt (employee)* entlassen; **dismissal** *n* Entlassung
f
disobedience *n* Ungehorsam
m; **disobedient** *adj* ungehorsam; **disobey** *vt* nicht gehorchen + *dat*
disorder *n (mess)* Unordnung
f; *(riot)* Aufruhr *m*; MED Störung *f*, Leiden *nt*
disorganized *adj* chaotisch
disparaging *adj* geringschät-
zig
dispatch *vt* abschicken, aber-
tigen
dispensable *adj* entbehrlich;
dispense *vt* verteilen; **dispense with** *vt* verzichten
auf + *acc*; **dispenser** *n* Automat *m*
disperse *vi* sich zerstreuen
display 1. *n (exhibition)* Ausstellung *f*, Show *f*; *(of goods)*
Auslage *f*, TECH Anzeige *f*,
Display *nt* 2. *vt* zeigen;
(goods) ausstellen
disposable *adj (container, razor etc)* Wegwerf-; **~ nappy**
Wegwerfwindel *f*; **disposal**
n Loswerden *nt*; *(of waste)*
Beseitigung *f*; **be at sb's ~**
jdm zur Verfügung stehen;
dispose of *vt* loswerden;

(waste etc) beseitigen
dispute 1. *n* Streit *m*; *(industrial)* Auseinandersetzung *f*
2. *vt* bestreiten
disqualification *n* Disqualifi-
kation *f*; **disqualify** *vt* disqualifizieren
disregard *vt* nicht beachten
disreputable *adj* verrufen
disrespect *n* Respektlosig-
keit *f*
disrupt *vt* stören; *(interrupt)*
unterbrechen; **disruption** *n*
Störung *f*; *(interruption)* Unterbrechung *f*
dissatisfied *adj* unzufrieden
dissent *n* Widerspruch *m*
dissolve 1. *vt* auflösen 2. *vi*
sich auflösen
dissuade *vt (davon abbringen)* **~ sb from doing sth**
jdn davon abbringen, etw
zu tun
distance *n* Entfernung *f*; **in
the/ from a ~** in/ aus der Ferne; **distant** *adj (a. in time)*
fern; *(relative etc)* entfernt;
(person) distanziert
distaste *n* Abneigung *f (for
gegen)*
distil *vt* destillieren; **distillery**
n Brennerei *f*
distinct *adj* verschieden;
(clear) klar, deutlich; **dis-
tinction** *n (difference)* Unterschied *m*; *(in exam etc)*
Auszeichnung *f*; **distinctive**
adj unverkennbar; **distinctly**
adv deutlich
distinguish *vt* unterscheiden

(*sth from sth* etw von etw)

distort *vt* verzerren; (*truth*) verdrehen

distract *vt* ablenken; **distraction** *n* Ablenkung *f*; (*diversion*) Zerstreuung *f*

distress 1. *n* (*need, danger*) Not *f*; (*suffering*) Leiden *nt*; (*mental*) Qual *f*; (*worry*) Kummer *m* 2. *vt* mitnehmen, erschüttern; **distressed area** *n* Notstandsgebiet *nt*

distribute *vt* verteilen; COMM (*goods*) vertreiben; **distribution** *n* Verteilung *f*; COMM (*of goods*) Vertrieb *m*; **distributor** *n* AUTO Verteiler *m*; COMM Händler(in) *m(f)*

district *n* Gegend *f*; (*administrative*) Bezirk *m*; **district attorney** *n* (*US*) Staatsanwalt *m*, Staatsanwältin *f*

distrust 1. *vt* misstrauen + *dat* 2. *n* Misstrauen *nt*

disturb *vt* stören; (*worry*) beunruhigen; **disturbance** *n* Störung *f*; **disturbing** *adj* beunruhigend

ditch 1. *n* Graben *m* 2. *vt fam* (*person*) den Laufpass geben + *dat*; (*plan etc*) verwerfen

ditto *n* dito, ebenfalls

dive 1. *n* (*into water*) Kopfsprung *m*; AVIAT Sturzflug *m*; *fam* zwielichtiges Lokal 2. *vi* (*under water*) tauchen; **diver** *n* Taucher(in) *m(f)*

diverse *adj* verschieden; **diversion** *n* (*of traffic*) Umleitung *f*; (*distraction*) Ablen-

kung *f*; **divert** *vt* ablenken; (*traffic*) umleiten

divide 1. *vt* teilen; (*in several parts, between people*) aufteilen 2. *vi* sich teilen; **dividend** *n* Dividende *f*

divine *adj* göttlich

diving *n* (Sport)tauchen *nt*; (*jumping in*) Springen *nt*; SPORT (*from board*) Kunstspringen *nt*; **diving board** *n* Sprungbrett *nt*; **diving goggles** *npl* Taucherbrille *f*; **diving mask** *n* Tauchmaske *f*

division *n* Teilung *f*; MATH Division *f*; (*department*) Abteilung *f*; SPORT Liga *f*

divorce *n* Scheidung *f* 2. *vt* sich scheiden lassen von; **divorced** *adj* geschieden; **get~** sich scheiden lassen; **divorcee** *n* Geschiedene(r) *mf*

DIY *abbr* = **do-it-yourself**; **DIY centre** *n* Baumarkt *m*

dizzy *adj* schwindlig

DJ 1. *abbr* = **disc jockey**; Diskjockey *m*, DJ *m* 2. *abbr* = **dinner jacket**; Smoking *m*

do 1. *v aux* (*in negatives*) **I don't know** ich weiß es nicht; **he didn't come** er ist nicht gekommen; (*in questions*) **does she swim?** schwimmt sie?; (*for emphasis*) **he does like talking** er redet sehr gern; (*replacing verb*) **they drink more than we do** sie trinken mehr als wir; **please don't!** bitte tun Sie/du das nicht!; (*in ques-

tion tags) **you know him, don't you?** du kennst ihn doch, oder? **2.** *vt* tun, machen; (*clean: room etc*) saubermachen; (*study*) studieren; AUTO (*speed*) fahren; (*distance*) zurücklegen; **she has nothing to ~** sie hat nichts zu tun; **~ the dishes** abwaschen; **you can't ~ Cambridge in a day** Cambridge kann man nicht an einem Tag besichtigen **3.** *vi* (*get on*) vorankommen; (*be enough*) reichen; **~ well/ badly** gut/schlecht vorankommen; (*in exam etc*) gut/schlecht abschneiden; **how are you doing?** wie geht's denn so?; **that (much) should ~** das dürfte reichen **4.** *n* (*party*) Party *f*; **do away with** *vt* abschaffen; **do up** *vt* (*fasten*) zumachen; (*parcel*) verschnüren; (*renovate*) wieder herrichten; **do with** *vt* (*need*) brauchen; **I could ~ a drink** ich könnte einen Drink gebrauchen; **do without** *vt* auskommen ohne; **I can ~ your comments** auf deine Kommentare kann ich verzichten

dock *n* Dock *nt*; LAW Anklagebank *f*; **dockyard** *n* Werft *f*

doctor *n* Arzt *m*, Ärztin *f*; (*in title, also academic*) Doktor *m*

document *n* Dokument *nt*;

documentary *n* Dokumentarfilm *m*; **documentation** *n* Dokumentation *f*

docusoap *n* Reality-Serie *f*, Dokusoap *f*

dodgy *adj* nicht ganz in Ordnung; (*dishonest, unreliable*) zwielichtig; **he has a ~ stomach** er hat sich den Magen verdorben

dog *n* Hund *m*; **doggie** *n* Tüte oder Box *f*, in der Essensreste aus dem Restaurant mit nach Hause genommen werden können

do-it-yourself 1. *n* Heimwerken *nt*, Do-it-yourself *nt* **2.** *adj* Heimwerker-; **do-it-yourselfer** *n* Bastler(in) *m(f)*, Heimwerker(in) *m(f)*

doll *n* Puppe *f*

dollar *n* Dollar *m*

dolphin *n* Delphin *m*

domain *n* Domäne *f*; IT Domain *f*

dome *n* Kuppel *f*

domestic *adj* häuslich; (*within country*) Innen-, Binnen-; **domesticated** *adj* (*person*) häuslich; (*animal*) zahm; **domestic flight** *n* Inlandsflug *m*

domicile *n* (ständiger) Wohnsitz

dominant *adj* dominierend, vorherrschend

dominoes *npl* Domino(spiel) *nt*

donate *vt* spenden; **donation** *n* Spende *f*

done 1. pp of **do 2.** adj (cooked) gar; **well ~** durchgebraten

döner (kebab) n Döner (Kebab) m

donkey n Esel m

donor n Spender(in) m(f)

don't contr of **do not**

door n Tür f; **doorbell** n Türklingel f; **door handle** n Türklinke f; **doorknob** n Türknauf m; **doormat** n Fußabtreter m; **doorstep** n Türstufe f; **right on our ~** direkt vor unserer Haustür

dope SPORT **1.** n (for athlete) Aufputschmittel nt **2.** vt dopen; **dopey** adj fam bekloppt; (from drugs) benebelt; (sleepy) benommen

dormitory n Schlafsaal m; (US) Studentenwohnheim nt

dosage n Dosierung f; **dose 1.** n Dosis f **2.** vt dosieren

dot n Punkt m; **on the ~** auf die Minute genau

double 1. adj, adv doppelt; **~ the quantity** die zweifache Menge, doppelt so viel **2.** vt verdoppeln **3.** n (person) Doppelgänger(in) m(f); FILM Double nt; **double bass** n Kontrabass m; **double bed** n Doppelbett nt; **double-click** vt IT doppelklicken; **double cream** n Sahne mit hohem Fettgehalt; **double-decker** n Doppeldecker m; **double glazing** n Doppelverglasung f; **double-park**

vi in zweiter Reihe parken; **double room** n Doppelzimmer nt; **doubles** npl SPORT (also match) Doppel nt

doubt 1. n Zweifel m; **no ~** ohne Zweifel, zweifellos, wahrscheinlich; **have one's ~s** Bedenken haben **2.** vt bezweifeln; (statement, word) anzweifeln; **I~ it** das bezweifle ich; **doubtful** adj zweifelhaft, zweifelnd; **it is ~ whether ...** es ist fraglich, ob ...; **doubtless** adv ohne Zweifel, sicherlich

dough n Teig m; **doughnut** n Donut m (rundes Hefegebäck)

dove n Taube f

down 1. n Daunen pl; (fluff) Flaum m **2.** adv unten; (motion) nach unten; (towards speaker) herunter; (away from speaker) hinunter; **~ here/ there** hier/dort unten; (downstairs) **they came ~ for breakfast** sie kamen zum Frühstück herunter **3.** prep (towards speaker) herunter; (away from speaker) hinunter; **drive ~ the hill/ road** den Berg/ die Straße hinunterfahren; (along) **walk ~ the street** die Straße entlang gehen; **he's ~ the pub** fam er ist in der Kneipe **4.** vt fam (drink) runterkippen **5.** adj niedergeschlagen, deprimiert

downcast adj niedergeschla-

dreamt

gen; **downfall** n Sturz m;
down-hearted adj entmutigt; **downhill** adv bergab
download vt downloaden, herunterladen; **down payment** n Anzahlung f; **downs** npl Hügelland nt; **downsize 1.** vt (business) verkleinern **2.** vi sich verkleinern

Down's syndrome n MED Downsyndrom nt

downstairs adv unten; (motion) nach unten; **downstream** adv flussabwärts; **downtown** adv (be, work etc) in der Innenstadt; (go) in die Innenstadt **2.** adj (US) in der Innenstadt; **~ Chicago** die Innenstadt von Chicago; **down under** adv fam (in/to Australia) in/nach Australien; (in/to New Zealand) in/nach Neuseeland; **downwards** adv, adj nach unten; (movement, trend) Abwärts-
doze 1. vi dösen **2.** n Nickerchen nt
dozen n Dutzend nt
DP abbr = **data processing**; DV f
draft n (outline) Entwurf m; (US) MIL Einberufung f
drag 1. vt schleppen **2.** n fam **be a ~** (boring) stinklangweilig sein; (laborious) ein ziemlicher Schlauch sein; **drag on** vi sich in die Länge ziehen
dragon n Drache m; **dragon-**

fly n Libelle f
drain 1. n Abfluss m **2.** vt (water, oil) ablassen; (vegetables etc) abgießen; (land) entwässern, trockenlegen **3.** vi (of water) abfließen; **drainpipe** n Abflussrohr nt
drama n Drama nt; **dramatic** adj dramatisch
drank pt of **drink**
drapes npl (US) Vorhänge pl
drastic adj drastisch
draught n (Luft)zug m; **there's a ~** es zieht; (beer) vom Fass; **draughts** nsing Damespiel nt; **draughty** adj zugig
draw 1. vt (pull) ziehen; (crowd) anlocken, anziehen; (picture) zeichnen **2.** vi SPORT unentschieden spielen **3.** n SPORT Unentschieden nt; (attraction) Attraktion f; (for lottery) Ziehung f; **draw out** vt herausziehen; (money) abheben; **draw up 1.** vt (formulate) entwerfen; (list) erstellen **2.** vi (car) anhalten; **drawback** n Nachteil m
drawer n Schublade f
drawing n Zeichnung f; **drawing pin** n Reißzwecke f
drawn pp of **draw**
dread 1. n Furcht f (of vor + dat) **2.** vt sich fürchten vor + dat; **dreadful** adj furchtbar; **dreadlocks** npl Rastalocken pl
dream 1. vt, vi träumen (about von) **2.** n Traum m; **dreamt**

pt, pp of **dream**

dreary *adj (weather, place)* trostlos; *(book etc)* langweilig

drench *vt* durchnässen

dress 1. *n* Kleidung *f; (garment)* Kleid *nt* **2.** *vt* anziehen; MED *(wound)* verbinden; **get ~ed** sich anziehen; **dress up** vi sich fein machen; *(in costume)* sich verkleiden (**as** als); **dress circle** *n* THEAT erster Rang; **dresser** *n* Anrichte *f; (US, dressing table)* (Frisier)kommode *f*; **dressing** *n* GASTR Dressing *nt*, Soße *f*; MED Verband *m*; **dressing gown** *n* Morgenmantel *m*; **dressing room** *n* SPORT Umkleideraum *m*; THEAT Künstlergarderobe *f*; **dressing table** *n* Frisierkommode *f*; **dress rehearsal** *n* THEAT Generalprobe *f*

drew *pt of* **draw**

dried *adj* getrocknet; *(milk, flowers)* Trocken-; ~ **fruit** Dörrobst *nt*; **drier** *n →* **dryer**

drift 1. *vi* treiben **2.** *n (of snow)* Verwehung *f; fig* Tendenz *f*; **if you get my ~** wenn du mich richtig verstehst

drill 1. *n* Bohrer *m* **2.** *vt, vi* bohren

drink 1. *vt, vi* trinken **2.** *n* Getränk *nt; (alcoholic)* Drink *m*; **drink-driving** *n (Brit)* Trunkenheit *f* am Steuer; **drinking water** *n* Trinkwas-

drip 1. *n* Tropfen *m* **2.** *vi* tropfen; **dripping 1.** *n* Bratenfett *nt* **2.** *adj* ~ **(wet)** tropfnass

drive 1. *vt (car, person in car)* fahren; *(force: person, animal)* treiben; TECH antreiben; ~ **sb mad** jdn verrückt machen **2.** *vi* fahren **3.** *n* Fahrt *f; (entrance)* Einfahrt *f*, Auffahrt *f*; IT Laufwerk *nt*; **drive away**, **drive off** *vt* vertreiben; **drive-in** *adj* Drive-in-; ~ **cinema** *(US)* Autokino *nt*; **driven** *pp of* **drive**

driver *n* Fahrer(in) *m(f)*; IT Treiber *m*; ~'**s license** *(US)* Führerschein *m*; ~'**s seat** Fahrersitz *m*; **driving** *n* (Auto)fahren *nt; (Brit)* Fahrstunde *f*; **driving lesson** *n* Fahrstunde *f*; **driving licence** *n (Brit)* Führerschein *m*; **driving school** *n* Fahrschule *f*; **driving seat** *n (Brit)* Fahrersitz *m*; **driving test** *n* Fahrprüfung *f*

drizzle 1. *n* Nieselregen *m* **2.** *vi* nieseln

drop 1. *n (of liquid)* Tropfen *m; (fall in price etc)* Rückgang *m* **2.** *vt a. fig (give up)* fallen lassen **3.** *vi (fall)* herunterfallen; *(figures, temperature)* sinken, zurückgehen; **drop by**, **drop in** *vi* vorbeikommen; **drop off** *vi (to sleep)* einnicken; **drop out** *vi (withdraw)* aussteigen; *(university)* das Studium abbrechen; **dropout** *n*

Aussteiger(in) *m(f)*

drove *pt of* **drive**

drown 1. *vi* ertrinken **2.** *vt* ertränken

drowsy *adj* schläfrig

drug 1. *n* MED Medikament *nt*, Arznei *f*; *(addictive)* Droge *f*; *(narcotic)* Rauschgift *nt*; **be on ~s** drogensüchtig sein **2.** *vt* (mit Medikamenten) betäuben; **drug addict** *n* Rauschgiftsüchtige(r) *m(f)*; **drug dealer** *n* Drogenhändler(in) *m(f)*; **druggist** *n* (US) Drogist(in) *m(f)*; **drugstore** *n* (US) Drogerie *f*

drum *n* Trommel *f*; **~s** *pl* Schlagzeug *nt*

drunk 1. *pp of* **drink 2.** *adj* betrunken; **get~** sich betrinken **3.** *n* Betrunkene(r) *m/f*; *(alcoholic)* Trinker(in) *m(f)*; **drunk-driving** *n* (US) Trunkenheit *f* am Steuer; **drunken** *adj* betrunken, besoffen

dry 1. *adj* trocken **2.** *vt* trocknen; *(dishes, oneself, one's hands etc)* abtrocknen **3.** *vi* trocknen, trocken werden; **dry out** *vi* trocknen; **dry-clean** *vt* chemisch reinigen; **dry-cleaning** *n* chemische Reinigung *f*; **dryer** *n* Trockner *m*; *(for hair)* Föhn *m*; *(over head)* Trockenhaube *f*

DTP *abbr* = **desktop publishing**; DTP *nt*

dual *adj* doppelt; **dual carriageway** *n* *(Brit)* zweispurige Schnellstraße *f*; **~ nationali-**

~ty doppelte Staatsangehörigkeit; **dual-purpose** *adj* Mehrzweck-

dubbed *adj* *(film)* synchronisiert

dubious *adj* zweifelhaft

duchess *n* Herzogin *f*

duck *n* Ente *f*

dude *n* (US) *fam* Typ *m*; **a cool ~** ein cooler Typ

due 1. *adj* *(time)* fällig; *(fitting)* angemessen; **in ~ course** zu gegebener Zeit; **~ to** infolge *+ gen*, wegen *+ gen* **2.** *adv* **~ south/north etc** direkt nach Norden/Süden etc

dug *pt*, *pp of* **dig**

duke *n* Herzog *m*

dull *adj* *(colour, light, weather)* trübe; *(boring)* langweilig

duly *adv* ordnungsgemäß; *(as expected)* wie erwartet

dumb *adj* stumm; *fam (stupid)* doof, blöde

dumb-bell *n* Hantel *f*

dummy 1. *n* *(sham)* Attrappe *f*; *(in shop)* Schaufensterpuppe *f*; *(Brit, teat)* Schnuller *m*; *fam (person)* Dummkopf *m* **2.** *adj* unecht, Schein-; **~ run** Testlauf *m*

dump 1. *n* Abfallhaufen *m*; *fam (place)* Kaff *nt* **2.** *vt lit*, *fig* abladen; *fam* **he ~ed her** er hat mir ihr Schluss gemacht

dumpling *n* Kloß *m*, Knödel *m*

dune *n* Düne *f*

dung n Dung m; (manure) Mist m

dungeon n Kerker m

duplex n zweistöckige Wohnung; (US) Doppelhaushälfte f

duplicate 1. n Duplikat nt **2.** vt (make copies of) kopieren; (repeat) wiederholen

durable adj haltbar; **duration** n Dauer f

during prep (time) während + gen

dusk n (time) Abenddämmerung f

dust 1. n Staub m **2.** vt abstauben; **dustbin** n (Brit) Mülleimer m; **dustcart** n (Brit) Müllwagen m; **duster** n Staubtuch nt; **dustman** n (Brit) Müllmann m; **dustpan** n Kehrschaufel f; **dusty** adj staubig

Dutch 1. adj holländisch **2.** n (language) Holländisch nt;

speak/talk double ~ fam Quatsch reden; **the ~** pl die Holländer; **Dutchman** n Holländer m; **Dutchwoman** n Holländerin f

duty n Pflicht f; (task) Aufgabe f; (tax) Zoll m; **on/off ~** im Dienst/nicht im Dienst; **be on ~** Dienst haben; **duty-free** adj zollfrei; **~ shop** Dutyfreeshop m

duvet n Federbett nt

DVD n abbr = **digital versatile disk**; DVD f

dwarf n Zwerg(in) m(f)

dwelling n Wohnung f

dye 1. n Farbstoff m **2.** vt färben

dynamo n Dynamo m

dyslexia n Legasthenie f; **dyslexic** adj legasthenisch; **be ~** Legastheniker(in) sein

dyspepsia n Verdauungsstörung f

E

E111 form n ≈ Auslandskrankenschein m

each 1. adj jeder/jede/jedes **2.** pron jeder/jede/jedes; **I'll have one of ~** ich nehme von jedem eins; **they ~ have a car** jeder von ihnen hat ein Auto; **~ other** einander, sich; **for/against ~ other** füreinander/gegeneinander **3.** adv je; **they cost 10 dollars ~** sie kosten 10 Dollar das

Stück

eager adj eifrig; **be ~ to do sth** darauf brennen, etw zu tun

eagle n Adler m

ear n Ohr nt; **earache** n Ohrenschmerzen pl; **eardrum** n Trommelfell nt

earl n Graf m

early adj, adv früh; **be 10 minutes ~** 10 Minuten zu früh kommen; **at the earliest** frühestens; **in ~ June/2008** Anfang Juni / 2008; ~ *retirement* vorzeitiger Ruhestand; ~ *warning system* Frühwarnsystem nt

earn vt verdienen; **earnings** npl Verdienst m, Einkommen nt

earphones npl Kopfhörer m; **earplug** n Ohrenstöpsel m, Ohropax® nt; **earring** n Ohrring m

earth 1. n Erde f; *what on ~ ...?* was in aller Welt ...? **2.** vt erden; **earthquake** n Erdbeben nt

ease 1. vt (pain) lindern **2.** n (easiness) Leichtigkeit f; *feel at ~* sich wohl fühlen; *feel ill at ~* sich nicht wohl fühlen; **easily** adv leicht; *he is ~ the best* er ist mit Abstand der Beste

east 1. n Osten m; *to the ~ of* östlich von **2.** adv (go, face) nach Osten **3.** adj Ost-; ~ *wind* Ostwind m; **eastbound** adj (in) Richtung Osten

Easter n Ostern nt; *at ~* zu Ostern; **Easter egg** n Osterei nt; **Easter Sunday** n Ostersonntag m

eastern adj Ost-, östlich; *Eastern Europe* Osteuropa nt; **East Germany** n Ostdeutschland nt; **eastwards** adv nach Osten

easy adj leicht; (task, solution) einfach; (life) bequem; (manner) ungezwungen;

easy-care adj pflegeleicht; **easy-going** adj gelassen

eat vt essen; (animal) fressen; **eat out** vi zum Essen ausgehen; **eat up** vt aufessen

eaten pp of **eat**

eavesdrop vi (heimlich) lauschen; ~ *on sb* jdn belauschen

eccentric adj exzentrisch

echo 1. n Echo nt **2.** vi widerhallen

ecological adj ökologisch; ~ *disaster* Umweltkatastrophe f; **ecology** n Ökologie f

economic adj wirtschaftlich, Wirtschafts-; **economical** adj wirtschaftlich; (person) sparsam; **economics** nsing or pl Wirtschaftswissenschaft f; **economist** n Wirtschaftswissenschaftler(in) m(f); **economize** vi sparen (on an + dat); **economy** n (of state) Wirtschaft f; (thrift) Sparsamkeit f; **economy class** n AVIAT Economyclass f

ecstasy n Ekstase f; (drug) Ecstasy f

eczema n Ekzem nt

edge n Rand m; (of knife) Schneide f; *on ~* nervös; **edgy** adj nervös

edible adj essbar

Edinburgh n Edinburg nt

edit vt (series, newspaper etc) herausgeben; (text) redigieren; (film) schneiden; IT editieren; **edition** n Ausgabe f; **editor** n Redakteur(in) m(f);

(of series etc) Herausgeber(in) m(f)

educate vt *(child)* erziehen; *(at school, university)* ausbilden; *(public)* aufklären; **educated** adj gebildet; **education** n Erziehung f; *(studies, training)* Ausbildung f; *(subject of study)* Pädagogik f; *(system)* Schulwesen nt; *(knowledge)* Bildung f; **educational** adj pädagogisch; **~ television** Schulfernsehen nt

eel n Aal m

eerie adj unheimlich

effect n Wirkung f *(on auf + acc)*; **come into ~** in Kraft treten; **effective** adj wirksam, effektiv

efficiency n Leistungsfähigkeit f; *(of method)* Wirksamkeit f; **efficient** adj TECH leistungsfähig; *(method)* wirksam, effizient

effort n Anstrengung f; *(attempt)* Versuch m; **make an ~** sich anstrengen; **effortless** adj mühelos

eg abbr = **exempli gratia (for example)**; z. B.

egg n Ei nt; **eggcup** n Eierbecher m; **eggplant** n *(US)* Aubergine f; **eggshell** n Eierschale f

ego n Ich nt; *(self-esteem)* Selbstbewusstsein nt

Egypt n Ägypten nt; **Egyptian 1.** adj ägyptisch **2.** n Ägypter(in) m(f)

eiderdown n Daunendecke f

eight 1. num acht; **at the age of ~** im Alter von acht Jahren; **it's ~ (o'clock)** es ist acht Uhr **2.** n *(a. bus etc)* Acht f; *(boat)* Achter m; **eighteen 1.** num achtzehn **2.** n Achtzehn f; → **eighth; eighteenth** adj achtzehnte(r, s); → **eighth;** eighth **1.** adj achte(r, s); **the ~ of June** der achte Juni **2.** n *(fraction)* Achtel nt; **an ~ of a litre** ein Achtelliter; **eightieth** adj achtzigste(r, s); → **eighth; eighty 1.** num achtzig **2.** n Achtzig f; → **eight**

Eire n die Republik Irland

either 1. conj **~ ... or** entweder ... oder **2.** pron **~ of the two** eine(r, s) von beiden **3.** adj **on ~ side** auf beiden Seiten **4.** adv **I won't go ~** ich gehe auch nicht

elaborate 1. adj *(complex)* kompliziert; *(plan)* ausgeklügelt; *(decoration)* kunstvoll **2.** vi **could you ~ on that?** könntest du mehr darüber sagen?

elastic adj elastisch; **~ band** Gummiband nt

elbow n Ellbogen m

elder 1. adj *(of two)* älter **2.** n Ältere(r) mf; BOT Holunder m; **elderly 1.** adj ältere(r, s) **2.** n **the ~** die älteren Leute; **eldest** adj älteste(r, s)

elect vt wählen; **he was ~ chairman** er wurde zum Vorsitzenden gewählt; **election**

n Wahl *f*; **election campaign** *n* Wahlkampf *m*

electric *adj* elektrisch; (*car, motor, razor etc*) Elektro-; ~ **blanket** Heizdecke *f*; ~ **cooker** Elektroherd *m*; ~ **current** elektrischer Strom; ~ **shock** Stromschlag *m*; **electrical** *adj* elektrisch; ~ **goods/appliances** Elektrogeräte; **electrician** *n* Elektriker(in) *m(f)*; **electricity** *n* Elektrizität *f*; **electronic** *adj* elektronisch

elegant *adj* elegant

element *n* Element *nt*; **an ~ of truth** ein Körnchen Wahrheit; **elementary** *adj* einfach; (*basic*) grundlegend; ~ **stage** Anfangsstadium *nt*; ~ **school** (*US*) Grundschule *f*; ~ **maths/French** Grundkenntnisse in Mathematik/ Französisch

elephant *n* Elefant *m*

elevator *n* (*US*) Fahrstuhl *m*

eleven 1. *num* elf **2.** *n* (*team, bus etc*) Elf *f* → **eight**; **eleventh 1.** *adj* elfte(r, s) **2.** *n* (*fraction*) Elftel *nt* → **eighth**

eligible *adj* in Frage kommend; (*for grant etc*) berechtigt; ~ **bachelor** begehrter Junggeselle

eliminate *vt* ausschließen (*from* aus), ausschalten; (*problem etc*) beseitigen

elm *n* Ulme *f*

elope *vi* durchbrennen (*with sb* mit jdm)

eloquent *adj* redegewandt

else *adv* **anybody/anything** ~ (*in addition*) sonst (noch) jemand/etwas; (*other*) ein anderer/etwas; **somebody** ~ jemand anders; **everyone** ~ alle anderen; *or* ~ sonst; **elsewhere** *adv* anderswo, woanders; (*direction*) woandershin

ELT *abbr* = **English Language Teaching**

e-mail E-Mail **1.** *vi, vt* mailen (*sth to sb* jdm etw) **2.** *n* E-Mail *f*; **e-mail address** *n* E-Mail-Adresse *f*

embankment *n* Böschung *f*; (*for railway*) Bahndamm *m*

embargo *n* Embargo *nt*

embark *vi* an Bord gehen

embarrass *vt* in Verlegenheit bringen; **embarrassed** *adj* verlegen; **embarrassing** *adj* peinlich

embassy *n* Botschaft *f*

embrace 1. *vt* umarmen **2.** *n* Umarmung *f*

embroider *vt* sticken; **embroidery** *n* Stickerei *f*

embryo *n* Embryo *m*

emerge *vi* auftauchen; **it ~d that** ... es stellte sich heraus, dass ...

emergency 1. *n* Notfall *m* **2.** *adj* Not-; ~ **exit** Notausgang *m*; ~ **room** (*US*) Notaufnahme *f*; ~ **service** Notdienst *m*; ~ **stop** Vollbremsung *f*

emigrate *vi* auswandern

emotion *n* Emotion *f*, Gefühl

nt; **emotional** *adj* (*person*) emotional; (*experience, moment, scene*) ergreifend

emperor *n* Kaiser *m*

emphasis *n* Betonung *f*; **emphasize** *vt* betonen; **emphatic**, **emphatically** *adj*, *adv* nachdrücklich

empire *n* Reich *nt*

employ *vt* beschäftigen; (*hire*) anstellen; (*use*) anwenden; **employee** *n* Angestellte(r) *mf*; **employer** *n* Arbeitgeber(in) *m(f)*; **employment** *n* Beschäftigung *f*; (*position*) Stellung *f*

empress *n* Kaiserin *f*

empty 1. *adj* leer **2.** *vt* (*contents*) leeren; (*container*) ausleeren

enable *vt* ~ **sb to do sth** es jdm ermöglichen, etw zu tun

enamel *n* Email *nt*; (*of teeth*) Zahnschmelz *m*

enchanting *adj* bezaubernd

enclose *vt* einschließen; (*in letter*) beilegen (*in, with* dat); **enclosure** *n* (*for animals*) Gehege *nt*; (*in letter*) Anlage *f*

encore *n* Zugabe *f*

encounter 1. *n* Begegnung *f* **2.** *vt* (*person*) begegnen + *dat*; (*difficulties*) stoßen auf + *acc*

encourage *vt* ermutigen; **encouragement** *n* Ermutigung *f*

encyclopaedia *n* Lexikon *nt*, Enzyklopädie *f*

end 1. *n* Ende *nt*; (*of film, play*

etc) Schluss *m*; (*purpose*) Zweck *m*; **at the ~ of May** Ende Mai; **in the ~** schließlich; **come to an ~** zu Ende gehen **2.** *vt* beenden **3.** *vi* enden; **end up** *vi* enden

endanger *vt* gefährden; **~ed species** vom Aussterben bedrohte Art

ending *n* (*of book*) Ausgang *m*; (*last part*) Schluss *m*; (*of word*) Endung *f*

endive *n* Endiviensalat *m*

endless *adj* endlos; (*possibilities*) unendlich

endurance *n* Ausdauer *f*; **endure** *vt* ertragen

enemy 1. *n* Feind(in) *m(f)* **2.** *adj* feindlich

energetic *adj* energiegeladen; (*active*) aktiv; **energy** *n* Energie *f*

enforce *vt* durchsetzen; (*obedience*) erzwingen

engage *vt* (*employ*) einstellen; (*singer, performer*) engagieren; **engaged** *adj* verlobt; (*toilet, telephone line*) besetzt; **get ~** sich verloben (*to* mit); **engaged tone** *n* (*Brit*) TEL Belegzeichen *nt*; **engagement** *n* (*marry*) Verlobung *f*

engine *n* AUTO Motor *m*; RAIL Lokomotive *f*; **~ failure** AUTO Motorschaden *m*; **~ trouble** AUTO Defekt *m* am Motor; **engineer** *n* Ingenieur(in) *m(f)*; (*US*) RAIL Lokomotivführer(in) *m(f)*; **engineering**

n Technik *f*; (*mechanical engineering*) Maschinenbau *m*; (*subject*) Ingenieurwesen *nt*; **engine immobilizer** *n* AUTO Wegfahrsperre *f*

England *n* England *nt*; **English 1.** *adj* englisch; **he's ~** er ist Engländer; **the ~ Channel** der Ärmelkanal **2.** *n* (*language*) Englisch *nt*; **in ~** auf Englisch; **translate into ~** ins Englische übersetzen; (*people*) **the ~pl** die Engländer; **Englishman** *n* Engländer *m*; **Englishwoman** *n* Engländerin *f*

engrave *vt* eingravieren; **engraving** *n* Stich *m*

engrossed *adj* vertieft (*in sth* in etw *acc*)

enjoy *vt* genießen; **I ~ reading** ich lese gern; **he ~s teasing her** es macht ihm Spaß, sie aufzuziehen; **did you ~ the film?** hat dir der Film gefallen?; **enjoyable** *adj* angenehm; (*entertaining*) unterhaltsam; **enjoyment** *n* (*stronger*) Freude *f* (*of an + dat*)

enlarge *vt* vergrößern; (*expand*) erweitern; **enlargement** *n* Vergrößerung *f*

enormous, enormously *adj, adv* riesig, ungeheuer

enough 1. *adj* genug; **that's ~** das reicht!; (*stop it*) Schluss damit!; **I've had ~** das hat mir gereicht!; (*eat*) ich bin satt **2.** *adv* genug, genügend

enquire *vi* sich erkundigen (*about* nach); **enquiry** *n* (*question*) Anfrage *f*; (*for information*) Erkundigung *f* (*about* über + *acc*); (*investigation*) Untersuchung *f*; '**Enquiries**' „Auskunft"

enrol *vi* sich einschreiben; (*for course, school*) sich anmelden; **enrolment** *n* Einschreibung *f*, Anmeldung *f*

en suite *adj*, *n* **room with ~** (*bathroom*) Zimmer *nt* mit eigenem Bad

ensure *vt* sicherstellen

enter 1. *vt* eintreten in + *acc*, betreten; (*drive into*) einfahren in + *acc*; (*country*) einreisen in + *acc*; (*in list*) eintragen; IT eingeben; (*race, contest*) teilnehmen an + *dat* **2.** *vi* (*towards speaker*) hereinkommen; (*away from speaker*) hineingehen

enterprise *n* COMM Unternehmen *nt*

entertain *vt* (*guest*) bewirten; (*amuse*) unterhalten; **entertaining** *adj* unterhaltsam; **entertainment** *n* (*amusement*) Unterhaltung *f*

enthusiasm *n* Begeisterung *f*; **enthusiastic** *adj* begeistert (*about* von)

entire, entirely *adj, adv* ganz

entitle *vt* (*qualify*) berechtigen (*to* zu); (*name*) betiteln

entrance *n* Eingang *m*; (*for vehicles*) Einfahrt *f*; (*entering*) Eintritt *m*; THEAT Auftritt *m*; **entrance exam** *n* Aufnahmeprüfung *f*; **entrance fee** *n* Eintrittsgeld *nt*

entrust *vt* ~ **sb with sth** jdm etw anvertrauen

entry *n* (*way in*) Eingang *m*; (*entering*) Eintritt *m*; (*in vehicle*) Einfahrt *f*; (*into country*) Einreise *f*; (*admission*) Zutritt *m*; (*in diary, accounts*) Eintrag *m*; **'no ~'** „Eintritt verboten"; (*for vehicles*) „Einfahrt verboten"; **entry phone** *n* Türsprechanlage *f*

envelope *n* (Brief)umschlag *m*

enviable *adj* beneidenswert; **envious** *adj* neidisch

environment *n* Umgebung *f*; (*ecology*) Umwelt *f*; **environmental** *adj* Umwelt-; **environmentalist** *n* Umweltschützer(in) *m(f)*

envy 1. *n* Neid *m* (*of* auf +*acc*) **2.** *vt* beneiden (*sb sth* jdn um etw)

epidemic *n* Epidemie *f*

epilepsy *n* Epilepsie *f*; **epileptic** *adj* epileptisch

episode *n* Episode *f*; TV Fortsetzung *f*, Folge *f*

epoch *n* Ära *f*, Epoche *f*

equal 1. *adj* gleich (*to* +*dat*) **2.** *n* Gleichgestellte(r) *mf* **3.** *vt* gleichen; (*match*) gleichkommen +*dat*; **two times two ~s four** zwei mal zwei ist vier; **equality** *n* Gleichheit *f*; (*equal rights*) Gleichbe-

rechtigung *f*; **equalize** *vi* SPORT ausgleichen; **equalizer** *n* SPORT Ausgleichstreffer *m*;

equally *adv* gleich; (*on the other hand*) andererseits

equation *n* MATH Gleichung *f*

equator *n* Äquator *m*

equilibrium *n* Gleichgewicht *nt*

equip *vt* ausrüsten; (*kitchen*) ausstatten; **equipment** *n* Ausrüstung *f*; (*for kitchen*) Ausstattung *f*; **electrical ~** Elektrogeräte *pl*

equivalent 1. *adj* gleichwertig (*to dat*); (*corresponding*) entsprechend (*to dat*) **2.** *n* Äquivalent *nt*; (*amount*) gleiche Menge; (*in money*) Gegenwert *m*

era *n* Ära *f*, Zeitalter *nt*

erase *vt* ausradieren; (*tape, disk*) löschen; **eraser** *n* Radiergummi *m*

erect 1. *adj* aufrecht **2.** *vt* (*building, monument*) errichten; (*tent*) aufstellen; **erection** *n* Errichtung *f*; ANAT Erektion *f*

erotic *adj* erotisch

err *vi* sich irren

erratic *adj* (*behaviour*) unberechenbar; (*bus line etc*) unregelmäßig; (*performance*) unbeständig

error *n* Fehler *m*; **error message** *n* IT Fehlermeldung *f*

erupt *vi* ausbrechen

escalator *n* Rolltreppe *f*

escalope n Schnitzel nt

escape 1. n Flucht f; (from prison etc) Ausbruch m; **there's no ~** es gibt keinen Ausweg; **have a narrow ~** gerade noch davonkommen **2.** vt (pursuers) entkommen + dat; (from prison etc) entgehen + dat **3.** vi (from pursuers) entkommen (from dat); (from prison etc) ausbrechen (from dat); (leak: gas) ausströmen; (water) auslaufen

escort 1. n (companion) Begleiter(in) m(f); (guard) Eskorte f **2.** vt (lady) begleiten

especially adv besonders

espionage n Spionage f

essay n Aufsatz m; (literary) Essay m

essential 1. adj (necessary) unentbehrlich, unverzichtbar; (basic) wesentlich **2.** n **the ~s** pl das Wesentliche; **essentially** adv im Wesentlichen

establish vt (set up) gründen; (introduce) einführen; (relations) aufnehmen; (prove) nachweisen; **~ that ...** feststellen, dass ...; **establishment** n Institution f; (business) Unternehmen nt

estate n Gut nt; (housing ~) Siedlung f; (country house) Landsitz m; **estate agent** n (Brit) Grundstücksmakler(in) m(f), Immobilienmakler(in) m(f); **estate car** n (Brit) Kombiwagen m

estimate 1. n Schätzung f; COMM (of price) Kostenvoranschlag m **2.** vt schätzen

estuary n Mündung f

etching n Radierung f

eternal adj, adv ewig; **eternity** n Ewigkeit f

ethical adj ethisch; **ethics** npl Ethik f

Ethiopia n Äthiopien nt

ethnic adj ethnisch; (clothes etc) landesüblich; **~ minority** ethnische Minderheit

EU abbr = **European Union**; EU f

euro n FIN Euro m; **Eurocheque** n Euroscheck m; **Europe** n Europa nt; **European 1.** adj europäisch; **~ Parliament** Europäisches Parlament; **~ Union** Europäische Union **2.** n Europäer(in) m(f); **Eurosceptic** n Euroskeptiker(in) m(f); **Eurotunnel** n Eurotunnel m

evacuate vt (place) räumen; (people) evakuieren

evaluate vt auswerten

evaporate vi verdampfen; fig verschwinden; **~d milk** Kondensmilch f

even 1. adj (flat) eben; (regular) gleichmäßig; (equal) gleich; (number) gerade; **the score is ~** es steht unentschieden **2.** adv sogar; **~ you** selbst (or sogar) du; **~ if** selbst wenn, wenn auch; **~ though** obwohl; **not ~** nicht

einmal; **~ better** noch besser;
even out vi (prices) sich ein-
pendeln

evening n Abend m; **in the ~**
abends, am Abend; **this ~**
heute Abend; **evening class**
n Abendkurs m; **evening
dress** n (generally) Abend-
kleidung f; (woman's)
Abendkleid nt

evenly adv gleichmäßig

event n Ereignis nt; (organized) Veranstaltung f; SPORT
(discipline) Disziplin f; **in
the ~ of** im Falle + gen

eventual adj (final) letztend-
lich; **eventually** adv (at last)
am Ende; (given time)
schließlich

ever adv (at any time) je(mals);
don't ~ do that again tu das
ja nie wieder; **he's the best ~**
er ist der Beste, den es je gegeben hat; **have you ~ been
to the States?** bist du schon
einmal in den Staaten gewesen?; **for ~** (für) immer; **for ~
and ~** auf immer und ewig; **~
so** fam äußerst ...; **~ so
drunk** ganz schön betrunken

every adj jeder / jede / jedes;
~ day jeden Tag; **~ other day**
jeden zweiten Tag; **~ five
days** alle fünf Tage; **I have
~ reason to believe that ...**
ich habe allen Grund anzunehmen, dass ...; **everybody**
pron jeder, alle pl; **everyday**
adj (commonplace) alltäg-
lich; (clothes, language etc)

Alltags-; **everyone** pron jeder, alle pl; **everything** pron
alles; **everywhere** adv überall; (with direction) überall-
hin

evidence n Beweise pl; (single
piece) Beweis m; (testimony)
Aussage f; **evident**, **evident-
ly** adj, adv offensichtlich

evil 1. adj böse **2.** n Böse(s) nt

evolution n Entwicklung f;
(of life) Evolution f; **evolve**
vi sich entwickeln

ex- pref Ex-, ehemalig; **~wife**
frühere Frau, Exfrau f; **ex**
n fam Verflossene(r) mf,
Ex mf

exact adj genau; **exactly** adv
genau; **~ not ~ fast** nicht gerade schnell

exaggerate vt, vi übertreiben;
exaggerated adj übertrieben; **exaggeration** n Übertreibung f

exam n Prüfung f; **examination** n MED (etc) Untersuchung f, Prüfung f; (at university) Examen nt; (at customs etc) Kontrolle f; **examine** vt untersuchen (for auf
+ acc); (check) kontrollieren,
prüfen; **examiner** n Prü-
fer(in) m(f)

example n Beispiel nt; **for ~**
zum Beispiel

excavation n Ausgrabung f

exceed vt überschreiten,
übertreffen; **exceedingly**
adv äußerst

excel 1. vt übertreffen **2.** vi

sich auszeichnen (*in* in + *dat*, *at* bei); **excellent, excellently** *adj, adv* ausgezeichnet

except 1. *prep* ~ außer + *dat*; ~ **for** abgesehen von 2. *vt* ausnehmen; **exception** *n* Ausnahme *f*; **exceptional, exceptionally** *adj, adv* außergewöhnlich

excess *n* Übermaß *nt* (*of* an + *dat*); **excess baggage** *n* Übergepäck *nt*; **excess fare** *n* Nachlösegebühr *f*; **excessive, excessively** *adj, adv* übermäßig; **excess weight** *n* Übergewicht *nt*

exchange *n* Austausch *m* (*for* gegen); (*of bought items*) Umtausch *m* (*for* gegen); FIN Wechsel *m*; TEL Vermittlung *f*, Zentrale *f* 2. *vt* austauschen; (*goods*) tauschen; (*bought items*) umtauschen (*for* gegen); (*money, blows*) wechseln; **exchange rate** *n* Wechselkurs *m*

excited *adj* aufgeregt; **exciting** *adj* aufregend; (*book, film*) spannend

exclamation *n* Ausruf *m*; **exclamation mark, exclamation point** (*US*) *n* Ausrufezeichen *nt*

exclude *vt* ausschließen; **exclusion** *n* Ausschluss *m*; **exclusive** *adj* (*select*) exklusiv; (*sole*) ausschließlich; **exclusively** *adv* ausschließlich

excruciating *adj* fürchterlich, entsetzlich

excursion *n* Ausflug *m*

excuse 1. *vt* entschuldigen; ~ **me** Entschuldigung! **2.** *n* Entschuldigung *f*, Ausrede *f*

ex-directory *adj* (*Brit*) TEL nicht im Telefonbuch stehen

execution *n* (*killing*) Hinrichtung *f*; **executive** *n* leitender Angestellter, leitende Angestellte

exemplary *adj* beispielhaft

exercise *n* (*in school, sports*) Übung *f*; (*movement*) Bewegung *f*; **get more** ~ mehr Sport treiben

exert *vt* (*influence*) ausüben; **exhaust** *n* (*fumes*) Abgase *pl*; AUTO Auspuff *m*; **exhausted** *adj* erschöpft; **exhausting** *adj* anstrengend

exhibit *n* (*in exhibition*) Ausstellungsstück *nt*; **exhibition** *n* Ausstellung *f*

exhilarating *adj* belebend, erregend

exile 1. *n* Exil *nt*; (*person*) Verbannte(r) *mf* **2.** *vt* verbannen

exist *vi* existieren; (*live*) leben (*on* von); **existence** *n* Existenz *f*; **come into** ~ entstehen; **existing** *adj* bestehend

exit *n* Ausgang *m*; (*for vehicles*) Ausfahrt *f*

exotic *adj* exotisch

expand 1. *vt* ausdehnen, erweitern **2.** *vi* sich ausdehnen; **expansion** *n* Expansion *f*, Erweiterung *f*

expect 1. *vt* erwarten; (*sup-*

pose) annehmen; **he ~s me
to do it** er erwartet, dass
ich es mache; **I ~** *it'll rain*
es wird wohl regnen; **I ~ so**
ich denke schon **2.** *vi* **be
~ing** ein Kind erwarten

expenditure *n* Ausgaben *pl*

expense *n* Kosten *pl*; *(single
cost)* Ausgabe *f*; *(business)*
~s *pl* Spesen *pl*; **at sb's ~**
auf jds Kosten; **expensive**
adj teuer

experience 1. *n* Erfahrung *f*;
(particular incident) Erlebnis *nt*; **by/from ~** aus Erfahrung **2.** *vt* erfahren, erleben;
(hardship) durchmachen;
experienced *adj* erfahren

experiment 1. *n* Versuch *m*,
Experiment *nt* **2.** *vi* experimentieren

expert 1. *n* Experte *m*, Expertin *f*; *(professional)* Fachmann *m*, Fachfrau *f*; LAW
Sachverständige(r) *mf* **2.**
adj fachmännisch; **expertise**
n Sachkenntnis *f*

expire *vi (end)* ablaufen; **expiry date** *n* Verfallsdatum *nt*

explain *vt* erklären *(sth to sb*
jdm etw)*; **explanation** *n* Erklärung *f*

explicit *adj* ausdrücklich,
deutlich

explode *vi* explodieren

exploit *vt* ausbeuten

explore *vt* erforschen

explosion *n* Explosion *f*; **explosive 1.** *adj* explosiv **2.** *n*
Sprengstoff *m*

export 1. *vt, vi* exportieren **2.** *n*
Export *m* **3.** *adj (trade)* Export-

expose *vt (to danger etc)* aussetzen *(to* dat)*; *(uncover)*
freilegen; *(imposter)* entlarven; **exposed** *adj (position)*
ungeschützt; **exposure** *n*
MED Unterkühlung *f*; PHOT
(time) Belichtung(szeit) *f*;
24 ~s 24 Aufnahmen

express 1. *adj (speedy)* Express-, Schnell-; **~ delivery**
Eilzustellung *f* **2.** *n* RAIL
Schnellzug *m* **3.** *vr* ausdrücken **4.** *vr* **~ oneself** sich ausdrücken; **expression** *n*
(phrase) Ausdruck *m*; *(look)*
Gesichtsausdruck *m*; **expressway** *n (US)* Schnellstraße *f*

extend *vt (arms)* ausstrecken;
(lengthen) verlängern;
(building) vergrößern, ausbauen; *(business, limits)* erweitern; **extension** *n*
(lengthening) Verlängerung
f; *(of building)* Anbau *m*;
TEL Anschluss *m*; **extensive**
adj (knowledge) umfangreich; *(use)* häufig; **extent** *n*
(length) Länge *f*; *(size)* Ausdehnung *f*; *(scope)* Umfang
m, Ausmaß *nt*; **to a certain/ large ~** in gewissem/
hohem Maße

exterior *n* Äußere(s) *nt*

external *adj* äußere(r, s), Außen-; **externally** *adv* äußerlich

extinct adj (species) ausge-
storben

extinguish vt löschen; extinguisher n Löschgerät nt

extra 1. adj zusätzlich; ~
charge Zuschlag m; ~ time
SPORT Verlängerung f 2. adv
besonders; ~ large (clothing)
übergroß 3. npl ~s zusätzli-
che Kosten pl; (food) Beilagen pl; (accessories) Zubehör
nt; (for car etc) Extras pl

extract 1. vt herausziehen
(from aus); (tooth) ziehen
2. n (from book etc) Auszug
m

extraordinary adj außerordentlich; (unusual) unge-
wöhnlich; (amazing) er-
staunlich

extreme 1. adj äußerste(r, s);

(drastic) extrem 2. n Extrem
nt; extremely adv äußerst,
höchst; extreme sports npl
Extremsportarten pl; ex-
tremist 1. adj extremistisch
2. n Extremist m

extrovert adj extrovertiert

exultation n Jubel m

eye 1. n Auge nt; keep an ~ on
sb/sth auf jdn/etw aufpassen 2. vt mustern; eyebrow
n Augenbraue f; eyelash n
Wimper f; eyelid n Augenlid
nt; eyeliner n Eyeliner m;
eyeopener n that was an ~
das hat mir die Augen geöffnet; eyeshadow n Lidschatten m; eyesight n Sehkraft f;
eyesore n Schandfleck m;
eye witness n Augenzeuge
m, Augenzeugin f

F

fabric n Stoff m

fabulous adj sagenhaft

façade n Fassade f

face 1. n Gesicht nt; (of clock)
Zifferblatt nt; (of mountain)
Wand f; in the ~ of trotz
+ gen; be ~ to ~ (people) einander gegenüberstehen 2.
vt, vi (person) gegenüberstehen + dat; (at table) gegen-
übersitzen + dat; ~ north
(room) nach Norden gehen;
~ (up to) the facts den Tatsa-
chen ins Auge sehen; be ~d
with sth mit etw konfrontiert

sein; face cream n Gesichts-
creme f

facet n fig Aspekt m

face value n Nennwert m

facial 1. adj Gesichts- 2. n fam
(kosmetische) Gesichtsbe-
handlung

facilitate vt erleichtern

facility n (building etc to be
used) Einrichtung f, Mög-
lichkeit f

fact n Tatsache f; as a matter
of ~, in ~ eigentlich, tatsächlich

factor n Faktor m

factory n Fabrik f; **factory outlet** n Fabrikverkauf m

factual adj sachlich

faculty n Fähigkeit f; (at university) Fakultät f; (US, teaching staff) Lehrkörper m

fade vi verblassen

fag n (Brit) fam (cigarette) Kippe f; (US) fam pej Schwule(r) m

Fahrenheit n Fahrenheit

fail 1. vt (exam) nicht bestehen **2.** vi versagen; (plan, marriage) scheitern; (student) durchfallen; (eyesight) nachlassen; **words ~ me** ich bin sprachlos; **failure** n (person) Versager(in) m(f); (act) Versagen nt; (of engine etc) Ausfall m; (of plan, marriage) Scheitern nt

faint 1. adj schwach; (sound) leise; fam **I haven't the ~est (idea)** ich habe keine Ahnung **2.** vi ohnmächtig werden (with vor + dat); **faintness** n MED Schwächegefühl (nt)

fair 1. adj (hair) blond; (skin) hell; (just) gerecht, fair; (reasonable) ganz ordentlich; (in school) befriedigend; (weather) schön; (wind) günstig; **a ~ number/ amount of** ziemlich viele/ viel **2.** adv **play ~** fair spielen; **fig** fair sein; **~ enough** in Ordnung! **3.** n (fun~) Jahrmarkt m; COMM Messe f; **fair-haired** adj

blond; **fairly** adv (honestly) fair; (rather) ziemlich

fairy n Fee f; **fairy tale** n Märchen nt

faith n (trust) Vertrauen nt (in sb zu jdm); REL Glaube m; **faithful, faithfully** adj, adv treu; **Yours ~ly** Hochachtungsvoll

fake 1. n (thing) Fälschung f **2.** adj vorgetäuscht **3.** vt fälschen

fall 1. vi fallen; (from a height, badly) stürzen; **~ ill** krank werden; **~ asleep** einschlafen; **~ in love** sich verlieben **2.** n Fall m; (accident) Sturz m; (decrease) Sinken nt (in + gen); (US, autumn) Herbst m; **fall apart** vi auseinanderfallen; **fall behind** vi zurückbleiben; (with work, rent) in Rückstand geraten; **fall down** vi (person) hinfallen; **fall off** vi herunterfallen; (decrease) zurückgehen; **fall out** vi herausfallen; (quarrel) sich streiten; **fall over** vi hinfallen; **fall through** vi (plan etc) ins Wasser fallen

fallen pp of **fall**

false adj falsch; (artificial) künstlich; **false alarm** n blinder Alarm; **false start** n SPORT Fehlstart m; **false teeth** npl (künstliches) Gebiss

fame n Ruhm m

familiar adj vertraut, bekannt; **be ~ with** vertraut sein mit,

gut kennen; **familiarity** n
Vertrautheit f

family n Familie f; *(including
relations)* Verwandtschaft f;
family man n Familienvater
m; **family name** n Familienname m, Nachname m

famine n Hungersnot f

famous adj berühmt

fan n *(hand-held)* Fächer m;
ELEC Ventilator m; *(admirer)*
Fan m

fanatic n Fanatiker(in) m(f)

fancy 1. adj *(elaborate)* kunstvoll; *(unusual)* ausgefallen **2.**
vt *(like)* gern haben; **he fancies her** sie steht auf sie; ~
that stell dir vor!, so was!;
fancy dress n Kostüm nt,
Verkleidung f

fan heater n Heizlüfter m

fantasise vi träumen *(about*
von); **fantastic** adj fantastisch; **that's** ~ fam das ist ja
toll!; **fantasy** n Fantasie f

far 1. adj weit; **the ~ end of the
room** das andere Ende des
Zimmers; **the Far East** der
Ferne Osten *2.* adv weit; ~
better viel besser; **by ~ the
best** bei weitem der/die/
das Beste; **as ~ as ...** bis
zum or zur ...; *(with place
name)* bis nach ...; **as ~ as
I'm concerned** was mich betrifft, von mir aus; **so ~** soweit; bisher; **faraway** adj
weit entfernt; *(look)* ver-
träumt

fare n Fahrpreis m

farm n Bauernhof m, Farm f;
farmer n Bauer m, Bäuerin f,
Landwirt(in) m(f); **farm-
house** n Bauernhaus nt;
farming n Landwirtschaft
f; **farmland** n Ackerland
nt; **farmyard** n Hof m

far-reaching adj weit rei-
chend; **far-sighted** adj weitsichtig

fart 1. n fam Furz m; **old ~** fam
(person) alter Sack **2.** vi
furzen

farther adj, adv comparative of
far; → **further**; **farthest**
adj, adv superlative of **far**;
→ **furthest**

fascinating adj faszinierend;
fascination n Faszination f

fashion n *(clothes)* Mode f;
(manner) Art (und Weise)
f; **be in** ~ (in) Mode sein;
out of ~ unmodisch; **fashionable, fashionably** adj,
adv *(clothes, person)* modisch

fast 1. adj schnell; *(dye)* wasch-
echt; **be** ~ *(clock)* vorgehen
2. adv schnell; *(firmly)* fest;
be ~ **asleep** fest schlafen **3.**
n Fasten nt **4.** vi fasten

fasten vt *(attach)* befestigen
(to an + dat); *(do up)* zumachen; **your seatbelts** bitte
anschnallen; **fastener, fastening** n Verschluss m

fast food n Fast Food nt; **fast
forward** n *(for tape)* Schnell-
vorlauf m; **fast lane** n Überholspur f

fat 1. adj dick; (meat) fett **2.** n
Fett m
fatal adj tödlich
fate n Schicksal nt
fat-free adj (food) fettfrei
father 1. n Vater m; (priest)
Pfarrer m **2.** vt (child) zeu-
gen; **Father Christmas** n
der Weihnachtsmann; **fa-
ther-in-law** n Schwiegervater m
fatigue n Ermüdung f
fattening adj **be ~** dick machen; **fatty** adj (food) fettig
faucet n (US) Wasserhahn m
fault n Fehler m; TECH Defekt
m; ELEC Störung f; (blame)
Schuld f; **it's your ~** du bist
daran schuld; **faulty** adj fehlerhaft; TECH defekt
favor (US), **favour 1.** n (approval) Gunst f; (kindness)
Gefallen m; **in ~ of** für; **I'm
in ~ (of going)** ich bin dafür,
dass wir gehen); **do sb a ~**
jdm einen Gefallen tun **2.**
vt (prefer) vorziehen; **favourite 1.** n Liebling m, Favo-
rit(in) m(f) **2.** adj Lieb-
lings-
fax 1. vt faxen **2.** n Fax nt; **fax
number** n Faxnummer f
FBI abbr = **Federal Bureau of
Investigation**; FBI nt
fear 1. n Angst f (of vor + dat)
2. vt befürchten; **I ~ that
most** davor habe ich am
meisten Angst; **fearful** adj
(timid) ängstlich, furchtsam;
(terrible) fürchterlich

feasible adj machbar
feast n Festessen nt
feather n Feder f
feature 1. n (facial) (Ge-
sichts)zug m; (of characteristic)
Merkmal nt; (of car etc) Aus-
stattungsmerkmal nt; (in the
press) Feature nt **2.** vt bringen, (als Besonderheit) zeigen; **feature film** n Spielfilm
m
February n Februar m; →
September
fed pt, pp of **feed**
federal adj Bundes-; **the Federal Republic of Germany**
die Bundesrepublik
Deutschland
fed-up adj **be ~ with sth** etw
satt haben; **I'm ~** ich habe
die Nase voll
fee n Gebühr f; (of doctor,
lawyer) Honorar nt
feeble adj schwach
feed 1. vt (baby, animal) füttern; (support) ernähren **2.**
n (for baby) Mahlzeit f;
(for animals) Futter nt; (in
paper ~) Zufuhr f; **feed in**
vt (information) eingeben;
feedback n (information)
Feed-back nt
feel 1. vt (sense) fühlen; (pain)
empfinden; (think) meinen
2. vi (person) sich fühlen; **I
~ cold** mir ist kalt; **do you
~ like a walk?** hast du Lust,
spazieren zu gehen?; **feeling**
n Gefühl nt
feet pl of **foot**

fell 1. *pt of* **fall 2.** *vt* (*tree*) fällen

fellow *n* Kerl *m*, Typ *m*; **~ citizen** Mitbürger(in) *m(f)*

felt 1. *pt, pp of* **feel 2.** *n* Filz *m*; **felt tip, felt-tip pen** *n* Filzstift *m*

female 1. *n* (*of animals*) Weibchen *nt* **2.** *adj* weiblich; **~ doctor** Ärztin *f*; **~ dog** Hündin *f*; **feminine** *adj* weiblich

fence *n* Zaun *m*

fencing *n* SPORT Fechten *nt*

fender *n* (*US*) AUTO Kotflügel *m*

fennel *n* Fenchel *m*

fern *n* Farn *m*

ferocious *adj* wild

ferry 1. *n* Fähre *f* **2.** *vt* übersetzen

festival *n* REL Fest *nt*; ART, MUS Festspiele *pl*; (*pop music*) Festival *nt*; **festive** *adj* festlich; **festivities** *n* Feierlichkeiten *pl*

fetch *vt* holen; (*collect*) abholen; (*in sale, money*) einbringen; **fetching** *adj* reizend

fetish *n* Fetisch *m*

fetus *n* (*US*) Fötus *m*

fever *n* Fieber *nt*; **feverish** *adj* MED fiebrig; *fig* fieberhaft

few *adj, pron pl* wenige *pl*; **a ~** *pl* ein paar; **fewer** *adj* weniger; **fewest** *adj* wenigste(r, s)

fiancé *n* Verlobte(r) *m*; **fiancée** *n* Verlobte *f*

fiber (*US*), **fibre** *n* Faser *f*; (*material*) Faserstoff *m*

fiction *n* (*novels*) Prosaliteratur *f*; **fictional, fictitious**

adj erfunden

fiddle 1. *n* Geige *f*; (*trick*) Betrug *m* **2.** *vt* (*accounts, results*) frisieren; **fiddle with** *vt* herumfummeln an + *dat*

fidelity *n* Treue *f*

fidget *vi* zappeln; **fidgety** *adj* zappelig

field *n* Feld *nt*; (*grass-covered*) Wiese *f*; *fig* (*of work*) (Arbeits)gebiet *nt*

fierce *adj* heftig; (*animal, appearance*) wild; (*criticism, competition*) scharf

fifteen 1. *num* fünfzehn **2.** *n* Fünfzehn *f*; → **eight**; **fifteenth** *adj* fünfzehnte(r, s); → **eighth**; **fifth 1.** *adj* fünfte(r, s) **2.** *n* (*fraction*) Fünftel *nt*; → **eighth**; **fifty 1.** *num* fünfzig **2.** *n* Fünfzig *f*; → **eight**; **fiftieth** *adj* fünfzigste(r, s); → **eighth**

fig *n* Feige *f*

fight 1. *vi* kämpfen (*with, against* gegen, *for, over* um) **2.** *vt* (*person*) kämpfen mit; *fig* (*disease, fire etc*) bekämpfen **3.** *n* Kampf *m*; (*brawl*) Schlägerei *f*; (*argument*) Streit *m*; **fight back** *vi* zurückschlagen; **fight off** *vt* abwehren

figurative *adj* übertragen

figure 1. *n* Gestalt *f*; (*of person*) Figur *f*; (*number*) Zahl *f*, Ziffer *f*; (*amount*) Betrag *m*; **a four-figure sum** eine vierstellige Summe **2.** *vt* (*US, think*) glauben **3.** *vi* (*ap-*

pear) erscheinen; **figure out** _vt_ (_work out_) herausbekommen; **I can't figure him out** ich werde aus ihm nicht schlau; **figure skating** _n_ Eiskunstlauf _m_

file 1. _n_ (_tool_) Feile _f_; (_dossier_) Akte _f_; IT Datei _f_; (_folder_) Aktenordner _m_; **on ~** in den Akten **2.** _vt_ (_metal, nails_) feilen; (_papers_) ablegen (_under_ unter)

fill _vt_ füllen; (_tooth_) plombieren; (_post_) besetzen; **fill in** _vt_ (_hole_) auffüllen; (_form_) ausfüllen; (_tell_) informieren (_on_ über); **fill out** _vt_ (_form_) ausfüllen; **fill up** _vi_ AUTO voll tanken

fillet _n_ Filet _nt_

filling _n_ GASTR Füllung _f_; (_for tooth_) Plombe _f_; **filling station** _n_ Tankstelle _f_

film 1. _n_ Film _m_ **2.** _vt_ (_scene_) filmen; **film star** _n_ Filmstar _m_; **film studio** _n_ Filmstudio _nt_

filter 1. _n_ Filter _m_; (_traffic lane_) Abbiegespur _f_ **2.** _vt_ filtern

filth _n_ Dreck _m_; **filthy** _adj_ dreckig

fin _n_ Flosse _f_

final 1. _adj_ letzte(r, s); (_stage, round_) End-; (_decision, version_) endgültig; **~ score** Schlussstand _m_ **2.** _n_ SPORT Endspiel _nt_; (_competition_) Finale _nt_; **~s** _pl_ Abschlussexamen _nt_; **finalize** _vt_ die endgültige Form geben

+ _dat_; **finally** _adv_ (_lastly_) zuletzt; (_eventually_) schließlich, endlich

finance 1. _n_ Finanzwesen _nt_; **~s** _pl_ Finanzen _pl_ **2.** _vt_ finanzieren; **financial** _adj_ finanziell; (_adviser, crisis, policy_ etc) Finanz-

find _vt_ finden; **he was found dead** er wurde tot aufgefunden; **I ~ myself in difficulties** ich befinde mich in Schwierigkeiten; **she ~s it difficult/easy** es fällt ihr schwer/leicht; **find out** _vt_ herausfinden; **findings** _npl_ LAW Ermittlungsergebnis _nt_; MED Befund _m_

fine 1. _adj_ (_thin_) dünn, fein; (_good_) gut; (_splendid_) herrlich; (_weather_) schön; **I'm ~** es geht mir gut; **that's ~** das ist OK **2.** _adv_ (_well_) gut **3.** _n_ LAW Geldstrafe _f_ **4.** _vt_ LAW mit einer Geldstrafe belegen; **fine arts** _npl_ **the ~** die schönen Künste _pl_

finger 1. _n_ Finger _m_ **2.** _vt_ herumfingern an + _dat_; **fingernail** _n_ Fingernagel _m_; **fingerprint** _n_ Fingerabdruck _m_; **fingertip** _n_ Fingerspitze _f_

finicky _adj_ (_person_) pingelig; (_work_) knifflig

finish 1. _n_ Ende _nt_; SPORT Finish _nt_; (_line_) Ziel _nt_; (_of product_) Verarbeitung _f_ **2.** _vt_ beenden; (_book_ etc) zu Ende lesen; (_food_) aufessen; (_drink_) austrinken **3.** _vi_ zu

Ende gehen; (song, story) enden; (person) fertig sein; (stop) aufhören; **have you ~ed?** bist du fertig?; **~ first/ second** SPORT als erster/zweiter durchs Ziel gehen; finishing line n Ziellinie f

Finland n Finnland nt; **Finn** n Finne m, Finnin f; **Finnish 1.** adj finnisch **2.** n (language) Finnisch nt

fir n Tanne f

fire n Feuer nt; (house etc) Brand m; **set ~ to sth** etw in Brand stecken; **be on ~** brennen **2.** vt (bullets, rockets) abfeuern; fam (dismiss) feuern **3.** vi AUTO (engine) zünden; **at sb** auf jdn schießen; fire alarm n Feuermelder m; fire brigade n Feuerwehr f; fire engine n Feuerwehrauto nt; fire escape n Feuerleiter f; fire extinguisher n Feuerlöscher m; firefighter n Feuerwehrmann m, Feuerwehrfrau f; fireman n Feuerwehrmann m; fireplace n (offener) Kamin; fireproof adj feuerfest; fire station n Feuerwache f; fireworks npl Feuerwerk nt

firm 1. adj fest; (person) **be ~** entschlossen auftreten **2.** n Firma f

first 1. adj erste(r, s) **2.** adv at (at first) zuerst; (finally) erstens; (arrive, finish) als erste(r); (happen) zum ersten Mal; **~**

of all zuallererst **3.** n (person) Erste(r) mf; AUTO (gear) erster Gang; **at ~** zuerst, anfangs; first aid n erste Hilfe; first-class **1.** adj erstklassig; (compartment, ticket) erster Klasse; **~ mail** (Brit) bevorzugt beförderte Post **2.** adv (travel) erster Klasse; first floor n (Brit) erster Stock; (US) Erdgeschoss nt; first lady n (US) Frau f des Präsidenten; firstly adv erstens; first name n Vorname m; first night n THEAT Premiere f; first-rate adj erstklassig

fir tree n Tannenbaum m

fish 1. n Fisch m **2.** vi fischen; (with rod) angeln; **go ~ing** fischen/angeln gehen

fishbone n Gräte f; fish farm n Fischzucht f; fish finger n (Brit) Fischstäbchen nt; fishing n Fischen nt; (with rod) Angeln nt; fishing boat n Fischerboot nt; fishing line n Angelschnur f; fishing rod n Angelrute f; fishmonger n Fischhändler(in) m(f); fish stick n (US) Fischstäbchen nt; fish tank n Aquarium nt; fishy adj fam (suspicious) faul

fist n Faust f

fit 1. adj MED gesund; SPORT in Form, fit; **keep ~** sich in Form halten **2.** vt passen + dat; (attach) anbringen (to an + dat); (install) einbauen (in in + acc) **3.** vi passen; (in space, gap) hineinpassen

4. n (of clothes) Sitz m; MED Anfall m; **it's a good ~** es passt gut; **fit in 1.** vt (accommodate) unterbringen; (find time for) einschieben **2.** vi (in space) hineinpassen; (plans, ideas) passen; **he doesn't ~ (here)** er passt nicht hierher; **~ with sb's plans** sich mit jds Plänen vereinbaren lassen; **fitness** n MED Gesundheit f; SPORT Fitness f; **fitted carpet** n Teppichboden m; **fitted kitchen** n Einbauküche f; **fitting 1.** adj passend **2.** n (of dress) Anprobe f; **~s** pl Ausstattung f

five 1. num fünf **2.** n Fünf f; → **eight**; **fiver** n (Brit) fam Fünfpfundschein m

fix vt befestigen (to an + dat); (settle) festsetzen; (date, time) ausmachen; (repair) reparieren; **fixer** n (drug addict) Fixer(in) m(f); **fixture** n **~s (and fittings)** pl Ausstattung f

fizzy adj sprudelnd; **~ drink** Limo f

flabbergasted adj fam platt
flabby adj (fat) wabbelig
flag n Fahne f
flake 1. n Flocke f **2.** vi **~ (off)** abblättern
flamboyant adj extravagant
flame n Flamme f; (person) **an old ~** eine alte Liebe f
flan n (fruit ~) Obstkuchen m
flannel 1. n Flanell m; (Brit,

face **~**) Waschlappen m **2.** vi herumlabern

flap 1. n Klappe f; fam **be in a ~** rotieren **2.** vt (wings) schlagen mit **3.** vi flattern
flared adj (trousers) mit Schlag; **flares** npl Schlaghose f
flash 1. n Blitz m; (news ~) Kurzmeldung f; PHOT Blitzlicht nt; **in a ~** im Nu **2.** vi **~ one's (head)lights** die Lichthupe betätigen **3.** vi (brightly) aufblinken; (brightly) aufblitzen; **flashback** n Rückblende f; **flashlight** n PHOTO Blitzlicht nt; (US, torch) Taschenlampe f; **flashy** adj grell, schrill; pej protzig
flat 1. adj flach (surface) eben; (drink) abgestanden; (tyre) platt; (battery) leer; (refusal) glatt **2.** n (Brit, rooms) Wohnung f; AUTO Reifenpanne f; **flat screen** n IT Flachbildschirm m; **flatten** vt platt machen, einebnen
flatter vt schmeicheln (sb + dat); **flattering** adj schmeichelhaft
flatware n (US) Besteck nt
flavor (US), **flavour 1.** n Geschmack m **2.** vt Geschmack geben + dat; (with spices) würzen; **flavouring** n Aroma nt
flaw n Fehler m; **flawless** adj fehlerlos; (complexion) makellos
flea n Floh m

fled pt, pp of **flee**
flee vi fliehen
fleece n (of sheep) Vlies nt; (soft material) Fleece m; (jacket) Fleecejacke f
fleet n Flotte f
flesh n Fleisch nt
flew pt of **fly**
flex n (Brit) ELEC Schnur f
flexibility n Biegsamkeit f; fig Flexibilität f; **flexible** adj biegsam; (plans, person) flexibel; **flexitime** n gleitende Arbeitszeit, Gleitzeit f
flicker vi flackern; TV flimmern
flies pl of **fly 2**
flight 1. n Flug m; (escape) Flucht f; **~ of stairs** Treppe f; **flight attendant** n Flugbegleiter(in) m(f); **flight recorder** n Flugschreiber m
flimsy adj leicht gebaut, nicht stabil; (thin) hauchdünn; (excuse) fadenscheinig
fling 1. vt schleudern 2. n **have a ~** eine (kurze) Affäre haben
flint n Feuerstein m
flip vt schnippen; **~ a coin** eine Münze werfen; **flip through** vt (book) durchblättern; **flipchart** n Flipchart f
flipper n Flosse f
flirt vi flirten
float vi schwimmen; (in air) schweben
flock n (of sheep) Herde f; (of birds) Schwarm m; (of people) Schar f

flood 1. n Hochwasser nt, Überschwemmung f; fig Flut f 2. vt überschwemmen; **floodlight** n Flutlicht nt; **floodlit** adj (building) angestrahlt
floor n Fußboden m; (storey) Stock m; **ground ~** (Brit), **first ~** (US) Erdgeschoss nt; **first ~** (Brit), **second ~** (US) erster Stock
flop 1. n fam (failure) Reinfall m, Flop m 2. vi misslingen, floppen
floppy disk n Diskette f
Florence n Florenz nt
flounder n (fish) Flunder f
flour n Mehl nt
flourish 1. vi gedeihen; (business) gut laufen; (boom) florieren 2. vt (wave about) schwenken; **flourishing** adj blühend
flow 1. n Fluss m; **go with the ~** mit dem Strom schwimmen 2. vi fließen
flower 1. n Blume f 2. vi blühen; **flower bed** n Blumenbeet nt; **flowerpot** n Blumentopf m
flown pp of **fly**
flu n fam Grippe f
fluent adj (Italian etc) fließend; **be ~ in German** fließend Deutsch sprechen
fluid 1. n Flüssigkeit f 2. adj flüssig
flung pt, pp of **fling**
flush 1. n (lavatory) Wasserspülung f; (blush) Röte f 2.

flute 392

vi (lavatory) spülen

flute n Flöte f

fly 1. vt, vi fliegen; **how time flies** wie die Zeit vergeht! **2.** n (insect) Fliege f; **~ flies** pl (on trousers) Hosenschlitz m; **fly-drive** n Urlaub m mit Flug und Mietwagen; **flyover** n (Brit) Straßenüberführung f, Eisenbahnüberführung f; **flysheet** n Überzelt nt

foal n Fohlen nt

foam 1. n Schaum m **2.** vi schäumen

focus 1. n Brennpunkt m; **in/out of ~** (photo) scharf/unscharf **2.** vt (camera) scharf stellen **3.** vi sich konzentrieren (on auf + acc)

foetus n Fötus m

fog n Nebel m; **foggy** adj neblig; **fog light** n AUTO (at rear) Nebelschlussleuchte f

foil n Folie f

fold 1. vt falten **2.** vi fam (business) eingehen **3.** n Falte f; **fold up 1.** vt (map etc) zusammenfalten; (chair etc) zusammenklappen **2.** vi (business) fam eingehen; **folder** n (portfolio) Aktenmappe f; (pamphlet) Broschüre f; IT Ordner m; **folding** adj zusammenklappbar; (bicycle, chair) Klapp-

folk n Leute pl; MUS Folk m; **my ~s** pl fam meine Leute **2.** adj Volks-

follow vt folgen + dat; (pur-

sue) verfolgen; (understand) folgen können + dat; (career, news etc) verfolgen; **as ~s** wie folgt **2.** vi (result) sich ergeben (from aus); **follow up** vt (request, rumour) nachgehen + dat, weiter verfolgen; **follower** n Anhänger(in) m(f); **following 1.** adj folgend; **the ~ day** (darauf) folgenden Tag **2.** prep nach

fond adj **be ~ of** gern haben; **fondly** adv (with love) liebevoll; **fondness** n Vorliebe f; (for people) Zuneigung f

fondue n Fondue f

font n Taufbecken nt; TYPO Schriftart f

food n Essen nt, Lebensmittel pl; (for animals) Futter nt; **food poisoning** n Lebensmittelvergiftung f; **food processor** n Küchenmaschine f; **foodstuff** n Lebensmittel nt

fool 1. n Idiot m, Narr m; **make a ~ of oneself** sich blamieren **2.** vt (deceive) hereinlegen **3.** vi **~ around** herumalbern; (waste time) herumtrödeln; **foolish** adj dumm; **foolproof** adj idiotensicher

foot 1. n Fuß m; (measure) Fuß m (30,48 cm); **on ~** zu Fuß **2.** vt (bill) bezahlen; **foot-and-mouth disease** n Maul- und Klauenseuche f; **football** n Fußball m; (US) Football m; **footballer** n Fußballspieler(in) m(f); **footbridge** n Fußgängerbrücke f; **footing** n (hold) Halt m; **footnote** n Fußnote f; **footpath** n Fußweg m; **footprint** n Fußabdruck m; **footwear** nt Schuhwerk nt

for 1. prep für; **I'm all** ~ **it** ich bin ganz dafür; (purpose) **what** ~? wozu?; ~ **pleasure** zum Vergnügen; **what's** ~ **lunch?** was gibt es zum Mittagessen?; (destination) **the train** ~ **London** der Zug nach London; (because of?) ~ **this reason** aus diesem Grund; **famous** ~ bekannt für, berühmt wegen; (with time) **we talked** ~ **two hours** wir redeten zwei Stunden lang; (up to now) **we have been talking** ~ **two hours** wir reden seit zwei Stunden; (with distance) ~ **miles (and miles)** meilenweit; **bends** ~ **2 miles** kurvenreich auf 2 Meilen; **as** ~ ... was ... betrifft **2.** conj denn

forbade pt of **forbid**

forbid vt verbieten

force 1. n Kraft f, Gewalt f; **come into** ~ in Kraft treten; **the Forces** pl die Streitkräfte **2.** vt zwingen; **forced** adj (smile) gezwungen

forceps npl Zange f

forearm n Unterarm m

forecast 1. n voraussagen; (weather) vorhersagen **2.** n Vorhersage f

forefinger n Zeigefinger m

foreground n Vordergrund m

forehand n SPORT Vorhand f

forehead n Stirn f

foreign adj ausländisch; **foreigner** n Ausländer(in) m(f); **foreign exchange** n Devisen pl; **foreign language** n Fremdsprache f; **foreign minister**, **foreign secretary** n Außenminister(in) m(f)

foremost adj erste(r, s); (leading) führend

forerunner n Vorläufer(in) m(f)

foresee irr vt vorhersehen; **foreseeable** adj absehbar

forest n Wald m; **forestry** n Forstwirtschaft f

forever adv für immer

forgave pt of **forgive**

forge 1. n Schmiede f **2.** vt schmieden; (fake) fälschen; **forgery** n Fälschung f

forget vt, vi vergessen; ~ **about sth** etw vergessen; **forgetful** adj vergesslich; **forget-me-not** n Vergissmeinnicht nt

forgive irr vt verzeihen; ~ **sb for sth** jdm etw verzeihen

forgot pt of **forget**

forgotten pp of **forget**

fork 1. n Gabel f; (in road) Gabelung f **2.** vi (road) sich gabeln

form 1. n (shape) Form f, Klasse f; (document) Formular nt; (person) **be in** (good)

~ in Form sein 2. *vt* bilden

formal *adj* förmlich, formell; **formality** *n* Formalität *f*

format 1. *n* Format *nt* 2. *vt* IT formatieren

former *adj* frühere(r, s); (*opposite of latter*) erstere(r, s); **formerly** *adv* früher

formula *n* Formel *f*

forth *adv* **and so ~** und so weiter; **forthcoming** *adj* kommend, bevorstehend

fortieth *adj* vierzigste(r, s); → *eighth*

fortnight *n* vierzehn Tage *pl*

fortress *n* Festung *f*

fortunate *adj* glücklich; *I was ~* ich hatte Glück; **fortunately** *adv* zum Glück; **fortune** *n* (*money*) Vermögen *nt*; *good ~* Glück *nt*; **fortune-teller** *n* Wahrsager(in) *m(f)*

forty 1. *num* vierzig 2. *n* Vierzig *f*; → *eight*

forward 1. *adv* vorwärts 2. *n* SPORT Stürmer(in) *m(f)* **3.** *vt* (*send on*) nachsenden; IT weiterleiten; **forwards** *adv* vorwärts

foster child *n* Pflegekind *nt*; **foster parents** *npl* Pflegeeltern *pl*

fought *pt, pp of* **fight**

foul 1. *adj* (*weather*) schlecht; (*smell*) übel *n* SPORT Foul *nt*

found1 *pt, pp of* **find** 2. *vt* (*establish*) gründen; **foundations** *npl* Fundament *nt*

fountain *n* Springbrunnen *m*;

fountain pen *n* Füller *m*

four 1. *num* vier 2. *n* Vier *f*; → *eight*; **fourteen 1.** *num* vierzehn 2. *n* Vierzehn *f*; → *eight*; **fourteenth** *adj* vierzehnte(r, s); → *eighth*; **fourth** *adj* vierte(r, s); → *eighth*

four-wheel drive *n* Allradantrieb *m*; (*car*) Geländewagen *m*

fowl *n* Geflügel *nt*

fox *n* Fuchs *m*

fraction *n* MATH Bruch *m*; (*part*) Bruchteil *m*; **fracture 1.** *n* MED Bruch *m* 2. *vt* brechen

fragile *adj* zerbrechlich

fragment *n* Bruchstück *nt*

fragrance *n* Duft *m*; **fragrant** *adj* duftend

frail *adj* gebrechlich

frame 1. *n* Rahmen *m*; (*of spectacles*) Gestell *nt*; *~ of mind* Verfassung *f* 2. *vt* einrahmen; **framework** *n* Rahmen *m*, Struktur *f*

France *n* Frankreich *nt*

frank *adj* offen

frankfurter *n* (Frankfurter) Würstchen *nt*

frankly *adv* offen gesagt; *quite ~* ganz ehrlich

frantic *adj* (*activity*) hektisch; (*effort*) verzweifelt; *~ with worry* außer sich vor Sorge

fraud *n* (*trickery*) Betrug *m*; (*person*) Schwindler(in) *m(f)*

freak 1. *n* Anomalie *f*; (*ani-*

mal, person) Missgeburt *f*; *fam (fan)* Fan *m*, Freak *m* **2.** *adj (conditions)* außergewöhnlich, seltsam; **freak out** *vi fam* ausflippen

freckle *n* Sommersprosse *f*

free 1. *adj, adv* frei; (*without payment*) gratis, kostenlos; **for** ~ umsonst **2.** *vt* befreien; **freebie** *n fam* Werbegeschenk *nt*; **freedom** *n* Freiheit *f*; **freephone** *adj* **a** ~ **number** eine gebührenfreie Nummer; **free kick** *n* SPORT Freistoß *m*

freelance 1. *adj* freiberuflich tätig; (*artist*) freischaffend **2.** *n* Freiberufler(in) *m(f)*

free-range *adj* (*hen*) frei laufend; ~ **eggs** *pl* Freilandeier *pl*

freeway *n* (*US*) (gebührenfreie) Autobahn

freeze 1. *vi* (*feel cold*) frieren; (*of lake etc*) zufrieren; (*water etc*) gefrieren **2.** *vt* Tiefkühltruhe *f*; (*in fridge*) Gefrierfach *nt*; **freezing** *adj* eiskalt; **I'm** ~ mir ist eiskalt; **freezing point** *n* Gefrierpunkt *m*

freight *n* (*goods*) Fracht *f*; (*money charged*) Frachtgebühr *f*; **freight car** *n* (*US*) Güterwagen *m*; **freight train** *n* (*US*) Güterzug *m*

French 1. *adj* französisch **2.** *n* (*language*) Französisch *nt*; **the** ~ *pl* die Franzosen; **French bean** *n* grüne Boh-

ne; **French bread** *n* Baguette *f*; **French dressing** *n* Vinaigrette *f*; **French fries** (*US*) *npl* Pommes frites *pl*; **French kiss** *n* Zungenkuss *m*; **Frenchman** *n* Franzose *m*; **French toast** *n* (*US*) in Ei und Milch getunktes gebratenes Brot; **French window(s)** *n(pl)* Balkontür *f*, Terrassentür *f*; **Frenchwoman** *n* Französin *f*

frequency *n* Häufigkeit *f*; PHYS Frequenz *f*; **frequent** *adj* häufig; **frequently** *adv* häufig

fresco *n* Fresko *nt*

fresh *adj* frisch; (*new*) neu; **freshen** *vi* ~ **up** (*person*) sich frisch machen; **freshman** *n* Erstsemester *nt*; **freshwater fish** *n* Süßwasserfisch *m*

Fri *abbr* = **Friday**; Fr

friction *n* Reibung *f*

Friday *n* Freitag *m*; → **Tuesday**

fridge *n* Kühlschrank *m*

fried *adj* gebraten; ~ **potatoes** Bratkartoffeln *pl*; ~ **egg** Spiegelei *nt*; ~ **rice** gebratener Reis

friend *n* Freund(in) *m(f)*; (*less close*) Bekannte(r) *mf*; **make** ~**s with sb** sich mit jdm anfreunden; **we're good** ~**s** wir sind gut befreundet; **friendly 1.** *adj* freundlich **2.** *n* SPORT Freundschaftsspiel *nt*; **friendship** *n* Freundschaft f

fright n Schrecken m; **frighten** vt erschrecken; **be ~ed** Angst haben; **frightening** adj beängstigend

frill n Rüsche f; **~s** fam Schnickschnack

fringe n (edge) Rand m; (on shawl etc) Fransen pl; (hair) Pony m

frizzy adj kraus

frog n Frosch m

from prep von; (place, out of) aus; (with date, time) ab; **travel ~ A to B** von A nach B fahren; **the train ~ Bath** der Zug aus Bath; **where does she come ~?** woher kommt sie?; **it's ten miles ~ here** es ist zehn Meilen von hier (entfernt); **~ May 5th** (onwards) ab dem 5. Mai

front 1. n Vorderseite f; (of house) Fassade f; (in war, of weather) Front f; (at seaside) Promenade f; **in ~, at the ~** vorne; **in ~ of** vor; **up ~** (in advance) vorher, im Voraus 2. adj vordere(r, s); Vorder-; (first) vorderste(r, s); **~ door** Haustür f; **~ page** Titelseite f; **~ seat** Vordersitz m; **~ wheel** Vorderrad nt

frontier n Grenze f

front-wheel drive n AUTO Frontantrieb m

frost n Frost m; (white ~) Reif m; **frosting** n (US) Zuckerguss m; **frosty** adj frostig

froth n Schaum m

frown vi die Stirn runzeln

froze pt of **freeze**

frozen 1. pp of **freeze 2.** adj (food) tiefgekühlt, Tiefkühl-

fruit n (as collective, a. type) Obst nt; (single ~) Frucht f; **fruit machine** n Spielautomat m; **fruit salad** n Obstsalat m

frustrated adj frustriert; **frustration** n Frustration f, Frust m

fry vt braten; **frying pan** n Bratpfanne f

fuchsia n Fuchsie f

fuck vt vulg ficken; **~ off** verpiss dich!; **fucking** adj vulg Scheiß-

fudge n ≈ weiche Karamellsüßigkeit

fuel n Kraftstoff m; (for heating) Brennstoff m; **fuel consumption** n Kraftstoffverbrauch m; **fuel gauge** n Benzinuhr f

fugitive n Flüchtling m

fulfil vt erfüllen

full adj voll; (person: satisfied) satt; (member, employment) Voll(zeit)-; (complete) vollständig; **~ of ...** voller ..., gen; **full beam** n AUTO Fernlicht nt; **full moon** n Vollmond m; **full stop** n Punkt m; **full-time** adj **~ job** Ganztagsarbeit f; **fully** adv völlig; (recover) voll und ganz; (discuss) ausführlich

fumble vi herumfummeln (with, at an + dat)

fumes *npl* Dämpfe *pl*; *(of car)* Abgase *pl*

fun *n* Spaß *m*; **for ~** zum Spaß; **it's ~** es macht Spaß; **make ~ of** sich lustig machen über + *acc*

function 1. *n* Funktion *f*; *(event)* Feier *f*; *(reception)* Empfang *m* **2.** *vi* funktionieren

fund *n* Fonds *m*; **~s** *pl* Geldmittel *pl*

fundamental *adj* grundlegend; **fundamentally** *adv* im Grunde

funding *n* finanzielle Unterstützung

funeral *n* Beerdigung *f*

funfair *n* Jahrmarkt *m*

fungus *n* Pilz *m*

funnel *n* Trichter *m*; *(of steamer)* Schornstein *m*

funny *adj* *(amusing)* komisch, lustig; *(strange)* seltsam

fur *n* Pelz *m*; *(of animal)* Fell *nt*

furious *adj* wütend (**with** *sb* *or* jdn)

furnished *adj* möbliert; **furniture** *n* Möbel *pl*; **piece of ~** Möbelstück *nt*

further *comparative of* **far 1.** *adj* weitere(r, s); **~ education** Weiterbildung *f*; **until ~ notice** bis auf weiteres **2.** *adv* weiter; **furthest** *superlative of* **far 1.** *adj* am weitesten entfernt **2.** *adv* am weitesten

fury *n* Wut *f*

fuse 1. *n* ELEC Sicherung *f* **2.** *vi* ELEC durchbrennen; **fuse box** *n* Sicherungskasten *m*

fuss *n* Theater *nt*; **make a ~** ein Theater machen; **fussy** *adj* *(difficult)* schwierig, kompliziert; *(attentive to detail)* pingelig

future 1. *adj* künftig **2.** *n* Zukunft *f*

fuze *(US)* → **fuse**

fuzzy *adj* *(indistinct)* verschwommen; *(hair)* kraus

G

gable *n* Giebel *m*

gadget *n* Vorrichtung *f*, Gerät *nt*

Gaelic 1. *adj* gälisch **2.** *n* *(language)* Gälisch *nt*

gain 1. *vt* *(obtain, win)* gewinnen; *(advantage, respect)* sich verschaffen; *(wealth)* erwerben; *(weight)* zunehmen **2.** *vi* *(improve)* gewinnen *(in*

an + *dat*); *(clock)* vorgehen **3.** *n* Gewinn *m* *(in* an + *dat)*

gale *n* Sturm *m*

gall bladder *n* Gallenblase *f*

gallery *n* Galerie *f*, Museum *nt*

gallon *n* Gallone *f*; *(Brit)* 4,546 *l* *(US)* 3,79 *l*

gallop 1. *n* Galopp *m* **2.** *vi* galoppieren

gallstone n Gallenstein m

Gambia n Gambia nt

gamble 1. vi um Geld spielen, wetten **2.** n **it's a ~** es ist riskant; **gambling** n Glücksspiel nt

game n Spiel nt; (animals) Wild nt; **~s** (in school) Sport m

gammon n geräucherter Schinken

gang n (of criminals, youths) Bande f, Gang f, Clique f

gangster n Gangster m

gangway n (Brit, aisle) Gang m, Gangway f

gap n (hole) Lücke f; (in time) Pause f; (in age) Unterschied m

gape vi (mit offenem Mund) starren

gap year n Jahr zwischen Schulabschluss und Studium, das oft zu Auslandsaufenthalten genutzt wird

garage n Garage f; (for repair) (Auto)werkstatt f

garbage n (US) Müll m; fam (nonsense) Quatsch m; **garbage can** n (US) Mülleimer m; (outside) Mülltonne f; **garbage truck** n (US) Müllwagen m

garbled adj (story) verdreht

garden n Garten m; (public) **~s** Park m; **garden centre** n Gartencenter nt; **gardener** n Gärtner(in) m(f); **gardening** n Gartenarbeit f

gargle vi gurgeln

gargoyle n Wasserspeier m

garlic n Knoblauch m; **garlic bread** n Knoblauchbrot nt; **garlic butter** n Knoblauchbutter f

gas n Gas nt; (US, petrol) Benzin nt; **step on the ~** Gas geben; **gas cooker** n Gasherd m; **gas cylinder** n Gasflasche f; **gas fire** n Gasofen m

gasket n Dichtung f

gas lighter n (for cigarettes) Gasfeuerzeug nt; **gas mask** n Gasmaske f; **gas meter** n Gaszähler m

gasoline n (US) Benzin nt

gasp vi keuchen; (in surprise) nach Luft schnappen

gas pedal n (US) Gaspedal nt; **gas pump** n (US) Zapfsäule f; **gas station** n (US) Tankstelle f; **gas tank** n (US) Benzintank m

gastric adj Magen-; **~ flu** Magen-Darm-Grippe f; **~ ulcer** Magengeschwür nt

gasworks n Gaswerk nt

gate n Tor nt; (barrier) Schranke f, AVIAT Gate nt, Flugsteig m

gateau n Torte f

gateway n Tor nt

gather 1. vt (collect) sammeln; **~ speed** beschleunigen **2.** vi (assemble) sich versammeln; (understand) schließen (from aus); **gathering** n Versammlung f

gauge n Meßgerät nt

gauze n Gaze f; (for bandages) Mull m

gave pt of **give**

gay adj (homosexual) schwul

gaze 1. n Blick m **2.** vi starren

GCSE abbr = **general certificate of secondary education**, ; Abschlussprüfung f der Sekundarstufe, ≈ mittlere Reife

gear n AUTO Gang m; (equipment) Ausrüstung f; (clothes) Klamotten pl; **change ~** schalten; **gearbox** n Getriebe nt; **gear change**, **gear shift** (US) n Gangschaltung f; **gear lever**, **gear stick** (US) n Schalthebel m

geese pl of **goose**

gel 1. n Gel nt **2.** vi gelieren; **they really ~led** sie verstanden sich auf Anhieb

gelatine n Gelatine f

gem n Edelstein m; fig Juwel nt

Gemini nsing ASTR Zwillinge pl

gender n Geschlecht nt

gene n Gen nt

general adj allgemein; **~ knowledge** Allgemeinbildung f; **~ election** Parlamentswahlen pl; **generalize** vi verallgemeinern; **generally** adv im Allgemeinen

generation n Generation f; **generation gap** n Generationsunterschied m

generosity n Großzügigkeit f; **generous** adj großzügig;

(portion) reichlich

genetic adj genetisch; **genetically modified** adj gentechnisch verändert, genmanipuliert; → **GM**

Geneva n Genf nt; **Lake ~** der Genfer See

genitals npl Geschlechtsteile pl

genius n Genie nt

gentle adj sanft; (touch) zart; **gentleman** n Herr m; (polite man) Gentleman m

gents n '~' (lavatory) „Herren"; **the ~** pl die Herrentoilette

genuine adj echt

geographical adj geografisch; **geography** n Geografie f; (at school) Erdkunde f

geometry n Geometrie f

geranium n Geranie f

germ n Keim m; MED Bazillus m

German 1. adj deutsch; **she's ~** sie ist Deutsche; **~ shepherd** Deutscher Schäferhund m **2.** n (person) Deutsche(r) mf; (language) Deutsch nt; **in ~** auf Deutsch; **German measles** n sg Röteln pl; **Germany** n Deutschland nt

gesture n Geste f

get 1. vt (receive) bekommen, kriegen; **~ a cold/ flu** sich erkälten/ eine Grippe bekommen; (buy) kaufen; (obtain) sich besorgen; (to keep) sich anschaffen; **~ sb sth** jdm etw besorgen; (*fetch*) jdm etw holen; **where did you ~ that (from)?** woher hast du das?; **~ a taxi** ein Taxi nehmen; (*persuade*) **~ sb to do sth** jdn dazu bringen, etw zu tun; (*manage*) **~ sth to work** etw zum Laufen bringen; **~ sth done** (*oneself*) etw machen; (*by sb else*) etw machen lassen; (*bring*) **this isn't ~ting us anywhere** so kommen wir nicht weiter; (*understand*) **don't ~ me wrong** versteh mich nicht falsch! **2.** *vi* (*become*) werden; **~ old** alt werden; **it's ~ting dark** es wird dunkel; **~ dressed/washed** sich anziehen/waschen; **I'll ~ ready** ich mache mich fertig; **~ lost** sich verirren; (*arrive*) **we got to Dover at 5** wir kamen um 5 in Dover an; **~ somewhere/nowhere** *fig* (*in career*) zu etwas/nichts bringen; (*with task, discussion*) weiterkommen/nicht weiterkommen; **get about** *vi* ~ **sth** über etw *acc* kommen; **get sth across** (*communicate*) etw klarmachen; **get along** *vi* (*manage*) zurechtkommen; (*people*) gut auskommen; (*with* mit); **get at** *vt* (*reach*) kommen an + *acc*; **what are you getting at?** worauf wollen Sie hinaus?, was meinst du damit?; **get away** *vi* (*leave*)

wegkommen; (*escape*) entkommen (*from* dat); **he got away with it** er kam ungeschoren davon; **get back 1.** *vi* zurückkommen; TEL. **~ to s.o.** jdn zurückrufen **2.** *vt* **get sth back** etw zurückbekommen; **get by** *vi* (*manage*) auskommen (*on* mit); **get down 1.** *vi* herunterkommen; **~ to business** zur Sache kommen **2.** *vt* **get sth down** (*write*) etw aufschreiben; **it gets me down** *fam* es macht mich fertig; **get in** *vi* (*arrive home*) heimkommen; (*into car etc*) einsteigen; **get into** *vt* (*car, bus etc*) einsteigen in + *acc*; (*rage, panic etc*) geraten in + *acc*; **~ trouble** in Schwierigkeiten kommen; **get off** *vi* (*train etc*) aussteigen (*aus*); (*horse*) absteigen (*aus*); *fam* (*be enthusiastic*) **~ on sth** auf etw abfahren; **get on 1.** *vi* (*progress*) vorankommen; (*be friends*) auskommen (*with* mit); **be getting ~** *alt* werden **2.** *vi,* (*train etc*) einsteigen in + *acc*; (*horse*) aufsteigen (*auf* + *acc*); **get out 1.** *vi* herauskommen; (*of vehicle*) aussteigen (*of* aus); **~ !** raus! **2.** *vt* (*take out*) herausholen; (*stain, nail*) herausbekommen; **get over** *vt* (*recover from*) hinwegkommen über + *acc*; (*illness*) sich erholen von; (*loss*) sich abfinden mit; **get through** vi durchkommen; **get up** vi aufstehen; **get-together** n Treffen nt

Ghana n Ghana nt

gherkin n Gewürzgurke f

ghetto n Ghetto nt

ghost n Gespenst nt; (of sb) Geist m

giant 1. n Riese m **2.** adj riesig

giblets npl Geflügelinnereien pl

Gibraltar n Gibraltar nt

giddy adj schwindlig

gift n Geschenk nt; (talent) Begabung f; **gifted** adj begabt; **giftwrap** vt als Geschenk verpacken

gigantic adj riesig

giggle 1. vi kichern **2.** n Gekicher nt

gill n (of fish) Kieme f

gimmick n (for sales, publicity) Gag m

gin n Gin m

ginger 1. n Ingwer m **2.** adj (colour) kupferrot; (cat) rötlichgelb; **ginger ale** n Gingerale nt; **ginger beer** n Ingwerlimonade f; **gingerbread** n Lebkuchen m (mit Ingwergeschmack); **ginger(-haired)** adj rotblond; **gingerly** adv (move) vorsichtig

giraffe n Giraffe f

girl n Mädchen nt; **girlfriend** n (feste) Freundin f; **girl guide** n (Brit), **girl scout** (US) Pfadfinderin f

gist n **get the ~** (of it) das Wesentliche verstehen

give 1. vt geben; (as present) schenken (to sb jdm); (state: name etc) angeben; (speech) halten; (blood) spenden; **~ sb sth** jdm etw geben/ schenken **2.** vi (yield) nachgeben; **give away** vt (give free) verschenken; (secret) verraten; **give back** vt zurückgeben; **give in** vi aufgeben; **give up** vt, vi aufgeben; **give way** vi (collapse, yield) nachgeben; (traffic) die Vorfahrt beachten

given 1. pp of **give 2.** adj (fixed) festgesetzt; (certain) bestimmt; **~ name** (US) Vorname m **3.** conj **~ that ...** angesichts der Tatsache, dass ...

glacier n Gletscher m

glad adj froh (about über); **I was ~ (to hear) that ...** es hat mich gefreut, dass ...; **gladly** adv gerne

glance 1. n Blick m **2.** vi einen Blick werfen (at auf + acc)

gland n Drüse f; **glandular fever** n Drüsenfieber nt

glare 1. n grelles Licht; (stare) stechender Blick **2.** vi (angrily) **~ at sb** jdn böse anstarren

glass n Glas nt; **~es** pl Brille f

glen n (Scot) (enges) Bergtal nt

glide vi gleiten; (hover) schweben; **glider** n Segelflugzeug nt; **gliding** n Segelfliegen *nt*

glimpse *n* flüchtiger Blick

glitter *vi* glitzern; (*eyes*) funkeln

glitzy *adj fam* glanzvoll, Schickimicki-

global *adj* global, Welt-; ~ **warming** die Erwärmung der Erdatmosphäre; **globe** *n* (*sphere*) Kugel *f*; (*world*) Erdball *m*; (*map*) Globus *m*

gloomily, gloomy *adv, adj* düster

glorious *adj* (*victory, past*) ruhmreich; (*weather, day etc*) herrlich; **glory** *n* Herrlichkeit *f*

gloss *n* (*shine*) Glanz *m*

glossary *n* Glossar *nt*

glossy 1. *adj* (*surface*) glänzend **2.** *n* (*magazine*) Hochglanzmagazin *nt*

glove *n* Handschuh *m*; **glove compartment** *n* Handschuhfach *nt*

glow *vi* glühen

glucose *n* Traubenzucker *m*

glue 1. *n* Klebstoff *m* **2.** *vt* kleben

glutton *n* Vielfraß *m*; **a ~ for punishment** *fam* Masochist *m*

GM *abbr* = **genetically modified**; Gen-; ~ **foods** gentechnisch veränderte Lebensmittel

GMT *abbr* = **Greenwich Mean Time**; WEZ *f*

go 1. *vi* gehen; (*in vehicle, travel*) fahren; (*plane*) fliegen; (*road*) führen (*to* nach); (*depart: train, bus*) (ab)fahren; (*person*) (fort)gehen; (*disappear*) verschwinden; (*time*) vergehen; (*function*) gehen, funktionieren; (*machine, engine*) laufen; (*fit, suit*) passen (*with zu*); (*fail*) nachlassen; **I have to ~ to the doctor/to London** ich muss zum Arzt/nach London; ~ **shopping** einkaufen gehen; **for a walk/swim** spazieren/schwimmen gehen; **has he gone yet?** ist er schon weg?; **the wine ~es in the cupboard** der Wein kommt in den Schrank; **get sth ~ing** etw in Gang setzen; **keep ~ing** weitermachen; (*machine etc*) weiterlaufen; **how's the job ~ing?** wie macht der Job?; ~ **deaf/mad/grey** taub/verrückt/grau werden **2.** *v aux* be **~ing to do sth** etw tun werden; **I was ~ing to do it** ich wollte es tun **3.** *n* (*attempt*) Versuch *m*; **can I have another~?** darf ich noch mal (probieren)?; **it's my ~** ich bin dran; **in one ~** auf einen Schlag; (*drink*) in einem Zug; **go after** *vt* nachlaufen + *dat*; (*in vehicle*) nachfahren + *dat*; **go ahead** *vi* (*start*) anfangen; (*start*) anfangen; **go away** *vi* weggehen; (*on holiday, business*) verreisen; **go back** *vi* (*return*) zurückgehen; **go by 1.** vi vorbeigehen; (vehicle) vorbeifahren; (years, time) vergehen **2.** vt (judge by) gehen nach; **go down** vi (sun, ship) untergehen; (flood, temperature) zurückgehen; (price) sinken; **~ well/badly** gut/schlecht ankommen; **go in** vi hineingehen; **go into** vt (enter) hineingehen in + acc; (crash) fahren gegen, hineinfahren in + acc; **~ teaching/politics/the army** Lehrer werden/in die Politik gehen/zum Militär gehen; **go off 1.** vi (depart) weggehen; (in vehicle) wegfahren; (lights) ausgehen; (milk etc) sauer werden; (gun, bomb, alarm) losgehen **2.** vt (dislike) nicht mehr mögen; **go on** vi (continue) weitergehen; (lights) angehen; **~ with or doing sth** etw weitermachen; **go out** vi (leave house) hinausgehen; (fire, light, person socially) ausgehen; **~ for a meal** essen gehen; **go up** vi (temperature, price) steigen; (lift) hochfahren; **go without** vt verzichten auf + acc; (food, sleep) auskommen ohne

go-ahead 1. adj (progressive) fortschrittlich **2.** n grünes Licht

goal n (aim) Ziel nt; SPORT Tor nt; **goalie, goalkeeper** n Torwart m; **goalpost** n Torpfos-

ten m

goat n Ziege f

gob 1. n (Brit) fam Maul nt; **shut your ~** halt's Maul! **2.** vi spucken; **gobsmacked** fam (surprised) platt

god n Gott m; **thank God** Gott sei Dank; **godchild** n Patenkind nt; **goddaughter** n Patentochter f; **goddess** n Göttin f; **godfather** n Pate m; **godmother** n Patin f; **godson** n Patensohn m

goggles npl Schutzbrille f; (for skiing) Skibrille f; (for diving) Taucherbrille f

going adj (rate) üblich; **goings-on** npl Vorgänge pl

go-kart n Gokart m

gold 1. n Gold nt **2.** adj golden; **goldfish** n Goldfisch m; **gold-plated** adj vergoldet

golf n Golf nt; **golf ball** n Golfball m; **golf club** n Golfschläger m; (association) Golfklub m; **golf course** n Golfplatz m

gone 1. pp of **go**; **he's ~** er ist weg **2.** prep **just ~ three** gerade drei Uhr vorbei

good 1. n (benefit) Wohl nt; (morally good things) Gute(s) nt; **it's for your own ~** es ist zu deinem Besten or Vorteil; **it's no ~** (doing sth) es hat keinen Sinn or Zweck; (thing) es taugt nichts; **for ~** für immer **2.** adj (gut; (suitable) passend; (thorough) gründlich; (well-behaved)

brav; (kind) nett, lieb; **be ~ at
sport/ maths** gut in Sport/
Mathe sein; **be no ~ at
sport/maths** schlecht in
Sport/Mathe sein; **too ~ to
be true** zu schön, um wahr
zu sein; **this is just not ~
enough** so geht das nicht;
a ~ three hours gute drei
Stunden; **~ morning/ evening** guten Morgen/Abend;
~ night gute Nacht; **have a ~
time** sich gut amüsieren

goodbye interj auf Wiedersehen

Good Friday n Karfreitag m

good-looking adj gut aussehend

goods npl Waren pl, Güter pl;
goods train n (Brit) Güterzug m

goose n Gans f; **gooseberry**
n Stachelbeere f; **goose
bumps** n, **goose pimples**
npl Gänsehaut f

gorge n Schlucht f

gorgeous adj wunderschön;
he's ~ er sieht toll aus

gorilla n Gorilla m

gossip 1. n (talk) Klatsch m;
(person) Klatschtante f **2.**
vi klatschen, tratschen

got pt, pp of **get**

gotten (US) pp of **get**

govern vt regieren; (province
etc) verwalten; **government**
n Regierung f; **governor** n
Gouverneur(in) m(f); **govt**
abbr = **government**; Regierung f

gown n Abendkleid nt; (academic) Robe f

GP abbr = **General Practitioner**; praktischer Arzt

GPS n abbr = **global posi-
tioning system**; GPS nt

grab vt packen; (person)
schnappen

graceful adj anmutig

grade n Niveau nt; (of goods)
Güteklasse f; (mark) Note f;
(US, year) Klasse f; **make
the ~** es schaffen; **grade
crossing** n (US) Bahnübergang m; **grade school** n
(US) Grundschule f

gradient n (upward) Steigung
f; (downward) Gefälle nt

gradual, gradually adj, adv
allmählich

graduate 1. n Uniabsol-
vent(in) m(f), Akademi-
ker(in) m(f) **2.** vi einen akademischen Grad erwerben

grain n (cereals) Getreide nt;
(of corn, sand) Korn nt

gram n Gramm nt

grammar n Grammatik f;
grammar school n (Brit) ≈
Gymnasium nt

gran n fam Oma f

grand 1. adj hochnäsig;
(posh) vornehm **2.** n fam
1000 Pfund bzw. 1000 Dollar

grand(d)ad n fam Opa m;
granddaughter n Enkelin
f; **grandfather** n Großvater
m; **grandma** n fam Oma f;
grandmother n Großmutter
f; **grandpa** n fam Opa m;

grandparents npl Großeltern pl; **grandson** n Enkel m

grandstand n SPORT Tribüne f

granny n fam Oma f

grant 1. vt gewähren (sb sth jdm etw); **take sb/ sth for ~ed** jdn/etw als selbstverständlich hinnehmen **2.** n Subvention f, finanzielle Unterstützung f; (for university) Stipendium n

grape n Weintraube f; **grapefruit** n Grapefruit f; **grape juice** n Traubensaft m

graph n Diagramm n; **graphic** adj grafisch; (description) anschaulich

grasp vt ergreifen; (understand) begreifen

grass n Gras nt; (lawn) Rasen m; **grasshopper** n Heuschrecke f

grate 1. n Feuerrost m **2.** vi kratzen **3.** vt (cheese) reiben

grateful, gratefully adj, adv dankbar

grater n Reibe f

gratifying adj erfreulich

gratitude n Dankbarkeit f

grave 1. n Grab nt **2.** adj ernst; (mistake) schwer

gravel n Kies m

graveyard n Friedhof m

gravity n Schwerkraft f; (seriousness) Ernst m

gravy n Bratensoße f

gray adj (US) grau

graze 1. vi (of animals) grasen **2.** vt (touch) streifen; MED abschürfen **3.** n MED Abschür-

fung f

grease 1. n (fat) Fett nt; (lubricant) Schmiere f **2.** vt einfetten; TECH schmieren; **greasy** adj fettig; (hands, tools) schmierig; fam (person) schleimig

great adj groß; fam (good) großartig, super; **a ~ deal of** viel; Great Britain n Großbritannien nt; **great-grandfather** n Urgroßvater m; **great-grandmother** n Urgroßmutter f; **greatly** adv sehr; **~ disappointed** zutiefst enttäuscht

Greece n Griechenland nt

greed n Gier f (for nach); (for food) Gefräßigkeit f; **greedy** adj gierig; (for food) gefräßig

Greek 1. adj griechisch **2.** n (person) Grieche m, Griechin f; (language) Griechisch nt

green 1. adj grün **2.** n (colour, for golf) Grün nt; (village ~) Dorfwiese f; **~s** (vegetables) grünes Gemüse; **the Greens, the Green Party** POL die Grünen; **green card** n (US, work permit) Arbeitserlaubnis f; (Brit, for car) grüne Versicherungskarte f; **greengage** n Reneklode f; **greengrocer** n Obst- und Gemüsehändler(in) m(f); **greenhouse** n Gewächshaus nt; **~ effect** Treibhauseffekt m; Greenland n Grönland *nt*; **green pepper** *n* grüner Paprika; **green salad** *n* grüner Salat

greet *vt* grüßen; **greeting** *n* Gruß *m*

grew *pt of* **grow**

grey *adj* grau; **grey-haired** *adj* grauhaarig; **greyhound** *n* Windhund *m*

grid *n* Gitter *nt*; **gridlock** *n* Verkehrsinfarkt *m*; **gridlocked** *adj* (roads) völlig verstopft; (talks) festgefahren

grief *n* Kummer *m*; (over loss) Trauer *f*

grievance *n* Beschwerde *f*

grieve *vi* trauern (for um)

grill 1. *n* (on cooker) Grill *m* **2.** *vt* grillen

grim *adj* (face, humour) grimmig; (situation, prospects) trostlos

grin 1. *n* Grinsen *nt* **2.** *vi* grinsen

grind *vt* mahlen; (sharpen) schleifen; (US, meat) durchdrehen

grip 1. *n* Griff *m*; **get a ~** nimm dich zusammen!; **get to ~s with sth** etw in den Griff bekommen **2.** *vt* packen

gristle *n* Knorpel *m*

groan *vi* stöhnen (with vor + dat)

grocer *n* Lebensmittelhändler(in) *m(f)*; **groceries** *npl* Lebensmittel *pl*

groin *n* ANAT Leiste *f*; **groin strain** *n* MED Leistenbruch *m*

groom 1. *n* Bräutigam *m* **2.** *vt*

well ..ed gepflegt

groovy *adj fam* cool

grope 1. *vi* tasten **2.** *vt* (sexually harrass) befummeln

gross *adj* (coarse) derb; (extreme: negligence, error) grob; (disgusting) ekelhaft; COMM brutto; **~ salary** Bruttogehalt *nt*

grotty *adj fam* mies, vergammelt

ground 1. *pt, pp of* **grind 2.** *n* Boden *m*, Erde *f*; SPORT Platz *m*; **~s** *pl* (around house) (Garten)anlagen *pl*; (reasons) Gründe *pl*; (of coffee) Satz *m*; **on** (the) **~s of** aufgrund von; **ground floor** *n* (Brit) Erdgeschoss *nt*; **ground meat** *n* (US) Hackfleisch *nt*

group *n* Gruppe *f*

grouse 1. *n* (bird) Schottisches Moorhuhn; (complaint) Nörgelei *f*

grow 1. *vi* wachsen; (increase) zunehmen (in an); (become) werden; **~ old** alt werden; **~ into ...** sich entwickeln zu ... **2.** *vt* (crop, plant) ziehen; (commercially) anbauen; **I'm ~ing a beard** ich lasse mir einen Bart wachsen; **grow up** *vi* aufwachsen; (mature) erwachsen werden; **growing** *adj* wachsend; **a ~ number of people** immer mehr Leute

growl *vi* knurren

grown *pp of* **grow**

grown-up 1. adj erwachsen **2.** n Erwachsene(r) mf; **growth** n Wachstum nt; (increase) Zunahme f; MED Wucherung f

grubby adj schmuddelig

grudge 1. n Abneigung f (against gegen) **2.** vt ~ **sb sth** jdm etw nicht gönnen

gruelling adj aufreibend; (pace) mörderisch

gruesome adj grausig

grumble vi murren (about über + acc)

grumpy adj fam mürrisch, grantig

grunt vi grunzen

G-string n ≈ Tanga m

guarantee 1. n Garantie f (of für) **2.** vt garantieren

guard 1. n (sentry) Wache f; (in prison) Wärter(in) m(f); (Brit) RAIL Schaffner(in) m(f) **2.** vt bewachen

guardian n Vormund m; ~ **angel** Schutzengel m

guess 1. n Vermutung f; (estimate) Schätzung f; **have a** ~ rate mal! **2.** vt, vi raten; (estimate) schätzen; **I** ~ **you're right** du hast wohl recht; **I** ~ **so** ich glaube schon; **guesstimate** n fam grobe Schätzung

guest n Gast m; **be my** ~ nur zu!; **guest-house** n Pension f; **guest room** n Gästezimmer nt

guidance n (direction) Leitung f; (advice) Rat m;

(counselling) Beratung f; **for your** ~ zu Ihrer Orientierung; **guide 1.** n (person) Führer(in) m(f); (tour) Reiseleiter(in) m(f); (book) Führer m **2.** vt führen; **guidebook** n Reiseführer m; **guide dog** n Blindenhund m; **guided tour** n Führung f (of durch); **guidelines** npl Richtlinien pl

guilt n Schuld f; **guilty** adj schuldig (of gen); (look) schuldbewusst; **have a ~ conscience** ein schlechtes Gewissen haben

guinea pig n Meerschweinchen nt; (person) Versuchskaninchen nt

guitar n Gitarre f

gulf n Golf m; **Gulf States** npl Golfstaaten pl

gull n Möwe f

gullible adj leichtgläubig

gulp 1. n (kräftiger) Schluck **2.** vi schlucken

gum 1. n (around teeth, usu pl) Zahnfleisch nt; (chewing ~) Kaugummi m

gun n Schusswaffe f; (rifle) Gewehr nt; (pistol) Pistole f; **gunfire** n Schüsse pl; **gunpowder** n Schießpulver nt

gush vi (heraus)strömen (from aus)

gut n Darm m; ~**s** pl (intestines) Eingeweide; (courage) Mumm m

gutter n (for roof) Dachrinne f; (in street) Rinnstein m,

Gosse f

guy n (man) Typ m, Kerl m; **~s** pl (US) Leute pl
gym n Turnhalle f; (for working out) Fitnesscenter nt; **gymnasium** n Turnhalle f; **gymnastics** nsing Turnen

nt; **gym-toned** adj durchtrainiert

gynaecologist n Frauenarzt m, Frauenärztin f, Gynäkologe m, Gynäkologin f; **gynaecology** n Gynäkologie f

H

habit n Gewohnheit f; **habitual** adj gewohnt; (drinker, liar) gewohnheitsmäßig
hack vt hacken; **hacker** n IT Hacker(in) m(f)
had pt, pp of **have**
haddock n Schellfisch m
hadn't contr of **had not**
haemophiliac, hemophiliac (US) n Bluter(in) m(f); **haemorrhage, hemorrhage** (US) **1.** n Blutung f **2.** vi bluten; **haemorrhoids, hemorrhoids** (US) npl Hämorrhoiden pl
haggis n (Scot) mit gehackten Schafsinnereien und Haferschrot gefüllter Schafsmagen
hail 1. n Hagel m **2.** vi hageln **3.** vt **~ sb as sth** jdn als etw feiern; **hailstone** n Hagelkorn nt; **hailstorm** n Hagelschauer m
hair n Haar nt, Haare pl; **get one's ~ cut** sich dat die Haare schneiden lassen; **hairbrush** n Haarbürste f; **hair conditioner** n Haarspülung f; **haircut** n Haarschnitt m;

hairdo n Frisur f; **hairdresser** n Friseur m, Friseuse f; **hairdryer** n Haartrockner m; (hand-held) Fön® m; (over head) Trockenhaube f; **hair gel** n Haargel nt; **hair remover** n Enthaarungsmittel nt; **hair spray** n Haarspray nt; **hair style** n Frisur f; **hairy** adj haarig, behaart; fam (dangerous) brenzlig
hake n Seehecht m
half 1. n Hälfte f; sport (of game) Halbzeit f; **cut in ~** halbieren **2.** adj halb; **three and a ~ pounds** dreieinhalb Pfund; **~ an hour, a ~ hour** eine halbe Stunde; **one and a ~** eineinhalb, anderthalb **3.** adv halb, zur Hälfte; **~ asleep** fast eingeschlafen; **~ as big (as)** halb so groß (wie); **half board** n Halbpension f; **half fare** n halber Fahrpreis; **half-hearted** adj halbherzig; **half-hour** n halbe Stunde f; **half moon** n Halbmond m; **half pint** n ≈ Viertelliter m or nt; **half**

price n (**at**) ~ zum halben Preis; **half-term** n (at school) Ferien pl in der Mitte des Trimesters; **half-time** n Halbzeit f; **halfway** adv auf halbem Wege; **halfwit** n fam Trottel m

halibut n Heilbutt m

hall n (building) Halle f; (for audience) Saal m; (entrance hall) Flur m; (large) Diele f; **~ of residence** (Brit) Studentenwohnheim nt

hallo interj hallo

halt 1. n Pause f, Halt m; **come to a** ~ zum Stillstand kommen 2. vt, vi anhalten

halve vt halbieren

ham n Schinken m

hamburger n GASTR Hamburger m

hammer 1. n Hammer m 2. vt, vi hämmern

hammock n Hängematte f

hamper 1. vt behindern 2. n (as gift) Geschenkkorb m; (for picnic) Picknickkorb m

hamster n Hamster m

hand 1. n Hand f; (of clock, instrument) Zeiger m; (in card game) Blatt nt; **~s off!** Finger weg!; **on the one ~ ...**, **on the other ~...** einerseits ..., andererseits ...; **give sb a ~** jdm helfen (with bei); **it's in his ~s** er hat es in der Hand; **be in good ~s** gut aufgehoben sein; **get out of ~** außer Kontrolle geraten 2. vt (pass) reichen (to sb jdm); hand

down vt (tradition) überliefern; (heirloom) vererben; **hand in** vt einreichen; (at school, university etc) abgeben; **hand out** vt verteilen; **hand over** vt übergeben

handbag n Handtasche f; **handbook** n Handbuch nt; **handbrake** n (Brit) Handbremse f; **hand cream** n Handcreme f; **handcuffs** npl Handschellen pl; **handheld PC** n Handheld m

handicap 1. n Behinderung f, Handikap nt 2. vt benachteiligen; **handicapped** adj behindert; **the ~** die Behinderten

handicraft n Kunsthandwerk nt

handkerchief n Taschentuch nt

handle 1. n Griff m; (of door) Klinke f; (of cup etc) Henkel m; (for winding) Kurbel f 2. vt (touch) anfassen; (deal with: matter) sich befassen mit; (people, machine etc) umgehen mit; (situation, problem) fertig werden mit; **handlebars** npl Lenkstange f

hand luggage n Handgepäck nt; **handmade** adj handgefertigt; **be ~** Handarbeit sein; **handout** n (sheet) Handout nt, Thesenpapier nt; **handset** n Hörer m; **please replace the** ~ bitte legen Sie auf; **hands-free phone** n

handshake

Freisprechanlage f; **handshake** n Händedruck m

handsome adj (man) gut aussehend

hands-on adj praxisorientiert; ~ **experience** praktische Erfahrung

handwriting n Handschrift f

handy adj (useful) praktisch

hang 1. vt (auf)hängen; (execute: hanged, hanged) hängen **2.** vi hängen **3.** n **he's got the ~ of it** er hat den Dreh raus; **hang about** vi sich herumtreiben, rumhängen; **hang on** vi sich festhalten (to an + dat); fam (wait) warten; **~ to sth** etw behalten; **hang up 1.** vi TEL auflegen **2.** vt aufhängen

hanger n Kleiderbügel m

hang glider n (Flug)drachen m; (person) Drachenflieger(in) m(f); **hang-gliding** n Drachenfliegen nt

hangover n (bad head) Kater m; (relic) Überbleibsel nt

hankie n fam Taschentuch nt

happen vi geschehen; (sth strange, unpleasant) passieren; **if anything should ~ to me** wenn mir etwas passieren sollte; **it won't ~ again** es wird nicht wieder vorkommen; **I ~ed to be passing** ich kam zufällig vorbei; **happening** n Ereignis nt

happily adv fröhlich, glücklich; (luckily) glücklicherweise; **happiness** n Glück

nt; **happy** adj glücklich; (satisfied) ~ **with sth** mit etw zufrieden; (willing) **be ~ to do sth** etw gerne tun; **Happy Christmas** fröhliche Weihnachten!; **Happy New Year** ein glückliches Neues Jahr!; **Happy Birthday** herzlichen Glückwunsch zum Geburtstag!; **happy hour** n Happy Hour f

harass vt (ständig) beläsigen; **harassment** n Belästigung f; (at work) Mobbing nt; **sexual ~** sexuelle Beläsigung

harbor (US), **harbour** n Hafen m

hard 1. adj hart; (difficult) schwer, schwierig; (harsh) hart(herzig); **don't be ~ on him** sei nicht zu streng zu ihm; **it's ~ to believe** es ist kaum zu glauben **2.** adv (work) schwer; (run) schnell; (rain, snow) stark; **try ~/~er** sich dat große / mehr Mühe geben; **hardback** n gebundene Ausgabe; **hard-boiled** adj (egg) hart gekocht; **hard copy** n IT Ausdruck m; **hard disk** n IT Festplatte f; **harden 1.** vt härten **2.** vi hart werden; **hardly** adv kaum; ~ **ever** fast nie; **hardship** n Not f; **hard shoulder** n (Brit) Standspur f; **hardware** n IT Hardware f, Haushalts- und Eisenwaren pl; **hard-working** adj fleißig, tüchtig

hare n Hase m

harm 1. n Schaden m; (bodily) Verletzung f; **it wouldn't do any ~** es würde nicht schaden **2.** vt schaden + dat; (person) verletzen; **harmful** adj schädlich; **harmless** adj harmlos

harp n Harfe f

harsh adj (climate, voice) rau; (light, sound) grell; (severe) hart, streng

harvest 1. n Ernte f; (time) Erntezeit f **2.** vt ernten

has pres of **have**

hash n GASTR Haschee nt; fam (hashish) Haschisch nt; **make a ~ of** etw vermasseln; **hash browns** npl (US) ≈ Kartoffelpuffer pl

hassle n **1.** Ärger m; (fuss) Theater nt; **no ~** kein Problem **2.** vt bedrängen

hasn't abbr of **has not**

haste n Eile f; **hastily, hasty** adv, adj hastig; (rash) vorschnell

hat n Hut m

hatch n NAUT Luke f; (in house) Durchreiche f; **hatchback** n (car) Wagen m mit Hecktür

hate 1. vt hassen; **I ~ doing this** ich mache das sehr ungern **2.** n Hass m (of auf + acc)

haul 1. vt ziehen, schleppen **2.** n (booty) Beute f; **haulage** n Transport m; (trade) Spedition f

haunted adj a **~ house** ein Haus, in dem es spukt

have 1. vt haben; (possess) **~ you got** or **do you ~ a light?** haben Sie Feuer?; (receive) **I've just had a letter from ...** ich habe soeben einen Brief von ... erhalten; **~ a baby** ein Kind bekommen; (to eat/drink) **what are you having?** was willst du (essen/trinken)?; **I had too much wine** ich habe zu viel Wein getrunken; **~ lunch/dinner** zu Mittag/Abend essen; (hold) **~ a party** eine Party geben; (take) **~ a bath/shower** ein Bad nehmen/duschen; (causative) **~ sth done** etw machen lassen; **they had a good time** sie haben sich gut amüsiert; (phrases with 'it') **I won't ~ it** das lasse ich mir nicht bieten!; **we've had it** fam wir sind geliefert **2.** v aux (forming perfect tenses) haben/sein; **he has seen it** er hat es gesehen; **she has come** sie ist gekommen; (expressing compulsion) **~ (got) to do sth** etw tun müssen; **you don't ~ to go** du musst nicht gehen; (in tag questions) **you've been there, ~n't you?** du bist mal dort gewesen, nicht wahr?; **have on** vt (be wearing) anhaben; (have arranged) vorhaben; (Brit) **you're having me on**

das meinst du nicht ernst

Hawaii n Hawaii nt

hawk n Habicht m

hay n Heu nt; **hay fever** n Heuschnupfen m

hazard n Gefahr f; (risk) Risiko nt; **hazardous** adj gefährlich; **~ waste** Sondermüll m; **hazard warning lights** npl Warnblinkanlage f

haze n Dunst m

hazelnut n Haselnuss f

hazy adj (misty) dunstig; (vague) verschwommen

he pron er

head 1. n Kopf m; (leader) Leiter(in) m(f); (at school) Schulleiter(in) m(f); (of state) Staatsoberhaupt nt; (tossing coin) **~s or tails?** Kopf oder Zahl? **2.** adj (leading) Ober-; **~ boy** Schulsprecher m; **~ girl** Schulsprecherin f **3.** vt anführen; (organization) leiten; **head for** vt steuern auf + acc; **he's heading for trouble** er wird Ärger bekommen

headache n Kopfschmerzen pl, Kopfweh nt; **header** n (soccer) Kopfball m; (dive) Kopfsprung m; **headfirst** adj kopfüber; **headhunt** vt COMM abwerben; **heading** n Überschrift f; **headlamp**, **headlight** n Scheinwerfer m; **headline** n Schlagzeile f; **headmaster** n Schulleiter m; **headmistress** n Schulleiterin f; **headphones** npl

Kopfhörer m; **headquarters** npl (of firm) Zentrale f; **headrest**, **head restraint** n Kopfstütze f; **headscarf** n Kopftuch nt; **head teacher** n Schulleiter(in) m(f)

heal vt, vi heilen

health n Gesundheit f; **good/bad for one's** ~ gesund/ ungesund; **health centre** n Ärztezentrum nt; **health club** n Fitnesscenter nt; **health food** n Reformkost f; **~ store** Bioladen m; **health insurance** n Krankenversicherung f; **health service** n Gesundheitswesen nt; **healthy** adj gesund

heap 1. n Haufen m; **~s of** fam jede Menge **2.** vt, vi häufen

hear vt, vi hören; **~ about sth** von etw erfahren; **I've ~d of it/him** ich habe schon davon/von ihm gehört; **hearing** n Gehör nt; LAW Verhandlung f; **hearing aid** n Hörgerät nt; **hearsay** n **from** ~ vom Hörensagen

heart n Herz nt; **loose/take** ~ den Mut verlieren/Mut fassen; **learn by** ~ auswendig lernen; (cards) **~s** Herz nt; **queen of** ~s Herzdame f; **heart attack** n Herzanfall m; **heartbeat** n Herzschlag m; **heartbreaking** adj herzzerreißend; **heartbroken** adj todunglücklich; untröstlich; **heartburn** n Sodbrennen nt; **heart failure** n Herzversagen *nt*; **heartfelt** *adj* tief empfunden; **heart-throb** *n fam* Schwarm *m*; **heart-to-heart** *n* offene Aussprache; **hearty** *adj* (*meal*, *appetite*) herzhaft; (*welcome*) herzlich

heat 1. *n* Hitze *f*; (*pleasant*) Wärme *f*; (*temperature*) Temperatur *f*; SPORT Vorlauf *m* **2.** *vt* (*house*, *room*) heizen; **heat up 1.** *vi* warm werden **2.** *vt* aufwärmen; **heated** *adj* beheizt; *fig* hitzig; **heater** *n* Heizofen *m*; AUTO Heizung *f*

heath *n* (*Brit*) Heide *f*; **heather** *n* Heidekraut *nt*

heating *n* Heizung *f*; **heatstroke** *n* Hitzschlag *m*

heaven *n* Himmel *m*; **heavenly** *adj* himmlisch

heavily *adv* (*rain*, *drink etc*) stark; **heavy** *adj* schwer; (*rain*, *traffic*, *smoker etc*) stark

Hebrew 1. *adj* hebräisch **2.** *n* (*language*) Hebräisch *nt*

hectic *adj* hektisch

he'd *contr* of **he had**; **he would**

hedge *n* Hecke *f*

hedgehog *n* Igel *m*

heel *n* ANAT Ferse *f*; (*of shoe*) Absatz *m*

hefty *adj* schwer; (*person*) stämmig; (*fine*, *amount*) saftig

height *n* Höhe *f*; (*of person*) Größe *f*

heir *n* Erbe *m*; **heiress** *n* Erbin *f*

held *pt*, *pp* of **hold**

helicopter *n* Hubschrauber *m*; **heliport** *n* Hubschrauberlandeplatz *m*

hell *n* Hölle *f*; **go to ~** scher dich zum Teufel; **that's a ~ of a lot of money** das ist verdammt viel Geld **2.** *interj* verdammt

he'll *contr* **he will**; **he shall**

hello *interj* hallo

helmet *n* Helm *m*

help 1. *n* Hilfe *f* **2.** *vt*, *vi* helfen + *dat* (*with* bei); **~ sb (to) do sth** jdm helfen, etw zu tun; **can I ~?** kann ich (Ihnen) behilflich sein?; **I couldn't ~ laughing** ich musste einfach lachen; **I can't ~ it** ich kann nichts dafür; **~ yourself** bedienen Sie sich; **helpful** *adj* (*person*) hilfsbereit; (*useful*) nützlich; **helping** *n* Portion *f*; **helpless** *adj* hilflos

hem *n* Saum *m*

hemophiliac *n* (*US*) Bluter *m*; **hemorrhage** *n* (*US*) Blutung *f*; **hemorrhoids** *npl* (*US*) Hämorrhoiden *pl*

hen *n* Henne *f*

hen night *n* (*Brit*) Junggesellinnenabschied

hence *adv* (*reason*) daher

Hepatitis *n* Hepatitis *f*

her 1. *adj* ihr; **she's hurt ~ leg** sie hat sich *dat* das Bein verletzt **2.** *pron* (*direct object*) sie; (*indirect object*) ihr; **do you know ~?** kennst du

sie?; *can you help ~?* kannst du ihr helfen?; *it's ~* sie ist's
herb n Kraut nt
herd n Herde f
here adv hier; (*to this place*) hierher; *come ~* komm her; *I won't be ~ for lunch* ich bin zum Mittagessen nicht da
hereditary adj erblich; **hereditary disease** n Erbkrankheit f; **heritage** n Erbe nt
hernia n Leistenbruch m, Eingeweidebruch m
hero n Held m
heroin n Heroin nt
heroine n Heldin f
herring n Hering m
hers pron ihre(r, s); *this is ~* das gehört ihr; *a friend of ~* ein Freund von ihr
herself pron (*reflexive*) sich; *she's bought ~ a flat* sie hat sich eine Wohnung gekauft; (*emphatic*) *she did it ~* sie hat es selbst gemacht; (*all*) *by ~* allein
he's contr of **he is**; **he has**
hesitate vi zögern; *don't ~ to ask* fragen Sie ruhig; **hesitation** n Zögern nt; *without ~* ohne zu zögern
heterosexual adj heterosexuell
hi interj hi, hallo
hiccup n Schluckauf m
hid pt of **hide**
hidden pp of **hide**
hide 1. vt verstecken (*from* vor + dat); (*feelings, truth*) ver-

bergen; (*cover*) verdecken 2. vi sich verstecken (*from* vor + dat)
hideous adj scheußlich
hiding (*beating*) Tracht f Prügel; (*concealment*) *be in ~* sich versteckt halten; **hiding place** n Versteck nt
hi-fi n Hi-Fi nt; (*system*) Hi-Fi-Anlage f
high 1. adj hoch; (*wind*) stark; (*on drugs*) high 2. adv hoch 3. n METEO Hoch nt; **highchair** n Hochstuhl m; **higher** adj höher; **higher education** n Hochschulbildung f; **high heels** npl Stöckelschuhe pl; **high jump** n Hochsprung m; **Highlands** npl (*schottisches*) Hochland f; **highlight** 1. n (*in hair*) Strähnchen nt; fig Höhepunkt m 2. vt (*with pen*) hervorheben; **highlighter** n Textmarker m; **highly** adj hoch, sehr; *~ paid* hoch bezahlt; *I think ~ of him* ich habe eine hohe Meinung von ihm; **high pressure** n Hochdruck m; **high school** n (*US*) Highschool f, ≈ Gymnasium nt; **high-speed** adj Schnell-; *~ train* Hochgeschwindigkeitszug m; **high street** n Hauptstraße f; **high tech** 1. adj Hightech- 2. n Hightech nt; **high tide** n Flut f; **highway** n (*US*) Autobahn f; (*Brit*) Landstraße f
hijack vt entführen, hijacken;

hobo

hijacker n Entführer(in) m(f), Hijacker m

hike 1. vi wandern 2. n Wanderung f; hiker n Wanderer m, Wanderin f; hiking n Wandern nt

hilarious adj zum Schreien komisch

hill n Hügel m; (higher) Berg m; hilly adj hügelig

him pron (direct object) ihn; (indirect object) ihm; do you know ~? kennst du ihn?; can you help ~? kannst du ihm helfen?; it's ~ er ist's; ~ too er auch

himself pron (reflexive) sich; he's bought ~ a flat er hat sich eine Wohnung gekauft; (emphatic) he did it ~ er hat es selbst gemacht; (all) by ~ allein

hinder vt behindern; hindrance n Behinderung f

Hindu 1. adj hinduistisch 2. n Hindu m; Hinduism n Hinduismus m

hinge n Scharnier nt; (on door) Angel f

hint 1. n Wink m, Andeutung f 2. vi andeuten (at acc)

hip 1. n Hüfte f 2. adj (trend) hip, trendy

hippopotamus n Nilpferd nt

hire 1. vt (worker) anstellen; (car, bike etc) mieten 2. n Miete f; for ~ (taxi) frei; hire(d) car n Mietwagen m; hire purchase n Ratenkauf m

his 1. adj sein; he's hurt ~ leg er hat sich dat das Bein verletzt 2. pron seine(r, s); it's ~ es gehört ihm; a friend of ~ ein Freund von ihm

historic adj (significant) historisch; historical adj (monument etc) historisch; (studies etc) geschichtlich; history n Geschichte f

hit 1. n (blow) Schlag m; (on target) Treffer m; (success) Erfolg m; MUS Hit m 2. vt schlagen; (ball, stone etc) treffen; the car ~ the tree das Auto fuhr gegen einen Baum; ~ one's head on sth sich dat den Kopf an etw dat stoßen; ~ (up)on sth stoßen auf + acc; hit-and-run adj ~ accident Unfall m mit Fahrerflucht

hitch-hike vi trampen; hitch-hiker n Tramper(in) m(f); hitchhiking n Trampen nt

HIV abbr = human immunodeficiency virus; HIV nt; ~ positive/negative HIV-positiv/negativ

hive n Bienenstock m

HM abbr = His/Her Majesty

HMS abbr = His/Her Majesty's Ship

hoarse adj heiser

hoax n Streich m, Jux m; (false alarm) blinder Alarm

hob n (of cooker) Kochfeld nt

hobble vi humpeln

hobby n Hobby nt

hobo n (US) Penner(in) m(f)

hockey n Hockey nt; (US)
Eishockey nt

hold 1. vt halten; (contain) enthalten; (be able to contain)
fassen; (post, office) innehaben; (value) behalten; (meeting) abhalten; (person as prisoner) gefangen halten; ~
one's breath den Atem anhalten; ~ hands Händchen
halten; ~ the line TEL bleiben
Sie am Apparat 2. vi halten;
(weather) sich halten 3. n
(grasp) Halt m; (of ship, aircraft) Laderaum m; hold
back vt zurückhalten; (keep
secret) verheimlichen; hold
on vi sich festhalten; TEL
dranbleiben; ~ to sth vt festhalten; hold out 1. vt ausstrecken; (offer) hinhalten; (offer) bieten 2. vi durchhalten;
hold up vt hochhalten; (support) stützen; (delay) aufhalten; holdall n Reisetasche f;
holder n (person) Inhaber(in)
m(f); holdup n (in traffic)
Stau m; (robbery) Überfall m

hole n Loch nt; (of fox, rabbit)
Bau m; ~ in the wall (cash
dispenser) Geldautomat m

holiday n (day off) freier Tag;
(public ~) Feiertag m; (vacation) Urlaub m; (at school)
Ferien pl; on ~ im Urlaub;
go on ~ Urlaub machen; holiday camp n Ferienlager nt;
holiday home n Ferienhaus
nt; (flat) Ferienwohnung f;
holidaymaker n Urlau-

ber(in) m(f); holiday resort
n Ferienort m

Holland n Holland nt

hollow 1. adj hohl; (words)
leer 2. n Vertiefung f

holly n Stechpalme f

holy adj heilig; Holy Week n
Karwoche f

home 1. n (of person, family,
country) Heimat f; (institution) Heim nt; at ~ zu Hause;
make oneself at ~ es sich dat
bequem machen; away from
~ verreist sein 2. adv go ~ nach
Hause gehen/fahren; home
address n Heimatadresse
f; home country n Heimatland nt; home game n SPORT
Heimspiel nt; homeless adj
obdachlos; homely adj häuslich; (US, ugly) unscheinbar;
home-made adj selbst gemacht; Home Office n (Brit)
Innenministerium nt

homeopathic adj (US) → homoeopathic

home page n IT Homepage f;
Home Secretary n (Brit) Innenminister(in) m(f); homesick adj be ~ Heimweh haben; homework n Hausaufgaben pl

homicide n (US) Totschlag m

homoeopathic adj homöopathisch

homosexual adj homosexuell

Honduras n Honduras nt

honest adj ehrlich; honesty n
Ehrlichkeit f

honey n Honig m; honeydew

melon n Honigmelone f;
honeymoon n Flitterwochen pl

Hong Kong n Hongkong nt

honor (US) → honour;
honorary adj (member, title etc)
Ehren-, ehrenamtlich; honour 1. vt ehren; (cheque) einlösen; (contract) einhalten 2. n Ehre f; in ~ of zu Ehren von; honourable adj ehrenhaft; honours degree n akademischer Grad mit Prüfung im Spezialfach

hood n Kapuze f; AUTO Verdeck nt; (US) AUTO Kühlerhaube f

hoof n Huf m

hook n Haken m; hooked adj (keen) besessen (on von); (drugs) abhängig (on von)

hooligan n Rowdy m

hoot vi AUTO hupen

Hoover® n Staubsauger m; hoover vi, vt staubsaugen

hop 1. vi hüpfen 2. n BOT Hopfen m

hope 1. vi, vt hoffen (for auf + acc); I ~ so/ ~ not hoffentlich / hoffentlich nicht; I ~ (that) we'll meet ich hoffe, dass wir uns sehen werden 2. n Hoffnung f; there's no ~ es ist aussichtslos; hopeful adj hoffnungsvoll; hopefully adv (full of hope) hoffnungsvoll; (I hope so) hoffentlich; hopeless adj hoffnungslos; (incompetent) miserabel

horizon n Horizont m; horizontal adj horizontal

hormone n Hormon nt

horn n Horn nt; AUTO Hupe f

hornet n Hornisse f

horny adj fam geil

horoscope n Horoskop nt

horrible, horribly adj, adv schrecklich; horrid, horribly adj, adv abscheulich; horrify vt entsetzen; horror n entsetzen nt; ~s (things) Schrecken pl

hors d'oeuvre n Vorspeise f

horse n Pferd nt; horse chestnut n Rosskastanie f; horsepower n Pferdestärke f, PS nt; horse racing n Pferderennen nt; horseradish n Meerrettich m; horse riding n Reiten nt; horseshoe n Hufeisen nt

hose, hosepipe n Schlauch m

hospitable adj gastfreundlich

hospital n Krankenhaus nt

hospitality n Gastfreundschaft f

host 1. n Gastgeber m; TV (of show) Moderator(in) m(f); Talkmaster(in) m(f) 2. vt (party) geben; TV (TV show) moderieren

hostage n Geisel f

hostel n Wohnheim nt; (youth hostel) Jugendherberge f

hostess n (of a party) Gastgeberin f

hostile adj feindlich; hostility n Feindseligkeit f

hot adj heiß; (drink, food, wa-

ter) warm; (*spiced*) scharf;
I'm (feeling) ~ mir ist heiß;
hot dog *n* Hotdog *nt*
hotel *n* Hotel *nt*; **hotel room** *n*
Hotelzimmer *nt*
hothouse *n* Treibhaus *nt*;
hotline *n* Hotline *f*; **hotplate**
n Kochplatte *f*; **hotpot** *n*
Fleischeintopf *mit Kartoffel-
einlage*; **hot-water bottle** *n*
Wärmflasche *f*
hour *n* Stunde *f*; **wait for ~s**
stundenlang warten; **~s** *pl*
(*of shop etc*) Geschäftszeiten *pl*; **hourly** *adj* stündlich
house 1. *n* Haus *nt*; **at my** ~
bei mir (zu Hause); **to my**
~ zu mir (nach Hause); **on
the** ~ auf Kosten des Hauses;
**the House of Commons/
Lords** das britische Unter-
haus/Oberhaus; **the Houses
of Parliament** das britische
Parlamentsgebäude **2.** *vt* unterbringen; **houseboat** *n*
Hausboot *nt*; **household** *n*
Haushalt *m*; ~ **appliance**
Haushaltsgerät *nt*; **house-
husband** *n* Hausmann *m*;
housekeeping *n* Haushal-
tung *f*; (*money*) Haushalts-
geld *nt*; **house-trained** *adj*
stubenrein; **house-warming
(party)** *n* Einzugsparty *f*;
housewife *n* Hausfrau *f*;
house wine *n* Hauswein *m*;
housework *n* Hausarbeit *f*
housing *n* (*houses*) Wohnun-
gen *pl*; (*house building*)
Wohnungsbau *m*; **housing**

benefit *n* Wohngeld *nt*;
housing development,
housing estate (*Brit*) *n*
Wohnsiedlung *f*
hover *vi* schweben; **hover-
craft** *n* Luftkissenboot *nt*
how *adv* wie; ~ **many** wie viele; ~ **much** wie viel; ~ **are
you?** wie geht es Ihnen?; ~
are things? wie geht's?; **~'s
work?** was macht die Ar-
beit?; ~ **about ...?** wie wäre
es mit ...?; **however 1.** *conj*
(*but*) jedoch, aber **2.** *adv*
(*no matter how*) wie ... auch;
~ **much it costs** wie viel es
auch kostet
howl *vi* heulen; **howler** *n fam*
grober Schnitzer
HQ *abbr* = **headquarters**
hubcap *n* Radkappe *f*
hug 1. *vt* umarmen **2.** *n* Umarmung *f*
huge *adj* riesig
hum *vi, vt* summen
human 1. *adj* menschlich; ~
rights Menschenrechte *pl*
2. *n* ~ (*being*) Mensch *m*; **hu-
manitarian** *adj* humanitär;
humanity *n* Menschheit *f*;
(*kindliness*) Menschlichkeit
f; **humanities** Geisteswissenschaften *pl*
humble *adj* demütig; (*modest*) bescheiden
humid *adj* feucht; **humidity** *n*
(*Luft*)feuchtigkeit *f*
humiliate *vt* demütigen; **hu-
miliation** *n* Erniedrigung *f*,
Demütigung *f*

humor (US) → **humour**; **humorous** adj humorvoll; (story) lustig, witzig; **humour** n Humor m; **sense of ~** Sinn m für Humor

hump n Buckel m

hundred num **one ~, a ~** (ein-)hundert; **a ~ and one** hundert(und)eins; **two ~** zweihundert; **hundredth 1.** adj hundertste(r, s) **2.** n (fraction) Hundertstel nt; **hundredweight** n Zentner m (50,8 kg)

hung pt, pp of **hang**

Hungarian 1. adj ungarisch **2.** n (person) Ungar(in) m(f); (language) Ungarisch nt; **Hungary** n Ungarn nt

hunger n Hunger m; **hungry** adj hungrig; **be ~** Hunger haben

hunk n fam gut aussehender Mann

hunt 1. n Jagd f; (search) Suche f (for nach) **2.** vt, vi jagen; (search) suchen (for nach); **hunting** n Jagen nt, Jagd f

hurdle n a. fig Hürde f; **the 400m ~s** der 400m-Hürdenlauf

hurl vt schleudern

hurray interj hurra

hurricane n Orkan m

hurried adj eilig; **hurry 1.** n Eile f; **be in a ~** es eilig haben; **there's no ~** es eilt nicht **2.** vi sich beeilen; **~ (up)** mach

schnell! **3.** vt antreiben

hurt 1. vt wehtun + dat; (wound: person, feelings) verletzen; **I've ~ my arm** ich habe mir am Arm wehgetan **2.** vi wehtun; **my arm ~s** mir tut der Arm weh

husband n Ehemann m

husky 1. adj rau **2.** n Schlittenhund m

hut n Hütte f

hyacinth n Hyazinthe f

hybrid n Kreuzung f

hydroelectric adj **~ power station** Wasserkraftwerk nt

hydrofoil n Tragflächenboot nt

hydrogen n Wasserstoff m

hygiene n Hygiene f; **hygienic** adj hygienisch

hymn n Kirchenlied nt

hypermarket n Großmarkt m; **hypersensitive** adj überempfindlich

hyphen n Bindestrich m

hypnosis n Hypnose f; **hypnotize** vt hypnotisieren

hypochondriac n eingebildete(r) Kranke(r)

hypocrisy n Heuchelei f; **hypocrite** n Heuchler(in) m(f)

hypodermic adj, n **~ (needle)** Spritze f

hypothetical adj hypothetisch

hysteria n Hysterie f; **hysterical** adj hysterisch; (amusing) zum Totlachen

I

I *pron* ich

ice 1. *n* Eis *nt* **2.** *vt* (cake) glasieren; **iceberg** *n* Eisberg *m*; **icebox** *n* (US) Kühlschrank *m*; **icecold** *adj* eiskalt; **ice cream** *n* Eis *nt*; **ice cube** *n* Eiswürfel *m*; **iced** *adj* eisgekühlt; (coffee, tea) Eis-; (cake) glasiert; **ice hockey** *n* Eishockey *nt*

Iceland *n* Island *nt*; **Icelander** *n* Isländer(in) *m(f)*; **Icelandic 1.** *adj* isländisch **2.** *n* (language) Isländisch *nt*

ice lolly *n* (Brit) Eis *nt* am Stiel; **ice rink** *n* Kunsteisbahn *f*; **ice skating** *n* Schlittschuhlaufen *nt*

icing *n* (on cake) Zuckerguss *m*

icon *n* Ikone *f*, IT Icon *nt*, Programmsymbol *nt*

icy *adj* (slippery) vereist; (cold) eisig

I'd *contr of* **I would; I had**

ID *abbr* = **identification**; Ausweis *m*

idea *n* Idee *f*; (I've) no ~ (ich habe) keine Ahnung; **that's my** ~ **of** ... so stelle ich mir ... vor

ideal 1. *n* Ideal *nt* **2.** *adj* ideal; **ideally** *adv* ideal; (before statement) idealerweise

identical *adj* identisch; ~ **twins** eineiige Zwillinge

identify *vt* identifizieren; **identity** *n* Identität *f*; **identity card** *n* Personalausweis *m*

idiom *n* Redewendung *f*; **idiomatic** *adj* idiomatisch

idiot *n* Idiot(in) *m(f)*

idle *adj* (doing nothing) untätig; (lazy) faul; (promise, threat) leer

idol *n* Idol *nt*; **idolize** *vt* vergöttern

idyllic *adj* idyllisch

i.e. *abbr* = **id est**; d. h.

if *conj* wenn, falls; (whether) ob; ~ **so** wenn ja; ~ **I were you** wenn ich du wäre; **I don't know** ~ **he's coming** ich weiß nicht, ob er kommt

ignition *n* Zündung *f*; **ignition key** *n* AUTO Zündschlüssel *m*

ignorance *n* Unwissenheit *f*; **ignorant** *adj* unwissend; **ignore** *vt* ignorieren, nicht beachten

I'll *contr of* **I will; I shall**

ill *adj* krank; ~ **at ease** unbehaglich

illegal *adj* illegal

illegitimate *adj* unzulässig; (child) unehelich

illiterate *adj* **be** ~ Analphabet(in) sein

illness *n* Krankheit *f*

illuminate *vt* beleuchten; **illuminating** *adj* (remark) aufschlussreich

illusion n Illusion f; *be under the ~ that ...* sich einbilden, dass ...

illustrate vt illustrieren; **illustration** n Abbildung f, Bild nt

I'm contr of *I am*

image n Bild nt; (*public ~*) Image nt; **imagination** n Fantasie f; (*mistaken*) Einbildung f; **imaginative** adj fantasievoll; **imagine** vt sich vorstellen; (*wrongly*) sich einbilden; *~! stell dir vor!*

imitate vt nachahmen, nachmachen; **imitation 1.** n Nachahmung f **2.** adj imitiert; *~ leather* Kunstleder nt

immaculate adj tadellos; (*spotless*) makellos

immature adj unreif

immediate adj unmittelbar; (*instant*) sofortig; (*reply*) umgehend; **immediately** adv sofort

immense, immensely adj, adv riesig, enorm

immersion heater n Boiler m

immigrant n Einwanderer m, Einwanderin f; **immigration** n Einwanderung f; (*facility*) Einwanderungskontrolle f

immobilize vt lähmen; **immobilizer** n AUTO Wegfahrsperre f

immoral adj unmoralisch

immortal adj unsterblich

immune adj MED immun (*from, to* gegen); **immune**

system n Immunsystem nt

impact n Aufprall m; (*effect*) Auswirkung f (*on* auf + acc)

impatience n Ungeduld f; **impatient, impatiently** adj, adv ungeduldig

impede vt behindern

imperfect adj unvollkommen; (*goods*) fehlerhaft

imperial adj kaiserlich, Reichs-; **imperialism** n Imperialismus m

impertinence n Unverschämtheit f, Zumutung f; **impertinent** adj unverschämt

implant n MED Implantat nt

implausible adj unglaubwürdig

implement 1. n Werkzeug nt, Gerät nt **2.** vt durchführen

implication n Folge f, Auswirkung f; (*logical*) Schlussfolgerung f; **implicit** adj implizit, unausgesprochen; **imply** vt (*indicate*) andeuten; (*mean*) bedeuten; *are you ~ing that...* wollen Sie damit sagen, dass ...

impolite adj unhöflich

import 1. vt einführen, importieren **2.** n Einfuhr f, Import m

importance n Bedeutung f; *of no ~* unwichtig; **important** adj wichtig (*to sb* für jdn); (*significant*) bedeutend; (*influential*) einflussreich

import duty n Einfuhrzoll m; **import licence** n Einfuhrge-

nehmigung f
impose vt (conditions) auferlegen (on dat); (penalty, sanctions) verhängen (on gegen); **imposing** adj eindrucksvoll, imposant
impossible adj unmöglich
impotence n Machtlosigkeit f; (sexual) Impotenz f; **impotent** adj machtlos; (sexually) impotent
impractical adj unpraktisch; (plan) undurchführbar
impress vt beeindrucken; **impression** n Eindruck m; **impressive** adj eindrucksvoll
imprison vt inhaftieren; **imprisonment** n Inhaftierung f
improper adj (indecent) unanständig; (use) unsachgemäß
improve vt verbessern 2. vi sich verbessern, besser werden; (patient) Fortschritte machen; **improvement** n Verbesserung f (in + gen; on gegenüber); (in appearance) Verschönerung f
improvise vt, vi improvisieren
impulse n Impuls m; **impulsive** adj impulsiv
in 1. prep in + dat; (expressing motion) in + acc; (in the case of) bei; **put it ~ the drawer** tu es in die Schublade; **~ the army** beim Militär; **~ itself** an sich; (time) **~ the morning/ afternoon/ evening** am Morgen/ Nachmittag/ Abend; **at three ~ the afternoon** um drei Uhr nachmit-

tags; **~ 2007** (im Jahre) 2007; **~ July** im Juli; **~ a week** in einer Woche; **~ writing** schriftlich; **~ German** auf Deutsch; **one ~ ten** einer von zehn, jeder zehnte; **~ all** insgesamt 2. adv (go) hinein; (come) herein; **be ~** zu Hause sein; (in fashion) in sein, modisch sein; (arrived) angekommen sein; **sb is ~ for sth** jdm steht etw bevor; (sth unpleasant) jmd kann sich auf etw acc gefasst machen; **be ~ on sth** an etw dat beteiligt sein
inability n Unfähigkeit f
inaccessible adj a. fig unzugänglich
inaccurate adj ungenau
inadequate adj unzulänglich
inappropriate adj unpassend; (clothing) ungeeignet; (remark) unangebracht
incapable adj unfähig (of zu); **be ~ of doing sth** nicht imstande sein, etw zu tun
incense n Weihrauch m
incentive n Anreiz m
incessant, incessantly adj, adv unaufhörlich
incest n Inzest m
inch n Zoll m (2,54 cm)
incident n Vorfall m; (disturbance) Zwischenfall m; **incidentally** adv nebenbei bemerkt, übrigens
inclination n Neigung f; **inclined** adj **be ~ to do sth** dazu neigen, etw zu tun

include *vt* einschließen; *(on list, in group)* aufnehmen; **including** *prep* einschließlich (+ *gen*); **not ~ service** Bedienung nicht inbegriffen; **inclusive** *adj* einschließlich (*of* + *gen*); *(price)* Pauschal-

incoherent *adj* zusammenhanglos

income *n* Einkommen *nt*; *(from business)* Einkünfte *pl*; **income tax** *n* Einkommensteuer *f*; *(on wages, salary)* Lohnsteuer *f*; **incoming** *adj* ankommend; *(mail)* eingehend

incompatible *adj* unvereinbar; *(people)* unverträglich; **IT** nicht kompatibel

incompetent *adj* unfähig

incomplete *adj* unvollständig

incomprehensible *adj* unverständlich

inconceivable *adj* unvorstellbar

inconsiderate *adj* rücksichtslos

inconsistency *n* Inkonsequenz *f*; *(contradictory)* Widersprüchlichkeit *f*; **inconsistent** *adj* inkonsequent; *(contradictory)* widersprüchlich; *(work)* unbeständig

inconvenience *n* Unannehmlichkeit *f*; *(trouble)* Umstände *pl*; **inconvenient** *adj* ungünstig, unbequem; *(time)* **it's ~ for me** es kommt mir ungelegen; **if it's not too**

~ for you wenn es dir passt

incorporate *vt* aufnehmen *(into* in + *acc)*; *(include)* enthalten

incorrect *adj* falsch; *(improper)* inkorrekt

increase 1. *n* Zunahme *f (in* an + *dat)*; *(in amount, speed)* Erhöhung *f (in* + *gen)*; **~ in size** Vergrößerung *f* **2.** *vt (price, taxes, salary, speed etc)* erhöhen; *(wealth)* vermehren; *(number)* vergrößern **3.** *vi* zunehmen *(in* an + *dat)*; *(prices)* steigen; *(in size)* größer werden; *(in number)* sich vermehren; **increasingly** *adv* zunehmend

incredible *adj*, **incredibly** *adv* unglaublich; *(very good)* fantastisch

incredulous *adj* ungläubig, skeptisch

incriminate *vt* belasten

incubator *n* Brutkasten *m*

incurable *adj* unheilbar

indecent *adj* unanständig

indecisive *adj (person)* unentschlossen; *(result)* nicht entscheidend

indeed *adv* tatsächlich; *(as answer)* allerdings; **very hot ~** wirklich sehr heiß

indefinite *adj* unbestimmt; **indefinitely** *adv* endlos; *(postpone)* auf unbestimmte Zeit

independence *n* Unabhängigkeit *f*; **independent** *adj* unabhängig (*of* von); *(per-*

son) selbstständig

indescribable *adj* unbeschreiblich

index *n* Index *m*, Verzeichnis *nt*; **index finger** *n* Zeigefinger *m*

India *n* Indien *nt*; **Indian 1.** *adj* indisch; *(Native American)* indianisch **2.** *n* Inder(in) *m(f)*; *(Native American)* Indianer(in) *m(f)*; **Indian Ocean** *n* Indischer Ozean; **Indian summer** *n* Spätsommer *m*, Altweibersommer *m*

indicate 1. *vt (show)* zeigen; *(instrument)* anzeigen; *(suggest)* hinweisen auf *+ acc* **2.** *vi* AUTO blinken; **indication** *n (sign)* Anzeichen *nt (of* für); **indicator** *n* AUTO Blinker *m*

indifferent *adj (not caring)* gleichgültig *(to, towards* gegenüber); *(mediocre)* mittelmäßig

indigestible *adj* unverdaulich; **indigestion** *n* Verdauungsstörung *f*

indignity *n* Demütigung *f*

indirect, indirectly *adj, adv* indirekt

indiscreet *adj* indiskret

indispensable *adj* unentbehrlich

indisposed *adj* unwohl

indisputable *adj* unbestreitbar; *(evidence)* unanfechtbar

individual 1. *n* Einzelne(r) *mf* **2.** *adj* einzeln; *(distinctive)* eigen, individuell; **~ case**

Einzelfall *m*; **individually** *adv (separately)* einzeln

Indonesia *n* Indonesien *nt*

indoor *adj (shoes)* Haus-; *(plant, games)* Zimmer-; SPORT *(soccer, championship, record etc)* Hallen-; **indoors** *adv* drinnen, im Haus

indulge *vi* **~ in sth** sich *dat* etw gönnen; **indulgence** *n* Nachsicht *f*; *(enjoyment)* (übermäßiger) Genuss; *(luxury)* Luxus *m*; **indulgent** *adj* nachsichtig *(with* gegenüber)

industrial *adj* Industrie-, industriell; **~ estate** Industriegebiet *nt*; **industry** *n* Industrie *f*

inedible *adj* nicht essbar, ungenießbar

ineffective *adj* unwirksam, wirkungslos; **inefficient** *adj* unwirksam; *(use, machine)* unwirtschaftlich; *(method etc)* unrationell

inequality *n* Ungleichheit *f*

inevitable *adj* unvermeidlich; **inevitably** *adv* zwangsläufig

inexcusable *adj* unverzeihlich

inexpensive *adj* preisgünstig

inexperience *n* Unerfahrenheit *f*; **inexperienced** *adj* unerfahren

inexplicable *adj* unerklärlich

infallible *adj* unfehlbar

infamous *adj (person)* berüchtigt *(for* wegen); *(deed)* niederträchtig

infancy n frühe Kindheit; **infant** n Säugling m; (small child) Kleinkind nt; **infant school** n Vorschule f

infatuated adj vernarrt or verknallt (**with** in + acc)

infect vt (person) anstecken; (wound) infizieren; **infection** n Infektion f; **infectious** adj ansteckend

inferior adj (in quality) minderwertig; (in rank) untergeordnet; **inferiority** n Minderwertigkeit f

infertile adj unfruchtbar

inflame vt MED entzünden; **inflammation** n MED Entzündung f

inflatable adj aufblasbar; **inflate** vt aufpumpen; (by blowing) aufblasen; (prices) hochtreiben

inflation n Inflation f

inflexible adj unflexibel

in-flight adj (catering, magazine) Bord-

influence 1. n Einfluss m (on auf + acc) **2.** vt beeinflussen; **influential** adj einflussreich

influenza n Grippe f

inform vt informieren (of, about über + acc); **keep sb ~ed** jdn auf dem Laufenden halten

informal adj zwanglos, ungezwungen

information n Auskunft f, Informationen pl; **for your ~** zu Ihrer Information; **further ~** weitere Informationen, weiteres; **information desk** n Auskunftsschalter m; **information technology** n Informationstechnik f; **informative** adj aufschlussreich

infra-red adj infrarot

infrastructure n Infrastruktur f

infuriate vt wütend machen; **infuriating** adj äußerst ärgerlich

infusion n (herbal tea) Aufguss m; MED Infusion f

ingenious adj (person) erfinderisch; (device) raffiniert; (idea) genial

ingredient n GASTR Zutat f

inhabit vt bewohnen; **inhabitant** n Einwohner(in) m(f)

inhale vt einatmen; (cigarettes) MED inhalieren; **inhaler** n Inhalationsgerät nt

inherit vt erben; **inheritance** n Erbe nt

in-house adj intern

inhuman adj unmenschlich

initial 1. adj anfänglich; **~ stage** Anfangsstadium nt **2.** vt mit Initialen unterschreiben; **initially** adv anfangs; **initials** npl Initialen pl

initiative n Initiative f

inject vt (drug etc) einspritzen; **~ sb with sth** jdm etw (ein)spritzen; **injection** n Spritze f, Injektion f

injure vt verletzen; **~ one's leg** sich dat das Bein verletzen; **injury** n Verletzung f

injustice n Ungerechtigkeit f

ink n Tinte f; **ink-jet printer** n Tintenstrahldrucker m

inland 1. adj Binnen- **2.** adv landeinwärts; **inland revenue** n (Brit) Finanzamt nt

in-laws npl fam Schwiegereltern pl

inline skates npl Inlineskates pl, Inliner pl

inmate n Insasse m

inn n Gasthaus nt

inner adj innere(r, s); **~ city** Innenstadt f

innocence n Unschuld f; **innocent** adj unschuldig

innovation n Neuerung f

innumerable adj unzählig

inoculate vt impfen (against gegen); **inoculation** n Impfung f

in-patient n stationärer Patient, stationäre Patientin

input n (contribution) Beitrag m; IT Eingabe f

inquire → **enquire**; **inquiry** → **enquiry**

insane adj wahnsinnig; MED geisteskrank; **insanity** n Wahnsinn m

insatiable adj unersättlich

inscription n (on stone etc) Inschrift f

insect n Insekt nt

insecure adj (person) unsicher; (shelves) instabil

insensitive adj unempfindlich (to gegen); (unfeeling) gefühllos

inseparable adj unzertrennlich

insert 1. vt einfügen; (coin) einwerfen; (key etc) hineinstecken **2.** n (in magazine) Beilage f; **insertion** n (in text) Einfügen nt

inside 1. the ~ das Innere; (surface) die Innenseite; **from the ~** von innen **2.** adj innere(r, s), Innen-; **~ lane** AUTO Innenspur f; SPORT Innenbahn f **3.** adv (place) innen; (direction) hinein; **go ~** hineingehen **4.** prep (place) in + dat; (into) in + acc ... hinein; (time, within) innerhalb + gen; **inside out** adv verkehrt herum; (know) in- und auswendig; **insider** n Eingeweihte(r) mf, Insider(in) m(f)

insight n Einblick m (into in + acc)

insincere adj unaufrichtig, falsch

insinuation n Andeutung f

insist vi darauf bestehen; **~ on sth** auf etw akk bestehen; **insistent** adj hartnäckig

insomnia n Schlaflosigkeit f

inspect vt prüfen, kontrollieren; **inspection** n Prüfung f; (check) Kontrolle f; **inspector** n (police) Inspektor(in) m(f); (senior) Kommissar(in) m(f); (on bus etc) Kontrolleur(in) m(f)

inspiration n Inspiration f; **inspire** vt (respect) einflößen (in dat); (person) inspirieren

install vt (software) installieren

installment. **instalment** n Rate f; (of story) Folge f; **pay in ~s** auf Raten zahlen; **installment plan** n (US) Ratenkauf m

instance n (of discrimination) Fall m; (example) Beispiel nt; **for ~** zum Beispiel

instant 1. n Augenblick m **2.** adj sofortig; **instant coffee** n Instantkaffee m; **instantly** adv sofort

instead adv stattdessen; **instead of** prep (an)statt + gen

instinct n Instinkt m; **instinctive**. **instinctively** adj, adv instinktiv

institute n Institut nt; **institution** n (organisation) Institution f, Einrichtung f; (home) Anstalt f

instruct vt anweisen; **instruction** n (teaching) Unterricht m; (command) Anweisung f; **~s for use** Gebrauchsanweisung f; **instructor** n Lehrer(in) m(f); (US) Dozent(in) m(f)

instrument n Instrument nt; **instrument panel** n Armaturenbrett nt

insufficient adj ungenügend

insulate vt ELEC isolieren; **insulating tape** n Isolierband nt; **insulation** n Isolierung f

insulin n Insulin nt

insult 1. n Beleidigung f **2.** vt beleidigen; **insulting** adj beleidigend

insurance n Versicherung f; **~ company** Versicherungsgesellschaft f; **~ policy** Versicherungspolice f; **insure** vt versichern (against gegen)

intake n Aufnahme f

integrate vt integrieren (into in + acc)

integrity n Integrität f, Ehrlichkeit f

intellect n Intellekt m; **intellectual** adj intellektuell; (interests etc) geistig

intelligence n (understanding) Intelligenz f; **intelligent** adj intelligent

intend vt beabsichtigen; **~ to do sth** vorhaben, etw zu tun

intense adj intensiv; (pressure) enorm; (competition) heftig; **intensity** n Intensität f; **intensive** adj intensiv; **intensive care unit** n Intensivstation f

intention n Absicht f; **intentional**, **intentionally** adj, adv absichtlich

interact vi aufeinander einwirken; **interaction** n Interaktion f, Wechselwirkung f; **interactive** adj interaktiv

interchange n (of motorways) Autobahnkreuz nt; **interchangeable** adj austauschbar

intercity n Intercityzug m, IC m

intercom n (Gegen)sprechanlage f

intercourse n (sexual) Geschlechtsverkehr *m*

interest 1. *n* Interesse *nt*; FIN (*on money*) Zinsen *pl*; COMM (*share*) Anteil *m*; **be of ~** von Interesse sein (*to* für) **2.** *vt* interessieren; **interested** *adj* interessiert (*in* an + *dat*); **be ~ed in** sich interessieren für; **are you ~ in coming?** hast du Lust, mitzukommen?; **interesting** *adj* interessant; **interest rate** *n* Zinssatz *m*

interface *n* Schnittstelle *f*

interfere *vi* (*meddle*) sich einmischen (*with*, *in* in + *acc*); **interference** *n* Einmischung *f*; TV, RAD Störung *f*

interior 1. *adj* Innen- **2.** *n* Innere(s) *nt*; (*of car*) Innenraum *m*; (*of house*) Innenausstattung *f*

intermediate *adj* Zwischen-

intermission *n* Pause *f*

intern *n* Assistent(in) *m(f)*

internal *adj* innere(r, s); (*flight*) Inlands-; **~ revenue** (*US*) Finanzamt *nt*; **internally** *adv* innen; (*in body*) innerlich

international 1. *adj* international; **~ match** Länderspiel *nt*; **~ flight** Auslandsflug *m* **2.** *n* SPORT (*player*) Nationalspieler(in) *m(f)*

Internet *n* IT Internet *nt*; **Internet banking** *n* Onlinebanking *nt*; **Internet café** *n* Internetcafé *nt*; **Internet provider** *n* Internetprovider *m*

interpret *vi*, *vt* (*translate*) dolmetschen; (*explain*) interpretieren; **interpretation** *n* Interpretation *f*; **interpreter** *n* Dolmetscher(in) *m(f)*

interrogate *vt* verhören; **interrogation** *n* Verhör *nt*

interrupt *vt* unterbrechen; **interruption** *n* Unterbrechung *f*

intersection *n* (*of roads*) Kreuzung *f*

interstate *n* (*US*) zwischenstaatlich; **~ highway** ≈ Bundesautobahn *f*

interval *n* (*space*, *time*) Abstand *m*; (*theatre etc*) Pause *f*

intervene *vi* eingreifen (*in* in); **intervention** *n* Eingreifen *nt*; POL Intervention *f*

interview 1. *n* Interview *nt*; (*for job*) Vorstellungsgespräch *nt* **2.** *vt* interviewen; (*job applicant*) ein Vorstellungsgespräch führen mit; **interviewer** *n* Interviewer(in) *m(f)*

intestine *n* Darm *m*; **~s** *pl* Eingeweide *pl*

intimate *adj* (*friends*) vertraut, eng; (*atmosphere*) gemütlich; (*sexually*) intim

intimidate *vt* einschüchtern; **intimidation** *n* Einschüchterung *f*

into *prep* in + *acc*; (*crash*) gegen; **translate ~ French** ins Französische übersetzen; **be ~ sth** *fam* auf etw *acc* stehen

intolerable *adj* unerträglich
intolerant *adj* intolerant
intoxicated *adj* betrunken; *fig* berauscht
intricate *adj* kompliziert
intrigue *vt* faszinieren; **intriguing** *adj* faszinierend, fesselnd
introduce *vt* (*person*) vorstellen (*to sb* jdm); (*sth new*) einführen (*to* in + *acc*); **introduction** *n* Einführung *f* (*to* in + *acc*); (*to book*) Einleitung *f* (*to* zu); (*to person*) Vorstellung *f*
introvert *n* Introvertierte(r) *mf*
intuition *n* Intuition *f*
invade *vt* einfallen in + *acc*
invalid 1. *n* Kranke(r) *mf*; (*disabled*) Invalide *m* **2.** *adj* (*not valid*) ungültig
invaluable *adj* äußerst wertvoll, unschätzbar
invariably *adv* ständig; (*every time*) jedes Mal, ohne Ausnahme
invasion *n* Invasion *f* (*of* in + *acc*)
invent *vt* erfinden; **invention** *n* Erfindung *f*; **inventor** *n* Erfinder(in) *m(f)*
inverted commas *npl* Anführungszeichen *pl*
invest *vt, vi* investieren (*in* in + *acc*)
investigate *vt* untersuchen; **investigation** *f* Untersuchung *f* (*into* + *gen*)
investment *n* Investition *f*;

it's a good ~ es ist eine gute Anlage
invigorating *adj* erfrischend, belebend; (*tonic*) stärkend
invisible *adj* unsichtbar
invitation *n* Einladung *f*; **invite** *vt* einladen
invoice *n* (*bill*) Rechnung *f*
involuntary *adj* unbeabsichtigt
involve *vt* verwickeln (*in sth* in etw *acc*); (*entail*) zur Folge haben; **be ~d in sth** (*participate in*) an etw *dat* beteiligt sein; *I'm not ~d* (*affected*) ich bin nicht betroffen
inward *adj* innere(r, s); **inwardly** *adv* innerlich; **inwards** *adv* nach innen
iodine *n* Jod *nt*
IOU *abbr* = **I owe you**; Schuldschein *m*
IQ *abbr* = **intelligence quotient**; IQ *m*
Iran *n* der Iran
Iraq *n* der Irak
Ireland *n* Irland *nt*
iris *n* (*flower*) Schwertlilie *f*; (*of eye*) Iris *f*
Irish 1. *adj* irisch; **~ coffee** Irishcoffee *m*; **~ Sea** die Irische See **2.** *n* (*language*) Irisch *nt*; **the ~** *pl* die Iren *pl*; **Irishman** *n* Ire *m*; **Irishwoman** *n* Irin *f*
iron 1. *n* Eisen *nt*; (*for ironing*) Bügeleisen *nt* **2.** *adj* eisern **3.** *vt* bügeln
ironic(al) *adj* ironisch
ironing board *n* Bügelbrett *nt*

irony n Ironie f

irrational adj irrational

irregular adj unregelmäßig

irrelevant adj belanglos, irrelevant

irreplaceable adj unersetzlich

irresistible adj unwiderstehlich

irresponsible adj verantwortungslos

irretrievable adv unwiederbringlich; (loss) unersetzlich

irritable adj reizbar; **irritate** vt (annoy) ärgern; (deliberately) reizen; **irritation** n (anger) Ärger m; MED Reizung f

is present of **be**; ist

Islam n Islam m; **Islamic** adj islamisch

island n Insel f; **Isle** n (in names) **the ~ of Man** die Insel Man; **the British ~s** die Britischen Inseln

isn't contr of **is not**

isolate vt isolieren; **isolated** adj (remote) abgelegen; **isolation** n Isolierung f

Israel n Israel nt; **Israeli 1.** adj israelisch **2.** n Israeli m or f

issue 1. n (matter) Frage f; (problem) Problem nt; (subject) Thema nt; (of newspaper etc) Ausgabe f; **that's not the ~** darum geht es nicht **2.** vt ausgeben; (document) ausstellen; (orders) erteilen; (book) herausgeben

it pron (as subject) er/sie/es;

(as direct object) ihn/sie/es; (as indirect object) ihm/ihr/ihm; **the worst thing about ~** das Schlimmste daran; **who is ~?** ~**'s me/**~**'s him** wer ist da? ich bin's/er ist's; ~**'s your turn** du bist dran; **that's ~** ja genau!; ~**'s raining** es regnet; ~**'s Charlie here**, hier spricht Charlie

IT abbr = **information technology**; IT f

Italian 1. adj italienisch **2.** n Italiener(in) m(f); (language) Italienisch nt

italic 1. adj kursiv **2.** npl **in ~s** kursiv

Italy n Italien nt

itch 1. n Juckreiz m; **I have an ~** mich juckt es **2.** vi jucken; **he is ~ing to ...** es juckt ihn, zu ...; **itchy** adj juckend

it'd contr of **it would; it had**

item n (article) Gegenstand m; (in catalogue) Artikel m; (on list, in accounts) Posten m; (on agenda) Punkt m; (in news) Bericht m; TV (radio) Meldung f

itinerary n Reiseroute f

it'll contr of **it will; it shall**

its pron sein; (feminine form) ihr

it's contr of **it is; it has**

itself pron (reflexive) sich; (emphatic) **the house ~ is OK** das Haus selbst or an sich ist in Ordnung; **by ~** allein; **the door closes (by) ~**

Tür schließt sich von selbst
I've contr of **I have**

ivory n Elfenbein nt
ivy n Efeu m

J

jab 1. vt (needle, knife) stechen
(into in + acc) **2.** n fam Spritze f

jack n AUTO Wagenheber m,
Bube m; **jack in** vt fam aufgeben, hinschmeißen; **jack
up** vt (car etc) aufbocken

jacket n Jacke f; (of man's
suit) Jackett nt; (of book)
Schutzumschlag m; **jacket
potato** ® n (in der Schale) gebackene Kartoffel

jack-knife 1. n Klappmesser
nt **2.** vi (truck) sich quer stellen

jacuzzi® n (bath) Whirlpool®
m

jail 1. n Gefängnis nt **2.** vt einsperren

jam 1. n Konfitüre f, Marmelade f; (traffic ~) Stau m **2.** vt
(street) verstopfen; **be ~med**
(stuck) klemmen; **~ on the
brakes** eine Vollbremsung
machen

Jamaica n Jamaika nt
jam-packed adj proppenvoll
janitor n (US) Hausmeister(in) m(f)
January n Januar m
Japan n Japan nt; **Japanese
1.** adj japanisch **2.** n (person)
Japaner(in) m(f); (language)
Japanisch nt

jar n Glas nt
jaundice n Gelbsucht f
javelin n Speer m; SPORT
Speerwerfen nt
jaw n Kiefer m
jazz n Jazz m
jealous adj eifersüchtig (of
auf + acc); **don't make me
~** mach mich nicht neidisch;
jealousy n Eifersucht f
jeans npl Jeans pl
jelly n Gelee nt; (dessert) Götterspeise f; (US, jam) Marmelade f; **jelly baby** n (sweet)
Gummibärchen nt; **jellyfish**
n Qualle f

jeopardize vt gefährden
jerk n Ruck m; fam (idiot)
Trottel m **2.** vt ruckartig bewegen **3.** vi (rope) rucken;
(muscles) zucken
Jerusalem n Jerusalem nt
jet n (of water etc) Strahl m;
(nozzle) Düse f; (aircraft)
Düsenflugzeug nt; **jet foil** n
Tragflächenboot nt; **jetlag**
n Jetlag m (Müdigkeit nach
langem Flug)
jetty n Landesteg m; (larger)
Landungsbrücke f
Jew n Jude m, Jüdin f
jewel n Edelstein m; (esp fig)
Juwel nt; **jeweller, jeweler**
(US) n Juwelier(in) m(f);

jewellery, jewelery (US) n Schmuck m.

Jewish adj jüdisch; **she's ~** sie ist Jüdin

jigsaw (puzzle) n Puzzle nt

jilt vt den Laufpass geben + dat

jitters npl fam **have the ~** Bammel haben; **jittery** adj fam ganz nervös

job n (piece of work) Arbeit f; (task) Aufgabe f; (occupation) Stellung f, Job m; **what's your ~?** was machen Sie beruflich?; **jobcentre** n Arbeitsvermittlungsstelle f, Arbeitsamt nt; **job-hunting** n **go ~** auf Arbeitssuche gehen; **jobless** adj arbeitslos; **job seeker** n Arbeitssuchende(r) m/f; **jobseeker's allowance** n Arbeitslosengeld nt; **job-sharing** n Arbeitsplatzteilung f

jockey n Jockey m

jog 1. vt (person) anstoßen 2. vi (run) joggen; **jogging** n Jogging nt; **go ~** joggen gehen

john n (US) fam Klo nt

join 1. vt (put together) verbinden (to mit); (club etc) beitreten + dat; **~ sb** sich jdm anschließen; (sit with) sich zu jdm setzen 2. vi (unite) sich vereinigen; (rivers) zusammenfließen; **join in** vi, vt mitmachen (bei)

joinery n Schreinerei f

joint 1. n (of bones) Gelenk nt;

(in pipe etc) Verbindungsstelle f; (of meat) Braten m; (marijuana) Joint m 2. adj gemeinsam; **joint account** n Gemeinschaftskonto nt; **jointly** adv gemeinsam

joke 1. n Witz m; (prank) Streich m; **for a ~** zum Spaß; **it's no ~** das ist nicht zum Lachen 2. vi Witze machen; **you must be joking** das ist ja wohl nicht dein Ernst!

jolly adj lustig, vergnügt

Jordan n (country) Jordanien nt; (river) Jordan m

jot down vt sich notieren; **jotter** n Notizbuch nt

journal n (diary) Tagebuch nt; (magazine) Zeitschrift f; **journalism** n Journalismus m; **journalist** n Journalist(in) m(f)

journey n Reise f; (esp on stage, by car, train) Fahrt f

joy n Freude f (at über + acc); **joystick** n IT Joystick m; AVIAT Steuerknüppel m

judge 1. n Richter(in) m(f); SPORT Punktrichter(in) m(f) 2. vt beurteilen (by nach) 3. vi urteilen (by nach); **judg(e)ment** n LAW Urteil nt; (opinion) Ansicht f; **an error of ~** Fehleinschätzung f

judo n Judo nt

jug n Krug m

juggle vi jonglieren (with mit)

juice n Saft m; **juicy** adj saftig

July n Juli m; **→ September**

jumble 1. n Durcheinander nt

2. *vt* ~ (**up**) durcheinander werfen; (*facts*) durcheinander bringen; **jumble sale** *n* (*for charity*) Wohltätigkeitsbasar *m*

jump 1. *vi* springen; (*nervously*) zusammenzucken; ~ **to conclusions** voreilige Schlüsse ziehen **2.** *vt* (*omit*) überspringen; ~ **the lights** bei Rot über die Kreuzung fahren; ~ **the queue** sich vordrängen **3.** *n* Sprung *m*; (*for horses*) Hindernis *nt*; **jumper** *n* Pullover *m*; (*US, dress*) Trägerkleid *nt*; (*person, horse*) Springer(in) *m(f)*; **jumper cables** *npl* (*US*); **jump leads** *npl* (*Brit*) AUTO Starthilfekabel *nt*

junction *n* (*of roads*) Kreuzung *f*; RAIL Knotenpunkt *m*

June *n* Juni *m*; → **September**

jungle *n* Dschungel *m*

junior 1. *adj* (*younger*) jünger; (*lower position*) untergeordnet (*to sb* jdm) **2.** *adj* **she's two years my** ~ sie ist zwei Jahre jünger als ich; **junior high (school)** *n* (*US*) ≈ Mittelschule *f*; **junior school** *n* (*Brit*) Grundschule *f*

junk *n* (*trash*) Plunder *m*; **junkfood** *n* Nahrungsmittel *pl* mit geringem Nährwert,

Junkfood *nt*; **junkie** *n fam* Junkie *m*, Fixer(in) *m(f)*; *fig* (*fan*) Freak *m*; **junk mail** *n* Reklame *f*; IT Junkmail *f*; **junk shop** *n* Trödelladen *m*

jury *n* Geschworene *pl*; (*in competition*) Jury *f*

just 1. *adj* gerecht **2.** *adv* (*recently*) gerade; (*exactly*) genau; ~ **as expected** genau wie erwartet; ~ **as nice** genauso nett; (*barely*) ~ **in time** gerade noch rechtzeitig; (*immediately*) ~ **before/after ...** gleich vor/nach ...; (*small distance*) ~ **round the corner** gleich um die Ecke; (*a little*) ~ **over an hour** etwas mehr als eine Stunde; (*only*) ~ **the two of us** nur wir beide; ~ **a moment** Moment mal; (*absolutely, simply*) **it was** ~ **fantastic** es war einfach klasse; ~ **about** so etwa; (*more or less*) mehr so oder weniger; ~ **about ready** fast fertig

justice *n* Gerechtigkeit *f*; **justifiable** *adj* berechtigt; **justifiably** *adv* zu Recht; **justify** *vt* rechtfertigen

juvenile *n* **1.** *adj* Jugend-, jugendlich **2.** *n* Jugendliche(r) *mf*

K

k *abbr* = **thousand**; **15k** 15 000

K *abbr* = **kilobyte**; KB

kangaroo *n* Känguru *nt*

karaoke *n* Karaoke *nt*

karate *n* Karate *nt*

kart *n* Gokart *m*

kayak *n* Kajak *m or nt*

Kazakhstan *n* Kasachstan *nt*

kebab *n* (*shish ~*) Schaschlik *nt or m*; (*doner ~*) Kebab *m*

keel *n* NAUT Kiel *m*; **keel over** *vi* (*boat*) kentern; (*person*) umkippen

keen *adj* begeistert (*on* von); (*hardworking*) eifrig; (*mind, wind*) scharf; (*interest, feeling etc*) stark; **be ~ on sb** von jdm angetan sein; **she's ~ on riding** sie reitet gern; **be ~ to do sth** darauf erpicht sein, etw zu tun

keep 1. *vt* (*retain*) behalten; (*secret*) für sich behalten; (*observe*) einhalten; (*promise*) halten; (*run: shop, diary, accounts*) führen; (*animals*) halten; (*support, family etc*) unterhalten, versorgen; (*store*) aufbewahren; **~ sb waiting** jdn warten lassen; **~ sb from doing sth** jdn davon abhalten, etw zu tun; **~ sth clean/ secret** etw sauber/geheim halten; **'~ clear'** „(bitte) freihalten"; **~ this to yourself** behalten Sie das für sich **2.** *vi* (*food*) sich halten; (*remain, with adj*) bleiben; **~ quiet!** sei ruhig!; **~ left** links fahren; **~ doing sth** (*repeatedly*) etw immer wieder tun; **~ at it** mach weiter so!; **it ~s happening** es passiert immer wieder; **keep back 1.** *vi* zurückbleiben **2.** *vt* zurückhalten; (*information*) verschweigen (*from* sb jdm); **keep off** *vt* (*person, animal*) fernhalten; **'~ the grass'** „Betreten des Rasens verboten"; **keep on 1.** *vi* weitermachen; (*walking*) weitergehen; (*in car*) weiterfahren; **~ doing sth** (*persistently*) etw immer wieder tun **2.** *vt* (*coat etc*) anbehalten; **keep out 1.** *vt* nicht hereinlassen **2.** *vi* draußen bleiben; **'~'** (*on sign*) Eintritt verboten; **keep to** *vt* (*road, path*) bleiben auf + *dat*; (*plan etc*) sich halten an + *acc*; **~ the point** bei der Sache bleiben; **keep up 1.** *vi* Schritt halten (*with* mit) **2.** *vt* (*maintain*) aufrechterhalten; (*speed*) halten; **~ appearances** den Schein wahren; **keep it up!** *fam* weiter so!

keeper *n* (*museum etc*) Aufseher(in) *m(f)*; (*goalkeeper*)

Torwart m; (*zoo keeper*) Tierpfleger(in) m(f); **~-fit** n Fitnesstraining nt; **~ exercises** Gymnastik f

kennel n Hundehütte f; **kennels** n Hundepension f

Kenya n Kenia nt

kept pt, pp of **keep**

kerb n Randstein m

kerosene n (US) Petroleum nt

ketchup n Ket(s)chup nt or m

kettle n Kessel m

key 1. n Schlüssel m; (*of piano, computer*) Taste f; MUS Tonart f; (*for map etc*) Zeichenerklärung f 2. vt **~ (in)** IT eingeben 3. adj entscheidend; **keyboard** n (*of piano, computer*) Tastatur f; **keyhole** n Schlüsselloch nt; **keypad** n IT Nummernblock m; **keyring** n Schlüsselring m

kick 1. n Tritt m; SPORT Stoß m 2. vt, vi treten; **kick out** vt fam rausschmeißen (*of* aus); **kick-off** n SPORT Anstoß m

kid 1. n (*child*) Kind nt 2. vt (*tease*) auf den Arm nehmen 3. vi Witze machen; **you're ~ding** das ist doch nicht dein Ernst!; **no ~ding** aber echt!

kidnap vt entführen; **kidnapper** n Entführer(in) m(f); **kidnapping** n Entführung f

kidney n Niere f; **kidney machine** n künstliche Niere

kill vt töten; (*esp intentionally*) umbringen; (*weeds*) vernich-

ten; **killer** n Mörder(in) m(f)

kilo n Kilo nt; **kilobyte** n Kilobyte nt; **kilogramme** n Kilogramm nt; **kilometer** n (US), **kilometre** n Kilometer m; **~s per hour** Stundenkilometer pl; **kilowatt** n Kilowatt nt

kilt n Schottenrock m

kind 1. adj nett, freundlich (*to* zu) 2. n Art f; (*of coffee, cheese etc*) Sorte f; **what ~ of ...?** was für ein(e) ...?; **this ~ of** so ein(e) ...; **~ of** (+ adj) fam irgendwie

kindergarten n Kindergarten m

kindly 1. adj nett, freundlich 2. adv liebenswürdigerweise

king n König m; **kingdom** n Königreich nt; **king-size** adj im Großformat; (*bed*) extra groß

kipper n Räucherhering m

kiss 1. n Kuss m; **~ of life** Mund-zu-Mund-Beatmung f 2. vt, vi küssen

kit n (*equipment*) Ausrüstung f; fam Sachen pl; (*sports kit*) Sportsachen pl; (*for building sth*) Bausatz m

kitchen n Küche f; **kitchen foil** n Alufolie f; **kitchen scales** n Küchenwaage f; **kitchenware** n Küchengeschirr nt

kite n Drachen m

kitten n Kätzchen nt

kiwi n (*fruit*) Kiwi f

km abbr = **kilometres**; km

knack n Dreh m, Trick m;

get / have got the ~ den Dreh herauskriegen / herausheben; **knackered** adj (Brit) fam fix und fertig, kaputt

knee n Knie nt; **kneecap** n Kniescheibe f; **knee-jerk** adj (reaction) reflexartig; **kneel** vi knien; (action, kneel down) sich hinknien

knelt pt, pp of **kneel**

knew pt of **know**

knickers npl (Brit) Schlüpfer m

knife n Messer nt

knight n Ritter m; (in chess) Pferd nt, Springer m

knit vt, vi stricken; **knitting** n (piece of work) Strickarbeit f; (activity) Stricken nt; **knitwear** n Strickwaren pl

knob n (on door) Knauf m; (on radio etc) Knopf m

knock 1. vt (with hammer etc) schlagen; (accidentally) stoßen; **~ one's head** sich dat den Kopf anschlagen **2.** vi klopfen (on, at an + acc) **3.** n (blow) Schlag m; (on door) Klopfen nt; **there was a ~** (at the door) es hat geklopft; **knock down** vt (object) umstoßen; (person) niederschlagen; (with car) anfahren; (building) abreißen; **knock out** vt (stun) bewusstlos schlagen; (boxer) k.o.

schlagen

knot n Knoten m

know vt, vi wissen; (be acquainted with: people, places) kennen; (recognize) erkennen; (language) können; **I'll let you ~** ich sage dir Bescheid; **I ~ some French** ich kann etwas Französisch; **get to ~ sb** jdn kennen lernen; **be ~n as** bekannt sein als; **know of** vt kennen; **not that I ~** nicht dass ich wüsste; **know-all** n fam Klugscheißer m; **know-how** n Kenntnis f, Know-how nt; **knowing** adj wissend; (look, smile) vielsagend; **knowledge** n Wissen nt; (of a subject) Kenntnisse pl; **to (the best of) my ~** meines Wissens

known pp of **know**

knuckle n (Finger)knöchel m; GASTR Hachse f; **knuckle down** vi sich an die Arbeit machen

Koran n Koran m

Korea n Korea nt

Kosovo n der Kosovo

kph abbr = **kilometres per hour**; km / h

Kremlin n **the ~** der Kreml

Kurd n Kurde m, Kurdin f; **Kurdish** adj kurdisch

Kuwait n Kuwait nt

L

L abbr (Brit) AUTO = **learner**

LA abbr of **Los Angeles**

lab n fam Labor nt

label 1. n Etikett nt; (tied) Anhänger m; (adhesive) Aufkleber m; (record ~) Label nt **2.** vt etikettieren; pej abstempeln

laboratory n Labor nt

laborious adj mühsam

labor (US), **labour 1.** n Arbeit f; MED Wehen pl; **be in ~** Wehen haben **2.** adj POL Labour-; **~ Party** Labour Party f; **labor union** n (US) Gewerkschaft f; **labourer** n Arbeiter(in) m(f)

lace 1. n (fabric) Spitze f; (of shoe) Schnürsenkel m **2.** vt **~ (up)** zuschnüren

lack 1. vt, vi **be ~ing** fehlen; **we ~ the time** uns fehlt die Zeit **2.** n Mangel m; **for ~ of** aus Mangel an + dat

lacquer n Lack m; (Brit, hair lacquer) Haarspray nt

lad n Junge m

ladder n Leiter f; (in tight) Laufmasche f

laddish adj (Brit) machohaft

laden adj beladen (with mit)

ladies, ladies' room n Damentoilette f; **lady** n Dame f; (as title) Lady f; **ladybird**, **ladybug** (US) n Marienkäfer m

lag 1. vi **(behind)** zurückliegen **2.** vt (pipes) isolieren

lager n helles Bier; **~ lout** betrunkener Rowdy

laid pt, pp of **lay**; **laid-back** adj fam cool, gelassen

lain pp of **lie**

lake n See m

lamb n Lamm nt; (meat) Lammfleisch nt; **lamb chop** n Lammkotelett nt

lame adj lahm; (excuse) faul; (argument) schwach

lament 1. n Klage f **2.** vt beklagen

laminated adj beschichtet

lamp n Lampe f; (in street) Laterne f; (in car) Licht nt, Scheinwerfer m

land 1. n Land nt **2.** vi (from ship) an Land gehen; AVIAT landen; **landing** n Landung f; (on stairs) Treppenabsatz m; **landing stage** n Landesteg m; **landing strip** n Landebahn f

landlady n Hauswirtin f, Vermieterin f; **landlord** n (of house) Hauswirt m, Vermieter m; (of pub) Gastwirt m; **landowner** n Grundbesitzer(in) m(f); **landscape** n Landschaft f; (format) Querformat nt; **landslide** n GEO Erdrutsch m

lane n (in country) enge Landstraße, Weg m; (in town) Gasse f; SPORT Bahn f; **get in** ~ (in car) sich einordnen

language n Sprache f

lantern n Laterne f

lap n **1.** Schoß m; (in race) Runde f **2.** vt (in race) überholen

lapse n **1.** (mistake) Irrtum m; (moral) Fehltritt m **2.** vi ablaufen

laptop n Laptop m

large adj groß; **by and** ~ im Großen und Ganzen; **largely** adv zum größten Teil; **large- -scale** adj groß angelegt, Groß-

lark n (bird) Lerche f

larynx n Kehlkopf m

laser n Laser m; **laser printer** n Laserdrucker m

lash vt peitschen; **lash out** vi (with fists) um sich schlagen; (spend money) sich in Unkosten stürzen (**on** für)

lass n Mädchen nt

last adj letzte(r, s); **the~ but one** der/die/das vorletzte; ~ **night** gestern Abend; ~ **but not least** nicht zuletzt **2.** adv zuletzt; (last time) das letzte Mal; **at** ~ endlich **3.** n (person) Letzte(r) mf; (thing) Letzte(s) nt; **he was the** ~ **to leave** er ging als Letzter **4.** vi (continue) dauern; (remain in good condition) durchhalten; (remain good) sich halten; (money)

ausreichen; **lasting** adj dauerhaft; (impression) nachhaltig; **lastly** adv schließlich; **last-minute** adj in letzter Minute; **last name** n Nachname m

late adj spät; (after proper time) zu spät; (train etc) verspätet; (dead) verstorben; **be** ~ zu spät kommen; (train etc) Verspätung haben **2.** adv spät; (after proper time) zu spät; **late avaiility flight** n Last-Minute-Flug m; **lately** adv in letzter Zeit; **late opening** n verlängerte Öffnungszeiten pl; **later** adj, adv später; **see you** ~ bis später; **latest 1.** adj späteste(r, s); (most recent) neueste(r, s) **2. the** ~ (news) das Neueste; **at the** ~ spätestens

Latin 1. n Latein nt **2.** adj lateinisch; **Latin America** n Lateinamerika nt; **Latin-American 1.** adj lateinamerikanisch **2.** n Lateinamerikaner(in) m(f)

latitude n GEO Breite f

latter adj (second of two) letztere(r, s); (last: part, years) letzte(r, s), später

Latvia n Lettland f

laugh 1. n Lachen nt; **for a** ~ aus Spaß **2.** vi lachen (at, about über + acc); ~ **at** sich lustig machen über; **it's no ~ing matter** es ist nicht zum Lachen; **laughter**

n Gelächter *nt*

launch 1. *n* (*launching, of ship*) Stapellauf *m*; (*of rocket*) Abschuss *m*; (*of product*) Markteinführung *f*; (*event*) Eröffnungsfeier *f* **2.** *vt* (*ship*) vom Stapel lassen; (*rocket*) abschießen; (*product*) einführen; (*project*) in Gang setzen

laundrette *n* (*Brit*), **laundromat** *n* (*US*) Waschsalon *m*; **laundry** *n* (*place*) Wäscherei *f*; (*clothes*) Wäsche *f*

lavatory *n* Toilette *f*

lavender *n* Lavendel *m*

lavish *adj* verschwenderisch; (*furnishings etc*) üppig; (*gift*) großzügig

law *n* Gesetz *nt*; (*system*) Recht *nt*; (*for study*) Jura; (*of sport*) Regel *f*; **against the ~** gesetzwidrig; **law-abiding** *adj* gesetzestreu; **law court** *n* Gerichtshof *m*; **lawful** *adj* rechtmäßig

lawn *n* Rasen *m*; **lawnmower** *n* Rasenmäher *m*

lawsuit *n* Prozess *m*; **lawyer** *n* Rechtsanwalt *m*, Rechtsanwältin *f*

laxative *n* Abführmittel *nt*

lay 1. *pt* of **lie 2.** *vt* legen; (*table*) decken; (*vulg*) poppen, bumsen; (*egg*) legen **3.** *adj* Laien-; **lay down** *vt* hinlegen; **lay on** *vt* (*provide*) anbieten; (*organize*) veranstalten, bereitstellen; **layabout** *n* Faulenzer(in) *m(f)*

layer *n* Schicht *f*

layman *n* Laie *m*

layout *n* Gestaltung *f*; (*of book etc*) Lay-out *nt*

laze *vi* faulenzen; **laziness** *n* Faulheit *f*; **lazy** *adj* faul; (*day, time*) gemütlich

lb *abbr* = **pound**; Pfd.

lead **1.** *n* Blei *nt* **2.** *vi* führen; (*group etc*) leiten; **~ the way** vorangehen **3.** *n* (*race*) Führung *f*; (*distance, time ahead*) Vorsprung *m* (*over* vor + *dat*); THEAT Hauptrolle *f*; (*dog's*) Leine *f*; ELEC (*flex*) Leitung *f*; **lead astray** *vt* irreführen; **lead away** *vt* wegführen; **lead back** *vi* zurückführen; **lead to** *vt* (*street*) hinführen nach; (*result in*) führen zu; **lead up to** *vt* (*drive*) führen zu

leaded *adj* (*petrol*) verbleit

leader *n* Führer(in) *m(f)*; (*of party*) Vorsitzende(r) *mf*; (*of project, expedition*) Leiter(in) *m(f)*, SPORT (*in race*) der/die Erste; (*in league*) Tabellenführer *m*; **leadership** *n* Führung *f*

lead-free *adj* (*petrol*) bleifrei

leading *adj* führend, wichtig

leaf *n* Blatt *nt*; **leaflet** *n* Prospekt *m*; (*pamphlet*) Flugblatt *nt*; (*with instructions*) Merkblatt *nt*

league *n* Bund *m*; SPORT Liga *f*

leak 1. *n* (*gap*) undichte Stelle; (*escape*) Leck *nt* **2.** *vi* (*pipe etc*) undicht sein; (*liquid* *etc*) auslaufen; **leaky** *adj* undicht

lean 1. *adj* (*meat*) mager **2.** *vi* (*not vertical*) sich neigen; (*rest*) ~ **against sth** sich an etw *acc* lehnen; (*support oneself*) ~ **on sth** sich auf etw *acc* stützen **3.** *vt* lehnen (*on, against* an + *acc*); **lean back** *vi* sich zurücklehnen; **lean towards** *vt* tendieren zu
leant *pt, pp of* **lean**
leap 1. *n* Sprung *m* **2.** *vi* springen; **leap year** *n* Schaltjahr *nt*
learn *vt, vi* lernen; (*find out*) erfahren; ~ (**how**) **to swim** schwimmen lernen; **learned** *adj* gelehrt; **learner** *n* Anfänger(in) *m(f)*; (*Brit, driver*) Fahrschüler(in) *m(f)*
learnt *pt, pp of* **learn**
lease 1. *n* (*of land, premises etc*) Pacht *f*; (*contract*) Pachtvertrag *m*; (*of house, car etc*) Miete *f*; (*contract*) Mietvertrag *m* **2.** *vt* pachten; (*house, car etc*) mieten; **lease out** *vt* vermieten; **leasing** *n* Leasing *nt*
least 1. *adj* wenigste(r, s); (*slightest*) geringste(r, s) **2.** *adv* am wenigsten; ~ **expensive** billigste(r, s) **3.** *n* **the** ~ das Mindeste; **not in the** ~ nicht im geringsten; **at** ~ wenigstens; (*with number*) mindestens
leather 1. *n* Leder *nt* **2.** *adj* ledern, Leder-

leave 1. *n* (*time off*) Urlaub *m*; **on** ~ auf Urlaub; **take one's** ~ Abschied nehmen (*of* von) **2.** *vt* (*place, person*) verlassen; (~ *behind: message, scar etc*) hinterlassen; (*after death*) hinterlassen (*to sb* jdm); (*entrust*) überlassen (*to sb* jdm); **be left** (*remain*) übrig bleiben; ~ **me alone** lass mich in Ruhe!; **don't** ~ **it to the last minute** warte nicht bis zur letzten Minute **3.** *vi* (*weg*)gehen, (*weg*)fahren; (*on journey*) abreisen; (*bus, train*) abfahren (*for* nach); **leave behind** *vt* zurücklassen; (*scar etc*) hinterlassen; **leave out** *vt* auslassen; (*person*) ausschließen (*of* von)
leaves *pl of* **leaf**
leaving do *n* Abschiedsfeier *f*
Lebanon *n* **the** ~ der Libanon
lecture *n* Vortrag *m*; (*at university*) Vorlesung *f*; **give a** ~ einen Vortrag/eine Vorlesung halten; **lecturer** *n* Dozent(in) *m(f)*; **lecture theatre** *n* Hörsaal *m*
led *pt, pp of* **lead**
LED *abbr* = **light-emitting diode**; Leuchtdiode *f*
leek *n* Lauch *m*
left 1. *pt, pp of* **leave 2.** *adj* linke(r, s) **3.** *adv* (*position*) links; (*movement*) nach links **4.** *n* (*side*) linke Seite; **the Left** POL die Linke; **on/to the** ~ links (*von*); **left-**

-hand adj linke(r, s); ~ **bend** Linkskurve f; ~ **drive** Linkssteuerung f; **left-handed** adj linkshändig; **left-hand side** n linke Seite
left-luggage locker n Gepäckschließfach nt; **left-luggage office** n Gepäckaufbewahrung f
left-overs npl Reste pl
left wing n linker Flügel; **left-wing** adj POL linksgerichtet
leg n Bein nt; (of meat) Keule f
legacy n Erbe nt, Erbschaft f
legal adj Rechts-, rechtlich; (allowed) legal; (limit, age) gesetzlich; ~ **aid** Rechtshilfe f; **legalize** vt legalisieren; **legally** adv legal
legible, legibly adj, adv leserlich
legislation n Gesetze pl
legitimate adj rechtmäßig, legitim
legroom n Platz m für die Beine
leisure 1. n (time) Freizeit f 2. adj Freizeit-; ~ **centre** Freizeitzentrum nt; **leisurely** adj gemächlich
lemon n Zitrone f; **lemonade** n Limonade f; **lemon curd** n Brotaufstrich aus Zitronen, Butter, Eiern und Zucker; **lemon juice** n Zitronensaft m; **lemon sole** n Seezunge f
lend vt leihen; ~ **sb sth** jdm etw leihen
length n Länge f; **4 metres in**

~ 4 Meter lang; **what** ~ **is it?** wie lange ist es?; **lengthy** adj sehr lange; (dragging) langwierig
lenient adj nachsichtig
lens n Linse f; PHOT Objektiv nt
lent pt, pp of **lend**
Lent n Fastenzeit f
lentil n BOT Linse f
Leo n ASTR Löwe m
leopard n Leopard m
lept pt, pp of **leap**
lesbian 1. adj lesbisch 2. n Lesbe f
less adj, adv n weniger; ~ **and** ~ immer weniger; (~ **often**) immer seltener; **lessen** 1. vi abnehmen, nachlassen 2. vt verringern; (pain) lindern; **lesser** adj geringer; (amount) kleiner
lesson n (at school) Stunde f; (unit of study) Lektion f; fig Lehre f; REL Lesung f; ~**s start at 9** der Unterricht beginnt um 9
let vt lassen; (lease) vermieten; ~ **sb have sth** jdm etw geben; ~**'s go** gehen wir; ~ **go (of sth)** (etw) loslassen; **let down** vt herunterlassen; (fail to help) im Stich lassen; (disappoint) enttäuschen; **let in** vt hereinlassen; **let out** vt hinauslassen; (secret) verraten; (scream etc) ausstoßen
lethal adj tödlich
let's abbr = **let us**
letter n (of alphabet) Buchsta-

be m; (message) Brief m; (official letter) Schreiben nt; **letterbox** n Briefkasten m

lettuce n Kopfsalat m

leukaemia, **leukemia** (US) n Leukämie f

level 1. adj (horizontal) waagerecht; (ground) eben; (two things, two runners) auf selber Höhe; **~ on points** punktgleich **2.** adv (run etc) auf gleicher Höhe, gleich auf; **draw ~** (in race) gleichziehen (with mit); (in game) ausgleichen **3.** n (altitude) Höhe f; (standard) Niveau nt; **be on a ~ with** auf gleicher Höhe sein mit **4.** vt (ground) einebnen; **level crossing** n (Brit) (schienengleicher) Bahnübergang m; **level-headed** adj vernünftig

lever n Hebel m; fig Druckmittel nt; **lever up** vt hochstemmen

liability n Haftung f; (burden) Belastung f; (obligation) Verpflichtung f; **liable** adj **be ~ for sth** (responsible) für etw haften

liar n Lügner(in) m(f)

liberal adj (generous) großzügig; (broad-minded) liberal; **Liberal Democrat 1.** n (Brit) POL Liberaldemokrat(in) m(f) **2.** adj liberaldemokratisch; **the ~ Party** die Liberaldemokratische Partei

liberate vt befreien; **liberation** n Befreiung f

liberty n Freiheit f

Libra n ASTR Waage f

library n Bibliothek f; (lending library) Bücherei f

Libya n Libyen nt

lice pl of **louse**

licence n (permit) Genehmigung f; COMM Lizenz f; (driving ~) Führerschein m; **licence 1.** n (US) → **licence 2.** vt genehmigen; **licensed** adj (restaurant etc) mit Schankerlaubnis; **license plate** n (US) AUTO Nummernschild nt; **licensing hours** npl Ausschankzeiten pl

lick 1. vt lecken **2.** n Lecken nt

licorice n Lakritze f

lid n Deckel m; (eye~) Lid nt

lie n Lüge f; **~ detector** n Lügendetektor m **2.** vi lügen; **~ to sb** jdn belügen **3.** vi (rest, be situated) liegen; (lie down) sich legen; (snow) liegen bleiben; **be lying third** an dritter Stelle liegen; **lie about** vi herumliegen; **lie down** vi sich hinlegen

lie in n **have a ~** ausschlafen

life n Leben nt; **get ~** lebenslänglich bekommen; **life assurance** n Lebensversicherung f; **lifebelt** n Rettungsring m; **lifeboat** n Rettungsboot nt; **lifeguard** n Bademeister(in) m(f), Rettungsschwimmer(in) m(f); **life insurance** n Lebensversicherung f; **life jacket** n

limit

Schwimmweste f; **lifeless** adj (dead) leblos; **lifelong** adj lebenslang; **life preserver** n (US) Rettungsring m; **life-saving** adj lebensrettend; **life-size(d)** adj in Lebensgröße; **life span** f; **life style** n Lebensstil m; **lifetime** n Lebenszeit f

lift 1. vt (hoch)heben; (ban) aufheben 2. n (Brit, elevator) Aufzug m, Lift m; **give sb a ~** jdn im Auto mitnehmen; **lift up** vt hochheben

ligament n Band nt

light 1. vt beleuchten; (fire, cigarette) anzünden 2. n Licht nt; (lamp) Lampe f; **~s** pl AUTO Beleuchtung f; (traffic lights) Ampel f; **in the ~ of** angesichts + gen 3. adj (bright) hell; (not heavy, easy) leicht; (punishment) milde; (taxes) niedrig; **~ blue/green** hellblau/hellgrün; **light up 1.** vt (illuminate) beleuchten 2. vi (a. eyes) aufleuchten

light bulb n Glühbirne f

lighten 1. vi hell werden 2. vt (give light to) erhellen; (make less heavy) leichter machen; fig erleichtern

lighter n (cigarette lighter) Feuerzeug nt

light-hearted adj unbeschwert; **lighthouse** n Leuchtturm m; **lighting** n Beleuchtung f; **lightly** adv leicht; **light meter** n PHOT Belichtungsmesser m

lightning n Blitz m

like 1. vt mögen, gern haben; **he ~s swimming** er schwimmt gern; **would you ~ ...?** hätten Sie gern ...?; **I'd ~ to go home** ich möchte nach Hause (gehen); **I don't ~ the film** der Film gefällt mir nicht 2. prep wie; **what's it/he ~?** wie ist es/er?; **he looks ~ you** er sieht dir ähnlich; **~ this/this** so; **likeable** adj sympathisch

likelihood n Wahrscheinlichkeit f; **likely** adj wahrscheinlich; **the bus is ~ to be late** der Bus wird wahrscheinlich Verspätung haben

like-minded adj gleich gesinnt

likewise adv ebenfalls; **do ~** das Gleiche tun

liking n (for person) Zuneigung f; (for type, things) Vorliebe f (for für)

lilac 1. n Flieder m 2. adj fliederfarben

lily n Lilie f; **~ of the valley** Maiglöckchen nt

limb n Glied nt

limbo n **in ~** (plans) auf Eis gelegt

lime n (tree) Linde f; (fruit) Limone f; (substance) Kalk m; **lime juice** n Limonensaft m; **limelight** n fig Rampenlicht nt; **limestone** n Kalkstein m

limit 1. n Grenze f; (for pollu-

tion etc) Grenzwert *m*; *drive over the ~* das Tempolimit überschreiten; *that's the ~* jetzt reicht's!, das ist die Höhe! **2.** *vt* beschränken (*to* auf + *acc*); (*freedom, spending*) einschränken; **limitation** *n* Beschränkung *f*; (*of freedom, spending*) Einschränkung *f*; **limited** *adj* begrenzt; *~ liability company* Gesellschaft *f* mit beschränkter Haftung, GmBH *f*; *public ~ company* Aktiengesellschaft *f*

limp 1. *vi* hinken **2.** *adj* schlaff

line 1. *n* Linie *f*; (*written*) Zeile *f*; (*on face*) Falte *f*; (*row*) Reihe *f*; (*US, queue*) Schlange *f*; RAIL Bahnlinie *f*; TEL Leitung *f*; (*range of items*) Kollektion *f*; *hold the ~* bleiben Sie am Apparat; *stand in ~* Schlange stehen; *something along those ~s* etwas in dieser Art; *drop me a ~* schreib mir ein paar Zeilen; *~s* THEAT Text *m* **2.** *vt* (*clothes*) füttern; (*streets*) säumen; **lined** *adj* (*paper*) liniert; (*face*) faltig; **line up** *vi* sich aufstellen; (*US, form queue*) sich anstellen

linen *n* Leinen *nt*; (*sheets etc*) Wäsche *f*

liner *n* Überseedampfer *m*, Passagierschiff *nt*

linesman *n* SPORT Linienrichter *m*

lingerie *n* Damenunterwäsche *f*

lining *n* (*of clothes*) Futter *nt*; (*brake* ~) Bremsbelag *m*

link 1. *n* (*connection*) Verbindung *f*; (*of chain*) Glied *nt*; (*relationship*) Beziehung *f* (*with* zu); (*between events*) Zusammenhang *m*; (*Internet*) Link *m* **2.** *vt* verbinden

lion *n* Löwe *m*

lip *n* Lippe *f*; **lipstick** *n* Lippenstift *m*

liqueur *n* Likör *m*

liquid 1. *n* Flüssigkeit *f* **2.** *adj* flüssig

liquor *n* Spirituosen *pl*

liquorice *n* Lakritze *f*

Lisbon *n* Lissabon *nt*

lisp *vt, vi* lispeln

list 1. *n* Liste *f* **2.** *vt* auflisten, aufzählen; *~ed building* unter Denkmalschutz stehendes Gebäude

listen *vi* zuhören; **listen to** *vt* (*person*) zuhören + *dat*; (*radio*) hören; (*advice*) hören auf; **listener** *n* Zuhörer(in) *m(f)*; (*to radio*) Hörer(in) *m(f)*

lit *pt, pp of* **light**

liter *n* (*US*) Liter *m*

literacy *n* Fähigkeit *f* zu lesen und zu schreiben; **literal** *adj* (*translation, meaning*) wörtlich; (*actual*) buchstäblich; **literally** *adv* (*translate, take sth*) wörtlich; **literary** *adj* literarisch; (*critic, journal etc*) Literatur-; **literature** *n* Literatur *f*; (*brochures etc*)

Informationsmaterial nt
Lithuania n Litauen nt
litre n Liter m
litter 1. n Abfälle pl; (of animals) Wurf m 2. vt be ~ed with übersät sein mit; litter bin n Abfalleimer m
little 1. adj klein; (in quantity) wenig; a ~ while ago vor kurzer Zeit 2. adv, n wenig; a ~ ein bisschen, ein wenig; as ~ as possible so wenig wie möglich; for as ~ as £5 ab nur 5 Pfund; I see very ~ of them ich sehe sie sehr selten; ~ by ~ nach und nach; little finger n kleiner Finger
live 1. adj lebendig; ELEC geladen, unter Strom; TV (radio, event) live; ~ broadcast Direktübertragung f 2. vi leben; (not die) überleben; (dwell) wohnen; you ~ and learn man lernt nie aus 3. vt (life) führen; live on 1. vi weiterleben 2. vt ~ sth von etw leben; (feed) sich von etw ernähren; earn enough to ~ genug verdienen, um davon zu leben; live together vi zusammenleben; live up to vt (reputation) gerecht werden + dat; (expectations) entsprechen + dat; live with vt (parents etc) wohnen bei; (partner) zusammenleben mit; (difficulty) you'll just have to ~ it du musst dich eben damit abfinden
liveliness n Lebhaftigkeit f;

lively adj lebhaft
liver n Leber f
lives pl of life
livestock n Vieh nt
living 1. n Lebensunterhalt m; what do you do for a ~? was machen Sie beruflich? 2. adj lebend; living room n Wohnzimmer nt
lizard n Eidechse f
load 1. n Last f; (cargo) Ladung f; TECH fig Belastung f; ~s of fam massenhaft; it was a ~ of rubbish fam es war grottenschlecht 2. vt (vehicle) beladen; IT laden; (film) einlegen
loaf n ~ (of bread) Brot nt
loaf about vi faulenzen
loan 1. n (item leant) Leihgabe f; FIN Darlehen nt; on ~ geliehen 2. vt leihen (to sb jdm)
loathe vt verabscheuen
loaves pl of loaf
lobby n Vorhalle f; POL Lobby f
lobster n Hummer m
local 1. adj (traffic, time etc) Orts-; (radio, news, paper) Lokal-; (government, authority) Kommunal-; (anaesthetic) örtlich; ~ call TEL Ortsgespräch nt; ~ elections Kommunalwahlen pl; ~ time Ortszeit f; ~ train Nahverkehrszug m; the ~ shops die Geschäfte am Ort 2. n (pub) Stammlokal nt; the ~s pl die Ortsansässigen pl;
locally adv örtlich, am Ort

locate vt (find) ausfindig machen; (establish) errichten; **be ~d** sich befinden (in, at in + dat); **location** n (position) Lage f; FILM Drehort m

loch n (Scot) See m

lock 1. n Schloss nt; NAUT Schleuse f; (of hair) Locke f 2. vt (door etc) abschließen 3. vi (door etc) sich abschließen lassen; (wheels) blockieren; **lock in** vt einschließen, einsperren; **lock out** vt aussperren; **lock up** vt (house) abschließen; (person) einsperren

locker n Schließfach nt; **locker room** n (US) Umkleideraum m

locksmith n Schlosser(in) m(f)

locust n Heuschrecke f

lodge 1. n (small house) Pförtnerhaus nt; (porter's lodge) Pförtnerloge f 2. vi in Untermiete wohnen (with bei); **lodger** n Untermieter(in) m(f); **lodging** n Unterkunft f

loft n Dachboden m

log n Klotz m; NAUT Log nt; **keep a ~ of sth** über etw Buch führen; **log in** vi IT sich einloggen; **log off** vi IT sich ausloggen; **log on** vi IT sich einloggen; **log out** vi IT sich ausloggen

logic n Logik f; **logical** adj logisch

logo n Logo nt

loin n Lende f

loiter vi sich herumtreiben

lollipop n Lutscher m; **~ man/lady** (Brit) Schülerlotse m, Schülerlotsin f

lolly n Lutscher m; fam (money) Knete f

London n London nt

loneliness n Einsamkeit f; **lonely, lonesome** (esp US) adj einsam

long 1. adj lang; (distance) weit; **it's a ~ way** es ist weit (to nach); **for a ~ time** lange; **how ~ is the film?** wie lange dauert der Film?; **in the ~ run** auf die Dauer 2. adv lange; **not for ~** nicht lange; **~ ago** vor langer Zeit; **before ~** bald; **all day ~** den ganzen Tag; **no ~er** nicht mehr; **as ~ as** solange 3. vi sich sehnen (for nach); (be waiting) sehnsüchtig warten (for auf); **long-distance call** n Ferngespräch nt; **long drink** n Longdrink m; **long-haul flight** n Langstreckenflug m; **longing** n Sehnsucht f (for nach); **longingly** adv sehnsüchtig; **longitude** n Länge f; **long jump** n Weitsprung m; **long-life milk** n H-Milch f; **long-range** adj Langstrecken-, Fern-; **~ missile** n Langstreckenrakete f; **long-sighted** adj weitsichtig; **long-standing** adj alt, langjährig; **long-term** adj langfristig; (car park, effect _etc_) Langzeit-; **~ unemployment** Langzeitarbeitslosigkeit f

loo n (Brit) fam Klo nt

look 1. n Blick m; (_appearance_) **~(s)** pl Aussehen nt; **I'll have a ~** ich schau mal nach; **have a ~ at sth** sich _dat_ etw ansehen; **can I have a ~?** darf ich mal sehen? **2.** vi schauen, gucken; (_search_) nachsehen; (_appear_) aussehen; (**I'm) just ~ing** ich schaue nur; **it ~s like rain** es sieht nach Regen aus **3.** vt **~ what you've done** sieh dir mal an, was du da angestellt hast; (_appear_) **he ~s his age** man sieht ihm sein Alter an; **~ one's best** sehr vorteilhaft aussehen; **look after** vt (_care for_) sorgen für; (_keep an eye on_) aufpassen auf + acc; **look at** vt ansehen, anschauen; **look back** vi zurückblicken; _fig_ zurückblicken; **look down on** vt _fig_ herabsehen auf + acc; **look for** vt suchen; **look forward to** vt sich freuen auf + acc; **look into** vt (_investigate_) untersuchen; **look out** vi hinaussehen (_of the window_ zum Fenster); (_watch out_) Ausschau halten (_for_ nach); **~!** Vorsicht!; **look up 1.** vi nachsehen **2.** vt (_word etc_) nachschlagen; **look up to** vt aufsehen zu

loop n Schleife f

loose adj locker; (_knot, button_) lose; **loosen** vt lockern; (_knot_) lösen

loot n Beute f

lop-sided adj schief

lord n (_ruler_) Herr m; (Brit, _title_) Lord m; **the Lord (God)** Gott der Herr; **the (House of) Lords** (Brit) das Oberhaus

lorry n (Brit) Lastwagen m

lose 1. vt verlieren; **~ weight** abnehmen; **~ one's life** umkommen **2.** vi verlieren; (_clock, watch_) nachgehen; **loser** n Verlierer(in) m(f); **loss** n Verlust m; **lost 1.** pt, pp of **lose**; **we've ~** wir haben uns verlaufen **2.** adj verloren; **lost-and-found** (US), **lost property (office)** n Fundbüro nt

lot n (_batch_) fam Menge f, Haufen m; **a ~** viel(e); **a ~ of money** viel Geld; **~s of people** viele Leute; **the (whole)** **~** alles; (_people_) alle; (**parking) ~** (US) Parkplatz m

lotion n Lotion f

lottery n Lotterie f

loud adj laut; (_colour_) schreiend; **loudspeaker** n Lautsprecher m; (_of stereo_) Box f

lounge 1. n Wohnzimmer nt; (_in hotel_) Aufenthaltsraum m; (_at airport_) Warteraum m **2.** vi sich herumlümmeln

louse n Laus f; **lousy** adj fam lausig

lout n Rüpel m

lovable adj liebenswert

love 1. n Liebe f (of zu); (person, address) Liebling m, Schatz m; SPORT null; **be in ~** verliebt sein (with sb in jdn); **fall in ~** sich verlieben (with sb in jdn); **make ~** (sexually) sich lieben; **make ~ to** (or **with**) **sb** mit jdm schlafen; **give her my ~** grüße sie von mir; **~, Tom** liebe Grüße, Tom **2.** vt (person) lieben; (activity) sehr gerne mögen; **~ to do sth** etw für sein Leben gerne tun; **I'd ~ a cup of tea** ich hätte liebend gern eine Tasse Tee; **love affair** n (Liebes)verhältnis nt; **love letter** n Liebesbrief m; **love life** n Liebesleben nt; **lovely** adj schön, wunderschön; (charming) reizend; **we had a ~ time** es war sehr schön; **lover** n Liebhaber(in) m(f); **loving** adj liebevoll

low 1. adj niedrig; (level, note, neckline) tief; (quality, standard) schlecht; (not loud) leise; (depressed) niedergeschlagen; **we're ~ on petrol** wir haben kaum noch Benzin **2.** n METEO Tief nt; **low-calorie** adj kalorienarm; **low-emission** adj schadstoffarm; **lower 1.** adj niedriger; (storey, class etc) untere(r, s) **2.** vt herunterlassen; (eyes, price) senken; (pressure) verringern; **low-fat** adj fettarm; **low tide** n

Ebbe f

loyal adj treu; **loyalty** n Treue f

lozenge n Pastille f

Ltd abbr = **limited**; ≈ GmbH f

luck n Glück nt; **bad ~** Pech nt; **luckily** adv glücklicherweise, zum Glück; **lucky** adj (number, day etc) Glücks-; **be ~** Glück haben

ludicrous adj grotesk

luggage n Gepäck nt; **luggage compartment** n Gepäckraum m; **luggage rack** n Gepäcknetz nt

lukewarm adj lauwarm

lullaby n Schlaflied nt

lumbago n Hexenschuss m

luminous adj leuchtend

lump n Klumpen m; MED Schwellung f; (in breast) Knoten m; (of sugar) Stück nt; **lump sum** n Pauschalsumme f

lunacy n Wahnsinn m; **lunatic 1.** adj wahnsinnig **2.** n Wahnsinnige(r) mf

lunch, luncheon n Mittagessen nt; **have ~** zu Mittag essen; **lunch break, lunch hour** n Mittagspause f; **lunchtime** n Mittagszeit f

lung n Lunge f

lurk vi lauern

lust n (sinnliche) Begierde f (for nach)

luster (US), **lustre** n Glanz m

Luxembourg n Luxemburg nt

luxurious adj luxuriös, Lu-

xus-; **luxury** n (a. luxuries pl)
Luxus m; **~ goods** Luxusgü-
ter pl

lynx n Luchs m
lyrics npl (words for song)
Liedtext m

M

m abbr = **metre**; m
M abbr = **Motorway**; A; (size)
= **medium**; M
ma n fam Mutti f
mac n (Brit) fam Regenmantel m
Macedonia n Mazedonien n
machine n Maschine f; **machine gun** n Maschinenge-
wehr nt; **machinery** n Ma-
schinen pl; fig Apparat m
mackerel n Makrele f
macro n IT Makro nt
mad adj wahnsinnig, verrückt; (dog) tollwütig; (angry) wütend, sauer (at a.
+ acc); fam **~ about** (fond
of) verrückt nach; **work like
~** wie verrückt arbeiten; **are
you ~?** spinnst du?
madam n gnädige Frau
mad cow disease n Rinder-
wahnsinn m; **maddening**
adj zum Verrücktwerden
made pt, pp of **make**
made-to-measure adj nach
Maß; **~ suit** Maßanzug m
madly adv wie verrückt; (with
adj) wahnsinnig; **madman** n
Verrückte(r) m; **madwoman**
n Verrückte f; **madness** n
Wahnsinn m
magazine n Zeitschrift f

maggot n Made f
magic 1. n Magie f; (activity)
Zauberei f; fig (effect) Zauber m; **as if by ~** wie durch
Zauberei **2.** adj Zauber-;
(powers) magisch; **magician**
n Zauberer m, Zaub(r)erin f
magnet n Magnet m; **magnet-
ic** adj magnetisch
magnificent, magnificently
adj, adv herrlich, großartig
magnify vt vergrößern; **magnifying glass** n Vergrößerungsglas nt, Lupe f
magpie n Elster f
maid n Dienstmädchen nt;
maiden name n Mädchenname m; **maiden voyage** n
Jungfernfahrt f
mail 1. n Post f; (e-mail) Mail f
2. vt (post) aufgeben; (send)
mit der Post® schicken (to an
+ acc); **mailbox** n (US) Briefkasten m; IT Mailbox f; **mail-
ing list** n Adressenliste f;
mailman n (US) Briefträger
m; **mail order** n Bestellung f
per Post; **mail order firm** n
Versandhaus n
main 1. adj Haupt-; **~ course**
Hauptgericht n; **the ~ thing**
die Hauptsache **2.** n (pipe)
Hauptleitung f; **mainframe**

n Großrechner *m*; **mainland** *n* Festland *nt*; **mainly** *adv* hauptsächlich; **main road** *n* Hauptverkehrsstraße *f*; **main street** *n* (US) Hauptstraße *f*

maintain *vt* (keep up) aufrechterhalten; (machine, roads) instand halten; (service) warten; **maintenance** *n* Instandhaltung *f*; TECH Wartung *f*

maize *n* Mais *m*

majestic *adj* majestätisch; **majesty** *n* Majestät *f*; **his/her Majesty** seine/ihre Majestät *f*

major 1. *adj* (bigger) größer; (important) bedeutend; ~ **part** Großteil *m*; (role) wichtige Rolle; ~ **road** Hauptverkehrsstraße *f*; MUS **A** – A-Dur *nt* **2.** *vi* (US) ~ **in sth** etw als Hauptfach studieren

Majorca *n* Mallorca *nt*

majority *n* Mehrheit *f*; **be in the** ~ in der Mehrzahl sein

make 1. *n* Marke *f* **2.** *vt* machen; (manufacture) herstellen; (clothes) nähen; (soup) zubereiten; (bread, cake) backen; (tea, coffee) kochen; (speech) halten; (earn) verdienen; (decision) treffen; **it's made of gold**; es ist aus Gold; ~ **sb do sth** jdn dazu bringen, etw zu tun; (force) jdn zwingen, etw zu tun; **she made**

us wait sie ließ uns warten; **what ~s you think that?** wie kommen Sie darauf?; **he never really made it** er hat es nie zu etwas gebracht; **she didn't ~ it through the night** sie hat die Nacht nicht überlebt; (calculate) **I ~ it £5/a quarter to six** nach meiner Rechnung kommt es auf 5 Pfund/nach meiner Uhr ist es dreiviertel sechs; **he's just made for this job** er ist für diese Arbeit wie geschaffen; **make for** *vt* zusteuern auf + acc; **make of** *vt* (think of) halten von; **I couldn't ~ anything of it** ich wurde daraus nicht schlau; **make off** *vi* sich davonmachen (with mit); **make out** *vt* (cheque) ausstellen; (list) aufstellen; (understand) verstehen; (discern) ausmachen; ~ **(that)** ... es so hinstellen, als ob ...; **make up 1.** *vt* (team etc) bilden; (face) schminken; (invent: story etc) erfinden; ~ **one's mind** sich entscheiden; **make it up with sb** sich mit jdm aussöhnen **2.** *vi* sich versöhnen; **make up for** *vt* ausgleichen; (time) aufholen

make-believe *adj* Fantasie-; **makeover** *n* gründliche Veränderung, Verschönerung *f*; **maker** *n* COMM Hersteller(in) *m(f)*; **makeshift** *adj* behelfsmäßig; **make-up** *n* Make-up

nt, Schminke *f*; **making** *n*
Herstellung *f*

malaria *n* Malaria *f*

Malaysia *n* Malaysia *f*

male 1. *n* Mann *m*; *(animal)*
Männchen *nt* **2.** *adj* männlich; ~ **chauvinist** Chauvi
m, Macho *m*; ~ **nurse** Krankenpfleger *m*

malfunction 1. *vi* nicht richtig
funktionieren **2.** *n* Defekt *m*

malice *n* Bosheit *f*; **malicious**
adj boshaft; *(damage)* mutwillig

malignant *adj* bösartig

mall *n* *(US)* Einkaufszentrum
nt

malnutrition *n* Unterernäh-
rung *f*

malt *n* Malz *f*

Malta *n* Malta *nt*; **Maltese 1.**
adj maltesisch **2.** *n* *(person)*
Malteser(in) *m(f)*; *(language)* Maltesisch *nt*

maltreat *vt* schlecht behandeln; *(violently)* misshandeln

mammal *n* Säugetier *nt*

mammoth *adj* Mammut-,
Riesen-

man 1. *n* *(male)* Mann *m*; *(human race)* der Mensch, die
Menschen *pl*; *(in chess)* Figur *f* **2.** *vt* besetzen

manage 1. *vi* zurechtkommen;
can you ~? schaffst du es?; ~
without sth ohne etw auskommen, auf etw verzichten
können **2.** *vt* *(control)* leiten;
(musician, sportsman) managen; *(cope with)* fertig wer-

den mit; *(task, portion, climb
etc)* schaffen; ~ **to do sth** es
schaffen, etw zu tun; **man-
ageable** *adj* *(object)* handlich; *(task)* zu bewältigen

management *n* Leitung *f*;
(directors) Direktion *f*; *(subject)* Management *nt*, Be-
triebswirtschaft *f*; **management consultant** *n* Unter-
nehmensberater(in) *m(f)*;

manager *n* Geschäftsfüh-
rer(in) *m(f)*; *(departmental
manager)* Abteilungslei-
ter(in) *m(f)*; *(of branch,
bank)* Filialleiter(in) *m(f)*;
(of musician, sportsman) Ma-
nager(in) *m(f)*; **managing
director** *n* Geschäftsfüh-
rer(in) *m(f)*

mane *n* Mähne *f*

maneuver *(US)* → **manoeuvre**

mango *n* Mango *f*

man-hour *n* Arbeitsstunde *f*

manhunt *n* Fahndung *f*

mania *n* Manie *f*; **maniac** *n*
Wahnsinnige(r) *mf*; *(fan)* Fa-
natiker(in) *m(f)*

manicure *n* Maniküre *f*

manipulate *vt* manipulieren

mankind *n* Menschheit *f*

manly *adj* männlich

man-made *adj* *(product)*
künstlich

manner *n* Art *f*; **in this ~** auf
diese Art und Weise; **~s** *pl*
Manieren *pl*

manoeuvre 1. *n* Manöver *nt* **2.**
vt, vi manövrieren

manor n ~ (*house*) Herrenhaus m

manpower n Arbeitskräfte pl

mansion n Villa f; (*of old family*) Herrenhaus m

manslaughter n Totschlag m

manual **1.** adj manuell, Hand- **2.** n Handbuch m

manufacture **1.** vt herstellen **2.** n Herstellung f; manufacturer n Hersteller m

manure n Dung m; (*esp artificial*) Dünger m

many adj, pron viele; ~ oft; not ~ people nicht viele Leute; too ~ problems zu viele Probleme

map n Landkarte f; (*of town*) Stadtplan m

maple n Ahorn m

marathon n Marathon m

marble n Marmor m; (*for playing*) Murmel f

march **1.** vi marschieren **2.** n Marsch m; (*protest*) Demonstration f

March n März m; → September

mare n Stute f

margarine n Margarine f

margin n Rand m; (*extra amount*) Spielraum f; comm Gewinnspanne f; marginal adj (*difference etc*) geringfügig

marijuana n Marihuana f

marinade n gastr Marinade f; marinated adj mariniert

marine adj Meeres-

marital adj ehelich; ~ status

Familienstand m

maritime adj See-

marjoram n Majoran m

mark **1.** n (*spot*) Fleck m; (*at school*) Note f; (*sign*) Zeichen nt **2.** vt (*indicate*) markieren; (*schoolwork*) benoten, korrigieren, Flecken machen auf + acc; marker n (*in book*) Lesezeichen nt; (*pen*) Marker m

market **1.** n Markt m **2.** vt comm (*new product*) auf den Markt bringen; (*goods*) vertreiben; marketing n Marketing nt; market leader n Marktführer m; market place n Marktplatz m; market research n Marktforschung f

marmalade n Orangenmarmelade f

maroon adj rötlich braun

marquee n großes Zelt

marriage n Ehe f; (*wedding*) Heirat f (to mit); married adj (*person*) verheiratet

marrow n (*bone marrow*) Knochenmark m; (*vegetable*) Kürbis m

marry **1.** vt heiraten; (*join*) trauen **2.** vi ~ / get married heiraten

marsh n Marsch f, Sumpf m

marshal n (*at rally etc*) Ordner m; (*US, police*) Bezirkspolizeichef m

martial arts npl Kampfsportarten pl

martyr n Märtyrer(in) m(f)

marvel 1. *n* Wunder *nt* **2.** *vi* staunen (*at* über + *acc*); **marvellous, marvelous** (*US*) *adj* wunderbar

mascara *n* Wimperntusche *f*

mascot *n* Maskottchen *nt*

masculine *adj* männlich

mashed *adj* ~ **potatoes** *pl* Kartoffelbrei *m*, Kartoffelpüree *nt*

mask 1. *n* Maske *f* **2.** *vt* (*feelings*) verbergen

masochist *n* Masochist(in) *m(f)*

mason *n* (*stonemason*) Steinmetz(in) *m(f)*; **masonry** *n* Mauerwerk *nt*

mass *n* Masse *f*; (*of people*) Menge *f*; REL Messe *f*; **~es of** massenhaft

massacre *n* Blutbad *nt*

massage 1. *n* Massage *f* **2.** *vt* massieren

massive *adj* (*powerful*) gewaltig; (*very large*) riesig

mass media *npl* Massenmedien *pl*; **mass production** *n* Massenproduktion *f*

master 1. *n* Herr *m*; (*of dog*) Besitzer *m*, Herrchen *nt*; (*artist*) Meister *m* **2.** *vt* meistern; (*language etc*) beherrschen; **masterly** *adj* meisterhaft; **masterpiece** *n* Meisterwerk *nt*

masturbate *vi* masturbieren

mat *n* Matte *f*; (*for table*) Untersetzer *m*

match 1. *n* Streichholz *nt*; SPORT Wettkampf *m*; (*ball*

games) Spiel *nt*; (*tennis*) Match *nt* **2.** *vt* (*be like, suit*) passen zu; (*equal*) gleichkommen + *dat* **3.** *vi* zusammenpassen; **matchbox** *n* Streichholzschachtel *f*; **matching** *adj* (*one item*) passend; (*two items*) zusammenpassend

mate 1. *n* (*companion*) Kumpel *m*; (*of animal*) Weibchen *nt*/Männchen *nt* **2.** *vi* sich paaren

material *n* Material *nt*; (*for book etc, cloth*) Stoff *m*; **materialistic** *adj* materialistisch; **materialize** *vi* zustande kommen; (*hope*) wahr werden

maternal *adj* mütterlich; **maternity** *adj* ~ **dress** Umstandskleid *nt*; ~ **leave** Elternzeit *f* (*der Mutter*); ~ **ward** Entbindungsstation *f*

math *n* (*US*) *fam* Mathe *f*; **mathematical** *adj* mathematisch; **mathematics** *nsing* Mathematik *f*; **maths** *nsing* (*Brit*) *fam* Mathe *f*

matter 1. *n* (*substance*) Materie *f*; (*affair*) Sache *f*; *a personal* ~ eine persönliche Angelegenheit; *a* ~ *of taste* eine Frage des Geschmacks; *no* ~ *how/what* egal wie/was; *what is the* ~? was ist los?; *as a* ~ *of fact* eigentlich; *a* ~ *of time* eine Frage der Zeit **2.** *vi* darauf ankommen, wichtig sein; *it doesn't* ~ es macht nichts; **matter-of-fact** *adj* sachlich, nüchtern

mattress *n* Matratze *f*

mature 1. *adj* reif **2.** *vi* reif werden; **maturity** *n* Reife *f*

maximum 1. *adj* Höchst-, höchste(r, s); **~ speed** Höchstgeschwindigkeit *f* **2.** *n* Maximum *nt*

may *vaux* (*be possible*) können; (*have permission*) dürfen; *it ~ rain* es könnte regnen; *~ I smoke?* darf ich rauchen?; *we ~ as well go* wir können ruhig gehen

May *n* Mai *m*; → **September**

maybe *adv* vielleicht

mayo (*US*) *fam*, **mayonnaise** *n* Mayo *f*, Mayonnaise *f*, Majonäse *f*

mayor *n* Bürgermeister *m*

maze *n* Irrgarten *m*; *fig* Wirrwarr *nt*

MB *abbr* = **megabyte**; MB *nt*

me *pron* (*direct object*) mich; (*indirect object*) mir; *it's ~* ich bin's

meadow *n* Wiese *f*

meal *n* Essen *nt*, Mahlzeit *f*; *go out for a ~* essen gehen; **meal pack** *n* (*US*) tiefgekühltes Fertiggericht; **meal time** *n* Essenszeit *f*

mean 1. *vt* (*signify*) bedeuten; (*have in mind*) meinen; (*intend*) vorhaben; *I~ it* ich meine das ernst; *what do you ~ (by that)?* was willst du damit sagen?; *~ to do sth* etw tun wollen; *it was ~t for*

you es war für dich bestimmt (*or* gedacht); *it was ~t to be a joke* es sollte ein Witz sein **2.** *vi* es meint es gut **3.** *adj* (*stingy*) geizig; (*spiteful*) gemein (*to* zu); **meaning** *n* Bedeutung *f*; (*of life, poem*) Sinn *m*; **meaningful** *adj* sinnvoll; **meaningless** *adj* (*text*) ohne Sinn

means *n* Mittel *nt*; (*pl, funds*) Mittel *pl*; *by ~ of* durch, mittels; *by all ~* selbstverständlich; *by no ~* keineswegs; *~ of transport* Beförderungsmittel

meant *pt, pp of* **mean**

meantime *adv* **in the ~** inzwischen; **meanwhile** *adv* inzwischen

measles *nsing* Masern *pl*; **German ~** Röteln *pl*

measure 1. *vt, vi* messen **2.** *n* (*unit, device for measuring*) Maß *nt*; (*step*) Maßnahme *f*; *take ~s* Maßnahmen ergreifen; **measurement** *n* (*amount measured*) Maß *nt*

meat *n* Fleisch *nt*; **meatball** *n* Fleischbällchen *nt*

mechanic *n* Mechaniker(in) *m(f)*; **mechanical** *adj* mechanisch; **mechanics** *nsing* Mechanik *f*; **mechanism** *n* Mechanismus *m*

medal *n* Medaille *f*; (*decoration*) Orden *m*; **medalist** (*US*), **medallist** *n* Medaillengewinner(in) *m(f)*

media *npl* Medien *pl*

median strip n (US) Mittelstreifen m
mediate vi vermitteln
medical 1. adj medizinisch; (treatment etc) ärztlich; ~ **student** Medizinstudent(in) m(f) **2.** n Untersuchung f; **Medicare** n (US) Krankenkasse f für ältere Leute; **medication** n Medikamente pl; **be on** ~ Medikamente nehmen; **medicinal** adj Heil-; ~ **herbs** Heilkräuter pl; **medicine** n Arznei f; (science) Medizin f
medieval adj mittelalterlich
mediocre adj mittelmäßig
meditate vi meditieren; (fig) nachdenken (on über + acc)
Mediterranean n (sea) Mittelmeer nt; (region) Mittelmeerraum m
medium 1. adj (quality, size) mittlere(r, s); (steak) halbdurch; ~(**dry**) (wine) halbtrocken; ~ **sized** mittelgroß; ~ **wave** Mittelwelle f **2.** n Medium nt; (means) Mittel nt
meet 1. vt treffen; (by arrangement) sich treffen mit; (difficulties) stoßen auf + acc; (get to know) kennen lernen; (requirement, demand) gerecht werden + dat; (deadline) einhalten; **pleased to** ~ **you** sehr angenehm!; ~ **sb at the station** jdn vom Bahnhof abholen **2.** vi treffen; (by arrangement) sich treffen; (become acquainted) sich kennen lernen; **we've met**

(before) wir kennen uns schon; **meet up** vt sich treffen (with mit); **meet with** vt (group) zusammenkommen mit; (difficulties, resistance etc) stoßen auf + acc; **meeting** n Treffen nt; (business meeting) Besprechung f; (of committee) Sitzung f; (assembly) Versammlung f; **meeting place, meeting point** n Treffpunkt m
megabyte n Megabyte nt
melody n Melodie f
melon n Melone f
melt vt, vi schmelzen
member n Mitglied nt; (of tribe, species) Angehörige(r) mf; **Member of Parliament** Parlamentsabgeordnete(r) mf; **membership** n Mitgliedschaft f; **membership card** n Mitgliedskarte f
memo n Mitteilung f, Memo nt; **memo pad** n Notizblock m
memorable adj unvergesslich; **memorial** n Denkmal nt (to für); **memorize** vt sich einprägen, auswendig lernen; **memory** n Gedächtnis nt; IT (of computer) Speicher m; (sth recalled) Erinnerung f; **in** ~ **of** zur Erinnerung an + acc
men pl of **man**
menace n Bedrohung f; (danger) Gefahr f
mend 1. vt reparieren; (clothes) flicken **2.** n **be on**

the~ auf dem Wege der Besserung sein

meningitis n Hirnhautentzündung f

menopause n Wechseljahre pl

mental adj geistig; ~ *hospital* psychiatrische Klinik; **mentality** n Mentalität f; **mentally** adv geistig; ~ *handicapped* geistig behindert; ~ *ill* geisteskrank

mention 1. n Erwähnung f **2.** vt erwähnen (*to sb* jdm gegenüber); **don't** ~ **it** bitte sehr, gern geschehen

menu n Speisekarte f; IT Menü nt

merchandise n Handelsware f; **merchant** adj Handels-

merciful adj gnädig; **mercifully** adv glücklicherweise

mercury n Quecksilber nt

mercy n Gnade f

mere adj bloß; **merely** adv bloß, lediglich

merge vi verschmelzen; AUTO sich einfädeln; COMM fusionieren; **merger** n COMM Fusion f

meringue n Baiser nt

merit n Verdienst nt; (*advantage*) Vorzug m

merry adj fröhlich; *fam* (*tipsy*) angeheitert; *Merry Christmas* Fröhliche Weihnachten!; **merry-go-round** n Karussell nt

mess n Unordnung f; (*muddle*) Durcheinander nt; (*dirty*) Schweinerei f; (*trouble*) Schwierigkeiten pl; **in a** ~ (*muddled*) durcheinander; (*untidy*) unordentlich; *fig* (*person*) in der Klemme; *make a* ~ *of sth* etw verpfuschen; **mess about** vi (*tinker with*) herummurksen (*with* an + *dat*); (*play the fool*) herumalbern; (*do nothing in particular*) herumgammeln; **mess up** vt verpfuschen; (*make untidy*) in Unordnung bringen; (*dirty*) schmutzig machen

message n Mitteilung f, Nachricht f; *can I give him a* ~*?* kann ich ihm etwas ausrichten?; *please leave a* ~ (*on answerphones*) bitte hinterlassen Sie eine Nachricht; *I get the* ~ ich hab's verstanden

messenger n Bote m

messy adj (*untidy*) unordentlich; (*situation etc*) verfahren

met pt, pp of **meet**

metal n Metall nt; **metallic** adj metallisch

meteorology n Meteorologie f

meter n Zähler m; (*parking meter*) Parkuhr f; (*US*) → **metre**

method n Methode f

meticulous adj (*peinlich*) genau

metre n Meter m or nt; **metric** adj metrisch; ~ *system* Dezimalsystem nt

Mexico n Mexiko nt

mice pl of **mouse**

mickey n **take the ~ (out of sb)** fam (jdn) auf den Arm nehmen

microchip n IT Mikrochip m; **microphone** n Mikrofon nt; **microscope** n Mikroskop nt; **microwave (oven)** n Mikrowelle(nherd) f(m)

mid adj **in ~ January** Mitte Januar; **he's in his ~ forties** er ist Mitte vierzig

midday n Mittag m; **at ~** mittags

middle 1. n Mitte f; **in the ~ of** mitten in + dat; **be in the ~ of doing sth** gerade dabei sein, etw zu tun **2.** adj mittlere(r, s), Mittel-; **middle-aged** adj mittleren Alters; **Middle Ages** npl **the ~** das Mittelalter; **middle-class** adj mittelständisch; (bourgeois) bürgerlich; **middle classes** npl **the ~** der Mittelstand; **Middle East** n **the ~** der Nahe Osten; **middle name** n zweiter Vorname

Midlands npl **the ~** Mittelengland nt

midnight n Mitternacht f

midst n **in the ~ of** mitten in + dat

midsummer n Hochsommer m; **Midsummer's Day** Sommersonnenwende f

midway adv auf halbem Wege; **~ through the film** nach der Hälfte des Films;

midweek adj, adv in der Mitte der Woche

midwife n Hebamme f

midwinter n tiefster Winter

might 1. pt of **may**; (possibility) könnte; (permission) dürfte; (would) würde; **they ~ still come** sie könnten noch kommen; **I thought she ~ change her mind** ich dachte schon, sie würde sich anders entscheiden **2.** n Macht f, Kraft f

mighty adj gewaltig; (powerful) mächtig

migraine n Migräne f

migrant n (bird) Zugvogel m; **~ worker** Gastarbeiter(in) m(f); **migrate** vi abwandern; (birds) nach Süden ziehen

mike n fam Mikro nt

Milan n Mailand nt

mild adj mild; (person) sanft; **mildly** adv **put it ~** gelinde gesagt; **mildness** n Milde f

mile n Meile f (= 1,609 km); **for ~s (and ~s)** kilometerweit; **~s per hour** Meilen pro Stunde; **~s better than** hundertmal besser als; **mileage** n Meilen pl, Meilenzahl f; **mileometer** n Kilometerzähler m; **milestone** n a. fig Meilenstein m

militant adj militant; **military** adj Militär-, militärisch

milk 1. n Milch f **2.** vt melken; **milk chocolate** n Vollmilchschokolade f; **milkman** n Milchmann m; **milk shake**

n Milkshake *m*, Milchmixgetränk *m*

mill *n* Mühle *f*; (*factory*) Fabrik *f*

millennium *n* Jahrtausend *nt*

millet *n* Hirse *f*

milligramme *n* Milligramm *nt*; **millilitre** (*US*), **millilitre** *n* Milliliter *m*; **millimeter** (*US*), **millimetre** *n* Millimeter *m*

million *n* Million *f*; **five ~** fünf Millionen; **~s of people** Millionen von Menschen; **millionaire** *n* Millionär(in) *m(f)*

mime 1. *n* Pantomime *f* **2.** *vt*, *vi* mimen; **mimic 1.** *n* Imitator(in) *m(f)* **2.** *vt*, *vi* nachahmen; **mimicry** *n* Nachahmung *f*

mince 1. *vt* (zer)hacken **2.** *n* (*meat*) Hackfleisch *nt*; **mincemeat** *n* süße Gebäckfüllung aus Rosinen, Äpfeln, Zucker, Gewürzen und Talg; **mince pie** *n* mit 'mincemeat' gefülltes süßes Weihnachtsgebäck

mind 1. *n* (*intellect*) Verstand *m*; (*also person*) Geist *m*; **out of sight, out of ~** aus den Augen, aus dem Sinn; **he is out of his ~** er ist nicht bei Verstand; **keep sth in ~** etw im Auge behalten; **I've a lot on my ~** mich beschäftigt so vieles im Moment; **change one's ~** es sich *dat* anders überlegen **2.** *vt* (*look after*) aufpassen auf + *acc*;

(*object to*) etwas haben gegen; **~ you, ...** allerdings ...; **I wouldn't ~ ...** ich hätte nichts gegen ...; **'~ the step'** „Vorsicht Stufe!" **3.** *vi* etwas dagegen haben; **do you ~ if I ...** macht es Ihnen etwas aus, wenn ich ...; **I don't ~** es ist mir egal, meinetwegen; **never ~** macht nichts

mine 1. *pron* meine(r, s); **this is ~** das gehört mir; **a friend of ~** ein Freund von mir **2.** *n* (*coalmine*) Bergwerk *nt*; MIL Mine *f*

miner *n* Bergarbeiter *m*

mineral *n* Mineral *nt*; **mineral water** *n* Mineralwasser *nt*

mingle *vi* sich mischen (*with* unter + *acc*)

minibar *n* Minibar *f*; **minibus** *n* Kleinbus *m*; **minicab** *n* Kleintaxi *nt*

minimal *adj* minimal; **minimize** *vt* auf ein Minimum reduzieren; **minimum 1.** *n* Minimum *nt* **2.** *adj* Mindest-

mining *n* Bergbau *m*

miniskirt *n* Minirock *m*

minister *n* POL Minister(in) *m(f)*; REL Pastor(in) *m(f)*, Pfarrer(in) *m(f)*; **ministry** *n* POL Ministerium *nt*

minor *adj* kleiner; (*insignificant*) unbedeutend; (*operation, offence*) harmlos; **~ road** Nebenstraße *f*; MUS **A ~** a-Moll *nt* **2.** *n* (*Brit, under* 18) Minderjährige(r) *mf*; **minority** *n* Minderheit *f*

mint *n* Minze *f*; *(sweet)* Pfefferminz(bonbon) *nt*; **mint sauce** *n* Minzsoße *f*

minus *prep* minus; *(without)* ohne

minute 1. *adj* winzig; *in ~ detail* genauestens 2. *n* Minute *f*; *just a ~* Moment mal!; *any ~* jeden Augenblick; *~s pl (of meeting)* Protokoll *nt*

miracle *n* Wunder *nt*; **miraculous** *adj* unglaublich

mirage *n* Fata Morgana *f*, Luftspiegelung *f*

mirror *n* Spiegel *m*

misbehave *vi* sich schlecht benehmen

miscalculation *n* Fehlkalkulation *f*; *(misjudgement)* Fehleinschätzung *f*

miscarriage *n* MED Fehlgeburt *f*

miscellaneous *adj* verschieden

mischief *n* Unfug *m*; **mischievous** *adj* *(person)* durchtrieben; *(glance)* verschmitzt

misconception *n* falsche Vorstellung

misconduct *n* Vergehen *nt*

miser *n* Geizhals *m*

miserable *adj (person)* todunglücklich; *(conditions, life)* elend; *(pay, weather)* miserabel

miserly *adj* geizig

misery *n* Elend *nt*; *(suffering)* Qualen *pl*

misfit *n* Außenseiter(in) *m(f)*

misfortune *n* Pech *nt*

misguided *adj* irrig; *(optimism)* unangebracht

misinform *vt* falsch informieren

misinterpret *vt* falsch auslegen

misjudge *vt* falsch beurteilen

mislay *irr vt* verlegen

mislead *irr vt* irreführen; **misleading** *adj* irreführend

misprint *n* Druckfehler *m*

mispronounce *vt* falsch aussprechen

miss 1. *vt (fail to hit, catch)* verfehlen; *(not notice, hear)* nicht mitbekommen; *(be too late for)* verpassen; *(chance)* versäumen; *(regret the absence of)* vermissen; *I ~ you* du fehlst mir 2. *vi* nicht treffen; *(shooting)* danebenschießen; *(ball, shot etc)* danebengehen; **miss out** 1. *vt* auslassen 2. *vi* ~ **on sth** etw verpassen

Miss *n (unmarried woman)* Fräulein *nt*

missile *n* Geschoss *nt*; *(rocket)* Rakete *f*

missing *adj (person)* vermisst; *(thing)* fehlend; *be/go ~* vermisst werden, fehlen

mission *n* POL, MIL, REL Auftrag *m*, Mission *f*; **missionary** *n* Missionar(in) *m(f)*

mist *n (feiner)* Nebel *m*; *(haze)* Dunst *m*; **mist over**, **mist up** *vi* sich beschlagen

mistake 1. *n* Fehler *m*; *by ~*

aus Versehen **2.** *irr vt* (*misunderstand*) falsch verstehen; (*mix up*) verwechseln (*for* mit); **mistaken** *adj* (*idea, identity*) falsch; **be ~** sich irren, falsch liegen

mistletoe *n* Mistel *f*

mistreat *vt* schlecht behandeln

mistress *n* (*lover*) Geliebte *f*

mistrust 1. *n* Misstrauen *nt* (*of* gegen) **2.** *vt* misstrauen *+ dat*

misty *adj* neblig; (*hazy*) dunstig

misunderstand *irr vt, vi* falsch verstehen; **misunderstanding** *n* Missverständnis *nt*; (*disagreement*) Differenz *f*

mitten *n* Fausthandschuh *m*

mix 1. *n* (*mixture*) Mischung *f* **2.** *vt* mischen; (*blend*) vermischen (*with* mit); (*drinks, music*) mixen; **~ business with pleasure** das Angenehme mit dem Nützlichen verbinden **3.** *vi* (*liquids*) sich vermischen lassen; **mix up** *vt* (*mix*) zusammenmischen; (*confuse*) verwechseln (*with* mit); **mixed** *adj* gemischt; **a ~ bunch** eine bunt gemischte Truppe; **~ grill** Mixedgrill *m*; **~ vegetables** Mischgemüse *nt*; **mixer** *n* (*for food*) Mixer *m*; (*for drinks*) Mischung *f*; MED Saft *m*; **mix-up** *n* Durcheinander *nt*

ml *abbr* = **millilitre**; ml

mm *abbr* = **millimetre**; mm

moan 1. *n* Stöhnen *nt*; (*complaint*) Gejammer *nt* **2.** *vi* stöhnen; (*complain*) jammern, meckern (*about* über *+ acc*)

mobile 1. *adj* beweglich; (*on wheels*) fahrbar **2.** *n* (*phone*) Handy *nt*; **mobile phone** *n* Mobiltelefon *nt*, Handy *nt*

mobility *n* Beweglichkeit *f*

mock 1. *vt* verspotten **2.** *adj* Schein-; **mockery** *n* Spott *m*

mod cons *abbr* = **modern conveniences**; (moderner) Komfort

mode *n* Art *f*; IT Modus *m*

model 1. *n* Modell *nt*; (*example*) Vorbild *nt*; (*fashion*) Model *n* **2.** *adj* (*miniature*) Modell-; (*perfect*) Muster- **3.** *vt* (*make*) formen **4.** *vi* **she ~s for Versace** sie arbeitet als Model bei Versace

modem *n* Modem *nt*

moderate 1. *adj* mäßig; (*views, politics*) gemäßigt; (*income, success*) mittelmäßig **2.** *n* POL Gemäßigte(r) *mf* **3.** *vt* mäßigen

modern *adj* modern; **~ history** neuere Geschichte; **~ Greek** Neugriechisch *nt*; **modernize** *vt* modernisieren

modest *adj* bescheiden; **modesty** *n* Bescheidenheit *f*

modification *n* Abänderung *f*; **modify** *vt* abändern

moist *adj* feucht; **moisten** *vt* befeuchten; **moisture** *n* Feuchtigkeit *f*; **moisturizer**

n Feuchtigkeitscreme *f*

molar *n* Backenzahn *m*

mold (*US*) → **mould**

mole *n* (*spot*) Leberfleck *m*; (*animal*) Maulwurf *m*

molecule *n* Molekül *nt*

molest *vt* belästigen

molt (*US*) → **moult**

molten *adj* geschmolzen

mom (*US*) Mutti *f*

moment *n* Moment *m*, Augenblick *m*; **just a ~** Moment mal!; **at** (*or* **for**) **the ~** im Augenblick; **in a ~** gleich

momentous *adj* bedeutsam

Monaco *n* Monaco *nt*

monarch *n* Monarch(in) *m*(*f*)

monarchy *n* Monarchie *f*

monastery *n* (*for monks*) Kloster *nt*

Monday *n* Montag *m*; → **Tuesday**

monetary *adj* (*reform, policy, union*) Währungs-; **~ unit** Geldeinheit *f*

money *n* Geld *nt*

monitor 1. *n* (*screen*) Monitor *m* **2.** *vt* (*progress etc*) überwachen

monk *n* Mönch *m*

monkey *n* Affe *m*; **~ business** Unfug *m*

monsoon *n* Monsun *m*

monster 1. *n* (*animal, thing*) Monstrum *nt* **2.** *adj* Riesen-; **monstrosity** *n* Monstrosität *f*; (*thing*) Ungetüm *nt*

month *n* Monat *m*; **monthly 1.** *adj* monatlich; (*ticket, salary*) Monats- **2.** *adv* monatlich **3.** *n* (*magazine*) Monats-

(*zeit*)schrift *f*

monty *n* **go the full ~** *fam* (*strip*) alle Hüllen fallen lassen; (*go the whole hog*) aufs Ganze gehen

monument *n* Denkmal *nt* (*to* für); **monumental** *adj* (*huge*) gewaltig

mood *n* (*of person*) Laune *f*; (*a. general*) Stimmung *f*; **be in a good/bad ~** gute/schlechte Laune haben, gut/schlecht drauf sein; **be in the ~ for sth** zu etw aufgelegt sein; **moody** *adj* launisch

moon *n* Mond *m*; **be over the ~** *fam* überglücklich sein; **moonlight 1.** *n* Mondlicht *nt* **2.** *vi* schwarzarbeiten; **moonlit** *adj* (*night, landscape*) mondhell

moor 1. *n* Moor *nt* **2.** *vt, vi* festmachen; **moorings** *npl* Liegeplatz *m*; **moorland** *n* Moorland *nt*, Heideland *nt*

moose *n* Elch *m*

mop *n* Mopp *m*; **mop up** *vt* aufwischen

moped *n* (*Brit*) Moped *nt*

moral 1. *adj* moralisch; (*values*) sittlich **2.** *n* Moral *f*; **~s** *pl* Moral *f*; **morale** *n* Stimmung *f*, Moral *f*; **morality** *n* Moral *f*, Ethik *f*

more *adj, pron adv* mehr; (*additional*) noch; **three ~** noch drei; **some ~ tea?** noch etwas Tee?; **are there any ~?** gibt es noch welche?; **I don't**

go there any ~ ich gehe nicht mehr hin; (*forming comparative*) **~ important** wichtiger; **~ slowly** langsamer; **~ and ~** immer mehr; **~ and ~ beautiful** immer schöner; **~ or less** mehr oder weniger; **moreish** *adj* (*food*) **these crisps are really ~** ich kann mit diesen Chips einfach nicht aufhören; **moreover** *adv* außerdem

morgue *n* Leichenschauhaus *nt*

morning 1. *n* Morgen *m*; **in the ~** am Morgen, morgens; (*tomorrow*) morgen früh; **this ~** heute morgen **2.** *adj* Morgen-; (*early*) Früh-; (*walk etc*) morgendlich; **morning after pill** *n* die Pille danach; **morning sickness** *n* Schwangerschaftsübelkeit *f*

Morocco *n* Marokko *nt*

moron *n* Idiot(in) *m(f)*

morphine *n* Morphium *nt*

morsel *n* Bissen *m*

mortal 1. *adj* sterblich; (*wound*) tödlich **2.** *n* Sterbliche(r) *mf*; **mortality** *n* (*death rate*) Sterblichkeitsziffer *f*

mortgage 1. *n* Hypothek *f* **2.** *vt* mit einer Hypothek belasten

mosaic *n* Mosaik *nt*

Moscow *n* Moskau *nt*

Moslem *adj*, *n* → **Muslim**

mosque *n* Moschee *f*

mosquito *n* (Stech)mücke *f*; (*tropical*) Moskito *m*; **~ net** Moskitonetz *nt*

moss *n* Moos *nt*

most 1. *adj* meiste *pl*, die meisten; **in ~ cases** in den meisten Fällen **2.** *adv* (*with verbs*) am meisten; (*with adj*) ...ste; (*very*) äußerst, höchst; **he ate (the) ~** er hat am meisten gegessen; **the ~ beautiful/ interesting** der / die / das schönste / interessanteste; **~ interesting** hochinteressant! **3.** *n* das meiste, der größte Teil; (*people*) die meisten; **~ of the money/ players** das meiste Geld / die meisten Spieler; **for the ~ part** zum größten Teil; **five at the ~** höchstens fünf; **make the ~ of sth** etw voll ausnützen; **mostly** *adv* (*most of the time*) meistens; (*mainly*) hauptsächlich; (*for the most part*) größtenteils

MOT *abbr* = **Ministry of Transport**; **~ (test)** ≈ TÜV *m*

motel *n* Motel *nt*

moth *n* Nachtfalter *m*; (*wool-eating*) Motte *f*; **mothball** *n* Mottenkugel *f*

mother 1. *n* Mutter *f* **2.** *vt* bemuttern; **mother-in-law** *n* Schwiegermutter *f*; **mother-to-be** *n* werdende Mutter

motion *n* Bewegung *f*; (*in meeting*) Antrag *m*

motivate *vt* motivieren

motor 1. n Motor m; fam (car) Auto nt **2.** adj Motor-; **Motorail train®** n (Brit) Autoreisezug m; **motorbike** n Motorrad nt; **motorboat** n Motorboot nt; **motorcycle** n Motorrad nt; **motorist** n Autofahrer(in) m(f); **motor oil** n Motorenöl nt; **motor racing** n Autorennsport m; **motor scooter** n Motorroller m; **motor vehicle** n Kraftfahrzeug nt; **motorway** n (Brit) Autobahn f

mould 1. n Form f; (mildew) Schimmel m **2.** vt formen; **mouldy** adj schimmelig

mount 1. vt (horse) steigen auf + acc; (exhibition etc) organisieren; (painting) mit einem Passepartout versehen **2.** vi ~ **(up)** (an)steigen **3.** n Passepartout nt

mountain n Berg m; **mountaineer** n Bergsteiger(in) m(f); **mountaineering** n Bergsteigen nt; **mountainside** n Berghang m

mourn 1. vt betrauern **2.** vi trauern (for um); **mourning** n Trauer f; **be in** ~ trauern (for um)

mouse n a. IT Maus f; **mouse mat**, **mouse pad** (US) n Mauspad nt; **mouse trap** n Mausefalle f

mousse n GASTR Creme f; (styling ~) Schaumfestiger m

moustache n Schnurrbart m

mouth n Mund m; (of animal) Maul nt; (of cave) Eingang m; (of bottle etc) Öffnung f; (of river) Mündung f; **keep one's ~ shut** fam den Mund halten; **mouthful** n (of drink) Schluck m; (of food) Bissen m; **mouth organ** n Mundharmonika f; **mouthwash** n Mundwasser nt; **mouthwatering** adj appetitlich, lecker

move 1. n (movement) Bewegung f; (in game) Zug m; (step) Schritt m; (moving house) Umzug m; **make a ~** (in game) ziehen; (leave) sich auf den Weg machen; **get a ~ on (with sth)** sich (mit etw) beeilen **2.** vt bewegen; (object) rücken; (car) wegfahren; (transport: goods) befördern; (people) transportieren; (in job) versetzen; (emotionally) bewegen, rühren; **I can't ~ it** (stuck, too heavy) ich bringe es nicht von der Stelle; **~ house** umziehen **3.** vi sich bewegen; (change place) gehen; (vehicle, ship) fahren; (move house, town etc) umziehen; (in game) ziehen; **move about** vi sich bewegen; (travel) unterwegs sein; **move away** vi weggehen; (move town) wegziehen; **move in** vi (to house) einziehen; **move on** vi weitergehen; (vehicle) weiterfahren; **move out** vi ausziehen; **move up** vi (in queue *etc*) aufrücken; **movement** *n* Bewegung *f*

movie *n* Film *m*; **the ~s** (*the cinema*) das Kino

moving *adj* (*emotionally*) ergreifend, berührend

mow *vt* ≈ mähen; **mower** *n* (*lawn*≈) Rasenmäher *m*

mown *pp* of **mow**

Mozambique *n* Mosambik *nt*

MP *abbr* = **Member of Parliament**; Parlamentsabgeordnete(r) *mf*

mph *abbr* = **miles per hour**; Meilen pro Stunde

Mr *n* (*form of address*) Herr

Mrs *n* (*form of address*) Frau

Ms *n* (*form of address for any woman, married or unmarried*) Frau

Mt *abbr* = **Mount**; Berg *m*

much 1. *adj* viel; **we haven't got ~ time** wir haben nicht viel Zeit **2.** *adv* viel; (*with verb*) sehr; **~ better** viel besser; **I like it very ~** es gefällt mir sehr gut; **I don't like it ~** ich mag es nicht besonders; **thank you very ~** danke sehr; **~ as I like him** so sehr ich ihn mag; **we don't see them ~** wir sehen sie nicht sehr oft; **~ the same** fast gleich **3.** *n* viel; **as ~ as you want** so viel du willst; **he's not ~ of a cook** er ist kein großer Koch

muck *n fam* Dreck *m*; **muck about** *vi fam* herumalbern; **muck up** *vt fam* dreckig ma-

chen; (*spoil*) vermasseln; **mucky** *adj* dreckig

mucus *n* Schleim *m*

mud *n* Schlamm *m*

muddle 1. *n* Durcheinander *nt*; **be in a ~** ganz durcheinander sein **2.** *vt ≈* (*up*) durcheinander bringen; **muddled** *adj* konfus

muddy *adj* schlammig; (*shoes*) schmutzig; **mudguard** *n* Schutzblech *nt*

muesli *n* Müsli *nt*

muffin *n* Muffin *m*; (*Brit*) weiches, flaches Milchbrötchen aus Hefeteig, das meist getoastet und mit Butter gegessen wird

muffle *vt* (*sound*) dämpfen; **muffler** *n* (*US*) Schalldämpfer *m*

mug 1. *n* (*cup*) Becher *m*; *fam* (*fool*) Trottel *m* **2.** *vt* (*attack and rob*) überfallen; **mugging** *n* Raubüberfall *m*

mule *n* Maulesel *m*

mulled *adj* ≈ **wine** Glühwein *m*

multicolored (*US*), **multicoloured** *adj* bunt; **multicultural** *adj* multikulturell; **multi-grade** *adj* ≈ **oil** Mehrbereichsöl *nt*; **multilingual** *adj* mehrsprachig

multiple 1. *n* Vielfache(s) *nt* **2.** *adj* mehrfach; (*several*) mehrere; **multiple-choice** (*method*) *n* Multiple-Choice-Verfahren *nt*

multiplex *adj*, *n* ≈ (*cinema*)

Multiplexkino nt
multiply 1. vt multiplizieren (by mit) **2.** vi sich vermehren
multi-purpose adj Mehrzweck-; **multistorey** (car park) n Parkhaus nt
mum n fam (mother) Mutti f, Mami f
mumble vt, vi murmeln
mummy n (dead body) Mumie f; fam (mother) Mutti f, Mami f
mumps nsing Mumps m
munch vt, vi mampfen
Munich n München nt
municipal adj städtisch
murder 1. n Mord m; **the traffic was** ~ der Verkehr war die Hölle **2.** vt ermorden; **murderer** n Mörder(in) m(f)
murky adj düster; (water) trüb
murmur vt, vi murmeln
muscle n Muskel m; **muscular** adj (strong) muskulös; (cramp, pain etc) Muskel-
museum n Museum nt
mushroom n (essbarer) Pilz; (button ~) Champignon m
mushy adj breiig
music n Musik f; **musical 1.** adj (sound) melodisch; (person) musikalisch; ~ **instrument** Musikinstrument nt **2.** n (show) Musical nt; **musically** adv musikalisch; **musician** n Musiker(in) m(f)
Muslim n, adj moslemisch **2.** n (show) Moslem m, Muslime f
mussel n Miesmuschel f
must 1. vaux (need to) müs-

sen; (in negation) dürfen; **I ~n't forget that** ich darf das nicht vergessen; (certainty) **he ~ be there by now** er ist inzwischen bestimmt schon da; (assumption) **I ~ have lost it** ich habe es wohl verloren; **~ you?** muss das sein? **2.** n Muss nt
mustache n (US) Schnurrbart m
mustard n Senf m
mustn't contr of **must not**
mute adj stumm
mutter vt, vi murmeln
mutton n Hammelfleisch nt
mutual adj gegenseitig; **by ~ consent** in gegenseitigem Einvernehmen
my adj mein; **I've hurt ~ leg** ich habe mir das Bein verletzt
Myanmar n Myanmar nt
myself pron (reflexive) mich acc, mir dat; **I've hurt ~** ich habe mich verletzt; **I've bought ~ a flat** ich habe mir eine Wohnung gekauft; (emphatic) **I did it ~** ich habe es selbst gemacht; (all) **by ~** allein
mysterious adj geheimnisvoll, mysteriös; (inexplicable) rätselhaft; **mystery** n Geheimnis nt; (puzzle) Rätsel nt
myth n Mythos m; fig (untrue story) Märchen nt; **mythology** n Mythologie f

N

nag vt, vi herumnörgeln (sb an jdm); **nagging** n Nörgelei f

nail 1. n Nagel m **2.** vt nageln (to an); **nail down** vt festnageln; **nailbrush** n Nagelbürste f; **nail clippers** npl Nagelknipser m; **nailfile** n Nagelfeile f; **nail polish** n Nagellack m; **nail polish remover** n Nagellackentferner m; **nail scissors** npl Nagelschere f; **nail varnish** n Nagellack m

naive adj naiv

naked adj nackt

name 1. n Name m; **his ~ is ...** er heißt ...; **what's your ~?** wie heißen Sie?; (reputation) **have a good/ bad ~** einen guten / schlechten Ruf haben **2.** vt nennen (after nach); (sth new) benennen; (nominate) ernennen (as als / zu); **a boy ~d ...** ein Junge namens ...; **namely** adv nämlich; **name plate** n Namensschild nt

nan bread n (warm serviertes) indisches Fladenbrot

nanny n Kindermädchen nt

nap n **have a ~** ein Nickerchen machen

napkin n (at table) Serviette f

Naples n Neapel nt

nappy n (Brit) Windel f

narrow 1. adj eng, schmal; (victory, majority) knapp; **have a ~ escape** mit knap-

per Not davonkommen **2.** vi sich verengen; **narrow down** vt einschränken (to sth auf etw acc); **narrow-minded** adj engstirnig

nasty adj ekelhaft; (person) fies; (remark) gehässig; (accident, wound etc) schlimm

nation n Nation f; **national 1.** adj national; **~ anthem** Nationalhymne f; **National Health Service** (Brit) staatlicher Gesundheitsdienst; **~ insurance** (Brit) Sozialversicherung f; **~ park** Nationalpark m **2.** n Staatsbürger(in) m(f); **nationality** n Staatsangehörigkeit f, Nationalität f; **nationwide** adj, adv landesweit

native 1. adj einheimisch; (inborn) angeboren, natürlich; **Native American** Indianer(in) m(f); **~ country** Heimatland nt; **a ~ German** ein gebürtiger Deutscher, eine gebürtige Deutsche; **~ language** Muttersprache f; **~ speaker** Muttersprachler(in) m(f) **2.** n Einheimische(r) mf; (in colonial context) Eingeborene(r) mf

nativity play n Krippenspiel nt

NATO acr = **North Atlantic Treaty Organization**; Nato f natural adj natürlich; (law, science, forces etc) Natur-; (inborn) angeboren; ~ resources Bodenschätze pl; naturally adv natürlich; (by nature) von Natur aus

nature n Natur f; (type) Art f; by ~ von Natur aus; nature reserve n Naturschutzgebiet nt

naughty adj (child) ungezogen; (cheeky) frech

nausea n Übelkeit f

nautical adj nautisch; ~ mile Seemeile f

nave n Hauptschiff nt

navel n Nabel m

navigate vi navigieren; (in car) lotsen, dirigieren; navigation n Navigation f; (in car) Lotsen nt

navy n Marine f

near 1. adj nahe; my ~est relations meine nächsten Verwandten; in the ~ future in nächster Zukunft; that was a ~ miss (of thing) das war knapp; (with price) ... or ~est offer Verhandlungsbasis ... 2. adv in der Nähe; come ~ näher kommen; (event) näher rücken 3. prep ~ (to) (space) nahe an + dat; (vicinity) in der Nähe + gen; ~ the station in der Nähe des Bahnhofs, in Bahnhofsnähe; nearby 1. adj nahe gelegen 2. adv in der Nähe; nearly adv fast; near-sighted adj kurzsichtig

neat adj ordentlich; (work, writing) sauber; (undiluted) pur

necessarily adv notwendigerweise; not ~ nicht unbedingt; necessary adj notwendig, nötig; it's ~ to ... man muss ...; it's not ~ for him to come er braucht nicht mitzukommen; necessity n Notwendigkeit f; the bare necessities das absolut Notwendigste

neck n Hals m; (size) Halsweite f; necklace n Halskette f; necktie n (US) Krawatte f

nectarine n Nektarine f

née adj geborene

need 1. n (requirement) Bedürfnis n (for für); (necessity) Notwendigkeit f; (poverty) Not f; be in ~ of sth etw brauchen; if ~(s) be wenn nötig 2. vt brauchen; I ~ to speak to you ich muss mit dir reden; you ~n't go du brauchst nicht (zu) gehen, du musst nicht gehen

needle n Nadel f

needless, needlessly adj, adv unnötig; ~ to say selbstverständlich

negative 1. n LING Verneinung f; PHOT Negativ nt 2. adj negativ; (answer) verneinend

neglect 1. n Vernachlässigung f 2. vt vernachlässigen; negligence n Nachlässigkeit f; negligent adj nachlässig

negotiate vi verhandeln; ne-

gotiation n Verhandlung f
neigh vi (horse) wiehern
neighbor (US), **neighbour** n
Nachbar(in) m(f); **neigh-
bo(u)rhood** n Nachbarschaft
f

neighbo(u)ring adj benachbart
neither 1. adj, pron keine(r, s)
von beiden; ~ **of you/us** keiner von euch/uns beiden **2.**
adv ~ ... nor ... weder ... noch
... **3.** conj **I'm not going** - ~
am I ich gehe nicht - ich auch
nicht
nephew n Neffe m
nerd n fam Schwachkopf m;
he's a real computer ~ er
ist ein totaler Computer-
freak
nerve n Nerv m; **he gets on
my** ~**s** er gebt mir auf die
Nerven; (courage) **keep/
lose one's** ~ die Nerven be-
halten/verlieren; (cheek)
have the ~ **to do sth** die
Frechheit besitzen, etw zu
tun; **nerve-racking** adj ner-
venaufreibend; **nervous** adj
(apprehensive) ängstlich;
(on edge) nervös; **nervous
breakdown** n Nervenzusammenbruch m

nest 1. n Nest nt **2.** vi nisten
net 1. n Netz nt; **the Net** (Internet) das Internet; **on the** ~ im
Netz **2.** adj (price, weight)
Netto-; ~ **profit** Reingewinn
m
Netherlands npl **the** ~ die

Niederlande pl
network n Netz nt; TV, RADIO
Sendenetz nt; IT Netzwerk nt
neurosis n Neurose f; **neurotic** adj neurotisch
neuter adj BIO geschlechtslos;
LING sächlich
neutral adj neutral **2.** n
(gear in car) Leerlauf m
never adv nie(mals); ~ **before**
noch nie; ~ **mind** macht
nichts!; **never-ending** adj
endlos; **nevertheless** adv
trotzdem
new adj neu; **this is all** ~ **to me**
das ist für mich noch unge-
wohnt
New England n Neuengland
nt
Newfoundland n Neufund-
land nt
newly adv neu; ~ **made** (cake)
frisch gebacken; **newly-
-weds** npl Frischvermählte
pl; **new moon** n Neumond m
news nsing (item of ~) Nachricht f; RADIO, TV Nachrichten pl; **good** ~ ein erfreuliche
Nachricht; **what's the** ~?
was gibt's Neues?; **have
you heard the** ~? hast du
das Neueste gehört?; **news-
agent**, **news dealer** (US) n
Zeitungshändler(in) m(f);
news bulletin n Nachrich-
tensendung f; **news flash** n
Kurzmeldung f; **newsgroup**
n IT Diskussionsforum nt,
Newsgroup f; **newsletter** n
Mitteilungsblatt nt; **news-**

paper n Zeitung f

New Year n das neue Jahr; **Happy ~** (ein) frohes Neues Jahr!; **~'s Day** Neujahr nt, Neujahrstag m; **~'s Eve** Silvesterabend m; **~'s resolution** guter Vorsatz fürs neue Jahr

New York n New York nt

New Zealand 1. n Neuseeland nt 2. adj neuseeländisch; New Zealander n Neuseeländer(in) m(f)

next 1. adj nächste(r, s); **the week after ~** übernächste Woche; **~ time I see him** wenn ich ihn das nächste Mal sehe; **you're ~** du bist jetzt dran 2. adv als Nächstes; (then) dann, darauf; **~ to** hehen + dat; **~ to last** vorletzte(r, s); **~ to impossible** nahezu unmöglich; **the ~ best thing** das Nächstbeste; **~ door** nebenan

NHS abbr = National Health Service

Niagara Falls npl Niagarafälle pl

nibble vt knabbern a + dat; nibbles npl Knabberzeug nt

Nicaragua n Nicaragua nt

nice adj nett, sympathisch; (taste, food, drink) gut; (weather) schön; **have a ~ day** (US) schönen Tag noch!; nicely adv nett; (well) gut; **that'll do ~** das genügt vollauf

nick vt fam (steal) klauen

nickel n CHEM Nickel nt; (US, coin) Nickel m

nickname n Spitzname m

nicotine n Nikotin nt; **nicotine patch** n Nikotinpflaster nt

niece n Nichte f

Nigeria n Nigeria nt

night n Nacht f; (before bed) Abend m; **good ~** gute Nacht!; **at** (or **by**) **~** nachts; **have an early ~** früh schlafen gehen; nightcap n Schlummertrunk m; nightclub n Nachtklub m; nightdress n Nachthemd nt; nightie n fam Nachthemd nt

nightingale n Nachtigall f

night life n Nachtleben nt; nightly adv (every evening) jeden Abend; (every night) jede Nacht; nightmare n Albtraum m; nighttime n Nacht f; **at ~** nachts

nil n SPORT null

Nile n Nil m

nine 1. num neun; **~ times out of ten** so gut wie immer 2. n (a. bus etc) Neun f; → **eight**; nineteen 1. num neunzehn 2. n (a. bus etc) Neunzehn f; → **eight**; nineteenth adj neunzehnte(r, s); → **eighth**; ninetieth adj neunzigste(r, s); → **eighth**; ninety 1. num neunzig 2. n Neunzig f; → **eight**; ninth 1. adj neunte(r, s) 2. n (fraction) Neuntel nt; → **eighth**

nipple n Brustwarze f

nitrogen n Stickstoff m

no 1. adv nein; (after comparative) nicht; **I can wait ~ longer** ich kann nicht länger warten; **I have ~ more money** ich habe kein Geld mehr **2.** adj kein; **in ~ time** im Nu; **~ way** fam keinesfalls; **it's ~ use** (or **good**) es hat keinen Zweck; **~ smoking** Rauchen verboten **3.** n Nein nt

nobody 1. pron niemand; (emphatic) keiner; **~ knows** keiner weiß es; **~ else** sonst niemand, kein anderer **2.** n Niemand m

no-claims bonus n Schadenfreiheitsrabatt m

nod vi, vt nicken; **nod off** vi einnicken

noise n (loud) Lärm m; (sound) Geräusch nt; **noisy** adj laut; (crowd) lärmend

nominate vt (in election) aufstellen; (appoint) ernennen

non- pref Nicht-; (with adj) nicht-, un-; **non-alcoholic** adj alkoholfrei

none pron keine(r, s); **~ of them** keiner von ihnen; **~ of it is any use** nichts davon ist brauchbar; **there are ~ left** es sind keine mehr da; (with comparative) **be ~ the wiser** auch nicht schlauer sein

nonetheless adv nichtsdestoweniger

non-fiction n Sachbücher pl;

non-resident n **'open to ~s'** „auch für Nichthotelgäste"; **non-returnable** adj; **~ bottle** Einwegflasche f

nonsense n Unsinn m

non-smoker n Nichtraucher(in) m(f); **non-smoking** adj Nichtraucher-; **non-standard** adj nicht serienmäßig; **nonstop** adj (train) durchgehend; (flight) Nonstop-; **2.** adv (talk) ununterbrochen; (fly) ohne Zwischenlandung

noodles npl Nudeln pl

noon n Mittag m; **at ~** um 12 Uhr mittags

no one pron niemand; (emphatic) keiner; **~ else** sonst niemand, kein anderer

nor conj **neither ... ~ ...** weder ... noch ...; **I don't smoke, ~ does he** ich rauche nicht, er auch nicht

normal adj normal; **get back to ~** sich wieder normalisieren; **normally** adv (usually) normalerweise

north 1. n Norden m; **to the ~** (go, face) nach Norden **2.** adj Nord-; **North America** n Nordamerika nt; **northbound** adj (in Richtung Norden); **northeast 1.** n Nordosten m; **to the ~** (of) nordöstlich (von) **2.** adv (go, face) nach Nordosten **3.** adj Nordost-; **northern** adj nördlich; **~ France** Nordfrankreich *nt*; **Northern Ireland** *n* Nordirland *nt*; **North Pole** *n* Nordpol *m*; **North Sea** *n* Nordsee *f*; **northwards** *adv* nach Norden; **northwest** 1. *n* Nordwesten *m*; **to the ~ of** nordwestlich von 2. *adv* (*go, face*) nach Nordwesten 3. *adj* Nordwest-

Norway *n* Norwegen *nt*; **Norwegian** 1. *adj* norwegisch 2. *n* (*person*) Norweger(in) *m(f)*; (*language*) Norwegisch *nt*

nose *n* Nase *f*; **nosebleed** *n* Nasenbluten *nt*; **nose-dive** *n* Sturzflug *m*

nosey → **nosy**

nostril *n* Nasenloch *nt*

nosy *adj* neugierig

not *adv* nicht; **~ one of them** kein einziger von ihnen; **I told him ~ to** (**do it**) ich sagte ihm, er solle es nicht tun; **~ at all** überhaupt nicht, keineswegs; (*don't mention it*) gern geschehen; **~ yet** noch nicht

notable *adj* bemerkenswert; **note** 1. *n* (*written*) Notiz *f*; (*short letter*) paar Zeilen *pl*; (*comment on book etc*) Anmerkung *f*; (*bank-*) Schein *m*; MUS (*sign*) Note *f*; (*sound*) Ton *m*; **make a ~ of sth** sich *dat* etw notieren; **~s** (*of lecture etc*) Aufzeichnungen *pl*; **take ~s** sich *dat* Notizen machen; (*über* + *acc*) 2. *vt* (*notice*) bemerken (*that* dass); (*write down*) notieren;

notebook *n* Notizbuch *nt*; IT Notebook *nt*; **notepad** *n* Notizblock *m*; **notepaper** *n* Briefpapier *nt*

nothing *n* nichts; **~ but ...** lauter ...; **for ~** umsonst; **he thinks ~ of it** er macht sich nichts daraus

notice 1. *n* (*announcement*) Bekanntmachung *f*; (*on ~ board*) Anschlag *m*; (*attention*) Beachtung *f*; (*advance warning*) Ankündigung *f*; (*to leave job, flat etc*) Kündigung *f*; **at short ~** kurzfristig; **until further ~** bis auf weiteres; **give sb ~** jdm kündigen; **hand in one's ~** kündigen; **take** (**no**) **~ of** (**sth**) etw (nicht) beachten 2. *vt* bemerken; **noticeable** *adj* erkennbar; (*visible*) sichtbar; **be ~** auffallen; **notice board** *n* Anschlagtafel *f*

notification *n* Benachrichtigung *f* (*of* von); **notify** *vt* benachrichtigen (*of* von)

notorious *adj* berüchtigt

nought *n* Null *f*

noun *n* Substantiv *nt*

novel 1. *n* Roman *m* 2. *adj* neuartig; **novelty** *n* Neuheit *f*

November *n* November *m*; → **September**

novice *n* Neuling *m*

now *adv* (*at the moment*) jetzt; (*introductory phrase*) also; **right ~** jetzt gleich; **just ~** gerade; **by ~** inzwischen; **from**

~ **on** ab jetzt; ~ **and again** (or **then**) ab und zu; **nowadays** adv heutzutage

nowhere adv nirgends; **we're getting** ~ wir kommen nicht weiter; ~ **near** noch lange nicht

nozzle n Düse f

nuclear adj (energy etc) Kern-; ~ **power station** Kernkraftwerk nt

nude 1. adj nackt 2. n (person) Nackte(r) mf; (painting etc) Akt m; (quantity) (An)zahl f; **to be in the ~** nackt sein; Nudist(in) m(f), FKK-Anhänger(in) m(f); **nudist beach** n FKK-Strand m

nuisance n Ärgernis nt; (person) Plage f; **what a ~** wie ärgerlich!

numb 1. adj taub, gefühllos 2. vt betäuben

number 1. n Nummer f; MATH Zahl f; (quantity) (An)zahl f; **in small/large ~s** in kleinen/großen Mengen; **a ~ of times** mehrmals 2. vt (give a number to) nummerieren; (count) zählen (among zu); **his days are ~ed** seine Tage sind gezählt; **number plate** n (Brit) AUTO Nummernschild nt

numeral n Ziffer f; **numerical** adj numerisch; (superiority) zahlenmäßig; **numerous**

adj zahlreich

nun n Nonne f

Nuremberg n Nürnberg nt

nurse 1. n Krankenschwester f; (male ~) Krankenpfleger m 2. vt (patient) pflegen; (baby) stillen; **nursery** n Kinderzimmer nt; (for plants) Gärtnerei f; (tree) Baumschule f; **nursery rhyme** n Kinderreim m; **nursery school** n Kindergarten m; ~ **teacher** Kindergärtner(in) m(f), Erzieher(in) m(f); **nursing** n (profession) Krankenpflege f; ~ **home** n Privatklinik f

nut n Nuss f; TECH (for bolt) Mutter f; **nutcase** n fam Spinner(in) m(f); **nutcracker** n, **nutcrackers** npl Nussknacker m

nutmeg n Muskat m, Muskatnuss f

nutrition n Ernährung f; **nutritious** adj nahrhaft

nuts fam 1. adj verrückt; **be ~ about sth** nach etw verrückt sein 2. npl (testicles) Eier pl

nutshell n Nussschale f; **in a ~** kurz gesagt

nutter n fam Spinner(in) m(f); **nutty** adj fam verrückt

nylon® 1. n Nylon® nt 2. adj Nylon-

O

O n TEL Null f

oak 1. n Eiche f **2.** adj Eichen-

OAP abbr = **old-age pensioner**; Rentner(in) m(f)

oar n Ruder nt

oasis n Oase f

oath n (statement) Eid m

oats npl Hafer m; GASTR Haferflocken pl

obedience n Gehorsam m; **obedient** adj gehorsam; **obey** vt, vi gehorchen + dat

object 1. n Gegenstand m; (abstract) Objekt nt; (purpose) Ziel nt **2.** vi dagegen sein; (raise objection) Einwände erheben (to gegen); (morally) Anstoß nehmen (to an + dat); **do you ~ to my smoking?** haben Sie etwas dagegen, wenn ich rauche?; **objection** n Einwand m

objective 1. n Ziel nt **2.** adj objektiv; **objectivity** n Objektivität f

obligation n (duty) Pflicht f; (commitment) Verpflichtung f; **no ~** unverbindlich; **obligatory** adj obligatorisch; **oblige** vt **~ sb to do sth** jdn (dazu) zwingen, etw zu tun; **he felt ~d to accept the offer** er fühlte sich verpflichtet, das Angebot anzunehmen

oblong 1. n Rechteck nt **2.** adj rechteckig

oboe n Oboe f

obscene adj obszön

observation n (watching) Beobachtung f; (remark) Bemerkung f; **observe** vt (notice) bemerken; (watch) beobachten; (customs) einhalten

obsessed adj besessen (with an idea etc von einem Gedanken etc); **obsession** n Manie f

obsolete adj veraltet

obstacle n Hindernis nt (to für)

obstinate adj hartnäckig

obstruct vt versperren; (pipe) verstopfen; (hinder) behindern, aufhalten; **obstruction** n Blockierung f; (of pipe) Verstopfung f; (obstacle) Hindernis nt

obtain vt erhalten; **obtainable** adj erhältlich

obvious adj offensichtlich; **it was ~ to me that ...** es war mir klar, dass ...; **obviously** adj offensichtlich

occasion n Gelegenheit f; (special event) (großes) Ereignis nt; **on the ~ of** anlässlich + gen; **special ~** besonderer Anlass; **occasional**, **occasionally** adj, adv gelegentlich

occupant n (of house) Bewohner(in) m(f); (of vehicle) Insasse m, Insassin f; **occupation** n Beruf m; (pastime) Beschäftigung f; (of country etc) Besetzung f; **occupied** adj (country, seat, toilet) besetzt; (person) beschäftigt; **keep sb/oneself ~** jdn/sich beschäftigen; **occupy** vt (country) besetzen; (time) beanspruchen; (mind, person) beschäftigen

occur vi vorkommen; **~ to sb** jdm einfallen

ocean n Ozean m; (US, sea) das Meer nt

o'clock adv 5~ 5 Uhr; **at 10 ~** um 10 Uhr

octagon n Achteck nt

October n Oktober m; → **September**

octopus n Tintenfisch m

odd adj (strange) sonderbar; (not even) ungerade; (one missing) einzeln; **be the ~ one out** nicht dazugehören; **odds** npl Chancen pl; **against all ~** entgegen allen Erwartungen

odometer n (US) AUTO Meilenzähler m

odor (US), **odour** n Geruch m

of prep von; (material, origin) aus; **the name ~ the hotel** der Name des Hotels; **the works ~ Shakespeare** Shakespeares Werke; **a friend ~ mine** ein Freund von mir; **the fourth ~ June** der vierte Juni; (quantity) **a glass ~ water** ein Glas Wasser; **a litre ~ wine** ein Liter Wein; **a girl ~ ten** ein zehnjähriges Mädchen; (US, in time) **it's five ~ three** es ist fünf vor drei; (cause) **die ~ cancer** an Krebs sterben

off 1. adv (away) weg, fort; (free) frei; (switch) ausgeschaltet; (milk) sauer; **a mile ~** eine Meile entfernt; **I'll be ~ now** ich gehe jetzt; **have the day/Monday ~** heute/ Montag freihaben; **the lights are ~** die Lichter sind aus; **the concert is ~** das Konzert fällt aus; **I got 10% ~** ich habe 10% Nachlass bekommen **2.** prep (away from) von; (away) **jump/fall ~ the roof** vom Dach springen/fallen; **get ~ the bus** aus dem Bus aussteigen; **he's ~ work/ school** er hat frei/schulfrei; **take £20 ~ the price** den Preis um 20 Pfund herabsetzen

offence n (crime) Straftat f; (minor) Vergehen nt; (to feelings) Kränkung f; **cause/take ~** Anstoß erregen/nehmen; **offend** vt kränken; (eye, ear) beleidigen; **offender** n Straffällige(r) m/f; **offense** (US) → **offence**; **offensive 1.** adj anstößig; (insulting) beleidigend; (smell) übel, abstoßend **2.** n MIL Offensive f

offer 1. n Angebot nt; **on ~ comm** im Angebot nt. **2.** vt anbieten (to sb jdm); (money, a chance etc) bieten

offhand 1. adj lässig **2.** adv (say) auf Anhieb

office n Büro nt; (position) Amt nt; **doctor's ~** (US) Arztpraxis f; **office block** n Bürogebäude nt; **office hours** npl Dienstzeit f; (notice) Geschäftszeiten pl; **officer** n MIL Offizier(in) m(f); (official) Polizeibeamte(r) m, Polizeibeamtin f; **office worker** n Büroangestellte(r) mf; **official 1.** adj offiziell; (report etc) amtlich; **~ language** Amtssprache f **2.** n Beamte(r) m, Beamtin f, Repräsentant(in) m(f)

off-licence n (Brit) Wein- und Spirituosenhandlung f; **off-line** adj IT offline; **off-peak** adj außerhalb der Stoßzeiten; (rate, ticket) verbilligt; **off-putting** adj, abstoßend; **off-season** adj außerhalb der Saison

offshore adj küstennah, Küsten-; (oil rig) im Meer; **offside** n AUTO Fahrerseite f; SPORT Abseits nt f

often adv oft; **every so ~** von Zeit zu Zeit

oil n Öl nt **2.** vt ölen; **oil level** n Ölstand m; **oil painting** n Ölgemälde nt; **oil-rig** n (Öl)bohrinsel f; **oil slick** n Ölteppich m; **oil tanker** n

Öltanker m; (truck) Tankwagen m; **oily** adj ölig; (skin, hair) fettig

ointment n Salbe f

OK, okay adj fam okay, in Ordnung; **that's ~ by** (or **with**) **me** das ist mir recht

old adj alt; **old age** n Alter nt; **~ pensioner** Rentner(in) m(f); **old-fashioned** adj altmodisch; **old people's home** n Altersheim nt

olive n Olive f; **olive oil** n Olivenöl nt

Olympic adj olympisch; **the ~ Games, the ~s** pl die Olympischen Spiele pl, die Olympiade

omelette n Omelett nt

omit vt auslassen

on 1. prep (position) auf + dat; (with motion) auf + acc; (vertical surface, day) an + dat; (with motion) an + acc; **it's ~ the table** es ist auf dem Tisch; **hang it ~ the wall** häng es an die Wand; **I haven't got it ~ me** ich habe es nicht bei mir; **~ TV** im Fernsehen; **~ the left** links; **~ the right** rechts; **~ the train/bus** im Zug/Bus; **~ the twelfth** am zwölften; **~ Sunday** am Sonntag; **~ Sundays** sonntags **2.** adj (light etc) TV, ELEC an; **what's ~ at the cinema?** was läuft im Kino?; **I've nothing ~** (nothing arranged) ich habe nichts vor; (no clothes) ich habe nichts an; **leave the light ~** das Licht brennen lassen

once 1. adv (one time, in the past) einmal; **at ~** sofort; (at the same time) gleichzeitig; **~ more** noch einmal; **for ~** ausnahmsweise (einmal); **~ in a while** ab und zu mal **2.** conj wenn ... einmal; **you've got used to it** sobald Sie sich daran gewöhnt haben

oncoming adj entgegenkommend; **~ traffic** Gegenverkehr m

one 1. num eins **2.** adj ein, eine, ein; (only) einzige(r, s); **~ day** eines Tages; **the ~ and only ...** der/die unvergleichliche ... **3.** pron eine(r, s); (people, you) man; **the who/that ...** der/die(jenige), der/die/das(jenige), die/das(jenige), das ...; **this ~, that ~** dieser/diese/dieses; **the blue ~** der/die/das Blaue; **which ~?** welcher/welche/welches?; **~ another** einander; **one-off 1.** adj einmalig **2.** n a **~** etwas Einmaliges; **one-parent family** n Einelternfamilie f; **one-piece** adj einteilig; **oneself** pron (reflexive) sich; **~ cut ~** sich schneiden; **one-way** adj **~ street** Einbahnstraße f; **~ ticket** (US) einfache Fahrkarte

onion n Zwiebel f

on-line adj IT online; **~ banking** Homebanking nt

only 1. adv nur; (with time) erst; **~ yesterday** erst gestern; **he's ~ four** er ist erst vier; **~ just arrived** gerade erst angekommen **2.** adj einzige(r, s); **~ child** Einzelkind nt

o.n.o. abbr = **or nearest offer**; VB

onside adv SPORT nicht im Abseits

onto prep auf + acc; (vertical surface) an + acc

onwards adv voran, vorwärts; **from today ~** von heute an, ab heute

opaque adj undurchsichtig

open 1. adj offen; **in the ~ air** im Freien; **~ to the public** für die Öffentlichkeit zugänglich; **the shop is ~** das Geschäft hat den ganzen Tag offen **2.** vt öffnen, aufmachen; (meeting, account, new building) eröffnen; (road) dem Verkehr übergeben **3.** vi (door, window etc) aufgehen, sich öffnen; (shop, bank) öffnen, aufmachen; (begin) anfangen (with mit); **open day** n Tag m der offenen Tür; **opening** n Öffnung f; (beginning) Anfang m; (official, of exhibition etc) Eröffnung f; **~ hours** (or times) Öffnungszeiten pl; **openly** adv offen; **open-minded** adj aufgeschlossen; **open-**

-plan adj ~ office Großraumbüro nt

opera n Oper f; opera glasses npl Opernglas nt; opera house n Oper f, Opernhaus nt

operate 1. vt (machine) bedienen; (brakes, lights) betätigen 2. vi (machine) laufen; (bus etc) verkehren (between zwischen); ~ (on sb) MED (jdn) operieren; operating theatre n Operationssaal m; operation f (of machine) Bedienung f; MED Operation f (on an + dat); (undertaking) Unternehmen nt; in ~ (machine) in Betrieb; have an ~ operiert werden (for wegen)

opinion n Meinung f (on zu); in my ~ meiner Meinung nach

opponent n Gegner(in) m(f)

opportunity n Gelegenheit f

oppose vt sich widersetzen + dat; (idea) ablehnen; opposed adj be ~ to sth gegen etw sein; as ~ to im Gegensatz zu; opposing adj (team) gegnerisch; (points of view) entgegengesetzt

opposite 1. adj (house) gegenüberliegend; (direction) entgegengesetzt; the ~ sex das andere Geschlecht 2. adv gegenüber 3. prep gegenüber; ~ me mir gegenüber 4. n Gegenteil nt

opposition n Widerstand m

(to gegen); POL Opposition f

oppress vt unterdrücken

opt vi ~ for sth sich für etw entscheiden

optician n Optiker(in) m(f)

optimist n Optimist(in) m(f); optimistic adj optimistisch

optimum adj optimal

option n Möglichkeit f; COMM Option f; have no ~ keine Wahl haben; optional adj freiwillig; ~ extras AUTO Extras pl

or conj oder; (otherwise) sonst; hurry up, ~ (else) we'll be late beeil dich, sonst kommen wir zu spät

oral 1. adj mündlich; ~ sex Oralverkehr m 2. n (exam) Mündliche(s) nt

orange 1. n Orange f 2. adj orangefarben; orange juice n Orangensaft m

orbit 1. n Umlaufbahn f 2. vt umkreisen

orchard n Obstgarten m

orchestra n Orchester nt; (US) THEAT Parkett nt

orchid n Orchidee f

ordeal n Tortur f; (emotional) Qual f

order 1. n (sequence) Reihenfolge f; (good arrangement) Ordnung f; (command) Befehl m; LAW Anordnung f; (condition) Zustand m, Bestellung f; out of ~ (not functioning) außer Betrieb; (unsuitable) nicht angebracht; in ~ (items) richtig geordnet;

(*all right*) in Ordnung; **in~ to do sth** um etw zu tun **2.** *vt* (*arrange*) ordnen; (*command*) befehlen; **~ sb to do sth** jdm befehlen, etw zu tun; (*food, product*) bestellen; **order form** *n* Bestellschein *m*

ordinary *adj* gewöhnlich, normal

ore *n* Erz *nt*

organ *n* MUS Orgel *f*; ANAT Organ *nt*

organic *adj* organisch; (*farming, vegetables*) Bio-, Öko-; **~ farmer** Biobauer *m*, Biobäuerin *f*; **~ food** Biokost *f*

organization *n* Organisation *f*; (*arrangement*) Ordnung *f*; **organize** *vt* organisieren; **organizer** *n* (*elektronisches*) Notizbuch

orgasm *n* Orgasmus *m*

oriental *adj* orientalisch

orientation *n* Orientierung *f*

origin *n* Ursprung *m*; (*of person*) Herkunft *f*; **original 1.** *adj* (*first*) ursprünglich; (*painting*) original; (*idea*) originell **2.** *n* Original *nt*; **originally** *adv* ursprünglich

Orkneys *npl*, **Orkney Islands** *npl* Orkneyinseln *pl*

ornamental *adj* dekorativ

orphan *n* Waise *f*, Waisenkind *nt*; **orphanage** *n* Waisenhaus *nt*

orthodox *adj* orthodox

orthopaedic, orthopedic (*US*) *adj* orthopädisch

ostrich *n* ZOOL Strauß *m*

other *adj*, *pron* andere(r, s); **any ~ questions?** sonst noch Fragen?; **the~ day** neulich; **every ~ day** jeden zweiten Tag; **someone / something or ~** irgend jemand / irgend etwas; **otherwise** *adv* sonst; (*differently*) anders

OTT *adj abbr* = **over the top**; übertrieben

otter *n* Otter *m*

ought *vaux* (*obligation*) sollte; (*probability*) dürfte; (*stronger*) müsste; **you ~ to do that** Sie sollten das tun; **that ~ to do** das müsste (*oder* dürfte) reichen

ounce *n* Unze *f* (*28,35 g*)

our *adj* unser; **ours** *pron* unsere(r, s); **this is ~** das gehört uns; **a friend of ours** ein Freund von uns; **ourselves** *pron* (*reflexive*) uns; **we enjoyed ~** wir haben uns amüsiert; **we've got the house to ~** wir haben das Haus für uns; (*emphatic*) **we did it ~** wir haben es selbst gemacht; (*all*) **by ~** allein

out *adv* hinaus / heraus; (*not indoors*) draußen; (*not at home*) nicht zu Hause; (*not alight*) aus; (*unconscious*) bewusstlos; (*published*) herausgekommen; (*results*) bekannt gegeben; **have you been ~ yet?** waren Sie schon draußen?; **I was ~ when they called** ich war nicht da, als sie vorbeikamen; **be ~ and about** unterwegs sein; **the fire is ~** das Feuer ist ausgegangen

outback n (in Australia) **the ~** das Hinterland

outboard n **~ motor** Außenbordmotor m

outbreak n Ausbruch m

outcome n Ergebnis nt

outcry n (public protest) Protestwelle f (against gegen)

outdo irr vt übertreffen

outdoor adj Außen-; SPORT im Freien; **~ swimming pool** Freibad nt; **outdoors** adv draußen, im Freien

outer adj äußere(r, s); **outer space** n Weltraum m

outfit n Ausrüstung f; (clothes) Kleidung f

outgoing adj kontaktfreudig

outgrow irr vt (clothes) herauswachsen aus

outing n Ausflug m

outlet n Auslass m, Abfluss m; (US) Steckdose f; (shop) Verkaufsstelle f

outline n Umriss m; (summary) Abriss m

outlive vt überleben

outlook n Aussicht(en) f(pl); (attitude) Einstellung f (on zu)

outnumber vt zahlenmäßig überlegen sein + dat; **~ed** zahlenmäßig unterlegen

out of prep (motion, motive, origin) aus; (position, away from) außerhalb + gen; **~**

danger / sight / breath außer Gefahr / Sicht / Atem; **made ~ wood** aus Holz gemacht; **we are ~ bread** wir haben kein Brot mehr; **out-of-date** adj veraltet; **out-of-the-way** adj abgelegen

outpatient n ambulanter Patient, ambulante Patientin

output n Produktion f; (of engine) Leistung f; IT Ausgabe f

outrage n (great anger) Empörung f (at über); (wicked deed) Schandtat f; (crime) Verbrechen nt; (indecency) Skandal m; **outrageous** adj unerhört; (clothes, behaviour etc) unmöglich, schrill

outright 1. adv (killed) sofort **2.** adj total; (denial) völlig; (winner) unbestritten

outside 1. n Außenseite f; **on the ~** außen **2.** adj äußere(r, s), Außen-; (chance) sehr gering **3.** adv außen; **go ~** nach draußen gehen **4.** prep außerhalb + gen; **outsider** n Außenseiter(in) m(f)

outsize adj übergroß; (clothes) in Übergröße

outskirts npl (of town) Stadtrand m

outstanding adj hervorragend; (debts etc) ausstehend

outward adj äußere(r, s); **~ journey** Hinfahrt f; **outwardly** adv nach außen hin; **outwards** adv nach außen

oval adj oval

ovary n Eierstock m

ovation n Ovation f, Applaus m

oven n Backofen m; **oven-proof** adj feuerfest

over 1. prep (position) über + dat; (motion) über + acc; **they spent a long time ~ it** sie haben lange dazu gebraucht; **from all ~ England** aus ganz England; **~ £20** mehr als 20 Pfund; **~ the phone/radio** am Telefon/im Radio; **talk ~ a glass of wine** sich bei einem Glas Wein unterhalten; **~ the summer** während des Sommers **2.** adv (across) hinüber/herüber; (finished) vorbei; (match, play etc) zu Ende; (left) übrig; **~ there/in America** da drüben/drüben in Amerika; **~ to you** Sie sind dran; **it's (all) ~ between us** es ist aus zwischen uns; **~ and ~ again** immer wieder; **start (all) ~ again** noch einmal von vorn anfangen; **children of 8 and ~** Kinder von 8 Jahren und darüber

over- pref über-

overall 1. n (Brit) Kittel m **2.** adj (situation) allgemein; (length) Gesamt-; **~ majority** absolute Mehrheit **3.** adv insgesamt; **overalls** npl Overall m

overboard adv über Bord

overbooked adj überbucht

overcharge vt zu viel verlan-gen von

overcome irr vt überwinden; **~ by sleep/emotion** von Schlaf/Rührung übermannt

overcooked adj zu lange gekocht; (meat) zu lange gebraten

overcrowded adj überfüllt

overdo irr vt übertreiben; **you're ~ing it** du übertreibst es; **overdone** adj übertrieben; (food) zu lange gekocht; (meat) zu lange gebraten

overdose n Überdosis f

overdraft n Kontoüberziehung f; **overdrawn** adj überzogen

overdue adj überfällig

overestimate vt überschätzen

overexpose vt PHOT überbelichten

overflow vi überlaufen

overhead 1. adj AVIAT- **locker** Gepäckfach nt; **~ projector** Overheadprojektor m; **~ railway** Hochbahn f **2.** adv oben

overhear irr vt zufällig mit anhören

overheat vi (engine) heiß laufen

overjoyed adj überglücklich (at über)

overland 1. adj Überland- **2.** adv (travel) über Land

overlap vi (dates etc) sich überschneiden; (objects) sich teilweise decken

overload vt überladen

overlook vt (view from above)

überblicken; (*not notice*) übersehen; (*pardon*) hinwegsehen über + *acc*
overnight 1. *adj* (*journey, train*) Nacht-; ~ **stay** Übernachtung *f* **2.** *adv* über Nacht
overpass *n* Überführung *f*
overpay *vt* überbezahlen
overrule *vt* verwerfen; (*decision*) aufheben
overseas 1. *adj* Übersee-; (*from Auslands-; ~ **students** Studenten aus Übersee **2.** *adv* (*go*) nach Übersee; (*live, work*) in Übersee
oversee *irr vt* beaufsichtigen
overshadow *vt* überschatten
oversight *n* Versehen *nt*
oversimplify *vt* zu sehr vereinfachen
oversleep *irr vi* verschlafen
overtake *irr vt, vi* überholen
overtime *n* Überstunden *pl*
overturn *vt, vi* umkippen
overweight *adj* **be** ~ Übergewicht haben
overwhelm *vt* überwältigen;
overwhelming *adj* überwältigend
overwork 1. *n* Überarbeitung *f* **2.** *vi* sich überarbeiten;
overworked *adj* überarbeitet
owe *vt* schulden; ~ **sth to sb** (*money*) jdm etw schulden; (*favour etc*) jdm etw verdanken; **how much do I ~ you?** was bin ich Ihnen schuldig?; **owing to** *prep* wegen + *gen*
owl *n* Eule *f*
own 1. *vt* besitzen **2.** *adj* eigen; **on one's ~** allein; **he has a flat of his ~** er hat eine eigene Wohung; **owner** *n* Besitzer(in) *m(f)*; (*of business*) Inhaber(in) *m(f)*; **ownership** *n* Besitz *m*; **under new ~** unter neuer Leitung
ox *n* Ochse *m*; **oxtail** *n* Ochsenschwanz *m*; ~ **soup** Ochsenschwanzsuppe *f*
oxygen *n* Sauerstoff *m*
oyster *n* Auster *f*
oz *abbr* = **ounces**; Unzen *pl*
Oz *n fam* Australien *nt*
ozone *n* Ozon *nt*; ~ **layer** Ozonschicht *f*

P

p 1. *abbr* = **page**; S. **2.** *n abbr* = **penny, pence**
p.a. *abbr* = **per annum**
pace *n* (*speed*) Tempo *nt*; (*step*) Schritt *m*; **pacemaker** *n* MED Schrittmacher *m*
Pacific *n* **the ~** (**Ocean**) der Pazifik
pacifier *n* (*US, for baby*) Schnuller *m*
pack 1. *n* (*of cards*) Spiel *nt*; (*esp US, of cigarettes*) Schachtel *f*; (*gang*) Bande *f*; (*US, backpack*) Rucksack *m*

m **2.** *vt* (*case*) packen; (*clothes*) einpacken **3.** *vi* (*for holiday*) packen; **pack in** *vt* (*Brit*) *fam* (*job*) hinschmeißen; **package** *n* Paket *nt*; **package deal** *n* Pauschalangebot *nt*; **package holiday** *n* Pauschalreise *f*; **packaging** *n* (*material*) Verpackung *f*; **packed lunch** *n* (*Brit*) Lunchpaket *nt*; **packet** *n* Päckchen *nt*; (*of cigarettes*) Schachtel *f*

pad *n* (*of paper*) Schreibblock *m*; (*padding*) Polster *nt*; **padded envelope** *n* wattierter Umschlag *m*; **padding** *n* (*material*) Polsterung *f*

paddle 1. *n* (*for boat*) Paddel *nt* **2.** *vi* (*in boat*) paddeln; **paddling pool** *n* (*Brit*) Planschbecken *nt*

padlock *n* Vorhängeschloss *nt*

page *n* (*of book etc*) Seite *f*

pager *n* Piepser *m*

paid **1.** *pt, pp* of **pay 2.** *adj* bezahlt

pain *n* Schmerz *m*; **be in ~** Schmerzen haben; **she's a (real) ~** sie nervt; **painful** *adj* (*physically*) schmerzhaft; **painkiller** *n* schmerzstillendes Mittel

painstaking *adj* sorgfältig

paint 1. *n* Farbe *f* **2.** *vt* anstreichen; (*picture*) malen; **paintbrush** *n* Pinsel *m*; **painter** *n* Maler(in) *m(f)*; **painting** *n* (*picture*) Bild *nt*, Gemälde *nt*

pair *n* Paar *nt*; **a ~ of shoes** ein Paar Schuhe; **a ~ of scissors** eine Schere; **a ~ of trousers** eine Hose

pajamas *npl* (*US*) Schlafanzug *m*

Pakistan *n* Pakistan *nt*

pal *n* *fam* Kumpel *m*

palace *n* Palast *m*

pale *adj* (*face*) blass, bleich; (*colour*) hell

palm (*of hand*) Handfläche *f*; **~ (tree)** Palme *f*; **palmtop (computer)** *n* Palmtop(computer) *m*

pamper *vt* verhätscheln

pan *n* (*saucepan*) Topf *m*; (*frying pan*) Pfanne *f*; **pancake** *n* Pfannkuchen *m*; **Pancake Day** *n* (*Brit*) Fastnachtsdienstag *m*

panda *n* Panda *m*

pane *n* Scheibe *f*

panel *n* (*of wood*) Tafel *f*; (*in discussion*) Diskussionsteilnehmer *pl*

panic 1. *n* Panik *f* **2.** *vi* in Panik geraten; **panicky** *adj* panisch

pansy *n* (*flower*) Stiefmütterchen *nt*

panties *npl* (*Damen*)slip *m*

pantomime *n* (*Brit*) *um die Weihnachtszeit aufgeführte Märchenkomödie*

pants *npl* Unterhose *f*; (*esp US, trousers*) Hose *f*

pantyhose *npl* (*US*) Strumpfhose *f*; **panty-liner** *n* Slipeinlage *f*

paper 1. *n* Papier *nt*; (*newspa-*

per) Zeitung *f*; (*exam*) Klausur *f*; (*for reading at conference*) Referat *nt*; **~s** *pl* (*identity papers*) Papiere *pl*; **~ bag** Papiertüte *f*; **~ cup** Pappbecher *m* **2.** *vt* (*wall*) tapezieren; **paperback** *n* Taschenbuch *nt*; **paper clip** *n* Büroklammer *f*; **paper feed** *n* (*of printer*) Papiereinzug *m*; **paperwork** *n* Schreibarbeit *f*

parachute 1. *n* Fallschirm *m* **2.** *vi* abspringen

paracetamol *n* (*tablet*) Paracetamoltablette *f*

parade 1. *n* (*procession*) Umzug *m*; MIL Parade *f* **2.** *vi* vorbeimarschieren

paradise *n* Paradies *nt*

paragliding *n* Gleitschirmfliegen *nt*

paragraph *n* Absatz *m*

parallel 1. *adj* parallel **2.** *n* MATH Parallele *f*

paralyze *vt* lähmen; *fig* lahm legen

paranoid *adj* paranoid

paraphrase *vt* umschreiben; (*sth spoken*) anders ausdrücken

parasailing *n* Parasailing *nt*

parasol *n* Sonnenschirm *m*

parcel *n* Paket *nt*

pardon *n* LAW Begnadigung *f*; **~ me/I beg your~** verzeihen Sie bitte; (*objection*) aber ich bitte Sie; **I beg your~?/~ me?** wie bitte?

parent *n* Elternteil *m*; **~s** *pl* Eltern *pl*; **~s-in-law** *pl*

Schwiegereltern *pl*; **parental** *adj* elterlich, Eltern-

parish *n* Gemeinde *f*

park 1. *n* Park *m* **2.** *vt, vi* parken; **no parking** *n* Parken *nt*; **'no ~'** „Parken verboten"; **parking brake** *n* (US) Handbremse *f*; **parking disc** *n* Parkscheibe *f*; **parking fine** *n* Geldbuße *f* für falsches Parken; **parking lights** *npl* (US) Standlicht *nt*; **parking lot** *n* (US) Parkplatz *m*; **parking meter** *n* Parkuhr *f*; **parking place, parking space** *n* Parkplatz *m*; **parking ticket** *n* Strafzettel *m*

parliament *n* Parlament *nt*

parrot *n* Papagei *m*

parsley *n* Petersilie *f*

parsnip *n* Pastinake *f* (*längliches, weißes Wurzelgemüse*)

part 1. *n* Teil *m*; (*of machine*) Teil *nt*; THEAT Rolle *f* (US, *in hair*) Scheitel *m*; **take ~** teilnehmen (*in* an + *dat*); **for the most ~** zum größten Teil **2.** *adj* Teil- **3.** *vt* (*separate*) trennen; (*hair*) scheiteln **4.** *vi* (*people*) sich trennen

partial *adj* (*incomplete*) teilweise, Teil-; (*biased*) parteiisch

participant *n* Teilnehmer(in) *m(f)*; **participate** *vi* teilnehmen (*in* an + *dat*)

particular 1. *adj* (*specific*) bestimmt; (*exact*) genau; (*fussy*) eigen; **in ~** insbesondere **2.** ~**s** pl (details) Einzelheiten pl; (about person) Personalien pl; **particularly** adv besonders

parting n (farewell) Abschied m; (Brit, in hair) Scheitel m

partly adv teilweise

partner n Partner(in) m(f); **partnership** n Partnerschaft f

partridge n Rebhuhn nt

part-time 1. adj Teilzeit- **2.** adv work ~ Teilzeit arbeiten

party 1. n (celebration) Party f; POL, LAW Partei f; (group) Gruppe f **2.** vi feiern

pass 1. vt (go/reach past) vorbeigehen an + dat; (in car etc) vorbeifahren an + dat; (time) verbringen; (exam) bestehen; (law) verabschieden; ~ **sth to sb,** ~ **sb sth** jdm etw reichen; ~ **the ball to sb** jdm den Ball zuspielen **2.** vi (on foot) vorbeigehen; (in car etc) vorbeifahren; (years) vergehen; (in exam) bestehen **3.** n (document) Ausweis m; SPORT Pass m; **pass away** vi (die) verscheiden; **pass by 1.** vi (on foot) vorbeigehen; (in car etc) vorbeifahren **2.** vt (on foot) vorbeigehen an + dat; (in car etc) vorbeifahren an + dat; **pass on** vt weitergeben (to an + acc); (disease) übertragen (to auf + acc); **pass out** vi (faint) ohnmächtig werden; **pass round** vt he-

rumreichen

passage n (corridor) Gang m; (in book, music) Passage f; **passageway** n Durchgang m

passenger n Passagier(in) m(f); (on bus) Fahrgast m; (on train) Reisende(r) mf; (in car) Mitfahrer(in) m(f)

passer-by n Passant(in) m(f)

passion n Leidenschaft f; **passionate** adj leidenschaftlich; **passion fruit** n Passionsfrucht f

passive 1. adj passiv **2.** n ~ (**voice**) LING Passiv nt

passport n (Reise)pass m; **passport control** n Passkontrolle f

password n IT Passwort nt

past 1. n Vergangenheit f **2.** adv (by) vorbei; **it's five** ~ es ist fünf nach **3.** adj (years) vergangen; (president etc) ehemalig; **in the** ~ **two months** in den letzten zwei Monaten **4.** prep (telling time) nach; **it's half** ~ **10** es ist halb 11; **go** ~ **sth** an etw dat vorbeigehen / -fahren

pasta n Nudeln pl

paste 1. vt (stick) kleben; IT einfügen **2.** n (glue) Kleister m

pastime n Zeitvertreib m

pastry n Teig m; (cake) Stückchen nt

pasty n (Brit) Pastete f

patch 1. n (area) Fleck m; (for mending) Flicken m **2.** vt flicken

pâté n Pastete f

paternal adj väterlich; ~ **grandmother** Großmutter f väterlicherseits; **paternity leave** n Elternzeit f (des Vaters)

path n a. IT Pfad m; a. fig Weg m

pathetic adj (bad) kläglich, erbärmlich; **it's ~** es ist zum Heulen

patience n Geduld f; (Brit,) Patience f; **patient 1.** adj geduldig **2.** n Patient(in) m(f)

patio n Terrasse f

patriotic adj patriotisch

patrol car n Streifenwagen m; patrolman n (US) Streifenpolizist m

patron n (sponsor) Förderer m, Förderin f; (in shop) Kunde m, Kundin f

patronize vt (treat condescendingly) von oben herab behandeln; **patronizing** adj (attitude) herablassend

pattern n Muster nt

pause n Pause f **2.** vi (speaker) innehalten

pavement n (Brit) Bürgersteig m; (US) Pflaster nt

pay **1.** vt bezahlen; **he paid (me) £20 for it** er hat (mir) 20 Pfund dafür gezahlt; ~ **attention** Acht geben (to auf + acc); ~ **sb a visit** jdn besuchen **2.** vi zahlen; (be profitable) sich bezahlt machen; ~ **for sth** etw zahlen **3.** n Be-

zahlung f, Lohn m; **pay back** vt (money) zurückzahlen; **pay in** vt (into account) einzahlen; **payable** adj zahlbar; (due) fällig; **payday** n Zahltag m; **payee** n Zahlungsempfänger(in) m(f); **payment** n Bezahlung f; (money) Zahlung f; **pay phone** n Münzfernsprecher m

PC **1.** abbr = **personal computer**; PC m **2.** abbr = **politically correct**; politisch korrekt

PDA abbr = **personal digital assistant**; PDA m

PE abbr = **physical education**, ; Sport m

pea n Erbse f

peace n Frieden m; **peaceful** adj friedlich

peach n Pfirsich m

peacock n Pfau m

peak n (of mountain) Gipfel m; fig Höhepunkt m; **peak period** n Stoßzeit f; (season) Hochsaison f

peanut n Erdnuss f; **peanut butter** n Erdnussbutter f

pear n Birne f

pearl n Perle f

pebble n Kiesel m

pecan n Pekannuss f

peck n, vi picken; **peckish** adj (Brit) fam ein bisschen hungrig

peculiar adj (odd) seltsam; ~ **to** charakteristisch für; **peculiarity** n (singular quality) Besonderheit f; (strangeness)

Eigenartigkeit f

pedal n Pedal nt

pedestrian n Fußgänger(in) m(f); **pedestrian crossing** n Fußgängerüberweg m

pee vi fam pinkeln

peel 1. n Schale f **2.** vt schälen **3.** vi (paint etc) abblättern; (skin etc) sich schälen

peer 1. n Gleichaltrige(r) mf **2.** vi starren

peg n (for coat etc) Haken m; (for tent) Hering m; (clothes) ~ (Wäsche)klammer f

pelvis n Becken nt

pen n (ball-point) Kuli m, Kugelschreiber m; (fountain pen) Füller m

penalize vt (punish) bestrafen; **penalty** n (punishment) Strafe f; (in soccer) Elfmeter m

pence pl of **penny**

pencil n Bleistift m; **pencil sharpener** n (Bleistift)spitzer m

penetrate vt durchdringen; (enter into) eindringen in + acc

penfriend n Brieffreund(in) m(f)

penguin n Pinguin m

penicillin n Penizillin nt

peninsula n Halbinsel f

penis n Penis m

penknife n Taschenmesser nt

penny n (Brit) Penny m; (US) Centstück nt

pension n Rente f; (for civil servants, executives etc) Pension f; **pensioner** n Rentner(in) m(f); **pension plan**, **pension scheme** n Rentenversicherung f

penultimate adj vorletzte(r, s)

people npl (persons) Leute pl; (von Staat) Volk nt; (inhabitants) Bevölkerung f; **people carrier** n Minivan m

pepper n Pfeffer m; (vegetable) Paprika m; **peppermint** n (sweet) Pfefferminz nt

per prep pro; ~ **annum** pro Jahr; ~ **cent** Prozent nt

percentage n Prozentsatz m

percolator n Kaffeemaschine f

percussion n MUS Schlagzeug nt

perfect 1. adj perfekt; (utter) völlig **2.** vt vervollkommnen; **perfectly** adv perfekt; (utterly) völlig

perform 1. vt (task) ausführen; (play) aufführen; MED (operation) durchführen **2.** vi THEAT auftreten; **performance** n (show) Vorstellung f; (efficiency) Leistung f

perfume n Duft m; (substance) Parfüm nt

perhaps adv vielleicht

peril n Gefahr f

period n (length of time) Zeit f; (in history) Zeitalter nt, Stunde f; MED Periode f; (US, full stop) Punkt m; **for a ~ of three years** für einen Zeitraum von drei Jahren;

periodical n Zeitschrift f

peripheral n IT Peripheriegerät nt

perish vi (die) umkommen; (material) verderben

perjury n Meineid m

perm n Dauerwelle f

permanent, permanently adj, adv ständig

permission n Erlaubnis f; permit 1. n Genehmigung f 2. vt erlauben, zulassen; ~ sb to do sth jdm erlauben, etw zu tun

persecute vt verfolgen

perseverance n Ausdauer f

Persian adj persisch

persist vi (in belief etc) bleiben (in bei); (rain, smell) andauern; persistent adj beharrlich

person n Mensch m; (in official context) Person f; in ~ persönlich; personal adj persönlich; (private) privat; personality n Persönlichkeit f; personal organizer n Organizer m; personal stereo n Walkman® m; personnel n Personal nt

perspective n Perspektive f

perspire vi schwitzen

persuade vt überreden; (convince) überzeugen; persuasive adj überzeugend

perverse adj pervers; (obstinate) eigensinnig; pervert 1. n Perverse(r) mf 2. vt (morally) verderben

pessimist n Pessimist(in)

m(f); pessimistic adj pessimistisch

pest n (insect) Schädling m; fig (person) Nervensäge f; (thing) Plage f; pester vt plagen; pesticide n Schädlingsbekämpfungsmittel nt

pet n (animal) Haustier nt; (person) Liebling m

petition n Petition f

petrol n (Brit) Benzin nt; petrol pump n (at garage) Zapfsäule f; petrol station n Tankstelle f; petrol tank n Benzintank m

pharmacy n (shop) Apotheke f

phase n Phase f

PhD abbr = Doctor of Philosophy; Dr. phil; (dissertation) Doktorarbeit f; do one's ~ promovieren

pheasant n Fasan m

phenomenon n Phänomen nt

Philippines npl Philippinen pl

philosophical adj philosophisch; fig gelassen; philosophy n Philosophie f

phone 1. n Telefon nt 2. vt, vi anrufen; phone book n Telefonbuch nt; phone bill n Telefonrechnung f; phone booth, phone box (Brit) n Telefonzelle f; phonecall n Telefonanruf m; phonecard n Telefonkarte f; phone number n Telefonnummer f

photo n Foto nt; photo booth n Fotoautomat m; photo-

copier n Kopiergerät nt;
photocopy 1. n Fotokopie f
2. vt fotokopieren; photograph 1. n Fotografie f, Aufnahme f 2. vt fotografieren;
photographer n Foto-
graf(in) m(f); photography
n Fotografie f

phrase n (expression) Redewendung f, Ausdruck m;
phrase book n Sprachführer
m

physical 1. adj (bodily) körperlich, physisch 2. n ärztliche Untersuchung; physi-
cally adv (bodily) körperlich, physisch; ~ handi-
capped körperbehindert
physician n Arzt m, Ärztin f
physics nsing Physik f
physiotherapy n Physiothe-
rapie f
physique n Körperbau m
piano n Klavier nt

pick vt (flowers, fruit) pflücken; (choose) auswählen;
(team) aufstellen; pick out
vt auswählen; pick up vt (lift
up) aufheben; (collect) abholen; (learn) lernen
pickle 1. n (food) (Mixed) Pickles pl 2. vt einlegen
pickpocket n Taschendieb(in)
m(f)
picnic n Picknick nt
picture 1. n Bild nt 2. go to the
~s (Brit) ins Kino gehen 2. vt
(visualize) sich vorstellen;
picture book n Bilderbuch
nt; picturesque adj male-
risch

pie n (meat) Pastete f; (fruit)
Kuchen m
piece n Stück nt; (part) Teil nt;
(in chess) Figur f; (in
draughts) Stein m; a ~ of
cake ein Stück Kuchen; fall
to ~s auseinanderfallen
pier n Pier m
pierce vt durchstechen,
durchbohren; (cold, sound)
durchdringen; pierced adj
(part of body) gepierct;
piercing adj durchdringend
pig n Schwein nt
pigeon n Taube f
piggy adj fam verfressen; pigheaded adj dickköpfig; piglet n Ferkel nt; pigsty n
Schweinestall m; pigtail n
Zopf m
pile n (heap) Haufen m; (one
on top of another) Stapel
m; pile up vi (accumulate)
sich anhäufen
pile-up n AUTO Massenkarambolage f
pill n Tablette f; the ~ die (Anti-
baby)pille; be on the ~ die
Pille nehmen
pillar n Pfeiler m
pillow n (Kopf)kissen nt; pillowcase n (Kopf)kissenbe-
zug m
pilot n AVIAT Pilot(in) m(f)
pimple n Pickel m
pin 1. n (for fixing) Nadel f; (in
sewing) Stecknadel f; TECH
Stift m; I've got ~s and nee-
dles in my leg mein Bein ist

mir eingeschlafen **2.** vt (*fix with pin*) heften (**to** an + acc)

PIN acr = **personal identification number**; = (**number**) PIN f, Geheimzahl f

pincers npl (*tool*) Kneifzange f

pinch 1. n (*of salt*) Prise f **2.** vt zwicken; (*fam: steal*) klauen **3.** vi (*shoe*) drücken

pine n Kiefer f

pineapple n Ananas f

pink adj rosa

pint n Pint nt (*Brit: 0,57 l, US: 0,473l*); (*Brit, glass of beer*) Bier nt

pious adj fromm

pip n (*of fruit*) Kern m

pipe n (*for smoking*) Pfeife f; (*for water, gas*) Rohrleitung f

pirate n Pirat(in m)(f); **pirated copy** n Raubkopie f

Pisces nsing ASTR Fische pl; **she's a** ~ sie ist Fisch

piss 1. vi vulg pissen **2.** n vulg Pisse f; **take the** ~ **out of sb** jdn verarschen; **piss off** vi vulg sich verpissen; **pissed** adj (*Brit, fam, drunk*) sturzbesoffen; (*US, fam, annoyed*) stocksauer

pistachio n Pistazie f

piste n, Piste f

pistol n Pistole f

pit n (*hole*) Grube f; (*coal-mine*) Zeche f; **the** ~**s** (*in motor racing*) die Box; **be the** ~**s** fam grottenschlecht sein

pitch 1. n SPORT Spielfeld nt; MUS (*of instrument*) Tonlage f; (*of voice*) Stimmlage f **2.** vt (*tent*) aufschlagen; (*throw*) werfen; **pitch-black** adj pechschwarz

pitcher n (*US, jug*) Krug m

pitiful adj (*contemptible*) jämmerlich

pitta bread n Pittabrot nt

pity 1. n Mitleid nt; **what a** ~ wie schade; **it's a** ~ es ist schade **2.** vt Mitleid haben mit

pizza n Pizza f

place 1. n (*spot, in text*) Stelle f; (*town etc*) Ort; (*house*) Haus nt; (*position, seat, on course*) Platz m; ~ **of birth** Geburtsort m; **at my** ~ bei mir; **in third** ~ auf dem dritten Platz; **out of** ~ nicht an der richtigen Stelle; (*remark*) unangebracht; **in** ~ **of** anstelle von; **in the first** ~ (*firstly*) erstens; (*immediately*) gleich; (*in any case*) überhaupt **2.** vt (*put*) stellen, setzen; (*lay flat*) legen; (*advertisement*) setzen (**in** in + acc); COMM (*order*) aufgeben; **place mat** n Set nt

plague n Pest f

plaice n Scholle f

plain 1. adj (*clear*) klar, deutlich; (*simple*) einfach; (*not beautiful*) unattraktiv; (*yoghurt*) Natur-; (*Brit, chocolate*) (Zart)bitter- **2.** n Ebene f; **plainly** adv (*frankly*) offen; (*simply*) einfach; (*obviously*) eindeutig

plait 1. n Zopf m **2.** vt flechten

plan 1. n Plan m; (*for essay etc*) Konzept nt **2.** vt planen; **~ to do sth, ~ on doing sth** vorhaben, etw zu tun **3.** vi planen

plane n (*aircraft*) Flugzeug nt; (*tool*) Hobel m; MATH Ebene f

planet n Planet m

plank n Brett nt

plant 1. n Pflanze f; (*factory*) Werk nt **2.** vt (*tree etc*) pflanzen; **plantation** n Plantage f

plaque n Gedenktafel f; (*on teeth*) Zahnbelag m

plaster n (*Brit*) MED (*sticking plaster*) Pflaster nt; (*on wall*) Verputz m; **to have one's arm in ~** den Arm in Gips haben

plastered adj fam besoffen; **get (absolutely) ~** sich besaufen

plastic 1. n Kunststoff m; **pay with ~** mit Kreditkarte bezahlen **2.** adj Plastik-; **plastic bag** n Plastiktüte f; **plastic surgery** n plastische Chirurgie f

plate n (*for food*) Teller m; (*flat sheet*) Platte f; (*plaque*) Schild nt

platform n RAIL Bahnsteig m

platinum n Platin nt

play 1. n Spiel m; THEAT (Theater)stück nt **2.** vt spielen; (*another player or team*) spielen gegen; **~ the piano** Klavier spielen **3.** vi spielen; **play at** vt **what are you**

~ing at? was soll das?; **play back** vt abspielen; **play down** vt herunterspielen

playacting n Schauspielerei f; **playback** n Wiedergabe f; **player** n Spieler(in) m(f); **playful** adj (*person*) verspielt; (*remark*) scherzhaft; **playground** n Spielplatz m; (*in school*) Schulhof m; **playgroup** n Spielgruppe f; **playing card** n Spielkarte f; **playing field** n Sportplatz m; **playmate** n Spielkamerad(in) m(f); **playwright** n Dramatiker(in) m(f)

plc abbr = **public limited company**; AG f

plea n Bitte f (*for* um)

plead vi dringend bitten (*with sb* jdn); LAW **~ guilty** sich schuldig bekennen

pleasant, pleasantly adj, adv angenehm

please 1. adv bitte; **more tea? - yes,** noch Tee? - ja, bitte **2.** vt (*be agreeable to*) gefallen + dat; **~ yourself** wie du willst; **pleased** adj zufrieden; (*glad*) erfreut; **~ to meet you** freut mich, angenehm; **pleasing** adj erfreulich; **pleasure** n Vergnügen nt, Freude f; **it's a ~** gern geschehen

pledge 1. n (*promise*) Versprechen nt **2.** vt (*promise*) versprechen

plenty 1. n **~ of** eine Menge, viel(e); **be ~** genug sein, rei-

chen; *I've got* ~ ich habe
mehr als genug **2.** *adv* (*US*)
fam ganz schön

plimsolls *npl* (*Brit*) Turnschuhe *pl*

plonk 1. *n* (*Brit*) *fam* (*wine*)
billiger Wein **2.** *vt* ~ *sth*
(*down*) etw hinknallen

plot 1. *n* (*of story*) Handlung *f*;
(*conspiracy*) Komplott *nt*;
(*of land*) Stück *nt* Land,
Grundstück *nt* **2.** *vi* ein Komplott schmieden

plough (*US*) **1.** *n* Pflug
m **2.** *vt, vi* AGR pflügen;
ploughman's lunch *n* (*Brit*)
fam in einer Kneipe serviertes Gericht aus Käse, Brot, Mixed
Pickles etc

pluck *vt* (*eyebrows, guitar*)
zupfen; (*chicken*) rupfen;
pluck up ~ (*one's*) *courage* Mut aufbringen

plug 1. *n* (*for sink, bath*) Stöpsel *m*; ELEC Stecker *m*; AUTO
(*Zünd*)kerze *f*; *fam* (*publicity*) Schleichwerbung *f* **2.** *vt*
fam (*advertise*) Reklame machen für; **plug in** *vt* anschließen

plum 1. *n* Pflaume *f* **2.** *adj fam*
(*job etc*) Super-

plumber *n* Klempner(in) *m*(*f*)

plump *adj* rundlich

plunge 1. *vt* (*knife*) stoßen;
(*into water*) tauchen **2.** *vi*
stürzen; (*into water*) tauchen

plural *n* Plural *m*

plus 1. *prep* plus; (*as well as*)
und **2.** *adj* Plus-; *20* ~ mehr

als 20 **3.** *n* *fig* Plus *nt*

plywood *n* Sperrholz *nt*

pm *abbr* = *post meridiem*; *at
3* ~ um 3 Uhr nachmittags; *at
8* ~ um 8 Uhr abends

pneumonia *n* Lungenentzündung *f*

poached *adj* (*egg*) pochiert,
verloren

PO Box *abbr* = *post office
box*; Postfach *nt*

pocket 1. *n* Tasche *f* **2.** *vt* (*put
in* ~) einstecken; **pocket-
book** *n* (*US, wallet*) Brieftasche *f*; **pocket calculator** *n*
Taschenrechner *m*; **pocket
money** *n* Taschengeld *nt*

poem *n* Gedicht *nt*; **poet** *n*
Dichter(in) *m*(*f*); **poetic** *adj*
poetisch; **poetry** *n* (*art*)
Dichtung *f*; (*poems*) Ge-
dichte *pl*

point 1. *n* Punkt *m*; (*spot*) Stelle *f*; (*sharp tip*) Spitze *f*; (*moment*) Zeitpunkt *m*; (*pur-
pose*) Zweck *m*; (*idea*) Argument *nt*; (*decimal*) Dezimalstelle *f*; ~*s* *pl* RAIL Weiche *f*;
~ *of view* Standpunkt *m*;
three – *two* drei Komma
zwei; *at some* ~ irgendwann
(*mal*); *get to the* ~ zur Sache
kommen; *there's no* ~ hat
keinen Sinn; *I was on the* ~
of leaving ich wollte gerade
gehen **2.** *vt* (*gun etc*) richten
(*at auf* + *acc*); ~ *one's finger
at* mit dem Finger zeigen *auf*
+ *acc* **3.** *vi* (*with finger etc*)
zeigen (*at, to auf* + *acc*);

point out vt (*indicate*) aufzeigen; (*mention*) hinweisen auf + acc; **pointed** adj spitz; (*question*) gezielt; **pointer** n (*on dial*) Zeiger m; (*tip*) Hinweis m; **pointless** adj sinnlos

poison 1. n Gift nt **2.** vt vergiften; **poisonous** adj giftig

poke vt (*with stick, finger*) stoßen, stupsen; (*put*) stecken

Poland n Polen nt

polar adj Polar-, polar; **~ bear** Eisbär m

pole n Stange f; GEO, ELEC Pol m

Pole n Pole m, Polin f

pole vault n Stabhochsprung m

police n Polizei f; **police car** n Polizeiwagen m; **policeman** n Polizist m; **police station** n (Polizei)wache f; **policewoman** n Polizistin f

policy n (*plan*) Politik f; (*principle*) Grundsatz m; (*insurance policy*) Police f

polio n Kinderlähmung f

polish 1. n (*for furniture*) Politur f; (*for floor*) Wachs nt; (*for shoes*) Creme f; (*shine*) Glanz m; fig Schliff m **2.** vt polieren; (*shoes*) putzen; fig den letzten Schliff geben + dat

Polish 1. adj polnisch **2.** n Polnisch nt

polite adj höflich; **politeness** n Höflichkeit f

political, politically adj, adv politisch; **~ly correct** politisch korrekt; **politician** n Politiker(in) m(f); **politics** nsing or pl Politik f

poll n (*election*) Wahl f; (*opinion poll*) Umfrage f

pollen n Pollen m, Blütenstaub m; **pollen count** n Pollenflug m

polling station n Wahllokal nt

pollute vt verschmutzen; **pollution** n Verschmutzung f

pompous adj aufgeblasen; (*language*) geschwollen

pond n Teich m

ponder vt nachdenken über + acc

pony n Pony nt; **ponytail** n Pferdeschwanz m

pool 1. n (*swimming pool*) Schwimmbad nt; (*private*) Swimmingpool m; (*game*) Poolbillard nt **2.** vt (*money etc*) zusammenlegen

poor 1. adj arm; (*not good*) schlecht **2.** npl **the ~** die Armen pl; **poorly 1.** adv (*badly*) schlecht **2.** adj (Brit) krank

pop 1. n (*music*) Pop m; (*noise*) Knall m **2.** vt (*put*) stecken; (*balloon*) platzen lassen **3.** vi (*balloon*) platzen; (*cork*) knallen; **~ in** (*person*) vorbeischauen; **popcorn** n Popcorn nt

Pope n Papst m

poppy n Mohn m

Popsicle® n (US) Eis nt am

Stiel

popular *adj* (*well-liked*) beliebt (*with* bei); (*widespread*) weit verbreitet

population *n* Bevölkerung *f*; (*of town*) Einwohner *pl*

porcelain *n* Porzellan *nt*

porch *n* Vorbau *m*; (*US, verandah*) Veranda *f*

porcupine *n* Stachelschwein *nt*

pork *n* Schweinefleisch *nt*; **pork chop** *n* Schweinekotelett *nt*; **pork pie** *n* Schweinefleischpastete *f*

porn *n* Porno *m*; **pornographic** *adj* pornografisch; **pornography** *n* Pornografie *f*

porridge *n* Haferbrei *m*

port *n* (*harbour*) Hafen *m*; NAUT (*left side*) Backbord *nt*; (*wine*) Portwein *m*; IT Anschluss *m*

portable *adj* tragbar; (*radio*) Koffer-

portal *n* IT Portal *nt*

porter *n* Pförtner(in) *m(f)*; (*for luggage*) Gepäckträger *m*

porthole *n* Bullauge *nt*

portion *n* Teil *m*; (*of food*) Portion *f*

portrait *n* Porträt *nt*

Portugal *n* Portugal *nt*; **Portuguese 1.** *adj* portugiesisch **2.** *n* Portugiese *m*, Portugiesin *f*; (*language*) Portugiesisch *nt*

pose 1. *n* Haltung *f* **2.** *vi* posieren **3.** *vt* (*threat, problem*)

darstellen

posh *adj fam* piekfein

position 1. *n* Stellung *f*; (*place*) Position *f*, Lage *f*; (*job*) Stelle *f*; (*opinion*) Standpunkt *m*; **be in a ~ to do sth** in der Lage sein, etw zu tun **2.** *vt* aufstellen; IT (*cursor*) positionieren

positive *adj* positiv; (*convinced*) sicher; (*definite*) eindeutig

possess *vt* besitzen; **possession** *n* ~(*s pl*) Besitz *m*

possibility *n* Möglichkeit *f*; **possible** *adj* möglich; **if ~** wenn möglich; **as big/ soon as ~** so groß/bald wie möglich; **possibly** *adv* (*perhaps*) vielleicht; **I've done all I ~ can** ich habe mein Möglichstes getan

post 1. *n* (*mail*) Post *f*; (*pole*) Pfosten *m*; (*job*) Stelle *f* **2.** *vt* (*letters*) aufgeben; **keep sb ~ed** jdn auf dem Laufenden halten; **postage** *n* Porto *nt*; **postal** *adj* Post-; **postbox** *n* Briefkasten *m*; **postcard** *n* Postkarte *f*; **postcode** *n* (*Brit*) Postleitzahl *f*

poster *n* Plakat *nt*, Poster *m*

postgraduate *n* jmd, der seine Studien nach dem ersten akademischen Grad weiterführt

postman *n* Briefträger *m*; **postmark** *n* Poststempel *m*

postmortem *n* Autopsie *f*

post office *n* Post® *f*; **post of-**

fice box n Postfach nt

postpone vt verschieben (till auf + acc)

posture n Haltung f

pot 1. n Topf m; (teapot, coffee pot) Kanne f **2.** vt (plant) eintopfen

potato n Kartoffel f

potential 1. adj potenziell **2.** n Potenzial nt; **potentially** adv potenziell

pottery n (objects) Töpferwaren pl

potty 1. adj (Brit) fam verrückt **2.** n Töpfchen nt

poultry n Geflügel nt

pound 1. n (money) Pfund nt; (weight) Pfund nt (0,454 kg); **a ~ of cherries** ein Pfund Kirschen; **ten-~ note** Zehnpfundschein m

pour vt (liquid) gießen; (rice, sugar etc) schütten; **~ sb sth** (drink) jdm etw eingießen; **pouring** adj (rain) strömend

poverty n Armut f

powder n Pulver nt; (cosmetic) Puder m; **powder room** n Damentoilette f

power 1. n Macht f; (ability) Fähigkeit f; (strength) Stärke f; ELEC Strom f; **be in ~** an der Macht sein **2.** v betreiben, antreiben; **power-assisted steering** n Servolenkung f; **power cut** n Stromausfall m; **powerful** adj (politician etc) mächtig; (engine, government) stark; (argument) durchschlagend; **pow-**

erless adj machtlos; **power station** n Kraftwerk nt

p&p abbr = **postage and packing**

PR 1. abbr = **public relations 2.** abbr = **proportional representation**

practical, practically adj, adv praktisch; **practice 1.** n (training) Übung f; (custom) Gewohnheit f; (doctor's, lawyer's) Praxis f; **in ~** (in reality) in der Praxis; **out of ~** außer Übung; **put sth into ~** etw in die Praxis umsetzen **2.** vt, vi (US) → **practise**

practise 1. vt (instrument, movement) üben; (profession) ausüben **2.** vi üben; (doctor, lawyer) praktizieren

Prague n Prag nt

praise 1. n Lob nt **2.** vt loben

pram n (Brit) Kinderwagen m

prawn n Garnele f, Krabbe f; **prawn crackers** npl Krabbenchips pl

pray vi beten; **prayer** n Gebet nt

pre- pref vor-, prä-

preach vi predigen

precaution n Vorsichtsmaßnahme f

precede vt vorausgehen + dat; **preceding** adj vorhergehend

precinct n (Brit, pedestrian precinct) Fußgängerzone f; (Brit, shopping precinct) Einkaufsviertel nt; (US, district) Bezirk m

precious *adj* kostbar; **~ stone** Edelstein *m*

précis *n* Zusammenfassung *f*

precise, **precisely** *adj*, *adv* genau

precondition *n* Vorbedingung *f*

predecessor *n* Vorgänger(in) *m(f)*

predict *vt* voraussagen; **predictable** *adj* vorhersehbar; *(person)* berechenbar

predominant *adj* vorherrschend; **predominantly** *adv* überwiegend

preface *n* Vorwort *nt*

prefer *vt* vorziehen (to *dat*), lieber mögen (to *als*); **~ to do sth** etw lieber tun; **preferably** *adv* vorzugsweise, am liebsten; **preference** *n* *(liking)* Vorliebe *f*; **preferential** *adj* **get ~ treatment** bevorzugt behandelt werden

prefix *n* *(US)* TEL Vorwahl *f*

pregnancy *n* Schwangerschaft *f*; **pregnant** *adj* schwanger; **two months ~** im zweiten Monat schwanger

prejudice *n* Vorurteil *nt*; **prejudiced** *adj* *(person)* voreingenommen

preliminary *adj* *(measures)* vorbereitend; *(results)* vorläufig; *(remarks)* einleitend

premature *adj* vorzeitig; *(hasty)* voreilig

premiere *n* Premiere *f*

premises *npl* *(offices)* Räumlichkeiten *pl*; *(of factory, school)* Gelände *nt*

premium-rate *adj* TEL zum Höchsttarif

preoccupied *adj* **be ~ with sth** mit etw sehr beschäftigt sein

prepaid *adj* vorausbezahlt; *(envelope)* frankiert

preparation *n* Vorbereitung *f*;

prepare 1. *vt* vorbereiten *(for* auf + *acc)*; *(food)* zubereiten; **be ~d to do sth** bereit sein, etw zu tun 2. *vi* sich vorbereiten *(for* auf + *acc)*

prerequisite *n* Voraussetzung *f*

prescribe *vt* vorschreiben; MED verschreiben; **prescription** *n* Rezept *nt*

presence *n* Gegenwart *f*; **present 1.** *adj (in attendance)* anwesend *(at* bei); *(current)* gegenwärtig; **~ tense** Gegenwart *f*, Präsens *nt* **2.** *n* Gegenwart *f*; *(gift)* Geschenk *nt*; **at ~** zurzeit **3.** *vt* TV, RADIO präsentieren; *(problem)* darstellen; *(report etc)* vorlegen

present-day *adj* heutig; **presently** *adv* bald; *(at present)* zurzeit

preservative *n* Konservierungsmittel *nt*; **preserve** *vt* erhalten; *(food)* einmachen, konservieren

president *n* Präsident(in) *m(f)*; **presidential** *adj* Präsidenten-; *(election)* Präsidentschaftspress 1. n *(newspapers, machine)* Presse f 2. vt *(push)* drücken; **~ a button** auf einen Knopf drücken 3. vi *(push)* drücken; pressing adj dringend; press-stud n Druckknopf m; press-up n *(Brit)* Liegestütz m; pressure n Druck m; **be under ~** unter Druck stehen; **put ~ on sb** jdn unter Druck setzen; pressure cooker n Schnellkochtopf m; pressurize vt *(person)* unter Druck setzen

presumably adv vermutlich; presume vt, vi annehmen

presumptuous adj anmaßend

presuppose vt voraussetzen

pretend 1. vt *(claim)* vorgeben; **~ that** so tun als ob; **~ to do sth** vorgeben, etw zu tun 2. vi **she's ~ing** sie tut nur so

pretentious adj anmaßend; *(person)* protzig

pretty 1. adj hübsch 2. adv ziemlich

prevent vt verhindern; **~ sb from doing sth** jdn daran hindern, etw zu tun

preview n FILM Voraufführung f; *(trailer)* Vorschau f

previous, previously adj, adv früher

prey n Beute f

price 1. n Preis m 2. vt **it's ~d at £10** es ist mit 10 Pfund ausgezeichnet; priceless adj unbezahlbar; price list n

Preisliste f; price tag n Preisschild nt

prick 1. n Stich m; *vulg (penis)* Schwanz m; *vulg (person)* Arsch m 2. vt stechen in + acc; **~ one's finger** sich dat in den Finger stechen; prickly adj stachelig

pride 1. n Stolz m; *(arrogance)* Hochmut m 2. vt **~ oneself on sth** auf etw acc stolz sein

priest n Priester m

primarily adv vorwiegend; primary adj Haupt-; **~ school** Grundschule f

prime 1. adj Haupt-; *(excellent)* erstklassig 2. n **in one's ~** in den besten Jahren; prime minister n Premierminister(in) m(f); prime time n TV Hauptsendezeit f

primitive adj primitiv

prince n Prinz m; *(ruler)* Fürst m; princess n Prinzessin f; *(wife of ruler)* Fürstin f

principal 1. adj Haupt-, wichtigste(r, s) 2. n, Rektor(in) m(f)

principle n Prinzip nt; **in ~** im Prinzip; **on ~** aus Prinzip

print 1. n *(picture)* Druck m; PHOT Abzug m; *(made by feet, fingers)* Abdruck m; **out of ~** vergriffen 2. vt drucken; *(photo)* abziehen; print out vt IT ausdrucken; printed matter n Drucksache f; printer n Drucker m; printout n IT Ausdruck m

prior adj früher; **a ~ engage-**

ment eine vorher getroffene Verabredung

priority n (thing having precedence) Priorität f

prison n Gefängnis nt; **prisoner** n Gefangene(r) mf

privacy n Privatleben nt; **private 1.** adj privat; (confidential) vertraulich **2.** n einfacher Soldat; **in ~** privat; **privately** adv privat; (confidentially) vertraulich; **privatize** vt privatisieren

privilege n Privileg nt; **privileged** adj privilegiert

prize n Preis m; **prize money** n Preisgeld nt; **prizewinner** n Gewinner(in) m(f); **prizewinning** adj preisgekrönt

pro n (professional) Profi m; **the ~s and cons** pl das Für und Wider

pro- pref pro-

probability n Wahrscheinlichkeit f; **probable, probably** adj, adv wahrscheinlich

probation n Probezeit f; LAW Bewährung f

probe 1. n (investigation) Untersuchung f **2.** vt untersuchen

problem n Problem nt; **no ~** kein Problem!

procedure n Verfahren nt

proceed 1. vi (continue) fortfahren; (set about sth) vorgehen **2.** vt **~ to do sth** anfangen, etw zu tun; **proceedings** npl LAW Verfahren nt; **proceeds** npl Erlös m

process 1. n Prozess m, Vorgang m; (method) Verfahren nt **2.** vt (application etc) bearbeiten; (food, data) verarbeiten; (film) entwickeln

procession n Umzug m

processor n IT Prozessor m; GASTR Küchenmaschine f

produce 1. n AGR Produkte pl, Erzeugnisse pl **2.** vt (manufacture) herstellen, produzieren; (on farm) erzeugen; (film, play, record) produzieren; (cause) hervorrufen; **producer** n (manufacturer) Hersteller(in) m(f); (of film, play, record) Produzent(in) m(f); **product** n Produkt nt, Erzeugnis nt; **production** n Produktion f; THEAT Inszenierung f; **productive** adj produktiv; (land) ertragreich

prof n fam Professor(in) m(f)

profession n Beruf m; **professional 1.** n Profi m **2.** adj beruflich; (expert) fachlich; (sportsman, actor etc) Berufs-

professor n Professor(in) m(f); (US, lecturer) Dozent(in) m(f)

proficient adj kompetent (in in + dat)

profile n Profil nt; **keep a low ~** sich rar machen

profit 1. n Gewinn m **2.** vi profitieren (by, from von); **profitable** adj rentabel

profound adj tief; (idea, thinker) tiefgründig; (knowl-

edge) profund

program 1. n IT Programm nt; (US) → **programme 2.** vt IT programmieren; (US) → **programme**

programme 1. n Programm nt; TV, RADIO Sendung f **2.** vt programmieren; **programmer** n IT Programmierer(in) m(f); **programming** n IT Programmieren nt; ~ **language** Programmiersprache f

progress 1. n Fortschritt m; **make** ~ Fortschritte machen **2.** vi (work, illness etc) fortschreiten; (improve) Fortschritte machen; **progressive** adj (person, policy) fortschrittlich; **progressively** adv zunehmend

prohibit vt verbieten

project n Projekt nt

prolong vt verlängern

prom n (at seaside) Promenade f; (Brit, concert) Konzert nt (bei dem ein Großteil des Publikums im Parkett Stehplätze hat); (US, dance) Ball für die Schüler und Studenten von Highschools oder Colleges

prominent adj (politician, actor etc) prominent; (easily seen) auffallend

promiscuous adj promisk

promise 1. n Versprechen nt **2.** vt versprechen; ~ **sb sth** jdm etw versprechen; ~ **to do sth** versprechen, etw zu

tun **3.** vi versprechen; **promising** adj viel versprechend

promote vt (in rank) befördern; (help on) fördern; COMM werben für; **promotion** n (in rank) Beförderung f; COMM Werbung f (of für)

prompt 1. adj prompt; (punctual) pünktlich **2.** adv at two o'clock~ Punkt zwei Uhr **3.** vt THEAT (actor) soufflieren + dat

prone adj **be** ~ **to sth** zu etw neigen

pronounce vt (word) aussprechen; **pronunciation** n Aussprache f

proof n Beweis m; (of alcohol) Alkoholgehalt m

prop 1. n Stütze f; THEAT Requisit nt **2.** vt ~ **sth against sth** etw gegen etw lehnen; **prop up** vt stützen; fig unterstützen

proper adj richtig; (morally correct) anständig

property n (possession) Eigentum nt; (characteristic) Eigenschaft f

proportion n Verhältnis nt; (share) Teil m; ~pl (size) Proportionen pl; **in** ~ **to** im Verhältnis zu; **proportional** adj proportional; ~ **representation** Verhältniswahlrecht nt

proposal n Vorschlag m; ~ (of marriage) (Heirats)antrag m; **propose 1.** vt vorschlagen **2.** vi (offer marriage) einen

Heiratsantrag machen (*to sb* jdm)

proprietor *n* Besitzer(in) *m(f)*; (*of pub, hotel*) Inhaber(in) *m(f)*

prose *n* Prosa *f*

prosecute *vt* verfolgen (*for* wegen)

prospect *n* Aussicht *f*

prosperity *n* Wohlstand *m*; **prosperous** *adj* wohlhabend; (*business*) gut gehend

prostitute *n* Prostituierte(r) *mf*

protect *vt* schützen (*from, against* vor + dat, gegen); **protection** *n* Schutz *m* (*from, against* vor + dat, gegen); **protective** *adj* beschützend; (*clothing etc*) Schutz-

protein *n* Protein *nt*, Eiweiß *nt*

protest 1. *n* Protest *m*; (*demonstration*) Protestkundgebung *f* **2.** *vi* protestieren (*against* gegen); (*demonstrate*) demonstrieren

Protestant 1. *adj* protestantisch **2.** *n* Protestant(in) *m(f)*

proud, proudly *adj, adv* stolz (*of* auf + *acc*)

prove *vt* beweisen; (*turn out to be*) sich erweisen als

proverb *n* Sprichwort *nt*

provide *vt* zur Verfügung stellen; (*drinks, music etc*) sorgen für; (*person*) versorgen (*with* mit); **provide for** *vt* (*family etc*) sorgen für; **provided** *conj* ~ (*that*) vorausge-

setzt, dass; **provider** *n* IT Provider *m*

provision *n* (*condition*) Bestimmung *f*; **~s** *pl* (*food*) Proviant *m*

provoke *vt* provozieren; (*cause*) hervorrufen

proximity *n* Nähe *f*

prudent *adj* klug; (*person*) umsichtig

prudish *adj* prüde

prune 1. *n* Backpflaume *f* **2.** *vt* (*tree etc*) zurechtstutzen

PS *abbr* = **postscript**; PS *nt*

pseudo *adj* pseudo-, Pseudo-; **pseudonym** *n* Pseudonym *nt*

psychiatric *adj* psychiatrisch; (*illness*) psychisch; **psychiatrist** *n* Psychiater(in) *m(f)*; **psychiatry** *n* Psychiatrie *f*; **psychic** *adj* übersinnlich; **I'm not ~** ich kann keine Gedanken lesen; **psychoanalysis** *n* Psychoanalyse *f*; **psychoanalyst** *n* Psychoanalytiker(in) *m(f)*; **psychological** *adj* psychologisch; **psychology** *n* Psychologie *f*; **psychopath** *n* Psychopath(in) *m(f)*

pto *abbr* = **please turn over**; b.w.

pub *n* (*Brit*) Kneipe *f*

puberty *n* Pubertät *f*

public 1. *n the* (**general**) ~ die (breite) Öffentlichkeit; **in ~** in der Öffentlichkeit **2.** *adj* öffentlich; (*relating to the state*) Staats- *f*; **~ conveni-**

ence (*Brit*) öffentliche Toilette; ~ *holiday* gesetzlicher Feiertag; ~ *opinion* die öffentliche Meinung; ~ *relations* pl Öffentlichkeitsarbeit f, Public Relations pl; ~ *school* (*Brit*) Privatschule f; **publication** n Veröffentlichung f; **publicity** n Publicity f; (*advertisements*) Werbung f; **publish** vt veröffentlichen; **publisher** n Verleger(in) m(f); (*company*) Verlag m; **publishing** n Verlagswesen nt

pudding n (*course*) Nachtisch m

puddle n Pfütze f

puff vi (*pant*) schnaufen

puffin n Papageientaucher m

puff paste (*US*), **puff pastry** n Blätterteig m

pull 1. n Ziehen nt; **give sth a** ~ an etw dat ziehen **2.** vt (*cart, tooth*) ziehen; (*rope, handle*) ziehen an + dat; *fam* (*date*) abschleppen; ~ **a muscle** sich dat einen Muskel zerren; ~ **sb's leg** jdn auf den Arm nehmen **3.** vi ziehen; **pull apart** vt (*separate*) auseinander ziehen; **pull down** vt (*blind*) herunterziehen; (*house*) abreißen; **pull in** vi hineinfahren; (*stop*) anhalten; **pull off** vt (*clothes*) ausziehen; (*deal etc*) zuwege bringen; **pull on** vt (*clothes*) anziehen; **pull out 1.** vi (*car from lane*) aus-

scheren; (*train*) abfahren; (*withdraw*) aussteigen (*of* aus) **2.** vt herausziehen; (*tooth*) ziehen; (*troops*) abziehen; **pull up 1.** vt (*raise*) hochziehen; (*chair*) heranziehen **2.** vi anhalten

pullover n Pullover m

pulp n Brei m; (*of fruit*) Fruchtfleisch nt

pulpit n Kanzel f

pulse n Puls m

pump n Pumpe f; (*in petrol station*) Zapfsäule f; **pump up** vt (*tyre etc*) aufpumpen

pumpkin n Kürbis m

pun n Wortspiel nt

punch 1. n (*blow*) (Faust-)schlag m; (*tool*) Locher m; (*hot drink*) Punsch m; (*cold drink*) Bowle f **2.** vt (*strike*) schlagen; (*ticket, paper*) lochen

punctual, punctually adj, adv pünktlich

punctuation n Interpunktion f; **punctuation mark** n Satzzeichen nt

puncture n (*flat tyre*) Reifenpanne f

punish vt bestrafen; **punishment** n Strafe f; (*action*) Bestrafung f

pupil n, Schüler(in) m(f)

puppet n Puppe f; (*string puppet*) Marionette f

puppy n junger Hund

purchase 1. n Kauf m **2.** vt kaufen

pure adj rein; (*clean*) sauber;

(*utter*) pur; **purely** *adv* rein; **purify** *vt* reinigen; **purity** *n* Reinheit *f*

purple *adj* violett

purpose *n* Zweck *m*; (*of person*) Absicht *f*; **on ~** absichtlich

purr *vi* (*cat*) schnurren

purse *n* Geldbeutel *m*; (*US, handbag*) Handtasche *f*

pursue *vt* (*person, aim*) verfolgen; (*hobby, studies*) nachgehen + *dat*

pus *n* Eiter *m*

push 1. *n* Stoß *m* **2.** *vt* (*person*) stoßen; (*car, chair etc*) schieben; (*button*) drücken; (*drugs*) dealen **3.** *vi* (*in crowd*) drängeln; **push in** *vi* (*in queue*) sich vordrängeln; **push off** *vi fam* (*leave*) abhauen; **push on** *vi* (*with job*) weitermachen; **push up** *vt* (*prices*) hochtreiben; **pushchair** *n* (*Brit*) Sportwagen *m*; **pusher** *n* (*of drugs*) Dealer(in) *m(f)*; **push-up** *n* (*US*) Liegestütz *m*; **pushy** *adj fam* aufdringlich, penetrant

put *vt* tun; (*upright*) stellen; (*flat*) legen; (*express*) ausdrücken; (*write*) schreiben; **he ~ his hand in his pocket** er steckte die Hand in die Tasche; **he ~ his hand on her shoulder** er legte ihr die Hand auf die Schulter; **~ money into one's account** Geld auf sein Konto einzah-

len; **put aside** *vt* (*money*) zurücklegen; **put away** *vt* (*tidy away*) wegräumen; **put back** *vt* zurücklegen; (*clock*) zurückstellen; **put down** *vt* (*in writing*) aufschreiben; (*Brit, animal*) einschläfern; (*rebellion*) niederschlagen; **put the phone down** (den Hörer) auflegen; **put one's name down for sth** sich für etw eintragen; **put forward** *vt* (*idea*) vorbringen; (*name*) vorschlagen; **put off** *vt* (*switch off*) ausschalten; (*postpone*) verschieben; **put sb off doing sth** jdn davon abbringen, etw zu tun; **put on** *vt* (*switch on*) anmachen; (*clothes*) anziehen; (*hat, glasses*) aufsetzen; (*make-up, CD*) auflegen; **put the kettle on** Wasser aufsetzen; **put weight on** zunehmen; **put out** *vt* (*hand, foot*) ausstrecken; (*light, cigarette*) ausmachen; **put up** *vt* (*picture*) aufhängen; (*tent*) aufstellen; (*building*) errichten; (*price*) erhöhen; (*person*) unterbringen; **~ with** sich abfinden mit; **I won't ~ with it** das lasse ich mir nicht gefallen

putt *vi*, *vt* SPORT putten

puzzle 1. *n* Rätsel *nt*; (*toy*) Geduldsspiel *nt*; (*jigsaw*) ~ Puzzle *nt* **2.** *vt* vor ein Rätsel stellen; **it ~s me** es ist mir ein

Rätsel; **puzzling** adj rätselhaft

pyjamas npl Schlafanzug m

pylon n Mast m

pyramid n Pyramide f

Q

quack vi quaken

quaint adj (idea, tradition) kurios; (picturesque) malerisch

qualification n (for job) Qualifikation f; (from school, university) Abschluss m; **qualified** adj (for job) qualifiziert; **qualify 1.** vt (limit) einschränken; **be qualified to do sth** berechtigt sein, etw zu tun 2. vi (finish training) seine Ausbildung abschließen; sport sich qualifizieren

quality n Qualität f; (characteristic) Eigenschaft f

quantity n Menge f, Quantität f

quarantine n Quarantäne f

quarrel 1. n Streit m 2. vi sich streiten; **quarrelsome** adj streitsüchtig

quarter 1. n Viertel nt; (of year) Vierteljahr nt; (US, coin) Vierteldollar m; **a ~ of an hour** eine Viertelstunde 2. vt vierteln

quarter final n Viertelfinale nt

quartet n Quartett nt

quay n Kai m

queen n Königin f; (in cards, chess) Dame f

queer 1. adj (strange) seltsam, sonderbar; pej (homosexual) schwul 2. n pej Schwule(r) m

quench vt (thirst) löschen

query 1. n Frage f 2. vt in Frage stellen; (bill) reklamieren

question 1. n Frage f; **that's out of the ~** das kommt nicht in Frage 2. vt (person) befragen; (suspect) verhören; (express doubt about) bezweifeln; **questionable** adj zweifelhaft; (improper) fragwürdig; **question mark** n Fragezeichen nt; **questionnaire** n Fragebogen m

queue 1. n (Brit) Schlange f; **jump the ~** sich vordrängeln 2. vi ~ (up) Schlange stehen

quibble vi kleinlich sein; (argue) streiten

quiche n Quiche f

quick adj schnell; (short) kurz; **be ~** mach schnell!; **quickly** adv schnell

quid n (Brit) fam Pfund m

quiet 1. adj (not noisy) leise; (peaceful, calm) still, ruhig; **be ~** sei still!; **keep ~ about sth** über etw acc nichts sagen 2. n Stille f, Ruhe f; **quietly** adv leise; (calmly) ruhig

quilt n (Stepp)decke f

quit 1. *vt* (*leave*) verlassen; (*job*) aufgeben; **~ doing sth** aufhören, etw zu tun **2.** *vi* aufhören; (*resign*) kündigen

quite *adv* (*fairly*) ziemlich; (*completely*) ganz, völlig; **I don't ~ understand** ich verstehe das nicht ganz; **~ a few** ziemlich viele; **~ so** richtig!

quits *adj* **be ~ with sb** mit jdm quitt sein

quiver *vi* zittern

quiz *n* (*competition*) Quiz *nt*

quota *n* Anteil *m*; COMM, POL Quote *f*

quotation *n* Zitat *nt*; (*price*) Kostenvoranschlag *m*; **quotation marks** *npl* Anführungszeichen *pl*; **quote 1.** *vt* (*text, author*) zitieren; (*price*) nennen **2.** *n* Zitat *nt*; (*price*) Kostenvoranschlag *m*; **in ~s** in Anführungszeichen

R

rabbi *n* Rabbiner *m*

rabbit *n* Kaninchen *nt*

rabies *nsing* Tollwut *f*

raccoon *n* Waschbär *m*

race 1. *n* (*competition*) Rennen *nt*; (*people*) Rasse *f* **2.** *vt* um die Wette laufen/fahren **3.** *vi* (*rush*) rennen; **racecourse** *n* Rennbahn *f*; **racetrack** *n* Rennbahn *f*

racial *adj* Rassen-; **~ discrimination** Rassendiskriminierung *f*

racing (*horse*) ~ Pferderennen *nt*; (*motor*) ~ Autorennen *nt*; **racing car** *n* Rennwagen *m*

racism *n* Rassismus *m*; **racist 1.** *n* Rassist(in) *m(f)* **2.** *adj* rassistisch

rack 1. *n* Ständer *m*, Gestell *nt* **2.** *vt* **~ one's brains** sich *dat* den Kopf zerbrechen

racket *n* SPORT Schläger *m*; (*noise*) Krach *m*

radar *n* Radar *nt or m*

radiation *n* (*radioactive*) Strahlung *f*

radiator *n* Heizkörper *m*; AUTO Kühler *m*

radical *adj* radikal

radio *n* Rundfunk *m*, Radio *nt*

radioactivity *n* Radioaktivität *f*

radio alarm *n* Radiowecker *m*; **radio station** *n* Rundfunkstation *f*

radiotherapy *n* Strahlenbehandlung *f*

radish *n* Radieschen *nt*

radius *n* Radius *m*; **within a five-mile ~** im Umkreis von fünf Meilen (*of* um)

raffle *n* Tombola *f*; **raffle ticket** *n* Los *nt*

raft *n* Floß *nt*

rag *n* Lumpen *m*; (*for cleaning*) Lappen *m*

rage 1. *n* Wut *f*; **be all the ~** der letzte Schrei sein *f*; **2.** *vi* toben; *(disease)* wüten

raid 1. *n* Überfall *m* (on auf + acc); *(by police)* Razzia *f* (on gegen) **2.** *vt* (bank etc) überfallen; *(by police)* eine Razzia machen in + dat

rail *n* (on stairs, balcony etc) Geländer *nt*; *(of ship)* Reling *f*; RAIL Schiene *f*; railcard *n* (Brit) ≈ Bahncard® *f*; railing *n* Geländer *nt*; **~s** *pl* (fence) Zaun *m*; railroad *n* (US) Eisenbahn *f*; railroad station *n* (US) Bahnhof *m*; railway *n* (Brit) Eisenbahn *f*; railway station *n* Bahnhof *m*

rain 1. *n* Regen *m* **2.** *vi* regnen; **it's ~ing** es regnet; rainbow *n* Regenbogen *m*; raincoat *n* Regenmantel *m*; rainforest *n* Regenwald *m*; rainy *adj* regnerisch

raise 1. *n* (US, of wages / salary) Gehalts-/Lohnerhöhung *f* **2.** *vt* (lift) hochheben; *(increase)* erhöhen; *(family)* großziehen; *(livestock)* züchten; *(money)* aufbringen; *(objection)* erheben; **~ one's voice** (in anger) laut werden

raisin *n* Rosine *f*

rally *n* POL Kundgebung *f*; AUTO Rallye *f*

RAM *acr* = **random access memory**; RAM *m*

ramble 1. *n* Wanderung *f* **2.** *vi* (walk) wandern; (talk) schwafeln

ramp *n* Rampe *f*

ran *pt of* **run**

ranch *n* Ranch *f*

rancid *adj* ranzig

random 1. *adj* willkürlich **2.** *n* **at ~** (choose) willkürlich; (fire) ziellos

randy *adj* (Brit) fam geil, scharf

rang *pt of* **ring**

range 1. *n* (selection) Auswahl *f* (of an + dat); COMM Sortiment *nt* (of an + dat); (of missile, telescope) Reichweite *f*; (of mountains) Kette *f*; **in this price ~** in dieser Preisklasse **2.** *vi* **~ from ... to ...** (temperature, sizes, prices) liegen zwischen ... und ...

rank 1. *n* Rang *m*; (social position) Stand *m* **2.** *adj* stinkend **3.** *vi* **~ among** zählen zu

ransom *n* Lösegeld *nt*

rap *n* MUS Rap *m*

rape 1. *n* Vergewaltigung *f* **2.** *vt* vergewaltigen

rapid, rapidly *adj, adv* schnell

rapist *n* Vergewaltiger *m*

rare *adj* selten, rar; (especially good) vortrefflich; (steak) blutig; **rarely** *adv* selten; **rarity** *n* Seltenheit *f*

rash 1. *adj* unbesonnen **2.** *n* MED (Haut)ausschlag *m*

rasher *n* ~ (of bacon) (Speck-) scheibe *f*

raspberry *n* Himbeere *f*

rat *n* Ratte *f*

rate 1. *n* (proportion, frequency) Rate *f*; (speed) Tempo *nt*;

~ (*of exchange*) (Wechsel-)kurs *m*; **~ of interest** Zinssatz *m*; **at any ~** auf jeden Fall **2.** *vt* (*evaluate*) einschätzen (*as* als)

rather *adv* (*in preference*) lieber; (*fairly*) ziemlich; **I'd ~ stay here** ich würde lieber hier bleiben; **I'd ~ not** lieber nicht; **or ~** (*more accurately*) vielmehr

ratio *n* Verhältnis *nt*

rational *adj* rational; **rationalize** *vt* rationalisieren

rattle 1. *vt* (*toy*) Rassel *f* **2.** *vt* (*keys, coins*) klimpern mit; (*person*) durcheinander bringen **2.** *vi* (*window*) klappern; (*bottles*) klirren; **rattle off** *vt* herunterrasseln; **rattlesnake** *n* Klapperschlange *f*

rave 1. *vi* (*talk wildly*) fantasieren; (*rage*) toben; (*enthuse*) schwärmen (*about* von) **2.** *n* (*Brit, event*) Raveparty *f*

raven *n* Rabe *m*

raving *adv* **~ mad** total verrückt

ravishing *adj* hinreißend

raw *adj* (*food*) roh; (*skin*) wund; (*climate*) rau

ray *n* (*of light*) Strahl *m*; **~ of hope** Hoffnungsschimmer *m*

razor *n* Rasierapparat *m*; **razor blade** *n* Rasierklinge *f*

Rd *n abbr* = **road**; Str.

re *prep* betreffs + *gen*

reach 1. *n* **within/out of** (**sb's**) **~** in/außer (jds)

Reichweite; **within easy ~ of the shops** nicht weit von den Geschäften **2.** *vt* (*arrive at, contact*) erreichen; (*come down/up as far as*) reichen bis zu; (*contact*) **can you ~ it?** kommen Sie dran?; **reach for** *vt* greifen nach; **reach out** *vi* die Hand ausstrecken; **~ for** greifen nach

react *vi* reagieren (*to* auf + *acc*); **reaction** *n* Reaktion *f* (*to* auf + *acc*); **reactor** *n* Reaktor *m*

read 1. *vt* lesen; (*meter*) ablesen; **~ sth to sb** jdm etw vorlesen **2.** *vi* lesen; **~ to sb** jdm vorlesen; **it ~s well** es liest sich gut; **it ~s as follows** es lautet folgendermaßen; **read out** *vt* vorlesen; **read through** *vt* durchlesen; **read up on** *vt* nachlesen über + *acc*; **readable** *adj* (*book*) lesenswert; (*handwriting*) lesbar; **reader** *n* Leser(in) *m(f)*

readily *adv* (*willingly*) bereitwillig; **~ available** leicht erhältlich

reading *n* (*action*) Lesen *nt*; (*from meter*) Zählerstand *m*; **reading glasses** *npl* Lesebrille *f*; **reading lamp** *n* Leselampe *f*; **reading matter** *n* Lektüre *f*

readjust 1. *vt* (*mechanism etc*) neu einstellen **2.** *vi* sich wieder anpassen (*to* an + *acc*)

ready adj fertig, bereit; **be~ to
do sth** (willing) bereit sein,
etw zu tun; **are you ~ to
go?** bist du so weit?; **get
sth ~** etw fertig machen;
get (oneself) ~ sich fertig
machen; **ready cash** n Bargeld nt; **ready-made** adj
(product) Fertig-; (clothes)
Konfektions-; **~ meal** Fertiggericht nt

real 1. adj wirklich; (actual) eigentlich; (genuine) echt; (idiot etc) wirklich; (leather) echt;
this time it's for ~ diesmal
ist es ernst; **get ~** sei realistisch! **2.** adv fam (esp US)
echt

real estate n Immobilien pl

realistic, realistically adj,
adv realistisch; **reality** n
Wirklichkeit f; **in ~** in Wirklichkeit; **realization** n
(awareness) Erkenntnis f; **realize** vt (understand) begreifen; (plan, idea) realisieren; **I
~d (that)** ... mir wurde klar,
dass ...

really adv wirklich

real time n IT **in ~** in Echtzeit

realtor n (US) Grundstücksmakler(in) m(f)

reappear vi wieder erscheinen

rear 1. adj hintere(r, s), Hinter-
2. n (of building, vehicle) hinterer Teil; **at the ~ of** hinter
+ dat; (inside) hinten in
+ dat; **rear light** n AUTO Rücklicht nt

rearm vi wieder aufrüsten

rearrange vt (furniture, system) umstellen; (meeting)
verlegen (for auf + acc)

rear-view mirror n Rückspiegel m; **rear window** n AUTO
Heckscheibe f

reason 1. n (cause) Grund m
(for für); (ability to think)
Verstand m; (common sense)
Vernunft f; **for some~** aus irgendeinem Grund **2.** vi **~
with sb** mit jdm vernünftig
reden; **reasonable** adj (person, price) vernünftig; (offer)
akzeptabel; (chance) reell;
(food, weather) ganz gut;
reasonably adv vernünftig;
(fairly) ziemlich

reassure vt beruhigen; **she
~d me that ...** sie versicherte
mir, dass ...

rebel 1. n Rebell(in) m(f) **2.** vi
rebellieren; **rebellion** n Aufstand m

reboot vt, vi IT rebooten

rebuild irr vt wieder aufbauen

recall vt (remember) sich erinnern an + acc; (call back) zurückrufen

recap vt, vi rekapitulieren

receipt n (document) Quittung f; (receiving) Empfang
m; **~s** pl (money) Einnahmen pl

receive vt (news etc) erhalten,
bekommen; (visitor) empfangen; **receiver** n TEL Hörer
m; RADIO Empfänger m

recent adj (event) vor kurzem

stattgefunden; (*photo*) neueste(r,s); (*invention*) neu; in ~ **years** in den letzten Jahren; **recently** *adv* vor kurzem; (*in the last few days or weeks*) in letzter Zeit

reception *n* Empfang *m*; **receptionist** *n* (*in hotel*) Empfangschef *m*, Empfangsdame *f*; (*woman in firm*) Empfangsdame *f*; MED Sprechstundenhilfe *f*

recess *n* (*in wall*) Nische *f*; (*US, in school*) Pause *f*

recession *n* Rezession *f*

recharge *vt* (*battery*) aufladen; **rechargeable** *adj* wieder aufladbar

recipe *n* Rezept *nt* (*for* für)

recipient *n* Empfänger(in) *m(f)*

reciprocal *adj* gegenseitig

recite *vt* vortragen

reckless *adj* leichtsinnig; (*driving*) gefährlich

reckon 1. *vt* (*calculate*) schätzen; (*think*) glauben 2. *vi* ~ **with** rechnen mit

reclaim *vt* (*baggage*) abholen; (*expenses, tax*) zurückverlangen

recline *vi* (*person*) sich zurücklehnen; **reclining seat** *n* Liegesitz *m*

recognition *n* (*acknowledgement*) Anerkennung *f*; **in ~ of** in Anerkennung + *gen*;

recognize *vt* erkennen; (*approve officially*) anerkennen

recommend *vt* empfehlen;

recommendation *n* Empfehlung *f*

reconcile *vt* (*people*) versöhnen; (*facts*) (miteinander) vereinbaren

reconsider *vt* noch einmal überdenken

reconstruct *vt* wieder aufbauen; (*crime*) rekonstruieren

record 1. *n* MUS (Schall)platte *f*; (*best performance*) Rekord *m*; **keep a ~ of** Buch führen über + *acc* 2. *adj* (*time etc*) Rekord- 3. *vt* (*write down*) aufzeichnen; (*on tape etc*) aufnehmen; **~ed message** Ansage *f*; **recorded delivery** *n* (*Brit*) **by ~** per Einschreiben

recorder *n* MUS Blockflöte *f*; (**cassette**) ~ (Kassetten)rekorder *m*; **recording** *n* (*on tape etc*) Aufnahme *f*

recover 1. *vt* (*money, item*) zurückbekommen; (*appetite, strength*) wiedergewinnen 2. *vi* sich erholen

recreation *n* Erholung *f*; **recreational** *adj* Freizeit-; ~ **vehicle** (*US*) Wohnmobil *nt*

recruit 1. *n* MIL Rekrut(in) *m(f)*; (*in firm, organization*) neues Mitglied 2. *vt* MIL rekrutieren; (*members*) anwerben; (*staff*) einstellen; **recruitment agency** *n* Personalagentur *f*

rectangle *n* Rechteck *nt*; **rectangular** *adj* rechteckig

recuperate vi sich erholen

recyclable adj recycelbar, wieder verwertbar; **recycle** vt recyceln, wieder verwerten; **~d paper** Recyclingpapier nt; **recycling** n Recycling nt, Wiederverwertung f

red 1. adj rot **2.** n **in the ~** in den roten Zahlen; **red cabbage** n Rotkohl m; **redcurrant** n (rote) Johannisbeere

redeem vt COMM einlösen

red-handed adj **catch sb ~** jdn auf frischer Tat ertappen

redhead n Rothaarige(r) mf

redial vt, vi nochmals wählen

redirect vt (traffic) umleiten; (forward) nachsenden

red light n (traffic signal) rotes Licht; **go through the ~** bei Rot über die Ampel fahren

red meat n Rind-, Lamm-, Rehfleisch

redo irr vt nochmals machen

reduce vt reduzieren (to auf + acc, by um); **reduction** n Reduzierung f; (in price) Ermäßigung f

redundant adj überflüssig; **be made ~** entlassen werden

red wine n Rotwein m

reef n Riff nt

reel n Spule f; (on fishing rod) Rolle f; **reel off** vt herunterrasseln

ref n fam (referee) Schiri m

refectory n (at college) Mensa f

refer vt **~ sb to sb/sth** jdn an jdn/etw verweisen; **~ sth to sb** (query, problem) etw an jdn weiterleiten **2.** vi **~ to** (mention, allude to) sich beziehen auf + acc; (book) nachschlagen in + dat

referee n Schiedsrichter(in) m(f); (in boxing) Ringrichter m; (Brit, for job) Referenz f

reference n (allusion) Anspielung f (to auf + acc); (for job) Referenz f; (in book) Verweis m; **~ (number)** (in document) Aktenzeichen nt; **with ~ to** mit Bezug auf + acc; **reference book** n Nachschlagewerk nt

referendum n Referendum nt

refill 1. vt nachfüllen **2.** n (for ballpoint pen) Ersatzmine f

refine vt (purify) raffinieren; (improve) verfeinern; **refined** adj (genteel) fein

reflect 1. vt reflektieren; fig widerspiegeln **2.** vi nachdenken (on über + acc); **reflection** n (image) Spiegelbild nt; (thought) Überlegung f

reflex n Reflex m

reform 1. n Reform f **2.** vt reformieren; (person) bessern

refrain vi **~ from doing sth** es unterlassen, etw zu tun

refresh vt erfrischen; **refreshing** adj erfrischend; **refreshments** npl Erfrischungen pl

refrigerator n Kühlschrank m

refuel vt, vi auftanken

refuge n Zuflucht f (from vor

+ *dat*); **take** ~ sich flüchten (*from* vor + *dat*, *in* in + *acc*); **refugee** *n* Flüchtling *m*

refund 1. *n* (*of money*) Rückerstattung *f*; **get a** ~ **(on sth)** sein Geld (für etw) zurückbekommen **2.** *vt* zurückerstatten

refusal *n* (*to do sth*) Weigerung *f*; **refuse 1.** *n* Müll *m*, Abfall *m* **2.** *vt* ablehnen; ~ **sb sth** jdm etw verweigern; ~ **to do sth** sich weigern, etw zu tun **3.** *vi* sich weigern

regain *vt* wiedergewinnen, wiedererlangen

regard 1. *n* **with** ~ **to** in Bezug auf + *acc*; **in this** ~ in dieser Hinsicht; ~**s** (*at end of letter*) mit freundlichen Grüßen; **give my** ~**s to** ... viele Grüße an ... + *acc* **2.** *vt* ~ **sb/ sth as sth** jdn / etw als etw betrachten; **as** ~**s** ... was ... betrifft; **regarding** *prep* bezüglich + *gen*; **regardless 1.** *adj* ~ **of** ohne Rücksicht auf + *acc* **2.** *adv* trotzdem; **carry on** ~ einfach weitermachen

regime *n* POL Regime *nt*

region *n* (*of country*) Region *f*, Gebiet *nt*; **regional** *adj* regional

register 1. *n* Register *nt*, Namensliste *f* **2.** *vt* (*with an authority*) registrieren lassen; (*birth, death, vehicle*) anmelden **3.** *vi* (*at hotel, for course*) sich anmelden; (*at universi-*

ty) sich einschreiben; **registered** *adj* eingetragen; (*letter*) eingeschrieben; **by** ~ **post** per Einschreiben; **registration** *n* (*for course*) Anmeldung *f*; (*at university*) Einschreibung *f*; AUTO (*number*) (polizeiliches) Kennzeichen; **registration form** *n* Anmeldeformular *nt*; **registration number** *n* AUTO (polizeiliches) Kennzeichen; **registry office** *n* Standesamt *nt*

regret 1. *n* Bedauern *nt* **2.** *vt* bedauern; **regrettable** *adj* bedauerlich

regular 1. *adj* regelmäßig; (*size*) normal **2.** *n* (*client*) Stammkunde *m*, Stammkundin *f*; (*in bar*) Stammgast *m*; (*petrol*) Normalbenzin *nt*; **regularly** *adv* regelmäßig

regulate *vt* regulieren; (*using rules*) regeln; **regulation** *n* (*rule*) Vorschrift *f*

rehabilitation *n* Rehabilitation *f*

rehearsal *n* Probe *f*; **rehearse** *vt, vi* proben

reign 1. *n* Herrschaft *f* **2.** *vi* herrschen (*over* über + *acc*)

reimburse *vt* (*person*) entschädigen; (*expenses*) zurückerstatten

reindeer *n* Rentier *nt*

reinforce *vt* verstärken

reinstate *vt* (*employee*) wieder einstellen

reject 1. *n* COMM Ausschussartikel *m* **2.** *vt* ablehnen; **rejec-**

tion n Ablehnung f
relapse n Rückfall m
relate 1. vt (story) erzählen; (connect) in Verbindung bringen (to mit) 2. vi ~ **to** (refer) sich beziehen auf + acc; **related** adj verwandt (to mit); **relation** n (relative) Verwandte(r) mf; (connection) Beziehung f; **relationship** n (connection) Beziehung f; (between people) Verhältnis nt
relative 1. n Verwandte(r) mf 2. adj relativ; **relatively** adv relativ, verhältnismäßig
relax 1. vi sich entspannen; ~*l* reg dich nicht auf! 2. vt (grip, conditions) lockern; **relaxation** n (rest) Entspannung f; **relaxed** adj entspannt
release 1. n (from prison) Entlassung f; **new/recent** ~ (film, CD) Neuerscheinung f 2. vt (animal, hostage) freilassen; (prisoner) entlassen; (handbrake) lösen; (news) veröffentlichen; (film, CD) herausbringen
relent vi nachgeben; **relentless, relentlessly** adj, adv (merciless) erbarmungslos; (neverending) unaufhörlich
relevance n Relevanz f (to für); **relevant** adj relevant (to für)
reliable, reliably adj, adv zuverlässig; **reliant** adj ~ **on** abhängig von
relic n (from past) Relikt nt

relief n (from anxiety, pain) Erleichterung f; (assistance) Hilfe f; **relieve** vt (pain) lindern; (boredom) überwinden; (take over from) ablösen; **I'm ~d** ich bin erleichtert
religion n Religion f; **religious** adj religiös
relish 1. n (for food) würzige Soße f 2. vt (enjoy) genießen; **I don't ~ the thought of getting up early** der Gedanke, früh aufzustehen, behagt mir gar nicht
reluctant adj widerwillig; **be ~ to do sth** etw nur ungern tun; **reluctantly** adv widerwillig
rely on vt sich verlassen auf + acc; (depend on) abhängig sein von
remain vi bleiben; (be left over) übrig bleiben; **remainder** n a. MATH Rest m; **remaining** adj übrig; **remains** npl Überreste pl
remark 1. n Bemerkung f 2. vt ~ **that** bemerken, dass; **remarkable, remarkably** adj, adv bemerkenswert
remedy n Mittel nt (for gegen)
remember 1. vt sich erinnern an + acc; ~ **to do sth** daran denken, etw zu tun; **I must ~ that** das muss ich mir merken 2. vi sich erinnern
remind vt ~ **sb of/about sb/ sth** jdn an jdn/etw erinnern; ~ **sb to do sth** jdn daran er-

innern, etw zu tun; *that ~s me* dabei fällt mir ein ...; re- minder*n* (*to pay*) Mahnung *f*

remnant*n* Rest *m*

remote 1. *adj* (*place*) abgele- gen; (*slight*) gering **2.** *n* TV Fernbedienung *f*; **remote control** *n* Fernsteuerung *f*; (*device*) Fernbedienung *f*

removal *n* Entfernung *f*, (*Brit, move from house*) Um- zug *m*; **removal firm** *n* (*Brit*) Spedition *f*; **remove** *vt* ent- fernen; (*lid*) abnehmen; (*doubt, suspicion*) zerstreuen

rename *vt* umbenennen

renew *vt* erneuern; (*licence, passport, library book*) ver- längern lassen

renovate *vt* renovieren

renowned *adj* berühmt (*for* für)

rent 1. *n* Miete *f*; *for~* (*US*) zu vermieten **2.** *vt* (*as hirer, ten- ant*) mieten; (*as owner*) ver- mieten; *~ed car* Mietwagen *m*; **rent out** *vt* vermieten; **rental 1.** *n* Miete *f*; (*for car, TV etc*) Leihgebühr *f* **2.** *adj* Miet-

reorganize*vt* umorganisieren

rep*n* COMM Vertreter(in) *m(f)*

repair 1. *n* Reparatur *f* **2.** *vt* re- parieren; (*damage*) wieder gutmachen

repay *irr vt* (*money*) zurück- zahlen; *~ sb for sth* sich bei jdm für etw revanchieren

repeat 1. *n* RADIO, TV Wieder- holung *f* **2.** *vt* wiederholen;

repetition *n* Wiederholung *f*

replace *vt* ersetzen (*with* durch); (*put back*) zurück- stellen, zurücklegen; **re- placement** *n* (*thing, person*) Ersatz *m*; (*temporarily in job*) Vertretung *f*

replay 1. *n* (**action**) *~* Wieder- holung *f* **2.** *vt* (*game*) wieder- holen

replica *n* Kopie *f*

reply 1. *n* Antwort *f* **2.** *vi* ant- worten; *~ to sb/ sth* jdm /auf etw *acc* antworten **3.** *vt ~ that* antworten, dass

report 1. *n* Bericht *m*, Zeugnis *nt* **2.** *vt* (*tell*) berichten; (*give information against*) mel- den; (*to police*) anzeigen **3.** *vi* (*present oneself*) sich mel- den; *~ sick* sich krankmel- den; **report card** *n* (*US, in school*) Zeugnis *nt*; **reporter** *n* Reporter(in) *m(f)*

represent *vt* darstellen; (*speak for*) vertreten; **repre- sentation** *n* (*picture etc*) Darstellung *f*; **representa- tive 1.** *n* Vertreter(in) *m(f)*; (*US*) POL Abgeordnete(r) *mf* **2.** *adj* repräsentativ (*of* für)

reproduce 1. *vt* (*copy*) repro- duzieren **2.** *vi* sich fort- pflanzen; **reproduction** *n* (*copy*) Reproduktion *f*; BIO Fortpflanzung *f*

reptile *n* Reptil *nt*

republic *n* Republik *f*; **repub- lican 1.** *adj* republikanisch **2.**

n Republikaner(in) *m(f)*
repulsive *adj* abstoßend
reputation *n* Ruf *m*
request 1. *n* Bitte *f (for* um); **on~** auf Wunsch **2.** *vt* bitten um
require *vt (need)* brauchen; *(desire)* verlangen; **required** *adj* erforderlich; **requirement** *n (condition)* Anforderung *f; (need)* Bedingung *f*
rerun *n* Wiederholung *f*
rescue 1. *n* Rettung *f;* **come to sb's~** jdm zu Hilfe kommen **2.** *vt* retten
research 1. *n* Forschung *f* **2.** *vi* forschen *(into* über + *acc)* **3.** *vt* erforschen; **researcher** *n* Forscher(in) *m(f)*
resemblance *n* Ähnlichkeit *f (to* mit); **resemble** *vt* ähneln + *dat*
resent *vt* übel nehmen
reservation *n (booking)* Reservierung *f; (doubt)* Vorbehalt *m;* **I have a~** *(in hotel, restaurant)* ich habe reserviert; **reserve 1.** *n (store)* Vorrat *m (of* an + *dat); (manner)* Zurückhaltung *f;* SPORT Reservespieler(in) *m(f); (game* ~) Naturschutzgebiet *nt* **2.** *vt (book in advance)* reservieren; **reserved** *adj* reserviert
residence *n* Wohnsitz *m; (living)* Aufenthalt *m;* **~ permit** Aufenthaltsgenehmigung *f;* **~ hall** Studentenwohnheim *nt;* **resident** *n (in house)* Bewohner(in) *m(f); (in town,*

area) Einwohner(in) *m(f)*
resign 1. *vt (post)* zurücktreten von; *(job)* kündigen **2.** *vi (from post)* zurücktreten; *(from job)* kündigen; **resignation** *n (from post)* Rücktritt *m; (from job)* Kündigung *f*
resist *vt* widerstehen + *dat;* **resistance** *n* Widerstand *m (to* gegen)
resit *(Brit)* **1.** *irr vt* wiederholen **2.** *n* Wiederholungsprüfung *f*
resolution *n (intention)* Vorsatz *m; (decision)* Beschluss *m*
resolve *vt (problem)* lösen
resort 1. *n (holiday resort)* Urlaubsort *m;* **as a last~** als letzter Ausweg **2.** *vi* **~to** greifen zu; *(violence)* anwenden
resources *npl (money)* (Geld)mittel *pl; (mineral resources)* Bodenschätze *pl*
respect 1. *n* Respekt *m (for* vor + *dat); (consideration)* Rücksicht *f (for* auf + *acc);* **with ~ to** in Bezug auf + *acc;* **in this~** in dieser Hinsicht; **in all due~** bei allem Respekt **2.** *vt* respektieren; **respectable** *adj (person, family)* angesehen; *(district)* anständig; *(achievement, result)* beachtlich; **respected** *adj* angesehen
respective *adj* jeweilig; **respectively** *adv* **5% and 10% ~** 5% beziehungsweise

10%

respond vi antworten (*to* auf + *acc*); (*react*) reagieren (*to* auf + *acc*); (*to treatment*) ansprechen (*to* auf + *acc*); re**sponse** n Antwort f; (*reaction*) Reaktion f; **in ~ to** als Antwort auf + *acc*

responsibility n Verantwortung f; **that's her ~** dafür ist sie verantwortlich; re**sponsible** adj verantwortlich (*for* für); (*trustworthy*) verantwortungsbewußt; (*job*) verantwortungsvoll

rest 1. n (*relaxation*) Ruhe f; (*break*) Pause f; (*remainder*) Rest m; **have** (or **take**) **a ~** sich ausruhen; (*break*) Pause machen **2.** vi (*relax*) sich ausruhen; (*lean*) lehnen (*on, against* an + *dat, gegen*)

restaurant n Restaurant nt; **restaurant car** n (*Brit*) Speisewagen m

restful adj (*holiday etc*) erholsam, ruhig; **restless** adj unruhig

restore vt (*painting, building*) restaurieren; (*order*) wiederherstellen; (*give back*) zurückgeben

restrain vt (*person, feelings*) zurückhalten; **~ oneself** sich beherrschen

restrict vt beschränken (*to* auf + *acc*); **restricted** adj beschränkt; **restriction** n Einschränkung f (*on* + *gen*)

rest room n (*US*) Toilette f

result 1. n Ergebnis nt; (*consequence*) Folge f; **as a ~ of** infolge + *gen* **2.** vi **~ in** führen zu; **~ from** sich ergeben aus

resume vt (*work, negotiations*) wieder aufnehmen; (*journey*) fortsetzen

résumé n Zusammenfassung f; (*US, curriculum vitae*) Lebenslauf m

resuscitate vt wieder beleben

retail adv im Einzelhandel; **retailer** n Einzelhändler(in) m(f)

retain vt behalten; (*heat*) halten

rethink irr vt noch einmal überdenken

retire vi (*from work*) in den Ruhestand treten; (*withdraw*) sich zurückziehen; re**tired** adj (*person*) pensioniert; **retirement** n (*time of life*) Ruhestand m; **retirement age** n Rentenalter nt

retrain vi sich umschulen lassen

retreat 1. n Rückzug m (*from* aus); (*refuge*) Zufluchtsort m **2.** vi sich zurückziehen

retrieve vt (*recover*) wiederbekommen; (*rescue*) retten; (*data*) abrufen

retrospect n **in ~** rückblikkend

return 1. n (*going back*) Rückkehr f; (*giving back*) Rückgabe f; (*profit*) Gewinn m; (*Brit, returr ticket*) Rückfahrkarte f; (*plane ticket*)

Rückflugticket *nt*, Return *m*; **in ~** als Gegenleistung *(for* für); **many happy ~s (of the day)** herzlichen Glückwunsch zum Geburtstag! **2.** *vi (person)* zurückkehren; *(doubts, symptoms)* wieder auftreten **3.** *vt (give back)* zurückgeben; **I ~ed his call** ich habe ihn zurückgerufen;**returnable** *adj (bottle)* Pfand-;**return flight** *n (Brit)* Rückflug *m*; *(both ways)* Hin- und Rückflug *m*;**return key** *n* Eingabetaste *f*;**return ticket** *n (Brit)* Rückfahrkarte *f*; *(for plane)* Rückflugticket *nt*

reunification *n* Wiedervereinigung *f*;**reunion** *n (party)* Treffen *nt*;**reunite** *vt* wieder vereinigen

reveal *vt (make known)* enthüllen; *(secret)* verraten; **revealing** *adj* aufschlussreich; *(dress)* freizügig

revenge *n* Rache *f*; *(in game)* Revanche *f*; **take ~ on sb (for sth)** sich an jdm (für etw) rächen

revenue *n* Einnahmen *pl*

reverse 1. *n (back)* Rückseite *f*; *(opposite)* Gegenteil *nt*; AUTO ~ **(gear)** Rückwärtsgang *m* **2.** *adj* **in ~ order** in umgekehrter Reihenfolge **3.** *vt (order)* umkehren; *(decision)* umstoßen; *(car)* zurücksetzen **4.** *vi* rückwärts fahren

review 1. *n (of book, film etc)* Rezension *f*; **be under ~** überprüft werden **2.** *vt (book, film etc)* rezensieren; *(re-examine)* überprüfen

revise 1. *vt* revidieren; *(text)* überarbeiten; *(Brit, in school)* wiederholen **2.** *vi (Brit, in school)* den Stoff wiederholen; **revision** *n (of text)* Überarbeitung *f*; *(Brit)* Wiederholung *f*

revitalize *vt* neu beleben

revive *vt (person)* wieder beleben; *(tradition, interest)* wieder aufleben lassen

revolt *n* Aufstand *m*; **revolting** *adj* widerlich

revolution *n* POL *fig* Revolution *f*;**revolutionary 1.** *adj* revolutionär **2.** *n* Revolutionär(in) *m(f)*

revolve *vi* sich drehen *(around* um);**revolver** *n* Revolver *m*; **revolving door** *n* Drehtür *f*

reward *n* Belohnung *f* **2.** *vt* belohnen; **rewarding** *adj* lohnend

rewind *irr vt (tape)* zurückspulen

rheumatism *n* Rheuma *nt*

rhinoceros *n* Nashorn *nt*

Rhodes *n* Rhodos *nt*

rhubarb *n* Rhabarber *m*

rhyme **1.** *n* Reim *m* **2.** *vi* sich reimen *(with* auf + *acc)*

rhythm *n* Rhythmus *m*

rib *n* Rippe *f*

ribbon *n* Band *nt*

rinse

rice n Reis m; **rice pudding** n Milchreis m

rich 1. adj reich; (food) schwer **2.** npl **the ~** die Reichen pl

rickety adj wackelig

rid vt **get ~ of sb/sth** jdn/etw loswerden

ridden pp of **ride**

riddle n Rätsel nt

ride 1. vt (horse) reiten; (bicycle) fahren **2.** vi (on horse) reiten; (in vehicle, on bike) Fahrt f; (on horse) (Aus)ritt m; **go for a ~** (in car, on bike) spazieren fahren; (on horse) reiten gehen; **take sb for a ~** fam jdn verarschen; **rider** n (on horse) Reiter(in) m(f)

ridiculous adj lächerlich; **don't be ~** red keinen Unsinn!

riding 1. n Reiten nt **2.** adj Reit-

rifle n Gewehr nt

right 1. adj (correct, just) richtig; (opposite of left) rechte(r, s); (clothes, job etc) passend; **be ~** (person) Recht haben; (clock) richtig gehen; **that's ~** das stimmt! **2.** n Recht nt (to auf + acc); (side) rechte Seite; **the Right** POL die Rechte; **take a ~** AUTO rechts abbiegen; **on the ~** rechts (of von); **to the ~** nach rechts, rechts (of von) **3.** adv (towards the ~) nach rechts; (directly) direkt; (exactly) genau; **turn ~** AUTO rechts ab-

biegen; **~ away** sofort; **~ now** im Moment; **~** (immediately) sofort; **right angle** n rechter Winkel; **right-hand drive** n Rechtssteuerung f **2.** adj rechtsgesteuert; **right-handed** adj **he is ~** er ist Rechtshänder; **right-hand side** n rechte Seite; **on the ~** auf der rechten Seite; **rightly** adv zu Recht; **right of way** n **have ~** AUTO Vorfahrt haben; **right wing** n POL, SPORT rechter Flügel; **give sb a ~** rechter Flügel; **right-wing** adj Rechts-; **~ extremist** Rechtsradikale(r) mf

rigid adj (stiff) starr; (strict) streng

rim n (of cup etc) Rand m; (of wheel) Felge f

rind n (of cheese) Rinde f; (of bacon) Schwarte f; (of fruit) Schale f

ring 1. vt, vi (bell) läuten; TEL anrufen **2.** n (on finger, in boxing) Ring m; (circle) Kreis m; (at circus) Manege f; **give sb a ~** TEL jdn anrufen; **ring back** vt, vi zurückrufen; **ring up** vt, vi TEL jdn anrufen; **ringing tone** n TEL Rufzeichen nt

ring road n (Brit) Umgehungsstraße f

ringtone n Klingelton m

rink n (ice rink) Eisbahn f; (for roller-skating) Rollschuhbahn f

rinse vt spülen

riot n Aufruhr m

rip 1. n Riss m 2. vt zerreißen; **~ sth open** etw aufreißen 3. vi reißen; **rip off** vt fam (person) übers Ohr hauen; **rip up** vt zerreißen

ripe adj (fruit) reif; **ripen** vi reifen

rip-off n that's a **~** fam (too expensive) das ist Wucher

rise 1. vi (from sitting, lying) aufstehen; (sun) aufgehen; (prices, temperature) steigen; (ground) ansteigen 2. n (increase) Anstieg m (in + gen); (pay rise) Gehaltserhöhung f; (to power, fame) Aufstieg m (to zu); (slope) Steigung f; **risen** pp of **rise**

risk 1. n Risiko nt 2. vt riskieren; **risky** adj riskant

ritual n Ritual nt

rival n Rivale m, Rivalin f (for um); COMM Konkurrent(in) m(f); **rivalry** n Rivalität f; COMM, SPORT Konkurrenz f

river n Fluss m; **the River Thames** (Brit), **the Thames River** (US) die Themse; **riverside** 1. n Flussufer nt 2. adj am Flussufer

road n Straße f; fig Weg m; **on the ~** (travelling) unterwegs; **roadblock** n Straßensperre f; **roadmap** n Straßenkarte f; **road rage** n aggressives Verhalten im Straßenverkehr; **roadside** n **at** (or **by**) **the ~** am Straßenrand; **roadsign** n Verkehrsschild nt; **road**

tax n Kraftfahrzeugsteuer f; **roadworks** npl Straßenarbeiten pl; **roadworthy** adj fahrtüchtig

roar 1. n (of person, lion) Brüllen nt; (von Verkehr) Donnern nt 2. vi (person, lion) brüllen (with vor + dat)

roast 1. n Braten m 2. adj **~ beef** Rinderbraten m; **~ chicken** Brathähnchen nt; **~ pork** Schweinebraten m; **~ potatoes** pl im Backofen gebratene Kartoffeln 3. vt (meat) braten

rob vt bestehlen; (bank, shop) ausrauben; **robbery** n Raub m

robe n (US, dressing gown) Morgenrock m; (of judge, priest etc) Robe f, Talar m

robin n Rotkehlchen nt

robot n Roboter m

rock 1. n (substance) Stein m; (boulder) Felsbrocken m; MUS Rock m; **on the ~s** (drink) mit Eis; (marriage) gescheitert 2. vt, vi (swing) schaukeln; (dance) rocken; **rock climbing** n Klettern nt

rocket n Rakete f; (in salad) Rucola f

rocking chair n Schaukelstuhl m

rocky adj (landscape) felsig; (path) steinig

rod n (bar) Stange f; (fishing rod) Rute f

rode pt of **ride**

rogue n Schurke m

role n Rolle f; **role model** n Vorbild nt

roll 1. n (of film, paper etc) Rolle f; (bread ~) Brötchen nt **2.** vt (move by ~ing) rollen; (cigarette) drehen **3.** vi (move by ~ing) rollen; **roll out** vi (pastry) ausrollen; **roll over** vi (person) sich umdrehen; **roll up 1.** vi fam (arrive) antanzen **2.** vt (carpet) aufrollen; **roll one's sleeves up** die Ärmel hochkrempeln

roller n (hair ~) (Locken)wickler m; **roller coaster** n Achterbahn f; **roller skates** npl Rollschuhe pl; **roller-skating** n Rollschuhlaufen nt; **rolling pin** n Nudelholz nt; **roll-on** (deodorant) n Deoroller m

ROM acr = **read only memory;** ROM m

Roman 1. adj römisch **2.** n Römer(in) m(f); **Roman Catholic 1.** adj römisch-katholisch **2.** n Katholik(in) m(f)

romance n Romantik f; (love affair) Romanze f

Romania n Rumänien nt; **Romanian 1.** adj rumänisch **2.** n Rumäne m, Rumänin f; (language) Rumänisch nt

romantic adj romantisch

roof n Dach nt; **roof rack** n Dachgepäckträger m

rook n (in chess) Turm m

room n Zimmer nt, Raum m; (large, for gatherings etc) Saal m; (space) Platz m; fig Spielraum m; **make ~ for** Platz machen für; **room-mate** n Zimmergenosse m, Zimmergenossin f; (US, sharing apartment) Mitbewohner(in) m(f); **room service** n Zimmerservice m

root n Wurzel f; **root out** vt ausrotten; **root vegetable** n Wurzelgemüse nt

rope n Seil nt; **know the ~s** fam sich auskennen

rose 1. pt of **rise 2.** n Rose f

rosé n Rosé(wein) m

rot vi verfaulen

rotate 1. vt (turn) rotieren lassen **2.** vi rotieren; **rotation** n (turning) Rotation f; **in ~** abwechselnd

rotten adj (decayed) faul; (mean) gemein; (unpleasant) scheußlich; (ill) elend

rough 1. adj (not smooth) rau; (path) uneben; (coarse, violent) grob; (crossing) stürmisch; (without comforts) hart; (unfinished, makeshift) grob; (approximate) ungefähr; **~ draft** Rohentwurf m; **I have a ~ idea** ich habe eine ungefähre Vorstellung **2.** adv **sleep ~** im Freien schlafen **3.** vt **~ it** primitiv leben; **roughly** adv grob; (approximately) ungefähr

round 1. adj rund **2.** adv **all ~** (on all sides) rundherum; **I'll be ~ at 8** ich werde um acht Uhr da sein; **the other way ~** umgekehrt **3.** prep (sur-

rounding) um (... herum); ~ (*about*) (*approximately*) ungefähr; ~ **the corner** um die Ecke; **go ~ the world** um die Welt reisen; **she lives ~ here** sie wohnt hier in der Gegend **4.** *n* Runde *f*; (*of bread, toast*) Scheibe *f*; **it's my ~** (*of drinks*) die Runde geht auf mich **5.** *vt* (*corner*) biegen um; **round off** *vt* abrunden; **round up** *vt* (*number, price*) aufrunden

roundabout 1. *n* (*Brit*) AUTO Kreisverkehr *m*; (*Brit, merry-go-round*) Karussell *nt* **2.** *adj* umständlich; **round-the-clock** *adj* rund um die Uhr; **round trip** *n* Rundreise *f*; **round-trip ticket** *n* (*US*) Rückfahrkarte *f*; (*for plane*) Rückflugticket *nt*

route *n* Route *f*; (*bus, plane etc service*) Linie *f*; *fig* Weg *m*

routine 1. *n* Routine *f* **2.** *adj* Routine-

row **1.** *n* (*line*) Reihe *f*; **three times in a ~** dreimal hintereinander **2.** *vt, vi* (*boat*) rudern **3.** *n* (*noise*) Krach *m*; (*dispute*) Streit *m*

rowboat *n* (*US*) Ruderboot *nt*

row house *n* (*US*) Reihenhaus *nt*

rowing *n* Rudern *nt*; **rowing boat** *n* (*Brit*) Ruderboot *nt*; **rowing machine** *n* Rudergerät *nt*

royal *adj* königlich; **royalty** *n*

(*family*) Mitglieder *pl* der königlichen Familie; **royalties** *pl* (*from book, music*) Tantiemen *pl*

RSPCA *abbr* = **Royal Society for the Prevention of Cruelty to Animals**; britischer Tierschutzverein

RSVP *abbr* = **répondez s'il vous plaît**; u. A. w. g.

rub *vt* reiben; **rub in** *vt* einmassieren; **rub out** *vt* (*with eraser*) ausradieren

rubber *n* Gummi *m*; (*Brit, eraser*) Radiergummi *m*; (*US*) *fam* (*contraceptive*) Gummi *m*; **rubber stamp** *n* Stempel *m*

rubbish *n* Abfall *m*; (*nonsense*) Quatsch *m*; (*poor-quality thing*) Mist *m*; **don't talk ~** red keinen Unsinn!; **rubbish bin** *n* Mülleimer *m*; **rubbish dump** *n* Müllabladeplatz *m*

rubble *n* Schutt *m*

ruby *n* (*stone*) Rubin *m*

rucksack *n* Rucksack *m*

rude *adj* (*impolite*) unhöflich; (*indecent*) unanständig

rug *n* (*Teppich m*; (*next to bed*) Bettvorleger *m*; (*for knees*) Wolldecke *f*

rugby *n* Rugby *nt*

rugged *adj* (*coastline*) zerklüftet; (*features*) markant

ruin 1. *n* Ruine *f*; (*financial, social*) Ruin *m* **2.** *vt* ruinieren

rule 1. *n* Regel *f*; (*governing*) Herrschaft *f*; **as a ~** in der

Regel 2. *vt, vi* (*govern*) regieren; (*decide*) entscheiden; **ruler** *n* Lineal *nt*; (*person*) Herrscher(in) *m(f)*

rum *n* Rum *m*

rumble *vi* (*stomach*) knurren; (*train, truck*) rumpeln

rummage *vi* ~ (*around*) herumstöbern

rumor (*US*), **rumour** *n* Gerücht *nt*

run 1. *vt* (*race, distance*) laufen; (*machine, engine, computer program, water*) laufen lassen; (*manage*) leiten, führen; (*car*) unterhalten; **I ran her home** ich habe sie nach Hause gefahren **2.** *vi* laufen; (*move quickly*) rennen; (*bus, train*) fahren; (*path etc*) verlaufen; (*machine, engine, computer program*) laufen; (*flow*) fließen; (*colours, make-up*) verlaufen; **~ for President** für die Präsidentschaft kandidieren; **be ~ning low** knapp werden; **my nose is ~ning** mir läuft die Nase; **it ~s in the family** es liegt in der Familie **3.** *n* (*on foot*) Lauf *m*; (*in car*) Spazierfahrt *f*; (*series*) Reihe *f*; (*sudden demand*) Ansturm *m* (*on* auf + *acc*); (*in tights*) Laufmasche *f*; (*in cricket, baseball*) Lauf *m*; **go for a ~** laufen gehen; (*in car*) eine Spazierfahrt machen; **in the long ~** auf die Dauer; **on the ~** auf der Flucht (*from*

vor + *dat*); **run along** *vi* herumlaufen; **run away** *vi* weglaufen; **run down** *vt* (*with car*) umfahren; (*criticize*) heruntermachen; **be ~** (*tired*) abgespannt sein; **run into** *vt* (*meet*) zufällig treffen; (*problem*) stoßen auf + *acc*; **run off** *vi* weglaufen; **run out** *vi* (*person*) hinausrennen; (*liquid*) auslaufen; (*lease, time*) ablaufen; (*money, supplies*) ausgehen; **he ran ~ of money** ihm ging das Geld aus; **run over** *vt* (*with car*) überfahren; **run up** *vt* (*debt, bill*) machen

rung *pp of* **ring**

runner *n* (*athlete*) Läufer(in) *m(f)*; **do a ~** *fam* wegrennen; **runner beans** *npl* (*Brit*) Stangenbohnen *pl*

running 1. *n* SPORT Laufen *nt*; (*management*) Leitung *f*, Führung *f* **2.** *adj* (*water*) fließend; **~ costs** Betriebskosten *pl*; (*for car*) Unterhaltskosten *pl*; **3 days ~** 3 Tage hintereinander

runny *adj* (*food*) flüssig; (*nose*) laufend

runway *n* Start- und Landebahn *f*

rural *adj* ländlich

rush *n* Eile *f*; (*for tickets etc*) Ansturm *m* (*for* auf + *acc*); **be in a ~** es eilig haben; **there's no ~** es eilt nicht **2.** *vt* (*do too quickly*) hastig machen; (*meal*) hastig essen; ~

***sb* to hospital** jdn auf dem schnellsten Weg ins Krankenhaus bringen; **don't ~ me** dräng mich nicht **3.** *vi* (*hurry*) eilen; **rush hour** *n* Hauptverkehrszeit *f*

rusk *n* Zwieback *m*

Russia *n* Russland *nt*; **Russian 1.** *adj* russisch **2.** *n* Rus-se *m*, Russin *f*; (*language*) Russisch *nt*

rust 1. *n* Rost *m* **2.** *vi* rosten; **rustproof** *adj* rostfrei; **rusty** *adj* rostig

ruthless *adj* rücksichtslos; (*treatment, criticism*) schonungslos

rye *n* Roggen *m*

S

sabotage *vt* sabotieren

sachet *n* Päckchen *nt*

sack 1. *n* (*bag*) Sack *m*; **get the ~** *fam* rausgeschmissen werden **2.** *vt fam* rausschmeißen

sacred *adj* heilig

sacrifice 1. *n* Opfer *nt* **2.** *vt* opfern

sad *adj* traurig

saddle *n* Sattel *m*

sadistic *adj* sadistisch

sadly *adv* (*unfortunately*) leider

safe 1. *adj* (*free from danger*) sicher; (*out of danger*) in Sicherheit; (*careful*) vorsichtig; **have a ~ journey** gute Fahrt! **2.** *n* Safe *m*; **safeguard 1.** *n* Schutz *m* **2.** *vt* schützen (*against* vor + *dat*); **safely** *adv* sicher; (*arrive*) wohlbehalten; (*drive*) vorsichtig; **safety** *n* Sicherheit *f*; **safety belt** *n* Sicherheitsgurt *m*; **safety pin** *n* Sicherheitsnadel *f*

Sagittarius *n* ASTR Schütze *m*

Sahara *n* **the ~** (**Desert**) die (Wüste) Sahara

said *pt, pp of* **say**

sail 1. *n* Segel *nt*; **set ~** losfahren (*for* nach) **2.** *vi* (*in yacht*) segeln; (*on ship*) mit dem Schiff fahren; (*ship*) auslaufen (*for* nach) **3.** *vt* (*yacht*) segeln mit; (*ship*) steuern; **sailboat** *n* (*US*) Segelboot *nt*; **sailing** *n* **go ~** segeln gehen; **sailing boat** (*Brit*) Segelboot *nt*; **sailor** *n* Seemann *m*; (*in navy*) Matrose *m*

saint *n* Heilige(r) *mf*

sake *n* **for the ~ of** um + *gen* ... willen; **for your ~** deinetwegen, dir zuliebe

salad *n* Salat *m*; **salad cream** *n* (*Brit*) majonäseartige Salatsoße *f*; **salad dressing** *n* Salatsoße *f*

salary *n* Gehalt *nt*

sale *n* Verkauf *m*; (*at reduced prices*) Ausverkauf *m*; **for ~** zu verkaufen; **sales clerk** *n*

(US) Verkäufer(in) m(f);
salesman n Verkäufer m;
(rep) Vertreter m; **sales rep**
n Vertreter(in) m(f); **saleswoman** n Verkäuferin f;
(rep) Vertreterin f

saliva n Speichel m

salmon n Lachs m

saloon n (ship's lounge) Salon
m; (US, bar) Kneipe f

salt 1. n Salz nt **2.** vt (flavour)
salzen; (roads) mit Salz
streuen; **salt cellar**, **salt
shaker** (US) n Salzstreuer
m; **salty** adj salzig

same 1. adj the ~ (similar)
der/die/das gleiche, die
gleichen pl; (identical) der
/die/dasselbe, dieselben pl;
they live in the ~ house
sie wohnen im selben Haus
2. pron the ~ (similar) der/
die/das Gleiche, die Gleichen pl; (identical) der
/die/dasselbe, dieselben pl;
I'll have the ~ same ich
möchte noch mal das Gleiche; *all the ~* trotzdem; *the
~ to you* gleichfalls; *it's all
the ~ to me* es ist mir egal
3. adv the ~ gleich

sample 1. n Probe f; (of fabric) Muster nt **2.** vt probieren

sanctions npl POL Sanktionen pl

sanctuary n (refuge) Zuflucht
f; (for animals) Schutzgebiet
nt

sand n Sand m

sandal n Sandale f

sandwich n Sandwich nt

sandy adj (full of sand) sandig; ~ **beach** Sandstrand m

sane adj geistig gesund, normal; (sensible) vernünftig

sang pt of **sing**

sanitary adj hygienisch; **sanitary napkin** (US), **sanitary
towel** n Damenbinde f

sank pt of **sink**

Santa (Claus) n der Weihnachtsmann

sarcastic adj sarkastisch

sardine n Sardine f

sari n Sari m (von indischen
Frauen getragenes Gewand)

sat pt, pp of **sit**

Sat abbr = **Saturday**; Sa.

satellite n Satellit m; **satellite
dish** n Satellitenschüssel f

satin n Satin m

satisfaction n (contentment)
Zufriedenheit f; *is that to
your ~?* sind Sie damit zufrieden?; **satisfactory** adj
zufrieden stellend; **satisfied**
adj zufrieden (with mit); **satisfy** vt zufrieden stellen;
(conditions) erfüllen; (need,
demand) befriedigen; **satisfying** adj befriedigend

Saturday n Samstag m, Sonnabend m; → **Tuesday**

sauce n Soße f; **saucepan** n
Kochtopf m; **saucer** n Untertasse f

Saudi Arabia n Saudi-Arabien nt

sauna n Sauna f

sausage n Wurst f; **sausage**

roll n mit Wurst gefülltes Blätterteigröllchen

savage adj (person, attack) brutal; (animal) wild

save1. vt (rescue) retten (from vor + dat); (money, time, electricity etc) sparen; (strength) schonen; IT speichern; **~ sb's life** jdm das Leben retten **2.** vi sparen **3.** n (in soccer) Parade f; **save up** vi sparen (for auf + acc); **saving** n (of money) Sparen nt; **~s** npl Ersparnisse pl; **~s account** Sparkonto nt

savory (US), **savoury** adj (not sweet) pikant

saw1. vt, vi sägen **2.** n (tool) Säge f **3.** pt of **see**; **sawdust** n Sägemehl nt

saxophone n Saxophon nt

say1. vt sagen (to sb jdm); (prayer) sprechen; **what does the letter ~?** was steht im Brief?; **the rules ~ that ...** in den Regeln heißt es, dass ...; **he's said to be rich** er soll reich sein **2.** n **have a ~ in sth** bei etw ein Mitspracherecht haben **3.** adv zum Beispiel; **saying** n Sprichwort nt

scab n (on cut) Schorf m

scaffolding n (Bau)gerüst nt

scale n (of map etc) Maßstab m; (on thermometer etc) Skala f; (of pay) Tarifsystem nt; MUS Tonleiter f; (of fish, snake) Schuppe f; **to ~** maßstabsgerecht; **on a large/ small ~** in großem/kleinem

Umfang; **scales** npl (for weighing) Waage f

scalp n Kopfhaut f

scan 1. vt (examine) genau prüfen; (read quickly) überfliegen; IT scannen **2.** n MED Ultraschall m; **scan in** vt IT einscannen

scandal n Skandal m

Scandinavia n Skandinavien nt; **Scandinavian 1.** adj skandinavisch **2.** n Skandinavier(in) m(f)

scanner n Scanner m

scapegoat n Sündenbock m

scar n Narbe f

scarce adj selten; (in short supply) knapp; **scarcely** adv kaum

scare 1. n (general alarm) Panik f **2.** vt erschrecken; **be ~d** Angst haben (of von + dat)

scarf n Schal m; (on head) Kopftuch nt

scarlet adj scharlachrot; **scarlet fever** n Scharlach m

scary adj (film, story) gruselig

scatter vt verstreuen; (seed, gravel) streuen; (disperse) auseinander treiben

scene n (location) Ort m; (division of play) THEAT Szene f; (view) Anblick m; **make a ~** eine Szene machen; **scenery** n (landscape) Landschaft f; THEAT Kulissen pl; **scenic** adj (landscape) malerisch; **~ route** landschaftlich schöne Strecke

scent n (perfume) Parfüm nt;

(smell) Duft *m*

sceptical *adj (Brit)* skeptisch

schedule 1. *n (plan)* Programm *nt; (of work)* Zeitplan *m; (list)* Liste *f; (US, of trains, buses, air traffic)* Fahr-, Flugplan *m;* **on ~** planmäßig; **be behind ~ with sth** mit etw in Verzug sein **2.** *vt* **the meeting is ~d for next Monday** die Besprechung ist für nächsten Montag angesetzt; **scheduled** *adj (departure, arrival)* planmäßig; **~ flight** Linienflug *m*

scheme 1. *n (plan)* Plan *m; (project)* Projekt *nt; (dishonest)* Intrige *f* **2.** *vi* intrigieren

scholar *n* Gelehrte(r) *mf;* **scholarship** *n (grant)* Stipendium *nt*

school *n* Schule *f; (university department)* Fachbereich *m; (US, university)* Universität *f;* **school bag** *n* Schultasche *f;* **schoolbook** *n* Schulbuch *nt;* **schoolboy** *n* Schüler *m;* **schoolgirl** *n* Schülerin *f;* **schoolteacher** *n* Lehrer(in) *m(f);* **schoolwork** *n* Schularbeiten *pl*

sciatica *n* Ischias *m*

science *n* Wissenschaft *f; (natural science)* Naturwissenschaft *f;* **science fiction** *n* Sciencefiction *f;* **scientific** *adj* wissenschaftlich; **scientist** *n* Wissenschaftler(in) *m(f); (natural sciences)* Naturwissenschaftler(in) *m(f)*

scissors *npl* Schere *f*

scone *n kleines süßes Hefebrötchen mit oder ohne Rosinen, das mit Butter oder Dickrahm und Marmelade gegessen wird*

scoop 1. *n (exclusive story)* Exklusivbericht *m;* **a ~ of ice-cream** eine Kugel Eis **2.** *vt* **~ (up)** schaufeln

scooter *n (Motor)*roller *m; (toy)* (Tret)roller *m*

scope *n* Umfang *m; (opportunity)* Möglichkeit *f*

score 1. *n* SPORT Spielstand *m; (final result)* Spielergebnis *nt; (in quiz etc)* Punktestand *m;* MUS Partitur *f;* **keep (the) ~** mitzählen **2.** *vt (goal)* schießen; *(points)* machen **3.** *vi (keep score)* mitzählen

scoreboard *n* Anzeigetafel *f*

scorn *n* Verachtung *f;* **scornful** *adj* verächtlich

Scorpio *n* ASTR Skorpion *m*

scorpion *n* Skorpion *m*

Scot *n* Schotte *m*, Schottin *f;* **Scotch 1.** *adj* schottisch **2.** *n (whisky)* schottischer Whisky, Scotch *m*

Scotch tape® *n (US)* Tesafilm® *m*

Scotland *n* Schottland *nt;* **Scotsman** *n* Schotte *m;* **Scotswoman** *n* Schottin *f;* **Scottish** *adj* schottisch

scout *n (boy scout)* Pfadfinder *m*

scrambled eggs *npl* Rührei *nt*

scrap 1. n (bit) Stückchen nt, Fetzen m; (metal) Schrott m **2.** vt (car) verschrotten; (plan) verwerfen

scrape 1. n (scratch) Kratzer m **2.** vt (car) schrammen; (wall) streifen; **~ one's knee** sich das Knie schürfen; **scrape through** vi (exam) mit knapper Not bestehen

scrap heap n Schrotthaufen m; **scrap metal** n Schrott m; **scrap paper** n Schmierpapier nt

scratch 1. n (mark) Kratzer m; **start from ~** von vorne anfangen **2.** vt kratzen; (car) zerkratzen; **~ one's arm** sich am Arm kratzen

scream 1. n Schrei m **2.** vi schreien (with vor + dat); **~ at sb** jdn anschreien

screen 1. n TV, FILM Bildschirm m; FILM Leinwand f **2.** vt (film) zeigen; (applicants, luggage) überprüfen; **screenplay** n Drehbuch nt; **screen saver** n IT Bildschirmschoner m

screw 1. n Schraube f **2.** vt vulg (have sex with) poppen; **~ sth to sth** etw an etw acc schrauben; **~ off/on** (lid) ab-/aufschrauben; **screw up** vt (paper) zusammenknüllen; (make a mess of) vermasseln; **screwdriver** n Schraubenzieher m

scribble vt, vi kritzeln

script n (of play) Text m; (of film) Drehbuch nt; (style of writing) Schrift f

scroll down vi IT runterscrollen; **scroll up** vi IT raufscrollen; **scroll bar** n IT Scrollbar f

scrub vt schrubben

scruffy adj vergammelt

scuba-diving n Sporttauchen nt

sculptor n Bildhauer(in) m(f); **sculpture** n ART Bildhauerei f; (statue) Skulptur f

sea n Meer nt, See f; **seafood** n Meeresfrüchte pl; **sea front** n Strandpromenade f; **seagull** n Möwe f

seal 1. n (animal) Robbe f; (stamp, impression) Siegel nt; TECH Verschluss m; (ring etc) Dichtung f **2.** vt versiegeln; (envelope) zukleben

seam n Naht f

seaport n Seehafen m

search 1. n Suche f (for nach); **do a ~ for** IT suchen nach; **in ~ of** auf der Suche nach **2.** vi suchen (for nach) **3.** vt durchsuchen; **search engine** n IT Suchmaschine f

seashell n Muschel f; **seashore** n Strand m; **seasick** adj seekrank; **seaside** n **at the ~** am Meer; **seaside resort** n Seebad nt

season 1. n Jahreszeit f, Saison f; **high/low ~** Hoch-/Nebensaison f **2.** vt (flavour) würzen

seasoning n Gewürz nt

season ticket n RAIL Zeitkarte f; THEAT Abonnement nt; SPORT Dauerkarte f

seat 1. n (place) Platz m; (chair) Sitz m; **take a ~** setzen Sie sich **2.** vt **the hall ~s 300** der Saal hat 300 Sitzplätze; **please be ~ed** bitte setzen Sie sich; **remain ~ed** sitzen bleiben; **seat belt** n Sicherheitsgurt m

sea view n Seeblick m; **seaweed** n Seetang m

secluded adj abgelegen

second 1. adj (number r, s); **the~ of June** der zweite Juni **2.** adv (in second position) an zweiter Stelle; (secondly) zweitens; **he came ~** er ist Zweiter geworden **3.** n (of time) Sekunde f; (moment) Augenblick m; ~ (gear) der zweite Gang; (second helping) zweite Portion; **just a ~** (einen) Augenblick!; **secondary** adj (less important) zweitrangig; **~ school** weiterführende Schule; **second-class 1.** adj (ticket) zweiter Klasse; **~ stamp** Briefmarke f für nicht bevorzugt beförderte Sendungen **2.** adv (travel) zweiter Klasse; **secondhand** adj, adv gebraucht; (information) aus zweiter Hand; **secondly** adv zweitens; **second-rate** adj pej drittklassig

secret 1. n Geheimnis nt **2.** adj geheim; (admirer) heimlich

secretary n Sekretär(in) m(f); (minister) Minister(in) m(f); **Secretary of State** n (US) Außenminister(in) m(f)

secretive adj geheimnistuerisch; **secretly** adv heimlich

sect n Sekte f

section n (part) Teil m; (of document) Abschnitt m; (department) Abteilung f

secure 1. adj (safe) sicher (from von +dat); (firmly fixed) fest **2.** vt (make firm) befestigen; (window, door) fest verschließen; (obtain) sich sichern; **securely** adv fest; (safely) sicher; **security** n Sicherheit f

sedative n Beruhigungsmittel nt

seduce vt verführen; **seductive** adj verführerisch

see 1. vt sehen; (understand) verstehen; (check) nachsehen; (accompany) bringen; (visit) besuchen; (talk to) sprechen; **~ the doctor** zum Arzt gehen; **~ sb home** jdn nach Hause begleiten; **~ you** tschüs!; **~ you on Friday** bis Freitag! **2.** vi sehen; (understand) verstehen; (check) nachsehen; (you) ~ siehst du!; **we'll ~** mal sehen; **see about** vt (attend to) sich kümmern um; **see off** vt (say goodbye to) verabschieden; **see out** vt (show out) zur Tür bringen; **see through** vt **see sth through**

etw zu Ende bringen; **~ sb/ sth** jdn/etw durchschauen; **see to** vt sich kümmern um; **~ it that ...** sieh zu, dass ...

seed n (of plant) Samen m; (in fruit) Kern m; **seedless** adj kernlos

seek vt suchen; (fame) streben nach; **~ sb's advice** jdn um Rat fragen

seem vi scheinen; he **~s (to be) honest** er scheint ehrlich zu sein

seen pp of **see**

seesaw n Wippe f

segment n Teil m

seize vt packen; (confiscate) beschlagnahmen; (opportunity, power) ergreifen

seldom adv selten

select 1. adj (exclusive) exklusiv 2. vt auswählen; **selection** n Auswahl f (of an + dat)

self n Selbst nt, Ich nt; **he's his old ~ again** er ist wieder ganz der Alte; **self-adhesive** adj selbstklebend; **self-assured** n selbstsicher; **self-catering** adj für Selbstversorger; **self-centred** adj egozentrisch; **self-confidence** n Selbstbewusstsein nt; **self-confident** adj selbstbewusst; **self-conscious** adj befangen, verklemmt; **self-contained** adj (flat) separat; **self-control** n Selbstbeherrschung f; **self-defence** n Selbstverteidigung f; **self-**

-employed adj selbstständig

selfish adj, **selfishly** adj, adv egoistisch, selbstsüchtig

self-pity n Selbstmitleid nt; **self-respect** n Selbstachtung f; **self-service** 1. n Selbstbedienung f 2. adj Selbstbedienungs-

sell 1. vt verkaufen; **~ sb sth, ~ sth to sb** jdm etw verkaufen; **do you ~ postcards?** haben Sie Postkarten? 2. vi (product) sich verkaufen; **sell out** vt **be sold ~** ausverkauft sein; **sell-by date** n Haltbarkeitsdatum nt

Sellotape® n (Brit) Tesafilm® m

semi n (Brit, house) Doppelhaushälfte f; **semicircle** n Halbkreis m; **semicolon** n Semikolon nt; **semidetached (house)** n (Brit) Doppelhaushälfte f; **semifinal** n Halbfinale nt

seminar n Seminar nt

senate n Senat m; **senator** n Senator(in) m(f)

send vt schicken; **~ sb sth, ~ sth to sb** jdm etw schicken; **~ her my best wishes** grüße sie von mir; **send away** 1. vt wegschicken 2. vi **~ for** anfordern; **send back** vt zurückschicken; **send for** vt (person) holen lassen; (by post) anfordern; **send off** vt (by post) abschicken

sender n Absender(in) m(f)

senior 1. adj (older) älter

serve

(high-ranking) höher; (pupils) älter; **he is ~ to me** er ist mir übergeordnet **2.** adj **he's eight years my ~** er ist um acht Jahre älter als ich; **senior citizen** n Senior(in) m(f)

sensation n Gefühl nt; (excitement, person, thing) Sensation f; **sensational** adj sensationell

sense 1. n (faculty, meaning) Sinn m; (feeling) Gefühl nt; (understanding) Verstand m; **~ of smell/taste** Geruchs-/Geschmackssinn m; **have a ~ of humour** Humor haben; **make ~** (sentence etc) einen Sinn ergeben; (be sensible) Sinn machen; **in a ~** gewissermaßen **2.** vt spüren; **senseless** adj (stupid) sinnlos

sensible, **sensibly** adj, adv vernünftig

sensitive adj empfindlich (to gegen); (easily hurt) sensibel; (subject) heikel

sent pt, pp of **send**

sentence 1. n LING Satz m; LAW Strafe f **2.** vt verurteilen (to zu)

sentiment n (sentimentality) Sentimentalität f; (opinion) Ansicht f; **sentimental** adj sentimental

separate 1. adj getrennt, separat; (individual) einzeln **2.** vt trennen (from von); **they are ~d** (couple) sie leben ge-

trennt **3.** vi sich trennen; **separately** adv getrennt; (singly) einzeln

September n September m; **in ~** im September; **on the 2nd of ~** am 2. September; **at the beginning/in the middle/at the end of ~** Anfang/Mitte/Ende September; **last/next ~** letzten/nächsten September

septic adj vereitert

sequel n (to film, book) Fortsetzung f (to von)

sequence n (order) Reihenfolge f

Serb n Serbe m, Serbin f; **Serbia** n Serbien nt

sergeant n Polizeimeister(in) m(f); MIL Feldwebel(in) m(f)

serial 1. n TV Serie f; (in newspaper etc) Fortsetzungsroman m **2.** adj IT seriell; **~ number** Seriennummer f

series n sing Reihe f; TV, RADIO Serie f

serious adj ernst; (injury, illness, mistake) schwer; (discussion) ernsthaft; **are you ~?** ist das dein Ernst?; **seriously** adv ernsthaft; (hurt) schwer; **~?** im Ernst?; **take sb ~** jdn ernst nehmen

sermon n REL Predigt f

servant n Diener(in) m(f)

serve 1. vt (customer) bedienen; (food) servieren; (one's country etc) dienen + dat; (sentence) verbüßen; **I'm be-**

ing ~d ich werde schon bedient; *it ~s him right* es geschieht ihm recht **2.** *vi* dienen *(as* als), aufschlagen **3.** *n*, Aufschlag *m*

server *n* IT Server *m*

service 1. *n (in shop, hotel)* Bedienung *f; (activity, amenity)* Dienstleistung *f; (set of dishes)* Service *nt*; AUTO Inspektion *f*; TECH Wartung *f*; REL Gottesdienst *m*, Aufschlag *m*; *train/ bus ~* Zug-/Busverbindung *f*; *~ not included* „Bedienung nicht inbegriffen" **2.** *vt* AUTO, TECH warten; **service area** *n (on motorway)* Raststätte *f (mit* Tankstelle); **service charge** *n* Bedienung *f*; **service provider** *n* IT Provider *m*; **service station** *n* Tankstelle *f*

serving *n (portion)* Portion *f*

session *n (of court, assembly)* Sitzung *f*

set 1. *vt (place)* stellen; *(lay flat)* legen; *(arrange)* anordnen; *(table)* decken; *(trap, record)* aufstellen; *(time, price)* festsetzen; *(watch, alarm)* stellen *(for* auf + *acc)*; *~ sb a task* jdm eine Aufgabe stellen; *~ free* freilassen; *~ a good example* ein gutes Beispiel geben; *the novel is ~ in London* der Roman spielt London **2.** *vi (sun)* untergehen; *(become hard)* fest werden; *(bone)* zusam-

menwachsen **3.** *n (collection of things)* Satz *m*; *(of cutlery, furniture)* Garnitur *f*; *(group of people)* Kreis *m*; RADIO, TV Apparat *m*, Satz *m*; THEAT Bühnenbild *nt*; FILM (Film-) kulisse *f* **4.** *adj (agreed, prescribed)* festgelegt; *(ready)* bereit; *~ meal* Menü *nt*; **set aside** *vt (money)* beiseite legen; *(time)* einplanen; **set off 1.** *vi* aufbrechen *(for* nach) **2.** *vt (alarm)* auslösen; *(enhance)* hervorheben; **set out 1.** *vi* aufbrechen *(for* nach) **2.** *vt (chairs, chess-pieces etc)* aufstellen; *(state)* darlegen; *~ to do sth (intend)* beabsichtigen, etw zu tun; **set up 1.** *vt (firm, organization)* gründen; *(stall, tent, camera)* aufbauen; *(meeting)* vereinbaren **2.** *vi ~ as a doctor* sich als Arzt niederlassen

setback *n* Rückschlag *m*

settee *n* Sofa *nt*, Couch *f*

setting *n (of novel, film)* Schauplatz *m*; *(surroundings)* Umgebung *f*

settle 1. *vt (bill, debt)* begleichen; *(dispute)* beilegen; *(question)* klären; *(stomach)* beruhigen **2.** *vi ~ (down)* *(feel at home)* sich einleben; *(calm down)* sich beruhigen; **settle in** *vi (in place)* sich einleben; *(in job)* sich eingewöhnen; **settlement** *n (of bill, debt)* Begleichung *f*;

(*colony*) Siedlung *f*; **reach a ~** sich einigen

setup *n* (*organization*) Organisation *f*; (*situation*) Situation *f*

seven 1. *num* sieben **2.** *n* Sieben *f*; → **eight**; **seventeen 1.** *num* siebzehn **2.** *n* Siebzehn *f*; → **eight**; **seventeenth** *adj* siebzehnte(r, s); → **eighth**; **seventh 1.** *adj* siebte(r, s) **2.** *n* (*fraction*) Siebtel *nt*; → **eighth**; **seventieth** *adj* siebzigste(r, s); → **eighth**; **seventy 1.** *num* siebzig; **~one** einundsiebzig; **2.** *n* Siebzig *f*; **be in one's seventies** in den Siebzigern sein; → **eight**

several *adj, pron* mehrere

severe *adj* (*strict*) streng; (*serious*) schwer; (*pain*) stark; (*winter*) hart; **severely** *adv* (*harshly*) hart; (*seriously*) schwer

sew *vt, vi* nähen

sewage *n* Abwasser *nt*; **sewer** *n* Abwasserkanal *m*

sewing *n* Nähen *nt*; **sewing machine** *n* Nähmaschine *f*

sewn *pp* of **sew**

sex *n* Sex *m*; (*gender*) Geschlecht *nt*; **have ~** Sex haben (*with mit*); **sexism** *n* Sexismus *m*; **sexist 1.** *adj* sexistisch **2.** *n* Sexist(in) *m(f)*; **sex life** *n* Sex(ual)leben *nt*

sexual *adj* sexuell; **~ discrimination/ harassment** sexuelle Diskriminierung / Belästigung; **~ intercourse** Ge-

schlechtsverkehr *m*; **sexuality** *n* Sexualität *f*

sexy *adj* sexy

Seychelles *npl* Seychellen *pl*

shack *n* Hütte *f*

shade 1. *n* (*shadow*) Schatten *m*; (*for lamp*) (Lampen-)schirm *m*; (*colour*) Farbton *m*; **~s** (*US, sunglasses*) Sonnenbrille *f* **2.** *vt* (*from sun*) abschirmen; (*in drawing*) schattieren

shadow *n* Schatten *m*

shady *adj* schattig; *fig* zwielichtig

shake 1. *vt* schütteln; (*shock*) erschüttern; **~ hands with sb** jdm die Hand geben; **~ one's head** den Kopf schütteln **2.** *vi* (*tremble*) zittern; (*building, ground*) schwanken; **shake off** *vt* abschütteln; **shaken** *pp* of **shake**; **shaky** *adj* (*trembling*) zittrig; (*table, chair, position*) wackelig

shall *vaux* werden; (*in questions*) sollen; **I ~ do my best** ich werde mein Bestes tun; **~ I come too?** soll ich mitkommen?; **where ~ we go?** wo gehen wir hin?

shallow *adj* seicht; (*person*) oberflächlich

shame *n* (*feeling of ~*) Scham *f*; (*disgrace*) Schande *f*; **what a ~** wie schade!; **~ on you** schäm dich!; **it's a ~ that ...** schade, dass ...

shampoo 1. *n* Shampoo *nt*;

have a ~ and set sich die Haare waschen und legen lassen **2.** vt (hair) waschen; (carpet) schamponieren

shandy n Radler m, Alsterwasser nt

shan't contr of **shall not**

shape 1. n Form f; (unidentified figure) Gestalt f; **in the ~ of** in Form + gen; **be in good ~** (healthwise) in guter Verfassung sein; **take ~** (plan, idea) Gestalt annehmen **2.** vt (clay, person) formen; **-shaped** suf -förmig; **heart~** herzförmig

share n Anteil + dat (in, of an m); FIN Aktie f **2.** vt, vi teilen; **shareholder** n Aktionär(in) m(f)

shark n Haifisch m

sharp 1. adj scharf; (pin) spitz; (person) scharfsinnig; (pain) heftig; (increase, fall) abrupt; **C/F ~** MUS Cis/Dis nt **2.** adv **at 2 o'clock ~** Punkt 2 Uhr; **sharpen** vt (knife) schärfen; (pencil) spitzen; **sharpener** n (pencil sharpener) Spitzer m

shatter 1. vt zerschmettern; fig zerstören **2.** vi zerspringen; **shattered** adj (exhausted) kaputt

shave 1. vt rasieren **2.** vi sich rasieren **3.** n Rasur f; **that was a close ~** fig das war knapp; **shave off** vt **shave one's beard off** sich den Bart abrasieren; **shaven 1.**

pp of **shave 2.** adj (head) kahl geschoren; **shaver** n ELEC Rasierapparat m; **shaving brush** n Rasierpinsel m; **shaving foam** n Rasierschaum m

shawl n Tuch nt

she pron sie

shed 1. n Schuppen m **2.** vt (tears, blood) vergießen; (hair, leaves) verlieren

she'd contr of **she had; she would**

sheep n Schaf nt; **sheepdog** n Schäferhund m; **sheepskin** n Schaffell nt

sheer adj (madness) rein; (steep) steil; (transparent) hauchdünn; **by ~ chance** rein zufällig

sheet n (on bed) Bettuch nt; (of paper) Blatt nt; (of metal) Platte f; (of glass) Scheibe f

shelf n Bücherbord nt, Regal nt; **shelves** pl (item of furniture) Regal nt

she'll contr of **she will; she shall**

shell 1. n (of egg, nut) Schale f; (sea~) Muschel f **2.** vt (peas, nuts) schälen; **shellfish** n (as food) Meeresfrüchte pl

shelter 1. n (protection) Schutz m; (accommodation) Unterkunft f; (bus shelter) Wartehäuschen nt **2.** vt schützen (from vor + dat) **3.** vi sich unterstellen; **sheltered** adj (spot) geschützt; (life) behütet

shelve vt fig aufschieben;
shelves pl of **shelf**
shepherd n Schäfer m; **shepherd's pie** n Hackfleischauflauf mit Decke aus Kartoffelpüree
sherry n Sherry m
she's contr of **she is**; **she has**
shield 1. n Schild m; fig Schutz m 2. vt schützen (from vor + dat)
shift 1. n (change) Veränderung f; (period at work, workers) Schicht f; (on keyboard) Umschalttaste f 2. vt (furniture etc) verrücken; ~ **gear(s)** (US) AUTO schalten 3. vi (move) sich bewegen; (move up) rutschen; **shift key** n Umschalttaste f
shin n Schienbein nt
shine 1. vi (be shiny) glänzen; (sun) scheinen; (lamp) leuchten 2. vt (polish) polieren 3. n Glanz m
shingles nsing MED Gürtelrose f
shiny adj glänzend
ship 1. n Schiff nt 2. vt (send) versenden; (by ship) verschiffen; **shipment** n (goods) Sendung f; (sent by ship) Ladung f; **shipwreck** n Schiffbruch m; **shipyard** n Werft f
shirt n Hemd nt
shit n vulg Scheiße f; ~! Scheiße!; **shitty** adj fam beschissen
shiver vi zittern (with vor

+ dat)

shock 1. n (mental, emotional) Schock m; **be in** ~ unter Schock stehen; **get a** ~ ELEC einen Schlag bekommen 2. vt schockieren; **shock absorber** n Stoßdämpfer m; **shocked** adj schockiert (by über + acc); **shocking** adj schockierend
shoe n Schuh m; **shoelace** n Schnürsenkel m; **shoe polish** n Schuhcreme f
shone pt, pp of **shine**
shook pt of **shake**
shoot 1. vt (wound) anschießen; (kill) erschießen; FILM drehen; fam (heroin) drücken 2. vi (with gun, move quickly) schießen; ~ **at sb** auf jdn schießen 3. n (of plant) Trieb m; **shooting** n (exchange of gunfire) Schießerei f; (killing) Erschießung f
shop 1. n Geschäft nt, Laden m 2. vi einkaufen; **shop assistant** n Verkäufer(in) m(f); **shopkeeper** n Geschäftsinhaber(in) m(f); **shoplifting** n Ladendiebstahl m; **shopping** n (activity) Einkaufen nt; (goods) Einkäufe pl; **do the** ~ einkaufen; **go** ~ einkaufen gehen; **shopping bag** n Einkaufstasche f; **shopping cart** n (US) Einkaufswagen m; **shopping center** (US), **shopping centre** n Einkaufszentrum nt;

shopping list n Einkaufszettel m; **shopping trolley** n (Brit) Einkaufswagen m; **shop window** n Schaufenster nt

shore n Ufer nt; **on ~** an Land

short adj kurz; (person) klein; **be ~ of money** knapp bei Kasse sein; **be ~ of time** wenig Zeit haben; **~ of breath** kurzatmig; **cut ~** (holiday) abbrechen; **we are two ~** wir haben zwei zu wenig; **it's ~ for ...** das ist die Kurzform von ...; **shortage** n Knappheit f (of an + dat); **shortbread** n Buttergebäck nt; **short circuit** n Kurzschluss m; **shortcoming** n Unzulänglichkeit f; (of person) Fehler m; **shortcut** n (quicker route) Abkürzung f; IT Shortcut m; **shorten** vt kürzen; (in time) verkürzen; **shortlist** n **be on the ~** in der engeren Wahl sein; **short-lived** adj kurzlebig; **shortly** adv bald; **shorts** npl Shorts pl; **short-sighted** adj kurzsichtig; **short-sleeved** adj kurzärmelig; **short-stay car park** n Kurzzeitparkplatz m; **short story** n Kurzgeschichte f; **short-term** adj kurzfristig

shot n, pt, pp of **shoot 2.** n (from gun, in soccer) Schuss m; PHOT, FILM Aufnahme f; (injection) Spritze f; (of alcohol) Schuss m

should 1. pt of **shall 2.** vaux **I ~ go now** ich sollte jetzt gehen; **you ~n't have said that** das hättest du nicht sagen sollen; **that ~ be enough** das müsste reichen

shoulder n Schulter f

shouldn't contr of **should not**

should've contr of **should have**

shout 1. n Schrei m; (call) Ruf m **2.** vt rufen; (order) brüllen **3.** vi schreien; **~ at** anschreien

shove 1. vt (person) schubsen; (car, table etc) schieben **2.** vi (in crowd) drängeln

shovel 1. n Schaufel f **2.** vt schaufeln

show 1. vt zeigen; **~ sb sth**, **~ sth to sb** jdm etw zeigen; **~ sb in** jdn hereinführen; **~ sb out** jdn zur Tür bringen **2.** n FILM, THEAT Vorstellung f; TV Show f; (exhibition) Ausstellung f; **show off** vi pej angeben; **show round** vt herumführen; **show sb round the house/ the town** jdm das Haus/ die Stadt zeigen; **show up** vi (arrive) auftauchen

shower 1. n Dusche f; (rain) Schauer m; **have (or take) a ~** duschen **2.** vi (wash) duschen

showing n FILM Vorstellung f

shown pp of **show**

showroom n Ausstellungsraum m

shrank *pt of* **shrink**

shred 1. *n* (*of paper, fabric*) Fetzen *m* **2.** *vt* (*in shredder*) (im Reißwolf) zerkleinern; **shredder** *n* (*for paper*) Reißwolf *m*

shrimp *n* Garnele *f*

shrink *vi* schrumpfen; (*clothes*) eingehen

shrivel *vi* ~ (**up**) schrumpfen; (*skin*) runzlig werden

Shrove Tuesday *n* Fastnachtsdienstag *m*

shrub *n* Busch *m*, Strauch *m*

shrug *vt, vi* ~ (**one's shoulders**) mit den Achseln zucken

shrunk *pp of* **shrink**

shudder *vi* schaudern; (*ground, building*) beben

shuffle *vt, vi* mischen

shut 1. *vt* zumachen, schließen; ~ **your mouth** *fam* halt den Mund! **2.** *vi* schließen **3.** *adj* geschlossen; **we're** ~ wir haben geschlossen; **shut down 1.** *vt* schließen; (*computer*) ausschalten **2.** *vi* schließen; (*computer*) sich ausschalten; **shut in** *vt* einschließen; **shut out** *vt* (*lock out*) aussperren; **shut oneself out** sich aussperren; **shut up 1.** *vt* (*lock up*) abschließen; (*silence*) zum Schweigen bringen **2.** *vi* (*keep quiet*) den Mund halten; ~**!** halt den Mund!; **shutter** *n* (*on window*) (Fenster-)laden *m*; **shutter release** *n*

Auslöser *m*

shuttle bus *n* Shuttlebus *m*

shuttlecock *n* Federball *m*

shuttle service *n* Pendelverkehr *m*

shy *adj* schüchtern; (*animal*) scheu

Sicily *n* Sizilien *nt*

sick *adj* krank; (*joke*) makaber; **be** ~ (*Brit, vomit*) sich übergeben; **be off** ~ wegen Krankheit fehlen; **I feel** ~ mir ist schlecht; **be** ~ **of sb/sth** jdn/etw satt haben; **it makes me** ~ *fig* es ekelt mich an; **sickbag** *n* Spucktüte *f*; **sick leave** *n* **be on** ~ krankgeschrieben sein; **sickness** *n* Krankheit *f*; (*Brit, nausea*) Übelkeit *f*

side 1. *n* Seite *f*; (*of road*) Rand *m*; (*of mountain*) Hang *m*; sport Mannschaft *f*; **by my** ~ neben mir; **side by side** nebeneinander **2.** *adj* (*door, entrance*) Seiten- *m* Anrichte *f*; **sideboards**, **sideburns** (*US*) *npl* Koteletten *pl*; **side dish** *n* Beilage *f*; **side effect** *n* Nebenwirkung *f*; **side order** *n* Beilage *f*; **side road** *n* Nebenstraße *f*; **side street** *n* Seitenstraße *f*; **sidewalk** *n* (*US*) Bürgersteig *m*; **sideways** *adv* seitwärts

sieve *n* Sieb *nt*

sift *vt* (*flour etc*) sieben

sigh *vi* seufzen

sight *n* (*power of seeing*) Sehvermögen nt; (view, thing seen) Anblick m; **~s** pl (of city etc) Sehenswürdigkeiten pl; **have bad ~** schlecht sehen; **lose~of** us der Augen verlieren; **out of ~** außer Sicht; **sightseeing** n **go~** Sehenswürdigkeiten besichtigen; **~ tour** Rundfahrt f

sign1. n Zeichen nt; (notice, road ~) Schild nt **2.** vt unterschreiben **3.** vi unterschreiben; **~ for sth** den Empfang einer Sache gen bestätigen; **~ in/out** sich ein-/austragen; **sign up** vi (for course) sich einschreiben; MIL sich verpflichten

signal1. n Signal nt **2.** vi (car driver) blinken

signature n Unterschrift f

significant adj (important) bedeutend, wichtig; (meaning sth) bedeutend

sign language n Zeichensprache f; **signpost** n Wegweiser m

silence1. n Stille f; (of person) Schweigen nt; **~!** Ruhe! **2.** vt zum Schweigen bringen; **silent** adj still; (taciturn) schweigsam; **she remained ~** sie schwieg

silk1. n Seide f **2.** adj Seiden-

silly adj dumm, albern; **don't do anything ~** mach keine Dummheiten

silver1. n Silber nt; (coins) Silbermünzen pl **2.** adj Silber-, silbern; **silver wedding** n sil-

berne Hochzeit

similar adj ähnlich (to dat); **similarity** n Ähnlichkeit f (to mit); **similarly** adv (equally) ebenso

simple adj einfach; (unsophisticated) schlicht; **simplify** vt vereinfachen; **simply** adv einfach; (merely) bloß; (dress) schlicht

simulate vt simulieren

simultaneous adj, adv gleichzeitig

since1. adv seitdem; (in the meantime) inzwischen **2.** prep seit + dat; **ever ~ 1995** schon seit 1995 **3.** conj (time) seit, seitdem; (because) da, weil; **ever ~ I've known her** seit ich sie kenne; **it's ages ~ I've seen him** ich habe ihn seit langem nicht mehr gesehen

sincere adj aufrichtig; **sincerely** adv aufrichtig; **Yours ~** mit freundlichen Grüßen

sing vt, vi singen

Singapore n Singapur nt

singer n Sänger(in) m(f)

single1. adj (one only) einzig; (not double) einfach; (bed, room) Einzel-; (unmarried) ledig; (Brit, ticket) einfach **2.** n (Brit, ticket) einfache Fahrkarte; mus Single f; **single out** vt (choose) auswählen; **single-handed single-handedly** adv im Alleingang; **single parent** n Alleinerziehende(r) mf

singular adj Singular m

sinister adj unheimlich

sink1. vt (ship) versenken **2.** vi sinken **3.** n Spülbecken nt; (in bathroom) Waschbecken nt

sip vt nippen an + dat

sir n ja; ~ ja(, mein Herr); **can I help you, ~?** kann ich Ihnen helfen?; **Sir James** (title) Sir James

sister n Schwester f (Brit, nurse) Oberschwester f; **sister-in-law** n Schwägerin f

sit1. vi (be sitting) sitzen; (~ down) sich setzen; (committee, court) tagen **2.** vt (Brit, exam) machen; **sit down** vi sich hinsetzen; **sit up** vi (from lying position) sich aufsetzen

site n Platz m; (building site) Baustelle f; (website) Site f

sitting n (meeting, for portrait) Sitzung f; **sitting room** n Wohnzimmer nt

situated adj **be** ~ liegen

situation n (circumstances) Situation f, Lage f; (job) Stelle f; **~s vacant/wanted** (Brit) „Stellenangebote/Stellengesuche"

six1. num sechs **2.** n Sechs f; → **eight**; **sixpack** n (of beer etc) Sechserpack m; **sixteen 1.** num sechzehn **2.** n Sechzehn f; → **eight**; **sixteenth** adj sechzehnte(r, s); →

eighth; **sixth1.** adj sechste(r, s); ~ form (Brit) ≈ Oberstufe f **2.** n (fraction) Sechstel nt; → **eighth**; **sixtieth** adj sechzigste(r, s); → **eighth**; **sixty1.** num sechzig; **~one** einundsechzig **2.** n Sechzig f; **be in one's sixties** in den Sechzigern sein; → **eight**

size n Größe f; **what ~ are you?** welche Größe haben Sie?; **a ~ too big** eine Nummer zu groß

sizzle vi brutzeln

skate 1. n Schlittschuh m; (roller skate) Rollschuh m **2.** vi Schlittschuh laufen; (roller-skate) Rollschuh laufen; **skateboard** n Skateboard nt; **skating** n Eislauf m; (roller-skate) Rollschuhlauf m; **skating rink** n Eisbahn f; (for roller-skating) Rollschuhbahn f

skeleton n Skelett nt

skeptical n (US) → **sceptical**

sketch 1. n Skizze f; THEAT Sketch m **2.** vt skizzieren

ski1. n Ski m **2.** vi Ski laufen; **ski boot** n Skistiefel m

skid vi AUTO schleudern

skier n Skiläufer(in) m(f); **skiing** n Skilaufen nt; **go ~** Ski laufen gehen; **~ holiday** Skiurlaub m; **skiing instructor** n Skilehrer(in) m

skilful, (US) **skillfully** adj, adv geschickt

ski-lift n Skilift m

skill n Geschick nt; (acquired

technique) Fertigkeit *f*;
skilled *adj* geschickt *(at, in
in + dat)*; *(worker)* Fach-;
(work) fachmännisch

skim *vi* ~ **(off)** *(fat etc)* ab-
schöpfen; ~ **(through)** *(read)*
überfliegen; **skimmed milk**
n Magermilch *f*

skin *n* Haut *f*; *(fur)* Fell *nt*;
(peel) Schale *f*; **skinny** *adj*
dünn

skip 1. *vi* hüpfen; *(with rope)*
Seil springen **2.** *vt (miss
out)* überspringen; *(meal)*
ausfallen lassen; *(school, lesson)* schwänzen

ski pants *npl* Skihose *f*; **ski
pass** *n* Skipass *m*; **ski pole**
n Skistock *m*; **ski resort** *n*
Skiort *m*

skirt *n* Rock *m*

ski run *n* (Ski)abfahrt *f*; **ski
stick** *n* Skistock *m*; **ski tow**
n Schlepplift *m*

skittle *n* Kegel *m*; **~s** *(game)*
Kegeln *nt*

skive *vi* ~ **(off)** *(Brit) fam* sich
drücken; *(from school)*
schwänzen; *(from work)*
blaumachen

skull *n* Schädel *m*

sky *n* Himmel *m*; **skydiving** *n*
Fallschirmspringen *nt*; **sky-
light** *n* Dachfenster *nt*; **skyscraper** *n* Wolkenkratzer *m*

slam *vt (door)* zuschlagen;
slam on *vt* **slam the brakes
on** voll auf die Bremse treten

slander 1. *n* Verleumdung *f* **2.**
vt verleumden

slang *n* Slang *m*

slap 1. *n* Klaps *m*; *(across face)*
Ohrfeige *f* **2.** *vt* schlagen; ~
sb's face jdn ohrfeigen

slash 1. *n (punctuation mark)*
Schrägstrich *m* **2.** *vt (face,
tyre)* aufschlitzen; *(prices)*
stark herabsetzen

slate *n (rock)* Schiefer *m*;
(roof slate) Schieferplatte *f*

slaughter *vt (animals)*
schlachten; *(people)* ab-
schlachten

Slav 1. *adj* slawisch **2.** *n* Slawe
m, Slawin *f*

slave *n* Sklave *m*, Sklavin *f*;
slave away *vi* schuften;
slave-driver *n fam* Sklaven-
treiber(in) *m(f)*; **slavery** *n*
Sklaverei *f*

sleaze *n (corruption)* Korrup-
tion *f*; **sleazy** *adj (bar, district)* zwielichtig

sledge *n* Schlitten *m*

sleep 1. *vi* schlafen **2.** *n* Schlaf
m; **put to ~** *(animal)* einschläfern; **sleep in** *vi (lie
in)* ausschlafen; **sleeper** *n*
RAIL *(train)* Schlafwagenzug
m; *(carriage)* Schlafwagen
m; **sleeping bag** *n* Schlafsack *m*; **sleeping car** *n*
Schlafwagen *m*; **sleeping
pill** *n* Schlaftablette *f*; **sleep-
less** *adj* schlaflos; **sleepy** *adj*
schläfrig; *(place)* verschlafen

sleet *n* Schneeregen *m*

sleeve *n* Ärmel *m*; **sleeveless**
adj ärmellos

sleigh *n* (Pferde)schlitten *m*

slurred

slender *adj* schlank; *fig* gering
slept *pt, pp of* **sleep**
slice 1. *n* Scheibe *f*; (*of cake, tart, pizza*) Stück *nt* **2.** *vt* ~ (**up**) in Scheiben schneiden
slid *pt, pp of* **slide**
slide 1. *vt* gleiten lassen; (*push*) schieben **2.** *vi* gleiten; (*slip*) rutschen **3.** *n* PHOT Dia *nt*; (*in playground*) Rutschbahn *f*; (*Brit, for hair*) Spange *f*
slight *adj* leicht; (*problem, difference*) klein; **not in the ~est** nicht im Geringsten; **slightly** *adv* etwas; (*injured*) leicht
slim 1. *vt* (*person*) schlank; (*book*) dünn; (*chance, hope*) gering **2.** *vi* abnehmen
slime *n* Schleim *m*; **slimy** *adj* schleimig
sling 1. *vt* werfen **2.** *n* (*for arm*) Schlinge *f*
slip 1. *n* (*mistake*) Flüchtigkeitsfehler *m*; **~ of paper** Zettel *m* **2.** *vt* (*put*) stecken; **~ on/off** (*garment*) an-/ausziehen; **it ~ped my mind** ich habe es vergessen **3.** *vi* (*lose balance*) ausrutschen
slipper *n* Hausschuh *m*; **slippery** *adj* (*path, road*) glatt; (*soap, fish*) glitschig; **slip-road***n* (*Brit, onto motorway*) Auffahrt *f*; (*off motorway*) Ausfahrt *f*
slit 1. *vt* aufschlitzen **2.** *n* Schlitz *m*
slope 1. *n* Neigung *f*; (*side of*

hill) Hang *m* **2.** *vi* (*be sloping*) schräg sein; **slope down** *vi* (*land, road*) abfallen; **sloping** *adj* (*floor, roof*) schräg
sloppy *adj* (*careless*) schlampig
slot *n* (*opening*) Schlitz *m*; IT Steckplatz *m*; **we have a ~ free at 2** (*free time*) um 2 ist noch ein Termin frei; **slot machine** *n* Automat *m*; (*for gambling*) Spielautomat *m*
Slovak 1. *adj* slowakisch **2.** *n* (*person*) Slowake *m*, Slowakin *f*; (*language*) Slowakisch *nt*; **Slovakia** *n* Slowakei *f*
Slovene, Slovenian 1. *adj* slowenisch **2.** *n* (*person*) Slowene *m*, Slowenin *f*; (*language*) Slowenisch *nt*; **Slovenia** *n* Slowenien *nt*
slow *adj* langsam; (*business*) flau; **be ~** (*clock*) nachgehen; (*stupid*) begriffsstutzig sein; **slow down** *vi* langsamer werden; (*when driving/walking*) langsamer fahren/gehen; **slowly** *adv* langsam; **slow motion** *n* **in ~** in Zeitlupe
slug *n* ZOOL Nacktschnecke *f*
slums *n* Slums *pl*
slump 1. *n* Rückgang *m* (*in an + dat*) **2.** *vi* (*onto chair etc*) sich fallen lassen; (*prices*) stürzen
slung *pt, pp of* **sling**
slur *n* (*insult*) Verleumdung *f*; **slurred** *adj* undeutlich

slush n (snow) Schneematsch m; **slushy** adj matschig; fig schmalzig

slut n pej Schlampe f

smack 1. n Klaps m **2.** vt ~ **sb** jdm einen Klaps geben

small adj klein; **small ads** npl (Brit) Kleinanzeigen pl; **small change** n Kleingeld nt; **small letters** npl in ~ in Kleinbuchstaben; **smallpox** n Pocken pl; **small print** n the ~ das Kleingedruckte; **small-scale** adj (map) in kleinem Maßstab; **small talk** n Konversation f, Smalltalk m

smart adj (elegant) schick; (clever) clever; **smart card** n Chipkarte f; **smartly** adv (dressed) schick

smash 1. n (car crash) Zusammenstoß m, Schmetterball m **2.** vt (break) zerschlagen; fig (record) brechen, deutlich übertreffen **3.** vi (break) zerbrechen; ~ **into** (car) krachen gegen; **smashing** adj fam toll

smear 1. n (mark) Fleck m; MED Abstrich m **2.** vt (spread) schmieren; (make dirty) beschmieren; fig verleumden

smell 1. vt riechen **2.** vi riechen (of nach) **3.** n Geruch m; (unpleasant) Gestank m; **smelly** adj übel riechend

smelt pt, pp of **smell**

smile 1. n Lächeln nt **2.** vi lächeln; ~ **at** jdn anlächeln

smog n Smog m

smoke 1. n Rauch m **2.** vt rauchen; (food) räuchern **3.** vi rauchen; **smoke alarm** n Rauchmelder m; **smoked** adj (food) geräuchert; **smoke-free** adj (zone, building) rauchfrei; **smoker** n Raucher(in) m(f); **smoking** n Rauchen nt; 'no ~' „Rauchen verboten"

smooth 1. adj glatt; (flight, crossing) ruhig; (movement) geschmeidig; (without problems) reibungslos; pej (person) aalglatt **2.** vt (hair, dress) glatt streichen; (surface) glätten; **smoothly** adv, reibungslos; **run ~** (engine) ruhig laufen

smudge n (writing, lipstick) verschmieren

smug adj selbstgefällig

smuggle vt schmuggeln; ~ **in/ out** herein-/herausschmuggeln

smutty adj (obscene) schmutzig

snack n Imbiss m; **have a ~** eine Kleinigkeit essen

snail n Schnecke f; **snail mail** n fam Schneckenpost f

snake n Schlange f

snap 1. n (photo) Schnappschuss m **2.** adj (decision) spontan **3.** vt (break) zerbrechen; (rope) zerreißen **4.** vi (break) brechen; (rope) reißen; (bite) schnappen (at nach); snap fastener n (US) Druckknopf m; snapshot n Schnappschuss m

snatch vt (grab) schnappen

sneak vi (move) schleichen; sneakers npl (US) Turnschuhe pl

sneeze vi niesen

sniff 1. vi schniefen; (smell) schnüffeln (at an + dat) 2. vt schnuppern an + dat; (glue) schnüffeln

snob n Snob m; snobbish adj versnobt

snog n küssen, vt knutschen

snooker n Snooker nt

snoop vi ~ (around) (herum-)schnüffeln

snooze n, vi (have a) ~ ein Nickerchen machen

snore vi schnarchen

snorkel n Schnorchel m; snorkelling n Schnorcheln nt

snout n Schnauze f

snow 1. n Schnee m 2. vi schneien; snowball n Schneeball m; snowboard n Snowboard nt; snowboarding n Snowboarding nt; snowdrift n Schneewehe f; snowflake n Schneeflocke f; snowman n Schneemann m; snowplough, snowplow (US) n Schneepflug m; snowstorm n Schneesturm m; snowy adj (region) schneereich; (landscape) verschneit

snug adj (person, place) gemütlich

snuggle up vi ~ to sb sich an jdn ankuscheln

so 1. adv so; ~ many/ much so viele/ viel; ~ do I ich auch; I hope ~ hoffentlich; 30 or ~ etwa 30; ~ what? na und?; and ~ on und so weiter 2. conj (therefore) also, deshalb

soak vt durchnässen; (leave in liquid) einweichen; I'm ~ed ich bin durchnässt; soaking adj ~ (wet) durchnässt

soap n Seife f; soap (opera) n Seifenoper f

sob vi schluchzen

sober adj nüchtern; sober up vi nüchtern werden

so-called adj so genannt

soccer n Fußball m

sociable adj gesellig

social adj sozial; (sociable) gesellig; socialist 1. adj sozialistisch 2. n Sozialist(in) m(f); socialize vi unter die Leute gehen; social security n (Brit) Sozialhilfe f; (US) Sozialversicherung f; society n Gesellschaft f; (club) Verein m

sock n Socke f

socket n ELEC Steckdose f

soda n (soda water) Soda f; (US, pop) Limo f

sofa n Sofa nt; sofa bed n Schlafcouch f

soft adj weich; (quiet) leise; (lighting) gedämpft; (kind) gutmütig; (weak) nachgiebig; **~ drink** alkoholfreies Getränk; **softly** adv sanft; (quietly) leise; **software** n rr Software f

soil n Erde f; (ground) Boden m

solar adj Sonnen-, Solar-

solarium n Solarium nt

sold pt, pp of **sell**

soldier n Soldat(in) m(f)

sole 1. n Sohle f; (fish) Seezunge f **2.** vt besohlen **3.** adj einzig; (owner, responsibility) alleinig; **solely** adv nur

solemn adj feierlich; (person) ernst

solicitor n (Brit) Rechtsanwalt m, Rechtsanwältin f

solid adj (hard) fest; (gold, oak etc) massiv; (solidly built) solide; (meal) kräftig; **three hours ~** drei volle Stunden

solitary adj einsam; (single) einzeln; **solitude** n Einsamkeit f

soluble adj löslich; (problem) lösbar; **solution** n Lösung f (to + gen); **solve** vt lösen

somber (US), **sombre** adj düster

some 1. adj etwas; (with plural nouns) einige; **~ woman (or other)** irgendeine Frau; **would you like ~ more (wine)?** möchten Sie noch etwas (Wein)? **2.** pron etwas; (plural) einige; **~ of the team** einige (aus) der Mannschaft **3.** adv **~ 50 people (or so)** et-

wa 50 Leute

somebody pron jemand; **~ (or other)** irgendjemand; **~ else** jemand anderes; **someday** adv irgendwann; **somehow** adv irgendwie; **someone** pron → **somebody**; **something 1.** pron etwas; **~ (or other)** irgendetwas; **~ else** etwas anderes; **~ nice** etwas Nettes; **would you like ~ to drink?** möchten Sie etwas trinken? **2.** adv **~ like 20** ungefähr 20; **sometime** adv irgendwann; **sometimes** adv manchmal; **somewhat** adv ein wenig; **somewhere** adv irgendwo; (to a place) irgendwohin; **~ else** irgendwo anders; (to another place) irgendwo anders hin; **~ around 6** ungefähr 6

son n Sohn m

song n Lied nt

son-in-law n Schwiegersohn m

soon adv bald; (early) früh; **too ~** zu früh; **as ~ as I ...** sobald ich ...; **as ~ as possible** so bald wie möglich; **sooner** adv (time) früher; (for preference) lieber

soot n Ruß m

soothe vt beruhigen; (pain) lindern

sophisticated adj (person) kultiviert; (machine) hoch entwickelt; (plan) ausgeklügelt

soppy adj fam rührselig

soprano n Sopran m

sore 1. adj **be ~** weh tun; **have a ~ throat** Halsschmerzen haben **2.** n wunde Stelle

sorrow n Kummer m

sorry adj (sight, figure) traurig; (I'm) (excusing) Entschuldigung!; **I'm ~** (regretful) es tut mir leid; **~?** wie bitte?; **I feel ~ for him** er tut mir leid

sort 1. n Art f; **what ~ of film is it?** was für ein Film ist das?; **a ~ of** eine Art + gen; **all ~s of things** alles Mögliche **2.** adv **~ of** irgendwie **3.** vt sortieren; **everything's ~ed** (dealt with) alles ist geregelt; **sort out** vt (classify etc) sortieren; (problems) lösen

sought pt, pp of **seek**

soul n Seele f

sound 1. adj (healthy) gesund; (safe) sicher; (sensible) vernünftig; (theory) stichhaltig; (thrashing) tüchtig **2.** adv **be ~ asleep** fest schlafen **3.** n (noise) Geräusch nt; MUS Klang m; TV Ton m **4.** vt **~ one's horn** hupen **5.** vi (seem) klingen (like wie); **soundcard** n IT Soundkarte f; **soundproof** adj schalldicht

soup n Suppe f

sour adj sauer; fig mürrisch

source n Quelle f; fig Ursprung m

sour cream n saure Sahne

south 1. n Süden m; **to the ~ of** südlich von **2.** adv (go, face) nach Süden **3.** adj Süd-; **South Africa** n Südafrika nt; **South African 1.** adj südafrikanisch **2.** n Südafrikaner(in) m(f); **South America** n Südamerika nt; **South American 1.** adj südamerikanisch **2.** n Südamerikaner(in) m(f); **southbound** adj (in) Richtung Süden; **southern** adj Süd-, südlich; **southwards** adv nach Süden

souvenir n Andenken nt (of an + acc)

sow 1. vt säen; (field) besäen **2.** n (pig) Sau f

soya bean n Sojabohne f

soy sauce n Sojasoße f

spa n (place) Kurort m

space n (room) Platz m, Raum m; (outer space) Weltraum m; (gap) Zwischenraum m; (for parking) Lücke f; **space bar** n Leertaste f; **spacecraft** n Raumschiff nt; **space shuttle** n Raumfähre f

spacing n (in text) Zeilenabstand m; **double ~** zweizeiliger Abstand

spacious adj geräumig

spade n Spaten m; **~s** Pik nt

spaghetti nsing Spaghetti pl

Spain n Spanien nt

spam n IT Spam m

Spaniard n Spanier(in) m(f); **Spanish 1.** adj spanisch **2.** n (language) Spanisch nt

spanner n (Brit) Schraubenschlüssel m
spare 1. adj (as replacement)
Ersatz-; **~ part** Ersatzteil
nt; **~ room** Gästezimmer
nt; **~ time** Freizeit f; **~ tyre**
Ersatzreifen m **2.** n (spare
part) Ersatzteil nt **3.** vt (lives,
feelings) verschonen; **can
you ~ (me) a moment?** hätten Sie einen Moment Zeit?
spark n Funke m; **sparkle** vi
funkeln; **sparkling wine** n
Schaumwein m, Sekt m;
spark plug n Zündkerze f
sparrow n Spatz m
sparse adj spärlich; **sparsely**
adv **~ populated** dünn besie-
delt
spasm n MED Krampf m
spat pt, pp of **spit**
speak vt sprechen; **can you
~ French?** sprechen Sie
Französisch?; **~ one's mind**
seine Meinung sagen **2.** vi
sprechen (to mit, zu); (make
speech) reden; **~ing** TEL am
Apparat; **so to ~** sozusagen;
speak up vi (louder) lauter
sprechen; **speaker** n Spre-
cher(in) m(f); (public speaker) Redner(in) m(f); (loudspeaker) Lautsprecher m
spear n Speer m
special 1. adj besondere(r, s),
speziell **2.** n (on menu) Tagesgericht nt; TV, RADIO Son-
dersendung f; **special delivery** n Eilzustellung f; **specialist** n Spezialist(in) m(f);

TECH Fachmann m, Fachfrau
f; MED Facharzt m, Fachärztin f; **speciality** n Spezialität
f; **specialize** vi sich spezialisieren (in auf + acc); **specially** adv besonders; (specifi-
cally) extra; **special offer** n
Sonderangebot nt; **specialty**
n (US) → **speciality**
species nsing Art f
specific adj spezifisch; (precise) genau; **specify** vt genau
angeben
specimen n (sample) Probe f;
(example) Exemplar nt
spectacle n Schauspiel nt
spectacles npl Brille f
spectacular adj spektaku-
lär
spectator n Zuschauer(in)
m(f)
sped pt, pp of **speed**
speech n (address) Rede f;
(faculty) Sprache f; **make a
~** eine Rede halten; **speech-
less** adj sprachlos (with vor
+ dat)
speed 1. vi rasen; **exceed ~
limit** zu schnell fahren **2.** n
Geschwindigkeit f; (of film)
Lichtempfindlichkeit f;
speed up 1. vt beschleunigen **2.** vi schneller werden/
fahren; **speedboat** n Renn-
boot nt; **speed bump** n Bo-
denschwelle f; **speed limit** n
Geschwindigkeitsbegren-
zung f; **speedometer** n Ta-
chometer m; **speed trap** n
Radarfalle f; **speedy** adj

schnell

spell 1. vt buchstabieren; **how do you ~ ...?** wie schreibt man ...? **2.** n (period) Weile f; **a cold/hot ~** (weather) ein Kälteeinbruch/eine Hitzewelle; (enchantment) Zauber m; **spellchecker** n IT Rechtschreibprüfung f; **spelling** n Rechtschreibung f; **~ mistake** Schreibfehler m

spelt pt, pp of **spell**

spend vt (money) ausgeben (on für); (time) verbringen

spent pt, pp of **spend**

sperm n Sperma nt

sphere n (globe) Kugel f; fig Sphäre f

spice n Gewürz nt; fig Würze f **2.** vt würzen; **spicy** adj würzig

spider n Spinne f

spike n (on railing etc) Spitze f; (on shoe, tyre) Spike m

spill vt verschütten

spin 1. vi (turn) sich drehen; (washing) schleudern; **my head is ~ning** mir dreht sich alles **2.** vt (turn) drehen; (coin) hochwerfen **3.** n (turn) Drehung f

spinach n Spinat m

spin-drier n Wäscheschleuder f

spine n Rückgrat nt; (of animal, plant) Stachel m; (of book) Rücken m

spiral 1. n Spirale f **2.** adj spiralförmig; **spiral staircase** n Wendeltreppe f

spire n Turmspitze f

spirit n (essence, soul) Geist m; (humour, mood) Stimmung f; (courage) Mut m; (verve) Elan m; **~s** pl (drinks) Spirituosen pl

spiritual adj geistig; REL geistlich

spit 1. vi spucken **2.** n (for roasting) (Brat)spieß m; (saliva) Spucke f; **spit out** vt ausspucken

spite n Boshaftigkeit f; **in ~ of** trotz + gen; **spiteful** adj boshaft

spitting image n **he's the ~ of you** er ist dir wie aus dem Gesicht geschnitten

splash 1. vt (person, object) bespritzen **2.** vi (liquid) spritzen; (play in water) planschen

splendid adj herrlich

splinter n Splitter m

split 1. vt (stone, wood) spalten; (share) teilen **2.** vi (stone, wood) sich spalten **3.** n (in stone, wood) Spalt m; (in clothing) Riss m; fig Spaltung f; **split up 1.** vi (couple) sich trennen **2.** vt (divide up) aufteilen; **split ends** npl (Haar)spliss m; **splitting** adj (headache) rasend

spoil 1. vt verderben; (child) verwöhnen **2.** vi (food) verderben

spoilt pt, pp of **spoil**

spoke 1. pt of **speak 2.** n Speiche f

spoken pp of **speak**

spokesperson n Sprecher(in) m(f)

sponge n (for washing) Schwamm m; **sponge cake** n Biskuitkuchen m

sponsor 1. n (of event, programme) Sponsor(in) m(f) 2. vt unterstützen; (event, programme) sponsern

spontaneous, spontaneously adj, adv spontan

spool n Spule f

spoon n Löffel m

sport n Sport m; **sports car** n Sportwagen m; **sports centre** n Sportzentrum nt; **sportsman** n Sportler m; **sportswear** n Sportkleidung f; **sportswoman** n Sportlerin f; **sporty** adj sportlich

spot 1. n (dot) Punkt m; (of paint, blood etc) Fleck m; (place) Stelle f; (pimple) Pickel m; **on the ~** vor Ort; (at once) auf der Stelle 2. vt (notice) entdecken; (difference) erkennen; **spotless** adj (clean) blitzsauber; **spotlight** n (lamp) Scheinwerfer m; **spotty** adj (pimply) pickelig

spouse n Gatte m, Gattin f

spout n Schnabel m

sprain vt **~ one's ankle** sich den Knöchel verstauchen

sprang pt of **spring**

spray 1. n (liquid in can) Spray nt or m; (spray can) Spraydose f 2. vt (plant, insects)

besprühen; (car) spritzen

spread 1. vt (open out) ausbreiten; (news, disease) verbreiten; (butter, jam) streichen 2. vi (news, disease, fire) sich verbreiten 3. n (of disease, religion etc) Verbreitung f; (for bread) Aufstrich m; **spreadsheet** n IT Tabellenkalkulation f

spring 1. vi (leap) springen 2. n (season) Frühling m; (coil) Feder f; (water) Quelle f; **springboard** n Sprungbrett nt; **spring onion** n (Brit) Frühlingszwiebel f; **spring roll** n (Brit) Frühlingsrolle f

sprinkle vt streuen; (liquid) sprengen; **~ sth with sth** etw mit etw bestreuen; **sprinkler** n (for lawn) Rasensprenger m; (for fire) Sprinkler m

sprint vi rennen; SPORT sprinten

sprout 1. n (of plant) Trieb m; (from seed) Keim m; (**Brussels**) **~s** pl Rosenkohl m 2. vi sprießen

sprung pp of **spring**

spun pt, pp of **spin**

spy 1. n Spion(in) m(f) 2. vi spionieren; **~ on sb** jdm nachspionieren

squad n SPORT Mannschaft f

square 1. n (shape) Quadrat nt; (open space) Platz m; (on chessboard etc)Feld $nt 2. adj (in shape) quadratisch; **2 ~ metres** 2 Quadratmeter;

2 metres ~ 2 Meter im Quadrat **3.** vt **3 ~d** 3 hoch 2

squash 1. n (drink) Fruchtsaftgetränk nt; SPORT Squash nt; (US, vegetable) Kürbis m **2.** vt zerquetschen

squeak vi (door, shoes etc) quietschen; (animal) quieken

squeal vi (person) kreischen (with vor + dat)

squeeze 1. vt drücken; (orange) auspressen **2.** vi **~ into the car** sich in den Wagen hineinzwängen

squid n Tintenfisch m

squirrel n Eichhörnchen nt

St 1. abbr = **saint**; St. **2.** abbr = **street**; Str.

stab vt (person) einstechen auf + acc; (to death) erstechen; **stabbing** adj (pain) stechend

stabilize 1. vt stabilisieren **2.** vi sich stabilisieren

stable 1. n Stall m **2.** adj stabil

stack 1. n (pile) Stapel m **2.** vt **~ (up)** (auf)stapeln

stadium n Stadion nt

staff n (personnel) Personal nt, Lehrkräfte pl

stag n Hirsch m; **stag night** n (Brit) Junggesellenabschied m

stage 1. n THEAT Bühne f; (of project, life etc) Stadium nt; (of journey) Etappe f; **at this ~** zu diesem Zeitpunkt **2.** vt THEAT aufführen, inszenieren; (demonstration) veran-

stalten

stagger 1. vi wanken **2.** vt (amaze) verblüffen; **staggering** adj (amazing) umwerfend; (amount, price) Schwindel erregend

stagnant adj (water) stehend; stagnate vi stagnieren

stain n Fleck m; **stained-glass window** n Buntglasfenster nt; **stainless steel** n rostfreier Stahl; **stain remover** n Fleck(en)entferner m

stair n (Treppen)stufe f; **~s** pl Treppe f; **staircase** n Treppe f

stake n (post) Pfahl m; (in betting) Einsatz m; FIN Anteil m (in an + dat); **be at ~** auf dem Spiel stehen

stale adj (bread) alt; (beer) schal

stalk 1. n Stiel m **2.** vt (wild animal) sich anpirschen an + acc; (person) nachstellen + dat

stall 1. n (in market) (Verkaufs)stand m; (in stable) Box f; **~s** pl THEAT Parkett nt **2.** vt (engine) abwürgen **3.** vi (driver) den Motor abwürgen; (car) stehen bleiben

stamina n Durchhaltevermögen nt

stammer vi, vt stottern

stamp 1. n (postage stamp) Briefmarke f; (for document) Stempel m **2.** vt (passport etc) stempeln; (mail) frankieren

stand 1. vi stehen; (as candidate) kandidieren **2.** vt (place) stellen; (endure) aushalten; **I can't~ her** ich kann sie nicht ausstehen **3.** n (stall) Stand m; (seats in stadium) Tribüne f; (for coats, bicycles) Ständer m; (for small objects) Gestell nt; **stand around** vi herumstehen; **stand by 1.** vi (be ready) sich bereithalten; (be inactive) danebenstehen **2.** vt (person) halten zu; (decision, promise) stehen zu; **stand for** vt (represent) stehen für; (tolerate) hinnehmen; **stand in for** vt einspringen für; **stand out** vi (be noticeable) auffallen; **stand up** vi (get up) aufstehen **2.** vt (girlfriend, boyfriend) versetzen; **stand up for** vt sich einsetzen für

standard 1. n (norm) Norm f; **~ of living** Lebensstandard m **2.** adj Standard-

standardize vt vereinheitlichen

stand-by 1. n (thing in reserve) Reserve f; **on ~** in Bereitschaft **2.** adj (flight, ticket) Standby-; **standing order** n (at bank) Dauerauftrag m; **standpoint** n Standpunkt m; **standstill** n Stillstand m; **come to a ~** stehen bleiben; fig zum Erliegen kommen

stank pt of **stink**

staple 1. n (for paper) Heft-

klammer f **2.** vt heften (to an + acc); **stapler** n Hefter m

star 1. n Stern m; (person) Star m **2.** vt **the film ~s Hugh Grant** der Film zeigt Hugh Grant in der Hauptrolle **3.** vi die Hauptrolle spielen

starch n Stärke f

stare vi starren; **~ at** anstarren

starfish n Seestern m

star sign n Sternzeichen nt

start 1. n (beginning) Anfang m, Beginn m; sport Start m; (lead) Vorsprung m; **from the~** von Anfang an **2.** vt anfangen; (car, engine) starten; (business, family) gründen; **~ to do sth, ~ doing sth** anfangen, etw zu tun **3.** vi (begin) anfangen; (car) anspringen; (on journey) aufbrechen; sport starten; (jump) zusammenfahren; **~ing from Monday** ab Montag; **start off 1.** n (discussion, process etc) anfangen, beginnen **2.** vi (begin) anfangen, beginnen; (on journey) aufbrechen; **start up 1.** n (in business) anfangen **2.** vt (car, engine) starten; (business) gründen; **starter** n (Brit, first course) Vorspeise f; auto Anlasser m; **starting point** n Ausgangspunkt m

startle vt erschrecken; **startling** adj überraschend

starve vi hungern; (to death) verhungern; **I'm ~ing** ich habe einen Riesenhunger

state 1. n (condition) Zustand m; POL Staat m; ~ **of health/ mind** Gesundheits-/Geisteszustand m; **the (United) States** die (Vereinigten) Staaten **2.** adj Staats-; (control, education) staatlich **3.** vt erklären; (facts, name etc) angeben; **stated** adj (fixed) festgesetzt; **statement** n (official declaration) Erklärung f; (to police) Aussage f; (from bank) Kontoauszug m; **state-of-the-art** adj hochmodern, auf dem neuesten Stand der Technik
static adj (unchanging) konstant
station 1. n (for trains, buses) Bahnhof m; (underground station) Station f; (police station, fire station) Wache f; TV, RADIO Sender m **2.** vt MIL stationieren
stationer's n ~ (shop) Schreibwarengeschäft nt; **stationery** n Schreibwaren pl
station wagon n (US) Kombiwagen m
statistics nsing (science) Statistik f; (figures) Statistiken pl
statue n Statue f
status n Status m; (prestige) Ansehen nt
stay 1. n Aufenthalt m **2.** vi bleiben; (with friends, in hotel) wohnen (with bei); ~ **the night** übernachten; **stay**

away vi wegbleiben; ~ **from sb** sich von jdm fern halten; **stay behind** vi zurückbleiben; (at work) länger bleiben; **stay in** vi (at home) zu Hause bleiben; **stay out** vi (not come home) wegbleiben; **stay up** vi (at night) aufbleiben
steady 1. adj (speed) gleichmäßig; (progress, increase) stetig; (job, income, girlfriend) fest; (worker) zuverlässig; (hand) ruhig; **they've been going ~ for two years** sie sind seit zwei Jahren fest zusammen **2.** vt (nerves) beruhigen
steak n Steak nt; (of fish) Filet nt
steal vt stehlen
steam 1. n Dampf m **2.** vt GASTR dämpfen; **steam up** vi (window) beschlagen; **steamer** n GASTR Dampfkochtopf m; (ship) Dampfer m
steel 1. n Stahl m **2.** adj Stahl-
steep adj steil
steeple n Kirchturm m
steer vt, vi steuern; (car, bike etc) lenken; **steering** n AUTO Lenkung f; **steering wheel** n Steuer nt, Lenkrad nt
stem n (of plant, glass) Stiel m
step 1. n Schritt m; (stair) Stufe f; (measure) Maßnahme f; ~ **by** ~ Schritt für Schritt **2.** vi treten; ~ **this way, please** hier entlang, bitte; **step**

down *vi (resign)* zurücktreten

stepbrother *n* Stiefbruder *m*; **stepchild** *n* Stiefkind *nt*; **stepfather** *n* Stiefvater *m*; **stepmother** *n* Stiefmutter *f*; **stepsister** *n* Stiefschwester *f*

stereo *n* **(system)** Stereoanlage *f*

sterile *adj* steril; **sterilize** *vt* sterilisieren

sterling *n* FIN das Pfund Sterling

stern 1. *adj* streng **2.** *n* Heck *nt*

stew *n* Eintopf *m*

steward *n (on plane, ship)* Steward *m*; **stewardess** *n* Stewardess *f*

stick 1. *vt (with glue etc)* kleben; *(pin etc)* stecken; *(fam (put)* tun **2.** *vi (get jammed)* klemmen; *(hold fast)* haften **3.** *n* Stock *m*; *(hockey stick)* Schläger *m*; *(of chalk)* Stück *nt*; *(of celery, rhubarb)* Stange *f*; **stick out** *vt* **stick one's tongue out (at sb)** (jdm) die Zunge herausstrecken **2.** *vi (protrude)* vorstehen; *(ears)* abstehen; *(be noticeable)* auffallen; **stick to** *vt (rules, plan etc)* sich halten an + *acc*; **sticker** *n* Aufkleber *m*; **sticky** *adj* klebrig; *(weather)* schwül; **~ label** Aufkleber *m*; **~ tape** Klebeband *nt*

stiff *adj* steif

stifle *vt (yawn etc, opposition)* unterdrücken; **stifling** *adj*

drückend

still 1. *adj* still; *(drink)* ohne Kohlensäure **2.** *adv (yet, even now)* (immer) noch; *(all the same)* immerhin; *(sit, stand)* still; **he ~ doesn't believe me** er glaubt mir immer noch nicht; **keep ~** halt still!; **bigger/better ~** noch größer/besser

stimulate *vt* anregen, stimulieren; **stimulating** *adj* anregend; **stimulus** *n (incentive)* Anreiz *m*

sting 1. *vt (wound with sting)* stechen **2.** *vi (eyes, ointment etc)* brennen **3.** *n (insect wound)* Stich *m*

stingy *adj fam* geizig

stink 1. *vi* stinken *(of nach)* **2.** *n* Gestank *m*

stir 1. *vt (mix)* (um)rühren; **stir up** *vt (mob)* aufhetzen; *(memories)* wachrufen; **~ trouble** Unruhe stiften; **stir-fry** *vt (unter Rühren)* kurz anbraten

stitch 1. *n (in sewing)* Stich *m*; *(in knitting)* Masche *f*; **have a ~ (pain)** Seitenstechen haben; **he had to have ~es** er musste genäht werden; **she had her ~es out** ihr wurden die Fäden gezogen; **be in ~es** *fam* sich kaputtlachen **2.** *vt (in sewing)* nähen; **stitch up** *vt (hole, wound)* nähen

stock 1. *n (supply)* Vorrat *m (of an + dat)*; *(of shop)* Bestand *m*; *(for soup etc)* Brühe *f*; **~s and shares** *pl* Aktien und Wertpapiere *pl*; **be in/ out of ~** vorrätig/nicht vorrätig sein; **take ~** Inventur machen; *fig* Bilanz ziehen **2.** *vt* (*keep in shop*) führen; stock up *vi* sich eindecken (*on, with* mit)

stockbroker *n* Börsenmakler(in) *m(f)*

stock cube *n* Brühwürfel *m*

stock exchange *n* Börse *f*

stocking *n* Strumpf *m*

stock market *n* Börse *f*

stole *pt of steal*, **stolen** *pp of steal*

stomach *n* Magen *m*; (*belly*) Bauch *m*; **on an empty ~** auf leeren Magen; **stomach-ache** *n* Magenschmerzen *pl*; **stomach upset** *n* Magenstimmung *f*

stone 1. *n* Stein *m*; (*seed*) Kern *m*, Stein *m*; (*weight*) *britische Gewichtseinheit* (*6,35 kg*) **2.** *adj* Stein-, aus Stein

stony *adj* (*ground*) steinig

stood *pt, pp of stand*

stool *n* Hocker *m*

stop 1. *n* Halt *m*; (*for bus, tram, train*) Haltestelle *f*; **come to a ~** anhalten **2.** *vt* (*vehicle, passer-by*) anhalten; (*put an end to*) ein Ende machen + *dat*; (*cease*) aufhören mit; (*prevent from happening*) verhindern; (*bleeding*) stillen; (*engine, machine*) abstellen; (*payments*)

einstellen; (*cheque*) sperren; **~ doing sth** aufhören, etw zu tun; **~ sb (from) doing sth** jdn daran hindern, etw zu tun; **~ it** hör auf (damit)! **3.** *vi* (*vehicle*) anhalten; (*during journey*) halten; (*pedestrian, clock, heart*) stehen bleiben; (*rain, noise*) aufhören; (*stay*) bleiben; **stop by** *vi* vorbeischauen; **stop over** *vi* Halt machen; (*overnight*) übernachten; **stopover** *n* (*on journey*) Zwischenstation *f*; **stopper** *n* Stöpsel *m*; **stop sign** *n* Stoppschild *nt*; **stopwatch** *n* Stoppuhr *f*

storage *n* Lagerung *f*; **store 1.** *n* (*supply*) Vorrat *m* (*of* an + *dat*); (*place for storage*) Lager *nt*; (*large shop*) Kaufhaus *nt*; (*US, shop*) Geschäft *nt* **2.** *vt* lagern; IT speichern; **storeroom** *n* Lagerraum *m*

storey *n* (*Brit*) Stock *m*, Stockwerk *nt*

storm 1. *n* Sturm *m*; (*thunderstorm*) Gewitter *nt* **2.** *vt, vi* (*with movement*) stürmen; **stormy** *adj* stürmisch

story *n* Geschichte *f*; (*plot*) Handlung *f*; (*US, of building*) Stock *m*, Stockwerk *nt*

stout *adj* (*fat*) korpulent; (*shoes*) fest

stove *n* Herd *m*; (*for heating*) Ofen *m*

stow *vt* verstauen; **stowaway** *n* blinder Passagier

straight 1. *adj* (*not curved*) ge-

rade; (hair) glatt; (honest)
ehrlich (with zu); fam (heterosexual) hetero **2.** adv (directly) direkt; (immediately)
sofort; (drink) pur; (think)
klar; **~ ahead** geradeaus;
go ~ on geradeaus weiter-
gehen/weiterfahren; **straightaway** adv sofort; **straightforward** adj einfach; (person) aufrichtig

strain 1. n Belastung f **2.** vt
(eyes) überanstrengen;
(rope, relationship) belasten;
(vegetables) abgießen; **~ a
muscle** sich einen Muskel
zerren; **strained** adj (relations) gespannt; **~ muscle**
Muskelzerrung f; **strainer** n
Sieb nt

strand 1. n (of wool) Faden m;
(of hair) Strähne f **2.** vt **be
(left) ~ed** (person) festsitzen

strange adj seltsam; (unfamiliar) fremd; **strangely**
adv seltsam; **~ enough** selt-
samerweise; **stranger** n
Fremde(r) mf

strangle vt (kill) erdrosseln

strap 1. n Riemen m; (on dress
etc) Träger m; (on watch)
Band n **2.** vt (fasten) fest-
schnallen (to an + dat);
strapless adj trägerlos

strategy n Strategie f

straw n Stroh nt; (drinking ~)
Strohhalm m

strawberry n Erdbeere f

stray 1. n streunendes Tier **2.**
adj (cat, dog) streunend **3.** vi

streunen

streak n (of colour, dirt) Streifen m; (in hair) Strähne f; (in
character) Zug m

stream 1. n (flow of liquid)
Strom m; (brook) Bach m **2.**
vi strömen

street n Straße f; **streetcar** n
(US) Straßenbahn f; **street
lamp**, **street light** n Straßen-
laterne f; **street map** n
Stadtplan m

strength n Kraft f, Stärke f;
strengthen vt verstärken;
fig stärken

strenuous adj anstrengend

stress 1. n Stress m; (on word)
Betonung f **2.** vt betonen;
(put under stress) stressen;
stressed adj **~ (out)** gestresst

stretch 1. n (of land) Stück nt;
(of road) Strecke f **2.** vt (material, shoes) dehnen; (rope,
canvas) spannen; (person in
job etc) fordern; **~ one's legs**
(walk) sich die Beine vertreten **3.** vi (person) sich strecken; (area) sich erstrecken
(to bis zu); **stretch out 1.** vt
ausstrecken **2.** vi (reach) sich
strecken; (lie down) sich ausstrecken; **stretcher** n Trag-
bahre f

strict, **strictly** adj, adv (se-
vere(ly)) streng; (exact(ly))
genau

strike 1. vt (match) anzünden;
(hit) schlagen; (find) finden;
it struck me as strange es
kam mir seltsam vor **2.** vi

stun

(*stop work*) streiken; (*attack*) zuschlagen; (*clock*) schlagen **3.** n (*by workers*) Streik m; **be on ~** streiken; **strike up** vt (*conversation*) anfangen; (*friendship*) schließen; **striking** adj auffallend; (*resemblance*) verblüffend

string n (*for tying*) Schnur f; MUS, TENNIS Saite f; **the ~s** pl (*section of orchestra*) die Streicher pl

strip 1. n Streifen m; (*Brit, of soccer player*) Trikot nt **2.** vt (*undress*) ausziehen **3.** vi (*undress*) sich ausziehen, strippen

stripe n Streifen m; **striped** adj gestreift

stripper n Stripper(in) m(f); (*paint stripper*) Farbentferner m

strive vi **~ to do sth** bemüht sein, etw zu tun; **~ for sth** nach etw streben

stroke n MED, TENNIS etc Schlag m; (*of pen, brush*) Strich m **2.** vt streicheln

stroll 1. n Spaziergang m **2.** vi spazieren; **stroller** n (*US, for baby*) Buggy m

strong adj stark; (*healthy*) robust; (*wall, table*) stabil; (*shoes*) fest; (*influence, chance*) groß; **strongly** adv stark; (*believe*) fest; (*constructed*) stabil

strove pt of **strive**

struck pt, pp of **strike**

structural, **structurally** adj

strukturell; **structure** n Struktur f; (*building, bridge*) Konstruktion f, Bau m

struggle 1. n Kampf m (*for* um) **2.** vi (*fight*) kämpfen (*for* um); (*do sth with difficulty*) sich abmühen; **~ to do sth** sich abmühen, etw zu tun

stub 1. n (*of cigarette*) Kippe f; (*of ticket, cheque*) Abschnitt m

stubble n Stoppeln pl

stubborn adj (*person*) stur

stuck 1. pt, pp of **stick 2.** adj **be ~** (*jammed*) klemmen; (*at a loss*) nicht mehr weiterwissen; **get ~** (*car in snow etc*) stecken bleiben

student n Student(in) m(f), Schüler(in) m(f)

studio n Studio nt

study 1. n (*investigation*) Untersuchung f; (*studying*) Studium nt; (*room*) Arbeitszimmer nt **2.** vt, vi studieren; **~ for an exam** sich auf eine Prüfung vorbereiten

stuff 1. n Zeug nt, Sachen pl **2.** vt (*push*) stopfen; (*room*) füllen; **~ oneself** fam sich voll stopfen; **stuffing** n GASTR Füllung f

stuffy adj (*room*) stickig; (*person*) spießig

stumble vi stolpern; (*when speaking*) stocken

stun vt (*shock*) fassungslos machen; **I was ~ned** ich war fassungslos (*or* völlig überrascht)

stung pt, pp of **sting**

stunk pp of **stink**

stunning adj (marvellous) fantastisch; (beautiful) atemberaubend; (very surprising, shocking) überwältigend; unfassbar

stupid adj dumm; **stupidity** n Dummheit f

sturdy adj robust; (building, car) stabil

stutter vi, vt stottern

stye n MED Gerstenkorn nt

style 1. n Stil m **2.** vt (hair) stylen; **styling mousse** n Schaumfestiger m; **stylish** adj elegant

subconscious 1. adj unterbewusst **2.** n **the** ~ das Unterbewusstsein

subject 1. n (topic) Thema nt; (in school) Fach nt; (citizen) Staatsangehörige(r) mf; (of kingdom) Untertan(in) m(f); LING Subjekt nt; **change the** ~ das Thema wechseln **2.** adj **be** ~ **to** (dependent on) abhängen von; (under control of) unterworfen sein + dat

subjective adj subjektiv

sublet irr vt untervermieten (to an + acc)

submarine n U-Boot nt

submerge 1. vt (put in water) eintauchen **2.** vi tauchen

submit 1. vt (application, claim) einreichen **2.** vi (surrender) sich ergeben

subordinate 1. adj unterge-

ordnet (to + dat) **2.** n Untergebene(r) mf

subscribe vi ~ **to** (magazine etc) abonnieren; **subscription** n (to magazine etc) Abonnement nt; (to club etc) (Mitglieds)beitrag m

subsequent adj nach(folgend); **subsequently** adv später, anschließend

subside vi (floods) zurückgehen; (storm) sich legen; (building) sich senken

substance n Substanz f

substantial adj beträchtlich; (improvement) wesentlich; (meal) reichhaltig

substitute 1. n Ersatz m; SPORT Ersatzspieler(in) m(f) **2.** vt ~ **A for B** B durch A ersetzen

subtitle n Untertitel m

subtle adj (difference, taste) fein; (plan) raffiniert

subtract vt abziehen (from von)

suburb n Vorort m; **suburban** adj vorstädtisch, Vorstadt-

subway n (Brit) Unterführung f; (US) RAIL U-Bahn f

succeed 1. vi erfolgreich sein; **he** ~**ed (in doing it)** es gelang ihm(, es zu tun) **2.** vt nachfolgen + dat; **succeeding** adj nachfolgend; **success** n Erfolg m; **successful** adj, adv erfolgreich

successive adj aufeinander folgend; **successor** n Nachfolger(in) *m(f)*

such **1.** *adj* solche(r, s); **~ a book** so ein Buch, ein solches Buch; *it was ~ a success that ...* es war solch ein Erfolg, dass ...; **~ as** wie **2.** *adv* so; **~ a hot day** so ein heißer Tag **3.** *pron* **as ~** als solche(r, s); **suchlike 1.** *adj* derartig **2.** *pron* dergleichen

suck *vt* (*toffee etc*) lutschen; (*liquid*) saugen; *it ~s* fam das ist beschissen

Sudan *n* (*the*) ~ der Sudan

sudden *adj* plötzlich; *all of a ~* ganz plötzlich; **suddenly** *adv* plötzlich

sue *vt* verklagen

suede *n* Wildleder *nt*

suffer **1.** *vt* erleiden **2.** *vi* leiden; **~ from** MED leiden an + *dat*

sufficient, sufficiently *adj, adv* ausreichend

suffocate *vt, vi* ersticken

sugar **1.** *n* Zucker *m* **2.** *vt* zuckern; **sugary** *adj* (*sweet*) süß

suggest *vt* vorschlagen; (*imply*) andeuten; *I ~ saying nothing* ich schlage vor, nichts zu sagen; **suggestion** *n* (*proposal*) Vorschlag *m*; **suggestive** *adj* vielsagend; (*sexually*) anzüglich

suicide *n* (*act*) Selbstmord *m*

suit **1.** *n* (*man's clothes*) Anzug *m*; (*lady's clothes*) Kostüm *nt*; (*cards*) Farbe *f* **2.** *vt* (*be*

convenient for) passen + *dat*; (*clothes, colour*) stehen + *dat*; (*climate, food*) bekommen + *dat*; **suitable** *adj* geeignet (*for* für)

suitcase *n* Koffer *m*

suite *n* (*of rooms*) Suite *f*; (*sofa and chairs*) Sitzgarnitur *f*

sulk *vi* schmollen; **sulky** *adj* eingeschnappt

sultana *n* (*raisin*) Sultanine *f*

sum *n* Summe *f*; (*money a.*) Betrag *m*; (*calculation*) Rechenaufgabe *f*

summarize *vt, vi* zusammenfassen; **summary** *n* Zusammenfassung *f*

summer *n* Sommer *m*; **summer camp** *n* (*US*) Ferienlager *nt*; **summertime** *n* **in** (*the*) ~ im Sommer

summit *n a.* POL Gipfel *m*

summon *vt* (*doctor, fire brigade etc*) rufen; (*to one's office*) zitieren; **summon up** (*courage, strength*) zusammennehmen

summons *nsing* LAW Vorladung *f*

sumptuous *adj* luxuriös; (*meal*) üppig

sun **1.** *n* Sonne *f* **2.** *vt* **~ oneself** sich sonnen

Sun *abbr* = **Sunday**; So.

sunbathe *vi* sich sonnen; **sunbed** *n* Sonnenbank *f*; **sunblock** *n* Sunblocker *m*; **sunburn** *n* Sonnenbrand *m*; **sunburnt** *adj* **be/ get ~** einen Sonnenbrand haben /

bekommen

sundae *n* Eisbecher *m*

Sunday *n* Sonntag *m*; → **Tuesday**

sung *pp of* **sing**

sunglasses *npl* Sonnenbrille *f*; **sunhat** *n* Sonnenhut *m*

sunk *pp of* **sink**

sunlamp *n* Höhensonne *f*; **sunlight** *n* Sonnenlicht *nt*; **sunny** *adj* sonnig; **sun protection factor** *n* Lichtschutzfaktor *m*; **sunrise** *n* Sonnenaufgang *m*; **sunroof** *n* AUTO Schiebedach *nt*; **sunscreen** *n* Sonnenschutzmittel *nt*; **sunset** *n* Sonnenuntergang *m*; **sunshade** *n* Sonnenschirm *m*; **sunshine** *n* Sonnenschein *m*; **sunstroke** *n* Sonnenstich *m*; **suntan** *n* (Sonnen)bräune *f*; **~ lotion** (or **oil**) Sonnenöl *nt*

super *adj fam* toll

superb, superbly *adj, adv* ausgezeichnet

superficial, superficially *adj, adv* oberflächlich

superfluous *adj* überflüssig

superior 1. *adj* (*better*) besser (*to* als); (*higher in rank*) höher gestellt (*to* als), höher **2.** *n* (*in rank*) Vorgesetzte(r) *mf*

supermarket *n* Supermarkt *m*

supersonic *adj* Überschall-

superstitious *adj* abergläubisch

supervise *vt* beaufsichtigen; **supervisor** *n* Aufsicht *f*; (*at*

university) Doktorvater *m*

supper *n* Abendessen *nt*; (*late-night snack*) Imbiss *m*

supplement 1. *n* (*extra payment*) Zuschlag *m*; (*of newspaper*) Beilage *f* **2.** *vt* ergänzen; **supplementary** *adj* zusätzlich

supplier *n* Lieferant(in) *m(f)*;

supply 1. *vt* (*deliver*) liefern; (*drinks, music etc*) sorgen für; **~ sb with sth** (*provide*) jdn mit etw versorgen **2.** *n* (*stock*) Vorrat *m* (*of* an + *dat*)

support 1. *n* Unterstützung *f*; TECH Stütze *f* **2.** *vt* (*hold up*) tragen, stützen; (*provide for*) ernähren, unterhalten; (*speak in favour of*) unterstützen; **he ~s Manchester United** er ist Manchester-United-Fan

suppose *vt* (*assume*) annehmen; **I ~ so** ich denke schon; **I ~ not** wahrscheinlich nicht; **you're not ~d to smoke here** du darfst hier nicht rauchen; **supposedly** *adv* angeblich

suppress *vt* unterdrücken

surcharge *n* Zuschlag *m*

sure 1. *adj* sicher; **I'm (not) ~** ich bin mir (nicht) sicher; **make ~ you lock up** vergiss nicht abzuschließen **2.** *adv* ~! klar!; **surely** *adv* ~ **you don't mean it?** das ist nicht dein Ernst, oder?

surf 1. *n* Brandung *f* **2.** *vi* SPORT surfen **3.** *vt* **~ the net** im Internet surfen

surface 1. *n* Oberfläche *f* **2.** *vi* auftauchen

surfboard *n* Surfbrett *nt*;

surfer *n* Surfer(in) *m(f)*;

surfing *n* Surfen *nt*

surgeon *n* Chirurg(in) *m(f)*;

surgery *n* (*operation*) Operation *f*; (*room*) Praxis *f*, Sprechzimmer *nt*; (*consulting time*) Sprechstunde *f*; **have ~** operiert werden

surname *n* Nachname *m*

surpass *vt* übertreffen

surprise 1. *n* Überraschung *f* **2.** *vt* überraschen; **surprising** *adj* überraschend; **surprisingly** *adv* überraschenderweise, erstaunlicherweise

surrender 1. *vi* sich ergeben (*to* + *dat*) **2.** *vt* (*weapon, passport*) abgeben

surround *vt* umgeben; (*stand all round*) umringen; **surrounding 1.** *adj* (*countryside*) umliegend **2.** *n* **~s** *pl* Umgebung *f*

survey 1. *n* (*opinion poll*) Umfrage *f*; (*of literature etc*) Überblick *m* (*of über* + *acc*); (*of land*) Vermessung *f* **2.** *vt* (*look out over*) überblicken; (*land*) vermessen

survive *vt, vi* überleben

suspect 1. *n* Verdächtige(r) *mf* **2.** *adj* verdächtig **3.** *vt* verdächtigen (*of* + *gen*); (*think likely*) vermuten

suspend *vt* (*from work*) suspendieren; (*payment*) vorübergehend einstellen; (*play-*

er) sperren; (*hang up*) aufhängen; **suspender** *n* (*Brit*) Strumpfhalter *m*; **~s** *pl* (*US, for trousers*) Hosenträger *pl*

suspense *n* Spannung *f*

suspicious *adj* misstrauisch (*of sb/sth* jdm/etw gegenüber); (*causing suspicion*) verdächtig

swallow 1. *n* (*bird*) Schwalbe *f* **2.** *vt, vi* schlucken

swam *pt of* **swim**

swamp *n* Sumpf *m*

swan *n* Schwan *m*

swap *vt, vi* tauschen; **~ sth for sth** etw gegen etw eintauschen

sway *vi* schwanken

swear *vi* (*promise*) schwören; (*curse*) fluchen; **~ at sb** jdn beschimpfen; **swear by** *vt* (*have faith in*) schwören auf + *acc*

sweat 1. *n* Schweiß *m* **2.** *vi* schwitzen; **sweater** *n* Pullover *m*; **sweaty** *adj* verschwitzt

swede *n* Steckrübe *f*

Swede *n* Schwede *m*, Schwedin *f*; **Sweden** *n* Schweden *nt*; **Swedish 1.** *adj* schwedisch **2.** *n* (*language*) Schwedisch *nt*

sweep *vt, vi* (*with brush*) kehren, fegen

sweet 1. *n* (*Brit, candy*) Bonbon *nt*; (*dessert*) Nachtisch *m* **2.** *adj* süß; (*kind*) lieb; **sweet-and-sour** *adj* süßsau

er; **sweetcorn** n Mais m;
sweeten vt (tea etc) süßen;
sweetener n (substance)
Süßstoff m

swell 1. vi ~ (**up**) (an)schwellen
2. adj (US) fam toll; swelling n MED Schwellung f

sweltering adj (heat) drückend

swept pt, pp of **sweep**

swift, swiftly adj, adv schnell

swim 1. vi schwimmen **2.** n **go
for a** ~ schwimmen gehen;
swimmer n Schwimmer(in)
m(f); swimming n Schwimmen nt; **go** ~ schwimmen gehen; **swimming cap** n (Brit)
Badekappe f; **swimming
costume** n (Brit) Badeanzug
m; **swimming pool** n
Schwimmbad nt; (private,
in hotel) Swimmingpool m;
swimming trunks npl (Brit)
Badehose f; **swimsuit** n Badeanzug m

swindle vt betrügen (out of
um)

swine n Schwein nt

swing 1. vt, vi (object) schwingen **2.** n (for child) Schaukel
f

swipe vt (credit card etc)
durchziehen; fam (steal)
klauen; **swipe card** n Magnetkarte f

Swiss 1. adj schweizerisch **2.** n
Schweizer(in) m(f)

vitch 1. n ELEC Schalter m **2.**
(change) wechseln; ~ **sth**
sth etw gegen etw eintau-

schen **3.** vi (change) wechseln (to zu); **switch off** vt abschalten, ausschalten;
switch on vt anschalten, einschalten; **switchboard** n TEL
Vermittlung f

Switzerland n die Schweiz

swivel 1. vi sich drehen **2.** vt
drehen

swollen 1. pp of **swell 2.** adj
MED geschwollen; (stomach)
aufgebläht

swop → **swap**

sword n Schwert nt

swore pt of **swear**

sworn pp of **swear**

swum pp of **swim**

swung pt, pp of **swing**

syllable n Silbe f

symbol n Symbol nt; **symbolic** adj symbolisch; **symbolize** vt symbolisieren

symmetrical adj symmetrisch

sympathetic adj mitfühlend;
(understanding) verständnisvoll; **sympathize** vi mitfühlen (with sb mit jdm); **sympathy** n Mitleid nt; (after
death) Beileid nt; (understanding) Verständnis nt

symphony n Sinfonie f

symptom n Symptom nt

synagogue n Synagoge f

synthetic adj (material) synthetisch

Syria n Syrien nt

syringe n Spritze f

system n System nt; **systematic** adj systematisch

T

tab n (*for hanging up coat etc*)
Aufhänger m; IT Tabulator
m; **pick up the ~** fam die
Rechnung übernehmen

table n Tisch m; (*list*) Tabelle
f; **~ of contents** Inhaltsver-
zeichnis nt; tablecloth n
Tischdecke f; tablespoon n
Servierlöffel m; (*in recipes*)
Esslöffel m

tablet n Tablette f

table tennis n Tischtennis nt;
table wine n Tafelwein m

tabloid n Boulevardzeitung f

taboo 1. n Tabu nt 2. adj tabu

tack n (*small nail*) Stift m; (*US,
thumbtack*) Reißzwecke f

tackle 1. n SPORT Angriff m;
(*equipment*) Ausrüstung f 2.
vt (*deal with*) in Angriff nehmen; SPORT angreifen; (*verbally*) zur Rede stellen
(*about* wegen)

tact n Takt m; tactful, tact-
fully adj, adv taktvoll; tac-
tic(s) n(pl) Taktik f; tact-
less, tactlessly adj, adv
taktlos

tag n (*label*) Schild nt; (*with
maker's name*) Etikett nt

tail n Schwanz m; **heads or
~s?** Kopf oder Zahl?; tail-
back n (*Brit*) Rückstau m;
taillight n AUTO Rücklicht nt

tailor n Schneider(in) m(f)

tailpipe n (*US*) AUTO Auspuffrohr nt

Taiwan n Taiwan nt

take vt nehmen; (*take along
with one*) mitnehmen; (*take
to a place*) bringen; (*list*)
abziehen (*from* von); (*capture: person*) fassen; (*gain,
obtain*) bekommen; FIN,
COMM einnehmen; (*train,
taxi*) nehmen, fahren mit;
(*trip, walk, holiday, exam,
course, photo*) machen;
(*bath*) nehmen; (*phone call*)
entgegennehmen; (*decision,
precautions*) treffen; (*risk*)
eingehen; (*advice, job*) annehmen; (*tablets*) nehmen;
(*heat, pain*) ertragen; (*react
to*) aufnehmen; **have room
for**) Platz haben für; **I'll ~ it
(*item in shop*)** ich nehme
es; **how long does it ~?**
wie lange dauert es?; **it ~s
4 hours** man braucht 4 Stunden; **I ~ it that ...** ich nehme
an, dass ...; **~ place** stattfinden; **take after** vt nachschlagen + dat; **take along** vt mitnehmen; **take apart** vt auseinander nehmen; **take away**
vt (*remove*) wegnehmen
(*from sb* jdm); (*subtract*) abziehen (*from* von); **take back**
vt (*return*) zurückbringen;
(*retract*) zurücknehmen;
take down vt (*picture, cur-

tains) abnehmen; (write down) aufschreiben; **take in** vt (understand) begreifen; (give accommodation to) aufnehmen; (deceive) hereinlegen; (include) einschließen; (show, film etc) mitnehmen; **take off 1.** vi (plane) starten **2.** vt (clothing) ausziehen; (hat, lid) abnehmen; (deduct) abziehen; **take a day off** sich einen Tag freinehmen; **take on** vt (undertake) übernehmen; (employ) einstellen; SPORT antreten gegen; **take out** vt (wallet etc) herausnehmen; (person, dog) ausführen; (insurance) abschließen; (money from bank) abheben; (book from library) ausleihen; **take over 1.** vt übernehmen **2.** vi **he took over (from me)** er hat mich abgelöst; **take to** vt **I've taken to her/it** ich mag sie/es; **doing sth** (begin) anfangen, etw zu tun; **take up** vt (carpet) hochnehmen; (space) einnehmen; (time) in Anspruch nehmen; (hobby) anfangen mit; (new job) antreten; (offer) annehmen

taken 1. pp of **take 2.** adj (seat) besetzt; **be ~ with** angetan sein von

takeoff n AVIAT Start m; **takeout** (US) → **takeaway**; **takeover** n COMM Übernahme f

tale n Geschichte f

talent n Talent nt; **talented** adj begabt

talk 1. n (conversation) Gespräch nt; (rumour) Gerede nt; (to audience) Vortrag m **2.** vi sprechen, reden; (have conversation) sich unterhalten; **~ to (or with) sb (about sth)** mit jdm (über etw acc) sprechen **3.** vt (language) sprechen; (nonsense) reden; (politics, business) reden über + acc; **~ sb into doing/ out of doing sth** jdn überreden/jdm ausreden, etw zu tun; **talk over** vt besprechen

talkative adj gesprächig

tall adj groß; (building, tree) hoch

tame 1. adj zahm **2.** vt (animal) zähmen

tampon n Tampon m

tan 1. n (on skin) (Sonnen-)bräune f; **get/have a ~** braun werden/sein **2.** vi braun werden

tangerine n Mandarine f

tango n Tango m

tank n Tank m; (for fish) Aquarium nt; MIL Panzer m

tanker n (ship) Tanker m; (vehicle) Tankwagen m

tanned adj (by sun) braun

Tanzania n Tansania nt

tap 1. n (for water) Hahn m **2.** vt, vi (strike) klopfen; **~ sb on the shoulder** jdm auf die Schulter klopfen; **tap-dance** vi steppen

tape 1. n (adhesive tape) Klebeband nt; (for tape recorder) Tonband nt; (cassette) Kassette f; (video) Video nt **2.** vt (record) aufnehmen;
tape up vt (parcel) zukleben; **tape measure** n Maßband nt; **tape recorder** n Tonbandgerät nt

tapestry n Wandteppich m

tap water n Leitungswasser nt

tar n Teer m

target n Ziel nt; (board) Zielscheibe f

tariff n (price list) Preisliste f; (tax) Zoll m

tart n (fruit tart) (Obst)kuchen m; (small) (Obst)törtchen nt; fam, pej (prostitute) Nutte f, Schlampe f

tartan n Schottenkaro m

tartar(e) sauce n Remouladensoße f

task n Aufgabe f; (duty) Pflicht f

Tasmania n Tasmanien nt

taste 1. n Geschmack m; (sense of taste) Geschmackssinn m; (small quantity) Kostprobe f; **it has a strange ~** es schmeckt komisch **2.** vt schmecken; (try) probieren **3.** vi (food) schmecken (of nach); **tasteful, tastefully** adj, adv geschmackvoll; **tasteless, tastelessly** adj, adv geschmacklos; **tasty** adj schmackhaft

taught pt, pp of **teach**

Taurus n ASTR Stier m

tax 1. n Steuer f (on auf + acc) **2.** vt besteuern; **taxation** n Besteuerung f; **tax bracket** n Steuerklasse f; **tax-free** adj steuerfrei

taxi 1. n Taxi nt **2.** vi (plane) rollen; **taxi rank** (Brit), **taxi stand** n Taxistand m

tax return n Steuererklärung f

tea n Tee m; (afternoon tea) ≈ Kaffee und Kuchen; (meal) frühes Abendessen; **teabag** n Teebeutel m; **tea break** n (Tee)pause f

teach 1. vt (person, subject) unterrichten; **~ sb (how) to dance** jdm das Tanzen beibringen **2.** vi unterrichten; **teacher** n Lehrer(in) m(f)

team n SPORT Mannschaft f, Team nt; **teamwork** n Teamarbeit f

teapot n Teekanne f

tear 1. n (in eye) Träne f

tear 1. vt zerreißen; **~ a muscle** sich einen Muskel zerren **2.** n (in material etc) Riss m; **tear down** vt (building) abreißen; **tear up** vt (paper) zerreißen

tearoom n Café, in dem in erster Linie Tee serviert wird

tease vt (person) necken (about wegen)

teaspoon n Teelöffel m; **tea towel** n Geschirrtuch nt

technical adj technisch; (knowledge, term, dictionary) Fach-; **technically** adv technisch; **technique** n

Technik *f*
techno *n* Techno *m*
technology *n* Technologie *f*
tedious *adj* langweilig
teen(age) *adj* (fashions etc)
Teenager-; teenager *n* Teenager *m*; teens *npl* **in one's ~** im Teenageralter
teeth *pl of* **tooth**
teetotal *adj* abstinent
telephone **1.** *n* Telefon *nt* **2.** *vi* telefonieren **3.** *vt* anrufen; telephone book *n* Telefonbuch *nt*; telephone booth, telephone box (Brit) *n* Telefonzelle *f*; telephone call *n* Telefonanruf *m*; telephone directory *n* Telefonbuch *nt*; telephone number *n* Telefonnummer *f*
telephoto lens *n* Teleobjektiv *nt*
telescope *n* Teleskop *nt*
television *n* Fernsehen *nt*; television set *n* Fernsehapparat *m*
tell *vt* (say, inform) sagen (sb sth jdm etw); (story) erzählen; (truth) sagen; (difference) erkennen; (reveal secret) verraten; **~ sb about sth** jdm von etw erzählen; **~ sth from sth** etw von etw unterscheiden **2.** *vi* (be sure) wissen; tell apart *vt* unterscheiden; tell off *vt* schimpfen
telling *adj* aufschlussreich
telly *n* (Brit) fam Glotze *f*; **on (the) ~** in der Glotze

temp **1.** *n* Aushilfskraft *f* **2.** *vi* als Aushilfskraft arbeiten
temper *n* (anger) Wut *f*; (mood) Laune *f*; **lose one's ~** die Beherrschung verlieren; temperamental *adj* (moody) launisch
temperature *n* Temperatur *f*; MED (high temperature) Fieber *nt*; **have a ~** Fieber haben
temple *n* Tempel *m*; ANAT Schläfe *f*
tempo *n* Tempo *nt*
temporarily *adv* vorübergehend; temporary *adj* vorübergehend; (road, building) provisorisch
tempt *vt* in Versuchung führen; temptation *n* Versuchung *f*; tempting *adj* verlockend
ten **1.** *num* zehn **2.** *n* Zehn *f*; → **eight**
tenant *n* Mieter(in) *m(f)*; (of land) Pächter(in) *m(f)*
tend *vi* **~ to do sth** (person) dazu neigen, etw zu tun; **~ towards** neigen zu; tendency *n* Tendenz *f*
tender *adj* (loving) zärtlich; (sore) empfindlich; (meat) zart
tendon *n* Sehne *f*
Tenerife *n* Teneriffa *f*
tenner *n* (Brit) fam (note) Zehnpfundschein *m*
tennis *n* Tennis *nt*; tennis court *n* Tennisplatz *m*; tennis racket *n* Tennisschläger *m*

thanks

tenor *n* Tenor *m*

tense *adj* angespannt; (*stretched tight*) gespannt; **tension** *n* Spannung *f*; (*strain*) Anspannung *f*

tent *n* Zelt *nt*

tenth **1.** *adj* zehnte(r, s) **2.** (*fraction*) Zehntel *nt*; → *eighth*

tent peg *n* Hering *m*; tent pole *n* Zeltstange *f*

term *n* (*in school, at university*) Trimester *nt*; (*expression*) Ausdruck *m*; **~s** *pl* (*conditions*) Bedingungen *pl*; *be on good ~s with sb* mit jdm gut auskommen; *come to ~s with sth* sich mit etw abfinden; *in the long/ short ~* langfristig/ kurzfristig; *in ~s of ...* was ... betrifft

terminal *n* **1.** (*bus terminal etc*) Endstation *f*; AVIAT Terminal *m*; IT Terminal *nt*; ELEC Pol *m* **2.** *adj* MED unheilbar; **terminally** *adv* (*ill*) unheilbar

terminate **1.** *vt* (*contract*) lösen; (*pregnancy*) abbrechen **2.** *vi* (*train, bus*) enden

terrace *n* (*of houses*) Häuserreihe *f*; (*in garden etc*) Terrasse *f*; **terraced** *adj* (*garden*) terrassenförmig angelegt; **terraced house** *n* (*Brit*) Reihenhaus *nt*

terrible *adj* schrecklich

terrific *adj* (*very good*) fantastisch

terrify *vt* erschrecken; *be terrified* schreckliche Angst ha-

ben (*of* vor + *dat*)

territory *n* Gebiet *nt*

terror *n* Schrecken *m*; POL Terror *m*; **terrorism** *n* Terrorismus *m*; **terrorist** *n* Terrorist(in) *m(f)*

test **1.** *n* Test *m*, Klassenarbeit *f*; (*driving test*) Prüfung *f*; *put to the ~* auf die Probe stellen **2.** *vt* testen, prüfen

Testament *n the Old/ New ~* das Alte/ Neue Testament

test-drive *vt* Probe fahren

testicle *n* Hoden *m*

testify *vi* LAW aussagen

test tube *n* Reagenzglas *nt*

tetanus *n* Tetanus *m*

text **1.** *n* Text *m*; (*of document*) Wortlaut *m*; (*sent by mobile phone*) SMS *f* **2.** *vt* (*message*) simsen, SMSen; *~ sb* jdm simsen, jdm eine SMS schicken; *I'll ~ it to you* ich schicke es dir per SMS

textbook *n* Lehrbuch *nt*

texting *n* SMS-Messaging *nt*; text message *n* SMS *f*

texture *n* Beschaffenheit *f*

Thailand *n* Thailand *nt*

Thames *n* Themse *f*

than *prep, conj* als; *bigger/ faster ~ me* größer/ schneller als ich

thank *vt* danken + *dat*; *~ you* danke; *~ you very much* vielen Dank; **thankful** *adj* dankbar; **thankfully** *adv* (*luckily*) zum Glück; **thanks** *adj* undankbar; **thanks** *npl* Dank *m*; *~ danke!*; *~ to* dank

+ *gen*

that 1. *adj* der/die/das; (*opposed to this*) jene(r, s); **who's ~ woman?** wer ist die Frau?; **I like ~ one** ich mag das da **2.** *pron* das; (*in relative clauses*) der/die/das, die *pl;* **~ is very good** das ist sehr gut; **the wine ~ I drank** der Wein, den ich getrunken habe; **~ is (to say)** das heißt **3.** *conj* dass; **I think ~ ...** ich denke, dass ... **4.** *adv* so; **~ good** so gut

that's *contr of* **that is; that has**

thaw 1. *vi* tauen; (*frozen food*) auftauen **2.** *vt* auftauen lassen

the *art* der/die/das, die *pl;* **Henry ~ Eighth** Heinrich der Achte; **by ~ hour** pro Stunde; **~ ... ~ better** je ..., desto besser

theater (*US*), **theatre** *n* Theater *nt;* (*for lectures etc*) Saal *m*

theft *n* Diebstahl *m*

their *adj* ihr; **they cleaned ~ teeth** sie putzten sich die Zähne; **someone has left ~ umbrella here** jemand hat seinen Schirm hier vergessen; **theirs** *pron* ihre(r, s); **it's ~** es gehört ihnen; **a friend of ~** ein Freund von ihnen; **someone has left ~ here** jemand hat seins hier liegen lassen

them *pron* (*direct object*) sie;

(*indirect object*) ihnen; **do you know ~?** kennst du sie?; **can you help ~?** kannst du ihnen helfen?; **it's ~** sie sind's; **if anyone has a problem you should help ~** wenn jemand ein Problem hat, solltest du ihm helfen

theme *n* Thema *nt;* MUS Motiv *nt;* **~ song** Titelmusik *f*

themselves *pron* sich; **they hurt ~** sie haben sich verletzt; **they ~ were not there** sie selbst waren nicht da; **they did it ~** sie haben es selbst gemacht; **(all) by ~** allein

then 1. *adv* (*at that time*) damals; (*next*) dann; (*therefore*) also; (*furthermore*) ferner; **from ~ on** von da an; **by ~** bis dahin **2.** *adj* damalig; **our ~ boss** unser damaliger Chef

theoretical, theoretically *adj, adv* theoretisch

theory *n* Theorie *f;* **in ~** theoretisch

therapy *n* Therapie *f*

there *adv* dort; (*to a place*) dorthin; **~ is/are** (*exists/exist*) es gibt; **it's over ~** es ist da drüben; **~ you are** (*when giving*) bitte schön; **thereabouts** *adv* (*approximately*) so ungefähr; **therefore** *adv* daher, deshalb

thermometer *n* Thermometer *nt*

Thermos® *n* ~ **(flask)** Thermosflasche® f

these *pron, adj* diese; **~ are not my books** das sind nicht meine Bücher

thesis *n (for PhD)* Doktorarbeit f

they *pron pl* sie; *(people in general)* man; *(unidentified person)* er/sie; **~ are rich** sie sind reich; **~ say that ...** man sagt, dass ...; **if anyone looks at this, ~ will see that ...** wenn jemand dies ansieht, wird er erkennen, dass ...

they'd *contr of* **they had; they would**

they'll *contr of* **they will; they shall**

they've *contr of* **they have**

thick *adj* dick; *(fog)* dicht; *(liquid)* dickflüssig; *fam (stupid)* dumm; **thicken** *vi (fog)* dichter werden; *(sauce)* dick werden

thief *n* Dieb(in) m(f)

thigh *n* Oberschenkel m

thimble *n* Fingerhut m

thin *adj* dünn

thing *n* Ding nt; *(affair)* Sache f; **how are you?** wie geht's?; **I can't see a ~** ich kann nichts sehen

think *vt, vi* denken; *(believe)* meinen; **I ~ so** ich denke schon; **I don't ~** ich glaube nicht; **think about** *vt* denken an + acc; *(reflect on)* nachdenken über + acc; *(have opinion of)* halten von; **think**

of *vt* denken an + acc; *(devise)* sich ausdenken; *(have opinion of)* halten von; *(remember)* sich erinnern an + acc; **think over** *vt* überdenken; **think up** *vt* sich ausdenken

third **1.** *adj* dritte(r, s) **2.** *n (fraction)* Drittel nt; *(in gear)* im dritten Gang; → **eighth**; **thirdly** *adv* drittens; **third-party insurance** *n* Haftpflichtversicherung f

thirst *n* Durst m *(for nach)*; **thirsty** *adj* **be ~** Durst haben

thirteen **1.** *num* dreizehn **2.** *n* Dreizehn f; → **eight**; **thirteenth** *adj* dreizehnte(r, s); → **eighth**; **thirtieth** *adj* dreißigste(r, s); → **eighth**; **thirty** **1.** *num* dreißig; **~one** einunddreißig **2.** *n* Dreißig f; **be in one's thirties** in den Dreißigern sein; → **eight**

this **1.** *adj* diese(r, s); **~ morning** heute Morgen **2.** *pron* das, dies; **~ is Mark** *(on the phone)* hier spricht Mark

thistle *n* Distel f

thorn *n* Dorn m, Stachel m

thorough *adj* gründlich; **thoroughly** *adv* gründlich; *(agree etc)* völlig

those **1.** *pron* die da, jene; **~ who** diejenigen, die **2.** *adj* die, jene

though **1.** *conj* obwohl; **as ~** als ob **2.** *adv* aber

thought **1.** *pt, pp of* **think 2.** *n* Gedanke m; *(thinking)*

Überlegung f; **thoughtful** adj (kind) rücksichtsvoll; (attentive) aufmerksam; (in Gedanken versunken) nachdenklich; **thoughtless** adj (unkind) rücksichtslos, gedankenlos

thousand num (one) ~, a ~ tausend; **five** ~ fünftausend; ~**s of** Tausende von

thrash vt (hit) verprügeln; (defeat) vernichtend schlagen

thread n Faden m 2. vt (needle) einfädeln; (beads) auffädeln

threat n Drohung f; (danger) Bedrohung f (to für); **threaten** vt bedrohen; **threatening** adj bedrohlich

three 1. num drei 2. n Drei f; → **eight**; **three-dimensional** adj dreidimensional; **three-quarters** npl drei Viertel pl

threshold n Schwelle f

threw pt of **throw**

thrifty adj sparsam

thrilled adj **be ~ (with sth)** sich (über etw acc) riesig freuen; **thrilling** adj aufregend

thrive vi gedeihen (on bei); (business) fig florieren

throat n Hals m, Kehle f

throbbing adj (pain, headache) pochend

thrombosis n Thrombose f

throne n Thron m

through 1. prep adv (time) während + gen; (because of) aus, durch; (US, up to and in-

cluding) bis 2. adv durch; **put sb ~** TEL jdn verbinden (to mit) 3. adj (ticket, train) durchgehend; ~ **flight** Direktflug m; **be ~ with sb/sth** mit jdm/etw fertig sein; **throughout** 1. prep (place) überall in + dat; (time) während + gen; ~ **the night** die ganze Nacht durch 2. adv überall; (time) die ganze Zeit

throw 1. vt werfen; (rider) abwerfen; (party) geben 2. n Wurf m; **throw away** vt wegwerfen; **throw in** vt (include) dazugeben; **throw out** vt (unwanted object) wegwerfen; (person) hinauswerfen (of aus); **throw up** vt, vi fam (vomit) sich übergeben

thrown pp of **throw**

thru (US) → **through**

thrush n Drossel f

thrust vt, vi (push) stoßen

thruway n (US) Schnellstraße f

thumb 1. n Daumen m 2. vt ~ **a lift** per Anhalter fahren; **thumbtack** n (US) Reißzwecke f

thunder 1. n Donner m 2. vi donnern; **thunderstorm** n Gewitter nt

Thur(s) abbr = **Thursday**; Do.

Thursday n Donnerstag m; → **Tuesday**

thus adv (in this way) so; (therefore) somit, also

thyme n Thymian m

Tibet n Tibet nt

tick 1. n (Brit, mark) Häkchen nt **2.** vt (name) abhaken; (box, answer) ankreuzen **3.** vi (clock) ticken

ticket n (for train, bus) (Fahr-)karte f; (plane ticket) Flugschein m, Ticket nt; (for theatre, match, museum etc) (Eintritts)karte f; (price ticket) (Preis)schild nt; (raffle ticket) Los nt; (for car park) Parkschein m; (for traffic offence) Strafzettel m; **ticket collector, ticket inspector** (Brit) n Fahrkartenkontrolleur(in) m(f); **ticket machine** n (for public transport) Fahrscheinautomat m; (in car park) Parkscheinautomat m; **ticket office** n RAIL Fahrkartenschalter m; THEAT Kasse f

tickle vt kitzeln; **ticklish** adj kitzlig

tide n Gezeiten pl; **the ~ is in/out** es ist Flut/Ebbe

tidy 1. adj ordentlich **2.** vt aufräumen; **tidy up** vt, vi aufräumen

tie 1. n (necktie) Krawatte f; SPORT Unentschieden nt; (bond) Bindung f **2.** vt (attach, do up) binden (to an + acc); (tie together) zusammenbinden; (knot) machen; **tie down** vt festbinden (to an + acc); fig binden; tie up vt (dog) anbinden; (parcel) verschnüren; (shoelace) bin-

den; (boat) festmachen

tiger n Tiger m

tight 1. adj (clothes) eng; (knot) fest (screw, lid) fest sitzend; (control, security measures) streng; (timewise) knapp; (schedule) eng **2.** adv (shut) fest; (pull) stramm; **hold ~** festhalten!; **tighten** vt (knot, rope, screw) anziehen; (belt) enger machen; (restrictions, control) verschärfen; **tights** npl (Brit) Strumpfhose f

tile n (on roof) Dachziegel m; (on wall, floor) Fliese f

till 1. n Kasse f **2.** prep, conj → **until**

tilt 1. vt kippen; (head) neigen **2.** vi sich neigen

time 1. n Zeit f; (occasion) Mal nt; MUS Takt m; **local ~** Ortszeit; **what ~ is it?, what's the ~?** wie spät ist es?, wie viel Uhr ist es?; **take one's ~ (over sth)** sich (bei etw) Zeit lassen; **have a good ~** Spaß haben; **in two weeks' ~** in zwei Wochen; **at ~s** manchmal; **at the same ~** gleichzeitig; **all the ~** die ganze Zeit; **by the ~ he ...** bis er ...; (in past) als er ...; **for the ~ being** vorläufig; **in ~** (not late) rechtzeitig; **on ~** pünktlich; **the first ~** das erste Mal; **this ~** diesmal; **five ~s six** fünf mal sechs; **four ~s a year** viermal im Jahr; **three**

at a ~ drei auf einmal **2.** *vt* (*with stopwatch*) stoppen; **you** ~**d that well** das hast du gut getimt; **time difference** *n* Zeitunterschied *m*; **timer** *n* Timer *m*; (*switch*) Schaltuhr *f*; **time-saving** *adj* Zeit sparend; **time switch** *n* Schaltuhr *f*; **timetable** *n* (*for public transport*) Fahrplan *m*; (*school*) Stundenplan *m*; **time zone** *n* Zeitzone *f*

timid *adj* ängstlich

timing *n* (*coordination*) Timing *nt*

tin *n* (*metal*) Blech *nt*; (*Brit, can*) Dose *f*; (*tinned*) in Alufolie *f*; **tinned** *adj* (*Brit*) aus der Dose; **tin opener** *n* (*Brit*) Dosenöffner *m*

tinsel *n* ≈ Lametta *nt*

tint *n* (*Farb*)ton *m*; (*in hair*) Tönung *f*; **tinted** *adj* getönt

tiny *adj* winzig

tip 1. *n* (*money*) Trinkgeld *nt*; (*hint*) Tipp *m*; (*end*) Spitze *f*; (*of cigarette*) Filter *m*; (*Brit, rubbish tip*) Müllkippe *f* **2.** *vt* (*waiter*) Trinkgeld geben + *dat*; **tip over** *vt, vi* (*overturn*) umkippen

tipsy *adj* beschwipst

tiptoe *n* **on** ~ auf Zehenspitzen

tire 1. *n* (*US*) → **tyre 2.** *vt* müde machen **3.** *vi* müde werden; **tired** *adj* müde; **be** ~ **of doing sth** es satt haben, etw zu tun; **tireless, tirelessly**

adv unermüdlich; **tiresome** *adj* lästig; **tiring** *adj* ermüdend

tissue *n* ANAT Gewebe *nt*; (*paper handkerchief*) Papier(taschen)tuch *nt*; **tissue paper** *n* Seidenpapier *nt*

tit *n* (*bird*) Meise *f*; *fam* (*breast*) Titte *f*

title *n* Titel *m*

to *prep* (*towards*) zu; (*with countries, towns*) nach; (*as far as*) bis; (*with infinitive of verb*) zu; ~ **Rome/ Switzerland** nach Rom/in die Schweiz; **I've been** ~ **London** ich war schon mal in London; **go** ~ **town/** ~ **the theatre** in die Stadt/ins Theater gehen; **from Monday** ~ **Thursday** von Montag bis Donnerstag; **he came** ~ **say sorry** er kam, um sich zu entschuldigen; **20 minutes** ~ **4** 20 Minuten vor 4; **they won by 4 goals** ~ **3** sie haben mit 4 zu 3 Toren gewonnen

toad *n* Kröte *f*; **toadstool** *n* Giftpilz *m*

toast 1. *n* (*bread, drink*) Toast *m*; **a piece** (*or slice*) **of** ~ eine Scheibe Toast; **propose a** ~ **to sb** einen Toast auf jdn ausbringen **2.** *vt* (*bread*) toasten; (*person*) trinken auf + *acc*; **toaster** *n* Toaster *m*

tobacco *n* Tabak *m*; **tobacconist's** *n* ~ (*shop*) Tabakladen *m*

toboggan *n* Schlitten *m*

today *adv* heute; **a week ~** heute in einer Woche; **~'s newspaper** die Zeitung von heute

toddler *n* Kleinkind *nt*

toe *n* Zehe *f*, Zeh *m*; **toenail** *n* Zehennagel *m*

toffee *n* (*sweet*) Karamellbonbon *nt*

tofu *n* Tofu *m*

together *adv* zusammen; **I tied them ~** ich habe sie zusammengebunden

toilet *n* Toilette *f*; **go to the ~** auf die Toilette gehen; **toilet bag** *n* Kulturbeutel *m*; **toilet paper** *n* Toilettenpapier *nt*; **toiletries** *npl* Toilettenartikel *pl*; **toilet roll** *n* Rolle *f* Toilettenpapier

token *n* Marke *f*; (*in casino*) Spielmarke *f*; (*voucher, gift token*) Gutschein *m*; (*sign*) Zeichen *nt*

Tokyo *n* Tokio *nt*

told *pt, pp of* **tell**

tolerant *adj* tolerant (*of* gegenüber); **tolerate** *vt* tolerieren; (*noise, pain, heat*) ertragen

toll *n* (*charge*) Gebühr *f*; **toll-free** *adj, adv* (*US*) TEL gebührenfrei; **toll road** *n* gebührenpflichtige Straße

tomato *n* Tomate *f*; **tomato juice** *n* Tomatensaft *m*; **tomato sauce** *n* Tomatensoße *f*; (*Brit, ketchup*) Tomatenket(s)chup *m* or *nt*

tomb *n* Grabmal *nt*; **tombstone** *n* Grabstein *m*

tomorrow *adv* morgen; **~ morning** morgen früh; **~ evening** morgen Abend; **the day after ~** übermorgen; **a week (from) ~/~ week** morgen in einer Woche

ton *n* (*Brit*) Tonne *f* (*1016 kg*); (*US*) Tonne *f* (*907 kg*); **~s of books** *fam* eine Menge Bücher

tone *n* Ton *m*; **toner** *n* (*for printer*) Toner *m*; **toner cartridge** *n* Tonerpatrone *f*

tongs *npl* Zange *f*; (*curling tongs*) Lockenstab *m*

tongue *n* Zunge *f*

tonic *n* MED Stärkungsmittel *nt*; **~ (water)** Tonic *nt*

tonight *adv* heute Abend; (*during night*) heute Nacht

tonsils *n* Mandeln *pl*; **tonsillitis** *n* Mandelentzündung *f*

too *adv* zu; (*also*) auch; **~ fast** zu schnell; **~ much / many** zu viel / viele; **me ~** ich auch; **she liked it ~** ihr gefiel es auch

took *pt of* **take**

tool *n* Werkzeug *nt*; **toolbar** *n* IT Symbolleiste *f*; **toolbox** *n* Werkzeugkasten *m*

tooth *n* Zahn *m*; **toothache** *n* Zahnschmerzen *pl*; **toothbrush** *n* Zahnbürste *f*; **toothpaste** *n* Zahnpasta *f*; **toothpick** *n* Zahnstocher *m*

top 1. *n* (*of tower, class, com-*

pany etc) Spitze *f*; *(of mountain)* Gipfel *m*; *(of tree)* Krone *f*; *(of street)* oberes Ende; *(of tube, pen)* Kappe *f*; *(of box)* Deckel *m*; *(of bikini)* Oberteil *nt*; *(sleeveless)* Top *nt*; **at the ~ of the page** oben auf der Seite; **at the ~ of the league** an der Spitze der Liga; **on ~** oben; **on ~ of** auf + *dat*; *(in addition to)* zusätzlich zu; **over the ~** übertrieben **2.** *adj (floor, shelf)* oberste(r, s); *(price, note)* höchste(r, s); *(best)* Spitzen-; *(pupil, school)* beste(r, s) **3.** *vt (exceed)* übersteigen; *(be better than)* übertreffen; *(league)* an erster Stelle liegen in + *dat*; **~ped with cream** mit Sahne obendrauf; **top up** *vt* auffüllen; **can I top you up?** darf ich dir nachschenken?

topic *n* Thema *nt*; **topical** *adj* aktuell

topless *adj, adv* oben ohne

topping *n (on top of pizza, ice-cream etc)* Belag *m*, Garnierung *f*

torch *n (Brit)* Taschenlampe *f*

tore *pt of* **tear**

torment *n* quälen

torn *pp of* **tear**

tornado *n* Tornado *m*

torrential *adj (rain)* sintflutartig

tortoise *n* Schildkröte *f*

torture 1. *n* Folter *f*; *fig* Qual *f* **2.** *vt* foltern

Tory *(Brit)* *n* Tory *m*, Konservative(r) *mf*

toss 1. *vt (throw)* werfen; *(salad)* anmachen; **~ a coin** eine Münze werfen **2.** *n* **I don't give a ~** *fam* es ist mir scheißegal

total 1. *n (of figures, money)* Gesamtsumme *f*; **a ~ of 30** insgesamt 30; **in ~** insgesamt **2.** *adj* total; *(sum etc)* Gesamt- **3.** *vt (amount to)* sich belaufen auf + *acc*; **totally** *adv* total

touch 1. *n (act of ~ing)* Berührung *f*; *(sense of ~)* Tastsinn *m*; *(trace)* Spur *f*; **be/keep in ~ with sb** mit jdm in Verbindung stehen/bleiben; **get in ~ with sb** sich mit jdm in Verbindung setzen **2.** *vt (feel)* berühren; *(emotionally)* bewegen; **touch on** *vt (topic)* berühren; **touchdown** *n* AVIAT Landung *f*; **touching** *adj (moving)* rührend; **touch screen** *n* Touchscreen *m*; **touchy** *adj* empfindlich, zickig

tough *adj* hart; *(material)* robust; *(meat)* zäh

tour 1. *n* Tour *f (of* durch); *(of town, building)* Rundgang *m (of* durch); *(of pop group etc)* Tournee *f* **2.** *vt* eine Tour / einen Rundgang / eine Tournee machen durch **3.** *vi (on holiday)* umherreisen; **tour guide** *n* Reiseleiter(in) *m(f)*

tourism *n* Tourismus *m*,

Fremdenverkehr m; **tourist** n Tourist(in) m(f); **tourist guide** n (book) Reiseführer m; (person) Fremdenführer(in) m(f); **tourist office** n Fremdenverkehrsamt nt

tournament n Turnier nt

tour operator n Reiseveranstalter m

tow vt abschleppen; (caravan, trailer) ziehen

towards prep – **me** mir entgegen, auf mich zu; **we walked ~ the station** wir gingen in Richtung Bahnhof; **my feelings ~ him** meine Gefühle ihm gegenüber

towel n Handtuch nt

tower n Turm m; **tower block** n (Brit) Hochhaus nt

town n Stadt f; **town center** (US), **town centre** n Stadtmitte f, Stadtzentrum nt; **town hall** n Rathaus nt

towrope n Abschleppseil nt; **tow truck** n (US) Abschleppwagen m

toxic adj giftig, Gift-

toy n Spielzeug nt; **toy with** vt spielen mit; **toyshop** n Spielwarengeschäft nt

trace 1. n Spur f; **without ~** spurlos **2.** vt (find) ausfindig machen; (draw) nachzeichnen; **tracing paper** n Pauspapier nt

track 1. n (mark) Spur f; (path) Weg m; RAIL Gleis nt; (on CD, record) Stück nt; **keep/lose ~ of sb/sth** jdn/etw im Auge behal-

ten/aus den Augen verlieren; **track down** vt ausfindig machen; **tracksuit** n Trainingsanzug m

tractor n Traktor m

trade 1. n (commerce) Handel m; (business) Geschäft m; (skilled job) Handwerk n **2.** vi handeln (in mit) **3.** vt (exchange) tauschen (for gegen); **trademark** n Warenzeichen nt; **tradesman** (shopkeeper) Geschäftsmann m; (workman) Handwerker m; **trade(s) union** n (Brit) Gewerkschaft f

tradition n Tradition f; **traditional, traditionally** adj, adv traditionell

traffic n Verkehr m; pej (trading) Handel m (in mit); **traffic circle** n (US) Kreisverkehr m; **traffic jam** n Stau m; **traffic lights** npl Verkehrsampel f; **traffic warden** n (Brit) ≈ Politesse f

tragedy n Tragödie f; **tragic** adj tragisch

trail 1. n Spur f; (path) Weg m **2.** vt (follow) verfolgen; (drag) schleppen; (drag behind) hinter sich herziehen; SPORT zurückliegen hinter + dat **3.** vi (hang loosely) schleifen; SPORT weit zurückliegen; **trailer** n Anhänger m; (US, caravan) Wohnwagen m; FILM Trailer m

train 1. n RAIL Zug m **2.** vt (teach) ausbilden; SPORT trainieren 3. *vi* SPORT trainieren; **~ as** (*or* **to be**) **a teacher** eine Ausbildung als Lehrer machen; **trained** *adj* (person, voice) ausgebildet; **trainee** *n* Auszubildende(r) *mf*; (academic, practical) Praktikant(in) *m(f)*; **trainer** *n* SPORT Trainer(in) *m(f)*; **~s** (Brit, shoes) Turnschuhe *pl*; **training** *n* Ausbildung *f*; SPORT Training *nt*; **train station** *n* Bahnhof *m*

tram *n* (Brit) Straßenbahn *f*

tramp *n* Landstreicher(in) *m(f)*

tranquillizer *n* Beruhigungsmittel *nt*

transaction *n* (piece of business) Geschäft *nt*

transatlantic *adj* transatlantisch; **~ flight** Transatlantikflug *m*

transfer 1. *n* (of money) Überweisung *f*; (US, ticket) Umsteigekarte *f* **2.** *vt* (money) überweisen (to sb an jdn); (patient) verlegen; (employee) versetzen; SPORT transferieren **3.** *vi* (on journey) umsteigen; **transferable** *adj* übertragbar

transform *vt* umwandeln; **transformation** *n* Umwandlung *f*

transfusion *n* Transfusion *f*

transistor *n* Transistor *m*

transition *n* Übergang *m* (from ... to von ... zu)

translate *vt, vi* übersetzen;

translation *n* Übersetzung *f*; **translator** *n* Übersetzer(in) *m(f)*

transmission *n* TV, RADIO Übertragung *f*; AUTO Getriebe *nt*

transparent *adj* durchsichtig

transplant MED **1.** *vt* transplantieren **2.** *n* (operation) Transplantation *f*

transport 1. *n* (of goods, people) Beförderung *f*; **public ~** öffentliche Verkehrsmittel *pl* **2.** *vt* befördern, transportieren; **transportation** *n* → **transport**

trap 1. *n* Falle *f* **2.** *vt* **be ~ped** (in snow, job etc) festsitzen

trash *n* (book, film etc) Schund *m*; (US, refuse) Abfall *m*; **trash can** *n* (US) Abfalleimer *m*; **trashy** *adj* (novel) Schund-

traumatic *adj* traumatisch

travel 1. *n* Reisen *nt* **2.** *vi* (journey) reisen **3.** *vt* (distance) zurücklegen; (country) bereisen; **travel agency** *n*, **travel agent** *n* (company) Reisebüro *nt*; **traveler** (US) → **traveller**; **traveler's check** (US) → **traveller's cheque** *n* Reisende(r) *mf*; **traveller's cheque** *n* (Brit) Reisescheck *m*

tray *n* Tablett *nt*; (for mail etc) Ablage *f*; (of printer, photocopier) Fach *nt*

tread *n* (on tyre) Profil *nt*; **tread on** *vt* treten auf + *acc*

treasure 1. n Schatz m **2.** vt schätzen

treat 1. n besondere Freude; **it's my ~** das geht auf meine Kosten **2.** vt behandeln; **~ sb (to sth)** jdn (zu etw) einladen; **~ oneself to sth** sich etw leisten; **treatment** n Behandlung f

treaty n Vertrag m

tree n Baum m

tremble vi zittern

tremendous adj gewaltig; fam (very good) toll

trench n Graben m

trend n Tendenz f; (fashion) Mode f, Trend m; **trendy** adj trendy

trespass vi **'no ~ing'** „Betreten verboten"

trial n LAW Prozess m; (test) Versuch m; **trial period** n (for employee) Probezeit f

triangle n Dreieck nt; MUS Triangel m; **triangular** adj dreieckig

tribe n Stamm m

trick 1. n Trick m; (mischief) Streich m **2.** vt hereinlegen

tricky adj (difficult) schwierig; (situation) heikel

trifle n Kleinigkeit f; (Brit) GASTR Trifle nt (Nachspeise aus Biskuit, Wackelpudding, Obst, Vanillesoße und Sahne)

trigger 1. n (of gun) Abzug m **2.** vt ~ (off) auslösen

trim 1. vt (hair, beard) nachschneiden; (nails) schneiden; (hedge) stutzen **2.** n just

a ~, please nur etwas nachschneiden, bitte; **trimmings** npl (decorations) Verzierungen pl; (extras) Zubehör nt; GASTR Beilagen pl

trip 1. n Reise f; (outing) Ausflug m **2.** vi stolpern (over über + acc)

triple 1. adj dreifach **2.** adv ~ **the price** dreimal so teuer **3.** vi sich verdreifachen; **triplets** npl Drillinge pl

tripod n Stativ nt

trite adj banal

triumph n Triumph m

trivial adj trivial

trod pt of **tread**

trodden pp of **tread**

trolley n (Brit, in shop) Einkaufswagen m; (for luggage) Kofferkuli m; (serving trolley) Teewagen m

trombone n Posaune f

troops npl MIL Truppen pl

trophy n Trophäe f

tropical adj tropisch

trouble 1. n (problems) Schwierigkeiten pl; (worry) Sorgen pl; (effort) Mühe f; (unrest) Unruhen pl; MED Beschwerden pl; **be in ~** in Schwierigkeiten sein; **get into ~** (with authority) Ärger bekommen; **make ~** Schwierigkeiten machen **2.** vt (worry) beunruhigen; (disturb) stören; **sorry to ~ you** ich muss dich leider kurz stören; **troubled** adj (worried) beunruhigt; **trouble-free** adj problemlos; **troublemaker** *n* Unruhestifter(in) *m(f)*; **troublesome** *adj* lästig

trousers *npl* Hose *f*; **trouser suit** *n* (*Brit*) Hosenanzug *m*

trout *n* Forelle *f*

truck *n* Lastwagen *m*; (*Brit*) RAIL Güterwagen *m*; **trucker** *n* (*US, driver*) Lastwagenfahrer(in) *m(f)*

true *adj* (*factually correct*) wahr; (*genuine*) echt; **come ~** wahr werden

truly *adv* wirklich; **Yours ~** (*in letter*) mit freundlichen Grüßen

trump *n* Trumpf *m*

trumpet *n* Trompete *f*

trunk *n* (*of tree*) Stamm *m*; ANAT Rumpf *m*; (*of elephant*) Rüssel *m*; (*piece of luggage*) Überseekoffer *m*; (*US*) AUTO Kofferraum *m*; **trunks** *npl* (*swimming*) Badehose *f*

trust **1.** *n* (*confidence*) Vertrauen *nt* (*in zu*) **2.** *vt* vertrauen + *dat*; **trusting** *adj* vertrauensvoll; **trustworthy** *adj* vertrauenswürdig

truth *n* Wahrheit *f*; **truthful** *adj* ehrlich; (*statement*) wahrheitsgemäß

try **1.** *n* Versuch *m* **2.** *vt* (*attempt*) versuchen; (*try out*) ausprobieren; (*sample*) probieren; LAW (*person*) vor Gericht stellen; (*courage, patience*) auf die Probe stellen **3.** *vi* versuchen; (*make effort*) sich bemühen; **try on**

vt (*clothes*) anprobieren; **try out** *vt* ausprobieren

T-shirt *n* T-Shirt *nt*

tub *n* (*for ice-cream, margarine*) Becher *m*

tube *n* (*pipe*) Rohr *nt*; (*of rubber, plastic*) Schlauch *m*; (*for toothpaste, glue etc*) Tube *f*; **the Tube** (*in London*) die U-Bahn; **tube station** *n* U-Bahn-Station *f*

tuck *vt* (*put*) stecken; **tuck in 1.** *vt* (*shirt*) in die Hose stecken; (*person*) zudecken **2.** *vi* (*eat*) zulangen

Tue(s) *abbr* = **Tuesday**; Di.

Tuesday *n* Dienstag *m*; **on ~** (*am*) Dienstag; **on ~s** dienstags; **this/last/next** ~ diesen/letzten/nächsten Dienstag; **(on) ~ morning/afternoon/evening** (*am*) Dienstag Morgen/Nachmittag/Abend; **every ~** jeden Dienstag; **a week on ~/~ week** Dienstag in einer Woche

tug **1.** *vt* ziehen **2.** *vi* ziehen (*at* an + *dat*)

tuition *n* Unterricht *m*; (*US, fees*) Studiengebühren *pl*; **~ fees** *pl* Studiengebühren *pl*

tulip *n* Tulpe *f*

tumble *vi* (*person, prices*) fallen; **tumble dryer** *n* Wäschetrockner *m*

tummy *n fam* Bauch *m*

tumor (*US*), **tumour** *n* Tumor *m*

tuna n Thunfisch m

tune 1. n Melodie f; **be in/out of ~** (instrument) gestimmt/verstimmt sein; (singer) richtig/falsch singen **2.** vt (instrument) stimmen; (radio) einstellen (to auf + acc)

Tunisia n Tunesien nt

tunnel n Tunnel m; (under road, railway) Unterführung f

turbulence n AVIAT Turbulenzen pl; **turbulent** adj stürmisch

Turk n Türke m, Türkin f

turkey n Truthahn m

Turkey n die Türkei; **Turkish 1.** adj türkisch **2.** n (language) Türkisch nt

turmoil n Aufruhr m

turn 1. n (rotation) Drehung f; (performance) Nummer f; **make a left ~** nach links abbiegen; **at the ~ of the century** um die Jahrhundertwende; **it's your ~** du bist dran; **in ~, by ~s** abwechselnd; **take ~s** sich abwechseln **2.** vt (wheel, key, screw) drehen; (to face other way) umdrehen; (corner) biegen um; (page) umblättern; (transform) verwandeln (into in + acc) **3.** vi (rotate) sich drehen; (to face other way) sich umdrehen; (change direction: driver, car) abbiegen; (become) werden; (weather) umschlagen; **~ into sth** (become) sich in etw acc verwandeln; **~ cold/green** kalt/grün werden; **~ left/right** links/rechts abbiegen; **turn away** vt (person) abweisen; **turn back 1.** vi (go back) umkehren; **turn down** vt (refuse) ablehnen; (radio, TV) leiser stellen; (heating) kleiner stellen **1.** vi abbiegen **2.** vt (switch off) ausschalten; (tap) zudrehen; (engine, electricity) abstellen; **turn on** vt (switch on) einschalten; (tap) aufdrehen; (engine, electricity) anstellen; fam (person) anmachen, antörnen; **turn out 1.** vt (light) ausmachen; (pockets) leeren **2.** vi (develop) sich entwickeln; **as it turned out** wie sich herausstellte; **turn over 1.** vt onto other side, umdrehen; (page) umblättern **2.** vi (person) sich umdrehen; (car) sich überschlagen; TV umschalten (to auf + acc); **turn round 1.** vt (to face other way) umdrehen **2.** vi (person) sich umdrehen; (go back) umkehren; **turn to** vi sich zuwenden + dat; **turn up 1.** vi (person, lost object) auftauchen **2.** vt (radio, TV) lauter stellen; (heating) höher stellen; **turning** n (in road) Abzweigung f; **turning point** n Wendepunkt m

turnip n Rübe f

turnover n FIN Umsatz m

turnpike n (US) gebühren-pflichtige Autobahn

turquoise adj türkis

turtle n (Brit) Wasserschildkröte f; (US) Schildkröte f

tutor n (private) Privatlehrer(in) m(f); (Brit, at university) Tutor(in) m(f)

tuxedo n (US) Smoking m

TV n Fernsehen nt; (~ set) Fernseher m; **watch** ~ fernsehen; **on** ~ im Fernsehen 2. adj Fernseh-; ~ **programme** Fernsehsendung f

tweed n Tweed m

tweezers npl Pinzette f

twelfth adj zwölfte(r, s); → **eighth**; **twelve** 1. num zwölf 2. n Zwölf f; → **eight**

twentieth adj zwanzigste(r, s); → **eighth**; **twenty** 1. num zwanzig; → **eight**. 2. n Zwanzig f; **be in one's twenties** in den Zwanzigern sein; → **eight**

twice adv zweimal; ~ **as much/many** doppelt so viel/viele

twig n Zweig m

twilight n (in evening) Dämmerung f

twin 1. n Zwilling m 2. adj

(brother etc) Zwillings-; ~ **beds** zwei Einzelbetten

twinkle vi funkeln

twin room n Zweibettzimmer nt; **twin town** n Partnerstadt f

twist vt (turn) drehen, winden; (distort) verdrehen; **I've ~ed my ankle** ich bin mit dem Fuß umgeknickt

two 1. num zwei; **break sth in** ~ etw in zwei Teile brechen 2. n Zwei f; **the** ~ **of them** die beiden; → **eight**; **two-dimensional** adj zweidimensional; fig oberflächlich; **two-piece** adj zweiteilig; **two-way** adj ~ **traffic** Gegenverkehr

type n (sort) Art f; (typeface) Schrift(art) f; **he's not my** ~ er ist nicht mein Typ; **typeface** n Schrift(art) f; **typewriter** n Schreibmaschine f

typhoid n Typhus m

typhoon n Taifun m

typical adj typisch (of für)

typing error n Tippfehler m

tyre n (Brit) Reifen m; **tyre pressure** n Reifendruck m

Tyrol n **the** ~ Tirol nt

U

UFO acr = **unidentified flying object**; Ufo nt

Uganda n Uganda nt

ugly adj hässlich; (bad)

schlimm

UHT adj abbr = **ultra-heat treated**; ~ **milk** H-Milch f

UK abbr = **United Kingdom**;

Vereinigtes Königreich *nt*

Ukraine *n* **the ~** die Ukraine

ulcer *n* Geschwür *nt*

ultimate *adj* (*final*) letzte(r, s); (*authority*) höchste(r, s); **ultimately** *adv* letzten Endes; (*eventually*) schließlich; **ultimatum** *n* Ultimatum *nt*

ultra- *pref* ultra-

ultrasound *n* MED Ultraschall *m*

umbrella *n* Schirm *m*

umpire *n* Schiedsrichter(in) *m(f)*

umpteen *num fam* zig; **~ times** zigmal

un- *pref* un-

UN *nsing abbr* = **United Nations**; UNO *f*

unable *adj* **be ~ to do sth** etw nicht tun können

unacceptable *adj* unannehmbar

unaccustomed *adj* **be ~ to sth** etw nicht gewohnt sein

unanimous, unanimously *adj, adv* einmütig

unattached *adj* (*without partner*) ungebunden

unattended *adj* (*luggage, car*) unbeaufsichtigt

unauthorized *adj* unbefugt

unavailable *adj* nicht erhältlich; (*person*) nicht erreichbar

unavoidable *adj* unvermeidlich

unaware *adj* **be ~ of sth** sich einer Sache *gen* nicht bewusst sein; **I was ~ that ...** ich wusste nicht, dass ...

unbalanced *adj* unausgewogen

unbearable *adj* unerträglich

unbeatable *adj* unschlagbar

unbelievable *adj* unglaublich

uncertain *adj* unsicher

uncle *n* Onkel *m*

uncomfortable *adj* unbequem

unconditional *adj* bedingungslos

unconscious *adj* MED bewusstlos; **be ~ of sth** sich einer Sache *gen* nicht bewusst sein; **unconsciously** *adv* unbewusst

uncover *vt* aufdecken

undecided *adj* unschlüssig

undeniable *adj* unbestreitbar

under 1. *prep* (*beneath*) unter + *dat*; (*with motion*) unter + *acc*; **~ an hour** weniger als eine Stunde **2.** *adv* (*beneath*) unten; (*with motion*) darunter; **children aged eight and ~** Kinder bis zu acht Jahren; **under-age** *adj* minderjährig

undercarriage *n* Fahrgestell *nt*

underdog *n* Unterlegene(r) *mf*; (*outsider*) Außenseiter(in) *m(f)*

underdone *adj* GASTR nicht gar, durch

underestimate *vt* unterschätzen

underexposed *adj* PHOT unterbelichtet

undergo *irr vt* (*experience*)

durchmachen; *(operation, test)* sich unterziehen + *dat*
undergraduate *n* Student(in) *m(f)*
underground 1. *adj* unterirdisch **2.** *n (Brit)* U-Bahn *f*; **underground station** *n* U-Bahn-Station *f*
underlie *irr vt* zugrunde liegen + *dat*
underline *vt* unterstreichen
underlying *adj* zugrunde liegend
underneath 1. *prep* unter + *dat; (with motion)* unter + *acc* **2.** *adv* darunter
underpants *npl* Unterhose *f*; **undershirt** *n (US)* Unterhemd *nt*; **undershorts** *npl (US)* Unterhose *f*
understand *irr vt, vi* verstehen; *I ~ that ... (been told)* ich habe gehört, dass ...; *(sympathize)* ich habe Verständnis dafür, dass ...; **make oneself understood** sich verständlich machen; **understanding** *adj* verständnisvoll
undertake *irr vt (task)* übernehmen; *~ to do sth* sich verpflichten, etw zu tun; **undertaker** *n* Leichenbestatter(in) *m(f)*; *~'s (firm)* Bestattungsinstitut *nt*
underwater 1. *adv* unter Wasser **2.** *adj* Unterwasser-
underwear *n* Unterwäsche *f*
undo *irr vt (unfasten)* aufmachen; *(work)* zunichte machen; *vt* **rz** rückgängig machen

undoubtedly *adv* zweifellos
undress 1. *vt* ausziehen **2.** *vi* sich ausziehen
unearth *vt (dig up)* ausgraben; *(find)* aufstöbern
unease *n* Unbehagen *nt*; **uneasy** *adj (person)* unbehaglich; *I'm ~ about it* mir ist nicht wohl dabei
unemployed 1. *adj* arbeitslos **2.** *npl* **the ~** die Arbeitslosen *pl*; **unemployment** *n* Arbeitslosigkeit *f*; **unemployment benefit** *n* Arbeitslosengeld *nt*
unequal *adj* ungleich
uneven *adj (surface, road)* uneben; *(contest)* ungleich
unexpected *adj* unerwartet
unfamiliar *adj* **be ~ with sb/ sth** jdn/etw nicht kennen
unfasten *vt* aufmachen
unfit *adj* ungeeignet *(for* für); *(in bad health)* nicht fit
unforeseen *adj* unvorhergesehen
unforgettable *adj* unvergesslich
unforgivable *adj* unverzeihlich
unfortunate *adj (unlucky)* unglücklich; *it is ~ that ...* es ist bedauerlich, dass ...; **unfortunately** *adv* leider
unfounded *adj* unbegründet
unhappy *adj (sad)* unglücklich, unzufrieden
unhealthy *adj* ungesund
unheard-of *adj (unknown)* gänzlich unbekannt; *(outra-*

geous) unerhört

unhitch *vt* (*caravan, trailer*) abkoppeln

unhurt *adj* unverletzt

uniform 1. *n* Uniform *f* **2.** *adj* einheitlich

unify *vt* vereinigen

unimportant *adj* unwichtig

uninhabited *adj* unbewohnt

uninstall *vt* IT deinstallieren

unintentional *adj* unabsichtlich

union *n* (*uniting*) Vereinigung *f*; (*alliance*) Union *f*

unique *adj* einzigartig

unit *n* Einheit *f*; (*of system, machine*) Teil *nt*; (*in school*) Lektion *f*

unite 1. *vt* vereinigen; **the United Kingdom** das Vereinigte Königreich; **the United Nations** *pl* die Vereinten Nationen *pl*; **the United States** (**of America**) *pl* die Vereinigten Staaten (von Amerika) *pl* **2.** *vi* sich vereinigen

universe *n* Universum *nt*

university *n* Universität *f*

unkind *adj* unfreundlich (*to* zu)

unknown *adj* unbekannt (*to* + *dat*)

unleaded *adj* bleifrei

unless *conj* es sei denn, wenn ... nicht; **don't do it ~ I tell you to** mach das nicht, es sei denn, ich sage es dir; **~ I'm mistaken ...** wenn ich mich nicht irre ...

unlicensed *adj* (*to sell alco-*

hol) ohne Lizenz

unlike *prep* (*in contrast to*) im Gegensatz zu; **it's ~ her to be late** es sieht ihr gar nicht ähnlich, zu spät zu kommen; **unlikely** *adj* unwahrscheinlich

unload *vt* ausladen

unlock *vt* aufschließen

unlucky *adj* unglücklich; **be ~** Pech haben

unmistakable *adj* unverkennbar

unnecessary *adj* unnötig

unoccupied *adj* (*seat*) frei; (*building, room*) leer stehend

unpack *vt, vi* auspacken

unpleasant *adj* unangenehm

unplug *vt* **~ sth** den Stecker von etw herausziehen

unprecedented *adj* beispiellos

unpredictable *adj* (*person, weather*) unberechenbar

unreasonable *adj* unvernünftig; (*demand*) übertrieben

unreliable *adj* unzuverlässig

unsafe *adj* nicht sicher; (*dangerous*) gefährlich

unscrew *vt* abschrauben

unskilled *adj* (*worker*) ungelernt

unsuccessful *adj* erfolglos

unsuitable *adj* ungeeignet (*for* für)

until 1. *prep* bis; **not ~** erst; **from Monday ~ Friday** von Montag bis Freitag; **he didn't come home ~ midnight**

er kam erst um Mitternacht nach Hause; **~ then** bis dahin **2.** *conj* bis; **she won't come ~ you invite her** sie kommt erst, wenn du sie einlädst

unusual, unusually *adj, adv* ungewöhnlich

unwanted *adj* unerwünscht, ungewollt

unwell *adj* krank; **feel ~** sich nicht wohl fühlen

unwilling *adj* **be ~ to do sth** nicht bereit sein, etw zu tun

unwind *irr* **1.** *vt* abwickeln **2.** *vi* (*relax*) sich entspannen

unwrap *vt* auspacken

unzip *vt* den Reißverschluss aufmachen an + *dat*; IT entzippen

up 1. *prep* **climb~ a tree** einen Baum hinaufklettern; **go ~ the street/the stairs** die Straße entlanggehen/die Treppe hinaufgehen; **further ~ the hill** weiter oben auf dem Berg **2.** *adv* (*in higher position*) oben; (*to higher position*) nach oben; (*out of bed*) auf; **~ there** dort oben; **~ and down** (*walk, jump*) auf und ab; **what's ~?** fam was ist los?; **~ to £100** bis zu 100 Pfund; **what's she ~ to?** was macht sie da?; (*planning*) was hat sie vor?; **it's ~ to you** das liegt bei dir; **I don't feel ~ to it** ich fühle mich dem nicht gewachsen

upbringing *n* Erziehung *f*

update 1. *n* (*list etc*) Aktuali-

sierung *f*; (*software*) Update *nt* **2.** *vt* (*list etc, person*) aktualisieren

upgrade *vt* (*computer*) aufrüsten; **we were ~d** das Hotel hat uns ein besseres Zimmer gegeben

upheaval *n* Aufruhr *m*; POL Umbruch *m*

uphill *adv* bergauf

upon *prep* → **on**

upper *adj* obere(r, s); (*arm, deck*) Ober-

upright *adj, adv* aufrecht

uprising *n* Aufstand *m*

uproar *n* Aufruhr *m*

upset 1. *irr vt* (*overturn*) umkippen; (*disturb*) aufregen; (*sadden*) bestürzen; (*offend*) kränken; (*plans*) durcheinander bringen **2.** *adj* (*disturbed*) aufgeregt; (*sad*) bestürzt; (*offended*) gekränkt; **~ stomach** Magenverstimmung *f*

upside down *adv* verkehrt herum; *fig* drunter und drüber; **turn sth ~** (*box etc*) etw umdrehen/durchwühlen

upstairs *adv* oben; (*go, take*) nach oben

up-to-date *adj* modern; (*fashion, information*) aktuell; **keep sb ~** jdn auf dem Laufenden halten

upwards *adv* nach oben

urban *adj* städtisch, Stadt-

urge 1. *n* Drang *m* **2.** *vt* **~ sb to do sth** jdn drängen, etw zu tun; **urgent, urgently** *adj,*

adv dringend
urine *n* Urin *m*
us *pron* uns; **can he help ~?** kann er uns helfen?; **it's ~** wir sind's; **both of ~** wir beide
US, USA *n sing abbr* = **United States (of America)**; **USA** *f*
use 1. *n* (*using*) Gebrauch *m*; (*for specific purpose*) Verwendung *f*; **in/out of ~** in/außer Gebrauch; **no ~** (*doing that*) es hat keinen Zweck(, das zu tun); **it's (of) no ~ to me** das kann ich nicht brauchen **2.** *vt* benutzen, gebrauchen; (*for specific purpose*) verwenden; (*method*) anwenden; **use up** *vt* aufbrauchen
used 1. *adj* (*secondhand*) gebraucht **2.** *vaux* **be ~d to** ▸

sb/sth an jdn/etw gewöhnt sein; **get ~d to sb/sth** sich an jdn/etw gewöhnen; **she ~d to live here** sie hat früher mal hier gewohnt; **useful** *adj* nützlich; **useless** *adj* nutzlos; (*unusable*) unbrauchbar; (*pointless*) zwecklos; **user** *n* Benutzer(in) *m(f)*; **user--friendly** *adj* benutzerfreundlich
usual *adj* üblich, gewöhnlich; **as ~** wie üblich; **usually** *adv* normalerweise
utensil *n* Gerät *nt*
uterus *n* Gebärmutter *f*
utilize *vt* verwenden
utmost *adj* äußerst
utter 1. *adj* völlig **2.** *vt* von sich geben; **utterly** *adv* völlig
U-turn *n* AUTO Wende *f*; **do a ~** wenden

V

vacancy *n* (*job*) offene Stelle; (*room*) freies Zimmer; **vacant** *adj* (*room, seat*) frei; (*post*) offen; (*building*) leer stehend; **vacate** *vt* (*room, building*) räumen; (*seat*) frei machen
vacation *n* (*US*) Ferien *pl*, Urlaub *m*; (*at university*) (Semester)ferien *pl*; **go on ~** in Urlaub fahren
vaccinate *vt* impfen; **vaccination** *n* Impfung *f*; **~ card** Impfpass *m*

vacuum 1. *n* Vakuum *nt* **2.** *vt, vi* (staub)saugen; **vacuum cleaner** *n* Staubsauger *m*
vagina *n* Scheide *f*
vague *adj* (*imprecise*) vage; (*resemblance*) entfernt; **vaguely** *adv* in etwa, irgendwie
vain *adj* (*attempt*) vergeblich; (*conceited*) eitel; **vainly** *adv* (*in vain*) vergeblich
valid *adj* (*ticket, passport etc*) gültig; (*argument*) stichhaltig
valley *n* Tal *nt*
valuable *adj* wertvoll; (*time*)

kostbar; **valuables** *npl* Wertsachen *pl*

value 1. *n* Wert *m* **2.** *vt* (*appreciate*) schätzen; **value added tax** *n* Mehrwertsteuer *f*

valve *n* Ventil *nt*

van *n* AUTO Lieferwagen *m*

vanilla *n* Vanille *f*

vanish *vi* verschwinden

vanity *n* Eitelkeit *f*; **vanity case** *n* Schminkkoffer *m*

vapor (*US*), **vapour** *n* (*mist*) Dunst *m*; (*steam*) Dampf *m*

variable *adj* (*weather, mood*) unbeständig; (*quality*) unterschiedlich; (*speed, height*) regulierbar; **varied** *adj* (*interests, selection*) vielseitig; (*career*) bewegt; (*work, diet*) abwechslungsreich; **variety** *n* (*diversity*) Abwechslung *f*; (*assortment*) Vielfalt *f* (*of* an + *dat*); (*type*) Art *f*; **various** *adj* verschieden

varnish 1. *n* Lack *m* **2.** *vt* lackieren

vary 1. *vt* (*alter*) verändern **2.** *vi* (*be different*) unterschiedlich sein; (*fluctuate*) sich verändern; (*prices*) schwanken

vase (*US*) *n* Vase *f*

vast *adj* riesig; (*area*) weit

VAT *abbr* = **value added tax**, Mehrwertsteuer, MwSt.

Vatican *n* **the ~** der Vatikan

VCR *abbr* = **video cassette recorder**, Videorekorder *m*

veal *n* Kalbfleisch *nt*

vegan *n* Veganer(in) *m(f)*

vegetable *n* Gemüse *n*

vegetarian 1. *n* Vegetarier(in) *m(f)* **2.** *adj* vegetarisch

vehicle *n* Fahrzeug *nt*

veil *n* Schleier *m*

vein *n* Ader *f*

Velcro® *n* Klettband *nt*

velvet *n* Samt *m*

vending machine *n* Automat *m*

venereal disease *n* Geschlechtskrankheit *f*

venetian blind *n* Jalousie *f*

Venezuela *n* Venezuela *nt*

vengeance *n* Rache *f*

Venice *n* Venedig *nt*

venison *n* Rehfleisch *nt*

vent *n* Öffnung *f*

ventilate *vt* lüften; **ventilation** *n* Belüftung *f*; **ventilator** *n* (*in room*) Ventilator *m*; **be on a ~** MED künstlich beatmet werden

venture 1. *n* (*project*) Unternehmung *f*; COMM Unternehmen *nt* **2.** *vi* (*go*) (sich) wagen

venue *n* (*for concert etc*) Veranstaltungsort *m*

verb *n* Verb *nt*

verdict *n* Urteil *nt*

verge 1. *n* (*of road*) (Straßen)rand *m*; **be on the ~ of doing sth** im Begriff sein, etw zu tun **2.** *vi* **~ on** grenzen an + *acc*

verification *n* (*confirmation*) Bestätigung *f*; (*check*) Überprüfung *f*; **verify** *vt* (*confirm*) bestätigen; (*check*) überprüfen

vermin *npl* Schädlinge *pl*; *(insects)* Ungeziefer *nt*

verruca *n* Warze *f*

versatile *adj* vielseitig

verse *n (poetry)* Poesie *f*; *(stanza)* Strophe *f*

version *n* Version *f*

versus *prep* gegen; *(in contrast to)* im Gegensatz zu

vertical *adj* senkrecht, vertikal

very 1. *adv* sehr; **~ much** sehr **2.** *adj* **the ~ book I need** genau das Buch, das ich brauche; **at that ~ moment** gerade in dem Augenblick; **at the ~ top** ganz oben; **the ~ best** der/die/das Allerbeste

vest *n (Brit)* Unterhemd *nt*; *(US, waistcoat)* Weste *f*

vet *n* Tierarzt *m*, Tierärztin *f*

veto 1. *n* Veto *nt* **2.** *vt* sein Veto einlegen gegen

via *prep* über + *acc*

vibrate *vi* vibrieren; **vibration** *n* Vibration *f*

vicar *n* Pfarrer(in) *m(f)*

vice 1. *n (evil)* Laster *nt* **2.** *pref* Vize-; **~chairman** stellvertretender Vorsitzender; **~president** Vizepräsident(in) *m(f)*

vice versa *adv* umgekehrt

vicinity *n* **in the ~** in der Nähe *(of + gen)*

vicious *adj (violent)* brutal; *(malicious)* gemein; **vicious circle** *n* Teufelskreis *m*

victim *n* Opfer *nt*

victory *n* Sieg *m*

video 1. *adj* Video- **2.** *n* Video *nt*; *(recorder)* Videorekorder *m* **3.** *vt* (auf Video) aufnehmen; **video camera** *n* Videokamera *f*; **video cassette** *n* Videokassette *f*; **video clip** *n* Videoclip *m*; **video recorder** *n* Videorekorder *m*; **videotape 1.** *n* Videoband *nt* **2.** *vt* (auf Video) aufnehmen

Vienna *n* Wien *nt*

Vietnam *n* Vietnam *nt*

view 1. *n (sight)* Blick *m (of* auf + *acc)*; *(vista)* Aussicht *f*; *(opinion)* Meinung *f*; **in ~ of** angesichts + *gen* **2.** *vt (situation, event)* betrachten; *(house)* besichtigen; **viewer** *n (for slides)* Diabetrachter *m*; TV Zuschauer(in) *m(f)*

viewpoint *n fig* Standpunkt *m*

village *n* Dorf *nt*

villain *n* Schurke *m*; *(in film, story)* Bösewicht *m*

vinegar *n* Essig *m*

vineyard *n* Weinberg *m*

vintage *n (of wine)* Jahrgang *m*

violate *vt (treaty)* brechen; *(rights, rule)* verletzen

violence *n (brutality)* Gewalt *f*; *(of person)* Gewalttätigkeit *f*; **violent** *adj (brutal)* brutal; *(death)* gewaltsam

violet *n (colour)* Veilchen *nt*; Violett *nt*

violin *n* Geige *f*, Violine *f*

virgin n Jungfrau f
Virgo n ASTR Jungfrau f
virtual adj IT virtuell; **virtually** adv praktisch
virtue n Tugend f; **by ~ of** aufgrund + gen; **virtuous** adj tugendhaft
virus n MED, IT Virus nt
visa n Visum nt
visibility n METEO Sichtweite f; **good/poor ~** gute/ schlechte Sicht; **visible** adj sichtbar; (evident) sichtlich; **visibly** adv sichtlich
vision n (power of sight) Sehvermögen nt; (foresight) Weitblick m; (dream, image) Vision f
visit 1. n Besuch m; (stay) Aufenthalt m 2. vt besuchen; **visiting hours** npl Besuchszeiten pl; **visitor** n Besucher(in) m(f); **~'s book** Gästebuch nt
visual adj Seh-; (image, joke) visuell; **visualize** vt sich vorstelle; **visually** adv visuell; **~ impaired** sehbehindert
vital adj (essential) unerlässlich, wesentlich; (argument, moment) entscheidend; **vitality** n Vitalität f; **vitally** adv äußerst
vitamin n Vitamin nt
vivid adj (description) anschaulich; (memory) lebhaft
V-neck n V-Ausschnitt m
vocabulary n Wortschatz m, Vokabular nt
vocal adj (of the voice) Stimm-; (group) Gesangs-; (protest, person) lautstark
vocation n Berufung f; **vocational** adj Berufs-
vodka n Wodka m
voice 1. n Stimme f 2. vt äußern; **voice mail** n Voicemail f
void 1. n Leere f 2. adj LAW ungültig
volcano n Vulkan m
volt n Volt nt; **voltage** n Spannung f
volume n (of sound) Lautstärke f; (space occupied by sth) Volumen nt; (size, amount) Umfang m; (book) Band m; **volume control** n Lautstärkeregler m
voluntary, voluntarily adj, adv freiwillig; (unpaid) ehrenamtlich; **volunteer** 1. n Freiwillige(r) mf 2. vi sich freiwillig melden
voluptuous adj sinnlich
vomit vi sich übergeben
vote 1. n Stimme f; (ballot) Wahl f; (result) Abstimmungsergebnis nt; (right to vote) Wahlrecht nt 2. vt (elect) wählen; **they ~d him chairman** sie wählten ihn zum Vorsitzenden 3. vi wählen; **~ for/against sth** für/ gegen etw stimmen; **voter** n Wähler(in) m(f)
voucher n Gutschein m
vow n Gelöbnis nt
vowel n Vokal m
voyage n Reise f

vulgar *adj* vulgär, ordinär
vulnerable *adj* verwundbar;

(sensitive) verletzlich
vulture *n* Geier *m*

W

wade *vi* *(in water)* waten
wafer *n* Waffel *f*; REL Hostie *f*;
wafer-thin *adj* hauchdünn
waffle *n* Waffel *f*; *(Brit) fam*
(empty talk) Geschwafel *nt*
wag *vt* *(tail)* wedeln mit
wage *n* Lohn *m*
waggon *(Brit)*, **wagon** *n*
(horse-drawn) Fuhrwerk *nt*;
(Brit) RAIL Waggon *m*; *(US)*
AUTO Wagen *m*
waist *n* Taille *f*; **waistcoat** *n*
(Brit) Weste *f*; **waistline** *n*
Taille *f*
wait 1. *n* Wartezeit *f* 2. *vi* warten *(for* auf + *acc)*; **~ and see**
abwarten; **~ a minute** Moment mal!; **wait up** *vi* aufbleiben
waiter *n* Kellner *m*
waiting *n* 'no ~' „Halteverbot"; **waiting list** *n* Warteliste *f*; **waiting room** *n* MED
Wartezimmer *nt*; RAIL War-
tesaal *m*
waitress *n* Kellnerin *f*
wake 1. *vt* wecken 2. *vi* aufwachen; **wake up** 1. *vt* aufwecken 2. *vi* aufwachen;
wake-up call *n* TEL Weckruf
m
Wales *n* Wales *nt*
walk 1. *n* Spaziergang *m*;
(ramble) Wanderung *f*;

(route) Weg *m*; **go for a ~**
spazieren gehen; **it's only a
five-minute ~** es sind nur
fünf Minuten zu Fuß 2. *vi* gehen; *(stroll)* spazieren gehen;
(ramble) wandern 3. *vt* *(dog)*
ausführen; **walking** *n* **go ~**
wandern; **walking shoes**
npl Wanderschuhe *pl*
wall *n* *(inside)* Wand *f*; *(outside)* Mauer *f*
wallet *n* Brieftasche *f*
wallpaper 1. *n* Tapete *f*; IT
Bildschirmhintergrund *m* 2.
vt tapezieren
walnut *n* *(nut)* Walnuss *f*
waltz *n* Walzer *m*
wander *vi* *(person)* herum-
wandern
want 1. *n* *(lack)* Mangel *m* *(of
an* + *dat)*; *(need)* Bedürfnis
nt; **for ~ of** aus Mangel an
+ *dat* 2. *vt* *(desire)* wollen;
(need) brauchen; **he doesn't
~ to** er will nicht
WAP phone *n* WAP-Handy *nt*
war *n* Krieg *m*
ward *n* *(in hospital)* Station *f*;
(child) Mündel *nt*
warden *n* Aufseher(in) *m(f)*;
(in youth hostel) Herbergs-
vater *m*, Herbergsmutter *f*
wardrobe *n* Kleiderschrank
m

warehouse n Lagerhaus nt

warfare n Krieg m; (techniques) Kriegsführung f

warm 1. adj warm; (welcome) herzlich; **I'm ~** mir ist warm **2.** vt wärmen; (food) aufwärmen; **warm over** vt (US, food) aufwärmen; **warm up 1.** vt (food) aufwärmen; (room) erwärmen **2.** vi (food, room) warm werden; SPORT sich aufwärmen; **warmly** adv warm; (welcome) herzlich; **warmth** n Wärme f; (of welcome) Herzlichkeit f

warn vt warnen (of, against vor + dat); **~ sb not to do sth** jdn davor warnen, etw zu tun; **warning** n Warnung f; **warning light** n Warnlicht nt; **warning triangle** n AUTO Warndreieck nt

warranty n Garantie f

wart n Warze f

wary adj vorsichtig; (suspicious) misstrauisch

was pt of **be**

wash 1. n **have a ~** sich waschen; **it's in the ~** es ist in der Wäsche **2.** vt sich waschen; (plates, glasses etc) abwaschen; **~ the dishes** (das Geschirr) abwaschen **3.** vi (clean oneself) sich waschen; **wash off** vt abwaschen; **wash up** vi (Brit, wash dishes) abwaschen; (US, clean oneself) sich waschen; **washable** adj waschbar;

washbag n (US) Kulturbeutel m; **washbasin** n Waschbecken nt; **washcloth** n (US) Waschlappen m; **washer** n TECH Dichtungsring m; (washing machine) Waschmaschine f; **washing** n (laundry) Wäsche f; **washing machine** n Waschmaschine f; **washing powder** n Waschpulver nt; **washing-up** n (Brit) Abwasch m; **do the ~** abwaschen; **washing-up liquid** n (Brit) Spülmittel nt; **washroom** n (US) Toilette f

wasn't contr of **was not**

wasp n Wespe f

waste 1. n (materials) Abfall m; (wasting) Verschwendung f; **it's a ~ of time** das ist Zeitverschwendung **2.** adj (superfluous) überschüssig **3.** vt verschwenden (on an + acc); (opportunity) vertun; **waste bin** n Abfalleimer m; **wastepaper basket** n Papierkorb m

watch 1. n (timepiece) (Armband)uhr f **2.** vt (observe) beobachten; (guard) aufpassen auf + acc; (film, play, programme) sich dat ansehen; **~ TV** fernsehen **3.** vi zusehen; (guard) Wache halten; **~ for sb/sth** nach jdm/etw Ausschau halten; **~ out** pass auf!; **watchdog** n Wachhund m; **watchful** adj wachsam

water 1. n Wasser nt; **~s** pl (ter-

wedding dress

ritory) Gewässer *pl* **2.** *vt*
(plant) gießen **3.** *vi (eye)* tränen; *my mouth is ~ing* mir
läuft das Wasser im Mund
zusammen; water down *vt*
verdünnen; **watercolor**
(US), watercolour *n (paint-*
ing) Aquarell *nt*; *(paint)*
Wasserfarbe *f*; **watercress**
n (Brunnen)kresse *f*; **water-**
fall *n* Wasserfall *m*; **watering**
can *n* Gießkanne *f*; **water**
level *n* Wasserstand *m*; **wa-**
termelon *n* Wassermelone
f; **waterproof** *adj* wasserdicht; **water-skiing** *n* Was-
serskilaufen *nt*; **water**
sports *npl* Wassersport *m*;
watertight *adj* wasserdicht;
water wings *npl* Schwimmflügel *pl*; **watery** *adj* wässrig

wave 1. *n* Welle *f* **2.** *vt (move*
to and fro) schwenken;
(hand, flag) winken mit **3.**
vi (person) winken; *(flag)*
wehen; **wavelength** *n* Wellenlänge *f*; **wavy** *adj* wellig

wax *n* Wachs *nt*; *(in ear)* Oh-
renschmalz *nt*

way *n* Weg *m*; *(direction)*
Richtung *f*; *(manner)* Art *f*;
can you tell me the ~ to ...
? wie komme ich (am besten) zu ... ?; *we went the*
wrong ~ wir sind in die falsche Richtung gefahren /ge-
gangen; *lose one's ~* sich
verirren; *make ~ for sb/*
sth jdm/etw Platz machen;
get one's own ~ seinen Wil-

len durchsetzen; *'give ~'*
AUTO „Vorfahrt achten"; *the*
other ~ round andersherum;
one ~ or another irgendwie;
in a ~ in gewisser Weise; *in*
the ~ im Weg; *by the ~* übrigens; *'~ in' '*„Eingang"; *'~ out'*
„Ausgang"; *no ~ fam* kommt
nicht infrage!

we *pron* wir

weak *adj* schwach; **weaken 1.**
vt schwächen **2.** *vi* schwächer
werden

wealth *n* Reichtum *m*;
wealthy *adj* reich

weapon *n* Waffe *f*

wear 1. *vt (have on)* tragen **2.**
vi (become worn) sich abnutzen **3.** *n ~ (and tear)* Abnut-
zung *f*; **wear off** *vi (diminish)*
nachlassen; **wear out 1.** *vt*
abnutzen; *(person)* erschöp-
fen **2.** *vi* sich abnutzen

weary *adj* müde

weather *n* Wetter *nt*; **weather**
forecast *n* Wettervorhersage
f

weave *vt (cloth)* weben; *(bas-*
ket etc) flechten

web *n a. fig* Netz *nt*; *the Web*
das Web, das Internet; **web-**
cam *n* Webcam *f*; **web page**
n Webseite *f*; **website** *n*
Website *f*

we'd *contr of* **we had; we**
would

Wed *abbr* = *Wednesday*; Mi.

wedding *n* Hochzeit *f*; **wed-**
ding anniversary *n* Hochzeitstag *m*; **wedding dress**

n Hochzeitskleid *nt*; **wedding ring** *n* Ehering *m*; **wedding shower** *n* (*US*) Party für die zukünftige Braut

wedge *n* (*under door etc*) Keil *m*; (*of cheese etc*) Stück *nt*, Ecke *f*

Wednesday *n* Mittwoch *m*; → **Tuesday**

wee *adj*, klein

weed 1. *n* Unkraut *nt* **2.** *vt* jäten

week *n* Woche *f*; **twice a ~** zweimal in der Woche; **a ~ on Friday/Friday ~** Freitag in einer Woche; **in two ~s' time, in two ~s** in zwei Wochen; **weekday** *n* Wochentag *m*; **weekend** *n* Wochenende *nt*; **weekly** *adj*, *adv* wöchentlich; (*magazine*) Wochenzeitung *nt*

weep *vi* weinen

weigh *vt*, *vi* wiegen; **weigh up** *vt* abwägen; (*person*) einschätzen; **weight** *n* Gewicht *nt*; **lose/put on ~** abnehmen/zunehmen; **weightlifting** *n* Gewichtheben *nt*; **weight training** *n* Krafttraining *nt*

weird *adj* seltsam; **weirdo** *n* Spinner(in) *m(f)*

welcome 1. *n* Empfang *m* **2.** *adj* willkommen; (*news*) angenehm; **~ to London** willkommen in London! **3.** *vt* begrüßen; **welcoming** *adj* freundlich

welfare *n* Wohl *nt*; (*US, social security*) Sozialhilfe *f*; **wel-**

fare state *n* Wohlfahrtsstaat *m*

well 1. *n* Brunnen *m* **2.** *adj* (*in good health*) gesund; **are you ~?** geht es dir gut?; **feel ~** sich wohl fühlen **3.** *interj* nun; **~, I don't know** nun, ich weiß nicht **4.** *adv* gut; **~ done** gut gemacht!; **it may ~ be** das kann wohl sein; **as ~** (*in addition*) auch; **~ over 60** weit über 60

we'll *contr of* **we will; we shall**

well-behaved *adj* brav; **well-done** *adj* (*steak*) durchgebraten

wellingtons *npl* Gummistiefel *pl*

well-known *adj* bekannt; **well-off** *adj* (*wealthy*) wohlhabend; **well-paid** *adj* gut bezahlt

Welsh 1. *adj* walisisch **2.** *n* (*language*) Walisisch *nt*; **the ~ pl** die Waliser *pl*; **Welshman** *n* Waliser *m*; **Welshwoman** *n* Waliserin *f*

went *pt of* **go**

wept *pt*, *pp of* **weep**

were *pt of* **be**

we're *contr of* **we are**

weren't *contr of* **were not**

west 1. *n* Westen *m* **2.** *adv* (*go, face*) nach Westen **3.** *adj* West-; **westbound** *adj* (*in*) Richtung Westen; **western 1.** *adj* West-, westlich; **Western Europe** Westeuropa *nt* **2.** *n* FILM Western *m*; **West Germany** *n* Westdeutschland *nt*;

westwards *adv* nach Westen
wet 1. *vt* ~ **oneself** in die Hose machen **2.** *adj* nass, feucht; '~ **paint**' „frisch gestrichen"; **wet suit** *n* Taucheranzug *m*
we've *contr of* **we have**
whale *n* Wal *m*
wharf *n* Kai *m*
what 1. *pron, interj* was; ~'s **your name?** wie heißt du?; ~ **is the letter about?** worum geht es in dem Brief?; ~ **are they talking about?** worüber reden sie?; ~ **for?** wozu? **2.** *adj* welche(r, s); ~ **colour is it?** welche Farbe ist es?; **whatever** *pron* **I'll do** ~ **you want** ich tue alles, was du willst; ~ **he says** egal, was er sagt
what's *contr of* **what is; what has**
wheat *n* Weizen *m*
wheel 1. *n* Rad *nt*; *(steering wheel)* Lenkrad *nt* **2.** *vt (bicycle, trolley)* schieben; **wheelchair** *n* Rollstuhl *m*; **wheel clamp** *n* Parkkralle *f*
when 1. *adv (in questions)* wann; **on the day** ~ an dem Tag, als **2.** *conj* wenn; *(in past)* als; ~ **I was younger** als ich jünger war; **whenever** *adv (every time)* immer wenn; **come** ~ **you like** komm wann immer du willst
where 1. *adv* wo; ~ **are you going?** wohin gehst du?; ~ **are you from?** woher kommst du? **2.** *conj* wo; **that's** ~ **I**

used to live da habe ich früher gewohnt; **whereabouts 1.** *adv* wo **2.** *npl* Aufenthaltsort *m*; **whereas** *conj* während, wohingegen; **wherever** *conj* wo immer; ~ **that may be** wo immer das sein mag
whether *conj* ob
which 1. *adj* welche(r, s); ~ **car is yours?** welches Auto gehört dir?; ~ **one?** welche(r, s)? **2.** *pron (in questions)* welche(r, s); *(in relative clauses)* der / die / das, die *pl*; **it rained, ~ upset his plans** es regnete, was seine Pläne durcheinander brachte; **whichever** *adj, pron* welche(r, s) auch immer
while 1. *n a* ~ eine Weile; **for a** ~ eine Zeit lang; **a short ~ ago** vor kurzem **2.** *conj* während; *(although)* obwohl
whine *vi (person)* jammern
whip 1. *n* Peitsche *f* **2.** *vt (beat)* peitschen; ~**ped cream** Schlagsahne *f*
whirl *vt, vi* herumwirbeln; **whirlpool** *n (in river, sea)* Strudel *m*; *(pool)* Whirlpool *m*
whisk 1. *n* Schneebesen *m* **2.** *vt (cream etc)* schlagen
whisker *n (of animal)* Schnurrhaar *nt*; ~**s** *pl (of man)* Backenbart *m*
whisk(e)y *n* Whisky *m*
whisper *vi, vt* flüstern
whistle 1. *n* Pfiff *m*, Pfeife *f* **2.** *vt, vi* pfeifen

white 1. n (of egg) Eiweiß nt; (of eye) Weiße nt **2.** adj weiß; (with fear) blass; (coffee) mit Milch

white lie n Notlüge f; **white meat** n helles Fleisch; **white water rafting** n Rafting nt; **white wine** n Weißwein m

Whitsun n Pfingsten nt

who pron (in questions) wer; (in relative clauses) der/die/das, die pl; **~ did you see?** wen hast du gesehen?; **~ does that belong to?** wem gehört das?; **the people ~ live next door** die Leute, die nebenan wohnen; whoever pron wer auch immer; **~ you choose** wen auch immer du wählst

whole 1. adj ganz **2.** n Ganze(s) nt; **the ~ of my family** meine ganze Familie; **on the ~** im Großen und Ganzen; wholefood n (Brit) Vollwertkost f; wholeheartedly adv voll und ganz; wholemeal adj (Brit) Vollkorn-; wholesale adv (buy, sell) im Großhandel; wholesome adj gesund; wholewheat adj Vollkorn-; wholly adv völlig

whom pron (in questions) wen; (in relative clauses) den/die/das, die pl; **with ~ did you speak?** mit wem haben Sie gesprochen?

whooping cough n Keuchhusten m

whose 1. adj (in questions)

wessen; (in relative clauses) dessen/deren/dessen, deren pl **2.** pron (in questions) wessen; **~ is this?** wem gehört das?

why adv, conj warum; **that's ~** deshalb

wicked adj böse; fam (great) geil

wide 1. adj breit; (skirt, trousers) weit; (selection) groß **2.** adv weit; **wide-angle lens** n Weitwinkelobjektiv nt; **wide-awake** adj hellwach; **widely** adv weit; **~ known** allgemein bekannt; **widen** vt verbreitern; fig erweitern; **wide-open** adj weit offen; **widescreen TV** n Breitbildfernseher m; **widespread** adj weit verbreitet

widow n Witwe f; **widowed** adj verwitwet; **widower** n Witwer m

width n Breite f

wife n (Ehe)frau f

wig n Perücke f

wild 1. adj wild; (violent) heftig; (plan, idea) verrückt **2.** adv **in the ~** in freier Wildbahn; **wildlife** n Tier- und Pflanzenwelt f; **wildly** adv wild; (enthusiastic, exaggerated) maßlos

will 1. vaux he/they **~ come** er wird/sie werden kommen; **I won't be back until late** ich komme erst spät zurück; **the car won't start** das Auto will nicht anspringen; **~ you**

have some coffee? möchten Sie eine Tasse Kaffee? **2.** n Wille m; (*wish*) Wunsch m; (*document*) Testament nt; **willing** adj bereitwillig; **be ~ to do sth** bereit sein, etw zu tun; **willingly** adv gern(e)

willow n Weide f

wimp n Weichei nt

win 1. vt, vi gewinnen **2.** n Sieg m; **win over, win round** vt für sich gewinnen

wind vt (*rope, bandage*) wickeln; **wind down** vt (*car window*) herunterkurbeln; **wind up** vt (*clock*) aufziehen; (*car window*) hochkurbeln; (*meeting, speech*) abschließen; (*person*) aufziehen, ärgern

wind n Wind m; MED Blähungen pl

wind instrument n Blasinstrument nt; **windmill** n Windmühle f

window n Fenster nt; (*counter*) Schalter m; **windowpane** n Fensterscheibe f; **window-shopping** n **go ~** einen Schaufensterbummel machen; **windowsill** n Fensterbrett nt

windpipe n Luftröhre f; **windscreen** n (*Brit*) Windschutzscheibe f; **windscreen wiper** n (*Brit*) Scheibenwischer m; **windshield** n (*US*) Windschutzscheibe f; **windshield wiper** n (*US*) Scheibenwischer m; **wind-

surfer** n Windsurfer(in) m(f); (*board*) Surfbrett nt; **windsurfing** n Windsurfen nt

windy adj windig

wine n Wein m; **wine list** n Weinkarte f; **wine tasting** n (*event*) Weinprobe f

wing n Flügel m; (*Brit*) AUTO Kotflügel m

wink vi zwinkern; **~ at sb** jdm zuzwinkern

winner n Gewinner(in) m(f), Sieger(in) m(f); **winning 1.** adj (*team, horse etc*) siegreich **2.** n **~s** pl Gewinn m

winter n Winter m; **winter sports** npl Wintersport m; **wint(e)ry** adj winterlich

wipe vt abwischen; **~ one's nose** sich dat die Nase putzen; **wipe off** vt abwischen; **wipe out** vt (*destroy*) vernichten; (*data, debt*) löschen

wire 1. n Draht m; ELEC Leitung f; (*US, telegram*) Telegramm nt **2.** vt (*plug in*) anschließen; (*US*) TEL telegrafieren (*sb sth* jdm etw); **wireless** adj drahtlos

wisdom n Weisheit f; **wisdom tooth** n Weisheitszahn m

wise, wisely adj, adv weise

wish 1. n Wunsch m (*for* nach); **with best ~es** (*in letter*) herzliche Grüße **2.** vt wünschen, wollen; **~ sb good luck/Merry Christmas** jdm viel Glück / frohe

Weihnachten wünschen; **I ~ I'd never seen him** ich wünschte, ich hätte ihn nie gesehen

witch n Hexe f

with prep mit; (cause) vor + dat; **I'm pleased ~ it** ich bin damit zufrieden; **shiver ~ cold** vor Kälte zittern; **he lives ~ his aunt** er wohnt bei seiner Tante

withdraw irr **1.** vt zurückziehen; (money) abheben; (comment) zurücknehmen **2.** vi sich zurückziehen

wither vi (plant) verwelken

withhold irr vt vorenthalten (from sb jdm)

within prep innerhalb + gen; **~ walking distance** zu Fuß erreichbar

without prep ohne; **~ asking** ohne zu fragen

withstand irr vt standhalten + dat

witness 1. n Zeuge m, Zeugin f **2.** vt Zeuge sein +

witty adj geistreich

wives pl of **wife**

wobble vi wackeln; **wobbly** adj wackelig

wok n Wok m

woke pt of **wake**

woken pp of **wake**

wolf n Wolf m

woman n Frau f

womb n Gebärmutter f

women pl of **woman**

won pt, pp of **win**

wonder 1. n (marvel) Wunder

nt; (surprise) Staunen nt **2.** vt, vi (speculate) sich fragen; **I ~ what/if ...** ich frage mich, was/ob ...; **wonderful, wonderfully** adj, adv wunderbar

won't contr of **will not**

wood n Holz nt; **~s** Wald m; **wooden** adj Holz-; fig hölzern; **woodpecker** n Specht m

wool n Wolle f; **woollen, woolen** (US) adj Woll-

word 1. n Wort nt; (promise) Ehrenwort nt; **~s** pl (of song) Text m; **have a ~ with sb** mit jdm sprechen; **in other ~s** mit anderen Worten 2. vt formulieren; **word processor** n (program) Textverarbeitungsprogramm nt

wore pt of **wear**

work 1. n Arbeit f; (of art, literature) Werk nt; **~ of art** Kunstwerk nt; **he's at ~** er ist in/auf der Arbeit; **out of ~** arbeitslos **2.** vi arbeiten (at, on an + dat); (machine, plan) funktionieren; (medicine) wirken; (succeed) klappen **3.** vt (machine) bedienen; **work out 1.** vi (plan) klappen; (sum) aufgehen; (person) trainieren **2.** vt (price, speed etc) ausrechnen; (plan) ausarbeiten; **work up** vt **get worked up** sich aufregen; **workaholic** n Arbeitstier nt; **worker** n Arbeiter(in) m(f); **workman** n Handwerker m; **workout** n

SPORT Fitnesstraining *nt*, Konditionstraining *nt*; **work permit** *n* Arbeitserlaubnis *f*; **workplace** *n* Arbeitsplatz *m*; **workshop** *n* Werkstatt *f*; (*meeting*) Workshop *m*

world *n* Welt *f*; **world championship** *n* Weltmeisterschaft *f*; **World War** *n* ~ **I/II, the First/Second** ~ der Erste/Zweite Weltkrieg; **world-wide** *adj*, *adv* weltweit; **World Wide Web** *n* World Wide Web *nt*

worm *n* Wurm *m*

worn 1. *pp* of **wear 2.** *adj* (*clothes*) abgetragen; (*tyre*) abgefahren; **worn-out** *adj* abgenutzt; (*person*) erschöpft

worried *adj* besorgt; **worry 1.** *n* Sorge *f* **2.** *vt* Sorgen machen + *dat* **3.** *vi* sich Sorgen machen (*about* um); **don't** ~ keine Sorge!; **worrying** *adj* beunruhigend

worse 1. *adj comparative of* **bad**; schlechter; (*pain, mistake etc*) schlimmer **2.** *adv comparative of* **badly**; schlechter; **worsen 1.** *vt* verschlechtern **2.** *vi* sich verschlechtern

worship *vt* anbeten, anhimmeln

worst 1. *adj superlative of* **bad**; schlechteste(r, s); (*pain, mistake etc*) schlimmste(r, s) **2.** *adv superlative of* **badly**; am schlechtesten **3.** *n* **the** ~

is over das Schlimmste ist vorbei; *at* (*the*) ~ schlimmstenfalls

worth 1. *n* Wert *m* **2.** *adj* **it is** ~ **£50** es ist 50 Pfund wert; *seeing* sehenswert; **it's** ~ **it** (*rewarding*) es lohnt sich; **worthless** *adj* wertlos; **worthwhile** *adj* lohnend, lohnenswert; **worthy** *adj* (*deserving respect*) würdig; **be** ~ *of sth* etw verdienen

would *vaux if you asked he* ~ **come** würde er kommen; *I* ~ *have told you, but* ... ich hätte es dir gesagt, aber ...; ~ *you like a drink?* möchten Sie etwas trinken?; *he* ~*n't help me* er wollte mir nicht helfen

wouldn't *contr* of **would not**

would've *contr* of **would have**

wound 1. *n* Wunde *f* **2.** *vt* verwunden, verletzen **3.** *pt*, *pp* of **wind**

wove *pt* of **weave**

woven *pp* of **weave**

wrap 1. *vt* (*parcel, present*) einwickeln; **wrap up 1.** *vt* (*parcel, present*) einwickeln **2.** *vi* (*dress warmly*) sich warm anziehen; **wrapping paper** *n* Packpapier *nt*; (*giftwrap*) Geschenkpapier *nt*

wreath *n* Kranz *m*

wreck 1. *n* (*ship, plane, car*) Wrack *nt*; *a nervous* ~ ein Nervenbündel *nt* **2.** *vt* (*car*) zu Schrott fahren; *fig* zerstö-

ren; **wreckage** n Trümmer pl
wrench n (tool) Schraubenschlüssel m
wrestling n Ringen nt
wring out vt auswringen
wrinkle n Falte f
wrist n Handgelenk nt; **wrist-
watch** n Armbanduhr f
write 1. vt schreiben; (cheque)
ausstellen **2.** vi schreiben; ~
to sb jdm schreiben; **write
down** vt aufschreiben; **write
off** vt (debt, person) abschreiben; (car) zu Schrott fahren;
write out vt (name etc) ausschreiben; (cheque) ausstellen; **write-protected** adj IT
schreibgeschützt; **writer** n
Verfasser(in) m(f); (author)

Schriftsteller(in) m(f); **writing** n Schrift f; (profession)
Schreiben nt; **writing paper**
n Schreibpapier nt
wrong adj (incorrect) falsch;
(morally) unrecht; **you're** ~
du hast Unrecht; **what's** ~
with your leg? was ist mit
deinem Bein los?; **I dialled
the** ~ **number** ich habe mich
verwählt; **don't get me** ~ versteh mich nicht falsch; **go** ~
(plan) schief gehen; **wrongly**
adv falsch; (unjustly) zu Unrecht
wrote pt of **write**
WWW abbr = **World Wide
Web**; WWW

X

xenophobia n Ausländer-
feindlichkeit f
XL abbr = **extra large**; XL,
übergroß

Xmas n Weihnachten nt
X-ray 1. n (picture) Röntgenaufnahme f **2.** vt röntgen
xylophone n Xylophon nt

Y

yacht n Jacht f; **yachting** n
Segeln nt
yard n Hof m; (US, garden)
Garten m; (measure) Yard
nt (0,91 m)
yawn vi gähnen
yd abbr = **yard(s)**
year n Jahr nt; ~**s ago** vor Jahren; **a five-year-old** ein(e)

Fünfjährige(r); **yearly** adj,
adv jährlich
yearn vi sich sehnen (for nach
+ dat)
yeast n Hefe f
yell vi, vt schreien; ~ **at sb** jdn
anschreien
yellow adj gelb; ~ **fever** Gelb-
fieber nt; **the Yellow Pages®**

pl die Gelben Seiten *pl*

yes 1. *adv* ja; *(answering negative question)* doch; **say~ to sth** ja zu etw sagen **2.** *n* Ja *nt*

yesterday *adv* gestern; **the day before ~** vorgestern; **~'s newspaper** die Zeitung von gestern

yet 1. *adv (still)* noch; *(up to now)* bis jetzt; *(in a question: already)* schon; **he hasn't arrived ~** er ist noch nicht gekommen; **have you finished ~?** bist du schon fertig?; **~ again** schon wieder; **as ~** bis jetzt **2.** *conj* doch

yield 1. *n* Ertrag *m* **2.** *vt (result, crop)* hervorbringen; *(profit, interest)* bringen **3.** *vi* nachgeben *(to + dat)*; MIL sich ergeben *(to + dat)*; **'~'** *(US)* AUTO „Vorfahrt beachten"

yoga *n* Joga *nt*

yog(h)urt *n* Jog(h)urt *m*

yolk *n* Eigelb *nt*

Yorkshire pudding *n* gebackener Eierteig, der meist zum Roastbeef gegessen wird

you 1. *pron (as subject)* du/Sie/ihr; *(as direct object)* dich/Sie/euch; *(as indirect object)* dir/Ihnen/ihnen; **~ never can tell** man weiß nie

you'd *contr of* **you had; you would; ~ better leave** du solltest gehen

you'll *contr of* **you will; you shall**

young *adj* jung; **youngster** *n* Jugendliche(r) *mf*

your *adj (sg)* dein; *(polite form)* Ihr; *(pl)* euer; *(polite form)* Ihr; **have you hurt ~ leg?** hast du dir das Bein verletzt?

you're *contr of* **you are**

yours *pron (sg)* deine(r, s); *(polite form)* Ihre(r, s); *(pl)* eure(r, s); *(polite form)* Ihre(r, s); **is this ~?** gehört das dir/Ihnen?; **a friend of ~** ein Freund von dir/Ihnen; **~ ...,** dein/deine ..., Ihr/Ihre ...

yourself *pron sg* dich; *(polite form)* sich; **have you hurt ~?** hast du dich/haben Sie sich verletzt?; **did you do it ~?** hast du es selbst gemacht?; **(all) by ~** allein; **yourselves** *pron pl* euch; *(polite form)* sich; **have you hurt ~?** habt ihr euch/haben Sie sich verletzt?

youth *n (period)* Jugend *f*; **youth hostel** *n* Jugendherberge *f*

you've *contr of* **you have**

yucky *adj fam* eklig

Yugoslavia *n hist* Jugoslawien *nt*

yummy *adj* lecker

Z

zap 1. vt IT löschen; (*in computer game*) abknallen **2.** vi TV zappen; **zapper** n TV Fernbedienung f

zebra (*US*) n Zebra nt; **zebra crossing** n (*Brit*) Zebrastreifen m

zero n Null f

zest n (*enthusiasm*) Begeisterung f

zigzag 1. n Zickzack m **2.** vi (*person, vehicle*) im Zickzack gehen/fahren

zinc n Zink nt

zip 1. n (*Brit*) Reißverschluss m **2.** vt ~ (**up**) den Reißverschluss zumachen; IT zippen;

zip code n (*US*) Postleitzahl f; **Zip disk®** n IT ZIP-Diskette® f; **Zip drive®** n IT ZIP-Laufwerk® nt; **Zip file®** n IT ZIP-Datei® f; **zipper** n (*US*) Reißverschluss m

zodiac n Tierkreis m; **sign of the ~** Tierkreiszeichen nt

zone n Zone f; (*area*) Gebiet nt; (*in town*) Bezirk m

zoo n Zoo m

zoom 1. vi (*move fast*) brausen, sausen **2.** n ~ (*lens*) Zoomobjektiv nt; **zoom in** vi PHOT heranzoomen (*on* an + acc)

zucchini n (*US*) Zucchini f

Anhang

German irregular verbs

backen	backte	hat gebacken
befehlen	befahl	hat befohlen
beginnen	begann	hat begonnen
beißen	biss	hat gebissen
bergen	barg	hat geborgen
betrügen	betrog	hat betrogen
biegen	bog	hat/ist gebogen
bieten	bot	hat geboten
binden	band	hat gebunden
bitten	bat	hat gebeten
blasen	blies	hat geblasen
bleiben	blieb	ist geblieben
braten	briet	hat gebraten
brechen	brach	hat/ist gebrochen
brennen	brannte	hat gebrannt
bringen	brachte	hat gebracht
denken	dachte	hat gedacht
dringen	drang	ist gedrungen
dürfen	durfte	hat gedurft
empfangen	empfing	hat empfangen
empfehlen	empfahl	hat empfohlen
empfinden	empfand	hat empfunden
erschrecken	erschrak	ist erschrocken
essen	aß	hat gegessen
fahren	fuhr	hat/ist gefahren
fallen	fiel	ist gefallen
fangen	fing	hat gefangen
finden	fand	hat gefunden
flechten	flocht	hat geflochten
fliegen	flog	hat/ist geflogen
fließen	floss	ist geflossen
fressen	fraß	hat gefressen
frieren	fror	hat gefroren
geben	gab	hat gegeben
gehen	ging	ist gegangen
gelingen	gelang	ist gelungen
gelten	galt	hat gegolten

genießen	genoss	hat genossen
geschehen	geschah	ist geschehen
gewinnen	gewann	hat gewonnen
gießen	goss	hat gegossen
gleichen	glich	hat geglichen
gleiten	glitt	ist geglitten
graben	grub	hat gegraben
greifen	griff	hat gegriffen
haben	hatte	hat gehabt
halten	hielt	hat gehalten
hängen	hing	hat gehangen
hauen	haute	hat gehauen
heißen	hieß	hat geheißen
helfen	half	hat geholfen
kennen	kannte	hat gekannt
klingen	klang	hat geklungen
kneifen	kniff	hat gekniffen
kommen	kam	ist gekommen
können	konnte	hat gekonnt
kriechen	kroch	ist gekrochen
laden	lud	hat geladen
lassen	ließ	hat gelassen
laufen	lief	ist gelaufen
leiden	litt	hat gelitten
leihen	lieh	hat geliehen
lesen	las	hat gelesen
liegen	lag	hat gelegen
lügen	log	hat gelogen
mahlen	mahlte	hat gemahlen
meiden	mied	hat gemieden
messen	maß	hat gemessen
misslingen	misslang	ist misslungen
mögen	mochte	hat gemocht
müssen	musste	hat gemusst
nehmen	nahm	hat genommen
nennen	nannte	hat genannt
pfeifen	pfiff	hat gepfiffen
raten	riet	hat geraten
reiben	rieb	hat gerieben
reißen	riss	hat/ist gerissen

reiten	ritt	hat/ist geritten
rennen	rannte	ist gerannt
riechen	roch	hat gerochen
ringen	rang	hat gerungen
rufen	rief	hat gerufen
salzen	salzte	hat gesalzen
saufen	soff	hat gesoffen
saugen	sog/saugte	hat gesogen/gesaugt
schaffen	schuf	hat geschaffen
scheiden	schied	hat/ist geschieden
scheinen	schien	hat geschienen
scheißen	schiss	hat geschissen
schieben	schob	hat geschoben
schießen	schoss	hat/ist geschossen
schlafen	schlief	hat geschlafen
schlagen	schlug	hat geschlagen
schleichen	schlich	ist geschlichen
schleifen	schliff	hat geschliffen
schließen	schloss	hat geschlossen
schmeißen	schmiss	hat geschmissen
schmelzen	schmolz	ist geschmolzen
schneiden	schnitt	hat geschnitten
schreiben	schrieb	hat geschrieben
schreien	schrie	hat geschrie(e)n
schweigen	schwieg	hat geschwiegen
schwimmen	schwamm	hat/ist geschwommen
schwören	schwor	hat geschworen
sehen	sah	hat gesehen
sein	war	ist gewesen
senden	sandte	hat gesandt
singen	sang	hat gesungen
sinken	sank	ist gesunken
sitzen	saß	hat gesessen
spinnen	spann	hat gesponnen
sprechen	sprach	hat gesprochen
springen	sprang	ist gesprungen
stechen	stach	hat gestochen
stehen	stand	hat gestanden
stehlen	stahl	hat gestohlen
steigen	stieg	ist gestiegen

sterben	starb	ist gestorben
stinken	stank	hat gestunken
stoßen	stieß	hat/ist gestoßen
streichen	strich	hat gestrichen
streiten	stritt	hat gestritten
tragen	trug	hat getragen
treffen	traf	hat getroffen
treiben	trieb	hat getrieben
treten	trat	hat/ist getreten
trinken	trank	hat getrunken
tun	tat	hat getan
überwinden	überwand	hat überwunden
verderben	verdarb	hat/ist verdorben
vergessen	vergaß	hat vergessen
verlieren	verlor	hat verloren
verschwinden	verschwand	ist verschwunden
verzeihen	verzieh	hat verziehen
wachsen	wuchs	ist gewachsen
waschen	wusch	hat gewaschen
weisen	wies	hat gewiesen
wenden	wendete/wandte	hat gewandt/gewendet
werben	warb	hat geworben
werden	wurde	ist geworden
werfen	warf	hat geworfen
wiegen	wog	hat gewogen
wissen	wusste	hat gewusst
ziehen	zog	hat/ist gezogen
zwingen	zwang	hat gezwungen

Numbers

Cardinal Numbers

0	null *zero, nought*	30	dreißig *thirty*
1	eins *one*	40	vierzig *forty*
2	zwei *two*	50	fünfzig *fifty*
3	drei *three*	60	sechzig *sixty*
4	vier *four*	70	siebzig *seventy*
5	fünf *five*	80	achtzig *eighty*
6	sechs *six*	90	neunzig *ninety*
7	sieben *seven*	100	(ein)hundert
8	acht *eight*		a/*one hundred*
9	neun *nine*	101	hundert(und)eins
10	zehn *ten*		a *hundred and one*
11	elf *eleven*	200	zweihundert
12	zwölf *twelve*		*two hundred*
13	dreizehn *thirteen*	572	fünfhundert(und)zwei-
14	vierzehn *fourteen*		undsiebzig *five hundred*
15	fünfzehn *fifteen*		*and seventy-two*
16	sechzehn *sixteen*	1000	(ein)tausend
17	siebzehn *seventeen*		a/*one thousand*
18	achtzehn *eighteen*	1998	as year:
19	neunzehn *nineteen*		neunzehnhundertacht-
20	zwanzig *twenty*		undneunzig
21	einundzwanzig		*nineteen (hundred and)*
	twenty-one		*ninety-eight*
22	zweiundzwanzig	2000	zweitausend
	twenty-two		*two thousand*
23	dreiundzwanzig	2010	as year: zweitausendzehn
	twenty-three		*two thousand (and) ten*
24	vierundzwanzig	61 48 25	as phone number:
	twenty-four		einundsechzig acht-
25	fünfundzwanzig		undvierzig fünfund-
	twenty-five		zwanzig
26	sechsundzwanzig		*six one four eight*
	twenty-six		*two five*
27	siebenundzwanzig		
	twenty-seven	1,000,000	eine Million
28	achtundzwanzig		a/*one million*
	twenty-eight	2,000,000	zwei Millionen
29	neunundzwanzig		*two million*
	twenty-nine	1,000,000,000	eine Milliarde
			a/*one billion*

Ordinal numbers

1. erste *first*
2. zweite *second*
3. dritte *third*
4. vierte *fourth*
5. fünfte *fifth*
6. sechste *sixth*
7. siebte *seventh*
8. achte *eighth*
9. neunte *ninth*
10. zehnte *tenth*
11. elfte *eleventh*
12. zwölfte *twelfth*
13. dreizehnte *thirteenth*
14. vierzehnte *fourteenth*
15. fünfzehnte *fifteenth*
16. sechzehnte *sixteenth*
17. siebzehnte *seventeenth*
18. achtzehnte *eighteenth*
19. neunzehnte *nineteenth*
20. zwanzigste *twentieth*
21. einundzwanzigste
    twenty-first
22. zweiundzwanzigste
    twenty-second
23. dreiundzwanzigste
    twenty-third
24. vierundzwanzigste
    twenty-fourth
25. fünfundzwanzigste
    twenty-fifth
26. sechsundzwanzigste
    twenty-sixth
27. siebenundzwanzigste
    twenty-seventh
28. achtundzwanzigste
    twenty-eighth

29. neunundzwanzigste
    twenty-ninth
30. dreißigste *thirtieth*
40. vierzigste *fortieth*
50. fünfzigste *fiftieth*
60. sechzigste *sixtieth*
70. siebzigste *seventieth*
80. achtzigste *eightieth*
90. neunzigste *ninetieth*
100. (ein)hundertste *(one)
    hundredth*
101. hundert(und)erste
    (one) hundred and first
200. zweihundertste
    two hundredth
572. fünfhundert(und)zwei-
    undsiebzigste
    *five hundred and
    seventy-second*
1000. tausendste
    (one) thousandth
1998. neunzehnhundert(und)-
    achtundneunzigste
    *nineteen hundred and
    ninety-ninth*
2000. zweitausendste
    two thousandth
500 000. fünfhunderttausends-
    te *five hundred thou-
    sandth*
1 000 000. millionste
    (one) millionth
2 000 000. zweimillionste
    two millionth

Fractions, decimals and mathematical calculation methods

¹/₂	ein halb	*one/a half*
¹/₂ m	eine halbe Meile	*half a mile*
1 ¹/₂	anderthalb/eineinhalb	*one and a half*
2 ¹/₂	zweieinhalb	*two and a half*
¹/₃	ein Drittel	*one/a third*
²/₃	zwei Drittel	*two thirds*
¹/₄	ein Viertel	*one fourth, one/a quarter*
³/₄	drei Viertel	*three fourths, three quarters*
¹/₅	ein Fünftel	*one/a fifth*
3 ⁴/₅	drei vier Fünftel	*three and four fifths*
0,4	null Komma vier	*point four (.4)*
2,5	zwei Komma fünf	*two point five (2.5)*
1x	ein mal	*once*
2x	zwei mal	*twice*
3x	drei mal	*three times*
4x	vier mal	*four times*
7 + 8 = 15	sieben plus acht ist fünfzehn	*seven plus eight is fifteen*
10 − 3 = 7	zehn minus drei ist sieben	*ten minus three is seven*
2 x 3 = 6	zwei mal drei ist sechs/zwei multipliziert mit drei ist sechs	*two times three is six/two multiplied by three is six*
20 : 5 = 4	zwanzig (dividiert) durch fünf ist vier	*twenty divided by five is four*

European currency

Germany and Austria

1 euro (€) = 100 cent (ct)

coins	banknotes
1 ct	€ 5
2 ct	€ 10
5 ct	€ 20
10 ct	€ 50
20 ct	€ 100
50 ct	€ 200
€ 1	€ 500
€ 2	

Switzerland

1 Swiss franc (Sfr) = 100 Rappen (Rp) / centimes (c)

coins	banknotes
1 Rp	10 Sfr
5 Rp	20 Sfr
10 Rp	50 Sfr
20 Rp	100 Sfr
½ Sfr (50 Rp)	200 Sfr
1 Sfr	1,000 Sfr
2 Sfr	
5 Sfr	

States of the Federal Republic of Germany

Baden-Württemberg	Baden-Württemberg
Bayern	Bavaria
Berlin	Berlin
Brandenburg	Brandenburg
Bremen	Bremen
Hamburg	Hamburg
Hessen	Hesse
Mecklenburg-Vorpommern	Mecklenburg-Western Pomerania
Niedersachsen	Lower Saxony
Nordrhein-Westfalen	North Rhine-Westphalia
Rheinland-Pfalz	Rhineland-Palatinate
Saarland	*das Saarland* the Saarland
Sachsen	Saxony
Sachsen-Anhalt	Saxony-Anhalt
Schleswig-Holstein	Schleswig-Holstein
Thüringen	Thuringia

States of the Republic of Austria

Burgenland	*das Burgenland* the Burgenland
Kärnten	Carinthia
Niederösterreich	Lower Austria
Oberösterreich	Upper Austria
Salzburg	Salzburg
Steiermark	*die Steiermark* Styria
Tirol	Tyrol
Vorarlberg	Vorarlberg
Wien	Vienna

Cantons of the Swiss Confederation

Aargau	*der Aargau* the Aargau
Appenzell	Appenzell
Basel	Basel, Basle
Bern	Bern(e)
Freiburg	*French* Fribourg Fribourg
Genf	*French* Genève Geneva
Glarus	Glarus
Graubünden	Graubünden, Grisons
Jura	*der Jura* the Jura
Luzern	Lucerne

Neuenburg	*French* Neuchâtel Neuchâtel
Nidwalden	Nidwalden
Obwalden	Obwalden
Schaffhausen	Schaffhausen
Schwyz	Schwyz
Solothurn	Solothurn
St. Gallen	St Gallen, St Gall
Tessin	*Italian* Ticino **das Tessin** the Ticino
Thurgau	**der Thurgau** the Thurgau
Unterwalden	Unterwalden
Uri	Uri
Waadt	*French* Vaud Vaud
Wallis	*French* Valais **das Wallis**
	the Valais, Wallis
Zug	Zug
Zürich	Zurich

Temperatures

	°F (Fahrenheit)	°C (Celsius)
	400°	204°
	350°	177°
	300°	149°
boiling point	212°	100°
	100°	38°
	80°	27°
	60°	16°
	40°	4°
freezing point	32°	0°
	20°	– 7°
	0°	–18°

How to convert Celsius into Fahrenheit and vice versa

To convert Celsius into Fahrenheit

multiply by 9, divide by 5 and add 32.

To convert Fahrenheit into Celsius

subtract 32, multiply by 5 and divide by 9.